December 1, 2013

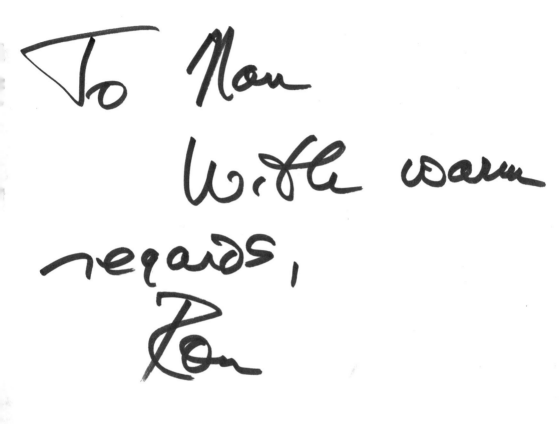

To Nan

With warm
regards,
Ron

Chief: The Quest for Justice in California

Chief: The Quest for Justice in California

Chief Justice Ronald M. George (retired)

Introduction by The Honorable Tani G. Cantil-Sakauye
Chief Justice of California

Based upon oral history interviews conducted
by Laura McCreery
California Supreme Court Oral History Project

2013
Berkeley Public Policy Press
Institute of Governmental Studies
University of California, Berkeley

Library of Congress Cataloging-in-Publication Data

George, Ronald M.
   Chief: the quest for justice in California / Chief Justice Ronald M. George (retired) ;
Introduction by The Honorable Tani G. Cantil-Sakauye, Chief Justice of California.
      pages cm
   "Based upon oral history interviews conducted by Laura McCreery, California Su-
preme Court Oral History Project"—title page.
   Includes index.
   ISBN 978-0-87772-444-5
   1. George, Ronald M. 2. Judges—California—Biography. 3. Justice, Administration
of—California—History. I. Title.
   KF373.G465A3 2013
   347.794'035092—dc23
   [B]
                                         2013015196

Dedication

To my wife, Barbara, who has been my constant source of inspiration, love, and support through these and others of life's adventures.

Contents

---

   * Researchers seeking more detail may consult a traditional oral-history Table of Contents beginning on page 779.

Preface

I admit being reluctant when the California Supreme Court Historical Society asked me, more than a year before I announced my intended retirement, whether I would provide a series of oral history interviews. After all, the lifetime habits of a sitting judge include constraints on speaking openly and publicly on issues that may appear before the courts.

But once retirement set in in earnest, my reluctance dissolved. Besides, as various memoirists have recognized, retrospective journeys are best undertaken while memories are fresh, before time and vanity rearrange facts.

With generous initial funding from the historical society, the oral history was undertaken as part of the ongoing California Supreme Court Oral History Project housed at UC Berkeley's Institute of Governmental Studies. I am deeply grateful for the excellent product that has resulted. I have donated the royalties earned by the sale of this book to the university.

Before the interviews commenced, I regarded the project largely as a matter of obligation—to preserve a record of my almost 15-year stewardship as Chief Justice of California, as well as of the 30 years of public service that preceded it. But once Project Director Laura McCreery undertook the interviews, I found the process rewarding and pleasurable; Laura's thorough preparation, insightful perspective and focus, and spirited manner added great enjoyment to our 20 sessions together, and I am extremely grateful to her for the ensuing 65 hours of recorded conversation.

My wife Barbara not only shared much of the experience of my 45 years of public service, but was also a true partner in the postinterview editing of the manuscript of these sessions, as was our eldest son, Eric. Our other two sons, Andrew and Chris, also offered valuable suggestions. The three of them bore not only the benefits but also many of the burdens of their father's judicial service during those busy and challenging years. I am deeply indebted as well to my parents, who instilled in me the values that helped guide me throughout my career in public service.

I also greatly appreciate the generosity of the persons and institutions separately acknowledged as supporters of this oral history project.

Finally, my thanks go also to Ethan Rarick and Maria Wolf for their valuable assistance in transforming the manuscript of these interviews into book form for the Berkeley Public Policy Press, the publishing arm of the Institute of Governmental Studies, and to Gale Tunnell and Mary DeRose for their very helpful secretarial assistance in preparing the manuscript in final form.

It is my hope that this oral history, which has provided me with a welcome and fulfilling sense of closure on a personal level, will be a useful resource for legal professionals as well as for others with a general interest in the history, functioning, and vital role played by our courts in American society.

Note on Oral History

Oral history is a method of collecting historical information through recorded interviews between a narrator with firsthand knowledge of historically significant events and an informed interviewer, with the goal of preserving substantive additions to the historical record.

The recordings for the *California Supreme Court Oral History Project* were transcribed, lightly edited for continuity and clarity, and reviewed in draft by the interviewee. The edited manuscript is published in book form by Berkeley Public Policy Press for the widest possible use, including collection by research libraries. The original recordings are preserved in the Digital Preservation Repository of the California Digital Library.

Because it is primary material, oral history is not intended to present the final, verified, or complete narrative of events. It is a spoken account, offered by the interviewee in response to questioning, and as such it is reflective, partisan, deeply involved, and irreplaceable.

All uses of this manuscript are covered by a legal agreement between the Regents of the University of California and Chief Justice Ronald M. George (signed by him on July 21, 2011). The manuscript is thereby made available for research purposes by the University of California, Berkeley. All literary rights in the manuscript, including the right to publish, are reserved to the Regents of the University of California. No part of the manuscript may be quoted for publication without the written permission of the director of the Institute of Governmental Studies, which serves as the steward for public access and use of the material.

Requests for permission to quote for publication should be addressed to: Director, Berkeley Public Policy Press, Institute of Governmental Studies #2370, University of California, Berkeley; Berkeley, California 94720-2370. Such requests should include identification of specific passages to be quoted, anticipated use of the passages, and identification of the user.

It is recommended that this oral history be cited as follows: Ronald M. George, "Chief: The Quest for Justice in California," an oral history conducted in 2011 by Laura McCreery, Institute of Governmental Studies, University of California, Berkeley; 2013.

Laura McCreery
Oral History Project Director

Introduction

In 1996, when Ronald M. George became Chief Justice of California, I was in my sixth year as a municipal court judge in Sacramento County. The Supreme Court and the Judicial Council were distant entities; sources of guidance, precedent and rules to be applied on the bench, but not entities that affected me personally. As Chief Justice George assumed his leadership position as head of the Judicial Branch and chair of the council, I anticipated that I would experience his influence as one of a large cadre of state judges whose courtroom work would reflect the decisions of the two bodies that he would now lead—whether administrative or jurisprudential. I knew that his visionary leadership in reorganizing and strengthening the court system and his keen intelligence and jurisprudential experience would be inspiring and beneficial. I underestimated.

Chief Justice George's leadership in the Judicial Branch has been nothing short of legendary. He saw a disjointed, sometimes struggling collection of individual courts and transformed them into a true judicial branch of government, powered by a deliberate balance between state oversight and local control. One might inquire why Chief George would undertake such a massive restructuring of the Judicial Branch. The answer is simple yet undeniable—Chief George was committed to access to justice for all. As I presided over courtrooms in my local court, I reaped the rewards of his endeavors. As Chief Justice, I have come to admire even more how his major structural reforms have enabled our courts to withstand the great California recession to the greatest degree possible. The judicial branch has struggled and continues to do so, but our courts would be in far worse shape had the changes he championed not been adopted.

My journey to becoming a lawyer and judge started when I was very young and experienced my mother returning home, feeling disrespected and disheartened, after going to court without counsel to protest the forced sale of our family home due to redevelopment. I learned a lesson that I have seen repeated time

1

and again: what courts do—and how they do it—has a profound effect on individual lives and rights. Chief Justice George thoroughly understood that. He demonstrated it in his unwavering focus on ensuring access and fairness for all, his efforts to encourage increased minority representation in the bar and bench, and in his sensitivity to how the sweeping history-making changes he led would have day-to-day consequences of enormous import to individual litigants. He believed in the power of the courts to effect change and it was clear he wanted the courts to exercise that power wisely and well.

In 1997, I was elevated to the Superior Court. There, I had the opportunity to create and then preside over Sacramento's first courtroom dedicated solely to domestic violence issues. I was part of a vanguard of judges looking to find more effective ways to serve the community by looking outside the courtroom doors—and our efforts were encouraged, enhanced, and supported every step of the way by the Judicial Council led by Chief Justice George and the Administrative Office of the Courts. California saw an increasing profusion of collaborative justice courts and became recognized as a national leader in seeking new partnerships to make court services more effective and beneficial not only to individuals, but to society as a whole.

This was just one area in which Chief Justice George's leadership made a difference. He promoted the basic premise that by focusing services on particular populations of court users whose appearance in criminal court often simply highlighted a broader problem, courts could prevent future criminality and mitigate potential dangers to society. My experience in advancing the use of domestic violence prevention programs caused me to greatly appreciate how Chief Justice George transformed and improved the court system. The difference between how courts operated at the time I first took the bench and how they function today is unmistakable—the courts are not limited to the strict confines of the cases that come before them but rather the courts now are partners responsive to the needs of the communities they serve.

I was elevated to the Court of Appeal in 2005, and in 2008, I was thrilled to be named to the Judicial Council. The branch had come alive and was exciting, and relevant in a way it had not been when I began practice. The expectations of all whom we served, the diversity of California, the challenges facing courts—all had expanded, morphed, and opened up new areas and perspectives.

My experience on the council brought even greater appreciation and respect for Chief Justice George's leadership and his dedication. It was a great privilege not only to be a beneficiary of his vision but to serve alongside him in continuing to make positive changes. He also appointed me to the Commission for Impartial Courts, an inclusive and wide-ranging study grappling with difficult issues centered on preserving and enhancing an impartial court system. As he recognized, too often the notion of "independence of the judiciary" was being confused with the concept of judges acting based on personal preferences. Chief George understood that it was essential that the public understand the value of a truly "independent" judicial branch that was not politically or in any other fashion reliant on or taking direction from any source other than the rule of law.

My appreciation for Ronald George and all that he has accomplished has grown exponentially since I succeeded him as Chief Justice. This position is not for the faint of heart or the easily fatigued. He has made it that way, not only by setting an example of strong leadership; the role of Chief Justice necessarily has had to greatly expand in order to accomplish his vision for the courts.

There is yet another wrinkle. The focus on the administration of justice, of course, is only part of the role. The Chief Justice of California also participates fully as a member of the Supreme Court, presides over oral argument and court conferences and meetings, produces one-seventh of the opinions, and handles internal administrative and policy issues. At this point, mentioning the intermittent but, nonetheless, very real demands of the role of chair of the Commission on Judicial Appointments, which reviews gubernatorial appointments to the Appellate and Supreme Courts, would seem like piling on.

When I arrived at the Supreme Court, I thought I was a reasonably seasoned appellate justice. I soon found that the work of the state's highest court is different in quantity and urgency to a degree that one really cannot comprehend from outside these chambers. This is all the more reason to marvel and appreciate the remarkable jurisprudential legacy from Chief Justice Ronald George. From his earliest days as an advocate before the United States Supreme Court for our state, to his 15 years presiding over one of the finest groups of justices one could hope to assemble on one bench, he has been a thoughtful principled jurist. His opinions have strengthened the rule of law and the foundation for the reputation of California's high court as one of the finest—indeed, studies have shown that opinions of our court are the most followed by high courts in other states.

Ronald George served with grace and wisdom, and he made it look deceptively easy. As I have grown to understand in greater detail the demands of the position and the complexity of being the leader of the third branch of government, my admiration and appreciation for him and his body of work continues to grow. Like him, I have spent my legal career in public service—and, like him, I believe there can be no higher calling. He set the bar very high—after helping to redesign a far more challenging playing field. Each day I uncover another reason to appreciate what he did, and each day I find another challenge to moving ahead. My hope is to serve with honor and to advance and improve the branch that George built. The foundation that he laid, the example that he set, the courage that he displayed, the vision that he demonstrated—and most of all the deeply felt, undiluted commitment to improving the administration of fair and impartial justice for all that he modeled—all light the way for those of us who follow. I thank him—and am most enthusiastic to join others in learning more about his history from the pages that follow.

The Honorable Tani G. Cantil-Sakauye
Chief Justice of California, August 2013

Biographical Summary

by Laura McCreery, Oral History Project Director,
Institute of Governmental Studies

Chief Justice Ronald M. George was born in Los Angeles in 1940. Although he and his younger sister were educated in the Beverly Hills public schools, in the 1950s they twice spent a full school year abroad at the International School in Geneva, Switzerland, receiving all instruction in French. After graduating from Beverly Hills High School, Ronald M. George took a bachelor's degree at Princeton's Woodrow Wilson School of Public and International Affairs and—disillusioned with his intended career of State Department diplomat—returned to California to pursue a law degree at Stanford.

Hired out of law school by Attorney General Stanley Mosk in 1964, he became a deputy attorney general in Los Angeles, specializing in representing the State of California in criminal matters on appeal. He appeared before the U.S. Supreme Court in six oral arguments, including the initial lead case on the constitutionality of the death penalty (*Aikens v. California*, 1972, mooted by *People v. Anderson* and replaced by *Furman v. Georgia* as lead case). He argued before the California Supreme Court in 11 cases, including *Anderson* and *People v. Sirhan Sirhan*, both in 1972. He handled more than 100 appeals and writs before the state and federal courts. Meanwhile, with his wife, Barbara, he made his home in southern California and raised three sons, Eric, Andrew, and Christopher.

In 1972, Governor Ronald Reagan appointed him at the age of 32 to the Los Angeles Municipal Court, where he later served as supervising judge of the West Los Angeles branch and of the criminal courts division. In 1977, Governor Jerry Brown elevated him to the Los Angeles Superior Court. There Judge

George presided over the notorious Hillside Strangler case, after denying the district attorney's motion to dismiss the murder charges against the defendant, Angelo Buono. Following a jury trial lasting a record-breaking two years and two days, Buono was convicted of nine murders.

In 1983, while serving as president of the California Judges Association concurrent with the Hillside Strangler trial, Judge George was named supervising judge of the superior court's criminal division. In 1985, at his request, he was assigned to the civil division, where he tried cases and served on the mandatory settlement panel.

In 1987, Governor George Deukmejian appointed Judge George to succeed Associate Justice John Arguelles on the California Court of Appeal for the Second Appellate District. In 1991, Governor Pete Wilson elevated Justice George to associate justice of the California Supreme Court. Upon the retirement of Chief Justice Malcolm M. Lucas in 1996, Governor Wilson again turned to Justice George, appointing him as the twenty-seventh Chief Justice of California. Unanimously rated "exceptionally well qualified" by the Commission on Judicial Nominees Evaluation, Chief Justice George took the oath of his new office on Law Day, May 1, 1996.

Just two weeks later, Chief Justice George announced in his first State of the Judiciary address to a joint session of the California Legislature that he would visit the courts in each of California's 58 counties, which he completed in a single year. Those visits, involving 13,000 miles of travels that were concluded in August 1997, had both immediate and lasting effects on Chief Justice George's views of, and advocacy for, a truly independent, co-equal judicial branch of California government. At the California Supreme Court, throughout the state judiciary, and to the executive and legislative branches in Sacramento, he expounded on the principle that full access to justice must extend to all Californians, not only in name but in practice.

On occasion Chief Justice George's trips to Sacramento coincided with those of his wife, who had budget and advocacy duties of her own as chair of the California Arts Council. Barbara George chaired the Civic Center Art Committee in San Francisco, which was responsible for art installations at the co-joined court and state buildings. Two books, *Art & Architecture—San Francisco Civic Center Complex* and *Court Houses of California*, an illustrated history, document the results of those efforts. She also contributed her talents to art selection for various other state buildings.

Walking the halls of the Capitol so often that Senate President pro Tem John Burton quipped that he should register as a lobbyist, Chief Justice George worked with all branches of government and with a wide array of "justice system partners"—the State Bar, the counties, judicial organizations, civil plaintiffs' and defense groups, as well as prosecution and criminal defense counsel groups—to pursue major reforms: the Trial Court Funding Act of 1997; unification of municipal and superior trial courts in each county (accomplished by constitutional amendment in 1998); and the Trial Court Facilities Act of 2002, which transferred more than 500 county court facilities to state ownership and judicial branch management, an undertaking eventually supplemented by a separately enacted $5 billion revenue bond measure to enable the construction and renovation of court facilities.

Leading the efforts of the Judicial Council and its staff, the Administrative Office of the Courts, Chief Justice George also pressed for jury reforms, expanded court interpreter services, obtained funding to increase judicial salaries, and worked to establish new judgeships, self-help centers for unrepresented litigants, and uniform court rules. Through it all, he carried his one-seventh share of the caseload on the California Supreme Court itself, steadfastly observing that his judicial duties, particularly the writing of opinions, were his favorite part of the job. Indeed, his judicial robe—a gift from his colleagues in the attorney general's office when he first took the bench in 1972—always hung in full view in his chambers, unless he was wearing it, as a constant reminder of that preference.

Although the decisions of the George Court did not consistently attract ideological labels or yield predictable voting patterns, Chief Justice George himself often held the center of the seven-member panel, authoring and casting deciding votes in such key cases as the 1997 rehearing of *American Academy of Pediatrics v. Lungren*, which invalidated, on the basis of the privacy provision of the state Constitution, the statutory parental-consent requirement for minors seeking an abortion. In the most closely watched decision of his tenure, Chief Justice George in 2008 authored the four-three majority in *In re Marriage Cases*, which held that statutory provisions defining marriage as "between a man and a woman" violated the constitutional right of all Californians to marry and denied them the equal protection of the laws. Known as a judicial moderate, he assigned the *Marriage Cases* and certain others to himself on the ground that, as Chief Justice, he should have the "broad shoulders" to withstand criticism of the court for rulings on controversial issues.

Chief Justice George spoke publicly about matters that in his view stymied the courts' ability to uphold their constitutional responsibilities. Citing the backlog, inefficiencies, delays, and spiraling costs of administering capital punishment, he famously told the *New York Times* in 2004 that a death row inmate in California was more likely to die of old age than by execution. He came to favor amending the state constitution to modify the automatic appeal of death cases to the California Supreme Court by sending a limited number of those cases instead to the courts of appeal. This proposal and others championed by the Commission on the Fair Administration of Justice (2005–2008) have not thus far swayed the legislative and executive branches to enact significant death penalty reforms.

Concerned by a sharp decline in civics education, Chief Justice George initiated annual special sessions of California Supreme Court proceedings in varying locations around the state, often arranging for high school, college, and law students to observe oral argument and ask questions of the justices. He spoke publicly about the importance of civics knowledge for all Californians, who are called upon to decide statewide ballot initiatives. He served on the steering committee of the "Sandra Day O'Connor Project on the State of the Judiciary" at Georgetown University, a three-year public education effort on civics and judicial independence that resulted in the highly successful iCivics website.

Chief Justice George announced in July 2010 that he would step down six months hence rather than seek retention for another 12-year term. After tending to myriad administrative and judicial matters in his final months, he was succeeded in the first days of 2011 by Chief Justice Tani Cantil-Sakauye, who was nominated by Governor Arnold Schwarzenegger for elevation from the California Court of Appeal for the Third Appellate District and approved by voters in the November 2010 general election.

Although Chief Justice George won dozens of awards and honors throughout his career, including induction into the American Academy of Arts and Sciences, he was traveling in Antarctica in December 2010 and did not immediately learn of one of the most notable tributes of all: Governor Arnold Schwarzenegger's executive order that San Francisco's Civic Center Complex would henceforth be known as the Ronald M. George State Office Complex in honor of "a superbly effective leader." The complex (the Earl Warren Building and the Hiram M. Johnson State Office Building, both of which retain their individual names) houses the California Supreme Court, the Court of Appeal for the First Appellate District, the Judicial Council, and the Administrative Office of the Courts, as well as various state executive and legislative branch offices.

Chief Justice George spent the early months of his retirement traveling, reading, and visiting with family members. He also has retained his ties with former colleagues from all three branches of California government and continues to promote civics education and government reforms, both independently and as a member of the Think Long Committee for California. More recently, after the conclusion of these oral history sessions, he accepted an invitation to serve as a member, with several world leaders, of the Commission on Global Ethics and Citizenship, to review the United Nations' Universal Declaration of Human Rights and recommend any revisions.

Chapter 1

Early Days
May 26, 2011

This is Laura McCreery speaking, and I'm here from the UC Berkeley Institute of Governmental Studies to conduct the first in a series of oral history interviews with the Honorable Ronald M. George, recently retired Chief Justice of California. Good afternoon, Chief Justice George.

Good afternoon. I've looked forward to our sessions, and I'm so glad that we are beginning the first one. I know it will be very productive and enjoyable for me.

Likewise. Would you start us off, please, by stating your date of birth and then saying a few words about where you were born?

I was born on March 11, 1940, in Los Angeles and went to public schools, interrupted by a couple of years of school in Geneva, Switzerland. I spent the bulk of my youth in Southern California until I went off to college back east.

When you were born, as the elder of two children, how long had your immediate family been in the Los Angeles area?

My father had a very interesting course that brought him to Los Angeles and caused me to be born as a Californian. He was born in 1904 in Paris, France, actually at his parents' apartment with the assistance of a midwife. He left Paris in the 1920s seeking his fortune—or his future, in any event—in the New World.

Those who have followed history closely may recall that there was a substantial French presence in Mexico, some of which arose out of the efforts of Napoleon III to develop a French empire in the Americas. That continued on, at least by way of commercial presence, into the 1920s. My father learned of an employment opportunity in Mexico City to be the assistant to the director of a French import-export company doing business in Mexico. He set off from France on an ocean steamer, I believe to Veracruz, and made his way to Mexico City. He was fairly assured of having this position but realized the night before the interview that it was assumed that he had fluent typing skills. He had never even touched a typewriter before, so he sought out an office supply company, even though it was the evening hours, and spent a good part of the night in front of the plate glass window memorizing the keyboard so that he was able to go in the next morning and get the position with the typing skills that were required.

He lived in Mexico from 1926 to 1928 and travelled around that country, sometimes on horseback, looking at various operations related to the company. We found in his effects some remarkable photographs. It was still in the recent aftermath of the revolution led by Pancho Villa, and there were some rather gruesome photographs of bandits lined up in front of firing squads.

He would go back to France periodically to visit his parents. One year he decided, due to a fascination with what he had heard about Southern California, that he would make his way up the coast and see what Los Angeles was all about. He did that and he fell in love with Southern California and Los Angeles. Then he continued his journey across the United States by train and left from New York to see his parents and eventually decided he wanted to settle in Southern California.

He had met my mother earlier. Her father had been in the fur business, as had his own father. My father had served as a young apprentice in her father's fur enterprise. My parents ended up getting married and settling in Los Angeles. I believe it was 1938. She was of Hungarian extraction. Two years after they moved there I was born in 1940 as a Californian. I might otherwise have turned out to be a French child experiencing the turmoil of World War II or a Mexican child. I describe myself as somewhat of a French goulash. I have a sister, Rita George Daughtry, who is four years junior to me, who was born in 1944. She's an artist in the Topanga area of Los Angeles and also has an art restoration business. My father brought his parents to the United States and, when he was able to, he purchased an apartment building and made his mother the manager. His father died before I was born. I have very fond memories of my French grandmother. She had some Basque heritage as well as family from the northern part of France. She never, despite all of her years in the United States, learned much English other than to say hello and goodbye and yet was an excellent building manager.

You mentioned that you were looking at boxes of family documents in Los Angeles and ran across a picture of your father's grandmother. What do you know of her life, if anything?

Nothing. It's not that my parents went out of their way to be private, but they just did not talk about their relatives, except for my grandparents who came to this country. Other relatives I never really learned that much about. It was a surprise, going through my parents' effects, to find the nineteenth century images of the grandparents of my father and of my mother. I hardly knew that photography existed at that time.

When my father arrived in Southern California he got into his trade, the fur business. He worked at I. Magnin and became head of the fur department in Los Angeles and had some management responsibilities over other branches, including Santa Barbara and San Francisco. As soon as he was able to, through his own investments, he ceased his employment there and began going to the stockbroker's office every day.

My father, who had come to the United States with little means, managed to make very shrewd investments with the savings that he accumulated. Very frankly, he was a speculator in the stock market. There is no better way to describe it. [Laughter] He took great chances. In those days you could put up 10 percent of the money and invest with 90 percent on margin, but you risked being sold out at market if you could not cover your losses within minutes. It caused, frankly, a fair amount of tension in my parents' marriage, because my father was very much of a risk taker. He did not approach the stock market with all of the analytical tools a lot of people employed. With him—he had very much of a Latin temperament—it was all instinct and intuition. If he just felt good about something he would go with it. I had to be careful when I came home from school to find out from my mother how the market had been that day. There were days to definitely avoid my father and not go near him, and other days when he would be quite exuberant. My mother happened to be far more conservative in her approach to investments, and it caused some friction, although they both were the beneficiaries of his gut instincts.

One of his investments was in Western Airlines, which of course later merged into other airlines. The conventional wisdom was that once World War II was over, domestic airlines would fold because they were so dependent upon war traffic. My father saw the potential for growth in the West and invested in Western Airlines and became a very large shareholder, perhaps the largest non-institutional shareholder at the time, and served on the board of directors of the company. He also invested in gold commodities. He saw the future of gold mining companies and did very well in that. He also acquired additional real estate holdings.

To what extent did your father talk with you directly about his work as an investor?

He did. He was very excited about these investments. In fact, I had a rather bizarre experience that you've just reminded me of.

My first visit to Europe was in conjunction with a year of schooling that my parents planned for me and my sister Rita at the International School of Geneva. They picked that school because it was one of the very few schools, at least at that time, that was coeducational. Geneva was, as it remains today, a hub of international activity with various international organizations that either have headquarters or subsidiary offices there. We were placed there in school for the year 1952–1953, when I was twelve and she was eight. During the summers preceding and following the school year we traveled to Paris and other locations. My parents loved to go to the French Riviera.

I should go back to why my parents wanted to put my sister and me in that school for a year. We were being raised in Beverly Hills, and I think my parents felt—and certainly rightly so, in retrospect—that in a way it was a very provincial upbringing, in the true sense of the word, for their children as residents of Beverly Hills to be focused on the immediate world around us—centered on the entertainment industry—to the exclusion of other places. It might be that people in small towns in the Midwest were less provincial because they had more of an interest in what was going on in other places—in New York and Hollywood and Washington. I think my parents felt it would be very good for us to have a broadening experience, especially since they were Europeans. They recognized what there was out there in the world that we were not being exposed to.

They often spoke French around the house. They also were fluent in German, and my father in Flemish and Dutch that he learned from when his father's fur business caused the family to spend some time in Belgium, Holland, and Germany. He knew some Spanish from his years in Mexico. Although my parents never bothered to have my sister and me learn to speak any foreign languages when we were at home, they did at some point arrive at the conclusion that we should go abroad to learn French. For all those reasons they enrolled us in the school, and it was an occasion that dovetailed with their desire to take off a year and just travel around the world. They wanted a safe place to park us.

I still remember arriving at the International School and my father and mother making some inquiries. It became apparent that we would be placed in the English-speaking division. That's where virtually all Americans, English, Canadians, and Australians were placed. They asked, "Our children are going to have exposure to the French language for only an hour or so every day. Is that right?" "Yes, that's true, except they'll be dealing socially with kids from all different nationalities." There were 50 different nationalities represented among the student body and the faculty there. My parents said, "We want them in the French-speaking division."

The Swiss schools, then and now, are quite strict and challenging. Even though I came from a public school system at that time rated among the top in the United States, it was no match for the Swiss schools. I was going to have to take subjects that were pretty challenging, yet my parents said, "No, he's going to be put in the French speaking division." This was eighth grade for me. I had to take subjects such as Swiss history, chemistry, algebra, German, which I also didn't speak—in French. The Swiss were not terribly sympathetic. I got my failing grade every week for a few weeks until I acquired a rudimentary knowledge of French.

My parents decided that my sister and I should have a second bout with the Swiss schools, so we went back in 1955–1956, when I was 15 and she was 11. It was more or less a similar experience. I don't recall exactly which countries they visited during that school year, except that I am certain that Russia was one of them. They were quite adventurous, and they went to all sorts of exotic places.

To get back to your question about discussing the stock market and business affairs—you're going to wonder, what could this school experience possibly have to do with it? When my parents decided that they were going to visit Russia, they were among the very first tourists in the post-Stalin period to travel there, outside of official delegations. My father, being leveraged like that in the stock market—people were amazed that he would take off and travel for a year, because he was in the broker's office every day. But at least he wanted to be aware of what was going on in the market. Before he left for Russia, every day he'd read the *International Herald Tribune* to learn how his investments were faring and what events might affect the stock market. But he knew he wouldn't have access to that information when he was in Russia.

Having kept me informed of all of his dealings in the market—as much as you would share with someone my age—he said, "Here are a bunch of postcards, and I want you to write me a postcard every day. Here's our itinerary in Russia. I want you to tell me how my key stocks are doing. The authorities in Russia may not be terribly receptive to an importation of Dow Jones data on a daily basis, [Laughter] so we're going to have a little bit of a code." He said, "Starting off, put the time of day." I'm pretty sure the Dow Jones industrials index was in the 500 range then. "You'll write for example 5:21, and you put a.m. if it went up for the day or p.m. if it went down. Then you'll write about the stocks I'm most interested in." I don't remember all the names, but I do recall, since his most important holding was Western Airlines, that this stock was referred to by me in my communications as "Willie." "Willie is doing fine but had some problems last week." Almost every day I was sending something.

This was, I'm sure, a very amateurish method of getting information into Communist Russia at that time, the 1950s. It turned out that my parents were not getting any of these postcards, which concerned them. And then they learned that President Eisenhower had had one of his two major health problems. I don't know if it was his intestinal surgery or his heart problem. My father, aside from an interest in how the president might be doing, felt that this could have a very severe impact on the stock market. He could no longer wait to find out how things were.

My parents said they wanted to phone me at the International School in Geneva, and they were told by Intourist, the government tourist bureau, "This is out of the question. We don't allow phone calls for nonemergency reasons." My mother then said, "Our son has been ill and we haven't heard from him." What made it more complicated was they were not in Moscow. They were in Kiev, and the Soviet Union was so overcentralized that everything, at least a phone call by a foreigner to someone outside the country, had to go through Moscow, which was several hundred miles out of the way, before being routed to Switzerland. The authorities relented and asked for the phone number. It was going to take two or three days to set up this phone call. My mother said, "We don't have the number, but it's the International School, the *Ecole Internationale*." "Oh, no. If you don't have the number we can't put the call through." My mother said, "Let me see. Maybe I do have it." She made up a phone number and figured, "They'll be working on this for two or three days. If I can just get someone on the other end, they can transfer me since it will go through an operator."

It was like some very cheesy type of Cold War drama, only over the stock market. [Laughter] As my mother would tell the story, it was quite amusing because this unfortunate woman in Geneva, whose number it happened to be, came on the line and said she had been getting these advance notices from the Swiss phone company. "A call is coming through to you from Russia." She said, *"Je ne connais personne . . ."* ("I don't know anyone in Russia. Please leave me alone.") But she was told, "Your number is the number they're trying to call." When my mother got to speak to this woman—the operator was still on the line—my mother intervened and asked the operator, "If this is not the International School, can you transfer me?"

I remember I was in the dining hall of the school when I was summoned out, being told there was a phone call from Kiev for me. My parents greeted me, and then they asked, "How is everything? We haven't gotten any mail from you. Please tell us how everybody is." I started with the routine about, "Willie is doing this, and Sally is doing this." After about a minute or so, we were cut off and that was the end of the conversation. [Laughter] I'm sure it was a deliberate cut-off by someone monitoring the call. That is a rather long-winded response to your question about my father discussing his stock market dealings with me.

That was some early training for you, wasn't it, in reading the stock pages and interpreting on his behalf. What was their interest in traveling to Russia in this first period of time when one could go as a tourist?

Just seeing the world. During those years they went to the Far East. They came back to see us over Christmas vacation and Easter, but otherwise for an entire year they traveled to places such as Lebanon, Syria, India, and the Far East.

You come from a family of great travelers?

It did instill in both my sister and me a great love of travel as a learning experience and often as an adventure as well.

You touched on your mother's side of the family. What do you know of her family life other than her father's fur trade?

She went to school in various countries—Switzerland, Germany, and France—attending the Sorbonne in Paris—and spent a year in England as an *au pair*, becoming fluent in English, French, and German with a slight taste of an accent in her English. My father never lost his heavy French accent. It was considered quite charming, and he sounded like a combination of Charles Boyer and Maurice Chevalier.

They married then and settled in Los Angeles around 1938. Before you went off to the International School, what do you remember about life in Los Angeles when you were a youngster in those immediate postwar years?

I remember how spread out Los Angeles was. If one went to the airport— that's L.A. International—there were actual bean fields, agricultural areas between the west side of town and the airport. I remember wonderful public transportation, with the little red cars that people wish they had today.[1]

I also remember Beverly Hills being very much oriented toward the entertainment industry. It didn't take me too long to develop a bit of an aversion to the excessive impact of the industry upon the school environment. Today I have many friends in the entertainment industry, and I have nothing against it, but it just seemed so predominant. There are other places where you have the entertainment industry, banking, various businesses, and government being considered equally significant interests, but in many ways Beverly Hills was a one-track town. I can see why my parents wanted me to be exposed to something beyond that.

I had been a B+ student in the Beverly Hills schools, which as I said were extremely competitive. After I came back, I was getting straight As with no effort. It was really an awakening to go to school in Switzerland, with its high academic demands. We also were awakened at dawn to run around the school park and then take cold showers. [Laughter] It was a very different kind of background, but one that was marvelous in retrospect. I don't mean to imply that the school was all grim hard work. There were a lot of wonderful outings, and athletics included skiing.

They even had, as I'm thinking back upon it now, what you might call a competitive treasure hunt with another school that included brief forays across the Swiss border. It started off with a clue to find a particular café in Geneva and to play something on the jukebox. That gave some coordinates to some other place. We had to take a mountain railway on the other side of Switzerland to get to the top, and that led to another location with the next clues. This was a three- or four-day adventure. We were let loose as 15- and 16-year-olds to do this with a Swiss train pass and our passports and no adult supervision. It ended with a welcoming banquet at the finish line in Lausanne.

I'm interested in how that experience might have changed you. What sort of child were you before you went to the International School?

I was narrowly focused upon my immediate environment, which involved friends who were mostly the offspring of people in the movie industry. When I got to Geneva, of course I was exposed to children from most of the continents and to a lot of different cultures. I became friendly with a couple of teachers, too, who really expanded my horizons. Due to their encouragement, as well as that of my parents, I developed an ambition to make my career in the Foreign

---

[1] Red Car lines of the Pacific Electric Railway.

Service of the U.S. State Department. I became very interested in international affairs. That focus stayed with me for quite a few years, until another experience got me off that career track. I went from someone who was very focused on the culture of Southern California to someone who was quite fascinated by world history and international relations.

How do you evaluate that whole time abroad, thinking back on it?

I would say it was one of the key elements in my upbringing. It certainly brought me an awareness and a tolerance, not just of different nationalities but different religions, different cultures, of people with diverse views. Although I haven't analyzed it, I'm sure it played a significant role in shaping my values, even as they ended up being manifested in a legal and judicial career.

You mentioned religion a moment ago. What was your own religious upbringing, if any?

My parents did not give me any specific religious upbringing. They felt, and I very much appreciate it, that one shouldn't be inculcated with a particular sectarian viewpoint but should be allowed to find his or her own way. That's what my sister and I did rather than being indoctrinated with a particular set of beliefs and then having to choose between following parental teachings or breaking away. They left it totally up to us. What was always most important to them were moral values and spiritual pursuits, and not the institution of a religious denominational faith as such. Certainly they instilled in me a tolerance for all major faiths, which were represented there in Geneva. I had a full panoply of good friends who were European, Asian, and Middle Eastern, as well as American and South American.

What did your parents want for you and your sister as the first generation born in the United States?

I think they wanted us to have the opportunity to do what we wanted to do, but with the cast of it being something socially worthwhile. As is so often the case, as immigrants to the United States they had a great appreciation of the values of our American system, our American way of life, perhaps more than many native-born Americans. To them these were very meaningful values, as they are, I think, to so many immigrants from all parts of the world. This may be what drew them to the United States to begin with, but they certainly appreciated everything this country has to offer. I think I benefited from having an immigrant's commitment and enthusiasm for these values instilled in me.

You said your sister was four years younger and had a career in art. Could you tell me more about your relationship with her over the years, both as you were growing up and living abroad but also later on?

We're very close, and we both share quite a sense of humor, certainly to the extent of pulling pranks on each other, even though professionally we've taken such very different directions—she's very much an artist in so many different ways, in terms of temperament and personality, as well as her actual vocation. I have absolutely zero artistic talent. I love all sorts of art and music, and my wife Barbara is very much into the arts field, but in terms of any creative ability, I have none. I couldn't draw a stick figure as well as my four-year-old grand-daughter.

My parents tried to instill in me some abilities in piano, and I did everything I could to evade my responsibilities there. In fact, there was a rather amusing story that you've just reminded me of. I was relegated to practicing the piano every evening after dinner. My parents, not by coincidence, planned their evening constitutional immediately after dinner so they wouldn't have to listen to me botching up my scales and the pieces, "Für Elise" and others, that I would traipse through on the keyboard.

Our family was assisted by a kind, elderly housekeeper who actually had had some training in music. It was among Emily's responsibilities to report on whether I had dutifully practiced during the time my parents chose to take their evening walk. They would come back, and Emily would say, "Mr. and Mrs. George, Ronnie," as I was known then, "practices dutifully every evening, but he doesn't seem to make much progress." The reason that she heard the same mistakes made over and over again was this. Being a Beverly Hills brat, I had a bunch of friends who were connected with the entertainment industry. The father of one friend was in the recording industry. My friend and I hatched a plan to record my piano practice—I actually cut a record on a device they had at home. I paid my little sister a penny each evening to be by the record player. The minute she would hear the front door open, she was supposed to lift the needle off. When I would hear that, I'd resume my stance at the piano. That's why Emily would say, "He seems to make the same mistakes over and over again." It was the same rendition repeated time and time again. [Laughter]

One evening my parents left on their walk, and it turned out to be a much cooler evening than my mother had anticipated. She had to come back for a warmer coat. My sister wasn't being terribly attentive because it was so early in my performance. She thought my parents were just starting off, so she didn't hear them come back. My parents walked down the hallway and passed by my door. I'm sitting on the bed reading a comic book, and they're hearing me play in the living room, so of course I was busted! [Laughter] But my parents were quite tolerant. They got quite a laugh out of it and a good story to tell.

What other community or political interests, locally, might your parents have had while you were in school?

My parents had virtually no political involvement. I don't want to sound harsh about this in any way, but even when I became a mature adult and they were getting on in years they never got much involved in the details of the American political process even though they had great respect for its underlying values. They were more focused on what was going on internationally. I never had any in-depth discussions with them about domestic politics or anything of that sort. That's probably something I didn't get terribly interested in myself until college.

My mother loved attending classical music concerts. My parents were total nonjoiners. They never joined any organizations—political, social, charitable, or whatever. They would make contributions, but they had absolutely zero involvement. It was really part of their personality that they did not get involved the way Barbara and I have gotten involved in certain activities. It was, I think, very much an American thing to be involved in community organizations and other things of that sort. That's a gross generalization, but I think it's not infrequent that you find Europeans, whether in Europe or here, who have not gotten involved in community organizations.

While you were not at the International School you were attending Beverly Hills High School. What can you tell me about your experiences there?

Having had exposure to the very different school life in Switzerland, I suppose I came back well equipped to cope with high school but looked somewhat askance at what I perceived as the occasional excesses of those of my classmates who I thought were a bit narrowly focused on Hollywood.

You had developed different sensibilities by that time through your own experiences.

Yes. But it's funny, because my parents did have some very close friends who were quite active in the film industry even though it wasn't, by any means, their exclusive focus. I think my mother was the closest friend of the actor Sydney Greenstreet. He was over frequently, and I have a wonderful inscribed photograph from him to me. There was a famous episode in our family history where he had come over for dinner. One new sensation was Reddi-Wip, whipped cream out of a can. This was a big deal, and Sydney Greenstreet expressed great interest in this. My father showed him how it worked, only my father wasn't terribly familiar with it either and proceeded to spray him from waist up to face level with whipped cream. [Laughter] Sydney Greenstreet got a big kick out of accusing my father of having done this deliberately out of jealousy for all the attention that Greenstreet was always paying to my mother. [Laughter] So my life was not, by any means, sequestered from the Hollywood experience.

You met your wife Barbara while still in elementary school. Tell me how you got to know her.

My sister Rita and Barbara were in first grade together, and they became close friends, partly due to fact that they both had European mothers—Barbara's mother, Marja, was Danish—who sent them to school in what they viewed as somewhat frumpy European clothing. I think they bonded over such things. My sister is as much of a foodie as I am and loved the fact that Barbara's mother would always have freshly baked Danish cookies and cakes waiting at home, at the end of the school day. Rita and Barbara were close, and Barbara and I would speak occasionally.

I was always considered the pesky older brother of Barbara's best friend. At some point, my next door neighbor started to date Barbara and would come to me for my advice, which he insists to this day was deliberately designed to sabotage their relationship. Barbara assured him that their relationship was over with, but he still had high hopes. I guess I got to know Barbara through his coming to me for advice. It just naturally evolved where, one day, I decided I would ask Barbara out. She was the only one of my sister's friends I ever asked out.

You decided to advise yourself for a change?

[Laughter] Yes, exactly. That's how it all began. I remember we went to Trader Vic's for our first date, and we hit it off right away. It progressed quite naturally to an engagement and then to marriage.

What year was that?

We got married on January 30, 1966, after becoming engaged the previous October.

You went off and did other things in the meantime, and we'll get to that. Before we finish your time growing up and in high school, which adults were most influential to you, either relatives or others?

Certainly my parents were, and I had a couple teachers at the International School in Geneva who were very influential in terms of my interest in international matters.

Who were they?

I remember, in particular, Paul Meyhoffer. He and his wife would have me over for dinner, and he helped instill a real interest in international affairs. At Beverly Hills High School I had a history teacher, Salvador Occhipinti, who made current affairs come alive and would grill us mercilessly about the latest events. I think those two teachers focused me on a career in international relations and in the Foreign Service. I also had some wonderful teachers who instilled in me a love of literature and of the English language. I actually enjoyed grammar and parsing sentences the way they probably don't teach anymore.

You graduated from Beverly Hills High in 1957. What were your plans at that time? What did you hope to do next?

I was quite focused on a career in the Foreign Service of the U.S. State Department, so I decided that my top two choices would be either the Georgetown University School of Foreign Service or Princeton University's Woodrow Wilson School of Public and International Affairs. I was admitted to both schools and chose to go to Princeton. I continued my language studies in French and added Russian, and then got into the Woodrow Wilson School my junior year and took a broad selection of courses crossing the departmental boundaries of history, political science, economics, and sociology. That was my focus, but I also took many courses in English, American, and comparative literature, in philosophy and art history.

One of my roommates was Darcy O'Brien, from Beverly Hills High School, who was the son of movie stars, George O'Brien—mainly from the silent screen days—and Marguerite Churchill. I couldn't quite get away from Hollywood. [Laughter]

What was your living situation when you first arrived?

Darcy and I had a few other roommates from the East and the Midwest. We ended up combining units. If you wanted to have five or six guys install bunk beds in one room so that you could make a lavish suite of the other rooms to impress all the visiting girls, that was quite okay. We had a very nice set of quarters. I was always the last one to turn in, and I am to this day—to the annoyance of Barbara—a fresh-air fiend, so I would open up the window when I'd go to bed and some mornings my roommates were displeased to find a little snowbank on the windowsill or a frozen bar of ice connecting the dripping water faucet to the sink. There was a lot of fun, a lot of pranks among a group of very different guys rooming together. We all learned a lot from each other in one way or the other.

Tell me about the school itself and your program of study.

The Woodrow Wilson School offered a major field of study crossing various departments. If you wanted to focus on African studies, which to a certain extent I did—I wrote my senior thesis on Africa's voice at the United Nations— you could take courses in sociology, international relations, history, economics, and political science focusing on all those different disciplines dealing with a subject such as Africa. There were these conferences where everyone would write a paper. I chaired one year's conference on disarmament. But my focus and my thesis were on Africa. I went up to the U.N. and interviewed diplomats and went through voting records to see whether African nations were truly voting as a bloc and, if so, on what issues. I did a lot of original research.

With that focus on Africa, I accepted an invitation of another friend at Princeton, Don Emmerson, to visit Africa in the summer of 1959, between my sophomore and junior years, before writing my thesis. The trip was basically a modified form of hitchhiking, finding out that a British colonial officer, or an African native, or a missionary, or an American diplomat was going to be traveling from one area to another and arranging to ride with them. I more or less hitchhiked with all of those categories of individuals and had some true adventures in the course of that summer.

I'd like to hear about that. How did you become interested in Africa to begin with?

I don't really have an answer, but it may have been through my friend Don Emmerson telling me about his parents' tour of duty there. His father, John Emmerson, was U.S. Consul General in Lagos, Nigeria, which was still a British colony. It might have been through that connection, plus just a sense of adventure.

You had not been to Africa yourself before then?

No, I had not, nor had my parents. They had been to Egypt, but they had not been to sub-Saharan Africa. My trip was quite an amazing experience, just from the standpoint of some occasionally dangerous encounters. There were places where I was informed that we were the first white persons ever to be seen in that village. People were, by and large, very friendly.

Where did you start?

We started the trip in Lagos, Nigeria. Nigeria is an interesting country from many standpoints. It's the most populous country in Africa, at least now. Geographically and ethnically it's quite diverse. The southern part is equatorial, and there's a central mountainous area, and the northern part includes the outer reaches of the Sahara Desert. I saw some camel caravans come down through there.

In a northern Nigerian city—I believe it was Sokoto in the Northwest—we were warned that just a couple of weeks before there had been an unsuccessful effort by the U.S. Information Agency to establish rapport between America and the African population, based upon an oversimplified view that native Africans would relate immediately to American jazz by seeing a film on the life of Louis Armstrong. Despite some connections, the thought in that instance was misguided, at least to the extent that the film was very much a flop when our government set up a movie screening area in a tent-like structure to show it in the central marketplace. There was absolutely no real interest in the film. People were watching without much reaction. Then, there's a point in the film where apparently the camera focuses on a close-up of Louis Armstrong, and his lip was quite ulcerated from blowing on the horn. Someone in the audience stood up, pointed at the screen, and said, "Leper. America. Leper." They tore the whole place apart running out. I was advised, "Lie low in this area. There's still some reaction to that."

I also went to Ghana, which had just become independent. This was 1959, and Kwame Nkrumah had led Ghana to independence in 1957, so it was quite wonderful to see the exuberance in the first independent sub-Saharan African state.

I had a very interesting experience in what was then two countries, the British and French Cameroons. They arose out of a German colony, Kamerun, that after World War I had been divided into respective British and French protectorates. Of course, now they're united into one country again, Cameroon. The Cameroons was a very interesting area located at a confluence of various tribal migrations that had occurred over the centuries, resulting in there being many kings, who were called *fons*. You'd go a few miles and you were in someone else's territory. I was traveling with a missionary at that point, quite a robust fellow. He said, "We're going into this area, and I have a bottle of gin because this is an offering that this *fon* would appreciate." [Laughter] "In this other area," he said, "I'm already a hero." There was a baboon that lived on the cliff above the village that would come down and terrorize the populace. He said, "I shot it dead off the cliff one day, so we're in good shape there."

This was a very fascinating area just about on the equator. Mt. Cameroon has many different climatic zones. The mountain is more than 13,000 feet in elevation, so right at the equator you go up into all these different zones. I didn't get to the top parts. We learned later that riots had occurred in a town that we had been visiting, although we had been totally unaware of this while we were there and could have been in jeopardy.

While we were there, someone came up to Don Emmerson and me and told us that we were summoned to Government House. Each of us got on our one decent set of clothes—I actually had a coat and tie—and went to Government House expecting to be dressed down for something we had done that was illegal or wrong or inappropriate. Instead we were greeted by the prime minister of the British Cameroons and his full cabinet, who had heard that there were these two American college students in the country. They were eager to meet us. We had a nice chat about what things were like in the United States. They were very courteous, and they gave us gifts. We then posed for a photograph standing on the steps of Government House, these two nineteen-year-olds and the prime minister and his cabinet in tribal robes. As a somewhat empty gesture, because I never thought anything would come of it, I did say upon parting that should the prime minister ever come to the United States and be in the vicinity of Princeton, I'd be very happy to see him. I thought, "That's the last I'm ever going to hear of that."

What else did you talk about with the prime minister and his cabinet, before the parting words you just described?

What we were studying and how the American form of government worked. I just have very general recollections.

But your presence there was rare enough that he was taking great interest in whatever you were doing?

He thought it would be worthwhile to chat with us. Aside from getting this nice photograph in the mail, that was the end of it until a few months later when an envelope arrived in my mail festooned with exotic stamps. I opened it up, and it contained a letter from the prime minister himself saying that indeed he would be coming to New York—I had made a point of telling him Princeton was only an hour's train ride away—and that he would appreciate, in conjunction with his visit to the United Nations, being able to come down to Princeton and give a talk. I believe his visit to the U.S. had something to do with preparations for the admission of his reunited nation to the U.N.

I was active, as was Don Emmerson, in a typically archaically worded institution at Princeton called the American Whig-Cliosophic Society. It was located in a mini-Parthenon type of structure and was the debating society, but also covered international affairs. We arranged for a talk by the prime minister, and that went well. Afterwards, we thought it would be appropriate to take him out to lunch at the Nassau Inn in Princeton.

There were a lot of southern boys who went to Princeton—and I say boys, as no women were admitted in those days. Given the history of Princeton back in the pre–Civil War days, when some of the attending students came from slave-owning families, the town had somewhat of a border-state mentality.

The prime minister, Don Emmerson, and I walked into the Nassau Inn to have lunch, and the *maître d'* looked up with some anxiety and then mentioned quietly, "You can't bring a black person in here." I said, "How could that be? He's in tribal attire. He's an African statesman." When I was told, "You can't," I replied, "This is going to be a terrible embarrassment for the university, our country, and certainly to me." He said, "No, I'm sorry. You can't."

The wheels went whirring around in my head for 30 seconds or so, and I said, "By any chance do you have a private room, and would that be all right?" He said, "Oh, sure. That would be no problem." I turned around to the prime minister, who had been unaware of this discussion, and said, "Mr. Prime Minister, they are so honored to have you here they have offered us a private room." He never realized what had happened, but to me this was quite a telling incident. It reinforced sentiments I already had that probably played a role in shaping some of my values.

My parents, before helping install me at Princeton, had done a road trip with me and my sister. We had visited Monticello, Mount Vernon, and other parts of Virginia. I was very shocked, as a Californian, to see establishments—restaurants, gas stations, and so forth—with designations of "No Negroes" or "Coloreds Only," for drinking fountains, restrooms, and other facilities. I think that, having come from a very tolerant, mixed, and diverse experience in Switzerland, this was an exposure to another side of life that I'm sure had some impact on the formulation of my thinking. It left quite an impression on me as a teenager.

You mentioned Princeton having a lot of students from down there. I wonder what you might have noticed about your fellow students from the South, if anything in particular.

There were some who were quite openly bigoted. I remember getting involved in debates and even writing a letter to the editor of the *Daily Princetonian* about a piece that someone had written. Those attitudes came mainly from classmates who were graduates of southern and some other prep schools. Coming from California or the Midwest, you almost felt you were the subject of a milder form of discrimination. You had to prove that you weren't someone who had just fallen off a turnip truck.

I'd like to spend a little more time on your summer trip to Africa. You've given other accounts and mentioned also today tailing these diplomats in various forms while you were there. How did you go about arranging contacts with those who were there in diplomatic roles?

Some of it was through my friend Don Emmerson's father, who was aware of people traveling to one place or the other. Other contacts were just persons we met while traveling. Part of the summer I was traveling with my friend, but he went off to a student conference in Europe, so the rest of the time I was traveling by myself. I would learn someone was going to the next town. We covered quite an expanse of Nigeria, a very large country.

What did you observe, and what interactions did you have directly, with those in diplomatic or consular roles?

These experiences had a major impact on me in terms of what ultimately caused me to change my viewpoint about a career in the Foreign Service, a certain disillusionment. Bear in mind that this was before the Peace Corps and before, perhaps, a more enlightened attitude in the Foreign Service. I think in many ways things were unchanged from the way they were in the 1920s and '30s. There were consular officials stuck in these remote places, some of them just drinking too much every night, wishing they were home and having little if any contact with the local community. There were two individuals who impressed me as clear exceptions. It turned out that one had just submitted his resignation, and the other was about to. They each told me they had sent reports back to Washington saying "if we only take such-and-such action we can be on the right side, or the winning side, of this particular development." Their reports were just ignored. These two persons clearly were disillusioned.

With all of that, going back to college, I really began to wonder if I wanted to devote my life to that type of service. I decided, not at all out of the purest of motives, to apply to law school as a way of postponing the decision of what to do with my life and perhaps leaving the broadest range of options open. That's what I did, and I chose to go to Stanford. I thought it was time to get back to California and just see where the law school training would take me.

Before we leave the Woodrow Wilson School, I wonder if you could say more about the school itself. That was one of your two choices as an undergraduate, to go there, specifically with a career in the Foreign Service in mind. What else did you get out of that program, even though you ended up changing your career plans?

I was quite enamored with the cross-departmental discipline that one could pursue. I was very impressed with the faculty, and I liked the conferences where everyone would write a paper on one aspect of a problem. Then two or three dozen students would get together and work things out, as if you were part of an international organization. I also took some courses in domestic political science. I was getting some background in that area as well.

You mentioned that you chaired a conference on disarmament while you were a student. How did you organize it and carry it out?

What I remember specifically was trying to get people together and come up with productive proposals. I guess that was sort of a preview of some later challenges I had as Chief Justice—taking a problem, getting different points of view, trying to blend them into policy recommendations. I'd say that what sticks with me—more than the actual substance—was the process and learning about process.

It sounds as if it did raise your political awareness to be there. What were your interests and pursuits in that arena while at Princeton?

I did have a couple of things that could be termed "college capers," one strictly not political but one that was political. One of my roommates and I decided that we would try to ride the rails and sneak on board a train. We did hop freight cars for a couple of days. That was quite an experience, including getting locked in a boxcar briefly, and being chased by a railroad detective. That created a bit of a stir.

Where did the idea spring from, do you recall?

I don't. It must have been some romanticized idea that came from reading something. I'll blame it on a book. [Laughter]

You have a scrapbook that shows there was newspaper coverage of your escapade?

Yes, both in the college paper and in the New Jersey newspaper then known as the *Trenton Evening Times*.

But the more significant caper was in the fall of 1960. As you'll recall, there was a series of debates between Richard M. Nixon and John F. Kennedy during the presidential campaign. One of those debates was held in New York,[2] and I thought because New York was just an easy one-hour train ride away—not by riding the rails, but this time buying a ticket—that it would be great fun to try to get up there and see this debate. I was planning to go there otherwise just to have a good time and look up some friends in New York and decided I would try to get into the debate. I immediately realized upon showing up at the ABC Studios, which I did in ample time because I thought seating might be scarce, that I was very naïve to think I could get in.

They said, "You have to be a member of the press." I said, "I am a member of the press. I work for a college newspaper." They explained that the credentials were being given out at the two campaign headquarters. Kennedy's was at the old Biltmore Hotel and I went there. People were standing in line, and when I got up to the counter, they asked for my name, and it wasn't on the list of course. I said, "My editor is going to be furious at me and at your campaign too. I've got to cover this story." They said, "There must have been a mistake" and asked what paper I was with, so I said I was from the *Yale Daily News* instead of the *Daily Princetonian*. [Laughter] I didn't want to leave too many tracks.

I got the credential and went back to the ABC Studios. I noticed there were special arrangements made for the photographic element of the press. There was a separate room, and they got to take pictures of the candidates going in and out. I had my camera, my little Brownie or whatever. I took out the camera and of course was looked at with total contempt by all of these professional photographers, who had elaborate equipment and runners who were ready to take their film back to the papers and wire services. I don't think I even had a flash. I had to synchronize taking my pictures with the flashbulbs that were going off. I got some pictures of Nixon and Kennedy and got to see the debate.

Then an announcement was made that the press bus was leaving for Madison Square Garden for a labor rally. It was pretty late in the evening by then. I

---

[2] The fourth and last of those debates took place on October 21, 1960 in New York City.

thought, "Why not see if this can work for the next step of the way?" I got on the bus, no problem, and went to the labor rally. The credential had Kennedy's picture on it and said underneath "press." I realized the ones for staff were identical except at the very bottom they said "staff" instead of "press." If it wasn't completely visible you could pass as staff, which I later used for my benefit.

You were making this up as you went along?

Oh, yes, and these were innocent days. Security precautions were rather minimal. The next announcement was, "The bus is now leaving for LaGuardia Airport." I thought to myself, should I try or not? This is really idiotic; I'm going to be stuck out on Long Island at the airport late at night. But I thought, nothing ventured, nothing gained. The bus went right up onto the tarmac, literally to the stairway. I got onto the press plane that was following Kennedy's plane. The doors closed, and it's the only time in my life that I had the experience of roaring down a runway and having absolutely no idea where the plane was headed.

The plane was filled with working press. In those days some of the reporters covering campaigns carried small typewriters. I figured, I've got to look as if I'm truly involved in the press. Maybe I can make use of my account of this adventure. I started writing up the experiences that I'd had that day. Pierre Salinger, who was press secretary, was going up and down the aisle. I tried to be very casual and said, "Pierre, I've lost my itinerary," because by then I was quite curious where the plane was headed. [Laughter] "Would you mind giving me another copy?"

The first stop was St. Louis, and I think the plane got there just in time for a couple hours' sleep, around six in the morning. I proceeded, with these credentials, to be able to enter buses that were part of the motorcades around St. Louis, Kansas City, Wichita, and the tri-state mining area that encompasses Joplin and part of Oklahoma. There were some incredible sights, such as the motorcade going by a convent with nuns jumping up and down, very enthused about the candidate.

At outdoor events, I could sit up there in the stands without performing press-type duties if I covered the lower part of the badge so I could pass as staff. I remember meeting Senator Stuart Symington; he's included in the photographs I took. In fact, I was seated near President Harry Truman in the stands there, and he said to me, "We've got a winner."

Finally I realized I had midterms coming up and really could not afford to stay any longer. I had to get my parents to wire me some money. I remember taking advantage of my campaign credentials and met some college girls there, who invited me to a couple parties. I had abandoned the campaign at that point and had to make my way back to school from Missouri. I recall the last part of it involved some hitchhiking. My funds again were rather low. My roommates, whom I had called so they wouldn't think I had vanished off the face of the earth, had told the school newspaper about my adventure. The *Daily Princetonian* ran a story and asked me to write two articles about the whole experience, which I did. A story also appeared November 7 on page 2 of the *Washington Post* headlined "Red Faces in Kennedy Camp" about the escapade.

The experience certainly heightened my interest in the domestic political process. Who knows? That, combined with my disillusionment with the prospect of a Foreign Service career, might have helped push me in the direction of law school—without being motivated yet as to what I would want to do with it—knowing that there were avenues other than the one I had been tracked on for so long, namely a career in international affairs.

Having just met all these illustrious politicians, including, I think, Vice President Nixon, along the way—

Yes. I met him just in the context of the press room where I could take photographs at the debate. I didn't get a chance to actually meet Nixon. My meeting with Kennedy was literally a handshake and a couple of words and getting his autograph.

I wonder what effect these various meetings had on you, if any, to come face to face with some of the top political figures and minds of the day.

It certainly made the American political process far more real than it had been to me. It had been a rather abstract academic experience to study the process and the election. Here were live candidates and, of course, all the excitement and thrill of a debate, of crowds, of this other cast of characters, from President Truman to Senator Symington. It was very intriguing.

There was a great emphasis at the time on that series of television debates between Kennedy and Nixon and the venue of television and what effect it might have had on the public's voting and so on. What was your own take on the importance of seeing the two go face to face live that way?

It really was spell-binding for me. We've now become a bit accustomed to presidential debates, which I think are rather sterile compared to this set of debates. The Nixon-Kennedy debates were the very first presidential debates and for me certainly are the most dramatic that have occurred to date. It was incredibly exciting to actually see the individuals parry back and forth. It was almost like watching a boxing match. There were hard blows, there were ducks, everything was happening.

You had done some debating yourself in college.

A bit, yes. But just to see the extent to which they had obviously both prepped themselves and assimilated mountains of detail—just to think they had only a few seconds to retrieve and explicate something in response to an inquiry and to retort—it was almost like a gladiator sport. It was one of the most exciting things I had ever seen.

Did it change your view of either candidate to see him in action that way?

Nixon did show a lot of knowledge about the issues, but he really did suffer in terms of physical appearance. I've read that of those who heard the debates on radio, a larger percentage of them thought Nixon had won, but those who saw it on television thought that Kennedy had won. Having seen the one debate in person, I could see why that would be true, and of course I was a young college student. A lot of us were identifying with the new generation of politicians and were quite caught up in the whole Kennedy mystique.

Upon rereading the two articles that you wrote for your school paper, how do those strike you now, knowing you were forming your own opinions and really coming of age practically at that moment?

Rereading them caused me to relive the excitement. I think there are elements that reflect the outlook, enthusiasm, and brashness of a 20-year-old, which I was at the time. [Laughter] I enjoyed the writing. I was pleased that I was able to wield a pen effectively at that age, before my legal training served to constrict my ability—or at least the appropriateness—of engaging in more colorful writing.

It certainly came in handy later on. Even the Washington Post *got a few licks in, suggesting the Kennedy campaign might be a little embarrassed that you had broken their ranks, and so on. That was quite an event that you pulled off.*

Yes, and my parents got to know that their son was a bit of an adventurer. I think they were surprised by the African adventure and then having heard about the political campaign, they really were. I had seen them the summer before this, when I came back from Africa.

That was a funny story too, because I had not realized that my visa for Nigeria was good for only one entry. When I went off to Ghana and returned to

Nigeria, I was told I was *persona non grata* and had to be out by midnight or I'd be arrested. I got out from Kano and flew to southern France, where my parents were about to arrive, believing I was still in Africa. I engaged in a ruse with Italian friends of my parents who were picking them up from the airport with their chauffeur. I substituted myself for the chauffeur and pulled the cap way down.

Our friends, the Bellinis, engaged my parents in a conversation about their new chauffeur. "Doesn't he drive poorly?" Finally, my parents said, "Yes. He's kind of erratic." With that I took my cap off, turned around, and said, "You can drive with someone else if you prefer." [Laughter] Those were fun days, and my parents got a big kick out of the African trip and later out of the Kennedy caper, as well.

In your own mind, what does it say about the young Ronald M. George that he would conceive of and pull off the Kennedy caper, even if it wasn't planned to such a great extent ahead of time?

Probably that I was—and maybe became and still am—more of a risk taker than some people might assume from a relatively quiet demeanor. However, even though, like my mother, I was a beneficiary of my father's speculation in the stock market, I shared her aversion to that type of risk taking and remained quite cautious when it came to investments. But I share my father's instinct for taking chances and seizing opportunities. I've always subscribed to the view of the French scientist Louis Pasteur that chance favors those who are prepared.

###

Chapter 2

Young Lawyer
June 3, 2011

We agreed that we would start today reviewing your reasons and thoughts about going to law school after you finished your degree at Princeton in 1961. What was in your mind about the next best step for your career?

As we discussed, I don't regard my motives for entering into the study of law as necessarily the most noble. I had had this idea of going into the Foreign Service of the U.S. State Department, an idea that I was pursuing for several years, and that was the focus of my undergraduate studies. Then I quickly became disillusioned with that prospect, so I decided upon an application to law school as a way of postponing the decision of what to do with my professional life, and as a way of leaving open the greatest number of options. That was what influenced me, and I thought it was time to come back to California. So I was very happy to be admitted to Stanford Law School and to commence my study of law at that time in the fall of 1961.

What do you recall about the process of applying for law school, which I gather was a bit different than it is today?

With a great amount of sympathy to today's students, I feel things were a lot easier back then. If you went to a fairly good school and you'd done fairly well, it was not at all as competitive as it seems to be today. Certainly, once you graduated as an undergraduate or from law school, there were many opportunities. I'm not saying you could just pick anything you might have wanted, but you had a broad array of possibilities.

How did you go about moving to Palo Alto and getting yourself set up to live there?

I could have stayed at what was then the law dorm, Crothers Hall, but I felt like having more independence. I managed to find a bungalow that had been the carriage house of a fine old home in the old part of Palo Alto. I believe it was 1166 Ramona Street, nestled under a gigantic oak tree. It was a very bucolic setting, near campus, and I resided there alone and enjoyed it. That was the bulk of my stay there.

What kind of a financial commitment was Stanford in those days?

All I recall is that it was just a mere fraction of what things are today. Some parents now spend more to send their children to preschool than some of us were paying for undergraduate and law school education back then.

By west coast standards Stanford was an old law school, even at that time, having gone back to the end of the 19th century. What did you hear about the school before you went there, in terms of its program?

All I really knew was that it had an outstanding faculty, as well as some very noted visiting scholars. It had a track record of luring faculty members out to teach for a year from back east and then, after putting them up in nice housing that was university owned, extending an offer to escape the eastern climate permanently. I think Stanford attracted a great number of very fine faculty members that way.

You must have had certain expectations about the study of law itself. How did those compare with what you found there?

I have to say that I didn't find everything of great interest. I was involved as an undergraduate in the study of very broad questions of public policy, both international and domestic. Much of the study of law struck me as involved in a lot of minutiae, so it was quite an adjustment for me and I can't say that I gravitated to all of it. Some of it I found boring and considered drudgery. Other things I found very interesting.

I think one of the main influences upon my career, really, was to study constitutional law with a noted scholar who had come out from Columbia, Professor

Gerald Gunther. He made me very interested in combining my long-term interest in public policy with my training in the law, which is in turn what ultimately caused me to apply to be a deputy attorney general in the California Department of Justice.

I don't mean to imply that he was the only person who imbued the study of law with policy considerations and made it interesting. I was surprised to truly enjoy my class in tax law because of my tax law professor, Joseph Sneed, who also served during his career as the No. 2 man in the U.S. Department of Justice, dean of the Duke University law school, and ultimately a very fine judge on U.S. Court of Appeals for the Ninth Circuit. Instead of just teaching a lot of I.R.S. regulations and provisions of the Internal Revenue Code, he made tax law come alive by pointing out the social, political, and economic policies that were furthered by changes in the tax law. That was a surprisingly interesting course for me. But it was Professor Gunther, who wrote a very fine biography of Judge Learned Hand after clerking for him, who really made the law come alive for me in terms of my interest in making it my career.

What was Professor Gunther's style of teaching and getting students excited about these areas?

He certainly covered constitutional law in a very broad sweep in terms of tying it to what was going on in the nation, explaining how the decisions of the U.S. Supreme Court—which were the primary ones focused on—blended with historical developments. He covered the human side of the actual litigants involved in the particular litigation. It was something that was very interesting to me on a historical, personal, and policy basis.

What opportunity did you have to get to know him personally outside the classroom?

Not all that much. He was not as approachable as some professors who would hang out in the student lounge and play poker with the students until the wee small hours. There were some faculty members who were very close in their contacts with the students, but I don't believe Professor Gunther was among them. He was someone whose class was very stimulating and whom people had a lot of respect for.

How soon did this idea sprout with you of applying to the California attorney general's office?

My recollection is that this took place in the second year of law school. I considered a number of public offices, but I was attracted to the office of the attorney general in the California Department of Justice because it offered a wide scope of public law practice and had a major focus on appellate practice, which was more in keeping with my particular interests from a policy standpoint.

It sounds as if policy came across rather strongly in your program. I don't know if that had any relationship to the person who was dean of the school at that time, who I gather had a lot of interests in international law?

Yes, Dean Carl Spaeth did have that interest, that's correct. He certainly made a point of trying to keep a broad range of curricula available to the students. I think he left his imprint on the law school that way.

What sort of force was he as a leader?

He left during my second year at the law school, so I didn't have much in the way of direct contact with him.

You described living alone in this former carriage house rather than mixing it up day and night with the other students. What were your study habits as a law student?

They were probably not the best. I know that some of my classmates would tease me about my trying to drag them off to see movies. I did my best studying late at night, so I'd come back to my little carriage house and burn the midnight oil and sometimes miss an early class if I'd been up too late. I wasn't as disciplined as so many of my classmates. Most fell into a certain stereotype. They seemed very, very serious, with a few exceptions.

Does that suggest you were not as pressed to the grindstone, shall we say?

Probably. Putting the situation in a more positive light, in terms of my classmates, I think they were better motivated. They had more definite ideas of what they wanted from law school and were able to really focus on that, whereas I was still somewhat at sea in terms of what I was going to do with a career. I think they all knew they wanted to be on the law review, and they wanted to earn a certain grade point average so they would be attractive candidates for the large law firms. I didn't have the sense, really, of what I wanted to do, at least at the beginning.

What about extracurricular activities?

There were some haphazard activities here and there, going out for the usual beer and that type of thing. I even wrote a little spoof in one of the student publications about the somewhat dreary and overly regimented life of my classmates, which I guess was an outlet for expressing my whimsical take on it.

Say more about your law school class. What was the makeup of that group, generally speaking?

It was a pretty broad mix nationally. We had people who were graduates of fine schools around the country and some from lesser known schools. There were some with whom I established friendships that extended beyond the law school years, but for the most part I think people sort of scattered afterwards. I've gone down to the school when asked to give a talk or participate in some event now and then, but I haven't been very involved in class postgraduation activities as such.

How do you evaluate the program at the time you went through it? How well did it prepare you to go on?

I think it did prepare me well, and it really caused me to think and speak and write as a lawyer. It's quite a transformation when all of a sudden you wake up and you say, maybe with a bit of trepidation, I'm really starting to think like a lawyer.

I remember taking hikes in the hills above the campus, walking up a field and seeing a row of oak trees gyrating quite a bit in the wind of a storm. I looked at these beautiful trees and started thinking about something from my torts class, as to who would be liable if one of the limbs were to come crashing down on me or someone else, depending upon where the trunk and the roots were on one side of the fence marking the property line, and the branch, maybe, being located on the other side of the fence. I thought, oh no. I'm beginning to think like a lawyer. [Laughter]

You talked about the importance of learning to write and how you focused on that as an undergraduate. How do you think that skill advanced while you were in law school?

I think it got honed down, just the need to express oneself clearly in writing. Also, with the Socratic method, having to think on your feet in a crowded classroom, occasionally with a rather difficult professor.

One of my professors was very much of a terror. His name was Moffatt Hancock. He was legally blind. When someone would respond to one of his questions and muddle up various concepts instead of approaching them totally analytically, the professor would say, "You're serving this up like a dog's dinner—throwing everything in and just mixing it all together." [Laughter] Being in his class was truly like something out of *The Paper Chase*. One fellow, who had been a veteran of the Korean War, was chewed out by the professor and questioned as to how he ever got into college, let alone law school, and was told he didn't belong in law school. He was told to leave the classroom, and I believe he never returned, period, not just to the class but to law school. I remember one occasion when the professor called on someone in the front row. Hancock thought this student was present and was deliberately taking advantage of the professor's lack of vision in not responding. Hancock went up to the seat, which contained only the jacket of another student. But the professor grabbed this jacket and shook it furiously. There was some subdued laughter, but people didn't dare laugh very much. Then Professor Hancock said, "That's what I *would* do if someone were seated there and were not answering."

Professor Hancock was always very concerned that the students in our large, first-year property class might be taking advantage of his visual handicap and not answering when in fact they were there, because people were so terrified at being called upon by him. In terms of Professor Hancock's vision, if you were at the periphery of the seating chart he could hold it up an inch or so away from his eye and spot your name and you would be called upon, whereas if you were in the center you were safe from being called. Students would take advantage and not respond.

Although Professor Hancock truly inspired terror in his students, he had a devilish sense of humor when he was teaching. I actually enjoyed his class very much in terms of the way he would convey otherwise deadly dull concepts of property law.

We had only four females in our graduating class, so that's an indication of how things have changed, because when I checked a couple years ago the majority of students in the most recent Stanford Law School class were female. But four was a number sufficient, still, to ensure the first-place standing in the class to one of our classmates, Brooksley Born. She went on to make quite a name for herself in terms of her role in the Clinton administration's policy regarding derivatives. She was head of an agency now known as the *Commodity Futures Trading Commission*. The late Judge Pam Rymer of the Ninth Circuit U.S. Court of Appeals was another one of those four women in our class. There was another woman who became a professor, and the fourth one, I believe, went into law practice.

As you say, he brought alive an area of the law that you might not otherwise have connected with. It sounds as if the women in your class fared all right?

They certainly did. They were quite outstanding, and of course Stanford had a history of women of achievement, including Justice Sandra Day O'Connor, who was several years earlier.

To finish up about your time in law school, how much of an emphasis or aware-ness was there among the students and in your classes of what was going on in California's own judicial system at the time?

This brings to mind a criticism that I developed, at least in later years. I don't know that it was on my mind when I was in law school. There is, I think, an insufficient focus in California law schools on the role of California law—and on the role of state court jurisprudence generally—in the overall formulation of law and of decision making. I don't know whether it's because our better schools like to see themselves—as they sometimes will actually put it—as "the Harvard of the West," but there's almost a snobbish attitude about federal deci-sions, even at the district court level, being more worthy of attention than the law of state courts, even our home courts in California.

Now, some of that has changed, and there was a symposium last year that Stanford gave on state constitutions. My remarks related to that subject were published as a foreword to an issue of the *Stanford Law Review*.[1] I want to be fair about that, but generally speaking if you look at where the emphasis has been, I think that state law has been very much neglected in our major law schools, at least in California, especially when you consider that roughly 95 per-cent of the cases filed in American courts are filed in state courts. I believe much more emphasis should be given to studying state court law, particularly because there are many areas that, under our U.S. Constitution, are clearly within the province of the states, so all of the law will be state-court law in those areas. I would like to see more of a balance in that regard. I will say that the University of California Berkeley School of Law a couple years ago had an all-day presen-tation on the California courts. I don't want to be extreme in my viewpoint here about the lack of balance. There are some very happy exceptions, but speaking in general terms I think that in our law schools, including our California law schools, there is an insufficient treatment of state law and its importance.

Even if not prompted to do so in your courses at Stanford, to what extent did you have California's system and its courts and its decisions on your radar screen? Were those developments reaching you at all?

---

[1] Keynote Address, *Symposium*, State Constitutions, 62 Stan. L. Rev. 1515 (2010).

They really weren't, so to the extent I was focused on obtaining employment after my graduation, it was more on having a career in public law and in particular, with regard to the attorney general's office, being able to practice appellate law, rather than the actual substance of what that law might be.

Coming back to California for law school after an absence, did it appear that California's political and social climate had changed much while you were away?

I didn't take note of this. But like most people, I recall where I was when I learned of President John F. Kennedy's assassination: That was while I was already back at Stanford. In terms of coming back to the West, I'd actually given some thought to going into politics, and with that in mind I certainly felt it would be better for me not to have seven years of undergraduate and professional studies all back East at Ivy League schools, but to reaffirm my California roots. That helped guide me to come back to California for law school. I ultimately chose not to pursue a political career, but it was something that was on my mind when I made the decision on where to go to law school.

May I ask what sorts of things you were considering?

Perhaps running for legislative office. I never focused on a particular office or a particular sequence, but I believe along with my disillusionment with the possibility of a career in the Foreign Service came an interest in domestic policy, so my academic and personal interests shifted from international policy to domestic policy, and with that came some thought about the possibility of running for political office. Once I had my experience in the attorney general's office, that in turn led me to consider a judicial career rather than a career in the executive or legislative branches, but I don't suppose I really thought about this at the time I started off in the attorney general's office. It just evolved somewhat spontaneously, not with a lot of forethought or plotting.

Since we talked about your brief experience with President Kennedy's campaign, would you tell me where you were at the time of his assassination and what you recall about that event from your own memory?

I remember driving up to the law school and hearing it on the radio and being, of course, stunned and totally shocked and then obsessed with the events of the subsequent days in terms of Lee Harvey Oswald and the funeral and other proceedings in Washington.

As you say, that did change our whole climate for some period of time, certainly over the long term but in the immediate aftermath.

It certainly did, and of course everything else going on in the 1960s including Reverend Martin Luther King, Jr.'s assassination and then Senator Robert Kennedy's assassination, which again—I remember where my wife and I were, in southern France. We had ordered breakfast room service, and the server brought it in and shared that news with us. Of course, I never could have imagined that I would ultimately end up handling the prosecution on appeal against Sirhan Sirhan for that assassination. It's a cliché to say it, but on those momentous occasions, I think most of us remember exactly where we were and what we were doing.

What else comes back to you about law school that you'd like to say, if anything, and its influences on you as a young person?

Again, although I've mentioned it, I think not so much the substance of the studies—apart from constitutional law, which really did tie into my later professional interests as a prosecutor and as a judge. It really was the process of dispute resolution, the process of learning how to think, and speak, and write in a persuasive, logical, and clear fashion. Those were invaluable lessons from law school that certainly influenced me throughout my professional life and to this day.

We've touched on how you became interested in the state attorney general's office, so walk me through, if you would, the close of law school and taking the bar exam in advance of beginning your professional career there.

Of course, the bar exam was something to prepare for and to be anxious about. Then, while the results were pending, I started work at the Los Angeles office of the attorney general, at first as a legal assistant and then ultimately as a deputy attorney general once I was admitted to the bar.

Working in that office was a wonderful event from the first day on, making the switch from purely academic or theoretical contemplation of the law to real-life disputes. I felt truly blessed by having several old timers there who were, many of them, acknowledged statewide as among the foremost appellate lawyers, and having my work reviewed by them. The head of criminal appeals was William E. James—Bill James, as he was known—and he was considered one of the very finest appellate lawyers in California. There was Gordon Ringer, who later became a superior court judge, Clark Moore, who also became a judge, and a host of others. In a way, it was a continuation of my learning process, only in a real rather than a theoretical world. I was placed in criminal appeals as my primary assignment, with a secondary assignment in criminal trials. Either the section head or one of the half dozen supervising attorneys would review the draft of the brief I would prepare. Each supervisor had his or her own style, and I was just soaking up all their individual wisdom and then ultimately crafting it into my own approach, in terms of analysis and writing style. But they each had something somewhat different to offer, and it was like having half a dozen professors teaching the same course on alternate sessions. I learned a lot from each of them.

I also learned a lot from my contemporaries in the office. We had a number of fine people in the office, some of whom went on to do other great things. In fact, as an interesting sign of the times, one of the persons working in the office was Sam Williams, who joined the attorney general's office because, as an African American, he could not obtain employment elsewhere, even though he was very well qualified. Showing how times changed over the coming years, he ultimately was elected president of the State Bar of California. But at that point, in the 1960s, he was unable to obtain employment in a law firm because of his race.

My assignment to trials as a secondary assignment involved two types of cases, basically. One was when, for some reason or other, the district attorney's office in a Southern California county was disqualified from prosecuting a case and had to recuse itself, perhaps because of some personal or professional tie between a member of the office and the parties to the litigation. Young deputy attorneys general would be sent to try these cases in Los Angeles or sometimes in outlying counties.

I remember trying several cases in Santa Maria in northern Santa Barbara County and in Imperial County, where in those days if you said you were from Los Angeles you might as well have come from the People's Republic of China. You were not welcome. [Laughter] That's a generality, but there's a lot of truth in it. I even remember signs on clerks' counters that read, "We don't care how you do it in Los Angeles. . . ."

I had a very interesting assignment in 1970. There were riots in Santa Barbara, at the University of California, Santa Barbara, at Isla Vista. In the course of those riots, a student named Kevin Moran was shot to death, apparently by a National Guardsman. Everybody ended up being disqualified on that case—the local bench and the D.A., who would have presented the evidence at a coroner's inquest. I was sent up there initially to give legal advice to the numerous law enforcement agencies that were involved in trying to put down the riots. There were several police departments and sheriff's departments and state entities. It was like a war zone, with helicopters and a lot of violent activity going on. Because of my role, when it came time to investigate the death of Kevin Moran, I was assigned to conduct the investigation with the assistance of California Department of Justice agents, and to present a coroner's inquest before a visiting Orange County judge, because the local judiciary was disqualified.

It was a fascinating case. It was established that the rifle of one of the National Guardsmen—who had arrived on the scene in a National Guard truck and had jumped off the bed of the vehicle—did discharge. Kevin Moran was on the steps of the Bank of America, which was one of those modular or trailer-type structures. He was fatally shot. No one could figure out whether the National Guardsman was really responsible or how he could have been, because it was established that his rifle was pointed upwards. There was also a fence between him and the Bank of America steps. Yet ballistic tests suggested that the fatal bullet was fired from his weapon. What the investigation ultimately concluded—and of course it's the forensic lab people who get the credit for resolving this—I was just the lawyer presenting the case—was the following.

In the course of this riot, students gathered rocks from the roofs of the flat-roofed apartment buildings in the vicinity—white limestone rocks that are often used as roofing insulation. The air was thick with these flying missiles being thrown at the bank. The ballistics examinations revealed that apparently the discharged bullet ricocheted off one of these numerous pieces of limestone rock that were flying through the air and then was deflected downward. When the bullet was analyzed, in the lead they found two things of interest. One was a fiber from the student who was standing immediately next to Kevin Moran. Apparently the bullet went through his shirt without wounding him but managed to collect a fiber and then went into Kevin Moran. Most significantly, there was an odd mineral deposit in the lead of the bullet that matched the limestone that was being thrown on that occasion.

That was quite a whodunit or at least a "how it happened" episode. The coroner's inquest was conducted in the tile-floored mural room of the wonderful old Santa Barbara courthouse with quite an audience. Because I was the sole attorney on the case, I was on my feet there for the better part of two or three days presenting this evidence. Of course, the determination had to be made by the judge sitting as the presiding officer as to whether there was a purposeful homicide or a negligent act or just a pure accident.

Which way did it go?

It was found to be accidental. I also believe that the safety was defective on the rifle, which caused it to discharge.

I had another unusual assignment, which was to accompany and advise Attorney General Evelle Younger in his brief testimony at the Charles Manson trial, concerning his prior offer—when he was L.A. District Attorney—of a possible plea agreement to one of Manson's codefendants.

In addition to the cases where the D.A. was disqualified, the other major category of cases where deputy attorneys general would conduct trial prosecutions in the criminal area was the auto forfeiture cases. The forfeiture law at the time caused the state attorney general's office rather than the D.A.'s office to bring these cases. They were technically civil, but they were criminal in nature and therefore we in the criminal division tried them. The issue would be whether a vehicle had been employed to transport contraband drugs. In those instances the attorney general's office would file a lawsuit typically entitled, *People of the State of California v. One 1959 Chevrolet.* [Laughter]

The law was quite harsh in some of its applications. In some instances, of course, it was clear that a drug dealer was transporting drugs and, one might say, deserved to lose his or her vehicle when that was established. But the law extended beyond that, to where the owner of the vehicle had loaned his or her car to someone without any knowledge of the purpose for which it would be used. I remember one case where a man even said to his daughter, "I know you haven't been well and you have to go to the pharmacy to get your medications. You can use the car for that purpose, but that's it, and no hitchhikers." She ended up loaning the vehicle to someone who had a passenger who lit up some sort of narcotic, and the father lost his car. Although I considered such proceedings harsh, I felt obliged to enforce them because the law at the time required it, but I had a couple of colleagues who just said, "I cannot prosecute this type of case." Those auto forfeiture cases often were jury trials and were where new deputies typically learned how to try a case. They were quite easy. They would take only a day or two, but they were something that kind of fell between the cracks. The D.A.'s office didn't handle them, and we were stuck with them. It was a training tool.

I take it there were quite a few of them?

Yes, there were in those days. But putting those aside, the other notable trial prosecution that I had in addition to the inquest was the following. One day I was called up to the office of Charles O'Brien, the chief deputy attorney general, the person immediately under the attorney general. He inquired, "Did you hear what the *Los Angeles Free Press* has done?" They were an underground newspaper. "They somehow obtained a roster of our 80 California Department of Justice Bureau of Narcotic Enforcement undercover agents and published the names, home addresses, and home phone numbers of these agents, putting them and their families at great risk." He said, "I want you to conduct an investigation. Although the horse is out of the barn, try through civil proceedings to stop any further dissemination of this information and, if you can, get back the actual roster—even though the information is out there. Second, see what criminal action can be taken against those responsible."

Why do you think Mr. O'Brien selected you?

I really don't know, because my primary experience was in appeals, although I'd handled some trials. The case did call for some creative approaches in coming up with civil and criminal complaints. Also, knowing that it was a delicate matter, maybe he thought I would deal with it tactfully. After all, going against a newspaper was something most public officials would not relish.

I was given a couple of agents to work with. I contacted the *Los Angeles Free Press* and indicated that the attorney general was very upset about this, that undoubtedly there were violations of the law involved in their apparent acquisition of this information and that, although the information was out, we wanted the roster back.

Ultimately, after making a couple of phone calls, I was approached by an attorney representing the *Los Angeles Free Press* and its publisher. I told him, "It would be important to get this roster back, and I can't make any promises to you but we need to have it back. We don't want an original roster floating around even though the information is out." I made arrangements for the attorney to come by the attorney general's office and hand it to me. As soon as he did, I promptly passed it on to one of the criminalists in the Department of Justice, who sprayed the roster with a substance called Ninhydrin. That immediately caused a series of fingerprints to appear as purple splotches on the document. The agents were able to track down those prints and identify them as belonging to Art Kunkin, the publisher, a reporter on the staff, Gerald Applebaum, and the thief, Jerry Reznick, an employee in the attorney general's mail room. He had apparently taken the roster from the mail and sold it to the *Los Angeles Free Press*.

Now that we had that evidence, I filed a civil action and obtained an injunction to prevent the *Los Angeles Free Press* and its officers and employees from disseminating this information to any other entity or persons and from further publishing it, although that was really beside the point at this juncture.

My instructions had been to also proceed criminally, so I worked with the district attorney's office, appeared before the Los Angeles County Grand Jury, and obtained an indictment against the newspaper and its personnel. We had to come up with an appropriate crime to charge. With regard to the thief this was easy. It is a crime to remove an official government document without permission from the governmental custodian. But with regard to the *Free Press* and its publisher and its reporter, we had to be more imaginative. I came up with the theory it was receiving stolen property, because the roster was a physical object that had been stolen and then acquired under circumstances indicating that the defendants knew it had been stolen. With that in mind, I proceeded to embark upon a jury trial that lasted about six weeks with cocounsel, a deputy D.A. The two of us ended up obtaining convictions against the *Free Press* and its personnel. Those convictions were upheld in the Court of Appeal. The *Free Press* then sought review in the California Supreme Court.

At the same time that this court was considering the *Free Press* case, there was a lot of stir in the media about the Pentagon Papers case involving Daniel Ellsberg. It became evident to me that the California Supreme Court might be very much concerned about what the implications might be in a less tawdry circumstance than that presented by a stolen roster of undercover narcotic officers' names and addresses. What about something that might present more of a justification for theft and publication despite the law being to the contrary? Ultimately, I believe motivated by that concern, the California Supreme Court in *People v. Kunkin*[2] granted review and reversed the convictions of the *Free Press* and its employees on the theory that the evidence was insufficient to establish the defendants' knowledge that the roster was stolen. My reaction at the time, and it probably is still my reaction today, was that reversing the convictions for insufficiency of the evidence was really just a means of dodging the First Amendment issue presented by the Pentagon Papers type of situation.

One account I read described it as reversing on a technicality and that there was certainly no question the material had been stolen to begin with. What was your response upon learning that? How did it change the overall picture in your mind?

I guess by then I had had enough experience with difficult cases—and sometimes losing them—that I took it in stride. I recognized that there were some rather legitimate issues being posed by the Pentagon Papers situation at the time. I felt that if I were to lose the case, I probably would have preferred to lose it on the First Amendment question and have that fascinating issue directly confronted by the court, rather than having the court duck out by the back door. That was probably my main sentiment.

Had that happened to you before?

---

[2] Citations for reported appellate court opinions are listed at the conclusion of this volume in the Index of Cases Cited.

Not exactly in that fashion, although when we get to my appellate practice I had some question in one of the death penalty cases about whether an issue was being directly confronted or not. On the other hand, there's an old maxim of constitutional law that I had occasion to quote on more than one occasion in authoring opinions for the California Supreme Court once I joined that court. It is that a court should, where possible, avoid resolving a case in a manner that would cast doubt upon the constitutionality of a statute, and should avoid constitutional issues where it is possible to do so and resolve the case on a narrower ground. I don't know that this approach would extend to coming up with something that I thought was not very justifiable as a basis for reversing the *Free Press* convictions, but rather if there were two bases for resolving a case, or two ways of interpreting a statute, one of which would render the statute subject to constitutional doubt and the other one not, that you go for the approach that would avoid that problem. I think this maxim is not one that I would have applied in my own review of the *Free Press* case. On other hand, I recognize that, especially at that time, it would have put the California Supreme Court in a very difficult position in terms of upholding this prosecution while having to come up with some very clear standards that would distinguish it from a case involving more legitimate free press issues. That might have been a task that the court wasn't yet willing or able to undertake.

Chief Justice Don Wright was leading that court by then. Do you have a particular view of him in all this?

I really did not at that point, although he ended up authoring the court's opinion in the *Free Press* case. I wasn't viewing things then in a way that focused so much on the individual propensities of the justices. I know Chief Justice Wright was considered a very practical, pragmatic individual, so this is something that I'm sure must have been on his mind, to avoid the rather difficult First Amendment issue.

We'll talk later about my appearance before him and his colleagues in matters concerning the death penalty as well as a meeting that I had with him in the wake of that. But at this point I didn't have any particular personal relationship with Chief Justice Wright.

The Los Angeles Free Press *case was a fascinating development for you personally. What do you think you took away from that that you could use later on?*

The whole process of decision making, up and down the spectrum of courts, was very interesting to me in terms of having a case—and it was the only such case I ever had—where I actually investigated the case, brought the charges specifically to a grand jury, then tried the case, and handled it on appeal. This was a unique experience for me, just seeing a case go from more or less a raw factual dispute, crystallize into discrete legal issues, and then see it make its course through various tribunals in our judicial system. Of course, it also gave me good experience in terms of trying a difficult and lengthy jury case before a wonderful trial judge, Harold Ackerman. He was a very learned and pleasant judge to try a case before.

I was interested when you said you were quickly assigned in the Los Angeles attorney general's office to criminal appeals as your primary assignment. What portion of that staff of deputy attorneys general was working in that area?

It's difficult for me to say. First of all, of course, the office was just a fraction of the size it is today. I'm fairly certain—because of an assignment I had in 1971—that the entire Los Angeles office then included 110 attorneys. We didn't have a San Diego office at that time; I believe we just had San Francisco, Sacramento, and Los Angeles. The reason I recall is that there were three divisions of the office: criminal, civil, and a third one now called the division of public rights. There was one deputy assigned to be in charge of the Los Angeles office on a rotating basis from each of the three divisions. For several months in 1971, it was my turn to be in charge of the day-to-day operations in the newly created position of administrative assistant in charge of the Los Angeles office. I would guess—and it really isn't much more than an approximation—that we probably had about 15 to 20 attorneys in the criminal appeals section. It could be a few less, it could be a few more.

I'm trying to get a sense of the big picture of that office and how the bulk of the workload was spread out. How were the assignments made on an individual basis within criminal appeals?

I don't know exactly how or why individuals were given particular assignments. I know that you could ask for assignments, but I'm sure that wasn't the beginning and end of it all.

Were you seeking that sort of assignment?

I did seek criminal because I knew that I would have the greatest opportunity to appear in the appellate courts and be involved in constitutional law, which I had found so interesting in law school, and to handle policy matters generally. There were sections such as tax law, where you might never get to court, or at least not more than once a year. There were some other sections where you got to court more frequently, torts and condemnation, but really in terms of being in court, criminal appeals was where it was at. That was my primary assignment. It involved being given the doghouse of a case—that's what they were called, these binders with the clerk's and reporter's transcripts and the appellant's opening brief. It was expected that you'd have your respondent's brief ready within a certain amount of time, depending upon the complexity and length of the trial proceedings. Then you'd bring your draft to whoever was assigned to be your reviewer on that case.

What was also exciting is once you had been there long enough, they would give you death penalty cases. These cases certainly came with their fallbacks—working on lengthy transcripts containing gruesome facts and many complex issues—but the attraction of those cases was that under our California Constitution, then and now, they're classified as automatic appeals that go directly to the California Supreme Court, bypassing our intermediate Courts of Appeal. So you have the experience, which I think was almost unique in any kind of law practice for a young or beginning lawyer, of arguing before the California Supreme Court.

I found myself having a number of death penalty cases. Ultimately there were 11 cases, some capital and some noncapital, that I argued before the California Supreme Court. That in turn lead me to the next step where, when I was 28 years old, a case I handled in the California Supreme Court was granted certiorari review by the U.S. Supreme Court. That was *Chimel v. California,* in which I made the first of six oral arguments before the high court.

Let's do talk about that. Fill me in, if you would, on the whole detail of being admitted to practice before the U.S. Supreme Court. What was the sequence of all these things happening?

I have in my scrapbook the telegram that I received from the clerk of the U.S. Supreme Court stating that certiorari was granted in *Chimel v. California.* "Letter to follow." Before I actually saw the telegram—which was addressed to the attorney general, not to me personally—Barbara and I were having dinner at a pizza parlor and heard the news over the radio that this case had been granted review. I could tell from the description of what was involved—the legal issues and the underlying facts—that the case involved someone who was a coin collection thief. My case of *People v. Chimel* had become *Chimel v. California.*

Fill me in, if you would, on People v. Chimel, *the lead-in to this.*

Maybe as a preface that is instructive on the often mispronounced name of this case, I'll mention that in a subsequent case called *Hill v. California,* one of the issues was a question of the retroactivity of the holding in *Chimel v. Califor-nia*. Justice Brennan inquired of me, because I had been counsel on the *Chimel* case, whether I could assist the court with "the official legal pronunciation" of the name of that case. I responded that, "although there have been about six dif-ferent variants," I had the official pronunciation "from the horse's mouth" or "at least according to Mr. Chimel,"[3] because there was a proceeding that the Orange County district attorney's office had asked me to participate in involving Mr. Chimel on remand from the U.S. Supreme Court. I actually learned that Mr. Chimel himself pronounced it "Shy Mel." A few weeks later, I was arguing a case before the California Supreme Court that did not involve the *Chimel* case—it didn't even involve search and seizure issues, as did *Chimel*—and I concluded my oral argument by saying, "If there are no further questions from the court, respondent will submit." Justice Mosk said he had read the account of the oral argument in *Hill v. California*, in which I was asked by Justice Brennan to elu-cidate on the pronunciation of the *Chimel* case. Mosk observed there had been differences among the justices of the California Supreme Court on that subject and asked me to clarify for them what I had shared with the U.S. Supreme Court, which I proceeded to do.

The issue in *Chimel* was whether a longstanding precedent of the U.S. Su-preme Court, *United States v. Rabinowitz*, should be overruled. That precedent recognized an exception to the general requirement of a search warrant to con-duct a search of premises. The exception was that when law enforcement offic-ers make an arrest and then conduct a search incident to that arrest—and those were the operative words, "incident to arrest"—the search may be conducted without the usual requirement of a warrant. There is always this overlying re-quirement of reasonableness of a police search, but it was deemed reasonable under those circumstances to not only search the person of the arrestee—his or her body and clothing—but also, if the arrest was to take place inside, let's say, the residence of the arrestee, the fact of an arrest would give the authorities the right to search, without a warrant, the entire residence, from attic down to base-ment, and that would be deemed reasonable, whereas otherwise if officers went to a residence and no arrest was involved, they would need a search warrant to conduct that same search. In fact, it was my understanding that often arrests were timed or calculated to take place so that there would be this right to con-duct the search of the entire residence without having to set forth probable cause in an affidavit seeking a search warrant. This type of warrantless search was a very basic tool of everyday law enforcement. Its validity was the issue.

---

[3] 6 *Crim. Law Reporter*, pp. 4133–4135 (Jan. 28, 1970).

In the six oral arguments that I ultimately had before the U.S. Supreme Court, there were some where there were almost unnerving periods of silence, with no questions. The other extreme, typified by the *Chimel* case, was when I would be barraged by questions. It seemed sometimes that all nine justices were firing away at the same time. *Chimel* was a very, very active oral argument. I remember an exchange with Justice Thurgood Marshall, who asked me, "Why couldn't the police just go get a warrant?" In effect, weren't they just being lazy? The object of Mr. Chimel's burglaries were collections of thousands of valuable coins, so my response was, no, the police were not being lazy. Under the U.S. Supreme Court's own decisions requiring great specificity in an application for a search warrant—requiring that each item to be seized be specified in detail so that it wouldn't just provide carte blanche for a roving search of whatever turned up—the authorities would have been required to describe each coin, in order to distinguish those that properly could be seized under the warrant from those that could not. My answer was, "This would have been like having to describe each grain of sand on the beach." This was the kind of interplay we had, so it was a very exciting oral argument.

You asked me about the process of being admitted to practice before the bar of the U.S. Supreme Court. This was a little ritual that I believe is unchanged today. It involves, at the beginning of an oral argument session, with the full court and counsel and observers in attendance, the Chief Justice calling forward each applicant to the bar of the U.S. Supreme Court by name, stating for example, "Will Mr. Jones from Cleveland, Ohio, step forward with his sponsor?" It is generally acknowledged that very few of the lawyers who have been admitted to the bar of the high court ever have the occasion to argue a case there. But the certificate of admission is a nice thing to have in the office, maybe to impress clients, maybe just to feel part of a continuing professional tradition. This is a ritual that takes a few minutes those mornings, the lawyers coming to Washington perhaps as part of a vacation trip and being sworn in with their families in attendance.

I wanted to focus on the *Chimel* argument without worrying about the process of being admitted to the bar of the high court, so I took care of that formality the day before in order to have it out of the way. Having been somewhat anxious, I had packed my best white shirt while forgetting that it required cufflinks, so I had to appear before the high court with my cuffs fastened by paperclips. On the following day, I'm seated at counsel table, because *Chimel* was the first case up on the docket that morning. I recall somewhat impatiently waiting for this traditional admissions ceremony to be over with since I no longer had any interest in it, having been admitted the day before, and hearing these names, and cities, and sponsors drone on. All of a sudden I was jolted out of my stupor. I'm shaken to hear Chief Justice Earl Warren say, "Will Barbara George,"—the

name of my wife, and she was in attendance in one of the spectators' rows—
"from Los Angeles step forward with her sponsor?"

I was absolutely horrified. I turned my head around and gave her this deadly
look, more or less asking her by my gaze, "How could you possibly do this to
me? I know we do little practical jokes on each other, but to unnerve me on this
day when I'm already anxious?" And what's more, it's probably a crime because she's not even a lawyer. How could she purport to be admitted to the bar
of the high court? It seemed endless, but finally, of all things, another Barbara
George from Los Angeles who was present stepped forward and was sworn in to
be a member of the bar of the U.S. Supreme Court. I hadn't even known that
such a person existed. After I returned home, I checked a directory put out by
the Los Angeles County Bar Association, and sure enough, on the same page
with me, was attorney Barbara George from Los Angeles.

*You might well have been nervous. How did you prepare, generally speaking,
for this first appearance there?*

That was one of the wonderful things about my experience in the attorney
general's office. If one had an important case before the California Supreme
Court and certainly before the U.S. Supreme Court, you were given the luxury
of being able to spend virtually whatever amount of time you needed to write
your brief. You weren't rushed, and you were able to research the case—really
do a complete job—and then when it came time for oral argument, to devote
yourself to preparing, trying to anticipate all the questions that might be asked.

A rule strictly followed, for the most part, by our California Courts of Appeal and the California Supreme Court is that an attorney is not allowed to go
outside the record—you're confined to the four corners of the transcript; however, the U.S. Supreme Court justices have no compunction about asking counsel
all sorts of things that they know very well are not in the record. "How often do
police officers do this?" "What are the usual kinds of problems they might encounter?" Or "What might their motives be in doing this or that?" Things you
would rarely if ever be asked by the California Supreme Court or by the Court
of Appeal, so you had to try to anticipate what you might have to answer. Or
statistical references. "How often does this type of case come up?" It was a
wonderful experience, as a very young attorney, being allowed to argue a case
before the U.S. Supreme Court.

I should mention, by the way, that it wasn't automatic that I got to argue
this case. I had not been in practice as many years as lawyers generally are when
they argue before the U.S. Supreme Court. There was some discussion in the
office concerning whether I should be permitted to argue the case or instead the

head of the criminal division should argue it. I had to advocate to keep it, but once they decided to let me handle the case, they gave me full support. To get a little ahead of the account here, I was told that my superiors were very pleased with the written and oral presentations that I made in the *Chimel* case. I ended up being given other cases to argue in that court that I had not previously handled before they got to the U.S. Supreme Court. My last three years there were spent primarily in preparing briefing and oral arguments in five additional matters before the U.S. Supreme Court. I should say, more accurately, there was a total of six oral arguments, but one case, *Hill v. California*, was reargued, so I went back to argue that matter a second time.

But on this first instance, when you had not made such an argument before, as you say you had to lobby a little bit to keep the case. How did you go about doing that, do you recall?

I not only, of course, had to tout my own qualifications, but also invoked how important it would be for the morale and spirit of the office and the reputation of the office to allow someone to follow his or her case straight through, wherever it went, and not have it taken away, in effect.

I assume that's a pretty compelling argument in its own right, seeing something through from the very beginning?

Yes, but I have to note objectively that I benefited from my superiors' actions in not strictly following that practice. The next five oral arguments I had before the high court were in cases that I had not previously handled before they reached that court. The stakes are so much higher once a case gets up there, in terms of establishing the law not only for California but nationwide with all of the consequences to other states as well, so one could also take the view that at that level only one of the most senior lawyers should handle the case.

In any event, once I had done the first one, they were sufficiently pleased so that I ended up having a fairly steady diet of it—six arguments before the U.S. Supreme Court by the time I was 31. I am extremely grateful to the attorney general's office for providing me with such an extraordinary experience.

This first argument in Chimel was March 27, 1969. You had just turned 29 years old. As you say, it was the first case to be heard that day. Tell a bit more about how it proceeded in your interaction with the justices. You were arguing before an illustrious group there.

Yes, they seemed to be barraging me with questions right and left. Justice Stewart was very active, and I told you about the pointed questions from Justice

Marshall. It was a very interesting experience being asked whether one of their own precedents, the *Rabinowitz* case, should be overruled. That's not something that the court did lightly. There was a lot of media interest too. I remember discussions with the press afterwards. The *Los Angeles Times* had a correspondent who was covering the U.S. Supreme Court, Ron Ostrow. My recollection is that either on the occasion of that argument or one of the subsequent ones, he had me over to his home and we discussed the case. I had very little experience with Washington before then, so of course it was quite exciting to combine an official visit there with the normal things that a tourist might do.

On that day when you made your argument, how did you think it went?

I was pretty sure that I was in trouble in terms of being able to sustain the state's position. There seemed to be a majority that was very dubious of employing a search incident to an arrest that took place in a residence as a rationale for searching the entire home from top to bottom. I did have doubts as to the likely outcome. That one was not a big surprise for me. But I knew then, and I know even better today, that it's quite dangerous to make predictions about how a court is going to rule based upon the oral arguments. I'm not sure whether it's even more hazardous to make such predictions when you're one of the attorneys on the case, or if it's then less hazardous. [Laughter] In either event, the justices often ask questions as a way of testing the outer limits of the argument being made by counsel. Sometimes the point of a question is directed not so much at the recipient attorney but rather at one of the justice's colleagues down the bench, in an attempt to make a point with that justice about the position taken by one of the advocates. Questions, whether hypothetical or not, are not always a good clue as to how that particular justice may be thinking about the case.

It sounds like you got quite a taste of the showmanship aspects during a very active argument. Were there any surprises there for you in how it went or the questions and answers?

I don't believe so. There were a couple of justices at both ends of the spectrum, where I either expected them to be definitely for me or definitely against my position, and a number in the middle where I was less inclined to guess. But had I been called upon to make a bet on the outcome, I would have expected to lose that case.

My feeling was—and I think people don't always give full thought to this— that the government, in this case the State of California, is entitled to the same forceful advocacy as the lowliest criminal charged with the worst type of offense, provided the government attorney acts in an ethical manner. There's a certain additional responsibility on prosecutors in terms of the search for the truth—which is not the equivalent of prevailing at any cost—but basically you don't have to always agree with the position of your client the State of California. That's always something that was foremost in my mind. My job wasn't to represent Ron George's views on each and every issue, but rather to see to it that the State of California had the best and most vigorous but ethical advocacy that I was capable of furnishing.

How well did you succeed on those grounds?

My track record, especially being a prosecutor in the late sixties and early seventies, wasn't bad. I lost the *Chimel* case. The *Hill* case, which I argued twice—those were the second and third arguments—I won that case. That involved two issues. One was the extent to which the *Chimel* ruling would be retroactively applied. The other issue, which resulted in the principal holding, was whether, when the police have grounds to believe that someone is the suspect but they're mistaken, although reasonably mistaken, and it turns out that the person arrested is someone other than the perpetrator—is the evidence seized in the search incident to that arrest admissible in court? The argument that I made for the prosecution was upheld there. Of course, under the *Chimel* ruling the scope of search incident to arrest is reduced to items that might be found on the person arrested or within his or her immediate reach, rather than from attic to basement. Next was the case of *McGautha v. California*, one of the two death penalty matters I argued before the high court. The issue was whether the absence of standards to guide the jury in selecting between the punishments of death and life in prison without possibility of parole itself rendered the death penalty unconstitutional as a denial of due process of law. I prevailed in that case. In another case, *Kirby v. Illinois*, the court directed me to argue as *amicus curiae*—or rather, California to argue as *amicus curiae*—on behalf of the State of Illinois.

How did that come about?

The issue there was whether the right to counsel attached at a police lineup prior to the filing of formal charges or whether it was only the filing of formal charges that would invoke the right to counsel. California had experience with the issue of counsel at the lineup stage and probably for that reason the U.S. Supreme Court thought it would be useful, in resolving the Illinois case, to obtain the perspective of California's practical experience. I was given the task of writing a brief and then having some of the oral argument time before the U.S. Supreme Court. Our position prevailed there.

Then the last case, which will probably be the subject of more extensive discussion between you and me, *Aikens v. California*, involved whether the death penalty itself was unconstitutional under the cruel *and* unusual punishment clause of the U.S. Constitution. The ruling of the California Supreme Court in *People v. Anderson*, which I briefed and argued, held that the death penalty violated the state's constitutional ban on cruel *or* unusual punishment. *Anderson* mooted out the U.S. Supreme Court case, so *Aikens*—the lead case on the cruel and unusual punishment issue before the U.S. Supreme Court—was just remanded without its becoming—as I'm convinced to this day it was intended to be—a case in which the high court would have upheld the death penalty. Basically my record before the high court on those cases where the court reached the merits was a 75 percent success rate, which as a prosecutor in that era I thought wasn't bad. [Laughter]

Before we try to launch into the Aikens *case and all the related things that happened, finish up for me the general work in the Los Angeles office of the attorney general. You mentioned getting the rotating assignment of supervision. What was involved in that role?*

It was more or less handling some of the fairly routine day-to-day questions that might come up or shuffling them off to the right section or individuals in the office. It was not a policymaking role but rather more or less a bureaucratic role. Because there were three divisions in the office, at that time it was thought best to rotate that assignment among individuals who had some sense of responsibility in the eyes of the powers that be.

Were you considered quite a young attorney to have that kind of position there?

Yes, I think I was and also to be arguing some of these cases, but it was a wonderful reflection on the office that they would give someone who was new and less experienced some of these major responsibilities.

I'm partly just exploring your own interest and proclivity for the leadership role. As a rotating assignment, maybe it wasn't such a strong measure of that. How was your thinking evolving about taking on additional duties, looking ahead to how your own career might develop?

Before going on the bench, this was probably my only real administrative type of assignment, that and mentoring or reviewing the work of—as I got a bit of seniority—some newer deputies, where I would review their draft briefs. It was probably just a first taste of it.

What view were you forming of the attorney general's office statewide, as a whole, now that you were a part of it? Knowing you were in the L.A. office, what interaction with or views did you form of the overall operation under Thomas Lynch as attorney general?

Tom Lynch was a very agreeable person, as was the other attorney general under whom I served, Evelle Younger. I had been hired by Stanley Mosk, and I don't know if we discussed on the record or just informally the relationship I had with Stanley Mosk?

We haven't done that yet, so please go ahead, if you would.

Not too long after I went to work in the attorney general's office, Mosk was appointed by Governor Pat Brown directly to the California Supreme Court. Mosk had been considered a strong possibility to run for the U.S. Senate, the position that Alan Cranston ultimately obtained. Whatever the political powers had in mind, I believe that although Attorney General Mosk was recognized for his own great abilities as a lawyer and as a superior court judge, his appointment to the high court also fit into the whole political framework that was being devised. When Stanley Mosk arrived at the California Supreme Court, I've been told, he was considered a masterful politician, which he was. But his intellectual ability was not yet truly recognized in terms of what a legal scholar and a fine jurist he was. What I have heard is that his fellow justices soon felt that they had had only a limited vision of him and that he certainly qualified as an exceptional justice of the court, more than they might have expected from his very active political career.

One thing that was interesting about my relationship with Stanley Mosk—as he would tell the story—was that there were five phases in his and my relationship. First, he hired me out of law school and was my boss in the attorney general's office. Second, when he was appointed to the California Supreme Court, I appeared before him as an advocate. Third, I became a judge, first a trial judge and then a Court of Appeal justice. As a justice of the Supreme Court, he would review my work when cases that I had handled made their way up to the court. Fourth, I was ultimately elevated to be an associate justice on the California Supreme Court, and we were colleagues on that court. Then, as he put it, fifth and finally I—upon becoming Chief Justice—became his boss. That was the course of our relationship over the period of 1964 to 1996, when I became chief.

Continuing for the rest of his time on that court until his death in 2003?

Yes. We had a wonderful relationship. Even though we were often on opposite sides of legal issues, I believe we each had a lot of respect for each other. He had some very generous things to say about my performance as Chief Justice.

I don't know what hand he had in your hiring at the attorney general's office back in 1964. What do you recall about the circumstances of meeting him for the first time?

I remember being ushered into his office and having an interview, which I recall was fairly short and very friendly. It's quite possible that he was just being asked to sign off on a decision that his chief deputy and others might have made. But that was my first contact.

He went so soon after that to the California Supreme Court. You may not have had any chance to interact with him as a member of his statewide office.

That's correct, though frankly it would be unusual for young deputies to have much contact with the attorney general himself.

As time went on in the Los Angeles office, assignments were coming thick and fast, many of them to cases before the U.S. Supreme Court, in a relatively short time. What did you see as your next step? Were you thinking ahead much?

I loved what I was doing, and oddly enough—and I'm not sure whether this rotating assignment of being administrative assistant in charge of the Los Angeles office in 1971 had much to do with it—as I acquired more experience, I was told that the powers that be wanted me to undertake more and more administrative duties and specifically not handle as much in the way of casework.

Who were the powers that be at that point?

Probably the chief deputy attorney general, Charlie O'Brien. Maybe the section heads who advised him. To a certain degree I saw the handwriting on the wall, indicating to me that what I most enjoyed doing I might not be able to do as much of. That certainly was not my main motivation in applying to the bench, but since you ask about my next step, this was a factor. I thought, I really like handling cases at whatever level, whether it's as an advocate or I'd like to handle them as a judge. I don't want to be an administrator or bureaucrat. Not that I would have been totally deprived of casework, but it was very clear to me that it was expected that I devote myself more to noncase-related work. It probably caused me to give earlier consideration than I otherwise would have to a career on the bench. I think that was basically it—that I might have been thinking about a judicial career as something further off in the future.

To look at it another way, you were exposed to watching a lot of other judges in action. I wonder who stands out as memorable or influential to you in their roles on the bench, while you were in the attorney general's office.

I remember that the most interesting group to appear before was Division Five of the Second District Court of Appeal. The justices on that panel were truly a lively bunch. They really kept you on your toes with their questions but they were very friendly. There was a rooftop cafe in our building—which is now demolished, but it was right across from the *Los Angeles Times*, between there and city hall—you'd go up there and have coffee. The justices would be there, and you could chat about things. There was a great sense of camaraderie, not a lot of distance or formality. The justices who were most active in interactions with the young deputy attorneys general were, especially, Justices Otto Kaus, who was later elevated to the California Supreme Court, Shirley Hufstedler, who went to the Ninth Circuit, and Clarke Stephens. They were in Division Five, and I really enjoyed the oral arguments there. I remember Gordon Files in Division Four being an exceptional jurist. I'm sure I'm omitting some others whom I found particularly interesting. Of course, it was quite exciting to appear before the California Supreme Court as well, which heard all the automatic appeals in the death penalty cases.

I don't mean to jump ahead too much to your own time as a judge, but I was thinking about the thought process that you might be going through about where all this was leading. This was some fairly heady stuff you were connecting up with.

It was, and certainly individuals such as the ones I've mentioned made the prospect of a career on the bench an attractive one, people who were intellectually gifted, active, and not just passive in their interaction with the counsel who were appearing before them, and approachable on a personal level.

We do want to talk about your argument and your whole preparation and process for the Aikens *case before the U.S. Supreme Court and its relation to* People v. Anderson *and that whole theme. It may be that we should put that off until next time.*

There is an amusing story I can tell involving a family member, namely my mother, and her desire to attend the *Aikens* argument that won't get us fully into the death penalty cases but that might be a suitable bridge.

My mother had intended to accompany Barbara and me to hear my argument in the U.S. Supreme Court. Something intervened and she couldn't, but she extracted a promise from me that when I was done with this momentous oral argument involving whether or not the death penalty was cruel and unusual punishment, I would give her a call and tell her how it had gone. It was January of 1972. Barbara and I left the U.S. Supreme Court after the oral argument, together with opposing counsel representing the ACLU and the NAACP, Professor Anthony Amsterdam, and second counsel on the case, Jerry Falk, who had worked on the brief with him but was not part of the argument. It was a cold, blustery day. There was snow in the air. At the bottom of the steps, parked on the street, were a couple of TV units with reporters ready to interview us about this important case. We gave our interviews, which were to be patched into the morning news. When Barbara and I got back to our hotel, I remembered that I was to dutifully call my mother and tell her how the argument had gone. I recall, still full of myself from being a participant in this major event, that I proceeded to launch into a description of my oral argument and what fine points I thought I had made. I barely got 20 or 30 seconds into it when my mother cut me off. She said, "I saw you on television, on the news, just a while ago. I saw the snow and the wind blowing. Don't you have enough sense to have your coat buttoned up? No scarf or hat?" Nothing like a mother to cut you off at the knees and put everything in perspective. [Laughter] That was an interesting sidelight.

There is a little sequel to that story, which I find amusing although it doesn't involve me directly. On a few occasions I've been asked over the years to attend the annual meeting of the California Academy of Appellate Lawyers, which takes place in Carmel or Ojai and has a full weekend of seminars and talks and social events. In the course of one of those meetings, I was asked to describe the experience of arguing before the U.S. Supreme Court. Along with sharing more substantive insights, I told the story of Barbara George's admission to the bar of the court, and I also related the phone conversation with my mother that I just described to you, and of course got a good laugh out of that.

Then Jerry Falk, who had been there on that day in 1972, said, "I have a sequel to that story." Years later, he said, he had occasion to appear on his own before the U.S. Supreme Court. He had asked his mother to go back with him, and she had been able to attend. He had also asked his father to attend, and the father had a business trip to take to Chicago and was unable to join them. Somehow Mr. and Mrs. Falk, Sr., coordinated their travels so that when Mrs. Falk flew back from Washington to San Francisco, Mr. Falk's arrival in San Francisco from Chicago more or less coincided with hers, and they met at the San Francisco airport and arranged to come back into town on the airport shuttle together. As Jerry Falk, who remained back East for a few more days, told the story, Mr. Falk, Sr., of course was quite interested to find out from Mrs. Falk how their son had fared in his first argument before the high court. She, being a typically proud mother, went on to describe Jerry's performance as brilliant, along the lines of his words falling like pearls from his lips. He couldn't say anything wrong; he made this point and that point. Then finally the father inquired what was the opposing counsel like, the government attorney? Apparently Mrs. Falk said to Mr. Falk something along the lines of the opposing counsel being inept and unable to get two words out straight without bungling them up. When the senior Falks got to the bus terminal in San Francisco and were struggling with their luggage, they were helped by a nice young man. Mrs. Falk said, "Thank you so much, young man." His response was, "Much obliged. I'm just sorry that you didn't like my oral argument, Mrs. Falk." [Laughter] A nice sequel to my own experience. The academy got a big kick out of Jerry Falk's story.

This may be a point where it's convenient for us to break and then proceed next time with the death penalty arguments before the U.S. Supreme Court and also the Sirhan Sirhan case in the California Supreme Court.

###

Chapter 3

Representing the State before the U.S. and California Supreme Courts
July 7, 2011

We've been talking about your time in the attorney general's office and the various arguments you made before the U.S. Supreme Court. Before we go into detail on cases, I wonder if you can talk about how—after the first case, Chimel—you were chosen to be the one to take those arguments forward to the U.S. Supreme Court?

The first one, *Chimel*, of course was rather serendipitous. It was a case I had previously handled in which the U.S. Supreme Court decided to review its longstanding precedents in *Harris v. United States* and *United States v. Rabinowitz* on the scope of search incident to arrest. The next case that came up, *Hill v. California,* did involve, among other issues, the retroactivity of the *Chimel* ruling. Therefore, there was a certain rationale for giving that case to me, although I had not argued it in the California Supreme Court or the lower court. Then, after that, it just seemed I developed a U.S. Supreme Court practice. I considered myself very fortunate. I was told, "You really did a fine job, and we want you to handle these cases." The five arguments I had before the U.S. Supreme Court following *Chimel* were all in cases in which I had no prior involvement. Like so many things in life, perhaps it was a combination of good luck and hard work, but it was a very exciting time to be arguing before the U.S. Supreme Court, when a lot of law was being made—an uphill battle, often, for

63

prosecutors. The *Chimel* opinion was issued on the last day of Earl Warren's tenure as Chief Justice.

In fact, there was a seventh case, *California v. Krivda*, that was another one I had not handled previously but in which I obtained approval for the State of California to file a petition seeking review in the U.S. Supreme Court. The case involved the issue whether there was a reasonable expectation of privacy, in terms of search and seizure law, in one's garbage, which is not a very glamorous sounding topic but one with a lot of ramifications, both for personal privacy and police investigations involving "dumpster diving." The petition I filed stated: "It would be a perversion of the maxim of constitutional law that 'a man's home is his castle' to make a man's garbage can an inviolable sanctuary."

The search of the Krivdas' garbage yielded evidence—obtained from the bin of a garbage truck—that was used against them in a marijuana possession prosecution. The petition for writ of certiorari, contesting the suppression of the evidence, was granted on April 3, 1972—shortly before my appointment to the bench later that month. So I never got to argue the case, but that would have been my seventh oral argument before the high court. After the oral argument, the case ended up being remanded to the state court for additional findings, so in the end there wasn't an opinion on the merits of the issue involved.

What was your process of deciding that you wanted to send that forward as a petition and then working through the attorney general's office to do so? Whom did you have to convince?

The head of the criminal appeals section, Bill James. We had had some rulings against us, including the *Krivda* case and others, that put a restriction on law enforcement that I considered of sufficient general interest in terms of California jurisprudence but also nationally. We had the support of the attorneys general of some other states. That met the test, and the high court thought it was significant enough to warrant review.

There was an interesting sidelight to the case relating to the various participants in the proceedings. I was not the only future California Chief Justice involved in the case. An *amicus curiae* brief was filed by Rose Elizabeth Bird on behalf of the California Public Defenders' Association. Another little bizarre twist: the attorney representing the defendants in the municipal court was one Jerry Brown, our former and now again current governor. The judge was Joan Dempsey Klein, who later became the senior presiding justice among the appellate justices of our state. That's an interesting juxtaposition of persons involved in this otherwise banal matter of garbage. The docket also reflects an unrelated "B. George" as court reporter.

Did you ever have occasion to speak with them about this later on?

No.

I felt very fortunate to have the luxury in the attorney general's office— as it was then a much smaller office, of course, with proportionately less of a case-load—to spend virtually as much time as I felt these cases merited without being concerned about billable hours or dealings with clients and satisfying their particular wishes of the moment, just spending the time necessary to write the briefs and prepare for oral argument.

It was exciting to have interaction, although across the bench, with these very notable justices, a couple of whom—Justices Black and Douglas—had been appointed to the high court before I was born. I remember being told a story about Justice Hugo Black, who could be quite unpredictable in some areas and predictable in others. When appointed by President Roosevelt, Black was a U.S. Senator from Alabama, but early in his career he had been a member of the Ku Klux Klan. The story that some prosecutors would tell, perhaps a bit direct and impolite, was that Hugo Black had spent the first half of his life wearing a white robe scaring black people and the second half of his life wearing a black robe scaring white people. We never knew what to expect, except that you could be in for tough questioning from Justice Black.

What was your own experience with him?

I don't think he was overbearing or unkind to counsel. I probably had the most sparring with Thurgood Marshall, although Justice Stewart could really bear down too. Others were less involved in the oral argument.

One nice reward after making those appearances was that although Barbara and I didn't have much in the way of funds to take exotic vacations in those days, Delta Airlines had something they called a triangle fare. For an additional $35 on the price of your Los Angeles round trip to Washington, D.C., you could go on to the Virgin Islands. We availed ourselves of that on a couple of occasions to take a little vacation at our own expense at a minimal cost.

We touched last time upon the McGautha *case as one of several you argued there. Perhaps we can use that today as a gateway into the* Aikens *case and the subject of the death penalty?*

The *McGautha* case involved an attack on the manner in which the death penalty was imposed by juries. According to the defendant, the existing procedure violated a basic principle of due process of law by not providing the jury

with sufficient standards to make the determination between life imprisonment—in California, life without possibility of parole—or the death penalty.
The defendant's argument was rejected by the high court, which upheld the procedures for imposing the death penalty. Our point was that sufficient guidance
was given to the jury and that you had to view the conduct of a capital trial in
the context of all of the applicable procedural rules, some of which were unique
to California, that guided the discretion of the jury; that guided the charging and
determination of special circumstances; that guided a trial judge in evaluating a
verdict rendered by the jury imposing the death penalty, and then, in turn, the
review afforded by the California Supreme Court in the automatic appeal. In
about 30 percent of the cases at that time, the death penalty or the underlying
conviction was set aside in the automatic appeal or in the accompanying habeas
corpus proceedings. I urged that these various safeguards were sufficient to meet
constitutional standards.

As a general matter, why were jury standards so significant?

The argument was made that the death penalty was capricious and that a jury might impose or not impose the death penalty for reasons that had little if any
relation to the particular defendant's conduct and life history. What I tried to
demonstrate was that the jury *was* directed toward things that were appropriate
to consider in making that determination.

There were a lot of points to try to weave into that argument. I remember
with that case, as with others, you couldn't set out to give a prepared speech.
The justices wouldn't appreciate it, and they wouldn't let you anyway. If you
selected the few major points that you wanted to make in your half-hour presentation—and it was always inadvisable to try to cover everything that was in your
brief or you would end up not covering anything very well—you might be met
right away with a question on maybe the second or third point you wanted to
make. You couldn't say, "I'll get to that later." What I found to be an effective
technique for surviving the half-hour up there and still being able to communicate what you felt you had to share with the justices was to answer the question
on that second or third point, weave in the rest of your argument on that second
or third point, and then go back to the first point. You could otherwise—and I
saw other counsel do that in cases that were argued while I was waiting to argue
my own—end up being very flustered and frustrated, never having been able to
make your basic points by the time the questions had subsided and the half-hour
was over with.

How did you figure this out?

Just by observation. Fortunately, you have an opportunity to observe those who argue before you, for better or for worse, and that got to be a technique I thought would get me through the time. That white light on the podium would go off when five minutes were left of your argument. When the red light went off you could be in the middle of a preposition and be told, "Your time is over." There were exceptions, but most of the time the Chief Justice would be quite strict in cutting you off.

Is there anything else you'd like to say about the McGautha *decision itself, which was 6–3 for California, the record shows?*

No. It's very risky to try to predict what's going to happen, but I had a fairly good feeling about the *McGautha* case. It was a case that was well argued all around. I'll immodestly include myself in that. I thought I was privileged to have a truly fine attorney, one of the top in the United States, Herman Selvin, on the other side, and also the solicitor general of the United States, Erwin Griswold, former dean of Harvard Law School, arguing as amicus curiae.

What was his style?

It was a bit academic, no histrionics. He was someone for whom I had a lot of respect. I had occasion to actually listen to the tape of the oral argument almost 40 years later. About 30 years ago, I ordered tapes of the six oral arguments in which I participated. I've only managed to listen to two of them so far. It was quite enjoyable to listen to the parrying back and forth among all the counsel and the members of the court in *McGautha*.

Did you come away with any particular tips that you picked up from hearing Mr. Selvin in action?

Just that one could make a very fine, pointed, and even passionate argument without a lot of histrionics. So often I saw, as an attorney and as a judge later on, the kind of overly emotional appeals that were probably a turnoff to the court. There was none of that, despite the high stakes involved here in this argument.

McGautha *was argued in November 1970, and then in January 1972 you returned for the* Aikens v. California *case. Perhaps before getting to the oral argument itself, you could set the stage for how that came to you and what was happening in California leading up to that.*

When *McGautha* came down there were about 98 individuals on death row in California, and there were more, of course, by the time *Aikens* reached the high court. The U.S. Supreme Court granted review in four cases. *Aikens v. California* was the lead case. The others were *Furman v. Georgia* and two more cases from the South. Specifically, an issue in all four cases was whether the death penalty itself inherently constituted cruel and unusual punishment under the Eighth Amendment to the U.S. Constitution not because of the way it was carried out, not because of the procedures, which more or less was the underlying issue in *McGautha*—whether the procedures lacked sufficient standards— but whether the death penalty itself, the act of the state putting someone to death because of his or her criminal conduct, constituted an unconstitutional deprivation of rights, regardless of the fairness of the proceedings.

I knew from my general awareness of U.S. Supreme Court jurisprudence and from my experience in the *McGautha* case that the high court, unlike our California Supreme Court in most instances, did not restrict counsel to what was strictly within the record of the case—to "the four corners of the transcript." In fact, the court was well known for posing questions that went way beyond anything that had been introduced as empirical evidence or otherwise brought to the attention of the lower courts. I knew one had to be prepared to respond to such questions. I also was aware, of course, that opponents of the death penalty had frequently made the assertion that the death penalty was cruel and unusual punishment because of the fact, in their view, that it was disproportionately imposed by juries and by courts upon individuals from a lower socio-economic level, individuals with a lower IQ level, and disproportionately upon members of racial minorities. I thought it best to try to prepare myself to meet such questions or even, in anticipation of those arguments, to try to refute them by including material in the brief that I would file on behalf of the State of California in the U.S. Supreme Court.

In addition to my research into case law and law review articles and other studies, I thought it would be useful to actually have data illustrating the manner in which the death penalty was imposed and on which persons death penalty judgments were being imposed in California. I wanted to distinguish California's situation from that of other states, not only because of the nature of the three cases from southern states that were companion cases to *Aikens*, but also because there were so many cases that reached the high court from states that I believe were much less mindful of due process and provided far fewer protections for persons charged with crimes, especially capital crimes. California, I felt, provided much higher protections—in some ways unique protections—for persons charged with capital offenses.

I had the impression, which I still do to this day, that this unusual grouping of cases was picked with a definite purpose on behalf of the U.S. Supreme Court, namely to use *Aikens* as an illustration of what *was* permissible and would justify rejecting the cruel and unusual punishment attack on the death penalty and, on other hand, the three other cases that didn't have those protections. *Aikens* was a highly unusual case in that the defendant had waived his right to jury trial on the issue of penalty. So you had a judge with incredible foresight—it was Judge Jerome Berenson from the Ventura County Superior Court—coming up with factors in aggravation and factors in mitigation that he thought should be considered in performing his task as a judge in deciding between the two alternate punishments of death and life without parole and then weighing those factors and coming out with the determination that death was the appropriate punishment. It's very unusual to have jury trial waived in a death penalty case, but those same factors are appropriate to guide a jury as well as a judge in making that determination. It's my view—and of course this does not amount to anything more than informed speculation—that *Aikens* was selected to provide a distinction between California's procedure—at least the procedure followed in that particular California case—and on the other hand the procedures that were standard in many other parts of the country. We'll later get into why the court ended up not making a ruling in the *Aikens* case when we discuss *People v. Anderson*. But I'm convinced that had the *Aikens* case not been rendered moot by the *Anderson* decision of the California Supreme Court, the U.S. Supreme Court would have upheld the death penalty in *Aikens*, having picked this very unusual case as the lead case in this quartet of cases.

Who, if anyone, shares your view that this was used in this manner?

I don't know. I haven't really had much occasion to discuss this, and I haven't come across any literature discussing it.

But you formed that view very much at the time, and you still have that view today?

I did, and I still do. This may become clearer when we talk about the *Aikens* decision and its chronology in relation to *People v. Anderson*.

I planned a visit to San Quentin prison, where all the male inmates on death row were housed. There was only one female defendant then under death sentence, who was kept at Frontera in Corona, and I made a separate visit there. I wanted first of all to observe the facilities on death row so that I could, if appropriate, refute any negative assertions about the actual conditions of confinement.

But most importantly, I wanted to examine the records of each of the individuals—I believe there were 102 individuals on death row then—so as to be able to determine on a pragmatic basis whether there was any merit in the assertions that the death penalty was being imposed in a discriminatory fashion upon persons from less advantaged groups and upon racial minorities. The prison authorities were, of course, quite cooperative, and they set me up in the maximum-confinement unit there with all the records. I was able to go through the file of each individual on death row, looking at the circumstances of the crime, the particular background—prior history, socio-economic background, employment, IQ, racial classification, and so forth, to see if there was any pattern.

I allocated three days for this chore, a Thursday, Friday, and Saturday, which were August 19, 20, and 21 of 1971. First I was shown through the death row area. By the way, not to get ahead of ourselves on the *Sirhan* case, but for some reason or other the associate warden taking me around saw fit to introduce me to Mr. Sirhan. "Hello. This is Mr. George from the attorney general's office." Sirhan replied, "Yes. Why do I want to talk to him? He's just trying to get me gassed." That was extent of our conversation.

I did go through all of death row, and it was rather interesting seeing some of these individuals who had been there for many years and whose cases I had cited in my briefs in various cases. They were almost legendary figures in criminal law, such as Gilbert in the famous *Gilbert v. California* high court ruling on the right to counsel at police lineups. Seeing them there, in the flesh, so to speak, was a rather bizarre experience.

I saw the conditions of confinement and then, more significantly, went through these reams and reams of files and came up with data that I set forth in various tables in the respondent's brief that I filed in the U.S. Supreme Court. This data, in my view, certainly did not suggest that the death penalty in California—and I stress California—was somehow imposed in a discriminatory manner. What I did was go through the percentage of individuals who, among those convicted of first-degree murder, then were brought to trial on the issue of penalty, in terms of the racial composition of the individuals who were convicted of first-degree murder compared to the racial composition of those individuals who actually received the death penalty. It was quite interesting to me that, in fact, there was no higher percentage of persons who were black who received the death penalty as compared to those black defendants who received a guilty verdict of first-degree murder. The same was true with regard to persons whose death sentences were commuted and those who were actually executed. There was no disproportion in terms of whites receiving more lenient treatment. That was true up and down the spectrum in terms of murder convictions and death penalties and commutations and executions actually carried out.

It was a worthwhile endeavor, though one of the most bizarre experiences in my professional career occurred on the third day that I was supposed to be there going through all of these records. It was frankly—I don't know a better word for it—creepy just being locked up there in the maximum confinement unit, spending hours and hours on that Thursday and Friday. I thought I'd just as soon not make a third day of it there. I decided to work late Friday evening so I wouldn't have to come back Saturday. On the third day I was supposed to be there, the infamous San Quentin riot and escape attempt took place—right in the maximum security area where I had been working—in what came to be known as the San Quentin Six when the case went to trial with the survivors. The riot that day, August 21, 1971, resulted in the death of three guards and three inmates and ultimately a trial that lasted 15 months, which was the longest criminal trial, I believe, in American history until surpassed by my Hillside Strangler trial that ended up holding that distinction in the Guinness Book of World Records for several years. It was quite strange to have been working right there the day before the riot occurred. Without referencing my own personal near proximity to these events, I did include an argument in my brief indicating that life terms do not fully protect society and that there can be violence in prison that puts at risk fellow prisoners and guards and civilian employees, in addition to whatever risk there might be of escape from prison.

That was part of my preparation for the case, with of course months of more mundane type of research. I should mention that I did go visit the one woman who was then on death row, Jean Carver, who was convicted of bludgeoning to death with a large rock an elderly female religious minister. I still remember that case because it was assigned to me. While I examined her file, the warden arranged to have Barbara be given a tour by an inmate around the women's prison, which didn't have a true death row, just one special area for this one female. When Barbara came back she said to the warden, "The inmate whom you had show me around was very informed and courteous. What's she in here for?" "Murder." She had killed her own child. Barbara had been in her sole immediate company for an hour or so, exchanging pleasantries while discussing life in the prison.

These visits had a pragmatic bearing upon my response to some of the arguments that were being made about the death penalty.

What was your preparation in terms of your colleagues in the office? How were you advised and guided in your preparation, and by whom?

I previously mentioned Bill James, who was the statewide head of the criminal appeals section and one of the foremost criminal appellate lawyers in California, if not nationwide. I had the benefit of his experience and also consulted other colleagues in terms of the experience they had had in handling their capital cases in order to have a more complete understanding of the scope of the issue. Of course, there was no dearth of literature on the subject.

What knowledge did you have of who would represent the other side on the Aikens *case and what preparations they might be involved with?*

The ACLU and the NAACP Legal Defense Fund had long sought to have the U.S. Supreme Court grant review on the cruel and unusual punishment issue, and I'm certain they sought review in numerous cases. It may have been dozens of cases across the United States, so of course they were understandably pleased that the court finally agreed to take up the issue. It was fairly apparent who would argue the case because the lead counsel was Professor Anthony Amsterdam, who was nationally recognized as a scholar and as someone very knowledgeable with regard to the issues involving the constitutionality of the death penalty. He did excellent work on the case, in the briefing and in the oral argument.

Did you have any personal hesitation about getting into this area?

Well, at one point in my life I had some doubts about the death penalty in terms of whether it was an appropriate form of punishment. During my experience in the attorney general's office, I came to develop my personal views. When friends would kid me about that, I said, "I've either been educated or corrupted, depending upon your point of view."

I felt that, first of all, my personal views were irrelevant, because the State of California was entitled to the same vigorous legal representation that any person charged with a crime, whether on death row or not, would be entitled to—obviously with certain limitations in terms of a prosecutor's duty always being to pursue the truth, to share information with the defense, and not to obtain convictions at any cost. The duty is not the same on the defense side as it is on the prosecution. Keeping in mind those constraints, I felt that the State of California should receive advocacy as forceful as what I knew Professor Amsterdam would provide to Mr. Aikens and others similarly situated. What was at stake were the lives of 550 individuals on death row nationally that would be affected by the high court's ruling.

When I say I was either educated or corrupted, by then I had enough experience handling death penalty cases before the California Supreme Court and reading materials in conjunction with representing the state in such matters that I felt the issue was basically this: is there sufficient justification for the death penalty that the people of the State of California—through their elected representatives or directly through the initiative process—can constitutionally choose to have the death penalty available as a punishment for the most serious of offenses? I personally concluded, by the time I acquired experience in the attorney general's office, that there was nothing unconstitutional about the people of the state having that option. Whether it should be imposed in a particular case, or even whether the death penalty *should* be on the books—whether the people should decide to have it and whether the legislature should decide to have it—was a separate question. But if the people wanted to have the death penalty, there was nothing in the federal or state constitution that would prevent their doing so.

I became convinced on the basis of the cases I was familiar with and the literature I had read that the death penalty did serve as a valid deterrent to murder in a certain number of cases. That doesn't mean that it always did, but it meant—in my view—that there were cases where the existence of the death penalty caused an armed robber, for example, not to kill his victim. There actually was a Los Angeles Police Department study that I read and cited in my brief that examined situations where armed robbers confronted solitary liquor store clerks or others—perhaps a bartender right before closing time at 2:00 a.m. or a pursuing police officer where the criminal had the draw on the officer. The criminal did not fire his loaded weapon when there was a clear opportunity to do so, or had armed himself with an unloaded firearm or a toy gun, or didn't even bring a firearm. Examination of the police reports seemed to bear out the fact that in a certain number of those cases, it was the thought of what was sometimes referred to by the criminal as "the little green room"—meaning the execution chamber—that was enough to have kept him from arming himself or using a lethal weapon. To me, this signified that in a certain number of cases, there were victims alive who would be dead but for the fact of a particular criminal being deterred by the existence of the death penalty.

Having said that, I came to believe that whatever deterrent resulted from having the death penalty, it ceased to have effect as the delays in carrying it out expanded more and more over the years to the point where, by the end of my term as Chief Justice, the delay was averaging 25 years on death row before a person would be executed, after countless judicial reviews. We'll talk when we get to my term as Chief Justice about procedures that I have urged to improve the process by which the death penalty is employed in California as long we do have a death penalty on the books. Whatever deterrent effect the death penalty has is, in my view, dependent upon it being carried out in a reasonably prompt fashion. I don't mean lickety-split the way they do in some of the southern states, but soon enough where the offender's expectation is not that he or she is more likely to die of old age than of the death penalty. To the extent that so much delay has been built into the process, I believe that the major justification for the death penalty—in terms of policy and perhaps also in terms of constitutional argument to a certain extent—has been undermined. There is a vastly reduced deterrent effect, in my view, if the expectation is that the death penalty will not be carried out for 25 or more years. I was convinced that the deterrent effect—certainly what existed to a far greater extent back then in the late 1960s and early 1970s—was an adequate justification, among others, for the people to choose to have the death penalty as an available option.

Was Aikens *the right case to take forward in this regard?*

I think it was the ideal case from a prosecutor's standpoint, and I remain convinced to this day that had the California Supreme Court's decision in *People v. Anderson* not intervened, the U.S. Supreme Court would have concluded this was the way to proceed properly: have standards of aggravation and mitigation to guide the jury and the judge in weighing evidence of the circumstances of the crime and of the defendant's background and criminal history in determining whether to impose the death penalty. All the circumstances of the *Aikens* case justified imposing the death penalty in that particular case. This was the situation where if one believed there are cases, even if they're more extreme, that justify the death penalty, one would say this was one of those cases. If you're going to have a death penalty, this would be a case where you would find it justified. The defendant was convicted of committing two charged murders in a particularly vicious manner on separate occasions during the course of rapes. He had a prior record of murder and violent assaults, and did not present any substantial evidence in mitigation.

What else stands out to you as you review the brief you prepared?

Certainly that I felt I had the luxury of all the time I needed to prepare this brief and prepare for oral argument. Actually, my brief also invoked a bit of original-meaning jurisprudence, even though later as a judge that was not a road I was prone to take. I did point out in both the brief and the oral argument that the wording of the federal constitution specifically contemplated the death penalty in the Fifth and Fourteenth Amendments' reference to not depriving an individual of "*life*, liberty, or property, without due process of law." There's also a reference in the Fifth Amendment to "*capital*" crimes. There, in those exact words, was a recognition that life *would* be taken under some circumstances. So although it may sound simplistic to some individuals, I felt that there was an argument worth making—and I did make it—that how could capital punishment be referred to in the Constitution and yet be unconstitutional in light of the Constitution specifically recognizing the existence of the death penalty?

There was a line of legal theory that Chief Justice Warren had evoked in the opinion he wrote in *Trop v. Dulles*, speaking of society's "evolving standards of decency." An argument I made was that this concept still could not detract from the actual wording of the Constitution and also that this was a dangerous road to take, because what would be the case if society's standards—being recognized under that doctrine as somewhat fluid—evolved in a negative way? Let's say it became acceptable to boil people in oil for committing crimes that are non-capital under today's jurisprudence, crimes that don't involve the death of the victim. If society's standards evolved to condone such punishments, would that render them no longer cruel and unusual? That was one of the arguments that I made and of course also made in the California Supreme Court. I don't know if you have anything more you want to ask about *Aikens* before we segue into *People v. Anderson*?

You set the stage with the anecdote about calling your mother after the Aikens *oral argument that blustery day in January. Maybe you could spend a few minutes talking about the actual act of being there and making the oral argument in this specific case. What stands out as you think back on those events?*

Of course for any lawyer, certainly including myself, appearing before the U.S. Supreme Court is a highlight of one's career and a very exciting day filled with both personal satisfaction and trepidation. Adding to that general circumstance was the fact that this was a case involving the fate of capital punishment and, literally, the lives of several hundred men and women on death row across the United States. The real buzz that you could feel even around the high court about the momentous arguments made it a very heady experience. I certainly consider appearing before the high court, and perhaps especially on that case, as one of the highlights of my career.

What about interaction with the justices, which is of course in the recorded oral argument. You mentioned a few minutes ago they were apt to bring up all sorts of other things, and you did a lot of special preparation. How much were you called upon to wander outside the record?

As I recall, there was a lot more listening and perhaps oddly enough—in light of the significance of the issues—less interruption in questioning than in some of the other arguments I had before the high court. I felt privileged to be able to get the points across that I wanted to, without the sense of frustration of being cut off by questions, although I never resented that when it happened. Any lawyer who appears before an appellate court should know that he or she is not there to give a prepared speech or address, but rather to satisfy the questions on the minds of the justices. I felt there was a lot of listening, and you could feel it was a momentous occasion in terms of everyone taking each participant's role quite seriously.

What happened next?

The U.S. Supreme Court had had the cruel and unusual punishment issue before it for some time. The briefs were filed in September 1971 in *Aikens*, and oral argument was originally set for the following month. But there were two vacancies that occurred on the U.S. Supreme Court, and I believe that was the reason for argument being postponed until January 17, 1972. What was quite fascinating is the fact that in the interim between the granting of certiorari, the filing of the briefs in *Aikens*, and the January 17 date of oral argument, the California Supreme Court took up a case, *People v. Anderson*, that had been languishing on its docket for some time. At that time, unlike today, the California Supreme Court felt it was not bound by the requirement in the California Constitution that all judges—whether at the trial or appellate level—decide any case within 90 days of submission. Except in unusual cases where a court orders supplemental briefing for some particular reason, submission normally occurs at the time of oral argument. Argument in the *Anderson* case had occurred in February of 1970, and the case still was awaiting decision a year and a half later.

What happened was quite unique. The California Supreme Court in December of 1971—which, of course, is after *Aikens* was supposed to have been argued but, because of the postponement, ended up being about a month before *Aikens* finally was argued—ordered that the *Anderson* case be re-argued. There wasn't time to file new briefs to cover anything that had happened in the lengthy period since the prior briefs had been filed a couple years before. What was highly unusual is that Professor Amsterdam and I were directed to file with the California Supreme Court copies of the briefs that we had filed in the U.S. Supreme Court and to argue on the basis of those briefs. We didn't even put new covers on them. We just submitted copies to the state court.

The California Supreme Court scheduled the re-argument in *Anderson* for January 6, 1972, more or less beating the U.S. Supreme Court to the punch by a couple of weeks. Then, in an extraordinary development, the California Supreme Court—which had had its case under submission for a year and a half—ended up rendering its opinion in *People v. Anderson* on February 18, 1972, just six weeks after the oral argument, in contrast to its prior unhurried review in *Anderson* and generally in all the other capital cases.

Before we expand on the opinion, what more can you tell me about the argument date itself in the California Supreme Court?

I just recall that it was more or less a dress rehearsal, in a way, for the U.S. Supreme Court. We made pretty much the same arguments, Professor Amsterdam and I. It was very bizarre, the same individuals arguing the same points on the West Coast and the East Coast within a couple weeks.

It came up later, yet you argued it first?

Yes. It gave the impression of the California Supreme Court having dug into its docket of cases that had been languishing at the court, rushing to restore the *Anderson* case on calendar, intending—I'll be blunt about it—to preempt the U.S. Supreme Court from ruling on the California case, *Aikens*, as an unusually favorable vehicle in which the federal high court could draw a distinction between what is permissible in a death penalty case under the cruel and unusual punishment clause and what is not.

Counsel for both sides did have the opportunity, which we exercised—or it might have been a directive—to file letter briefs in the state court on the one single aspect that differentiated *Anderson*, at least theoretically, from *Aikens*: the prohibition against cruel and unusual punishment contained in the Eighth Amendment to the federal constitution is phrased in the conjunctive—"cruel *and* unusual"—whereas the California constitutional provision is phrased in the disjunctive—"cruel *or* unusual." I filed a brief, needless to say, indicating the view of the State of California that this slight difference in wording had no significance and that the two clauses did not prescribe different standards; a death penalty that would pass muster under one Constitution's clause would pass muster under the other.

The rationale employed by the California Supreme Court in its *Anderson* opinion evoked a basis recognized in jurisprudence—when properly evoked—for a state court to render its decision premised on state constitutional or other provisions, thereby causing its decision to pass muster on independent state grounds that are not subject to review in a federal tribunal. The position that I took was that there were no independent state constitutional grounds here, at least none that would hinge upon the use of the word "or" as opposed to the use of the word "and."

As you say, the California Supreme Court delivered its opinion on February 18,
1972 in Anderson. *Tell me what you thought upon hearing how it came out.*

Chief Justice Donald Wright wrote the opinion for the court striking down
the death penalty as invalid under the state constitution's prohibition against
"cruel or unusual" punishment. Given the sequence, the chronology of events
I've described, I can't say I was shocked to see it come out the way it did, much
as I very much disagreed with the decision and particularly the rationale for it.
There were many things in the opinion that I took issue with.

I was directed by the attorney general personally to take a very hard-hitting
approach in a petition for rehearing. I was told specifically to "take off the kid
gloves." I wrote a petition for rehearing that I know some may have thought—
and some did, in fact, think—was overly assertive, but basically it took the California Supreme Court to task for, number one, rushing to judgment, basically
pulling the rug out from under the U.S. Supreme Court by resolving this issue
while it was under review by the high court in a California case. The U.S. Supreme Court had not yet done what I expected it to do and what it eventually
did, namely dismiss *Aikens* as moot given the fact that Mr. Aikens no longer
faced the death penalty because of the ruling in *Anderson.* I argued basically that
the state court should not have gone ahead while that issue was before the U.S.
Supreme Court and rendered the ruling that it did, and that despite its disclaimer,
the California Supreme Court was basically deciding the federal constitutional
issue.

I also attacked the state high court's reliance on the "and/or" terminology,
quoting Justice John Harlan's observation in an earlier opinion [*DeSylva* v. *Bal-*
lentine] that the word "or" is often used as a careless substitute for the word
"and," and that in statutory construction there's been such laxity in the use of the
terms that courts don't, in most instances, place any significance on the choice
of word. I argued that, in fact, the states were mixed in their constitutional prohibitions against cruel and unusual punishment—some used the word "or," and
many others used the word "and"—and no significance could be drawn from
that selection of terminology. I questioned whether North Carolina's use of the
word "or" might preclude enforcement of the death penalty in that state, while
South Carolina's choice of the word "and" might sanctify capital punishment in
that jurisdiction.

Where I'm certain I did annoy some members of the California Supreme
Court was in pointing out the following: the state court had, in part, concluded
that the death penalty was cruel by reason of the length of pre-execution confinement. I pointed out that a major portion, if not *the* major portion, of pre-
execution confinement delay resulted from the slow pace of the California Su-

preme Court's very own leisurely process of review and the fact that, when ultimately reviewed, so many of the cases had been reversed and sent back for new trials on penalty or on the issue of guilt. I urged that it was self-contradictory for the court to rely upon the results of its own actions in bringing about delay, as a justification for its conclusion that the death penalty was unconstitutionally "cruel."

As an illustration in the petition for rehearing, I pointed to what had happened in Mr. Anderson's case—namely the California Supreme Court's initial affirmance of the death judgment in 1966, followed by its 1968 opinion setting aside the defendant's death sentence, the filing of briefs in 1969, oral argument in 1970, followed by re-argument in 1972, and then this rush to judgment six weeks later in the *People v. Anderson* decision of February 18, 1972, after all of that delay. I cited other examples. One was the case of *People v. Thornton*, where the transcripts had been filed in 1968 with the California Supreme Court. The briefing had been completed in 1969, and as of 1972 when I filed the petition for rehearing in *Anderson*, the case hadn't even been set for oral argument. Another case I cited was *People v. Winhoven*, where the transcripts were filed in 1967, with briefing filed that same year, oral argument in 1968, followed by supplemental briefing later that year, and then nothing happened in 1969 and nothing in 1970. Finally, in September of 1971 the defendant died. These were illustrations that were meant to bring home the fact that the court had been dilatory and that its conclusion—that the delay in carrying out the death penalty rendered that punishment cruel—was somewhat circular and self-serving.

What, again, was very assertive was the reference, in my petition for rehearing, to the court's having invoked the doctrine that I mentioned a moment ago, the evolving standards of society. The petition stated that the court really had based its decision in *Anderson* on the court's own evolving standards rather than on society's evolving standards. I also said that the court, in effect, had made inappropriate and unsubstantiated legislative findings about deterrence not justifying the death penalty—and upon other subjects—and that those actions by the court violated basic concepts of separation of powers among the three branches of government. Then I concluded with an observation the court had made in its decision in *Anderson*, that it was not acting out of sympathy, of course, for those who had committed crimes of violence but rather was acting in part out of concern for a society that diminishes itself whenever it takes the life of one of its members. I sought to rebut that statement in the court's opinion by urging in our petition for rehearing that a society that professes to respect human life must protect the life of its citizens.

It was a hard hitting petition for rehearing, and word reached me through the grapevine that there were a couple members of the court who were so disturbed by the language in the petition for rehearing that they suggested I should be questioned about whether the language employed in the petition constituted contempt of the court. But I never heard anything formally.

Which members were those?

I never heard. What probably also annoyed the court was the circumstance that the attorney general wrote a letter to Justice McComb, who was the only dissenter in *Anderson*, urging that the justice do something that on occasion he had done before, namely incorporate—in an opinion dissenting from the denial of rehearing—substantial portions of our petition for rehearing if not the entirety of the petition. This incorporation never came to pass, but there were some other things going on between Chief Justice Wright and Justice McComb, who ultimately was removed from the bench because of—I can't put it more delicately than this—senility that had blemished an otherwise fine career. I believe these circumstances probably aggravated the situation in addition to the court's views concerning the tone of the petition for rehearing.

This was a suggestion that he incorporate the whole thing by reference?

Yes, and thereby have it appear in the official reports of the decisions of the California Supreme Court. This incorporation never occurred. Instead, I was called upon to assist in the drafting of an amendment to the California Constitution to provide that the death penalty is not cruel or unusual punishment, and to prospectively restore the death penalty in California.

What form did that request take for your involvement?

I was contacted by then-State Senator George Deukmejian and was asked to assist in drafting the language.

What happened?

I worked on it, and it was overwhelmingly passed by the electorate as Proposition 17 of 1972 reversing the *Anderson* decision.

Who else was involved in that, other than Senator Deukmejian?

The governor's office was working with Senator Deukmejian on it, specifically the governor's chief of staff and legal affairs secretary. Those were, respectively, Ed Meese and Herb Ellingwood. My contacts were primarily through Senator Deukmejian's office.

But the other two branches were working together on that. Talk a bit more, if you would, about Chief Justice Wright and his leadership of the court in this matter, which I think was a surprise to the governor who appointed him.

I'm sure that many presidents and many governors have been surprised by decisions rendered by judges they appointed, but probably no one more than Governor Ronald Reagan, who had appointed Donald Wright as Chief Justice. Certainly the people in his administration knew Donald Wright quite well. I believe that Wright, who was a Court of Appeal justice at the time of his elevation, had served on a committee that evaluated candidates for appointment to the bench by Governor Reagan, had worked well with Reagan's administration, and had been interviewed very extensively, I heard—even on the question of the death penalty—before his appointment to the high court. Also, I believe, the administration—based on a review of all of his opinions—considered him very much of a hardliner in the area of criminal law, so his authorship of the *Anderson* opinion certainly came as a major surprise.

I was told there was also some bad feeling between Reagan and Wright arising from the fact that the Chief Justice was otherwise ready to retire but insisted he would not do so before Justice McComb was removed from the California Supreme Court. That resulted in some rather acrimonious relations, but McComb ultimately was removed.

That's a process of the Commission on Judicial Performance?

Yes, Justice McComb was removed due to his inability to perform his duties [*McComb v. Commission on Judicial Performance*]. I will say, as an advocate who observed his demeanor on the bench, that there was no doubt in my view that he exhibited signs of senility in his behavior.

The final chapter in my relationship with Chief Justice Wright occurred when I had a personal meeting with him. I received a letter from the Chief Justice shortly after I was appointed to the Los Angeles Municipal Court. I don't know how usual it was to receive a letter from the Chief Justice on one's appointment, but this letter, in any event, was somewhat unusual. In fact, I have that letter, dated April 26, 1972. It reads: "Dear Mr. George, I was delighted to read of your appointment to the municipal court in Los Angeles. Having observed you in court, I am well acquainted with your conspicuous ability and I predict for you a most distinguished career on the bench. Please accept my sincere congratulations." Then here is the interesting part in this context: "If you are in the San Francisco area, please drop in. We will find it easier to converse than we did in the courtroom. With best personal regards." I knew and he knew that it would be customary for me to be in the San Francisco Bay Area as a new judge attending the California Judicial College, which in fact I did attend in July of that year, roughly three months after receiving that letter. I thought, well, not only can I or should I, but obviously I must pay the Chief Justice a visit. This is a command performance. [Laughter]

As a brand-new judge who had just turned 32, it was with some trepidation, of course, that I called up the Chief Justice's chambers and made an appointment to meet with him. I assumed this might be a five-minute meeting, just a courtesy call, but what amazed me was that it ended up being the better part of an hour. I was asked very direct questions by Chief Justice Wright, including some about various cases I had argued before the court. But he focused on the *Anderson* case and specifically on the petition for rehearing. How was it that I came to write such a strongly worded petition for rehearing? Did I just take it upon myself to do this? I said, "I'll be very candid with you. I'm not attempting to avoid responsibility, but I was directed to not give kid glove treatment to the petition for rehearing and to express our position quite forcefully. What I wrote was reviewed very carefully at all levels, by the attorney general himself." He was very interested and asked me quite a bit about all of that.

What next occurred was the somewhat troubling part of it. As I got up to leave—and this was in the old chambers of the Chief Justice located on the fourth floor of the McAllister Street building, what's now called the "ceremonial" chief's room because it's used for meetings but no longer as a chambers for the sitting chief—I walked by the windows that face out onto Civic Center Plaza. Partly but not fully concealed by the drapery was a tape recorder, one of those old spool-to-spool tape recorders. The tape and the spools were moving. Needless to say, I didn't comment on what I had observed. I don't believe it was apparent to Chief Justice Wright that I had seen this. The entire drive back to judges' college in Berkeley, I was going over in my mind each and every word that I might have uttered. Was there anything I said that I wish I hadn't said, especially if it had been recorded? That's all I can really say about the conversation. Although it was very cordial, it was a bit unnerving to be meeting the Chief Justice, let alone having those questions posed and realizing that our conversation appeared to have been recorded. But he was very polite and not unfriendly.

After I became chief, when I became aware of the archival material that is kept by the librarian of the California Judicial Center Library, which services the California Supreme Court and the First District Court of Appeal, I asked her whether there were any records that had been deposited in the archives from

Chief Justice Wright that might include a tape recording or a transcription of a tape recording of my meeting with him. He had given most of his material to the Huntington Library in Southern California, but she was unable to locate any record of the conversation there or elsewhere. There is no way of knowing for sure what happened with that tape, but I don't believe it was an unreasonable assumption on my part that the tape recorder had not been activated coincidentally for reasons unrelated to my visit. I think that the conversation must have been recorded—and for whatever purpose I'll never know. But the incident is a tantalizing bit of California Supreme Court history—of the Chief Justice surreptitiously recording a conversation with a future Chief Justice.

Neither of you could have known that you would be peers, in the annals of history at least. Did you have further personal interaction with Chief Justice Wright before his retirement some five years later?

No, not before his retirement, nor afterwards.

What else about the Anderson *case and your immediate involvement in that would you like to add before we move on?*

Of course, the case was something that received a lot of publicity. I received a letter from a deputy attorney general in the San Francisco office who I guess was involved with the *Anderson* case earlier on. The letter was dated the day of my appointment to the bench and was written in good humor. My colleague wrote that at first he resented that I had been given this case to argue and then thought afterwards how lucky it was for him that this happened. In the end he concluded with reference to himself, "pride goeth before a fall." Ron George gets appointed to the bench after losing the issue of the constitutionality of the death penalty. [Laughter]

The case certainly did bring me to the attention of the appointing authority, Governor Reagan, and I was not blamed by anyone for the outcome.

As you say, it did get a lot of attention. I don't know what your awareness was of public sentiment in the way this was playing out. Did any of that come back to you in any direct way?

There was a lot of correspondence I received, even telegrams and letters from legislators, about the arguments I had made, letters pro and con, depending upon whether the legislator did or did not favor the death penalty. It was a moment of much publicity and personal attention.

Do you want to finish the part about the U.S. Supreme Court making Furman v.
Georgia *its lead case and proceeding on that basis?*

Yes. Without the benefit of a live case, review in *Aikens* ended up being
dismissed by the U.S. Supreme Court. *Furman* then became the lead case, and it
did not pass muster the way I believe *Aikens* would have passed muster under
the standards set forth by the U.S. Supreme Court.

That decision didn't hold any great surprise for you?

No. Once the California Supreme Court concluded there was to be no death
penalty in California, it would have been contrary to all of the jurisprudence of
the U.S. Supreme Court to hold on to the *Aikens* case and render what would
have been basically an advisory opinion.

*It certainly had ramifications nationwide. You make the interesting distinction
between the southern cases and the situation in California.*

Yes because, again, I want to stress the highly unusual, almost unique, nature of *Aikens*. I felt, and I feel to this day, that it was not coincidental that this
particular case was picked out of hundreds of cases around the United States and
dozens of cases in California for review on the issue that was before the high
court. It is rare to have a jury waiver on the issue of penalty in a capital case and
still rarer to have had the trial judge engage in the prescient process followed by
Judge Jerome Berenson in setting out what later became the proper standard for
judges and juries in making determinations between the alternate punishments of
death and life without possibility of parole.

What did you know of Judge Berenson before that?

I met him once or twice, but only after I argued *Aikens*. He was a highly respected judge in Ventura. In fact, even though I believe he was considered a
somewhat tough judge, the fact that defense counsel would waive jury before
him in a capital case shows that they certainly considered him a fair judge as
well.

*Thank you for reflecting on that. We also want to talk about your involvement in
the case of Sirhan Sirhan and the assassination of Senator Robert Kennedy. You
mentioned that you and your wife were in France at the time the assassination
occurred in June of 1968 and that you learned the news from someone deliver-*

ing room service, little knowing of your coming involvement in the case. What happened that led it to come to you?

One day in the office—the transcript in the *Sirhan* case had been received, and I don't believe the appellant's brief had yet been received—I was summoned into the office of the head of the criminal appeals section and was told he would like me to handle the case. It was a very lengthy transcript. I remember they had to install a special metal bookcase in my office to handle the many thousands of pages of transcript. By the way, in the strong earthquake that occurred in 1971, that bookcase came crashing down on my desk. But it was at about six in the morning, so I wasn't at work yet. It was quite a chore going through the record, and of course the case was receiving a lot of attention. I devoted many months to preparing the brief. A lot of issues were raised. In fact, I learned years later that the attorney general's office subsequently printed extra copies of the brief, which covered many different issues and alternate arguments, to give to new deputies as a model brief. I consider that a great compliment by my alma mater.

A number of interesting issues were raised in the case. One of them was related to the issue raised in the *Krivda* case. In a pile of trash adjacent to the Sirhan residence, an envelope was observed on which were written the words: "RFK must soon die, die, die," repeated many, many times, and the issue was raised whether there was an expectation of privacy in the contents of one's trash that lies in plain view. Sirhan's lawyers also claimed he had a constitutional right to enter a plea of guilty to first-degree murder in exchange for a life sentence—without the prosecution's consent, which it did not give, instead seeking to obtain the death penalty, which it succeeded in doing. There were issues involving the effect of pretrial publicity, various issues relating to Sirhan's mental capacity, other search and seizure issues arising out of what was considered an emergency situation, there being some thought at the time that perhaps this assassination was part of a nationwide conspiracy to assassinate other public officials in addition to Robert Kennedy, who of course was a candidate for president of the United States at that time. And there were some more garden-variety issues as well.

How did your office instruct you to pursue this? Was there anything in the way of particular guidance in this instance?

No. Once you were experienced you were just handed a case file with the understanding, "Do your best job, and come back in a few weeks or a few months." Someone would be assigned to review your brief.

Again, you were being singled out for a very high-profile assignment.

Yes. I was quite awestruck to be handling a matter with such legal and historical significance and with an obviously high profile nationally. It was a great privilege.

The oral argument in the *Sirhan* case took place during a very busy month of April 1972—on April 7, four days after my petition for certiorari was granted by the U.S. Supreme Court in the *Krivda* case. My appointment to the bench came just two weeks after the *Sirhan* case was argued, so there were a lot of things happening toward the end. The opinion affirming the conviction came down after I had been appointed.

Actually, that was not the only involvement I had in the *Sirhan* matter, because during the pendency of the appeal there were attempts to reopen the case on the theory that conspiracies had been uncovered, that evidence had been concealed, and that some of the ballistics evidence had been tampered with. I was asked to participate with law enforcement agencies and the district attorney's office in an investigation. As an attorney who was primarily an appellate lawyer, my involvement in past cases assigned to me had more often than not been somewhat in the abstract in terms of evaluating broad legal issues. But here I was getting involved in the gritty aspects of the physical evidence, literally handling material intimately associated with the fatal shooting itself, and even examining autopsy photos which, in the case of a public person, were very difficult for me to look at—with the victim's face being peeled back to expose areas of the skull, and examining ballistics evidence, and so forth. This was, again, a very different kind of experience, given the fact that Robert Kennedy was a public figure.

As I mentioned, I had been introduced to Sirhan during my visit to death row in preparation for the death penalty arguments before the U.S. Supreme Court. In subsequent years, Sirhan has kept asserting his innocence and putting forth conspiracy theories. As an associate justice and then as Chief Justice, I had to recuse myself on the petitions filed by Sirhan in the California Supreme Court. Presumably he will continue to file others in the future. The same was true regarding filings by the two defendants in the Hillside Strangler case.

You had fairly abundant evidence in this case. I'm wondering, from a legal standpoint, what kinds of choices did you have to make about how to present on the appeal?

I had a lot of alternate arguments, and that's why, perhaps, they used this brief for training purposes. Where possible I would contest whether an issue could even be raised in terms of whether an adequate objection had been made and, if it could be raised, whether error had occurred, and if there was error, was the error nonprejudicial. But then, let's say, with reference to a search, if not justifiable on traditional grounds, was there some emergency circumstance here that would authorize the search, given the possibility of a national conspiracy to assassinate public officials? If not, with regard to the search of Sirhan's bedroom in the family home, did Sirhan's brother have authority to give a consent—which he purported to do—to the search? Then I tried to distinguish some of the cases that restricted the search of garbage, saying that they shouldn't be applied retroactively to cover Sirhan's search. So I had alternatives and I tried to argue on every conceivable theory.

My relatively short time in the attorney general's office was quite an interesting experience. But there was a lot that was not as glamorous as the death penalty and the *Sirhan* case. I don't want to give the impression that it was all such heady stuff.

What other kinds of more routine duties did you face?

There wasn't usually all that much trial work in the attorney general's office. If you wanted some trial experience—or if they wanted you to have some—you would have an assignment under the trials section. As I mentioned previously, the way we new deputies cut our teeth was to try auto forfeiture cases, which often had jury trials, and matters in which the attorney general's office substituted in because the D.A. had a conflict of interest.

There were also a number of cases where the State of California would be sued because of prison conditions, or a prisoner would file a habeas corpus petition, and I'd go into federal court—which is a very different experience from going into state court—and have to defend the state in terms of justifying a prisoner's continued incarceration or perhaps defend the state against a claim seeking damages. Some of those federal judges at that time were viewed by us state deputy attorneys general as somewhat tyrannical and not that receptive to arguments by lawyers representing the state.

There was a judge named Leon Yankwich, who had been appointed by President Franklin Roosevelt and was, needless to say, well on in years. I appeared before him on a couple of cases. I heard that on one occasion an attorney somewhat intemperately kept looking at his watch—even though he himself, I think, was late—and exclaimed, "I wonder when that little SOB is going to take the bench." Judge Yankwich was a very short man, and with that, up pops the chair behind the bench. He'd been reclining in his chair. [Laughter] So there were amusing experiences even in federal court.

How else did the federal courts differ? Did you get much of a sense of that?

Much more formal and very punctilious, more concerned with proper decorum. The state courts, for the most part, were less formal and did not demand strict adherence to specified procedures.

How were your skills as an advocate evolving?

Needless to say, one acquires some degree of self-confidence, having survived 11 arguments in the California Supreme Court and six in the U.S. Supreme Court, and appearances before a variety of trial judges, state and federal, some of whom were pretty hard on young lawyers. I learned to show the proper respect but how to bounce back and try not to be intimidated, and at the same time give my client, the State of California, vigorous representation.

Anything else about the attorney general's office?

I was involved in the rotating assignment I mentioned to you of being administrative assistant in charge of the L.A. office so that gave me some administrative experience.

We touched on that before but not in great depth. In practice, what kinds of actual duties did that involve?

Dealing with the press, to a certain degree; briefing the section heads on some problems and even the attorney general occasionally; dealing with the public and public complaints, and that type of thing. It wasn't anything all that significant, but it was probably my first exposure to some sort of administrative responsibility.

I should mention also, somehow I'd gotten involved as a member of the State Bar committee on criminal law and procedure, which had some members who became quite prominent in later years as justices, judges, district attorneys, and public defenders. This was the beginning of many statewide professional contacts I had with persons outside Los Angeles, which proved to be very instructive.

It gave you a bit of a view of the whole system?

Yes, the whole system and how things operated in different parts of the state.

The admonition I mentioned to you previously, that I was expected to focus less on major cases and handle more administrative matters, accelerated my interest in applying for a judicial appointment. I began to see a diminution of the opportunities that I was enjoying so much in the attorney general's office. The stars just seemed to be in the right alignment for an appointment to the bench. I was involved in a lot of high-profile cases, although not always on the winning side.

But you'd already run the table, in a way?

Yes. So I thought this might be the time to apply. I wrote a letter to Governor Reagan—and I actually mailed it from Los Angeles International Airport on my way to argue the *Aikens* case before the U.S. Supreme Court—asking to be considered for appointment to the bench.

You said you had already come to his attention?

Yes, I had come to his attention somewhat, but actually it was more after *Anderson* came down, so I don't know to what extent I had come to his attention or just to his office's. My letter was dated January 15, and the oral arguments in Washington took place January 17. I pecked out the letter myself at home on my Royal typewriter and put it in the mail at the airport.

I had never met Governor Reagan, but I just thought, this is the right time. I received a letter in reply dated January 24 that was probably a form letter, but it indicated—I believe the words were—"every possible consideration" would be given to my application. That was in the days before there was a Commission on Judicial Nominees Evaluation, known as the JNE ["Jenny"] Commission, so what a governor would do, whether it was an appointment to the municipal court or to the Supreme Court, would be to submit the names of the candidates to the board of governors of the State Bar, and they would evaluate them at their next meeting or the following one. Less than three months after receiving the letter from Governor Reagan, I received a telephone call from him appointing me to the bench.

He did call you himself?

He called me himself on April 20, 1972.

What did he say?

This truly sounds like vintage Ronald Reagan, but his exact words were, "I know about your fine work in the attorney general's office, and I've got some new chores for you." I felt as if I were being summoned to his ranch to clear brush or split logs. [Laughter] Those were his words. And he said some nice things about the work I had done.

His appointments secretary was Ned Hutchinson, with whom I had a conversation shortly after receiving the Governor's call. Hutchinson said that they were favorably impressed with my qualifications and that they had set out to appoint me to the superior court directly. Someone else also had made an inquiry on my behalf, where that possibility had been raised. When that possibility was passed on to me, I had said, "I can't be appointed to the superior court. I would love it, but the California Constitution says you must be a member of the State Bar for 10 years or more for appointment to the superior court or any higher court." And the constitution provided then, "and for municipal court, five years or more." Given my youthful age, I had not been a member for 10 years. So I had had to make that known, and Hutchinson confirmed this in our conversation. Looking at it in retrospect, I am very happy for the time I spent on municipal court. When we get into that phase of my career, I'll be able to share anecdotes and experiences that were not only highly enjoyable but that probably made me a better and more experienced judge.

That was my first direct contact with Ronald Reagan.[1] I remember the call came on a Thursday. It was customary for the person in charge of advising the governor on judicial appointments to notify the presiding judge that an appointment had just been made to his or her court and then for the presiding judge in turn to call the newly appointed judge. That Thursday afternoon, about an hour or so after my conversations with Governor Reagan and Mr. Hutchinson, I received a call from the presiding judge of the Los Angeles Municipal Court, a rather crusty judge named Alan Campbell. After he congratulated me and said he'd heard good things about me and all that, I started to conclude the conversation by saying, "I'll see you Monday morning, all set to get started." He said, "What do you mean? I expect you here at eight o'clock tomorrow morning. I'll swear you in, and I've got a jury trial for you at eight-thirty." On Friday morning. [Laughter]

Even though I had spent only about seven years in the attorney general's office, I still had a certain amount of packing up to do. I remember trying to get my affairs in order, closing up some correspondence and files, packing things into boxes. It took me until 2:00 a.m. getting everything out of my office, and it

---

[1] In fact, the only time I met Ronald Reagan in person was when I visited him in the early 1990s in his Los Angeles office after he had left the presidency. My eldest son Eric was with me, and Reagan shared a couple lawyer jokes with him.

seems as if I've been kind of catching my breath ever since then, moving from one thing to the other, without much of an interval of time to catch up. But this was really quite abrupt.

When he swore me in the next morning, Judge Campbell gave me the following advice: "Let me tell you something, young man. Don't ever forget that every time you render a decision as a judge you'll make one temporary friend and a permanent enemy. Now, put that aside and never let it influence your decision making." [Laughter]

That's having it both ways. [Laughter]

He swore me in, and there was my jury trial. Then, of course, at a later date there was the customary formal induction ceremony. The court would get a few judges together who were newly appointed during the past few months and have a ceremonial swearing in. I still remember, in reflecting upon the growth of the legal profession since then, that the president of the State Bar addressed the group of new judges—there were nine of us—in Division One, stating that he was conveying greetings on behalf of the 30,000 members of the State Bar of California. We now have more than 200,000.

Were you able to have family with you on that occasion?

Yes, with two of our three sons on their feet, the three-year-old and the one-year-old, and another one *in utero*. [Laughter] Barbara was quite visibly pregnant.

In fact, I recall Barbara and an equally pregnant friend dropping by my courtroom unscheduled several weeks later, shortly before the noon recess, during a jury trial. They had just had appointments with their gynecologist, whose office was located near the courthouse and near Tommy's, where they stopped to order chili burgers for an impromptu lunch in my chambers. I must have shown my embarrassment as the bailiff, with court in session, led these highly pregnant women carrying this fare past the jurors and into my chambers.

Maybe you can fill in a bit about your family life in these intervening years, about your three sons and also how your parents were doing?

My parents were doing quite well. Needless to say, they were very, very proud. I called my father, who was in Europe at the time, and he said, "You've been appointed a judge? What do you mean? What kind of judge?" I told him Los Angeles Municipal Court, and he was very pleased, as was my mother. It was a dream come true for them as immigrants to see their son argue in the U.S. Supreme Court and then be appointed to the bench.

There were some judges who were friends of our family serving on the Los Angeles bench. Going through files upon my retirement, I came across some of the congratulatory letters. It was rather surprising for me because I had forgotten about this, and rather heartwarming, to see a couple judicial family friends who actually wrote that this would only be the first of several appointments leading eventually to the California Supreme Court. One was Judge Emil Gumpert, a longstanding family friend, and another was Presiding Justice Lester Roth, a friend of my in-laws. I thought that was a very nice thing to say, but who could have ever believed it—and who knows how much they truly believed it. It was surprising to come across that old correspondence in the course of doing my latest packing and unpacking upon retiring.

And your own family?

The boys were too young to understand what was going on. Later that first year on the bench, our third child was born and we had three very active boys under the age of four.

Where were you living at this time?

We were living on the west side of L.A. County in Beverly Hills, and once I took the bench I was commuting to the main court building in downtown L.A. The courthouse was just two blocks up the street from the old state building where I had been working in the attorney general's office, on First Street, opposite the *Los Angeles Times*. Then as the result of earthquake damage, the entire building holding that office and the Court of Appeal had to be evacuated, never to be occupied again. It has been razed and is becoming part of the long-delayed civic center mall. My future judicial assignments to the Hall of Justice, the Criminal Courts Building, the Court of Appeal, and the Los Angeles quarters of the Supreme Court all were located within a three or four block radius of the main courthouse and where I had worked in the A.G.'s office.

Barbara, of course, was wonderfully supportive and so excited throughout all of these events in my career. She was with me for all of the oral arguments in Washington. She's been part and parcel of all of these experiences, including a lot of things I'll mention when we get to my time as chief, in terms of her role in bringing art and the display of historic memorabilia to the buildings housing the court and the Judicial Council.

By the way, I had kept my application for appointment to the bench quite secret from my colleagues at the attorney general's office.

What was your thinking there?

This may sound a bit odd, but because I was bearing the heavy burden of a high-profile caseload, I had the perspective—perhaps incorrect and unrealistic— that maybe one of my bosses would say, "We really need him to finish up his cases that are not yet final. He's young and he can wait." I think that was behind my thinking. So no one knew about my application. Attorney General Younger even asked me later why I had not sought his help in obtaining the appointment. My colleagues, both my superiors and my contemporaries, were quite startled and apparently extremely pleased at my appointment. It was heartwarming to experience the attitude, "Here's one of us. Look, we can get appointed to the bench from the ranks." Some of my contemporaries took me out to lunch at a Chinese restaurant in Chinatown in Los Angeles and presented me with my judicial robe. I had had to borrow one for my first several days on the bench. [Laughter] The robe they gave me was one that I continued to use during my entire thirty-eight-and-a-half-year career as a judge.

That is the robe that hung in your chambers at the Supreme Court?

Yes, with the initials in the inner collar. It's the same robe. If that robe could talk about all the things it's seen! It has stood me in good stead over the years and required very little mending—it just suffered a little fraying around the sleeves.

You've remarked on other occasions how that robe is symbolic in a personal way to you.

It is. It was my custom as Chief Justice to receive the newly appointed judges who were up for a one-week orientation conducted by the Judicial Council and the Administrative Office of the Courts. I would describe to them the procedures followed at the Supreme Court, what my duties were as chief, dealing with the three branches of government, and all that. On one occasion Fritz Ohlrich, the clerk/administrator of the court, brought a group of new judges to my chambers. When he invited questions, one of the new judges inquired of me, "Why do you keep your robe out here on the coat rack?" I said, "With all of the administrative responsibilities I have, running the largest judicial system in the world, I never want to forget that I am a judge. My first and foremost responsibility is to participate in the decision of cases, and it stands as a constant reminder to me to see my robe hanging in the corner of my chambers instead of being put away inside a closet."

The lunch celebrating my appointment to the municipal court was fun, needless to say, with my colleagues from the attorney general's office presenting the robe. Being at a Chinese restaurant, the obligatory fortune cookies were passed out. Of course, my colleagues were eager to see what mine said. I opened my fortune cookie and, quite dramatically, proclaimed, "Judge not, lest ye be judged." [Laughter] But they learned this was just a joke on my part.

That pretty much was the conclusion of my career as a deputy attorney general—a wonderful experience, a very heady time for a young lawyer, being able to argue important cases before those high courts at a time when there was a lot of change taking place in the law, and having a steady diet of constitutional issues, a great learning experience before embarking upon a career on the bench.

###

Chapter 4

To the Bench: The Municipal Court
July 13, 2011

We were talking last time about the preliminaries and ceremonials leading to your becoming a municipal court judge at the appointment of Governor Ronald Reagan in 1972. You mentioned going to Judges' College in Berkeley in the summer of 1972, as I gather all the new judges did. Tell me more about who was there and what was happening.

Judges' College was a wonderful experience, as it still is today for virtually everyone who attends, because there is a great amount of knowledge that's acquired, no matter how much knowledge one might have in the various substantive fields. Seeing it from the perspective of being on the bench, making rulings—evidentiary and other—on various matters, is very different from having studied or even practiced law in those areas. There's also a great sense of camaraderie among new judges and an opportunity, after having spent time—for most people it was a few weeks or a few months—in one's own court, to meet colleagues similarly situated but from around the state, giving one an exposure to a great variety of backgrounds and geographical and other variables in the practice of judging. It's an excellent experience, and after full days of study, there's an opportunity in the evenings to get together and socialize.

In terms of my own personal experience, I was told that I was apparently the youngest judge in the state. I got teased quite a bit about that, both from my fellow student judges and from the faculty. It also may have been because I believe I looked younger than my age, which was just 32 to begin with. I was referred to by some as the "boy judge," which was a moniker that followed me once I got back to the L.A. Municipal Court. The other basis for becoming better known than perhaps I wanted to be among my fellow student judges was that one of our instructors, Judge Arthur Alarcon, who was then a judge of the L.A. Superior Court—later to become a justice of the state Court of Appeal and then a judge of the U.S. Court of Appeals for the Ninth Circuit—made a point in his course on criminal law and procedure of illustrating various developments in the law by reference to particular cases that he would introduce as, "Here's another case that Ron George lost representing the State of California." [Laughter] He referred to at least three cases I recall. One was *Chimel v. California*, as upending the law of search and seizure. Another was *In re Tahl*, which caused a total revision in the procedure for taking pleas of guilty in criminal cases, in terms of advisement of rights and of consequences of the plea and taking waivers. Then, third, *People v. Anderson*, which held that the death penalty was cruel or unusual punishment under the state constitution. Judge Alarcon enjoyed pointing out that these were cases in which I had not prevailed.

Did you know Judge Alarcon before this time?

Not all that well, but we had had some contact. I was fairly well known in the Los Angeles legal and judicial community just from the very cases that I mentioned as well as from others where I did prevail. Of course, I took this teasing good-naturedly and put forth the explanation that apparently Governor Ronald Reagan had concluded I could do less damage as a judge of the municipal court than I had done as an advocate arguing on behalf of the people of the State of California. [Laughter] I did become somewhat notorious at Judges' College.

Who were your fellow new judges?

In addition to dozens of new judges from all over the state, there was the group of the nine of us from the L.A. Municipal Court who had all participated in a joint swearing in ceremony—so we called ourselves the Supreme Court of Los Angeles. Included in the group were Armand Arabian, who later was a fellow justice on the California Supreme Court; Robert Devich, who ultimately became a justice of the state Court of Appeal; and Dickran Tevrizian, who ultimately became a judge of the U.S. District Court for the Central District of California. Michael Sauer retired a couple years ago after serving 36 years on the municipal and superior courts. A former senior colleague from the attorney general's office, Warren Deering, also retired after serving on the municipal and superior courts. Everette Porter and Maurice Hindin completed their judicial careers on the municipal court. David Kennick was removed by the Commission on Judicial Performance from his position on the municipal court, due to his prolonged, unexcused absences from the bench and various acts of judicial misconduct.

After Judges' College you went back to Los Angeles and resumed your trial duties. Your presiding judge, Alan Campbell, had put you on a case early on your first day after swearing you in. Could you tell me a little of the early trials that you were asked to take on? Were you in a criminal division?

I was in a criminal courtroom, and had the usual assortment of misdemeanors. What was interesting was experiencing the transition from having made, late in the month of March, the last of my six appearances before the U.S. Supreme Court on a lofty constitutional issue, the right to counsel at police lineups, in *Kirby v. Illinois*, and April 7, arguing the *Sirhan* case before the California Supreme Court, and then basically a couple weeks after that, being right in the trenches of a crowded urban courthouse, immersed in presiding over the gritty practice of the law with an assortment of real-life people charged with a tawdry array of street crime. That really came to the fore a bit later when I was assigned to the master calendar court. It's there that I encountered high-volume court calendars and undertook my first administrative assignment as a judge. It was very interesting to go from the abstract, almost scholarly, practice of law as a deputy attorney general that same month down to the everyday stream of cases, mostly involving petty offenses, that I encountered as a municipal court judge.

How was the workload, in terms of numbers of trials? I know it's just a guess this much time later, but what kind of numbers do you think you were seeing?

Before my assignment to the master calendar court, it was pretty much one case trailing the other in a steady stream. There was a broad array of cases that I was hearing, anything that came up as a misdemeanor—mostly Penal Code violations but sometimes local ordinance violations, as well—with the city attorney prosecuting the misdemeanor cases. Very much in contrast to the more abstract type of legal issues I was encountering as a deputy attorney general. The building to which I was initially assigned was the main courthouse for both the superior court and the municipal court. Interestingly enough, there were separate lunchrooms for the judges of each court. As a municipal court judge you couldn't go into the superior court lunchroom unless you were invited by a superior court judge. It was almost like a caste system of some sort. Those distinctions later disappeared by the time the courts unified during my tenure as Chief Justice.

Soon the Criminal Courts Building would open, which was a nineteen-story, block-long edifice designated just for criminal matters in the downtown or central part of Los Angeles County. That structure supplemented and then replaced the Hall of Justice, which was a very decrepit building that housed jail facilities on the upper floors. Felony preliminary hearings were being held there, and that became my next assignment. I was transferred from the main courthouse to the Hall of Justice before the new Criminal Courts Building was fully operational. In any event, this leads me to talk about the assignment I had in the Hall of Justice, handling felony preliminary hearings, as opposed to the trial of misdemeanor matters.

May I ask you, before we do that, to talk about Presiding Judge Campbell and your fellow judges when you first arrived? What was the experience of working yourself into this group and getting to know them?

A lot of them seemed to know me or know of me through these high-profile cases I'd had as a deputy attorney general. Sometimes when I had a case that had substantial impact on the criminal law—which by definition would mean when I had lost, because if the status quo continued it wouldn't be that significant, at least in terms of the effect on judges in applying the law—I would be sent by the attorney general's office to give lectures and explain, for instance, the new procedure for taking a plea of guilty or the new rules affecting search and seizure incident to arrest. I somewhat whimsically viewed this as a form of penance. [Laughter] I had lost the case, so I would have to make the rounds and explain it to judges and district attorneys and defense counsel, which I did. I got involved in the lecture circuit, so I got to know a lot of them that way. Through my involvement in the Municipal Court Judges Association of Los Angeles County, I soon was asked to author a publication that summarized legal developments for the judges of the 24 municipal court districts and one justice court located in Los Angeles County. I found the 64 judges on my court, the Los Angeles Municipal Court, as well as those on the other lower courts in the county, to be very receptive and collegial.

What was Judge Campbell's style of leading that group and making assignments?

He was really a no-nonsense administrator, but very cordial and gentlemanly. I didn't encounter a single judge whom I considered unfriendly, and of course I got kidded somewhat about, "Now you're in the trenches after doing all these lofty arguments. Now you see where the law's really made," or where the rubber hits the road, so to speak. [Laughter]

What sort of staff and clerks did you have available to you at that point?

Very fine clerks and bailiffs. The 25 municipal and justice courts in L.A. County had their own deputy marshals who served, instead of deputy sheriffs, as the courtroom bailiffs. There was more of a personal relationship and closeness with staff at the municipal court level than there was at the superior court level, perhaps just by necessity, given the far larger operations of the superior court.

The municipal court was a wonderful place to learn the art of judging. I acquired my trial judge skills there in an environment where the consequences were not as substantial as they would be on the superior court level. If a municipal court judge was a bit rough around the edges or made a mistake, the consequences were not as significant as when those errors would occur with a judge at the superior court level. Maybe because of that and because the judges tended to be younger, there was a great amount of informality, and joking around, and even practical jokes that went on at the municipal court.

That was right up your alley, if I may say so?

Yes, I'm afraid so. [Laughter]

Do any examples come to mind?

There was a colleague, Judge Jack Goertzen, who had been one of my supervisors when I did trial work in the attorney general's office. He was known as a notorious practical joker. Before I came on the municipal court, he and another judge, Pat Mullendore, had done some outrageously funny things. For example, there was another judge—Irwin Nebron, who later became presiding judge—who was very fastidious about his chambers and everything being very much in order and clean and spic-and-span. Judge Goertzen and Judge Mullendore went down to the Grand Central Market a few blocks to the south of the courthouse, purchased a live chicken, and let it loose in Judge Nebron's chambers before he arrived one morning. [Laughter] He came in totally flabbergasted by the sight and presumably the smell of poultry feathers and droppings and ordered the bailiff to come and remove the chicken. The bailiff apparently chased it around the chambers and finally was commanded by Judge Nebron, "Shoot the darn thing!" Which did not take place. But this was an illustration of some of the hijinks that went on at the municipal court.

Judge Goertzen, by the time I came onto the municipal court, had advanced to the superior court. We knew each other quite well. Although he headed the criminal trials section in the attorney general's office, he had handled some appellate cases, including one appeal that went to the U.S. Supreme Court.

When I told him that I had ordered copies of the tape recordings of my six oral arguments before the high court, Judge Goertzen was very interested and asked me how to do it. I told him it was a bit complicated. You had to contact the clerk of the U.S. Supreme Court and then, through the marshal's office of that court, you could get the tapes from the Library of Congress. When that was all said and done he asked, "Why don't I just go ahead and borrow your correspondence?" He wrote a letter asking for the tape recording of his oral argument. The case he had argued, *Douglas v. California*, was the companion to the famous case of *Gideon v. Wainwright*. *Gideon*, of course, involved the constitutional right to counsel in criminal trial proceedings, and *Douglas v. California* involved whether that same right extended to an indigent criminal defendant at the appellate level.

I just couldn't resist pulling a prank on Judge Goertzen. What I did—and hopefully the statute of limitations has run on this—was make up a fake letter, with photocopied letterhead, from the office of the marshal of the U.S. Supreme Court, to Judge Goertzen in response to his request. The letter reads, as follows. "Dear Judge Goertzen, This will acknowledge your recent order of a copy of the tape recording of your oral argument in *Douglas v. California*, the landmark decision extending the constitutional right to counsel to proceedings on appeal. It may be of interest to you that during recent years we have prepared copies of the recorded oral arguments for two law schools which have, in turn, forwarded to us the articles which they prepared analyzing the oral arguments in *Douglas v. California*. For your information, reference is made to these scholarly works." The letter cited two contrived titles for articles that were never written. The first was listed in the letter as "Comment: '*Douglas v. California*: Did the unrepresented defendant on appeal receive legal representation superior to that afforded the State of California?,'" citing the *Arkansas Law Review*. Then the other title: "Note: 'The right to counsel as established by *Douglas v. California*: Do principles of estoppel preclude an incompetent deputy attorney general from arguing the alleged non-prejudicial effect of lack of defense counsel on appeal?,'" citing the *Idaho Law Journal*. Finally, concluding: "Trusting that this information will be of interest to you, I remain, very truly yours."

I assumed that Judge Goertzen, having borrowed the correspondence from me, would conclude that this was a practical joke. However, I received a phone call from his clerk, whom I had to let in on the joke because I couldn't easily come up with a fake envelope. The clerk usually gave him his correspondence opened, with the envelope. The clerk said to me, "He received the letter, and he's taking it for real. Do you want to talk to him?" I said, "No, I'll let him stew in it for a little bit." I received another call about 15 or 20 minutes later from the clerk, who reported that Judge Goertzen, who is always a happy-go-lucky kind of fellow, was in a very gruff mood. Judge Goertzen had inquired of his clerk whether the judges' library in the courthouse happened to carry issues of the Arkansas and Idaho law publications, and he was told that it did not.

Then I received a third call from the clerk about a half hour later informing me that the judge was prepared to cancel his afternoon court calendar because, he said, he had some important research to do at the county law library. With that, I said, "Tony, put Judge Goertzen on the line." I got on the phone with him, and instead of receiving the usual friendly greeting I heard, "Yes? What is it?"

I said, "Jack, I just called to say hello and tell you that I happen to have back issues of the Arkansas Law Review and Idaho Law Journal in case you're interested." There was a silence, and then the words, "You son of a bitch!" And then uproarious laughter. Happily my friendship with him survived that incident. This is symbolic in some ways of the levity that existed, not that our cases weren't serious, but there was a lot of fun at the same time.

I have to tell you, Judge Goertzen and Judge Mullendore invited me out for lunch as a new judge. At the time I was assigned to the master calendar court. It was a time when many people enjoyed two- or three-martini lunches. I'll never forget. I just had one strong drink, and I came back, horrified, to the sea of humanity in Division 40, thinking, "My gosh. Here's a microphone and all of these proceedings I have to go through and take pleas and waivers and rule on motions. I will never, ever have even one drink over the lunch hour when I have a court calendar to go through, certainly, at least, not in the master calendar court." Judge Mullendore, like Judge Clarence "Red" Stromwall, a former member of the much-feared, four-detective L.A. Police Department hat squad, was known for taking the D.A.s and the public defenders out for drinks at the end of the day and then having to drive them to their homes afterwards. But these two judges remained solid as a rock.

Before serving in the master calendar court, I was assigned to relieve a judge in a division in the Hall of Justice that handled felony preliminary hearings. I was told only that the judge would be absent for a while—it wouldn't be too long—and I believe a reference was made by someone, perhaps the court staff, to the judge being on vacation. But I knew better than that, because I was aware that the judge in question, the Honorable Leland Geiler, was the subject of a disciplinary proceeding pending before the Commission on Judicial Performance. I knew this because the attorney general's office acted as counsel for the commission, and while still working in that office I had become aware of the ongoing investigation of Judge Geiler. The episodes of judicial misconduct verified by the investigation illustrate the dark side of the humor, if you will, and the eccentricity of this member of the bench. Judge Geiler had a ribald approach to life that I believe would rival that of some of the more outrageous characters in Chaucer's *Canterbury Tales*. Many of these incidents are set forth in the opinion of the California Supreme Court removing him from office. I also heard more details because some of his staff, and some of the attorneys—D.A.s and public defenders—assigned to his courtroom were on the receiving end of his behavior there and were called as witnesses before the commission. The incidents were truly outrageous. My assignment to the very grimy Hall of Justice stretched longer and longer as these hearings went on.

There was one incident, which is set forth in the California Supreme Court's opinion, involving an item received in evidence as an exhibit in one of the preliminary hearings conducted by Judge Geiler. I'm getting a little off-color here, but I'm talking about things that are a matter of record. It was a battery-operated mechanical dildo. The judge invited the D.A. and the public defender in for a conference in chambers, emerged from behind a filing cabinet, and proceeded to chase the public defender around until he managed to give him a pretty good prod in the buttocks with the dildo. Back in open court, when that public defender would continue with cross-examination that the judge thought excessive, the judge would make on-the-record comments like, "I guess it's time for me to take out that exhibit." Then he'd turn to the clerk and say, "Power up the battery on that." There were repeated references to this item. The public defender would then just say, "All right. No more cross-examination, Your Honor." Truly outrageous judicial behavior.

The judge also had a salacious interest in any kind of case that involved sex or sexual language and would make a point of repeating lewd language from the testimony. One incident—and I don't think this one got into a finding that made its way to the California Supreme Court, but it was mentioned by court staff— occurred when a group of grade-school children were brought to court by their teacher to see the workings of our system of justice. As chance would have it, they wandered into Judge Geiler's courtroom, and as chance would also have it, a felony preliminary hearing involving pimping charges was underway. The teacher immediately realized this was not suitable fare for her charges and got up to leave with them, but they were directed by Judge Geiler to remain in the courtroom and listen. When the vice officer employed some terminology to describe in the vernacular an offered sex act, the judge made a point of explaining to the little boys and girls exactly, "This means such-and-such." Again, truly outrageous behavior.

There's another incident that is in the official decision of the California Supreme Court removing Judge Geiler from office that involved his approaching a court commissioner in a crowded hallway in the Hall of Justice, reaching from behind him, and grabbing the commissioner's testicles to the point where he almost passed out from pain. This was another basis for Judge Geiler's being disciplined. This was the first decision removing a judge from the California bench, as opposed to lesser forms of discipline. Geiler illustrated the dark side of the characters who were on the bench. Most were quite normal in their actions and sense of humor, but there were a few who were truly eccentric.

I ended up getting involved in a bit of a dispute with one of the other judicial eccentrics, Judge Noel Cannon. Her odd behavior included—and this is contained in the official opinion of the California Supreme Court upholding the commission's action removing her from the bench—having a mechanical canary in chambers whose chirping could be heard during court proceedings, and regularly keeping a small dog in her lap or under the bench. The word was that a couple of the D.A.s would surreptitiously blow a dog whistle, whose high pitch—although inaudible to the human ear—would agitate the dog, thereby disrupting the proceedings, much to Judge Cannon's consternation. She was very proud of the fact that she had managed to have the county redecorate her chambers in pink and invited the media in to make a show of that. A judge, whom she was never able to identify, infuriated her by arranging for the installation of a pink toilet seat cover (which became known in the court building as the pink fanny gasket) in her chambers bathroom facility. She also had a rather unusual judicial robe made of fur, as well as a habit of using profanity on the bench.

But perhaps her most outrageous action occurred after she was stopped on the way to court one morning by a police officer, who told her that she was using her horn excessively and that the person she was honking at was properly stopped at the intersection. She responded with profanity and said no one was going to tell her what to do about using her automobile horn. When she arrived in chambers—this is all documented in the Supreme Court opinion—she demanded of various individuals in the command of the L.A. Police Department that this officer be summoned before her immediately and that she was not going to take the bench until he appeared. She said that if he ever crossed her again, she would give him "a .38 caliber vasectomy" with her firearm. She said this openly, so he was summoned into court. When he appeared, she completely altered her demeanor and gave the officer some religious tracts to read, as she often would with prisoners who were in the lockup. Judge Cannon also threatened to shoot the manager of her apartment building, and she had public defenders taken into custody in her courtroom when they displeased her. Outside of court, public defenders often would refer to Judge Cannon as a judge of the Marsupial (as in kangaroo) Court.

My run-in with her involved her refusal to authorize the reimbursement of travel expenses for a witness who had come from the East Coast to testify concerning the theft of court records from the West L.A. courthouse. I was serving there as supervising judge, and the witness was a UCLA student intern working in the clerk's office. Despite the absence of any supporting facts, Judge Cannon imagined that this attractive young woman was an accomplice of the thief and was sexually interested in him. Judge Cannon instructed the D.A.'s investigator not to have an affair with the witness—and not to repeat the judge's remarks to anyone. The Commission on Judicial Performance found this incident to constitute prejudicial judicial conduct. I decided to countermand Judge Cannon's order and directed that the witness be reimbursed, which needless to say displeased the judge immensely. By the way, that intern is now a judge of the Santa Barbara County Superior Court.

As you say, if the Commission on Judicial Performance hadn't yet had occasion to exercise the power to remove a judge, it was an interesting test of that whole relatively new system.

Yes, it certainly was, and these were two prime examples upon which to build a foundation of precedent for dealing with conduct that is sufficiently extreme as to justify the most extreme sanction, namely removal from the bench.

What else can you tell me about substituting for Judge Geiler in the felony preliminary hearings? What was that experience like for you?

It seemed that everyone—the clerks, D.A.s, public defenders, and some of the private attorneys in the courtroom where I was assigned—ended up being called as witnesses in the disciplinary proceedings.

Also just serving in that building was an unforgettable experience. Parts of it looked somewhat dungeon-like. It was very, very grimy and quite a contrast from the marbled halls of the U.S. Supreme Court. [Laughter] This was a real change in venue for me, that's for sure, down to the reality of everyday legal practice and judicial decision making in a large metropolitan area.

Thinking mainly of your more normal assignments, I wonder how were you taking to actually being a judge?

It's interesting that many lawyers have their trial experience first and then their appellate experience. But having started as a lawyer whose practice was primarily appellate and only incidentally trial, I was very conscious as a judge of building a record, of making sure that if there was an objection it was clearly stated and on point when I was called upon to make a specific ruling on an objection, because I had spent most of my career as a lawyer having to evaluate claims of error on appeal. Aside from the substance of the claims of error, there was always the question of whether the point had been adequately preserved by way of objection or request for jury instruction or some other procedural prerequisite to being able to claim error on appeal. I was made very conscious of all of that by my experience in the appellate courts. I went out of my way, always, to build a very careful record and also to afford counsel the courtesy of an explanation for my rulings, even though the conventional wisdom—and it may be correct—is that the less you say the better off you may be as a judge in terms of having your ruling upheld. As an appellate lawyer, having been mystified sometimes by various claims and rulings made at the trial level, I felt there was a moral if not legal obligation to make the basis for my rulings quite apparent to the counsel for the parties who were appearing before me.

I wonder how you compare that practice of yours to offer an explanation—and also your thoughts about looking ahead to what might happen should there be an appeal—to what your colleagues in the municipal bench were doing. Did you have occasion to discuss this with them?

I'm sure I did. I wasn't going around giving advice to people, let alone those who had far more experience than I did on the trial bench, but to the extent we talked about these things I could give my perspective, not as an enlightened trial judge so much, but as someone who had experience as an appellate prosecutor in trying to have judgments sustained that trial judges were making. It was very helpful to have a basis for a ruling but certainly to require specific objections and other requests or assignments of error and to make sure that the record was fully developed, and sometimes to develop it a bit more yourself without taking over the case, but just to make sure that there was an adequate basis upon which a ruling could be premised.

Your colleagues may not have had the kind of experience that would allow them to do that in the same way, so it was an extra level of benefit on your part, in some sense?

I don't want to imply in any way that I came in there as some kind of expert. Some of these judges had decades of experience on the bench, and I was a neophyte. But many were interested in the perspective of someone who had done appellate work in the attorney general's office. I learned a great deal that was of practical use from them too, so it certainly was a bilateral exchange of information and views.

To ask another way about your early experiences, how did you like being a judge?

It was very enjoyable to be there actually making the decisions instead of just arguing your position, even though the arguments I had participated in had taken place at very high levels of our court system. On the other hand—and I know that many new judges have this experience—it was frustrating sometimes to see counsel for either the prosecution or the defense doing a woefully inadequate job. Sometimes when this would happen, it was so tempting to doff one's robe and jump off the bench and try the case for them. [Laughter] Of course, I'm talking figuratively, but more specifically a judge is capable of taking over a case from a lawyer who's not doing a good job, but that's not right. It's not fair to do that. However, there are particular issues that arise in the context of a party who is not represented by counsel. You don't want to hold someone inflexibly to the exact same standard that you would require of an attorney. On the other hand, it's not fair to lean over backwards so far to assist an unrepresented litigant, whether in a criminal or civil case, that you're being unfair to the represented side. That does make it more difficult. But putting aside those considerations, you have to learn—and I think you do after a few weeks or months—that sometimes you just have to sit on your hands, figuratively, and let the parties try their case without your taking control over it merely because you feel it could be done better. That's not your job as a judge. You get to make the decision but you don't get to try the case as well.

How common was it to see unrepresented litigants?

I saw them in other assignments later on that were civil in nature, and of course small-claims cases that I also ended up handling on occasion. In the criminal sphere there was, of course, the constitutional right to counsel. There were certain kinds of infraction-type offenses where we might see unrepresented litigants, or sometimes in more serious matters they would waive their right to counsel, which they had a right to do, and insist on representing themselves. Although they were technically acting as lawyers, one couldn't demand 100 percent performance as one might from a lawyer. That just wasn't realistic, even if they were technically held to the same standard.

What else can you tell me about the quality of advocacy you saw coming from the district attorney's office during that period?

The office was often understaffed, as was the city attorney's office. The cases in municipal court were trials of only misdemeanors or only preliminary hearings in felony matters and sometimes were basically last-minute handoffs from one deputy D.A. to another. Sometimes you wondered if there was a competition among D.A.s to see who could get through a preliminary hearing presenting the least amount of evidence to survive a Penal Code section 995 motion to set aside the information, the charging document in superior court. The D.A.s would refer to earning "a skinny award," just in terms of how little you could manage to put on and thereby divulge of your case, just to get by and have enough to be allowed to proceed to trial.

The public defenders were very much understaffed, as of course they continue to be. I was continuously amazed at the perception held by so many persons charged with crime that somehow the deputy P.D.s were inferior, just as a matter of course, to the average private criminal attorney. The popular phrase used by persons charged with crime was that the public defenders were "dump trucks," implying that they would just dump their cases through plea negotiations. By the way, I much prefer that term to the word "plea bargain." I try to avoid the word "bargain" when I can; it sounds too much like the marketplace. [Laughter] But there was that perception of public defenders dumping their cases, and that they were not really there to fight it out for the best interests of the defendant. I found that perception to be quite inaccurate. If I had to generalize from my own experience, I would say that the average deputy public defender handling misdemeanor cases and routine felonies was more than equal to the average privately retained attorney handling those types of case. Within the realities of caseload and the amount of time and resources to prepare, I was for the most part favorably impressed by the deputy public defenders, just as I was by the prosecutors, whether they were deputy D.A.s or deputy city attorneys.

Los Angeles had somewhat pioneered the concept of having a public defender, I think. That office certainly had an important history.

That's correct. I believe Clara Shortridge Foltz established the very first public defender's office in California.

You had other special assignments in the course of your municipal court career.

Yes. After doing my stint in preliminary hearings, I was assigned to what was known as Division 40, which was the misdemeanor master calendar court. I believe I served about 14 months in that assignment. It was quite an incredible place. It was a very large courtroom; I believe it seated more than 250 persons and sometimes had standing room only. The courtroom had a custody box that would hold at least 25 prisoners behind a glass partition. At that time, every misdemeanor criminal case that was not a traffic case—because there was a separate courthouse for those cases—in the central part of Los Angeles County passed through my courtroom, with the exception of those cases that had been disposed of right at the arraignment court located at the Bauchet Street jail.

The way the master calendar court worked in the municipal court was that a case would be set for trial and everybody had to appear in the master calendar court on the trial date, the prosecutor, the defense attorney, the defendant—who was out on bail or own recognizance or in that custody box—and the witnesses as well. The average was probably to have 80 to 90 trials set on my morning calendar there, with everyone packing the courtroom, standing in the back, sometimes spilling into the almost impassable hallways adjacent to the courtroom, and maybe 25 or 30 custodies in the box. There were days when I had more than 100 trials, and everyone was supposed to be in the courtroom, which was the size of a theater. I would call the calendar of cases first thing, and the prosecutors would be asked to announce whether they were ready for trial.

If they knew they weren't going to be able to proceed with the case they would indicate that, but that was rarely the case. Usually those cases that weren't ready would go off to a second call of the calendar, mid-morning. By a certain time, if the case was not ready—or unless we were to settle it—I would dismiss the case under section 1385 of the Penal Code if the prosecution was unable to proceed and lacked legal cause for a continuance. So there was a lot of scrambling to locate witnesses, and so forth. Sometimes I heard the explanation, when privately retained defense counsel had not been paid, that the witness on whom counsel was waiting was "Mr. Green." [Laughter] That was a euphemism for saying, "Please put the case over until my client gives me some cash." But the prosecution didn't have that type of excuse, of course, in light of the defendant's speedy-trial rights. Cases would be called and called again, and dismissed by late morning. If the defendant didn't show up, I'd have to issue a bench warrant for his or her arrest.

I had a panel of trial judges who were considered "murderers' row." They were all very, very tough—a lot of old-timers. The defendants and their counsel generally were afraid to be assigned out to one of those judges. They didn't want to take their chances in going to trial, or to have to dispose of the case in a trial court on very severe terms. Consequently, I was disposing of the vast majority of the cases. Most never left Division 40. The panel judges often were just sitting around for hours or days with little or nothing to do, and occasionally would come down to chat or say, "Hey, let's go out to lunch." I would say, "Are you kidding? I'm too busy here." [Laughter]

There were all sorts of really colorful types among the private defense counsel, too. I remember Gladys Towles Root, who was sort of notorious and somewhat on in years by then. She wore outrageous hats and would come into court very décolleté, and some of the trial judges would make her take a kerchief and cover up her cleavage. [Laughter] There were some fairly outrageous characters on the bench and in the bar. It was quite a different experience for me.

In addition to a caseload that could exceed 100 on the morning trial calendar—to be dismissed, bench warranted, disposed of by way of plea negotiation or, to a much lesser extent, sent out for trial—there was an afternoon calendar of often 40 or 50 matters that were cases that had been continued for sentencing, or that were bench warrant pick-ups, or involved pending motions or cases brought by various county agencies, as well as holdovers from the morning calendar. The courtroom gave one the impression of a tide in a sea of humanity that came rolling in every morning, and you'd finally finish with the last dozen or so of the persons in the courtroom very late in the day. If you were to spend just a few extra minutes on each case you'd be keeping your staff there into the evening hours, so you had to be efficient and very quick and yet grasp a lot of things going on simultaneously. It was like a multi-ring circus. Then, of course, the next morning the tide came in with hundreds of new people in a new bunch of cases.

Some of the colorful characters I dealt with were defendants charged with various street crimes. At that time, the authorities were prosecuting a lot of lewd behavior cases, section 647(a) Penal Code violations. Although I knew what the charge was and was aware that the defendant had a male name, when I'd call the case and this beautiful creature in female attire would step forward, I'd fall for it from time to time and announce, "No, not the witness. I want the defendant forward." Then I'd hear a deep voice from the person indicating that, in fact, this *was* the male defendant. [Laughter] So there was a parade of every kind of thing you could imagine, from minor drug cases to indecent exposure and prostitution offenses, weapons cases, some less-aggravated assaults, shoplifting, gambling violations—such a contrast to what I had been dealing with as an appellate lawyer. That made it very intriguing and a welcome change of pace, believe it or not, after handling very heady matters, to see that side of street life in the micro-cosm of this courtroom.

What an education for you. What do you think you took away from that that you didn't have before?

Certainly a more direct and personal appreciation for the foibles of human behavior, because it is different dealing with people as individuals whom you see in the flesh and blood in front of you, warts and all, with their excuses, their attempts to justify their behavior. That goes for not just the defendants but some of the witnesses and the victims, as opposed to seeing things as an abstraction on appeal in the cold record of a transcript. This was very edifying for me and, in an odd way, tended to humanize the process for me.

This Division 40 assignment sounds quite intense.

It truly was. There were days where it was quite exhausting, not only for me, but especially for the court clerks and the deputy marshals. You can't imag-ine the number of prosecutors, public defenders, and private counsel, all running around inside this courtroom, often trying to get the attention of one of the sev-eral clerks so their case could be called. It was the type of scene, bordering on pandemonium, that you see in a third-world marketplace or on the floor of the New York Stock Exchange when trading is going on—so many simultaneous side conversations, interruptions, and requests for priority, and occasionally in-cidents of acting out. I actually had occasion there, and to a much lesser degree sitting in a trial courtroom, to have to hold persons in contempt, including some attorneys, which I didn't do lightly, but the master calendar court provided an environment that led people to vent their frustrations from time to time. Again, it had its moments of great humor as well. What I liked is that the consequences were not life and death, although they were important to the defendants and their families or others close to them, as well as to the victims. It was a place to learn about judging and to see a vast parade of life come before you every day on this tide and then recede.

After that assignment was over, were you back to what you had done before?

I had had a trial assignment before this master calendar assignment and then again afterwards, which I'll mention before I cover the West Los Angeles seg-ment of my career on the municipal court. There were actually, I want to make clear, some very substantive matters that we dealt with on the municipal court. I had some cases involving criminal charges that were brought against nursing homes for violation of various codes and regulations. Some of this involved questions of first impression, where—and I would not do this lightly as a trial judge, let alone as a municipal court judge—I ended up writing a couple of opinions interpreting these statutes and regulations that had not previously been interpreted. I also remember holding a hearing on the admissibility of polygraph or lie detector evidence, even though it was settled that a judge did not have to admit such evidence. But a showing was made that perhaps there was a stronger than normal basis for admitting it in the case before me. After hearing expert testimony on both sides of that issue, I ended up not admitting the polygraph evidence.

Then, on the lighter side, I have to say that one of my first misdemeanor trials did involve a rather seedy incident of a young man who was caught in a converted movie theater on Skid Row that featured striptease acts, engaging in a sexual act with himself, and had the misfortune to be caught in the expanding circumference of the Klieg light, while a vice officer was stationed in a box seat, dutifully surveilling the scene. I had been a judge just a very short time, and my father decided to make his first visit to see me in court. At that point I was on the receiving end from the master calendar court, so I didn't know what case might be assigned to me, or I certainly wouldn't have encouraged my father to come that day. But he shows up with two cronies of his from the stockbroker's office where he spent much of his time. This case gets underway, and I can detect from my father's body language his acute embarrassment. Although obviously I couldn't hear the conversation, his body language was more or less showing that he's making excuses to his friends, "This wouldn't be the normal type of case that my son would be handling. His cases are much more significant than that." [Laughter]

Did you talk with him about it afterwards?

Yes. He said he felt somewhat embarrassed to have brought his friends downtown to see his son presiding over that kind of case. Actually, the day he was there, both sides agreed on something, unfortunately. It was that a "jury view" would be very helpful in this matter. I felt, although I had discretion over it, that if both sides wanted to visit the scene of the crime, I should agree to it. We scheduled a jury view for either the next day or a couple of days hence. Counsel, the court staff, and I traipsed down there to this seedy area of Skid Row, with the jurors in tow and the defendant present. In order to provide the jurors with the same visual conditions initially encountered by the vice officer, both sides wanted the jurors and everyone else to enter the theater in a darkened, hardly illuminated condition. Then, once we had had our view, the lights were turned on—and they did have a Klieg light display. After the jurors, who seemed to be comprised of an inordinate number of elderly women, saw what they had been stepping on—and I won't go into detail—there were shrieks of dismay and insistence that they be excused to go home for the day so they could clean up. I acceded to that. This case was not a high point in my judicial career. [Laughter] But both sides felt that a jury view would really illuminate what the vice officer could or could not see from the vantage point that he was at.

Since we're talking, now, about family visits to "my son, the new judge," soon after my appointment to the bench I invited my mother to the symphony at the music center, which was just up the street from the court that I was assigned to. She was eager to see my courtroom, and I showed it to her. We were then going to have dinner nearby and hear the symphony. I was explaining to her that each courtroom shared a lockup with the adjacent courtroom, and she expressed interest in seeing it. Here's my mother in her evening finery, who walks into the lockup, which is filled with graffiti. It was not very pleasant visually, nor was the smell, because it was large enough to accommodate quite a few prisoners. I attempt to show her how this is state of the art, that the barred doors to the lock-up close electronically. The doors slam shut, incarcerating my mother. Guess what happens? There was a short in the electrical circuit, and I can't liberate my mother, who's locked in there planning on dinner and the symphony. [Laughter] It was after hours, so it took some time to find a deputy sheriff in the building who was able to come up and open the cell manually.

So those were my parents' visits to their son, their respective first-time visits to me as a judge—maybe not the most edifying of experiences, in terms of the new career that their son had embarked upon. My mother ultimately had her revenge when I brought home my judicial robe to perform a wedding ceremony at a nearby hotel, and unbeknownst to me she managed to sew up the sleeves of the robe. My penchant for engaging in the occasional practical joke may be a trait inherited from her.

There are a few other incidental experiences—as a new judge I was on search warrant duty, and some nights there would be a call at two or three in the morning. Barbara would brew up some coffee, and officers would come over to our home and wait while I read over a search warrant application.

That duty is generally for the new judges, to get awakened during the night?

Yes. I had some other interesting encounters away from the courthouse. I remember being approached at a bank and the person saying, "I appeared before you." I was already expecting some "acting out" there. Instead I heard, "The best thing that could have happened to me, that changed my life, was to receive that sentence from you."

I also remember once trying to do a home plumbing repair. I had affixed a pipe onto the toilet and it had gotten jammed up. I had to end up taking the toilet into an establishment in a not too great part of town that would help you with your plumbing problems, and I certainly needed help. This very large man was eyeing me as I was standing there waiting my turn. I figured, this is probably someone I sent away, and he doesn't look too friendly. Finally, I thought I'd break the ice, and I asked, "Where do we know each other from? You look familiar." He said, "I'm attorney so-and-so." Like me, he was standing there in his jeans with his plumbing.

I said, "How funny to see you here." He replied, "Listen, five minutes ago, this man comes up to me who's a client and says, 'Counselor, what are you doing in a place like this?' and I said, 'What do you mean? That's nothing. That's the judge over there!'" [Laughter] It was a bit of a metaphor. We were all reduced to the same level.

Then I was walking down the Venice boardwalk, and it was like one of those scenes out of an old movie. There was someone in the first chair of the barbershop facing the boardwalk with lather all over his face and the door open. I don't know how many people get a real shave anymore at a barbershop, but this fellow turns to me, because I'm just about three feet away, and says, "I know you. Where is it that I know you from?" I took a good look at him and said, "Mr. Reznick, I prosecuted you for stealing the names of the narcotics agents and their home addresses in the *Los Angeles Free Press* case." [Laughter] All judges end up having these strange encounters from time to time.

I gather it was 1974 to 1975 that you were made supervising judge in West Los Angeles. How did that come about?

The L.A. Municipal Court had a new presiding judge, Joan Dempsey Klein. She was in the attorney general's office before I was and was appointed to the municipal court and later elevated to the superior court and ultimately to the appellate court, and she remains to this day the most senior of the presiding justices of our Courts of Appeal. When she became presiding judge of the L.A. Municipal Court, she concluded, as she put it, that it was "time to clean up the West L.A. branch." She did not like the way it was run. She thought it was inefficient. There were some practices that she thought were undesirable. I guess I had established a reputation for getting things done in running the master calendar court downtown, so she suggested—well, it really wasn't a suggestion—I was assigned out there to be supervising judge. [Laughter]

I still remember going out there the first time. Three of the judges assigned to West L.A. had been there for many, many years and viewed it as their fiefdom. Judge Leo Freund had been there the longest. I had never met him before, but I remember our meeting—coming out there prior to actually assuming my duties as supervising judge—and his first words were, after a brief greeting, "Tell me, young man, what year were you born?" I said, "1940." He said, "I want you to know something. I have been sitting as a judge of the Los Angeles Municipal Court since four years before you were even born." What was left unsaid was, "I like it just the way it is, and you're not about to change anything that I'm involved in." [Laughter] That was an interesting welcome.

As I paid this introductory visit to the West Los Angeles branch—which was on Purdue Avenue, a rather rundown facility—I was regaled with stories about Judge Freund. It was known that if you said you were a member of ZBT fraternity, or had ever been, you would be let off or be dealt with very leniently. That was all it took. But the most memorable story I was told involved Judge Freund's calling of the arraignment calendar. Both at the call of that calendar and in the trying of misdemeanor cases, he had a habit of reading the police report, which was stapled to the pink complaint form. But as a judge you were not supposed to consider the report unless it was a matter of setting bail. In a crowded courtroom, Judge Freund called a case in which the defendant had a Hispanic surname. The judge calls the case of *People v. Whatever-it-was* and starts reading the police report to himself. Then he says, "What? You did this? You said this to the officer?" He was scowling and getting quite annoyed and going on and on about it, reading it to himself but still voicing his reaction to it. Finally, the defendant interjects—because he didn't speak English—"No comprendo. No comprendo." Freund, who already was somewhat hard of hearing, cups his ear and says, "What's that? A plea of *nolo contendere*? All right. Ninety days in county jail."[1] No one in the courtroom could believe it, and then Judge Freund insisted that the bailiffs remand this fellow. Finally, during a recess, it was explained to Judge Freund what had happened and the defendant was released from custody. Freund appropriately proclaimed his guiding philosophy to be "Justice delayed is justice denied," but many of his actions were viewed as typifying the law west of the Pecos, or at least west of the San Diego Freeway.

One of the other things that went on in West L.A. was a very cozy relationship with the University of California, Los Angeles. It was customary for complimentary UCLA season tickets to football games and other athletic events to be delivered to all the judges. The problem was that, of course, UCLA not only is and was a public agency that was appearing before the judges in that court facility as a party, but university students and employees also appeared regularly before the court as complaining witnesses or defendants in misdemeanor or traffic matters, and as jurors. Additionally, various prosecutions were initiated by the UCLA campus police. So this practice really put the local judiciary in a compromising position, where there certainly was at the very least the appearance of impropriety. When my first batch of free tickets arrived, I sent them back to the chief of the UCLA police department with the indication that I didn't think it was proper for me to receive them, but that each judge would have to make his own determination. I copied the other judges on that correspondence, so they all begrudgingly returned their tickets. This did not endear me to some of the old-timers.

Judge Freund, though, soon was assigned to the Beverly Hills courthouse, not as a Beverly Hills municipal court judge but as a West L.A. judge sitting in a borrowed courtroom, because to run the master calendar and to deal with the caseload we needed an extra courtroom. Since he would be hearing felony arraignments and felony preliminary hearings, there was no legal problem in terms

---

[1] A plea of *nolo contendere* or no contest has the same legal effect in a criminal proceeding as a plea of guilty.

of where he could properly sit, unlike the situation that might arise where a defendant faced a jury trial and had the right to be tried by jurors from that vicinage. A couple of the newer judges came out to join me, and I did make quite a few changes and set up a master calendar system for the West Los Angeles branch. I was pleased with some other improvements I instituted there. Several weeks after his death in 1976, Judge Freund managed to win reelection to a new six-year term of office from the voters of Los Angeles.

Can you tell me about the master calendar operation and how you put that into place?

The benefit of it was that one person—whoever was sitting in the master calendar court, which happened to be myself as supervising judge—would be able to direct the flow of cases to a court that was open for trial, whereas what the judges frequently had been doing was arranging for long gaps between the cases that they themselves set for trial in their own courtrooms. Under the former system, called direct calendaring, a judge who might have an excess number of cases awaiting trial wouldn't have any ready way of dealing with them and they might face dismissal, whereas another judge might be sitting around with nothing to do. Establishing a master calendar court enabled a supervising judge to have a case sent over as soon as the trial judge finished one case and sent the jury out to deliberate. This cut down quite a bit on the backlog.

There are a couple other things I should mention about the West L.A. branch. To deal with the caseload, we had a modular unit brought out there, so we literally had a "trailer court." I sat in this improvised courtroom for a brief time. It was a terrible place to try to dispense justice, because you had the sound of the very noisy air conditioning, which interfered with the audibility of some of the proceedings. You'd turn it off and then when it got really hot you might have to declare a recess and turn the air conditioning back on. Sometimes departing defendants on motorcycles would deliberately make an extra loop or two around the trailer courtroom, which was situated in the middle of the parking lot. [Laughter]

On one occasion when I was working late in the main West L.A. facility attending to some of my supervising duties, I heard a pounding noise. I didn't know at first if it was the plumbing or air conditioning or something else. The incessant pounding continued. I went to explore what it was, and it turned out to be frenetic knocking by an alternate juror. The alternates, of course, are customarily kept separate from the jurors in most instances, once they start deliberating. He had been locked in a separate room. My happy-go-lucky bailiff had just forgotten about him after releasing the 12 regular jurors, and had gone home that Friday evening. If I hadn't been working late in the courthouse, this poor alternate juror probably would have spent the weekend there. Happily, I found a deputy from the sheriff's office who was awaiting the last pickup of prisoners to be brought back to the downtown jail. He managed to unlock the room where the alternate was kept. I remember telling my bailiff Monday morning, "Bruce, one of these days someone is going to unlock one of these doors and find 12 skeletons hunched around a jurors' table in a deliberation room." [Laughter]

But it was an early introduction to you to the matter of court facilities, which of course you dealt with in great depth later on as Chief Justice.

Yes, and we'll talk about some of the woefully inadequate facilities for jurors and others, once we get to the point where I was in more of a position to do something about them as Chief Justice.

I also set up a process for informal resolution of traffic matters, had court forms translated into the Spanish language, and instituted a judge pro tem program for attorneys to volunteer to sit as judges to handle small claims cases with the consent of the parties. So a lot of changes were made to try to get this very overburdened branch court into a more efficient type of operation.

Had some of these measures been done in other branches? Where did these ideas come from?

Of course we had a master calendar court downtown that I had presided over, so I thought a similar process would be useful out there. It was really just a matter of sort of shaking things up a bit. That occupied me through 1975.

It took a certain courage in Presiding Judge Klein's position to take on a long-standing system full of players who say, "This is the way we've always done it."

Yes. Speaking of long-standing practices and traditions, it was a uniform practice and tradition that the next person to be elected assistant presiding judge would be the one with the most seniority in service on the court. Then that person would be unopposed in running for presiding judge the year after.

There was a L.A. Municipal Court judge named Joe Grillo who was viewed as very erratic and cantankerous. Reports of his divorce proceedings disclosed that he would wear his judicial robe at family dinners and require his children to address him as "Your Honor." He reportedly told the superior court commissioner hearing Grillo's divorce case that Grillo would overrule the commissioner's ruling. I was urged by my younger colleagues to challenge the seniority system and run against Joe Grillo for the position of assistant presiding judge. I did that in September of 1975, when I was only 35. I lost by about three or four votes out of the 64 judges on the court. A lot of promises were made by my opponent, and many of the judges still adhered to the seniority approach.

How common was it even to have someone run against the anointed next person?

Very, very uncommon. After I lost, early next year I asked to be reassigned, to resume a downtown trial assignment. An incident soon occurred that became of great interest in the media and elsewhere. Judge Grillo did live up to the predictions that had preceded his election concerning how he would perform in an administrative position. As presiding judge, he ended up ordering a county employee to honor a travel claim involving Judge Grillo's request for reimbursement for his expenses in going to Sacramento to lobby for something that I'm sure he felt was for the benefit of the L.A. Municipal Court. The trip wasn't authorized by the county, and it may be that Grillo should have been reimbursed. I don't know very much about the underlying controversy. Maybe the county was wrong in directing that he not be reimbursed. But when an individual who was basically an underling in the county auditor's office on the orders of his superiors refused to write out a check to Presiding Judge Grillo, Grillo walked across the Civic Center mall with his bailiff, from the courthouse to the county hall of administration, and directed the officer to arrest the county employee for contempt of Judge Grillo's order. This caused a big to-do.

At a meeting convened in August of 1976 by the judges of the court, many of whom were quite upset about this action, I offered a resolution declaring that regardless of the merits of the underlying dispute over travel expenses, Grillo had not chosen a proper means of resolving the dispute. My resolution failed to prevail. Before the month was out, I found myself the subject of an unusual mid-year reassignment by Presiding Judge Grillo—to the San Fernando Valley. This in turn prompted a fair amount of outrage among many of the other judges. I managed to work my way back to a downtown assignment quite soon, so that was short-lived, but it was an interesting little experience.

Tell me about San Fernando, if you would. How did it differ?

Every branch has its own atmosphere, and there was nothing about the San Fernando Valley, being assigned out there, that I didn't like except for the fact that it was distant from my home and involved driving over the Santa Monica mountains through one of the canyons to get there, and the fact that I viewed it as a form of retribution for the views I had expressed. In retrospect, the short-lived reassignment became a humorous topic among my colleagues and myself. I suppose it was illustrative of the personality of Judge Grillo.

How did you go about getting back downtown?

I don't remember the details. Probably through a phone call or two from myself and others. He backed off pretty quickly. It didn't take a lot of effort. [Laughter]

What became of Judge Grillo?

He did not advance to the superior court, and once Judge Grillo had done his year running the L.A. Municipal Court, Judge Nebron became the presiding judge and created a brand-new position of supervising judge of the criminal division of our court, assigning me to occupy that position out of a trial department in what was then known as the Criminal Courts Building.

That was another layer in the structure, intended to—?

Just to coordinate the operations of the municipal court in that building because, in addition to the panel of misdemeanor trial judges and, of course, Division 40, where I had sat—the misdemeanor master calendar court—there was also Division 30, which was the master calendar for felony preliminary hearings, the preliminary hearing judges, and some other specialty courts. Everything was brought under the supervision of the newly created position of supervising judge for all the criminal operations.

How did you like the assignment of heading up that new function?

I enjoyed it. We were able to streamline the operations there although, having had a master calendar operation already, the change was probably less extreme than it had been in West Los Angeles.

Once you were back in Los Angeles as supervising judge of criminal under the leadership of Presiding Judge Nebron, how were your own judicial skills evolving by that point? Did you have much sense of a progression since you had started, and how were things changing, if at all?

Having had the additional experience now of conducting trials and preliminary hearings as a judge, in addition to the experience I had as a deputy attorney general—where, as I said before, trials were not my major assignment; it was mainly appeals—I now became increasingly interested in systemic issues and in how things would work. I began to focus not only on the resolution of legal issues in a given case but on problems of case flow and delay and efficiency, while at the same time preserving the requisite access to justice. I believe these assignments—in the master calendar court, supervising judge of the West L.A. branch, and then supervising judge of the criminal division—all were very useful experiences for me that I gained from and ultimately made use of as Chief Justice.

That pertained not only to administrative changes that I later sought to effectuate in the judicial system, but also to rulings that I made as a Court of Appeal and Supreme Court justice. It was important to have a down-to-earth real life understanding of how the promulgation of rules by an appellate court impacts the daily operations of our busy trial courts, the practice of attorneys, and the rights of parties in court. There was no amount of abstract study of those matters that would be as beneficial as actually being in them up to your elbows on a day-to-day basis and seeing what one could do in terms of improving the system. I put some of that to use in the supervising judge positions. I also was asked by the Municipal Court Judges Association of Los Angeles County—comprised of judges from all 25 municipal and justice courts in the county—to prepare and circulate occasional advisory legal commentaries. In fact, there was a publication that I started called "Case and Commentary," which was put out by the association and later taken over by the municipal courts' planning and research unit, summarizing recent case law developments. I also wrote a short paper at the request of the presiding judge on the inherent power of courts to compel the other branches of government to make adequate provision for sufficient funding to ensure the orderly operation of the courts.

I remember going out to the Santa Anita Judicial District. This is an illustration of the variety of courts that existed in Los Angeles County. The Santa Anita district was a one-judge court, and the judge at that time was Judge John Saunders, who was the chair of the Municipal Court Judges Association of Los Angeles County.

When I went out there to meet with him concerning some issues facing the association, I recalled that this was my first trip out to Santa Anita since I had been a boy, when my father brought me out there to more or less teach me about horse racing and the cautions involved in that activity. My father and one of his business associates took their then-twelve-year-old sons—myself, and my friend—out to the Santa Anita racetrack. This was before the days of the freeway, and it was customary to leave before the last race to try to beat the heavy traffic home. We left early, but the traffic was totally jammed. My father's friend advised, "Bypass the traffic. Hit the soft shoulder here." So my father did this, just brazenly committing a traffic violation, I'm afraid. Sure enough, very soon a motorcycle officer roared up, with blinking lights and siren, and proceeded to royally chew out my father, which my father, of course, deserved. Then the officer looks in the back seat and sees us twelve-year-olds back there. He takes it a step further and says, "You should be doubly ashamed to set such a poor example as a parent in front of these two boys. That's just terrible." My father, with his French temperament, took only a few seconds to explode and to answer the officer and proclaim, "Look, you can tell me anything you want about my driving but I pride myself on being an excellent parent." Just then, almost as if on cue—I'm listening on the car radio to the results of the eighth race, where I had bet two dollars—I interrupt and announce, "Dad, Sloppy Joe," or whatever its name was, "came in and paid so-much to win, so-much to place, and so-much to show." The officer, with his hands on his hips, just shook his head, and my father felt totally humiliated. [Laughter]

That was an early encounter with the law and my father's occasionally—how should I say—creative ways of trying to bring me up. It was my last visit to Santa Anita until I went there to meet with Judge Saunders, who did a fine job of organizing the municipal court judges. Even at that time there were stirrings of a movement to unify or consolidate or combine the 25 municipal and justice courts in Los Angeles County with each other and perhaps with the superior court.

Was the movement coming from the municipal side, in this case?

Yes, from the municipal, certainly not from the superior court side.

Had that L.A. county association existed for some time already? What was its genesis?

It had. I'm not sure when it came into being. The association engaged in many worthwhile efforts.

You had a couple of other auxiliary assignments. I saw some reference to your being a member of Project Safer California, appointed by Governor Reagan?

Yes. This was a body that was basically interbranch and was designed to try to come up with some improvements in the criminal justice system.

You mentioned funding a few moments ago. In these early years of your tenure what was your thought about how well the court system was funded? What were the pressures there?

The illustration with Judge Grillo that I gave you involving the contempt incident certainly illustrates that the so-called "good old days"—like most people's perceptions of good old days—were largely figments of nostalgic recollection. Even funding for the judicial lobbying effort in Sacramento was controlled by the county. The county had very little idea of the courts' needs or of necessary expenditures, and each court was on its own—certainly there was no statewide sense of responsibility or even awareness of what was adequate funding. The courts were very poorly funded at that time, and years later they incurred great benefits once they were able to coordinate funding on a branchwide basis, with the accountability to the Judicial Council that comes with that, and in turn with the Judicial Council becoming accountable to the governor, his department of finance, and the legislature for the state funds that now became available.

I think that's pretty much it in terms of the administrative or systemic issues that I confronted as a municipal court judge. As I said, it was a great place to learn a lot of things, both procedurally in terms of how to manage a courtroom and how to improve the system of justice at the municipal court level. Also how to oversee judicial colleagues, frankly, because you learn a lot as a supervising judge—whether it was in West L.A. or downtown—or by running the master calendar court, in terms of who is and who is not a good team player. Much of my experience in that vein was very educational and stood me in good stead for the time when, as a superior court judge, I acquired additional supervisory responsibilities.

Did you find your own views changing on anything as a result of this work?

I guess just getting back to what I said before about these experiences perhaps causing me to humanize my view of people's actions and their frailty in committing some of these petty offenses. Some things you just couldn't help but chuckle at. I remember a fellow in the master calendar court who was charged with some sort of thievery because he was selling mislabeled watches. They weren't Bulova watches, but they were labeled as such. He said, "But your honor, look carefully here." He had one passed up to me on the bench. "It doesn't say Bulova. There's a slight space between the bar in the letter B and the rest of the letter, making the numeral thirteen. My watches are '13 ulova.'" I mean, how could you even make up something like that? [Laughter] Some of the offenses that took place on the streets or in the bars—again, you see human behavior but, occasionally, with all of its comedic overtones as well.

May I ask which of your colleagues you were close to?

I think that group of nine, even though there was quite a disparity in age, in background, and ethnicity—somehow we came on as a larger than normal group being sworn in together. We went very different ways, most of us, but there was a certain esprit de corps, almost like a graduating class. I also remained close with my friend Judge Jack Goertzen, who by then had gone on to the superior court. He and I would catch up together and later become colleagues on the superior court, where he served as presiding judge, and ultimately we were appointed to the same division of the Court of Appeal.

I also remained close to another of my bosses, who had been the second in command of the criminal appeals section in the attorney general's Los Angeles office, S. Clark Moore. I had learned a lot from him. After I was elevated to the superior court, he ended up being appointed to that Santa Anita one-judge municipal court judicial district that you and I were speaking of a moment ago, after Judge Saunders retired. He loved it and never wanted to go on to the superior court. He said, "This really is the people's court." One of the things he liked was that he was not just a judge, he was *the* judge. During my visits out there I walked with him from the courthouse to one place or the other for lunch. Almost everyone on the street knew who he was. "Hello, Judge." "Hello, Your Honor." He was treated like royalty, and he reveled in it. Here was something very small town-ish right in the middle of Los Angeles County.

Who could you go to for help if you needed it?

There were a number of very experienced judges who were quite my senior in time on the bench and in age. A lot of them were members of the so-called murderers' row that defense counsel were afraid to go to for trial, so I don't know that they necessarily saw things the way I would, but it was always beneficial to exchange views with them. I certainly enjoyed that. They were very receptive to any requests for advice. No one was standoffish or lorded it over me, despite my being in some instances half their age.

There was another duty I had in downtown Los Angeles that was, on occasion, rather amusing. Previously, I mentioned search warrant duty. Another duty assigned to new judges was performing wedding ceremonies. At that time the category of individuals who were entitled by law to officiate at weddings was much more limited than it is today. Consequently, you had a great number of bridal couples who would show up, especially at the central courthouse, obtain a wedding license, and then and there seek to be married at the courthouse. I remember being assigned to wedding duty two or three times at six-month intervals or so. People would be lined up at the clerk's counter probably from about 8:00 a.m. on. They'd have to wait until the noon hour to be married. As is customary, the judicial noon recess was from twelve to one-thirty, so the drill was that the assigned judge would gobble down his or her sandwich and then report to a room set up in the clerk's area of the building. These couples would be lined up, sometimes accompanied by eager family members, and you would sit down at a desk in one room and sign all the wedding certificates in advance.

Then the clerk would tell you when everyone was ready. Each couple would appear, one at a time of course, in front of a purple curtain. You'd perform a wedding ceremony that—by reference to the old comic strip L'il Abner—was somewhat of a Dogpatch-type wedding. Talk about seeing different walks of life, as I did in the master calendar court! I remember during one of the ceremonies hearing a clerk's annoyed voice from behind the curtain saying, "Will couple No. 27 get back in line? Or you'll have to go to the end of the line." If they didn't have a ring, I was told, "Just ask them to join hands." When I asked a couple to join hands, the woman dropped a bundle of newspapers that she had in her arms. By then I wasn't thinking anything was terribly unusual about carrying a bundle of newspapers, only she retrieved it right before it hit the ground and out came the leg of a newborn baby, swaddled in newspapers. I thought, "Now I've probably seen just about everything." When a groom would not automatically kiss his bride, I stopped inviting or giving him permission to do so, because you would have thought in some instances that I had asked him to kiss the floor. [Laughter] It was just a matter of getting through these ceremonies lickety-split, in time to start up at one-thirty with the court calendar. I officiated at quite a few weddings that were not truly inspirational in terms of the institution of marriage.

But it's still an important function of the system. As you say, they didn't have so many alternatives in those days.

No, although I officiated at a bunch of daffy weddings that I did "off-campus" too, some of them involving senior participants and performed at the behest of friends or of members of my family. I remember performing a wedding for the actress Britt Ekland and her husband, Slim Jim Phantom of the Stray Cats, who was at least a decade younger than she, doing the wedding at her Bel Air home, and having her Swedish contingent all standing there wearing gray, and speaking lines that sounded as if they came out of an Ingmar Bergman film. The attendants included Slim Jim's group of pseudo-Brits from his music band, wearing pink cutaways—and I say "pseudo" because I found out he was really a guy from New Jersey. His two parents were present and urged me to take a walk and bow out of performing the ceremony. They seemed not to be too pleased about their son taking a wife that much older than himself.

I performed one wedding for a wild-animal veterinarian, who was the nephew of one of my mother's tennis partners. After making a house call, he had moved in with one of his patients—an ocelot—and the patient's owner and her mother. The vet was insulted when I suggested that the ceremony symbolically should take place on top of the zebra rug in his living room. He declined in no uncertain terms, noting that the zebra had been one of his favorite patients. Some of these weddings were just hysterical. One couple in their eighties told me, "Just make it short and snappy. Neither one of us is a virgin, you know. We've each been married quite a few times." [Laughter] I always thought that if I were to write a book, it probably would have been about the weddings that I performed. I had one wedding where the male and female pet terriers decided to go at it right in the middle of the ceremony and had to be uncoupled. [Laughter] I had a couple of weddings where the dog was the ring bearer, with a pillow around its neck.

Let's cover the transition to superior court. I might start by asking—knowing that Governor Reagan's people had tried to make you a superior court judge immediately back in 1972 but couldn't owing to the constitution—as you went through this time on the municipal court, when and how did you begin thinking about approaching that next level?

I felt that I had learned a great deal at the municipal court level and that if I had been able to carve out my own career path I certainly would have chosen, in retrospect, to start my judicial career on the municipal court, as I did. I thoroughly enjoyed it while I was there. After a while, though, I came to look for more challenges in terms of different types of cases, to handle the felonies and the issues I had been involved with as an advocate—as a deputy attorney general—and to preside over the significant civil cases that one is faced with as a superior court judge. I had had a few civil matters on the municipal court, but basically it was a criminal assignment. The criminal cases were misdemeanors, except for the felony preliminary hearings, which are not all that challenging, because they only involve the determination whether sufficient evidence exists to bring the defendant to trial. Usually there's no defense put on, and of course there were no felony jury trials, although I had plenty of jury trials as a judge handling misdemeanors.

I began to look at the possibility of applying for appointment to the superior court, but it happened that I attained the requisite 10 years' experience following my admission to the bar only after the governor who had appointed me, Governor Ronald Reagan, had left office. So I had to start, in effect, all over again with a new governor, Governor Jerry Brown. I applied, and by then there was a Commission on Judicial Nominees Evaluation. It got back to me—and I had a sense too—that the interview had gone well, that the process of evaluating me had gone well, but also that nothing was happening in terms of my elevation. I didn't know if there was any impediment or not, but I saw a lot of other individuals being appointed either straight to superior court or by way of elevation.

I felt somewhat frustrated, so I did something a bit unorthodox. I made an appointment to meet with Governor Brown's legal affairs secretary who was in charge of judicial appointments at that time, Anthony Kline, and who's now a presiding justice of the Court of Appeal.

Prior to having that meeting, I had organized a small campaign committee of friends, a few of whom were lawyers, and proceeded to raise some money. I then flew up to Sacramento one afternoon in the fall of 1977 and had my appointment with Tony Kline, whom I had not previously met but later came to know quite well. He asked, what did I want to meet with him about? I said, "I'd just like to have some indication of my prospects for elevation to the superior court." Kline replied, "You know, in Los Angeles County it's very hard. You have to be patient because we're finding that there's a great need to obtain more diversity on the bench, and we're really focusing on appointing minorities." There was no indication whether and when I might be elevated—and certainly he didn't owe me any explanation—but he did ask, "Why do you want to know?" I replied, "Because I'm going to run for it, and I've organized a committee." He said, "Oh, is there an open seat?" I said, "Not that I know of." He said, "Well, who are you going to run against?" I said, "I'll pick an incumbent to run against." That was the end of the conversation. It was very soon thereafter that I was appointed. In fact, I believe there were a couple of appointments in the works that were announced the following week or so, and then I was part of the next batch of appointments to the Los Angeles Superior Court.

How did you learn of the appointment?

I received a phone call from Senator Alan Sieroty, who represented the area where I resided, congratulating me very warmly. I said, "Alan, thank you so much, but for what?" I honestly had no idea. He said, "You've been elevated to the superior court." I said, "How can that be? I haven't learned of it." He said, "I have a press release in my hand from the governor's office." Ultimately I did receive a phone call from Tony Kline, but that's how I learned of it, from Senator Sieroty.

I received suggestions that I donate my campaign funds to a political candidate, and I declined. Donors to my campaign received back everything there was, less expenditures. I think it ended up being close to 90 cents on the dollar for each contribution. I had received a very cute note from our eldest son, Eric, who was nine years old at the time, enclosing several dollar bills and saying, "Dad, I want to contribute nine dollars to your campaign." I don't know if there was a certain symmetry with his age or why he picked the number nine, or if that was what was left in his piggy bank, but it was a very sweet gesture. That was my short-lived campaign in 1977 for the 1978 superior court election. I'll never know what went on in the minds of those involved in the appointment process, but I was very grateful to my friends for coming to the fore and engaging in this effort.

It took some creative steps, though, to find out what was going on, and you had a plan for taking alternative action. How did you think all that through and decide to do those things?

I guess I felt I had exhausted the other options and—something we talked about earlier—there being a bit of the risktaker from my father in me, balanced by the more conservative approach of my mother. It just seemed to be the thing to do. My wife Barbara was very enthusiastic about the whole process and encouraged me as well. I'm sure many wives would have been negative about the prospect of a political campaign, but Barbara was not.

###

Chapter 5

Elevation to the Los Angeles Superior Court
July 21, 2011

We talked last time about your time serving as a judge on the Los Angeles Municipal Court and the fact that, after five years on that court, you were elevated to the superior court by Governor Jerry Brown. The record shows you were appointed by Governor Brown on December 23, 1977, took your oath on January 20, 1978—at age 37—succeeding the retiring Judge Steven Weisman. Perhaps you could start off by giving details about where you were sworn in?

I remember being sworn in by the presiding judge, William Hogoboom, and our three boys, six, eight, and ten, being in attendance and being very, very active little fellows running around. The obligatory photograph with the presiding judge depicts mischievous grins on their faces and maternal fingernails keeping the rascals in line. It was definitely a family occasion. My parents were there, and my sister, my uncle, and Barbara's family as well. It was a very special day. It took place downtown, which was destined not to be the site of my first day on the bench as a superior court judge.

Where were you assigned?

I was assigned, as were two other new judges, namely Loren Miller, Jr., and Florence T. Pickard, to the East District, located in Pomona. All of us were residents of the west side of the county. This was not a punitive assignment by any means, but it reflected the fact that there was fairly strict adherence to the seniority system on the court. Although there were judges who resided within a few miles of the Pomona courthouse, they had seniority and preferred to be assigned to downtown Los Angeles. Therefore, those with the least seniority, the three of us, were relegated to fill those open spots in the East District. Actually, it was a marvelous assignment, a great variety of serious criminal cases and a master calendar system, so that one was really immersed in trials, often one murder trial trailing another murder trial, without having a morning calendar of various cases to contend with, because other matters were all handled in the master calendar court. From the standpoint of the quality of the judicial experience, particularly as training for a new superior court judge, it could not have been better.

The commute was something else, however. I recall that the winter months of 1977–78 were very rainy, exceptionally so. We had to make our way on various freeways, through heavy truck traffic. Each leg of the trip out or back would take one to one-and-a-half hours. I felt like sort of a traveling salesman dispensing justice. There was one exception to the difficulty of that commute, however. One day it was my turn to pick up Loren Miller. The two of us usually would commute together. I would pick him up in Cheviot Hills and we would get onto the Santa Monica Freeway before getting to downtown L.A. and then continue eastward on the San Bernardino or Pomona freeways. As I was getting ready to leave my home, I looked outside the front window and said to Barbara, "Look. There's one of the longest stretch limos I've ever seen. I wonder what it's doing on our street this early in the morning." She said, "That's a surprise birthday gift from Linda"—one of our closest friends, Linda Millard—"to commute in style to Pomona, at least for the day." I entered the limo, and when it arrived at Loren's house he was standing outside. The limo had shaded windows, so I could see that he was looking in wonderment at the vehicle parked in front of his house. I finally put down the window, and said, "Hey, Miller. Don't you want to get to work?" He said, "What is this?" I didn't let on right away. The driver had muffins and orange juice and the *Wall Street Journal* for us. Of course, after a few minutes I told him how this had come about. Having arrived in style in Pomona for a change, instead of with the old Chevy I had, people were asking, "Is it true? We heard that you arrived in a limo?"

The supervising judge out there made a point of coming to my courtroom—it was Judge Sam Cianchetti—and asking, "Is it true that you and Miller came out here in a limo?" I said, "Yes it is. The presiding judge, Bill Hogoboom, says he really appreciates the difficulty of our daily commute, especially with this inclement weather, and he's found a transportation fund that authorizes sending us out in style." He said, "Oh, come on. You're putting me on." I said, "If you doubt me, just show up at five o'clock and you'll see we're being picked up in this vehicle." So he was there seeing Miller and me off, and my parting words were, "Judge Hogoboom has also decided to redecorate our chambers out here too, again in appreciation of our efforts." This is sort of a Cinderella story of course, because the next day I arrived in the old Chevy, and we were back to our routine. The episode was appreciated by everyone, and it was a nice exception to the normal commute out there.

You had only been on a couple of months at that time, then, if that was indeed the first year, 1978. Tell me something about your colleagues in Pomona.

It was a very agreeable group. The environment was ideal for a new superior court judge. The East District had a lot of serious crime out there, so a very interesting caseload resulted from it at the Pomona courthouse.

Being a new arrival, I was assigned to one of the courtrooms that was less desirable, at least from one standpoint. As the noon recess hour would approach, there was an odor of food that began to permeate the courtroom that I was assigned to. It seemed to be pretty much the same odor every day, and I didn't quite understand it, because there was no cafeteria nearby. It was explained to me by the bailiffs that the major custody lockup was adjacent to my courtroom. The prisoners customarily were given ham and cheese sandwiches, which they didn't find terribly savory. They thought they could embellish their lunch by melting the cheese in the sandwiches. They would take the T-shirt of a less assertive inmate and, after flushing the communal toilet in the middle of the cell, insert the T-shirt so the water wouldn't fill up the bowl. They then would burn some newspapers, melting their fare of ham and cheese sandwiches. I christened this "*jambon fromage à la Pomona.*" [Laughter] Other than that, I think the facilities were okay.

Knowing you were at a different level of the court system now and, as you say, trying felony cases, how would you compare what you were seeing to the comparable thing downtown?

It was really heavy duty, quite unlike the petty street crime that predominated the municipal court caseload. It seemed that I had one murder trial after another, some of them murders for hire. There was one trial in particular—*People v. Humphries and Berry*—that went on for about four months. There was an attempt to contact some of the jurors, and I reluctantly had to sequester them and have them locked up every night. It soon became evident from their requests for the reading of testimony and instructions that they were having a very difficult time arriving at a verdict. I started receiving reports from the bailiff who was in charge of watching them at night at the hotel that there were curious comings and goings among some of the male and female jurors. He was trying to keep everything under control, but there was a certain amount of erratic behavior that he could ascertain. He tried to stop some of this traffic in and out of their rooms but was unsuccessful. He ended up, he said, burying his head in the Bible and reading, trying to get guidance or comfort. Sure enough, ultimately the jury did hang up. The younger, livelier jurors voted in favor of a "not guilty" verdict, and the older and more conservative-appearing jurors favored a "guilty" verdict. Each camp was livid with the other.

After I discharged them and the case was over, the jurors asked to meet with me in chambers, and I agreed to do so. They said, "We really want to know, Judge, was he guilty or not?" I said, "I'm going to tell you something that I'm really not supposed to tell you. But you've been discharged. You won't go on another case, certainly not this year. There was a confession to the charges, but I had to keep it out of evidence because, under the constitutional rules that govern the admission of evidence, this was inadmissible evidence." You can imagine the looks the ones on one side of the dispute gave to the other.

The bailiffs, who put a moniker on everything, christened this—in view of the deadlocked jury—the "well-hung jury." [Laughter] By the way, these bailiffs also told me about another episode involving a man who was calling the court all the time trying to find out when the sequestered jury would be released. He was eager to know when his wife would be coming home. The court staff kept saying, "Not yet. They're still locked up." Then there wasn't a call for a few days. Finally, they received another inquiry from him, and the bailiff had to say, "Sir, I'm very sorry to tell you, but your wife and the other jurors were sent home three days ago." [Laughter] So all sorts of things can and occasionally do happen with jurors when they are sequestered. It's something that I always tried to avoid unless absolutely necessary, and I only did it a very few times.

After declaring a mistrial in the *Humphries* case, I was faced with the situation of having to retry this case. It made sense for me to be the one stuck with it, because I had invested a lot of effort in becoming familiar with the evidence and the legal issues. But that would have kept me in Pomona well into the following year, and I was told that I'd be given the Pomona assignment for only one year.

The presiding judge said, "Look, clearly you've got to try this case." I said, "Any chance I could move it downtown?" He said, "We don't have any extra courtrooms for you until you would be regularly assigned there, which would have been as of January 1, 1979. Here it is the fall of 1978 and you're about to start the several-month retrial." But he added, "If you feel that you can persuade one of your former colleagues, and in particular the one who's now the presiding judge of the municipal court, to loan you a courtroom—she's someone who was on your panel when you were in Division 40—you can bring the case downtown with you." So I managed to work that out with Presiding Judge Mary Waters. I brought the Pomona case downtown. It was retried in a courtroom I managed to borrow from the municipal court. The defendants were found guilty on retrial. But I almost got stuck with what would have been pretty close to an extra half-year in Pomona because of the need to retry this case.

Talk about the staff that you had at Pomona for your trial work and how that may have compared to what you were accustomed to at the municipal court level.

They were very devoted, and my clerk and court reporter followed me from Pomona to my downtown assignment. The clerks with whom I was fortunate enough to work over the years—both on the municipal court and the superior court—were very adept at their work, very agreeable, and had a good sense of humor.

Their humor was illustrated by one event that occurred shortly after I transferred downtown with my Pomona staff. I had just taken the noon recess, and my clerk told me that there was a defendant picked up on a bench warrant who had just arrived in the lockup, and that it would facilitate matters for the sheriff's transportation if we could take care of that matter without delay. I came out and took the bench, and the sheriff's deputy had a woman in custody in the courtroom. The public defender was there, and the D.A., and the clerk. I later learned the courtroom doors had been locked. All of a sudden the woman jumps onto counsel table, does a tap dance, and sings me "Happy birthday." She was from a company called Live Wires, and my staff had commissioned her for this occasion. [Laughter]

Lest you take yourself too seriously. [Laughter] It's nice to hear there was that kind of atmosphere. Tell me about coming back downtown, not only this retrial but also getting started in that new setting?

It was a fairly heavy-duty dose of serious cases. As in Pomona, it seemed as if there was one murder trial after another. There was occasional drama, such as one case that inspired the *Los Angeles Times* in its early edition to have a banner headline across all of the front-page columns that read, "Just Like Perry Mason: Defendant Freed, Witness Implicated." It was a murder trial involving a female defendant. The prosecution put on a witness who turned out to have some major inconsistencies in his testimony. As a result of vigorous cross-examination, the prosecution's case totally fell apart, and the D.A. concluded that not only did he not have a case against the defendant but in fact the prosecution's star witness was the person who was guilty of the crime—and therefore the rather flamboyant headline in the *Los Angeles Times*. This is the only time I saw a prosecutor stand up in the middle of the trial and say, "We move to dismiss the charges and ask that the defendant be discharged." Right in mid-jury trial. It was quite extraordinary.

I had another case, *People v. Ullo and Connor*, that involved some mafia murders for hire. It was disconcerting that when one of the defendants was arrested, the police found on him a map of the house of the judge—not myself—to whom he was on probation, along with directions how to get there. This was a high-security case. You could see that the jurors were somewhat uneasy.

There was actually an amusing aspect even to this case. The prosecution's theory was that one of the victims—although shot to death in Los Angeles County—had been buried in the Mojave Desert in San Bernardino County. The critical evidence, given the length of time that had transpired and the obvious decay of the remains, was ballistics evidence that would tie a gun associated with the defendants to the fatal wound to the victim's skull. The D.A. was understandably anxious about something and informed me and defense counsel, "In some of these desert areas, not only is this another county, but they don't always have a permanent coroner or deputy coroner. There are local physicians who are deputized as 'acting coroners.'" He said, "Normally, this being key evidence, I would have had a meeting and discussions and seen the physical evidence that the acting deputy coroner, a Dr. Scott, would employ in presenting his testimony. But I have not had the chance to have anything but the briefest of phone conversations with him. I would really welcome a recess when I hear he has arrived. I've asked the bailiff to notify me—and would like to have a longer than normal recess so I can have my first real contact with the witness." I said that was fine. Toward the end of the recess, the deputy D.A.—of course, appropriately accompanied by opposing counsel—asked to see me in chambers. The D.A.'s facial appearance was somewhat blanched. He said, "I have to tell you something that was rather extraordinary about my meeting with Dr. Scott and particularly so given the crowded nature of the hallways here in the Criminal Courts Building," which were filled with bailout defendants, victims, families of victims, gang members, witnesses, and jurors. He continued, "When I was notified by the bailiff that Dr. Scott had arrived and was in the hallway, I signaled that this would be a welcome time for a recess in order to prepare my witness. I walked into the hallway and met someone who I gathered was Dr. Scott." The acting coroner said to the D.A., "Nice to meet you. I guess we can talk about my testimony." The first words out of the D.A.'s mouth were, "I hope you brought x-rays and diagrams. That will be crucial." Dr. Scott replies, "No." The D.A. says, "Well, what are we going to do?" With a smile on his face, Dr. Scott says, "I have something better." In the crowded hallway, he takes out a paper bag, reaches in, and pulls out the skull. The D.A. is rendered speechless, and Dr. Scott—with I suppose the macabre sense of humor that someone dealing with cadavers might have—says, "What? You don't recognize him? Was he taller?" And then lifts the victim's skull even higher toward the hallway ceiling, with looks of amazement emanating from everyone in sight. Many of the coroners had an odd way of looking at death. Sometimes their testimony in court would reflect that.

I wonder how your experiences, now that you were getting so deeply involved in the superior court work, really differed from what you were accustomed to?

I couldn't help but be struck by the seriousness of what was at stake in the superior court. Not that the matters in municipal court were by any means frivolous, but on a positive level you did have more of a chance there to make some difference in a defendant's future, for instance by getting him or her into a rehabilitative program, or even by imposing just a taste of jail time to maybe change someone's life around. In municipal court you weren't involved with basically warehousing people in order to protect society. There was a lot of that in superior court. I'd say the majority of individuals whom I encountered as defendants convicted of felony crimes were people who were beyond redemption in that sense. All you could do was protect society. You didn't have much of a hope that they would acquire skills or behavior modification in prison and come out a better and more productive member of society or less of a threat to the community.

Even the courtrooms where these cases were tried and the adjacent hallways in the Criminal Courts Building could be dangerous places. We had one courtroom in particular that had a thick wall of glass between the spectator section of the courtroom and the bench and the jury box and in which all sorts of precautions were taken against individuals who might act out violently in the courtroom. In fact, I had a lengthy jury trial going on in a rape case. The court staff got to know the jurors, as they normally would. There was one particularly kindly gentleman who made a point of sharing with the bailiff and the clerk the latest pictures of his granddaughter. One day in the course of the trial, when a 15-minute recess was declared, the juror went to the snack bar in the building and then, instead of using the jurors' private restroom adjacent to the jury deliberation room for that courtroom, he chose to use the public restroom immediately across the hallway from the courtroom. All of a sudden there was a scream, and the bailiffs rushed into the restroom. This elderly gentleman had been stabbed in the back while standing at the urinal and bled to death almost immediately. Here is a courthouse, which is supposed to be a place of deliberation and serenity in an otherwise hectic and violent world, instead turning into a crime scene. This incident certainly influenced me later as Chief Justice, in terms of my attitude toward courthouse security—ensuring adequate perimeter screening for courthouses and at the entrance to courtrooms.

In fact, during one of my several visits to the Los Angeles courts as Chief Justice, on my way to meet with the presiding judge, I stepped out of the eleva-

tor and encountered a crew mopping up blood from the hallway in the main
courthouse where a physician had shot his wife to death right after a hearing in
family court involving their marital dissolution. I ended up by coincidence writing the opinion for the Supreme Court in the case dealing with the legal issue,
whether the county was liable for the inadequate security that had permitted a
party to bring a loaded firearm into the building. The case is *Zelig v. County of
Los Angeles*. Both incidents provided graphic illustrations to me of the security
problems that exist in our court buildings.

On a less serious note—and this was when I was presiding in the master
calendar court, Department 100—one of the custody defendants was not pleased
with my ruling granting a continuance for trial, so on the way back into the
lockup—with a deputy sheriff nearby but not quite quick enough to prevent
this—the defendant lunged forward, grabbed a flowerpot off the clerk's counter,
and with a fine pitching arm hurled it at me on the bench. It was fortunate that
my reflexes were quick enough to deflect the flowerpot upwards with the file of
the next case I was calling, and it shattered on the wall behind the bench.

These are just illustrations of what I encountered personally. Most judges
could recount some breach or other of security and the inadequacy of our court
facilities, factors that led me to try to make a priority of improving the facilities
in which jurors, litigants, lawyers, court employees, and judges do their work—
with security being just one aspect of the inadequacy of those facilities.

*Not only, as you say, were the cases themselves much more serious, but all the
surrounding things that have to happen to carry those trials out. This reminds
me of your earlier point that the municipal court was such a good training
ground because the stakes were not so high for the parties involved. Can you
reflect on how the earlier experience prepared you for these more serious settings and matters?*

I think just doing one's learning, perhaps making mistakes and benefiting
from them, learning how to deal with a myriad of problems—even if it's just a
matter of when a continuance should or should not be granted—acquiring greater insight into the credibility of witnesses, being able to make rapid-fire rulings
on evidentiary objections when there isn't the time to ponder them. You could
always take a recess if there was a serious legal question and make sure you got
the answer right, but you couldn't be doing that constantly when the objections
were coming like artillery over the bench, or like balls that you had to swing at
or not after making a quick call. Your response to these various challenges has
to become somewhat intuitive, and municipal court in many ways was an ideal
place to learn how to cope with them.

How did you like the felony trial work, as a judge?

It was very challenging, involving legal questions that often would become major issues on appeal. I had the long-term perspective that came from having been an appellate advocate for the state whose job it was to try to sustain convictions, unless there was clear error that required reversal. I had a real preoccupation with developing an adequate record. It was one thing to lose on the merits, but to lose as a deputy attorney general because the trial judge had not developed a record sufficient to enable the deputy to make a tenable argument is an altogether different matter.

One area that was certainly a challenging one for me, as it is for many judges—especially because of the consequences on appeal, when a judgment is challenged—is the matter of jury instructions. There are all sorts of very arcane concepts, especially when commission of a homicide is alleged. The offense can be charged in one or two or several different ways: as, starting from the less serious, an involuntary manslaughter, a voluntary manslaughter, a second-degree murder—and of course there are different types of second-degree murders and all that, too. Even putting aside the distinctions in the different types of first-degree murder, that offense can be charged with one or more special circumstances, and if at least one is proved true and the D.A. is seeking the death penalty, this causes the case to go into a "penalty" phase in which the question of the proper punishment, namely life imprisonment without possibility of parole or the death penalty, is determined by the jury. The concepts of premeditation and deliberation and malice aforethought and felony murder of different types underlying a murder prosecution are difficult and certainly provide fertile ground for seeking reversal of a judgment of conviction. Not giving an instruction or giving the wrong instruction can easily lead to reversal for prejudicial error, so these were very challenging concepts, much more so than the jury instructions in misdemeanor cases.

Am I right that you served on the superior court committee that was reviewing such jury instructions, more or less your entire time on that court?

Yes. In fact, I was the sole municipal court representative when I was still on that court and then became a regular member as a superior court judge. I served with Judge Alarcon, whom I mentioned earlier, on the CALJIC [California Jury Instructions—Criminal] committee that published pattern instructions used by all California courts hearing criminal cases. We would debate—and sometimes it did seem as if we were counting how many angels could fit on the head of a pin—all sorts of niceties, such as where a comma should or should not go in the instruction, having a certain faith or at least commitment that minor choices in style, grammar, punctuation, and word choice would have a definite bearing upon the jury's determination in arriving at its verdict. That may be wishful thinking, although it may be inevitable that we have to make that assumption, whether it's accurate or not in real life experience. But our committee spent a lot of time poring over these jury instructions.

There was a delightful, elderly, and erudite gentleman who was a retired judge of the Los Angeles Superior Court named Phil Richards who served as the committee's advisor and was very insistent that the committee stick to the somewhat stilted, almost Victorian language in which the CALJIC instructions were and to a large degree still are written. I remember, as a new member of the committee, asking my seatmate at the table during one of these meetings, "Why do we have to write in such Victorian language?" What was whispered back to me was, "Our wonderful consultant grew up in Victorian times. He probably spoke at the breakfast table"—to use words from the reasonable doubt instruction—"in terms of 'moral certainty.'"

Speaking of that particular instruction, the legislature, in an unusual action while I was on the committee, passed a resolution asking the CALJIC committee—although it was a committee of the Los Angeles Superior Court, our jury instructions were used statewide by other courts—to reexamine the reasonable doubt instruction, which, of course, is the instruction given in each and every criminal case, misdemeanor or felony, to see whether it could be rewritten. The giving of that instruction had been the cause of many reversals on appeal. Judges realized when they'd see the puzzled look on the faces of jurors, as that instruction was routinely read to them, that it contained conceptual language that was very difficult for even a lawyer or a judge to fully understand or define, let alone the average lay juror. So judges, in a good faith, well-meaning effort, often would tinker with the reasonable doubt instruction and try to convert it into the vernacular. More times than not, the end result would be a reversal by an appellate court.

There were only two of us on the committee, Judge Norman Epstein, a colleague of mine—later to become presiding justice of Division Four of the Second Appellate District—and I who felt strongly that we could and should and owed a duty to jurors to provide a simpler definition of this very basic instruction that was integral to every verdict that a jury would render in a California criminal prosecution. The majority published a report that basically said, "No. This would more or less be like desecrating the Holy Grail. We have to stick with it. It has been enshrined in a statute, it's always been relied upon," and so forth. So the committee left it at that, and the report went out with a dissenting view expressed by Judge Epstein and myself.

Sometimes you have to wait many years to have the satisfaction of having the last word, and lo and behold the U.S. Supreme Court ultimately came down with a decision that criticized California's reasonable doubt instruction. They didn't go so far as to say it was invalid, because the logical consequence of that probably would have been to overturn just about every criminal conviction in the state, that being the type of ruling that you'd have to apply retroactively. You certainly couldn't have someone be incarcerated or restricted by other serious consequences of his or her conviction, bearing the consequences of a basic instruction that had incorrectly defined the jurors' function in rendering a verdict. The U.S. Supreme Court in the *Victor* case, which reversed judgments from California and Nebraska, stated that this standard instruction was quite problematic and should be revised. Subsequently, in the 1994 case of *People v. Freeman*, the California Supreme Court took note of the high court's opinion and indicated that some modification of the reasonable doubt instruction was in order.

Although I signed the majority opinion in Freeman, I made this an occasion for one of my infrequent concurring opinions. I dug up the old CALJIC report and the dissenting report appended to it, authored by Judge Epstein and myself, and incorporated that minority view into my concurring opinion to make sure it was enshrined in the official *California Reports*, as a recommendation to the legislature that it amend the statute specifying the wording of the reasonable doubt instruction. Of course, I could not resist sending Judge Alarcon a short missive pointing out that, after all these years, the position of Judge Epstein and myself had been vindicated. That's a nice sequel to his having been able to kid me as a brand-new judge in 1972 at Judges' College about the cases I'd lost as a deputy attorney general—subsequently serving with him on the CALJIC committee, and then as a Supreme Court justice being able to very mildly rub his nose in it a bit in terms of the ultimate resolution of our dispute going back to the days of the CALJIC committee's work. Judge Alarcon and I have had a wonderful relationship over the years.

Of course, that reasonable doubt jury instruction persists to this day. It will be nice to talk about how you might have taken it up again when looking at revising jury instructions at a later time. What prompted the U.S. Supreme Court to note California's instruction and suggest revision?

It was challenged on appeal, for valid reasons, on the ground it was a vague and ambiguous concept that might very easily mean different things to different people. It was almost endearing how some judges had tried to reduce the concept of reasonable doubt to basic homilies—experiences that men or women might encounter in their everyday activities in or out of the home. Much as these attempts made a lot of sense and were well intentioned, the efforts rarely passed muster with the reviewing appellate court.

How does this compare to the way other states handle this matter?

California's jury instruction, although containing some elements similar to what has appeared in the jury instructions of other states, had some additional verbiage that made it, as I recall, somewhat worse than what existed in the jurisprudence of most other states. It may have been the concept of "moral certainty." But in any event the California instruction, although still not ideal, has been improved to eliminate some of its worst features. We'll later get into the topic of refining jury instructions generally, which was one aspect of my efforts as Chief Justice to engage in various measures of jury reform.

Returning to your time on the Los Angeles Superior Court, now that you were back downtown how were things proceeding into the late seventies and early eighties in terms of your division assignments?

I was asked to be supervising judge of the criminal division, which I've alluded to already. This assignment for 1983 and 1984 involved responsibility over about three dozen courtrooms in the Criminal Courts Building, as well as some supervisory duties over the criminal departments in other districts throughout the county. I believe there was a total of about 80 courtrooms over which I had either direct supervisory authority—namely, those in the building—or some indirect supervisory authority in the sense of establishing policies courtwide, countywide, on certain matters and also transferring cases among the various districts in L.A. County.

There were, of course, cases that were last-day cases, meaning that under applicable constitutional and statutory law this would be a case that had to go to trial that very day or suffer a dismissal. In most situations a case that's dismissed can be refiled, but there are adverse consequences and refiling is not without limitation. You can't keep coming back and refiling a dismissed case, so there were very serious consequences if a case had to be dismissed. It was something to be avoided at all costs. In fact, there was somewhat of a tradition, unfortunately, of the supervising judge of the criminal division occasionally having to transfer cases not only out of the Criminal Courts Building to perhaps another district in the county handling criminal cases, but even, when the going got quite tough in terms of caseload, having to transfer a criminal matter to a *civil* department, which would, of course, cause that court not to be able to handle its civil caseload. The law requires that the trial of criminal cases be given priority over civil trials. Once in a while the situation was so urgent in terms of a criminal case facing dismissal that a civil trial would have to be interrupted and the parties and counsel and jurors sent home, while the judge would try the criminal case to avoid that case being dismissed.

The supervising judge and his or her staff had to monitor and coordinate the caseload of dozens of courtrooms. You learn a lot sitting in a master calendar court about who is a team player and who isn't. There were some judges with whom I was on very close and friendly terms, who were real buddies, but they would not cooperate with the master calendar court. They wouldn't call in when their courtroom became free. Let's say their pending trial finished up early. If you sent a jury out to deliberate, you were supposed to take the next trial. You weren't supposed to sit around and wait until the jury came back with its verdict in several hours or days. I'd have to send around the coordinator to more or less do an inspection in terms of who was busy, who was on the bench and who wasn't. Yet there were some other judges with whom I had, if anything, a distant relationship—not a particularly friendly one—who turned out to be real team players. I would be sitting in Department 100 trying to juggle these couple dozen cases, and there might be as many as 10 last-day cases, most of which might be murder trials. I'd look to the side, and kneeling next to me at the side of the bench would be a judge whispering to me, "I just opened up and can take a case. In fact, why don't you send me two and I'll really try to work one over, settle it, and try the other one." That was, again, part of the learning process, in terms of the lessons from working with other judges as colleagues but in somewhat of a supervisory role.

I will say with some pride that, through whatever efforts I undertook to improve the system in the Criminal Courts Building, I managed to bring a halt to the practice of sending cases over to the civil courthouse. Then, perhaps in a bit of bravado—when we managed to have a somewhat lighter caseload duty due to fortuitous circumstances or the hard-working efforts of the criminal panel's judges to settle their cases or expedite their trials—I would call over to the civil master calendar a few blocks away and say, "Can we take some of your civil cases?" For the first time in anyone's recollection, the criminal division ended up taking some civil trials.

What made you think of offering that the other way around?

I probably thought of it as a great morale booster for those judges, myself included, who were assigned to the Criminal Courts Building. The civil departments weren't desperate, and usually the consequences of delay in a civil case are less drastic than a dismissal, but I thought it would be fun to put the shoe on the other foot.

How was this plan received by both sides?

I know that the criminal court judges were pleased. I remember Judge Norman Epstein, whom I mentioned a moment ago, having a big grin on his face and referring to it in some later years as something worthy of mention. It was appreciated over there too and taken advantage of.

It was quite a job trying to juggle all of these cases and, at the same time, perform my other duties presiding in Department 100. As supervising judge, one's duties included being advisor to the grand jury—which had its quarters adjacent to my courtroom—and also receiving indictments rendered by the grand jury. If a case was initiated with the return of an indictment in Department 100, it often would stay in that courtroom for some time while various preliminary matters, motions, bail hearings, and so forth took place. It wasn't just a question of sending these cases out right away, which of course I would do when they ultimately were ready to go to trial, but of hearing motions that were sometimes rather complex. Some of the most notorious cases—whether they involved serial killers, government corruption, or other conspiracies—came through Department 100 upon the return of an indictment. One somewhat infamous case in which I held several hearings was the so-called McMartin Preschool case involving charges of sexual molestation. That case had all sorts of motions, including a bail hearing and a motion seeking dismissal. The defendants, having sought a postindictment preliminary hearing, went to municipal court—having started in superior court and having sought that type of hearing in order to have the opportunity to cross-examine some of the prosecution's witnesses. The magistrate determined that a portion of the preliminary hearing involving the testimony of expert witnesses should be closed to the public. I had to hold a hearing and wrote a fairly lengthy memorandum of opinion explaining why, under U.S. Supreme Court precedent, it was erroneous to exclude the public and the press from that portion of the preliminary hearing and that the magistrate had to open it up. Those were among the types of matters that I had to undertake in Department 100.

I was trying the Hillside Strangler case down the hallway in a trial department while I also presided in Department 100. I would be running back and forth between the two courtrooms, and every time we had a jury recess in the Hillside Strangler trial, I'd go back to Department 100, take the bench, see if I could dispose of some cases, maybe hear a motion here and there, and where appropriate send a case out to a trial department. It was quite hectic handling both courtrooms.

Then, as a third part of this multitasking—you've asked about my involvement in the California Judges Association—I was simultaneously serving as president of that organization. That task involved traveling around the state, testifying before legislative committees in Sacramento, making various appearances, and having meetings of one sort or another. It turned out that the attorneys in the Hillside Strangler case, both the prosecution and the defense, were urging me not to hold court sessions of the trial on Fridays, because they needed time to interview their 400-some witnesses in the case. I soon acceded to that, not too far into the trial. On Fridays, if I wasn't flying up to Sacramento or elsewhere for CJA, I'd have the full day in Department 100. On Monday through Thursday, I'd be spending time in that master calendar courtroom early, before the jury trial would start, as well as during those 15-minute breaks and much of the hour-and-a-half noon recess in the trial, and then at the end of the day too. It was perfect training for the multitasking responsibilities that I ultimately assumed as Chief Justice. [Laughter]

Who was the presiding judge who was assigning you all of these things?

I was assigned to the supervising judge position by the incoming presiding judge, Harry Peetris, in consultation with the outgoing presiding judge, David Eagleson, who later joined the California Supreme Court. At Judge Peetris' direction, I enrolled at the National Judicial College in Reno, Nevada, because that institution had an excellent course in judicial administration that related to the supervisory duties I was about to assume. That type of course now is given in our California judicial college and our continuing judicial studies programs, but was not available at that time.

Why do you think Judge Peetris singled you out for these high honors?

I guess I had established a reputation for being able to run a high-volume court in an efficient but hopefully fair manner from my time on the L.A. Municipal Court—in the Division 40 master calendar court, in my position as supervising judge in West Los Angeles, and then downtown as supervising judge of the criminal division. In the long run, those assignments were excellent training in many ways for the future, by exposing me to a variety of case-related and administrative duties. I benefited greatly from these supervisory assignments. As I said with reference to which judges turned out to be team players and all, just having this wide array of colleagues, having to motivate them and trying to get work out of them; dealing with the D.A.s, the public defenders, the private practitioners; trying to figure out what they were after and being fair to them and yet not letting them get away with things they shouldn't—all these responsibilities provided me with valuable experience, as did dealing with other judges in my capacity as president of the California Judges Association.

To what extent did you have to resort to disciplinary actions?

There were certain things you could say and do, but to quote Justice Mildred Lillie, who served for a while as the Administrative Presiding Justice of the

Second District Court of Appeal, "The problem with being a supervising or presiding judge is somewhat akin to that of being the caretaker at a cemetery. You have a lot of people under you, but they aren't listening and you can't do much about it if they're not." [Laughter] I tried to do my best as a supervising judge. Peer pressure among judges was a factor in supervising them, and certainly the presiding judge knew through me who was putting out the work and who wasn't, and that conceivably could have a bearing upon one's future assignment.

There were quite a few personalities on the superior court bench, many of the old-school variety. There was a preponderance of individuals who had been on the bench far longer than I had, some of whom were old enough to be one of my parents. There was a charming woman, Kathleen Parker, known as "Kay" Parker, who was more or less considered the grand lady of the criminal bench in Los Angeles. Although she had formally retired as an active superior court judge while I was still on the municipal court, from the day following her retirement she continued to sit as an assigned judge. She was an active member of my panel and was loved by all—her fellow judges, the D.A.s, and defense counsel. Her retirement event was organized by private defense counsel Marv Part, I believe, and was held on the lot of Twentieth Century Fox in one of the large soundstages. Judge Parker was dressed in exotic Indian attire and was brought into the assembled throng astride an elephant. Leading the elephant was Harry Weiss, one of the most colorful private criminal defense attorneys—much beloved by the judges, in part because he always dealt his cases and never went to trial. Weiss, a bald, diminutive figure, was attired in the costume of an Indian *mahout*, the person who guides or drives an elephant.

Those were days with a lot of courthouse personalities. Busy as things were, the courts certainly didn't engage in assembly-line justice—a mode into which many of today's judges are fearful of falling, despite their best efforts, given the difficulty posed by the courts' vastly increased caseload in the face of the declining resources made available to them.

Knowing of your earlier interest while on the municipal court in looking at things systemically, to what extent were you seeking out these kinds of roles central to the administration of the court itself?

I never applied for any such position. My most enjoyable time on the municipal and superior courts, in the sense of doing what I really wanted to do, was trying cases, making rulings on objections, instructing the jury, managing the conduct of a trial consistent with my duties as a judge, without assuming the advocate's position for either side. Similarly, when I joined the Supreme Court and ultimately became Chief Justice, my favorite part was and always remained working on opinions, in particular my role in crafting my own opinions. But having said that, there was in both contexts an enormous satisfaction, once assigned the task, derived from trying to improve the system—and I hate to even call it, in a way, a system because that makes it sound impersonal—and from providing more accessible and fair justice to all involved in the process, whether it was the parties, the lawyers, or the jurors. There was a tremendous sense of accomplishment in making those systemic improvements, either as an administrator in a judicial capacity or in serving as an advocate for the judiciary in Sacramento in trying to improve the process either through furthering or defeating, as the case might be, proposed legislation affecting the judicial process.

You've mentioned a few names, but I wonder who among your fellow judges was also interested in these things?

I'd say foremost would be now-Presiding Justice Norman Epstein, who replaced Presiding Justice Charles Vogel when Vogel retired following a distinguished career during which he made important contributions to the law and to court administration after serving as president of the State Bar. I have enormous respect for both of them. Justice Epstein is one of the foremost intellects presently on the bench in California and certainly would have acquitted himself very well as a justice of the California Supreme Court. In addition to his continuing accomplishments on a day-to-day basis, he has made valuable contributions as the author of various periodic publications. For example, he prepares a summary of recent criminal cases for the California Judges Association publication. Justice Walter Croskey, another fine jurist who has made many contributions to the administration of justice, summarizes the civil cases. Additionally, Justice Epstein was called upon by the preeminent authority on California law, B. E. Witkin or "Bernie Witkin," as he was known, to assist in the preparation of the treatise on criminal law and criminal procedure, which is a set of volumes among, I believe, more than 30 in different areas of the law that Bernie Witkin came to author. Justice Epstein provided great assistance, and Witkin graciously designated this publication as co-authored by Justice Epstein. I think Justice Epstein stands out among several jurists noted for their contributions to California's judicial process, but I hesitate to mention a few more individuals and then leave some others out who might deserve equal mention. I believe no one would disagree with me in saying that Justice Epstein was certainly at the top of the group of jurists with interest and ability in this area.

In fact, Justice Epstein—then-Judge Epstein—tried to buck the seniority system on the municipal court, as I had unsuccessfully. He was elected presiding judge of the L.A. Municipal Court, and I believe it was at this point that he was elevated to the superior court. He has a long history in the development of substantive law, in case management and administrative reform, and in judicial education, and has been a very effective administrator in running Division Four, my old stomping grounds when I was on the Second District. It was a pleasure serving with him when we both were associate justices in Division Four.

While we're talking about your colleagues, maybe you could say more about your colleagues downtown on the superior court and who you might have been close to at that point.

There were the nine of us who had been appointed to the municipal court at roughly the same time, and some of us sort of palled around. I also remained close to Judge Goertzen, of whom you'll hear more when you and I discuss my time on the Court of Appeal, because we found ourselves serving in Division Four together.

Among my extracurricular activities, I served from 1983 to 1990 as a member and later chair of Senator Pete Wilson's Judicial Selection Advisory Committee [JSAC], so I was able to provide some meaningful input with regard to some candidates for the federal bench whom I had come to know while serving on the state bench, as well as concerning candidates for the positions of U.S. Attorney and U.S. Marshal.

How did that body operate?

This was a committee for Southern California. There was one for Northern California as well. John Davies, who in later years became Governor Wilson's judicial appointments secretary, was the statewide coordinator for these local committees and would send the names to us. When I was chair I would assign a particular candidate to a subcommittee of two or three persons, who would conduct an in-depth evaluation. Senator Wilson would recommend to the president only those individuals who received the highest ratings from our committee, and the appointments received high praise in the press for their quality and diversity.

I'm glad to say, by the way, that Barbara's and my eldest son Eric has applied his experience to similar tasks. That experience included serving as an intern in the Reagan White House Office of Presidential Personnel, deputy legal affairs secretary to Governor Wilson, and deputy counsel to the U.S. Senate Judiciary Committee. With all this background, he was a natural to be appointed to various Judicial Selection Advisory Committees. He has served under four appointing authorities on such committees—on the federal level he was appointed by President George W. Bush to evaluate candidates for the federal judiciary and for the positions of U.S. attorney and marshal in Southern California. When the committee became a Democratic-appointed committee, Eric was nonetheless reappointed by Senator Barbara Boxer and continued to serve on the committee. On the state side, Governor Schwarzenegger had actually interviewed Eric for the position of legal affairs secretary or judicial appointments secretary. But Eric did not want to work in either capacity on a full-time basis which, it was made clear to him, it would have to be, so their discussions did not progress further. But he did end up serving on Governor Schwarzenegger's Judicial Selection Advisory Committee. When Governor Schwarzenegger left office, Governor Jerry Brown appointed Eric to that committee, so he has served on four of those committees.

My chairmanship of Senator Wilson's JSAC committee extended from my time on the superior court into my years on the Court of Appeal. Among my other extracurricular activities, I was quite active in judicial education, teaching at Judges' College and in the continuing judicial studies program, particularly on search-and-search issues and how to try death penalty cases.

In the related area of judicial education publications, I was the editor of four volumes that more or less were guides to judging in a criminal assignment. I want to make it clear I did not establish or found these publications. They were initiated by predecessors, in particular Judge William Keene of the L.A. Superior Court. There was the *Judges' Benchbook* and the *Judges' Deskbook*, which contained a lot of useful information, even scripts and case authority and statutory authority for tackling different kinds of procedures, all from the judge's perspective.

I also published the *Bench Blotter*, which was a very large piece of laminated cardboard containing a multitude of information, much of it in tiny symbols, setting forth the sentencing options and obligations of a criminal court judge in a felony court as to virtually every crime, and specifically what the range of sentencing options might be. That usually involved three ranges, low, middle, and upper term; restrictions on whether or not and, if so, under what circumstances, probation could be granted; the imposition of consecutive sentences; how allegation and proof of prior felony convictions of different types were to be handled in computing the sentence to be imposed—all sorts of complex data. It was presented in this format so the judge would have it on the bench, right in front of him or her, because no judge could hope to memorize all of that information. I also put out what was more or less a book-formatted version of the Bench Blotter, the *Determinate Sentencing Manual*.

In addition to that, I was asked to co-author, with a retired L.A. Superior Court judge, William Levit, a publication called *The California Judicial Retirement Handbook*, which contained matters of obvious interest to each and every judge, namely the computation of one's retirement benefit, the circumstances under which one could take different types of retirement related to service, as well as disability retirement, survivors' benefits, and so forth, under different options—a whole assemblage of very esoteric material, trying to make sense out of obscure sections of the Government Code of California and case law interpreting them, and attorney generals' opinions. This had to be constantly updated. Serving as co-author, of course, I was more or less on a hotline, being the recipient of phone calls, sometimes at home late at night, from judges or their spouses or dependents raising questions that were sometime fairly urgent relating to retirement options.

I also testified before a couple of congressional committees, once before a committee of the House of Representatives holding hearings in Los Angeles on the causes of crime. At the request of the U.S. Senate Judiciary Committee I went to Washington, D.C. to testify before that committee regarding a subject that I had a great deal of interest in, namely reforming the general process by which jurors are selected to serve on a particular case. I made an effort to further such reforms as CJA president.

Let's turn to CJA and maybe have a chronology of your involvement, which I know started while you were still on the municipal court.

I had just joined the municipal court when I was contacted by a San Francisco municipal court judge, Harry Low, who ultimately became a presiding justice of the First District Court of Appeal. We knew each other slightly because we both had a slight overlap in the attorney general's office. He'd been on the bench since the mid-sixties and had become editor of a publication of the California Judges Association then called the *California Courts Commentary.* He said, "As a new judge, you should really get involved in CJA. I'd like to have you on my committee, and specifically working on this publication. There's a great deal of interest in the judges' retirement system. Much of that interest focuses upon the fact that there is"—if I correctly remember the figure at the time—"well over $1 billion of unfunded liability." The system was not actuarially sound, and he told me it would be very useful if I were to write an article for the judges' publication pointing this out and what the current options were.

I ended up working on this problem of unfunded liability in different capacities over the years, and it turned out that the solution ultimately chosen by the legislature was, unfortunately, not to fund the judges' retirement system—at a time when they could have done so fairly easily. They managed to fund their own legislative retirement system before it was eliminated by the voters in the term-limits initiative, as they also did for the teachers and for state employees. But they just decided to postpone doing anything about the judges' retirement system until ultimately they didn't have much of an alternative but to let all of us under the old system just eventually die off as the legislature appropriated funds every year to cover the unfunded liability, and then set up a vastly inferior system for new judges appointed after November 1994, with greatly reduced benefits. This was a matter and remains a matter of real concern, because judges make a substantial sacrifice by going on the bench. Most of them could be earning far more as a lawyer. But at least having the security of a meaningful pension was a hedge against receiving a lower salary, and yet it turned out that this pension fund was in a very precarious situation.

Anyway, I wrote this article, and it was a matter of great interest and led to Harry Low telling me, "I have a second assignment for you. You should write a companion piece on judicial salaries and how they are woefully inadequate, and how the salaries of judges compare to those of other public officials trained in the law." I did some research and found all sorts of grade IV deputy city attorneys and deputy D.A.s who were earning more than the judges before whom they were appearing. This information caused a lot of outrage at the current situation and was something I was able to address later as Chief Justice.

These articles received a lot of attention. What happened next was that I was made an assistant editor of the *California Courts Commentary*—I believe that happened in 1973—and a couple years after was put on the CJA public information committee to disseminate information on what we were doing in this and other areas. Because I had become somewhat of an expert in the matter of judges' benefits and compensation, I was made a member and, soon, vice chair and in 1979 chair of a committee that I believe originally was called the judges' benefits and compensation committee but later came to be called the finance committee. It turned out that there were some bills that came up that would have had a very negative impact on the judges' retirement system. One of them would have upped our required contribution rate from 8 percent of salary to 11 percent. Other proposed legislation would have cut down on our benefits or eligibility for benefits. There were all sorts of harmful proposals. I found myself, at CJA's request, testifying at legislative hearings and managed to get these bills killed. CJA was very grateful and recognized my efforts in its periodical.

How did you accomplish that in Sacramento?

I made very forceful arguments—I felt I was back to my advocacy days in the A.G.'s office—about what the deleterious effect would be on the recruitment and retention of qualified judges to serve on the bench; and how we didn't want to attract only persons who would view a judicial appointment as a step *up* in salary—we needed to have people who were truly committed and a wide range of individuals, not just individuals who, like myself, had been civil servants as prosecutors or public defenders or county counsel or city attorneys, but also a mix from the private sector; and how all of them—and maybe especially so persons who were making the sacrifice of leaving a much more high-paying job as a private-sector attorney—needed the security of knowing that they would earn a decent pension.

You made these arguments, but as an aside, how widely held were those views among your colleagues in CJA, that there should be that kind of diversity in the recruiting and retention matters?

I don't recall this being controversial, and they certainly were in favor of any argument that would carry the day in raising judicial compensation. I know that one bill we opposed received only one or two affirmative votes out of a committee of maybe 10 or so. I ended up being very effective on this, and the reason I say this is not to toot my own horn here but to illustrate something else we've talked about—how one thing leads to another. In 1980 I was placed on the executive board of CJA in recognition of the work I had done as a member and then as chair of the committee.

You were now an expert?

Yes, on something I knew absolutely nothing about when Harry Low called me to write that initial article. This newly acquired expertise is also what led to my being asked to co-author the *Judicial Retirement Handbook* that I mentioned a moment ago.

The president of CJA has among his or her prerogatives the right to confer what's called the President's Award upon that judge who's done the most for the judiciary during the preceding year. I received that award in 1981 in recognition of my efforts in an area that judges have a lot of interest in, namely their benefits and compensation. That in turn led to my being urged to run for president of CJA.

Who urged you?

My fellow executive board members. I believe the class or year of which I was a part, on the board, were all potential candidates, but I was urged to run and was told there'd be no opposition if I did run. So I ran and was elected president of CJA and served during the year 1982–1983.

As a prelude to your own presidency, what kind of an organization was it by the time you reached that post? How would you characterize it?

I loved the disparity among the membership. You had all sorts of courts whose small population entitled them only to the bare constitutional minimum, which then was, in number of judges, one municipal or justice court judge for the entire county and one superior court judge for the entire county. Now after court unification, which we'll discuss at a later session, the minimum is still two judges, both of whom would be superior court judges. Some of those sparsely populated counties span a very large territory. It can be a couple hundred miles' drive from outlying areas to the county seat, with certain court services available only at the county seat. The variety of courts encompassed rural and urban areas, coastal and inland, mountainous and desert, all sorts of different judicial backgrounds and philosophies. San Bernardino County, with 20,000 square miles, is the largest county in the U.S. and larger than nine of the states. Other counties are tiny in geographical area and in population.

Judges' College had been somewhat of a mini experience in that kind of mingling with my colleagues statewide, but CJA was much more so. Again, this was good training for the future, gaining firsthand experience with the problems that are unique to the rural judge, who may be the only judge within hundreds of miles of another judge and face challenges that are totally different from those of the urban judge. This is not to elevate one type of situation over another, but just to point out what a broad variety there was. Although during my term as president of CJA I did not undertake as comprehensive a tour as I ended up doing as Chief Justice, I did get around the state quite a bit. It was a wonderful learning experience.

My term started at the annual meeting in the fall, when by custom the Chief Justice first swears in the incoming president of the State Bar and then immediately thereafter swears in the incoming president of CJA. The following story of my swearing-in is amusing but of no real historical significance. Tony Murray, who was a partner in a prominent law firm, was sworn in as State Bar president. He was on very close terms with Rose Elizabeth Bird, the Chief Justice, and I believe assumed a substantial role in her defense when she was the subject of recall efforts. At that time the oaths of office were administered in front of the whole conference of delegates, which was hundreds of people. Since then, the delegates have split off, and it's a smaller crowd. As I recall it, Tony was summoned to the dais, sworn in, and received a hearty greeting and a warm *abrazo* from Chief Justice Bird. Then I was called up to be sworn in as CJA president. For whatever reason, I received a handshake that was so perfunctory and distant, at least in contrast to the effusive greeting bestowed just moments ago, that when the ceremony concluded a country-boy judge, Bob Barclay—and again, illustrating the variety in the ranks of the California judiciary, someone who had been a justice of the peace and then became a municipal court judge in the County of Modoc—came up to me with a big grin on his face and said to me, "The Chief Justice, when she shook your hand, looked as if she had just picked up something deposited by a dog on her lawn." We had a good laugh out of it, with this rural type of humor injected into the formal ceremony. This incident certainly did not affect my tenure as CJA president or my relationship with the Chief Justice, but it's an interesting illustration of the personalities at different levels.

Had you had any previous occasion of meeting Chief Justice Bird in person?

No, I had not. There I was trying to perform my duties as CJA president and still wondering how I got to that position. I said to Barbara, "How could this ever be? All this, because I agreed to write an article." I said, "It reminds me of the libretto in Gilbert and Sullivan's *H.M.S. Pinafore*, that goes along the lines of, 'I polished up the handle of the big front door so carefully that now I am the ruler of the Queen's Navy.'" [Laughter]

There I was with many responsibilities at CJA, also trying to perform my regular day-to-day judicial duties, although it was a very valuable learning experience for me in terms of training to carry out my future duties as Chief Justice. This was so in various respects, first of all learning at CJA how to deal with other judges in finding out what their concerns were and what the solutions might be, in a variety of contexts quite different from my own experience in a very urbanized judicial venue. This also involved traveling around the state and dealing with the legislature. Second, there was running the master calendar court in Department 100 as supervising judge and finding out how to motivate judges, and who were the team players and who weren't, and just being able to juggle many things at the same time, even in that one courtroom—aside from my third set of responsibilities in presiding over the Hillside Strangler case.

Who were the movers and shakers in the legislature in matters relating to the judiciary?

I remember a couple people who were negative stumbling blocks. I don't know why I remember them probably better than the others. There was one big difference from today. As chief, years later, I often had to mount last-ditch efforts to find two or three well-informed lawyer members of the legislature to stop something from going through and to speak in favor of our interests: for example, Bill Lockyer, Phil Isenberg, Joe Dunn, Darrell Steinberg, Bob Hertzberg.

In those days the task, even when these things rose on the horizon, was much easier. Why? Because we had a vastly larger number of lawyers who were serving in the legislature. If you just went through some basic Jurisprudence 101 with them, the light would go on. They would understand that there are three branches of government, something I no longer could take for granted in the

1990s and the following decade. On later occasions, I sometimes had to deliver a rather basic civics lesson. Back then there were plenty of lawyers, and even if they hadn't recently practiced that much law, you could make an appeal to them as members of the legal profession. They'd be aware of the vital role played by the courts in our society. They would realize, from being in court themselves occasionally, that the judiciary needed adequate resources—in the form of funding, facilities, and judicial positions—in order to adequately serve the public. It was mainly a question, when I was CJA president, of just alerting them, opening their eyes to what they probably knew in a sense, even if it was dormant, as opposed to opening up a whole new world, as it later was.

Nowadays, the judiciary committees in both the senate and the assembly have a large number of nonlawyers because they can't find enough lawyers among the legislators to fill up those committees and the few that they have, most of them, are just paper lawyers. They've never actually been in a courtroom. Back then, lawyers were fighting to get onto the judiciary committees of both houses, so it was a different world. Although occasionally some of them might get annoyed at a judicial decision or something a judge had said, there was a basic understanding of our three branches of government and their respective roles, and you could rekindle or evoke that, as opposed to going up there and having to give a primer from scratch in many instances.

Another great difference of course was that there was much more continuity in service in those august bodies in Sacramento which, for better or worse, are so altered today owing to term limits.

That's very much the case. There used to be an institutional memory. There were people like Judge Bill Munnell, who had served several terms in the legislature. He would carry the day for us. Legislators knew him well and respected him. Even those legislators who were not lawyers, understood the significance of the judiciary and how it functioned. This would be something that, once taught, would stay with them, hopefully from year to year. But as you point out with your reference to term limits, someone is sent to Sacramento today and during his or her first term may be elected speaker of the Assembly because legislative colleagues know that, without taking such action, there will be little or no continuity in the speakership. That person's going to be limited to six years in the assembly. As an advocate for the judicial branch, you have to reinvent the wheel each and every legislative session and do so with far fewer lawyers in the two houses. That makes it a far more onerous task today.

Then, add onto that, the difficult economic times we are in today, with our boom-and-bust cycle in California, which is very much affected by the initiative process—enacting spending mandates together with restraints on spending and on tax increases, that render our state government dysfunctional, at least in challenging fiscal times. All of this makes for a brew—a perfect storm—that has led to a situation much more difficult to deal with today, for me during my years as Chief Justice, and for my successor—than was the case back then, when there would be shots across the bow that you could usually, through good advocacy, deflect. That's not as readily done today.

Thank you for taking a detour into the other branches of state government. This role as CJA president is fascinating for the exposure it gave you to things around the state, in Sacramento but also out in all those counties. What do you think you took away from that year as president?

I certainly felt a total commitment to the administration of justice and to fair and accessible justice not only in my courtroom but, beyond that immediate perspective—through the supervisory positions that I had held on the municipal and superior courts and then through the CJA presidency—to the statewide judicial branch. The views and the experience that I acquired became less parochial and more statewide through my CJA experience, seeing a multitude of different conditions and challenges that judges had to meet, the variety of unfulfilled needs of individual litigants, depending upon where in the state they resided, depending upon how well or poorly funded their particular court was, at the hands of the local governmental entity. All of these things were true eye-openers. I certainly took away a lot of valuable lessons learned from the experience of dealing with judges as personalities from a multitude of backgrounds. Also the ability to multitask, because as I was heading CJA I had these other responsibilities with the Hillside Strangler trial and the master calendar court, Department 100, and supervising the criminal division. I learned to challenge myself and was able to tackle more tasks than I would have given myself credit for being able to perform.

These are among the things that I think I took away from my year as CJA president, but also, of course, a great affection for the organization, even though I had my differences with it on occasion when I served as Chief Justice. These differences perhaps were inevitable because, as head of the Judicial Council, an official governmental body created by the constitution and charged with the responsibility of serving the public interest and overseeing the judicial branch, I was bound to have differences of opinion and strategy with the voluntary membership organization, which has—and not in any way to denigrate it—a different set of priorities. I found as chief that the cooperation between the two organizations was enhanced by my appointment of CJA leaders as members of the Judicial Council and of its advisory committees and task forces.

Although there were a couple rough spots, the Judicial Council and I had a close and very productive working relationship with the California Judges Association, certainly in my later years as Chief Justice. We've had some outstanding people serve in leadership positions at CJA. I think there was a good understanding on behalf of both the Judicial Council and CJA of the differing and yet complementary roles played by each of the organizations and the cooperative stance that we must assume in Sacramento, whenever possible. When the position of the judges of the state is divided, their interests inevitably suffer at the hands of the other two branches and particularly from individuals who may not have the best interests of the judiciary at heart. We've accomplished a lot. When we work together, it's been much more than just the sum of the parts.

At that time, to what extent was the "cooperative stance" approach shared by those other partners that you worked with?

One thing that, ironically enough, may have caused there to be less friction between the Judicial Council and CJA at that earlier time—although I think overall it served to diminish the voice of the judiciary in Sacramento—was the fact that the Judicial Council viewed its role then as far less comprehensive in matters of state judicial administration than it later did when I served as Chief Justice. Consequently, there were areas or niches carved out that were the exclusive roles of either the Judicial Council or on the other hand CJA.

A good example was the matter of judges' benefits and compensation. That was viewed as a matter that was totally outside the purview of the Judicial Council. The chief and the Judicial Council would not weigh in on these matters. When I became chief, the circumstance that judicial salaries were lagging so far behind not just the private sector but behind the salaries of other public law-trained officials no longer could be ignored. It had gotten to the point where I and many others felt that the woeful inadequacy of judicial salaries and retirement benefits was such that this was having a very negative impact on the ability to attract and retain the best and the brightest for careers in the judiciary. It no longer was something that could be sloughed off by the Judicial Council or the Chief Justice with the words, "Leave that to the members of the judges' association. It's no business of the statewide administration of justice." When I did get involved in this area as Chief Justice and chair of the Judicial Council, that was certainly one matter concerning which CJA and others had no complaint about the expansion of the Judicial Council's area of activity, because in addition to the automatic yearly increase in salary that was provided under the Government Code through the link to increases for "other state employees," I soon managed to obtain an 8.5 percent pay boost just for the judges, on top of that automatic adjustment, by producing data that showed how judges' salaries compared negatively with those of other public legal officials.

There were other areas where there was more friction between the Judicial Council and individual courts or CJA. We had our occasional differences on some matters—the promulgation of statewide rules of court, various reforms, and mandatory judicial education, that I'm sure we'll discuss when we cover my years as Chief Justice. But those were overcome for the most part.

Thank you for reflecting on that relationship. It's a fascinating one and, as you say, it changed over time, as is natural I suppose with the changes elsewhere and the ever-increasing complexities of our system: salaries, benefits, retirement, and all the other things.

Everything was and is constantly changing, whether it's the state's fiscal condition, the judicial branch, the needs and particular problems of individual courts, and the needs of the public that each of us serves. All of that, of course, caused the relationship between the Judicial Council and CJA to evolve, just as the council's role *vis-à-vis* the legislature and the governor also evolved to meet changing conditions.

As you pointed out, that was only one of many balls you were keeping in the air, even then. In your assignment on the superior court you were doing these three major things simultaneously. You had a very busy life as a trial judge in the thick of things and yet all these other administrative and oversight roles. In general, how were you holding up in those years?

I certainly would not have been able to hold up without the continuing love and support of my wife Barbara, who exhibited a lot of understanding and encouragement as I tried to get through these difficult years with multiple tasks and, at the same time, tried to be a decent husband and father to three young, active boys and have them comprehend the mysterious world of their father's employment downtown. Meanwhile, Barbara not only bore the major responsibility for raising our sons, but also was running her own interior design business.

Again, it was multitasking among my professional obligations but also multitasking professional obligations with family responsibilities as a husband, father, and son, while trying to still do the things that I always did like and still like to do, namely engage in reading outside the law, in travel, and in running. Those particular years on the superior court were very, very busy years that certainly were almost equal in their multifaceted dimensions to my years as chief, when I also felt I was engaged in a juggling match, although over many more hours of the day than I had experienced during my time on the superior court.

###

Chapter 6

Presiding over the "Hillside Strangler" Trial, and Civil Assignments
August 4, 2011

We've been talking about your time on the Los Angeles Superior Court and your oversight of Department 100. I want to spend some time today talking about the longest trial you ever presided over—the longest criminal trial in U.S. history at that time—the so-called Hillside Strangler case that came forward as People v. Buono. *How does your involvement in that whole story begin?*

My involvement began with being assigned the case by the supervising judge and then hearing various motions preceding the infamous motion by the prosecution to dismiss all the murder charges against the defendant Angelo Buono, a motion that of course was concurred in by the defense. Some of these other motions were quite substantial and required lengthy evidentiary hearings. Before I was assigned the case, the codefendant Kenneth Bianchi had been allowed to plead guilty to some of the murder charges and avoid the death penalty, in exchange for which he agreed to testify fully and truthfully against Buono.

One of the defense motions in the Hillside Strangler case focused on rulings by the California Supreme Court holding it was prejudicial to a defendant to be forced to face trial on serious charges, such as murder, together with lesser charges where the evidence on the lesser charges could prejudice the defendant's right to a fair trial on the murder charges. The defendant, Angelo Buono, was also charged with a number of pimping and pandering and related charges. I felt it would be risky, given the precedents I mentioned, to deny the defendant's motion to sever those other counts from the trial of the murder charges. The

D.A. felt that showing this earlier conduct and the negative attitude it reflected toward women in general, and particularly female prostitutes, would establish a course of conduct leading up to the defendant's decision to kill other female victims, some of whom were involved in prostitution.

We should, perhaps, note that the victims ranged in age from 12 years old up to near 30. Some were students, working women, and also some prostitutes—a whole range of different people represented.

Yes. The defense view was that admitting the evidence that related to prostitution activities would be prejudicial error under established case law, while the D.A. felt it was proper to bolster his case by showing what he viewed as a progression in terms of criminal behavior. I granted the motion to sever the trial of the lesser charges.

May I back up and flesh out what happened at the outset? In other words, how exactly were you assigned this case, and what were your thoughts about being asked to take on something that was a very high-profile matter in Los Angeles and elsewhere?

I had had a number of significant criminal trials assigned to me, but of course this was *the* big case. It was one that, even at the time it was assigned to me, must have appeared to be a case that would involve a lot of problems and legal rulings that would be challenging.

I believe some of the assignments I received, and perhaps this one, reflect the circumstance that I came to the bench with the reputation, whether deserved or not, of someone who had been given challenging assignments as a deputy attorney general and who had experience in dealing with complex legal issues. Perhaps that played a role in why I was given the case. I don't know.

I was pleased to receive the assignment, but the more I got into the case I became convinced that it was a case fraught with many, many problems. I probably came to look at it as sort of a can of worms, ultimately. [Laughter] I don't know if I ever reached the point where I regretted having been assigned the case, but I soon realized I was in for more than I had expected.

It seemed that as the case progressed, it became plagued with more and more difficulties. The D.A. even began, perhaps in anticipation of his forthcoming motion to dismiss the charges, to make disparaging statements to the press about the prosecution's own star witness, Kenneth Bianchi, a practice that—as I later pointed out in my opinion denying the motion to dismiss—is hazardous at best for a prosecutor and certainly lays the groundwork for such statements concerning the weakness of the prosecutor's case to become a self-fulfilling prophecy. Bianchi, a cousin of the defendant Buono, was a co-conspirator in the 10 charged murders and, prior to my involvement in the case, had entered into a plea agreement with the D.A.'s office to receive a life sentence in exchange for testifying fully and truthfully about the murders.

Let's go ahead and talk about how that motion to dismiss came up here in this whole lengthy pretrial phase.

The prosecution had been aware for months and months of the continuing inconsistencies in Kenneth Bianchi's accounts to law enforcement officers, to psychiatrists, and to others. But still, at one point when the defense made a motion for bail, the D.A. opposed the motion on the legal premise that bail can be denied in a capital case when the proof is "evident"—that's the archaic term used in the California Constitution. The D.A.'s position was that the evidence of the defendant's guilt was strong enough that the defendant was not entitled to bail.

Somehow the prosecution's confidence, or stated confidence, in its case deteriorated further without anything all that remarkable happening—only incrementally more inconsistencies of the same nature occurring in Bianchi's account of his involvement in the murders. The prosecutors ultimately came to the conclusion that they were unlikely to obtain a conviction. The District Attorney's office stated expressly that it was making this "motion for dismissal without the likelihood of refiling." They would reserve that right but could not foresee circumstances arising under which they would acquire new or additional proof. To me, that was an important consideration, along with other factors, in deciding whether or not to grant the motion to dismiss—whether this was a case that should instead run its course and have a jury make that determination of guilt or innocence, rather than have the D.A. be the final arbiter of the case, given the seriousness of the charges.

To what extent did you see this coming, this request to dismiss?

I suppose the negative statements made by the D.A. about his case foreshadowed that move, but when it actually occurred I was rather surprised by it. I say that because in ruling on various motions, I had had to review the transcript of the preliminary hearing, which had lasted weeks and weeks, and the transcripts of other hearings, some of which had been conducted before me.

So I knew what evidence there was, and my gut reaction was, I suppose, that the district attorney was unable to see the forest for the trees and was focused upon individual inadequacies in the proof but, when considered all together, the evidence was sufficient for the case to go to trial and to obtain a conviction and have it upheld on appeal.

I was very troubled by the situation confronting me as a judge in this motion to dismiss, because I had then, and I have to this day, a very strong commitment and belief in our separation of powers and in the principle that each of the three branches—executive, legislative, and judicial—should not intrude upon the proper function of another branch.

Here I was having to determine whether I should, in effect, second-guess the D.A.'s evaluation of his own case, and yet I had been privy to that case through the preceding motions and other hearings. The statute governing the dismissal of criminal cases, Penal Code section 1385, states specifically that on motion of the prosecution a court may grant a dismissal "in furtherance of justice." Of course, here was a motion joined in by the defense, so I had both sides urging dismissal. Who was I to second-guess that?

Yet I felt strongly that the words "in furtherance of justice" imposed an obligation on my part, in ruling on such a motion, not to be a rubber stamp for either the prosecution or for the defense and instead to exercise my own independent judgment, based upon various factors that included the protection of society.

I put the case over for one week to July 21, 1981, to research the law and review the record. Instead of ruling from the bench, I wanted to fully explore the legal issues and the evidence that had been brought before the court in different contexts in this case. I wanted to be able to make an informed decision in exercising the discretion that was conferred upon me as a trial judge.

The way I resolved this conflict in my mind between my obligation to act "in furtherance of justice" on the one hand, and on the other hand adherence to the principle of separation of powers and the fact that the D.A. was seeking to, in effect, abandon his own case—and shouldn't the D.A. be entitled to do that?—was the following, and the case law backed me up on this.

I did not locate any precedential case law dealing specifically with a prosecutor trying to have his or her case dismissed and a trial judge not permitting that, but there was enough in the law to convince me that section 1385 of the Penal Code did impose a duty on a trial judge to act in the interests of justice, whatever that might be. The immediately following section, 1386, of the Penal Code abolished the prosecutorial practice that the statute quotes in Latin, *nolle prosequi*, the declaration "we shall not prosecute"—a legislative prohibition on a prosecutor's being able to drop a case for whatever reason or for unstated reasons. Section 1386 made section 1385 the only permissible basis for a prosecution motion to dismiss.

I resolved in my mind these competing considerations by concluding that, under the separation of powers doctrine recognized in California's Constitution, the prosecutor has—with perhaps only the most extreme exceptions—the absolute and exclusive right, duty, and obligation to decide whether or not to file criminal charges and, if so, which particular charges to file. But once the prosecutor has filed certain charges, they were then lodged in a court of law, and it was no longer "just the prosecution's case." Instead—once something was lodged and filed in a court—it became a judicial function of the court as part of its authority over its own processes to decide how to deal with the charges that have been filed, and how to act on various motions made by the prosecution or the defense, but that it was not up to the D.A. to unilaterally take the position, "Well, it's my case, and I'm dropping it." The court has an independent obligation to make that determination, in the interest of justice, once the prosecutor has chosen to file charges with a court.

Given the conclusion I arrived at, I then went through the evidence that had been presented to me in conjunction with the motion to dismiss and in some of the other hearings that I had been called upon to preside over or that had been placed before me in transcripts of earlier proceedings conducted in municipal court before the magistrate. I concluded it would not further justice to allow the prosecutor to abandon the 10 murder charges, that this was a case—involving charges that were serious and with important consequences to the public—that should run the course of submission to a jury, and that although I was not going to substitute my views for those of a jury, particularly on the credibility of Kenneth Bianchi or on what a jury should or should not do, this case, in effect, demanded a jury trial as the case then existed before me. Whatever action the jury might take would be the appropriate outcome.

If the District Attorney was not prepared to proceed with his case—and I gave his office two weeks to absorb my ruling—I would turn the case over to the state Attorney General, who has the authority under California law to take over a case from the D.A. under unusual circumstances. In the event the Attorney General chose not to take up the case, I reserved my statutory authority to consider whether to appoint a special prosecutor. That was my ruling, and it was almost like a bomb going off in the courtroom, I can assure you.

Before we get to that, during the time you were considering what you would do and then doing the research and writing this out, how alone were you with the whole thing? Was there anyone you could consult or talk to?

No, I didn't think it would be appropriate to do so. There was no precedent directly on point, and whatever law there was that related to this situation was fairly minimal. Of course, no one really could be aware of the evidence the way I was, other than the lawyers who had presented it to me, so it was very much of a lonely decision.

Yet you did patch together from these different sources—the Penal Code and what case law there was—some pretty strong strings of logic that led you to the decision. How comfortable did you feel, at the end of all that, that you had made your case, as it were?

I felt very comfortable by the time I went through it. I immersed myself in this for a week and, as is so often the case, putting something down on paper is the best test of whether it stands up or not.

Describe to me the day that you went into court and actually read this opinion. You have a copy before you today. I saw one account that said it took more than an hour to read it. In the course of all this, what was the scene in the court-room?

I always have felt an obligation, generally speaking, to make a full explication of the basis for a ruling. Sometimes it's less hazardous in terms of appellate review just to come down with a ruling and not state one's reasons, but I always felt a moral obligation to make it very clear, and especially on something like this.

I made a point of reading the opinion to those present in the courtroom. I did not lightly write opinions as a trial judge, but I felt it was appropriate to do so in this instance to highlight the evidence and the legal authority I had relied upon. This was a 31-page opinion.

Interestingly enough, I thought in the aftermath of our last interview, Laura, which was on July 21st—and we were then already nibbling around the edges of the Hillside Strangler case—that it was literally 30 years, to the day, of the date I made that ruling.

I later heard that some people wondered why I didn't automatically grant the D.A.'s motion on the day it was made. The press speculation was, well, the judge really wants to create a record and be very clear as to the basis for his ruling.

In fact, Penal Code section 1385 explicitly requires a judge to have the clerk's minutes reflect the reasons for his or her ruling granting such a motion. The minutes can state that the motion was granted "for the reasons expressed in the memorandum of opinion on file," and my written opinion stated that the opinion was incorporated into the minutes by reference.

That being the law, I believe that even though people expected an automatic or rubber-stamp granting of the D.A.'s motion to dismiss, it was generally understood why a judge faced with such a motion in this type of case would want to prepare a more detailed statement setting forth the basis for his or her ruling.

It appeared to me from the scene in the courtroom and the reaction immediately afterwards that the parties—both the prosecution and the defense—were stunned by the ruling. I recall there were some media accounts that suggested this could be "George's folly." Who was this judge to require the D.A. to proceed with a case in which the D.A. had little faith and that would result in great expense to the county in proceeding with a trial that was essentially unwinnable? Under the headline "Judge not known for controversy," the *Los Angeles Times* described the ruling as "extraordinary."

But my view was, even were the jury to render a verdict of acquittal, this was a case that, given the state of the evidence available, had to go before a jury in order to preserve the public's confidence in its system of justice. These serial killings had been front-page news day after day, reflecting how the community was terrorized by the discovery every several days of another nude, strangled body on a hillside facing the civic center from different angles of a circumference.

In subsequent years, various persons—including one of our court administrators who was living in the Glendale area—have told me that women and girls were afraid to leave their homes, especially at night. What made it so insidious were the indications that the perpetrators might very well be a police officer or a couple of officers or individuals pretending to be law enforcement officers, because there had been some sightings of victims being stopped by what appeared to be plainclothes officers displaying badges. On one or more occasions, observations had been reported of police agency insignia affixed to the exterior of what could have been an undercover vehicle. People were afraid when they were approached by a police officer—not knowing if he was a police officer committing these crimes or someone pretending to be a police officer.

As you say, the media attention was enormous at all stages, including I think the expectation that you would dismiss, as nearly everyone seemed to expect. What effect did this have on you to see what the media did with it after you announced that you would not dismiss—"George's folly" and so on?

The reaction to my ruling was mixed. Some thought it was incredible for a judge to second-guess a prosecutor, and others of course were jubilant that Angelo Buono was going to have to face trial on the murder charges. I didn't let that affect me, of course. I felt in my mind and in my heart that I had done the right thing. Then of course, as I stated toward the end of my written opinion, if this court is wrong in its perception of its duty, let an appellate court so indicate. Appellate court review was sought by way of a writ, and the Court of Appeal declined to intervene.

I also offered to disqualify myself from hearing the trial, although I had not been asked to. But I took the initiative, observing that I had made certain determinations based on credibility—not ultimate ones on Buono's guilt or innocence, but I had expressed myself with regard to the credibility of the prosecution's main witness. I volunteered, without the filing of a motion seeking to disqualify me, to recuse myself on my own motion and transfer the case to another trial judge. Interestingly enough, neither the prosecution nor the defense took advantage of my offer. I didn't really expect I'd end up being the trial judge in this case. [Laughter] When the D.A. decided he would not proceed with the case, I turned it over to the state Attorney General, who was George Deukmejian.

When Attorney General Deukmejian received a copy of my ruling, he appointed four nationally known prosecutors to evaluate the case. I know one of the four had worked on the staff of the Warren Commission investigating President Kennedy's assassination. After they evaluated the case for a relatively short period of time, they unanimously advised the A.G. that there was a case for the prosecution here and that it was a winnable case.

Contrary to the advice of his four experts, Attorney General Deukmejian decided he would assign the case in-house to two of his deputies. I imagine this act of confidence by the A.G. in the staff of his office must have been a boost for office morale. The A.G.'s office specializes in the criminal area in appeals and had a much more limited role in taking over trials when there were conflicts of interest. But the attorney general felt that he had persons qualified to try this case and that he didn't have to go outside the office to hire people to perform this task.

At the next hearing, I met for the first time two individuals whom I came to know quite well, ultimately as judicial colleagues when they were appointed to the bench: Roger Boren, a deputy attorney general who now serves as the administrative presiding justice for the Second District Court of Appeal, and Michael Nash, who is a judge of the Los Angeles Superior Court and has been the presiding judge of the juvenile court and a leading national authority in dealing with juvenile dependency proceedings.

At the request of the deputy attorneys general, and over objection of the defense, I granted the new prosecutors two months to prepare their case. They had walked in cold of course, after the D.A.'s office had had the case for a couple years or so. I granted the request but indicated that was all the time I would give them, noting the defendant's speedy trial rights under the law. I did find that the transfer of the prosecution from the D.A. to the A.G. constituted "good cause" for allowing a continuance over defense objection. By a six-to-one vote, the California Supreme Court denied the defense's writ petition to dismiss the murder charges on speedy trial grounds. Following the continuance, the two new prosecutors came in fully prepared to go to trial. They subsequently developed evidence that already existed and found some new leads as well. In the fall of

1981, before the start of jury selection, there was a hearing that took several weeks of testimony concerning whether five witnesses, including Kenneth Bianchi, the codefendant who had entered into an agreement with the prosecution to testify truthfully and fully against the defendant Angelo Buono, had been hypnotized. The defense had moved to exclude the testimony of these witnesses on the theory that their forthcoming testimony had been rendered unreliable by attempts to restore their memory of the events through hypnosis. Attempts had been made to hypnotize Bianchi, and most of the psychiatrists who testified believed he had, in fact, been hypnotized. Under this theory, the consequence of his having been hypnotized would be to render him unavailable as a witness for the prosecution, and it's clear under any test that the prosecution could not have made its case against Angelo Buono without the testimony of Kenneth Bianchi.

A decision of the California Supreme Court, *People v. Shirley*, came down as an unwanted gift on my birthday, March 11, 1982, in the course of the trial, holding that the testimony of a witness who had been successfully hypnotized was unreliable and could not be admitted at trial. This decision posed a dilemma in our case, because there were other witnesses—prosecution and defense—in addition to Kenneth Bianchi who had been the subject of attempted hypnosis. The question would be in each instance, was the person actually hypnotized or not? Part of the problem was that after the California Supreme Court came down with its decision in *People v. Shirley*, a modification of the opinion issued in June 1982 expressly left open the question whether or not the ruling should be applied retroactively to persons who had been hypnotized prior to the Supreme Court's ruling.

I remember feeling that, as a trial judge faced with the situation of the prosecution's main witness having been the subject of attempted hypnosis and there being other prosecution and defense witnesses who may or may not have been successfully hypnotized, and further not knowing from the Supreme Court's opinion whether I was supposed to apply the court's ruling retroactively or not, it was going to be truly difficult to navigate my way through this legal minefield. Fortunately, I did manage to get through it and anticipate correctly how the California Supreme Court ultimately would rule.

Kenneth Bianchi's agreement with the district attorney of L.A. County and the district attorney of Whatcom County in the state of Washington provided that in exchange for testifying truthfully and fully against Angelo Buono in our proceedings, Bianchi would receive life sentences for two murders that he committed in the state of Washington as well as life sentences for some of the California murders—all sentences being with the possibility of parole. Other murder charges would be dismissed. I believe he was pleading guilty to five of the 10 murders alleged in our case.

Ultimately, the way the parties' agreement was drawn, the only consequence in the event Bianchi were to fail to testify fully and accurately would be for Bianchi not to be able to serve his life sentences in California but instead having to serve them in the state of Washington, I believe at Walla Walla penal institution, which was considered a worse venue for a prisoner to serve his time. But that's all that would befall him.

Bianchi did not have much of an incentive to testify truthfully. For whatever reasons, either to help his cousin, Angelo Buono, or out of fear of what Buono might through fellow prisoners be able to inflict on Bianchi, Bianchi chose to renege on his promise very soon after that agreement was entered into with the Washington State and California authorities.

What made the whole issue so interesting was that Bianchi had a rather high IQ and, unlike Buono, had many social skills. He even managed to persuade a practicing psychologist that he, Bianchi, was a fellow psychologist. They discussed different types of Gestalt therapy and other strategies to be employed with patients. Bianchi had some kind of credential in psychology printed up. This was one of the numerous scams that he pursued as a way of establishing contact with young women.

It was established that Bianchi had access, while in custody in the state of Washington, to the film *The Three Faces of Eve*, which dealt with multiple personalities. When Bianchi's home in the state of Washington was searched, upwards of 20 volumes were seized from his home that dealt with the subjects of psychiatry, psychology, multiple personalities, and hypnosis. He had become quite an expert in that field and was able to persuade the majority of the psychiatrists who examined him that he had in fact been hypnotized and that he had multiple personalities.

Dr. Martin Orne, an expert in hypnosis and multiple personality, headed an institute for experimental psychiatry at the University of Pennsylvania. He was convinced—from examining Bianchi and from examining videotapes of interviews that other psychiatrists, psychologists, and law-enforcement officers had had with Bianchi—that Bianchi was faking. Dr. Orne developed a series of tests that he administered in his interviews with Bianchi. Some were simple things, for instance making the suggestion that Bianchi's lawyer had entered the room and then watching how Bianchi acted or reacted to the presence of this lawyer, who obviously wasn't there. I can say, from having seen what was played in court, that at best it was Grade B acting, highly exaggerated and unnatural performances by Bianchi. Dr. Orne was able to establish that a person truly hypnotized would react in a way different from the way Bianchi was reacting. There were other tests that were less dramatic, like drawing an imaginary circle on the skin of Bianchi's wrist and saying, "You're going to feel extreme heat if I touch you here or there." Bianchi didn't react the way one normally would if hypnotized.

Perhaps most comically, after one or more sessions with Bianchi, the suggestion was made to him that indeed it was very unusual for someone with Bianchi's syndrome to have only one alternate multiple personality, and that inevitably there would be three or more. The very next morning, when Dr. Orne resumed his interviews, a new personality emerged. It was Billy, a little boy who proceeded to speak in a high-pitched tone. By the way, I should note that among the first two personalities there was one very well mannered, polite Kenneth Bianchi and another personality who was violent and profane. Every other word was a four-letter word. Now Billy was added to that assemblage of personalities. I believe there was a fourth personality, not quite as distinct, that ultimately emerged.

Dr. Orne came to the conclusion that Bianchi was faking it, a view supported by the circumstantial evidence provided by the extensive film and reading material available to Bianchi. One other psychiatrist joined in the opinion held by Dr. Orne, but the majority did not. The majority believed he was telling the truth, he had been hypnotized, and the multiple personalities were real.

I had to make an initial determination as a question of law, based upon the testimony at this hearing—because this was not a question for the jury—whether Bianchi would be able to testify or not. I stated that I believed Dr. Orne's conclusions over those of the majority of the psychiatrists and that Bianchi had not been hypnotized and did not have these multiple personalities. Accordingly that led to my conclusion that he could be called by the prosecution as a witness. Without that the case could not have proceeded.

How difficult was it for you to arrive at that ruling on your own, or was it pretty clear to you by then?

Once we got into the issue, the basis for such a ruling was fairly clear from the lay-type evidence of Bianchi's reading, the truly poor acting performance, and certainly the motive Bianchi possessed to pretend to be hypnotized and to have multiple personalities, as well as the fact that there was very little sanction available against his coming up with these prevarications. Once we got into the hearing, it was very easy for me to arrive at the conclusion I came to. It's hard for me to believe that anyone who watched the tapes and heard this evidence would truly believe that Bianchi had been hypnotized and had multiple personalities. Everyone, prosecution and defense, considered him a consummate liar.

Yet he'd managed to convince some professionals otherwise.

Exactly. That was rather ironic. One of the questions that had been posed in the motion to dismiss was, "Is there anything wrong, anything improper, with the prosecution putting on a witness who is totally self-contradictory and who has established himself as a consummate liar?"

The case authority that I discussed in my written memorandum of opinion denying the people's motion to dismiss indicates that there is nothing wrong with the prosecution's doing that. The obligation of the prosecution is to turn over any evidence that would be helpful to the defense, but that obligation does not preclude the prosecution from putting someone on the witness stand who is self-contradictory.

If the prosecution feels that the witness whom it's putting on has told lies or is committing perjury, the obligation of the prosecution is fulfilled by revealing this circumstance to the defense and to the court and making the contradictory evidence available to the defense, which in turn would be able to present such evidence to the jury. The defense was provided with the contradictory evidence in the course of the proceedings that led up to the prosecution's motion to dismiss. The irony, ultimately, was that the district attorney who relinquished the case, John Van de Kamp, ended up prosecuting it. He won the attorney general's race, and Attorney General Deukmejian moved on to be governor. When Mr. Van de Kamp became attorney general, he inherited the ongoing trial in a case that he had attempted to drop.

In his race for attorney general, Van de Kamp was attacked by his opponents for moving to dismiss the Hillside Strangler prosecution. But the case hadn't concluded yet, so that argument didn't really take hold, because the correctness of Van de Kamp's action could not yet be fully evaluated in light of the unresolved status of the case.

The next step in the political ramifications of the case came when Van de Kamp later ran for the Democratic nomination for governor, competing against Dianne Feinstein. His substantial lead evaporated once she began to air a blitz of political ads, including one criticizing him for his decision to move to dismiss the Hillside Strangler case. By then, the jury had found the defendant guilty on nine counts of first-degree murder.

I have known Mr. Van de Kamp for a number of years, and in fact we were both guests at a small dinner party just a few weeks before his office filed the motion to dismiss. I consider him a very honorable man and very qualified to hold the offices that he has held. I believe he received some very poor advice from, in particular, one of his deputies who was handling the case, Roger Kelly, who had a reputation of milking cases for a lot of publicity and then dealing them out. I consider Mr. Van de Kamp in some ways to have been the eleventh victim in the Hillside Strangler case. His deputy, faced with a very, very difficult case, no doubt, failed in my view to see the forest for the trees and misadvised Mr. Van de Kamp concerning the winnability of the case.

I know from some of the statements that Mr. Van de Kamp made that he initially thought I may have had some political motive in wanting to help the fortunes of one of the persons running against him for attorney general. I noticed, when we would run into each other, that for a while the relationship was a bit strained on his part. I don't in any way fault him for that, and I have to give him great credit for ultimately, in an interview a few years after my ruling, stating that he had come to the conclusion that the trial judge was right after all and that the motion to dismiss should not have been made. We ended up having a very good relationship. I appeared before the Commission on the Fair Administration of Justice that the legislature appointed and that he chaired, and I run into him from time to time.

There are accounts that various people told him at the time he was getting bad advice to try to drop the case. The police chief, Mr. Gates, was said to have stated the same thing to him. Yet, for whatever reason, it was perhaps usual? If the deputy involved suggested dropping a case, would the D.A. usually go along?

I can't say if there's a usual practice or not, but I believe that in a case of this notoriety and public interest, it's something that a D.A. would personally want to sign off on or reject, one way or the other. Dismissal of such a prosecution wouldn't just be handed to the D.A. as a *fait accompli*. I'm sure that the deputy D.A.s were able to make an argument that sounded convincing to their boss at the time.

I heard that there were some others on the D.A.'s staff, not directly involved in the case, who advised him against dismissing it. I believe the chief deputy's spot was vacant at that time, so Mr. Van de Kamp was dealing directly with the two deputies handling the case, Roger Kelly and Jim Hines, rather than going through a hierarchy of individuals who perhaps might have dissuaded Mr. Van de Kamp from proceeding in that manner.

What was the reaction in your judicial community when you denied the request to dismiss?

I explained to David Eagleson, the presiding judge of the L.A. Superior Court, the basis for my intended ruling and why I was going to proceed that way. He did not in any way question that. Generally, most judges are respectful of their colleagues' rulings. But I wanted to explain to the presiding judge what I was doing, given the fact that I was going to be committing the resources of one of his courtrooms for what was estimated to be a one-year trial. Maybe I should have known—always double what the attorneys estimate. [Laughter] The jury part of the case ended up lasting two years and two days. I did hear there were a couple judges in the Criminal Courts Building who raised their eyebrows and wondered, as one of them told me afterwards, "How could you second-guess the D.A. about his own case?"

Of course, my ruling was not based upon what was being reported about the case in the media. I had spent many days observing witnesses who had appeared before me on the case, and there were thousands and thousands of pages of transcript that I had had to review in conjunction with pretrial rulings I had made in the case. I researched the law and felt very confident I was doing the right thing, knowing of course that if the jury acquitted the defendant, I still would be blamed for having wasted a lot of the county's resources that funded the D.A.'s office, the court-appointed defense counsel and their investigators and experts, and the L.A. Superior Court as well.

But in terms of your larger view of what should rightfully happen, that was a risk you were perfectly willing to take?

Yes. I was comfortable with that and could live with those consequences, but it really would have weighed on me to have let the D.A. have his way on a case that I thought was winnable and should at least go to a jury, considering the consequences to the public, given the law's requirement that a criminal case be dismissed only "in furtherance of justice," as provided by the applicable statute.

If Mr. Buono had been convicted of all of the pimping and pandering charges and everything else involved in the nonmurder counts, he would be out on the streets in a little more than four years, with credit for time already served. Given that circumstance, I believe the interests of justice were served by at least having a jury make the determination whether he was guilty of the murders.

Of course, the trial validated the faith that I have, as a judge, in the jury system. The jury ended up convicting on nine of the 10 murder counts. The one count on which the jury acquitted was the weakest of the 10 counts, so this demonstrated the jury was quite discriminating in the performance of its duty.

To this day, I have enormous admiration for all of the individuals professionally involved in the trial. Roger Boren and Mike Nash came in and picked up this case basically cold and developed it with special agent Paul Tulleners from the Department of Justice, finding new leads. On the defense side, Gerald Chaleff and Katherine Mader both did a very fine job of advocating on behalf of Mr. Buono. All the court staff were truly extraordinary.

I should say before I leave the subject of the attorneys that it is so often the case that even in much, much shorter proceedings, tensions and antagonisms develop between the attorneys or between the attorneys and the bench. In contrast, I believe we all got along splendidly and were all part of a process that worked the way it was designed to.

We had a daily transcript so that every day, the attorneys and the court had a full verbatim record of the proceedings of the previous day. We had two court reporters who were outstanding, Charlene Howell and Katie Ingersoll, who approximately every half hour changed shifts with one entering the courtroom and seamlessly taking over from the other without interruption, and then dictating their notes and preparing a transcript that was proofread and presented to counsel and the court in time for the next day's proceedings—even going through this process when the court travelled to crime scenes for two weeks of jury views. This went on, as I say, for two years of proceedings.

The 12 jurors, as well as the alternate jurors, were quite extraordinary in their devotion to the case. Ten of the 12, if I recall correctly, were civil servants, because there aren't many employers who would agree to pay the wages of a juror during the estimated one-year—and, in fact, two-year and two-day—length of the jury proceedings. An eleventh juror worked for Kaiser Permanente, which is close to being a civil servant, I suppose. Then, as an interesting twist, a twelfth juror was a flight attendant for what was then Pan American Airways.

Because of the length of the proceedings, I was persuaded not to hold court on Fridays. In addition to all the witnesses and circumstantial evidence that had to be presented on the 10 murder charges, there was evidence of other murders that weren't part of the charges, including the two Washington State homicides committed by Bianchi. We also ended up with evidence of one or two murders allegedly committed by Bianchi in New York State. It was like having 13 or 14 separate murder trials back to back. Of course, Kenneth Bianchi was on the stand for cross-examination for weeks and weeks, with the defense going through all of his countless inconsistencies. There were, I believe, about 400 witnesses who were called, and the attorneys were very eager for me to let them have Fridays off so that they could interview their forthcoming witnesses. I agreed to the schedule they proposed, which also facilitated my attending to my various other duties. As president of the California Judges Association, I ended up frequently traveling to Sacramento and other places around the state on Fridays.

Meanwhile, I was still going back and forth to my other courtroom— Department 100, the master calendar court—hearing motions, engaging in case settlements, and assigning cases out. I remember an interruption in the Hillside Strangler proceedings from another case in Department 100 in which both the D.A. and the public defender had urged me to accept a disposition with the unusual provision that I would agree to the defendant's wish that I would perform a wedding ceremony for him at the time of his sentencing hearing, before he was to go off to serve a very lengthy prison term. With great reluctance—intuitively I sensed this wasn't going to work out well—I agreed to it, had the sentencing hearing put off once, then twice because the defendant's intended apparently wasn't quite ready to accept the marital part of the disposition, even if the D.A. and the public defender had agreed to it. Then finally, I had to throw up my hands in exasperation when the defendant explained the third time around, "Your Honor, please put it over one more time. I have another woman in mind now." The marriage component of the case settlement fell through, but this was the type of thing—sometimes momentous, sometimes a bit farcical—that was going on in department 100 at the same time that I was trying to preside over the very difficult Hillside Strangler proceedings.

This Monday-through-Thursday trial schedule had a bearing on the flight attendant juror, who—perhaps to maintain her seniority or other benefits—accepted assignments to fly while she was serving on the case. Thursday, when proceedings had concluded for the week, she'd emerge from the jury room and its attendant restroom in flight attendant attire, and fly off to Hong Kong or Frankfurt, and then be back Monday to resume the trial. This is a dramatic illustration of the dedication of all the jurors who served on the case.

The demands imposed on the jurors by this extraordinary case were further compounded when I found it necessary, unfortunately, to sequester the jury once it was sent out to deliberate. The reason I took this action was that some of the less responsible members of the press were seeking to speak with the jurors and had made forays out to their homes, ready to interview them at the conclusion of the presentation of the evidence and the arguments, before they were to start their deliberations.

The last thing in the world I wanted after everything that had gone on, including a couple years of trial with the jury, was to have a mistrial and have myself or someone else have to retry the case. Once these media intrusions became apparent, I directed that the jurors go home, get their personal effects, and report back to be sequestered, which they were.

Then I did something else that was somewhat controversial. I directed that if and when the jurors arrived at a verdict—and of course before they had a verdict they had some questions that had to be addressed; that often happens regarding the reading back of certain testimony or further instructions on the law—each verdict of guilty or not guilty was to be received and recorded one-by-one as determined, instead of waiting until the jurors had arrived at verdicts on all 10 murder counts.

I chose that course of action because there is case law indicating that if a juror becomes disqualified, by reason of illness or other reason, from continuing in deliberations that already have commenced, jury deliberations must commence anew after an alternate juror is substituted, so that the substituted juror participates in all the deliberations leading to the verdicts. I was concerned about what would happen if the jurors commenced their deliberations, one of them had a health problem or became otherwise disqualified, an alternate joined them, and they had to restart their deliberations, scrapping everything they had previously discussed and voted on. I was convinced that once a verdict on a particular murder count was rendered and recorded in open court, that verdict would be locked down and, in effect, inviolate, whether it was a guilty or not guilty verdict. The jurors then could go on to the other charges.

Sure enough, after a period of deliberation, one of the jurors thought she was having heart problems and was hospitalized for a day or two. Fortunately, it turned out not to be anything that serious, but deliberations had to be suspended, with the jurors still sequestered. I was thinking then, "I'm so glad I adopted this procedure," because to require the jurors to start their deliberations all over again would have been horrendous for them and for the whole process.

Ultimately the 12 jurors who commenced the deliberations were able, without regard to this illness, to return the 10 verdicts that they did, being discharged from the case two years and two days after the commencement of jury selection.

It's perhaps notable that you only had to call upon two alternates during the course of the whole two-year trial. I gather you had eight in waiting should you need them, and two were pressed into service. But it seems a relatively small number, given the length of the trial.

It really does, when you consider all of the vagaries that occur in people's lives over a period of a couple of years. But I was particularly eager, once the jury had actually started to deliberate, not to have to recommence deliberations with a reconstituted jury, and happily we were able to avoid that. Again, I have enormous admiration for the jurors, who gave two years of their lives to perform this duty, especially given the fact that they were subjected to, on occasion, extremely gruesome testimony that must have remained with them at home and during their confinement in hotel rooms at night during the last month of their service—and undoubtedly for years after they completed their service on the case. I was informed by the bailiffs that they developed a real esprit de corps, not only celebrating together the birthdays and other special occasions in their lives and the lives of their families during the course of the trial, but maintaining contact after the trial was over. Some of them also showed up for the sentencing hearing.

I note that there were a lot of other things that occurred over the course of the two years too. Was there not another motion to dismiss midway through, claiming that the police had withheld some evidence from the defense side?

That is correct, so we had to have a hearing, and I ended up preparing a written ruling on that too. I think it's fair to say that the case was truly a minefield, with legal issues and unexpected factual developments coming up right and left. Of course, I could not know how my rulings would be viewed on appeal and was very mindful of trying to create an adequate record, being an appellate lawyer by training, and anticipate what an appellate court would find to be an appropriate ruling in each instance.

You spoke of the toll on the individual jury members. What about the toll on Judge George? How did you hold up?

When this case was approaching trial, I received advice from an older judge on my panel at the Criminal Courts Building, Ross Bigelow. He asked, "What sort of exercise program are you into?" I said, "Nothing in particular. Why do you ask?" He said, "Let me tell you. Some of our colleagues have had their physical or emotional health severely impaired by these lengthy high-publicity serial-killer trials. I suggest you get yourself into an exercise routine." He mentioned Muharem Kurbegovic, the so-called Alphabet Bomber, and some other trials that had taken place in the downtown area of the L.A. Superior Court.

I considered this advice, having respected Ross Bigelow's views on other issues. I thought, "I'll take up running." I took a run for about a quarter of a mile from my home and was out of breath. I thought, I don't know if this is really for me. And yet there was a certain attraction to running in terms of flexibility of time and location, and I didn't have to depend upon anyone else, given all my other responsibilities. I pursued it and really came to like it. I started running most days.

I got into it enough where I was intrigued by the possibility of entering a 10 kilometer race. I did that and performed well, so I started entering more 10Ks. Then, of course, the ultimate pursuit came to be to train for a marathon and complete it. I started running longer distances, even up to 20 miles or so, and ultimately ran the first of four marathons. The marathons postdated the trial, but they all resulted from this advice and from my experience in getting through the ordeal of the Hillside Strangler trial by running. I ran the Big Sur to Carmel marathon, the San Francisco marathon, the New York marathon, where I qualified for the only marathon you have to qualify for, the Boston, and completed that one as well.

Running truly changed my life, and I owe it to this advice I received on how to get through the trial. Running enabled me to cope with many other things in my professional career that otherwise might have been unbearably stressful.

Sometimes in the course of a run I'd come to solutions to knotty legal problems, including some posed by the Hillside Strangler trial. Often complex matters would sort themselves out as I ran. So that was very beneficial advice and something that also stood me in good stead through my years as Chief Justice.

Are you still running today?

About two years ago on a cost-benefits basis, which is how I approach many matters, I realized that my knees were aching enough through most of my runs that this outweighed the pleasure and the benefit. I had to be three-fourths of the way through a run before it would become truly pleasurable. In addition to running the marathons, I had really abused my legs by doing lengthy runs through Death Valley and other challenging venues, and being part of a team that ran a 180-mile relay race from Mount Rainier to the Pacific. I particularly remember a group of my friends and I deciding that we would run the Grand Canyon. We started before dawn at the North Rim at about 8,500 feet, ran down to Phantom Ranch at 2,500 feet and then up Bright Angel Trail on the South Rim to about 6,500 feet elevation. As a result of all of these runs, my knees started telling me it probably was time to discontinue this type of activity. Barbara and I still enjoy hiking together and walking the hills of San Francisco. But I'm afraid my marathon days are over.

If you qualified for Boston, you're the real deal. [Laughter]

[Laughter] I had to break three and a half hours for my age group to qualify for Boston. That was a real joy, having my running time at the New York marathon qualify me to run the Boston marathon.

Thank you for telling me about that. I can imagine what a great toll this trial might have had on one's own life. It just goes on so long. What were the effects on your family, if any?

Barbara and I have three wonderful sons who were growing up hearing a certain amount about these horrendous proceedings. The boys were about 9, 11, and 13 at the time the trial began. Of course, the trial was being covered in the press, and I would hear that friends of our boys would bring it up. "Your father is doing the Hillside Strangler case. What's happening there?" I tried not to make the day's trial proceedings the subject of dinner conversation, but it was inevitable that the boys would know about some of my cases and how gruesome this particular case was. In fact, after one of the court visits by our boys, each of the three of them on their own decided when they got home to draw a picture of an inmate confined in the jail lockup of the master calendar court.

I remember one occasion in particular that involved the boys and the Hillside Strangler case. There was an exhibit that was too large to fit into the nearby exhibit room. It was an enormous cardboard placard that had pictures of each of the 10 victims in life and in death, accompanied by other photographs of the neck area where garroting or other tortures had been inflicted. The attorneys asked for convenience's sake, instead of having this exhibit brought up from the basement each day, could it be stored in a corner of my chambers, and I agreed. I kept it facing the wall backwards. But the kids came in and poked behind and saw all of this. I was concerned about the futility of trying to shield them totally from their father's experience, and the fact that they were always being asked about the case.

Actually, the worst or at least most personally embarrassing aspect of my sons' exposure to the case involved our youngest son Chris. At this point he was nine and had a fourth-grade teacher who was quite intrigued about the case because it was a matter of such public interest. She kept asking, through my wife, whether the class could come down to court because this would be a great learning experience. Barbara and I communicated to her that the case really was not proper fare for young children and involved very disturbing evidence. But she was so adamant in repeatedly bringing up the possibility of a class outing to the Hillside Strangler trial that I relented.

I chose a date for the visit when I knew there would be nothing troubling about the proceedings. The kids were probably too young to get much out of the trial. I picked a date when one of the forensic experts was going to appear and testify about the crucial fiber evidence. A couple of the victims were found with minuscule amounts of fiber on their eyelids, which was very significant. Angelo Buono operated an auto upholstery shop, which was located adjacent to his home, the location where most of the murders were believed to have taken place. Some of that auto upholstery fiber would be placed on the victims' eyes, and then their eyes would be taped shut. The adhesive caused a couple bits of fiber to be found on two of the victims. Apparently it was a very unusual type of fiber, so it was quite significant that this fiber found on the victims' bodies, which had been dumped on hillsides, could be linked to Angelo Buono's upholstery shop. The forensic expert was supposed to testify on the day of the scheduled class visit. I felt this anticipated testimony was suitably noncontroversial from the standpoint of not exposing the kids to evidence that they shouldn't be seeing or hearing.

The class traipses into the courtroom. Barbara was asked to accompany the teacher and the class because she would be familiar with the courthouse and the courtroom proceedings. The kids are all seated, along with the usual packed courtroom, when one of the two prosecutors stands up and says, "Your honor, we ask for permission to call a witness out of order because Mr. So-and-So, the forensic expert, has not yet concluded giving his testimony in another proceeding." My heart sank, and even more so when the next witness was summoned. She was an ex-wife of Angelo Buono, who was called to testify concerning things he had done to her in past years that paralleled things that were done to the murder victims. She testified to being hogtied to the four bedposts, and so forth. I'm hearing this testimony, hoping that the teacher is going to get up and leave with her class, but she doesn't. Then one of the prosecutors asks Mrs. Buono, "Did Mr. Buono say anything to you while he was doing this to you?" The answer was, "Yes, he called me something." "What did he call you?" With that, she repeats a very graphic and vulgar reference to part of the female anatomy. Next, one of the low moments of my career on the bench occurred when our son Chris leaned over in Barbara's direction—because she was not seated immediately next to him; I believe there were one or two persons in between—and in a stage whisper that reverberated enough around the courtroom that it reached me up on the bench, proceeded to ask, "Mom, what's a 'blank, blank, blank, blank'?" I felt like diving under the bench. Shortly thereafter, the teacher realized this wasn't the most appropriate fare for her fledglings, and they left the courtroom, but this was another memorable moment in court with a member of my family.

I regret that the testimony planned for the day changed, and I hope you all survived it after the fact. [Laughter]

Yes, but there even were some rather annoyed parents who spoke to Barbara and said, "Why did you bring the kids down?" Barbara had to give the history of how she'd undertaken every kind of resistance to that suggestion and then every precaution in terms of selecting a day when everything would have been quite okay. People understood, but it became a tale told among our community of friends and the parents of Chris' classmates.

Speaking of precautions, I wonder if there were any special measures you had to put into place around the courthouse itself to protect the personnel and the jurors over and above what one would usually do?

Security was a concern, but mainly in the sense of protecting the jurors from unwarranted contacts—and I don't mean hostile contacts. There was great interest in the welfare of the jurors and how they were coping with this lengthy, stressful experience. It wasn't like some other cases I had, where you really had to worry about threats to jurors from gang members or mafia types and attempts to deliberately influence them. The main effort, before I had to have the jurors sequestered, was trying to make sure they were able to safely get back to their vehicles in the adjacent parking lot without being approached. Again, my concern was that there not be any grounds for a mistrial.

As you said, you took the precaution of having the jury verdicts delivered as they were decided so you were, I'm sure, doing everything you could to make sure that conclusions would be reached.

Yes, I certainly was. There was another interesting aspect of it, which ended up with the publication of a book that I believe you're familiar with by Darcy O'Brien called *Two of a Kind*.[1] The book gives a rather full account of the trial and also of some of the ancillary aspects, the investigation and events that occurred apart from the trial.

Among the interesting aspects of the trial discussed in the book is an account of the jury views that we took of the crime scenes. Both the prosecution and the defense wanted the jury to be brought to various locations from which victims had been abducted and also—for want of a better word—to dump sites where bodies were left afterwards. Because most of these criminal acts took place at night, we went on the jury views during nighttime hours. It was quite a caravan, with the press trying to be right there, which they had a right to be. But no one wanted them too close, where they could potentially influence the observations made by the jurors.

The locations of victim abductions and body disposals formed somewhat of a giant circle around the downtown civic center area, including police headquarters, and extended to Elysian Park, Glendale, and Hollywood. We visited all those sites. The prosecution, because it was nighttime, very creatively used a helicopter with a giant spotlight—flying from one location that was being called to the jurors' and my attention to another location—to illuminate each site. It was like a giant flashlight on a giant display board. The jury views helped make sense of the prosecution's theory that these various sites figuratively were joined at the end of spokes that all came to a center, and the center was Angelo Buono's home and auto upholstery shop. That was a very interesting aspect of the circumstantial evidence. To this day, I can't help but react when I drive by one of the more publicly located crime scenes from the case.

You mentioned earlier that your old friend Darcy O'Brien had expressed interest in writing the book. Maybe you could say more about how it came to be and to what extent he consulted you directly during the course of writing it?

---

[1] *Two of a Kind: The Hillside Stranglers* (New York, N.Y., New American Library, 1985).

Darcy O'Brien was a friend of mine in high school and was one of a group of us who roomed together at Princeton, where I was enrolled in the Woodrow Wilson School of Public and International Affairs. He was an English major and was a great influence on me in terms of what I read. I often was reading more English and American literature than books in my own field of international relations. Even then he was busy working on the first of several of his books to be published, called *A Way of Life, Like Any Other*.[2] He was the son of two movie stars, primarily from the silent-picture era, George O'Brien and Marguerite Churchill. The book semifictionalized their experiences but was basically autobiographical. After he was turned down six times, a publisher accepted his book, and it promptly won the Ernest Hemingway Award for the best first novel of that year. It's a wonderful account of his experience growing up in Hollywood.

We had kept in touch while he was getting his Ph.D. at UC Berkeley and I was at Stanford Law School. Then ultimately we lost contact. After teaching at Claremont College in California, he joined the faculty of the University of Tulsa, where he was part of the creative writing program and taught English literature.

One evening—it was fairly late at night, and was between the time I denied the prosecution's motion to dismiss the charges and the commencement of the trial—there was a knock at the door. There was Barbara's and my friend Darcy O'Brien, who told us, "I no longer have the addresses and phone numbers of my friends, but I remembered where your house was and I'm out here. What's happening?" We had a reunion over a good portion of a bottle of scotch that night. When I told him about the case I was involved in and that I had denied the prosecution's motion to dismiss and the trial was soon going to start, he was fascinated. Then he told me about a book he was writing.

I next heard from him three or four days later when he was back in Tulsa. He told me, "I'm totally unable to work on my own book. I'm just mesmerized by your Hillside Strangler case. I'd like to come out, attend the trial, and write a book on it—I guess somewhat following Truman Capote's approach in *In Cold Blood*." Darcy had been writing more literary works, such as a book on James Joyce. He did end up coming out and writing *Two of a Kind* and received awards for this and other true crime books, as the genre is called. He later accused me of leading him to a life of crime, because he wrote three or four more fascinating books on actual criminal cases and trials.

When he came out for the trial, I told him, "You have to understand. I can't be talking to you about the case until it's over, but I can assure you that you'll get a seat in the courtroom, even when it's packed. The exhibits are available to

---

[2] London, Martin, Brian & O'Keeffe, 1977.

public view and you'll have access to them. Of course, you're on your own. You can speak to the attorneys and speak to the detectives and other witnesses to the extent they choose to talk to you." He spent the better part of the two years of the trial out here, renting an apartment and then flying back to Tulsa and taking care of his academic responsibilities, not covering every day of the proceedings but the most important parts. He received all sorts of very interesting background information from some of the detectives. The lead sheriff's investigator was Deputy Frank Salerno, who was a very dedicated law enforcement officer, as was his counterpart in the Los Angeles Police Department, Detective Bob Grogan, who was a very colorful fellow.

Anyone who reads O'Brien's book will hear some tales of outrageous behavior that I learned of only after the case was over, when I read the book—like Grogan's pulling Angelo Buono out of the window of a car he was upholstering and telling him that he had better talk to the detectives. Or telling Kenneth Bianchi on the private plane ride down from Washington State to Los Angeles that if there was any more guff from him, he would be shown the open door of the plane. Once, feeling very frustrated at an early point in the investigation, coming out of a cops' bar in downtown L.A., Grogan shot out the bulbs in some of the streetlight standards. This detective was physically huge, bigger than life, and quite a character.

I remember one incident I was privy to that occurred when the verdicts were in and the jury had convicted Buono on nine of the 10 counts. Grogan barged into my chambers without notice—a visit I wouldn't have authorized, because I couldn't see witnesses or attorneys from one side without the other side being present. Grogan burst in like a bull in a china shop, holding a bottle of champagne, with the effervescence spilling onto my carpet and a finger bleeding from a cut from the wire that held in the cork. He was exulting in the verdicts. I said, "Please, you have to get out of here!" [Laughter] So there are things like that in the book that are very colorful. Grogan now has retired to Sedona, Arizona, where he has mellowed out and occasionally plays jazz piano at a club.

You've described receiving the verdicts as they were rendered by the jury rather than all together as a group at the end. When and how were those verdicts announced to the public?

The verdicts were publicly announced in open court as each of them came in. The first verdict was rendered nine days after the case went to the jury. It was a "guilty" verdict on the Lauren Wagner murder. The next of the verdicts, rendered a few days later, was a "not guilty" on the Yolanda Washington murder. As I mentioned, nine of the ten counts resulted in "guilty" verdicts, and the remaining one, the weakest of the counts, was the "not guilty."

You've described your own reaction upon learning how the jury decided. I wonder what sort of reaction it got out there in the world, from your point of view. What did you note about the response in the community?

First of all, people showed up en masse in the courtroom every time there was an indication the jury was about to deliver another verdict. I know that the D.A.'s office was annoyed that the verdicts were being rendered one by one, because they felt it was prolonging their agony to have another public event refuting their decision to drop the charges each time there was another "guilty" verdict, but this was done entirely for the reasons I indicated—to avoid the possibility of requiring the jury to commence its deliberations anew in the event one or more alternate jurors had to replace an original juror.

There was quite a reaction in the press, needless to say. There were editorials, "A Triumph of Justice" and so forth, being quite charitable toward my prior ruling that had refused to dismiss the charges—and also toward our jury system, indicating why it had been important to have the case submitted to a jury and expressing great appreciation for the personal sacrifice made by the jurors and alternate jurors in sitting on such a difficult case and in being away from their family, loved ones, employment, and other pursuits for such a very lengthy period of time.

Persons complain, understandably, when they have to be absent a few days for a jury trial. But imagine serving for two years and two days with such very oppressive evidence, for the most part, shadowing your thoughts during all your waking hours. And being locked up at night in a hotel during the final month.

How did it feel to learn the verdicts and realize it really was over?

Although I had approached the trial with confidence that I had made the right ruling in refusing to dismiss the case, even if it had resulted in a "not guilty" verdict on all 10 counts, I can't deny that I felt a sense of relief that this had not been a futile or empty exercise and that it had resulted in the public being protected by the conviction of someone who was truly a danger to the community. I felt vindicated and ultimately, of course, further vindicated when the Court of Appeal affirmed the conviction.

Talk to me, if you would, about the sentencing. When and how were various options considered, and was there an earlier time when they might have faced the death penalty?

Bianchi, due to the plea agreement, had obviated any possibility of being at risk of receiving the death penalty, which is why he had no incentive to tell the truth other than his being able to determine the locale or venue where he would serve his sentences, which were—under the agreement made before I ever got involved in the case—sentences of life *with* the possibility of parole.

Buono, on the other hand, faced the possibility of the death penalty. After the verdicts of guilty of first-degree murder with special circumstances were rendered, we proceeded with the second part of the trial, the penalty phase, at which the jury was charged with making the determination between the alternate punishments of life *without* possibility of parole or the death penalty.

Those are the only alternatives when a first-degree verdict is accompanied by a finding of one or more special circumstances and the prosecutor seeks the death penalty. Those special circumstances, for example, include multiple murders and murder in the course of a kidnapping or rape.

At the penalty phase, the defense made the argument that Bianchi was at least as culpable as Buono, and why should Buono receive the death penalty when Bianchi had received life with the possibility of parole? Aside from whatever weight this argument carried, I believe the jury probably was influenced also by pure fatigue on its part, and I say this for the following reasons. The prosecution didn't have much additional evidence to present. Sometimes in death penalty cases there is additional violent behavior that is brought before the jury or mitigating evidence in favor of the defendant. But there really wasn't much additional evidence or argument available to the jury.

My view is that when the jurors went back and started to deliberate on the issue of punishment, if it would have been an easy and quick determination for all of them that he should receive the death penalty, they would have rendered that verdict. But I had the impression—and that's all it is—that the jurors probably were divided on that issue or wanted to give it further consideration. Once the case was over with, the bailiffs who had charge of the jury told me that the jurors truly had battle fatigue, very understandably, not only having been on the case more than two years but also having been sequestered at a downtown hotel for one month. In very quickly returning a penalty verdict of life imprisonment without the possibility of parole, I believe they just threw in the towel and basically felt that they had done their duty, that Buono would be locked up for life without possibility of parole, and that they should be permitted to go home. Again, I don't know this for a fact, but I have a sense that's what happened.

I nonetheless, as the trial judge, had the duty to formally impose punishment on Angelo Buono as determined by the jury. Perhaps out of some sense of symmetry, I thought it would be appropriate to also have Kenneth Bianchi brought back at the same time for the determination I had to make within the narrow confines of the options available under his plea agreement. Where would he serve the balance of his life sentences—in Washington State, or in California? That was really all that could be done and, as I said before, sending him back to Washington State was the only sanction available for his not having testified fully and truthfully. I had an easy time, as did anyone else who heard him, coming to the conclusion that Bianchi had not testified fully and accurately. He could not have, because of the total contradictions in his testimony.

Could there have been a challenge to the agreement of his plea bargain, that he didn't fulfill it?

I suppose there could have been, and there were some comments to that effect. He had his own attorney, deputy public defender Alan Simon. Bianchi didn't mount much of a challenge, as I recall, although this has not stopped him from being a jailhouse lawyer who every now and then files a writ petition in the California Supreme Court claiming that he's totally innocent or that this or that error occurred that requires his release from the obligations of his plea agreement and from custody. Just as when the Supreme Court continued to hear from Mr. Sirhan, in both instances, of course, I had to disqualify or recuse myself.

So I had Bianchi brought back for him and Buono to face each other one last time, on January 9, 1984. I went through a litany of how each of them had inflicted upon their victims just about every type of execution method—hanging or strangulation, electrocution, lethal injection—that was imposed upon defendants who were sentenced by a court to die. I noted they would be housed at public expense and fed and given health care for the duration of their natural lives, when not only their victims but other people in other walks of life would not have those benefits, and how I would have had absolutely no reluctance to impose a death sentence on either of them. That was basically it. It was a somewhat dramatic courtroom encounter, as the two of them glared at each other and went their separate ways, never to see each other again.

I sentenced Buono to life in prison without possibility of parole, in accordance with the jury's penalty-phase verdict, and ordered that Bianchi serve the balance of his life sentences in Washington State. While in prison, Buono and Bianchi each married. Buono died in prison of a heart attack in 2002. Bianchi is serving his sentence and still pens occasional writ petitions to the California Supreme Court and presumably to the Washington courts as well.

What's it like to look back so closely at these events almost 30 years later, and what in your thinking surprises you at this juncture, if anything?

One of the feelings I had—and it would recur from time to time when I'd be confronted with a jury verdict, either as a judge or just as a reader of a newspaper—was how, when all is said and done, by and large jurors come to the right result. It did validate my faith in the jury system, notwithstanding the occasional

odd verdict here and there. It also enhanced my confidence in my own judgment, because it was a difficult call to make, and gave me faith in my own physical endurance, I suppose, and my ability to multitask. It was a vast learning
experience, and it was a case that apparently, in the eyes of some in the legal
press, is still one of the defining points in my judicial career.

I continue to encounter questions about it. There have been, I believe, three
or four dramatizations of the case on television, including some that use tapes
from Bianchi's hypnotic or pseudo-hypnotic interviews. In fact, when I was
called upon to perform one of my various duties as Chief Justice, namely to address the Judges' College, the dean of the judicial college said:

> Customarily we hear from the chief on whatever topics he wishes to
> address to us about the current state of the judiciary and how it's faring
> in Sacramento *vis-à-vis* budget and policy initiatives, and we get to ask
> him questions. But I have something else I'm going to do this year. I
> haven't told the chief about it, but I would like him to tell us about his
> ruling denying the prosecution's motion to dismiss the Hillside Stran-
> gler case.

This occurred just about three years ago, so many years had passed since
that ruling, and this topic was raised with no prior notice. Everyone was apparently quite captivated with the story, and I had requests for copies of the written
memorandum of opinion I had written denying the motion to dismiss, which I
had to retrieve and send off.

I mention this only in response to your question relating to how this seems
to be a topic, a case, that does not die in the public's recollection or imagination,
especially in terms of people who were around then and there. It's something
that many persons have a lot of memories about, either from reading about the
events or even knowing one or more of the victims or their family members.
I've had people come up and say, "I'm a friend of the such-and-such family, and
their daughter was one of the victims."

*Certainly there is great interest by your colleagues in the motion to dismiss, in
particular, and your ruling on it.*

Yes, I've had requests over the years for copies of the opinion. A few here
and there would write back, saying basically: "I pulled a Ron George. I denied
the D.A.'s motion to dismiss." I don't think I ever learned about the circumstances of those cases, and again it's not a ruling I would have made lightly.
Only the most extreme or unusual situation would have led me to do what I did.

I can imagine you established some sort of precedent—perhaps that's too formal a word here, but you were doing something highly unusual and highly unexpected?

I guess it was precedential, but only in the sense of judicial folklore.

Is there anything else you'd like to say about the case or its aftermath in your busy career life?

Just to say again how admirably everyone conducted themselves in the case, whether it was the four attorneys, who all continued with distinguished careers as attorneys or judges; whether it was the court staff, or the jurors, whose praises I've sung already. It was truly a remarkable event and one of the highlights in my judicial career, even though I went on to other courts, and quite a learning experience, not just in the narrow sense of the judicial process but in terms of a life experience.

I understand you were still in the criminal division for a time on the Los Angeles Superior Court but then made a switch over to the civil side. Can you tell me how all of that came about, please?

I decided, after I had completed the lengthy trial and the two years as supervising judge of the criminal division, that I wanted to do something new. I had been on sort of a five-to-seven year cycle—if one looks at it that way—in terms of my career in the attorney general's office, my years as a municipal court judge, and my years assigned to the superior court's criminal division. I wanted to try something different and quite new. I requested assignment to the civil division of the L.A. Superior Court and was fortunate to receive that assignment.

Was there any surprise that you were asking for it?

I don't think so. Everyone must have felt that I was, if anything, close to burnout after my time in the criminal division. I wanted something fresh and intellectually stimulating in terms of a new assignment where I'd be learning more about certain areas of the law that I had not had that much experience with.

I had a number of interesting trials in my civil assignment, including products liability cases, major tort cases, condemnation cases, and construction defect cases. Then I was placed on what was called at the time the mandatory settlement panel. My term there was extended several more months because I somehow, despite my primarily criminal law background, ended up having a lot of success in settling major cases. Maybe this was an invocation of the old diplomatic skills that I had pursued many years before as a college undergraduate.

I have great satisfaction even now in being able to reflect upon the fact that there were some cases—matters that would have consumed many months of trial time and substantial resources of the parties and of the L.A. Superior Court's civil division—that I was able to bring to conclusion. I have a couple of documents here that I pulled from my files.

Just to set the stage a bit, if you would, could you describe the role of settlement, particularly on the civil side, and what percent of cases, roughly, we're talking about?

I'd be sent a case out of the master calendar court, Department 1. I would be assigned these cases for settlement purposes. All the attorneys would be present. I would engage in the customary technique—which you cannot do if you're going to end up hearing the case as a trial judge—of meeting with one side apart from the other side and trying to evaluate the case in terms of what a fair and equitable disposition would be and what the likelihood would be for a plaintiff's verdict or, on the other hand, a defense verdict.

With reference to one case, *Chapman Financial v. Compact Video Systems*, this document indicates that the case settled what would have been a nine-month trial, where I was the fourth settlement judge on the case—others had attempted unsuccessfully to settle it—and that the case settled for a seven-digit amount. We were involved in settlement negotiations for four-and-a-half lengthy days, and when I say "we," there were 27 attorneys involved in the settlement. This is one example. There were many other cases I settled in the seven-digit range. I still remember a case where we arrived at a settlement at about 8 p.m. The attorneys were like a bunch of schoolboys let out of class. They threw their papers up in the air in their joy at having avoided a several-month trial.

How did you succeed where the others had failed?

I don't know—sometimes it's good luck. Maybe they'd been worn down. I tried not to pressure people inordinately, but I gave them my best judgment or evaluation of how the case might turn out, what the risks were of not settling, and what their exposure was. I engaged in good-faith evaluations that seemed to work.

I have a letter in another interesting case, *Knepp v. Wood*, that I found in my files, where one of the attorneys wrote in afterwards: "I do not believe that there is another judge anywhere that I have appeared before who possessed the right blend of skills to meld multiple highly individualistic plaintiffs, attorneys, and defense attorneys and come up with a settlement in this complex a case."

This was a case in which a school bus operated by a Baptist church was involved in an accident, with serious injuries ensuing. The church's insurance did not cover what was deemed to be an appropriate amount of damages. The attorneys finally came around to a figure that I had recommended, but it would require not only the agreement of the insurance carrier, but of the church itself. I took the rather extraordinary step, at their urging, of going to the church for an evening meeting of the entire congregation. This was the First Baptist Church of Reseda in the San Fernando Valley. At the request of the attorneys, I addressed the congregation—which for want of a better site in the church ended up being from the pulpit, as suggested by the pastor. I didn't wear my black robe. I figured there might have been real confusion about my wearing garb that resembled clerical attire. [Laughter] I spoke to the congregation about why this settlement that we tentatively had worked out would be in everyone's interest. The congregation had to vote on it, because it came out of their church's funds. This effort succeeded in settling the case.

These two instances that I gave you took place in 1986 and 1987. The negotiations extended through lunch hours and into the evenings and provided, again, wonderful learning experiences. It brought me great satisfaction to know that I'd been able to bring something to conclusion that had festered for so long in the minds and hearts of the plaintiffs and in the leadership of the defendant church. The same was true regarding some major business disputes that I managed to settle.

At a bar association event, I encountered one attorney who told me that as a reward for obtaining a very favorable settlement of a major case with my assistance, his client had given him a bonus gift of a new Mercedes. I told him I was pleased for him, as well as for the psychic remuneration I had received. Of course, it was always rewarding to have saved the resources of the L.A. Superior Court the many, many months of having a courtroom occupied with a case that, after an intense four or five days' worth of negotiations, we were able to bring to conclusion to make way for the next case that the tide would bring in.

There is a great consideration of the court's resources. What is the proper role of settlement in the overall system, in your view?

I consider it a vital role, but one that I believe should not involve undue pressure from the judge because, much as resources are definitely an important factor to consider—the parties' resources as well as the court's—we should not engage in an assembly-line system of justice. I would not think it appropriate, although I know there are some private judges who do this, to twist arms to the extent that people feel that it was just an expedient result and that the parties' interest in justice was not served. I never wanted to be threatening or overbearing but just to try to enlighten the parties' and the attorneys' perception of their own self-interest to the point where they would willingly settle and then be pleased about the fact that they had settled and how they had settled. That was a very rewarding experience. I truly enjoyed the stimulation of the civil trials over which I presided, and all of the rather technical aspects of instructing a jury and ruling on motions in some of these cases. But I believe one of my greatest satisfactions was being able to bring parties to finality, to closure, by settling some of these civil cases—to the best interests of the parties but also of the judicial system.

You mentioned the part of the process in which you recommend a settlement figure. What kinds of considerations did you have in coming up with those figures?

Of course, best-case and worst-case scenarios, and sharing with the attorneys, sometimes, what my observations had been concerning other cases tried in my courtroom or before other judges—not just settlements but what juries had actually done—without being able to predict, obviously, because every jury is an unknown entity. Still, invoking the law of averages, being able to say, "Your case doesn't look as good as you think it does because of such-and-such."

I remember, in one important wrongful termination employment case, telling the plaintiff's lawyer—and again, obviously, this was outside the presence of the other side, given the nature of the discussions—"I can't say for sure, but when your client walked into the courtroom," and I hadn't been closer than probably 12 or 15 feet from him, "he looked like an obvious alcoholic. Does he have an alcohol problem? If I pick up on that, at least some of the jurors also will. This will discredit his testimony." It turned out that this executive did have an alcohol problem. I wasn't smelling liquor off his breath. It was just his physical appearance and demeanor. Even things like that can be helpful in bringing parties to settlement, pointing out that, "Sure, if everything went his way he might receive double what I'm recommending, but he could end up being totally discredited and getting nothing." The attorney would normally share those observations with the client and point out why it was in the client's interest to accept a portion of the loaf and not go for everything and end up, perhaps, with nothing.

Often the insurance companies also needed to be persuaded that way. What I was finding was that the insurance carriers often were willing to pay a small figure to anyone just to make them go away, even when the plaintiff's case was totally worthless and you could conclude almost with certainty that, after only a single court appearance on a motion, you could knock out the case on demurrer or summary judgment. The insurance company would feel it was cheaper for it to just give the person some walking-away money of twenty or thirty thousand dollars and not be bothered. When they had a really bad case against them, they might stand tough and not offer an appropriate settlement, while giving away a lot of money on worthless cases. In a case where the plaintiff lost an eye and fault wasn't that much at issue, they might be stubborn and not want to contribute what was merited by the injury. I often found a contradiction—in terms of supposedly saving money—between offering a multitude of unwarranted settlements and thereby probably being marked as an easy hit for walking-away money in relatively frivolous cases and, on the other hand, not getting rid of a case where they stood to be liable for much, much more than the amount they were being asked to contribute by way of settlement.

How big was the civil settlement panel at that time, and who else was on it?

I don't recall, because we were not all grouped together in the same part of the courthouse. Because I also ended up doing trials part of my time there, it's hard for me to differentiate how many judges were assigned to settlements.

It was good to learn the settlement business, it sounds like, and you were okay at it?

Yes, to my surprise, because it was a new experience for me. As a deputy attorney general I did not have much work in the civil area, and certainly not anything like the settlement of major litigation—tort cases, products liability, and wrongful termination. Again, it was a wonderful experience with a refreshing exposure to new areas of the law, educating me in an area where I really had a lot to learn and enjoyed learning it.

What is there to say about your civil trial work in that period?

I was fortunate to have some excellent attorneys appear before me. I remember a case of a truck that lost its brakes on the Ridge Route. I remember wrongful termination cases, product liability cases, a great variety of cases, construction defect cases. It was all a new world to me, but by and large the attorneys were excellent, and it was truly a pleasure sitting back and watching them try their cases.

Was this the proper antidote to your burnout on the criminal work?

It was absolutely perfect, it really was. It could not have been a better change. Frankly, it also was very good preparation for the next step, which was my years on the Court of Appeal, because a good portion of the appellate caseload is civil. By virtue of having had day-to-day experience trying civil cases, I was in a much better position to perform my duties as an appellate justice in reviewing the actions of other judges who had tried civil cases in the lower courts.

*That sounds like the perfect subject for our next meeting. Is there anything you'd
like to add about the superior court?*

I would just say, as a little tag-on comment to the last one I made, that this
civil experience gave me some helpful insights into the operations of the civil
justice system that later bore upon my responsibilities as Chief Justice, when I
would meet every year with both the plaintiffs' bar and the civil defense bar. I
believe that the real-life experience I had as a trial and settlement judge in the
civil division helped give me a better appreciation for what their concerns were,
that is, those of the plaintiffs and the civil defense attorneys, and about possible
ways of meeting those concerns and, in the process, improving the civil justice
system.

###

Chapter 7

The California Court of Appeal
August 10, 2011

After talking about your time on the Los Angeles Superior Court, we both thought of things to add to what we discussed last time.

Reflecting upon our having basically completed our discussions on the superior court years, I thought I would mention that, in addition to the other assignments I had, while I was assigned to the civil division I did relieve a judge who was on vacation for two or three weeks and sat in his law and motion courtroom by direction of the presiding judge. That was quite a learning experience, with 20 to 30 highly complex matters every day on a calendar that was exclusively law and motion, mainly demurrers, summary judgments, and ancillary writs and motions—a very intense caseload. Fortunately, I had the assistance—as did the judges permanently assigned there—of a law clerk, but it was still quite a bit of heavy homework to bring home every night.

Interestingly enough, someone whom I met then was Martha Escutia, who ultimately was elected to the state senate and became the chair of the judiciary committee and a great ally of ours in some of the court reform measures that the Judicial Council and I got through. She was a brand-new law clerk at that time, and when we met again years later she described our relationship in some detail, frankly in greater detail than I remembered, because I was so busy mastering this complex task, even if for only two or three weeks. But she looked favorably upon our relationship at the superior court, which helped me persuade her to be of assistance to us in her later role as a leading legislator.

I also had an assignment of two or three weeks to the juvenile court, which of course is a division of the superior court. But that assignment was actually as a municipal court judge sitting on assignment as a judge of the superior court. That gave me a brief exposure to one more facet of the wide range of cases that one hears as a trial judge.

What sense did you get in that short amount of time of particular challenges facing the juvenile system?

I felt that there really wasn't enough time, given the heavy calendars, to do what most judges assigned to the juvenile court would want to do, which was so very, very important in terms of actually having a true opportunity to have a substantial bearing upon the future of the person before you. This was unlike serving in the criminal division of the superior court, where unfortunately one felt very often that all you could do was warehouse the person in order to protect society and that it was more the rare exception than the rule where you might actually have a rehabilitative effect on the life of the convicted defendant through your rulings and the sentence you imposed. In contrast, in the juvenile court you really felt there was that opportunity—and it was so important to be able to take the interest, time, and care—to fashion a disposition that might make a law-abiding and productive person out of that youthful offender. It was therefore so important to provide adequate resources to the juvenile courts.

One other broad matter of importance during your time on the superior court was the changes in the sentencing laws. Determinate sentencing went into effect in California in 1977. What are your thoughts generally about the effect of that change on our system?

It's interesting to me from the standpoint of history—and that goes beyond merely the law—how cyclical many things are over the years. Originally there was determinate sentencing in California, and it was thought to be rather harsh and not take into account the variations in the commission of a crime, nor perhaps the variations in the course of criminal conduct and adult behavior on the part of an offender. Because of this reaction to the determinate type of sentencing that existed in colonial America and in Britain—where x crime merited y punishment automatically—indeterminate sentencing was enacted in California as a means designed to have the punishment fit the criminal and not just the crime. The idea was that a parole board authority would have the ability to weigh the various factors involved in the commission of the crime and, most importantly, the factors involved in the defendant's life, positive and negative, and then set an appropriate term.

However, after a while that too was thought to be harsh, this time because it left the offender without specific information or notice of how long he or she would be serving in custody. This system was thought in some instances to permit disparate sentences among similarly situated defendants caused by the individual actions of the parole board. Because indeterminate sentencing, although a well-intended reform, was thought to be too harsh, we went back to a form of determinate sentencing, although with a variation. In almost every instance, the new determinate sentencing law enacted in 1977 fixed a lower, a middle, and an upper term. The judge, for reasons that had to be stated on the record, could deviate from the middle term, either downward or upward to a specified lower term or upper term. Likewise, when consecutive sentences were being imposed, the judge was obliged to make certain factual determinations.[1] This innovation was thought once again to be a progressive change in the law, but it interested me and to a certain extent amused me to see the cyclical change over the many years in how we approach matters and how we went back to some of the things that had been abandoned earlier as harsh or unfair.

I believe the current determinate sentencing law, despite those observations, does by and large work well in California. I'm glad it doesn't operate like the federal sentencing guidelines, which I question in their present form even though, due to a high court ruling, they are no longer mandatory. I really think those guidelines are so restrictive in terms of the options open to a sentencing judge that they unduly limit the judge's discretion and probably cause some sentences to be imposed that are unfair, certainly that federal district court judges have expressed concern about and have indicated they are imposing only because of the sentencing guidelines. I believe legitimate arguments can be made that when sentencing guidelines are so rigid as to impose very severe limits upon a judge's exercise of discretion in imposing an appropriate sentence, a basic judicial function is being impaired to the point where a constitutional issue of separation of powers might very well arise. One can legitimately inquire whether Congress has the right to involve itself in the sentencing process to that degree.

There are other things I wonder about in terms of Congress' role in prescribing various procedures that affect federal judges, for example, the proposed regulation of televising courtroom proceedings. I believe many things are better and more appropriately left to the judicial branch to determine for itself—matters that should reside in the individual discretion of a judge, rather than being superimposed by the executive and/or legislative branches.

How widely is your view of that federal sentencing law held, do you know?

---

[1] The U.S. Supreme Court has determined that most factual findings enhancing a sentence must be submitted to the jury for determination. Cunningham v. California (2007) 549 U.S. 270.

I don't really know except that I have read and personally heard federal district court and circuit court judges express frustration at how rigid those guidelines are. I sense a fair degree of dissatisfaction with the guidelines even in their current form.

Again, speaking at the federal level, what would be the avenue for addressing that separation of powers issue?

Certainly an attempt could be made to have Congress render them more flexible. Another avenue would be for someone, either a judge or a litigant, to challenge those guidelines in court on constitutional separation-of-powers grounds, although the high court's ruling has removed much of the force behind such an argument.

By contrast, you think the determinate sentencing law as it is set up in California works well?

I believe it does, by and large, because it permits enough flexibility that a judge feels in most instances that he or she can come to a fair result—and by a fair result I mean one that's fair both to the defendant and to the public—provided certain findings can be made that affect the length of the prison term and sometimes the defendant's eligibility for probation. There are some instances where there is no eligibility for probation, period. But in most situations the option of probation exists or, if it's generally disallowed, the option of probation can be invoked provided the judge makes certain specific findings. Also there's flexibility in terms of consecutive sentences, generally speaking.

I'm not indicating that I believe it's wrong for the legislative body to express its preferences or even some guidelines, but when they become rigid and inflexible, problems not only of fairness but of impairment of judicial discretion arise. Considering those concerns, I believe California's system is superior to what exists on the federal level.

Again, among your colleagues, generally speaking, is that view shared that California compares favorably in that regard?

It's difficult, of course, to speak for the judiciary of about 1,700 judges plus subordinate judicial officers, but I don't sense the degree of dissatisfaction or frustration with the determinate sentencing law in California courts that I do in the sentiments expressed by federal judges. It seems that when a recurring problem arises under the California sentencing law, the legislature in most instances has been responsive and willing to modify the sentencing options available for a given offense.

That's in a sense a different relation between the two branches than you're de-scribing on the federal level.

Somewhat, in the matter of sentencing laws.

That matter of judicial discretion is an interesting one. It's one thing to speak of it broadly but another thing when you're running up against it on a particular case.

That's true. I don't want to hold California out as necessarily a model in terms of leaving to judicial discretion what *should* be left to judicial discretion. I just find that in the area of determinate sentencing, there has been much more appropriate deference to the judiciary than there is in the federal system.

As a practical matter, what direct effect if any did the change to determinate sentencing in 1977 have on your own casework?

Once I became a superior court judge, the change was already in effect. The Determinate Sentencing Act was passed in 1976 and became effective July 1, 1977. I was confronted with it when I joined the superior court, although we had a transitional period, of course, when there were pre-DSA offenses that came before the court that still required sentencing under the old law. I felt I had much more leeway in imposing a sentence under the determinate sentencing law, not just because of the three ranges of low, medium, and upper terms, but also be-cause one had a sense of what that upper term would mean as far as the number of years to be served. There were offenses that under the old indeterminate sen-tencing law had a range from a minimum of one year to a maximum of life im-prisonment. I'm sure that many judges, including myself, had trepidations in some situations—where, let's say, the offense was less aggravated than most—about imposing an indeterminate sentence on such a defendant who, at least the-oretically, would be subject to a possible life sentence. I felt more at ease impos-ing a prison sentence if I knew specifically what the range of years would be, obviously making allowance for the "good behavior time" and "work time" credits that would be calculated against service of the full term.

I believe there were cases in which defendants who were eligible for proba-tion received a probationary sentence because of that concern on the part of the trial judge—which, in effect, led the judge to conclude, "I really feel this person should serve a few years in state prison, but I would be very troubled by his or her serving a life sentence. Rather than take that risk, I'm going to put that per-son on probation with the maximum allowable time in county jail," which is one year. That person might have otherwise received, let's say, a three- or four-year sentence to state prison, except for the lingering concern of the trial judge that an indeterminate term might result in a life sentence. But it wasn't always a concern that someone would serve too much time. The sentencing judge's concern might be that the person would instead serve too little time. I believe providing more notice to the court, the defendant, and the prosecution of the likely period of actual incarceration was certainly a positive aspect of the determinate sentencing law.

We touched before on the fact that you served as editor for various publications, including the sentencing handbook and the accompanying desk blotter with the summary of all those laws. How did that editorial experience affect your views of the big picture of sentencing in California?

My editorial role in these publications certainly made me aware of the sentencing situation in areas beyond my own individual experience as a sentencing judge. By necessity, in editing this publication I had to become aware of all the various sentencing options, some of which had their own idiosyncrasies. The *Bench Blotter* that I mentioned previously was in the most literal sense the big picture setting forth all these options.

Thank you. To finish up that period of time perhaps we'll just touch on a couple of extracurricular things you were doing while on the superior court.

I served on Attorney General George Deukmejian's Crime Victims Commission as a judge of the superior court and also on something called the Los Angeles Countywide Criminal Justice Coordinating Committee. What I found particularly worthwhile about the latter assignment was that it brought together the District Attorney of L.A. County, the Public Defender of L.A. County, the supervising judge of the criminal division, which was myself, and other partners in the criminal justice system to look at things systemically and see where we might work together to improve both the fairness and the efficiency of the criminal justice system in Los Angeles County. That was a theme that certainly followed me as I moved to other courts and one that I attempted to pursue as Chief Justice, getting the various components in the criminal justice system—some of whose roles were by law and by definition antagonistic to each other in the sense of being adversaries—to come together and recognize common problems and try to fashion mutually acceptable solutions for the betterment of the justice system.

Certainly, as you say, bringing together the D.A., the public defender, and other interested parties is quite a lesson in diplomacy and process, too. What stands out about the process of working together?

Everyone was very professional and very receptive in those meetings, and despite the fact that seeing the D.A.s and the public defenders in the courtroom made one sometimes feel like a referee in a boxing match, when they got together outside the courtroom I found them much more understanding of each other's respective positions and mindful of the need to work together to improve the justice system.

I don't know how closely you worked with Attorney General Deukmejian in serving on his committee, but can you summarize his interest in these criminal matters, as you saw it then, while he was attorney general?

I didn't work directly with him. At this time there was beginning to be a real interest in the impact of the criminal justice system on crime victims, and a sense that it wasn't just a matter of the people of the state being represented by the D.A., and the public defender or private counsel representing the defendant, but that there was this other entity out there, crime victims, who should be listened to, sometimes formally in the course of the sentencing proceedings. This committee, I believe, was designed to give recognition to that component and to explore ways in which the system could be improved accordingly.

Indeed, Mr. Deukmejian ran for governor the first time on something of a victims' rights platform. What do you recall about that period when he was running in 1982?

I don't have too much of a recollection of that campaign. I had worked with former State Senator Deukmejian in restoring the death penalty to California after I failed to prevail in the case of *People v. Anderson*, involving the ruling by the California Supreme Court that the death penalty was cruel or unusual punishment. I know that he enjoyed a reputation throughout his career—as a senator, as attorney general, and as a governor—of being an extremely diligent and fair-minded person whose word you could always count on. Even persons who disagreed with his views on certain issues often expressed the opinion that he was exceedingly fair and reasonable in negotiating with them on matters involving the budget or policy when he was governor. Of course, my contact with him, although indirect, also involved his decision to take over the Hillside Strangler prosecution. Again, he didn't do it on a reflexive level. He appointed, as we discussed before, four nationally renowned experts and made a reasoned evaluation based upon their findings. That typifies the kind of individual he was and is.

Perhaps that's a good transition into talking about your own appointment to the Court of Appeal in 1987. As you were serving on the superior court, however, how early did you begin thinking about possible advancement to the appeals level?

I was very eager to broaden my experience as a trial judge to include the civil assignments that we discussed last time, both civil trials and, as I added today, a bit of law and motion, and the time I spent on the mandatory settlement panel as it was called in those days. Without in any way indicating that I had learned everything there was to learn in my civil assignment, I felt satisfied that I had achieved the goal of acquiring a meaningful background in the civil area. My training from my first days as a lawyer had been, of course, as an appellate lawyer, so I was attracted to the possibility of a career as a justice on the Court of Appeal. I did put in my application, and I was by the way interviewed for that position by Governor Deukmejian's then-appointments secretary, Marvin Baxter, who ended up being a colleague of mine on the California Supreme Court.

How did you decide the timing of that application in 1987?

I may have put in for it before that, because it was an elevation that did not occur right away. I recall that I had applied for appointment to the Court of Appeal and saw to my disappointment that there were others—and I won't say in any way that they were less deserving—whose names were circulated roughly at the same time who achieved elevation before I did. I don't recall exactly when I applied, but I recall having to wait a while before it came through. When it did, I was very pleased to fill the position held by Justice John Arguelles, a long-time friend of mine who had been elevated to the Supreme Court. I ended up ultimately having the Commission on Judicial Appointments hearing for my appointment to the Court of Appeal presided over by Justice Edward Panelli, another friend of mine, because Chief Justice Lucas was unavailable to chair the commission. I believe he was recuperating from surgery at that time.

To back up just a moment, if I might, what was the nature of your conversations with Marvin Baxter in his role then as the appointments secretary for Governor Deukmejian? Did you meet with him in person, and what did he say?

I met with him in person, and I remember the conversation being rather brief, very friendly but somewhat matter of fact, factual inquiries, verifying certain things and not of a philosophical nature. Now, I suppose that, due to my history as a deputy attorney general and municipal and superior court judge, certain questions probably had been answered already just by virtue of the governor's office having checked with persons who were familiar with my career. I recall the meeting did not delve deeply into my views on any subjects.

As you say, you had Justice Panelli presiding over your hearing. What do you remember about that day?

The other two members of the Commission were Presiding Justice Lester Roth and Attorney General John Van de Kamp. Van de Kamp inquired of me during the hearing whether I was considered ambitious. My reply was that I considered ambition to be a positive trait, and that if I had not been ambitious, I would still be writing briefs in the attorney general's office. My parents and my sister attended the hearing, along with members of Barbara's family, and of course Barbara was there with the three boys. Justice Panelli administered the oath of office.

You mentioned being located in the Wilshire building at the time. Tell me something about your physical set up there, your chambers and so on.

The leased quarters in a commercial building located in the mid-Wilshire area of Los Angeles were quite nice, especially for something that was viewed as temporary housing. The Court of Appeal along with the Supreme Court, the Attorney General's office, and other agencies had had to vacate the old State Building, which was found to have suffered structural damage from the 1971 quake and had to be demolished. Ultimately, all of these entities were moved to the new Ronald Reagan State Office Building located about three blocks from their original location.

The appellate court provided a major change in my professional environment to the extent that, in both my criminal and civil assignments as a trial judge, I was used to crowded courtrooms and hallways, jurors and witnesses on the next case poking their heads into the courtroom wondering when their matter would be called to follow the case that was just being concluded, and the pressure of knowing that the master calendar court had so many cases and would be checking in through the coordinator periodically during the day to see how soon you could finish up and take the next case.

It was quite a contrast being placed in this somewhat rarefied atmosphere that called for and encouraged reflection—having the luxury of spending perhaps not quite as much time as one ideally wanted to, but fairly close to that in most situations—and if there was the exceptional case you could put it over and spend more time on it as needed. Having the opportunity to work with research attorneys and to do your own research, to examine your own drafts and the drafts of your colleagues, to deliberate with your own staff and then with the other justices on the case, and to have extended oral argument if it was called for in the case—all of that was a luxury in terms of being able to reflect and ponder legal issues. Often the situation had arisen at the trial court level—both in criminal and civil assignments—where I would take a hurried recess and look up some case law or statutory provisions, but I felt that I really would have benefited had I been able to spend several days really getting into the problem. But that was not something that was normally feasible under the circumstances. So I viewed it as a real luxury to expend whatever time and effort I might need to delve into matters at the appellate level. I love to engage in the details of legal writing, and of course this was a daily pursuit at the appellate level as opposed to just the occasional effort one might make, where appropriate, in the trial court. I found these to be very welcome changes after having had 15 years as a trial judge and again, in a cyclical way, being back at the appellate level and serving on a court that I had argued before as a deputy attorney general.

You have previously described your interest in legal research and writing, and yet you're describing a major change of environment. Were friends or colleagues able to help you smooth the way, or how did you go about making that adjustment on a personal level?

I found it a fairly easy adjustment in that, having been an advocate, having written briefs and argued cases before the Court of Appeal—which was 90 percent of my practice as a deputy attorney general—it did not seem all that difficult to make the transition and to consider the briefs of both sides and then work on drafts of opinions with my two research attorneys. It was nice to be on the other side of the bench and be asking the questions instead of having them fired at me.

But the change was substantial in terms of professional transition and certainly in terms of lifestyle and in the flexibility of the hours in my workday brought about by this change. I put in long hours, but they were not necessarily confined to a nine-to-five schedule. You could come in late and work on things late into the evening, or at home just as well as you could in chambers, unlike the vast bulk of your work as a trial judge, where you had to be there to interact with counsel and the jurors.

I'd like to return to oral argument, but perhaps first we could talk about your colleagues in your new position, starting with the presiding justice.

The presiding justice was Arleigh Woods, who is a delightful person and did a fine job of running the division, at the same time accommodating the idiosyncrasies of her three associate justices, who in addition to myself comprised Eugene McCloskey—who was a very friendly and bright individual with a great sense of humor—and Robert Kingsley, with whom I didn't get to work very much, because he retired early in 1988 and then died at the end of that year. His position was filled by Jack Goertzen, whom we've talked about before, who was my boss to the extent I did trials and investigations work as a deputy attorney general. Jack went on to the municipal court before I did, and then on to the superior court. He was elevated in the spring of 1988 and, happily, was appointed to Division Four, where I was serving. So we were back working together again, which led to a lot of professional accomplishments and fun.

It wasn't all shenanigans?

It wasn't all shenanigans although, since you bring up shenanigans, there certainly was one on my part. Again, Jack Goertzen was and is a person who just invites practical jokes and good humor.

I recall that I was about to take a vacation with Barbara and our three sons to Alaska. I mentioned to him that we were going to do some salmon fishing, and Jack made a point of saying how he adored wild King salmon, and could I see fit to bring some back for him? I probably would have just left it at that and forgotten it, but he proceeded for some reason or other to be quite insistent and repetitive in reminding me. "Don't forget to bring me some salmon." He must have mentioned it three or four times, so of course this awakened my sense of taking humorous advantage of the situation.

On the first day of fishing, I managed to catch a very nice-sized salmon. I believe it was 26 pounds. At the fishing lodge, they would immediately chop the head off and fillet the fish for you, and flash freeze it so you could bring it back home in good shape. This salmon, like others once they get on in years, had developed somewhat of a prehensile appearance, almost like the beak of a predatory bird, with large bulging eyes. I told the people processing the fish not to throw away the head of that salmon and to freeze it separately. I brought the frozen salmon head back to Los Angeles.

Division Four would, two or three times a week, have a writs conference in the chambers of the presiding justice when at least two or three writ petitions would have accumulated that we had to act on. I alerted Arleigh Woods to the fact that I had a practical joke to play on Jack Goertzen, and I asked her, "See if you can get a couple of cases together to merit calling us into your chambers." We'd usually do that in the morning shortly after nine o'clock, which I wanted to do before this fish head would thaw. Jack had a habit of drinking large quantities of coffee, which always caused him to ask to be momentarily excused not long after these conferences would start at 9:00 a.m.

I managed to go to his chambers bathroom facility right when this conference was supposed to start, and I took this very large frozen salmon head and stuffed it into his toilet bowl, with just the beady eyes and the beak protruding above the waterline and the rest of it appearing to emerge out of the drain of the toilet bowl. Then I proceeded to join the conference in Presiding Justice Woods' chambers. It was like counting the minutes until Jack would ask to be excused, which he did, and as he made his way back to his chambers it was like counting the seconds for a time bomb to be detonated. Sure enough, after a number of seconds this bellowing scream echoed through the chambers of Division Four.

Of course, the court staff was unaware of what was happening, so staff attorneys and secretaries came running to the most private part of Justice Goertzen's chambers, thinking that perhaps he was undergoing a heart attack or some other calamity, only to see him staring in disbelief at this monster from the deep that had just surfaced in his toilet facility. [Laughter] Given the history of practical jokes back and forth between Jack Goertzen and myself, I didn't feel too badly about the temporary discomfort I had caused him. He got a big kick out of it, with his wonderful sense of humor. As you can see, although I took my official duties seriously, I tried not to take myself too seriously.

Thank you for that fish story. It sounds as if Eugene McCloskey and Jack Goertzen were your two fellow associate justices on your panel for quite a period of time when you started out. You mentioned oral argument a few moments ago. Can you describe the style that the three of you might have displayed in conducting those sessions?

I remember Justice McCloskey having a wonderful sense of humor, being irreverent, and asking provocative questions—something I enjoyed. Presiding Justice Woods kept things nicely under control in an informal but properly authoritative way, without letting us get off track. I enjoyed being able to ask questions that would explore the ramifications of the decision being urged by the advocate, the impact on the system and on nonparties, because that was always a concern of mine as an appellate advocate—or at least I knew I had to be prepared to respond to those concerns expressed by justices of the state and U.S. Supreme Courts. I enjoyed the interplay between counsel and the bench and the opportunity to explore the full ramifications of the rulings that we were being urged to render.

In general, how active a questioner were you compared to Justices McCloskey and Goertzen?

I'd say probably average. Unlike what transpires in the California Supreme Court, the Court of Appeal doesn't expect counsel to take the full time allotted. The attorneys will sometimes ask for it, but often they'll just ask for a very few minutes, so it usually wasn't the same kind of involved dialogue that took place at the Supreme Court level.

We've talked about the other members of Division Four, but I should note that during my tenure Justice McCloskey retired. Justice Norman Epstein, whom we spoke of earlier, joined our division. That was a wonderful addition, because he brings so much to any gathering that he is a part of, whether it's the deliberations of an appellate panel, a committee, or some other group. He would often, in his oral and written work, uncover issues that had not been raised—or not been raised with full awareness of the ramifications. I felt we truly had an outstanding and very collegial division.

I also had two very fine staff attorneys, Greg Wolff, who came from heading the appellate division of the Los Angeles city attorney's office and had been recommended to me by Justice Elwood Lui, and Darien Pope, who had clerked for Justice Arguelles. Both staff attorneys, when I was elevated to the Supreme Court, moved up to the Bay Area and joined me on the staff of the high court.

That says a lot about your ability to work well with them. Can you say a bit more about how you were able to use their talents to advance your work?

In most instances, I had the benefit of having them do the research and then draft proposed dispositions for my consideration. For reasons of quality control, I also had them review each other's drafts. When I wrote a dissent, I had the luxury of doing something that I later found I could do only rarely at the Supreme Court level and that is do some original writing on my own. At the Supreme Court level there were portions of an opinion that I would write myself rather than using a draft. At the Court of Appeal, I would occasionally write an opinion myself from scratch. I generally wrote the dissents from scratch. That was something I truly enjoyed doing, having my hands in the writing process right from the outset.

What was your philosophical view of dissents? What would it take for you to go that route and prepare a formal opinion differing from the majority?

That's a very interesting question that I have given some thought to over the years. It's a question upon which reasonable minds can and do differ. I believe that often an appellate justice—and I include Supreme Court justices as well—will write a separate opinion when it might be better not to bother doing so. I believe this to be especially true of concurring opinions. My reasons for saying this echo those in Witkin's treatise on appellate opinion writing.[2] Sometimes the writing of a separate opinion, especially a concurring opinion, really amounts to no more than venting one's spleen and proclaiming, "I would use this language instead of what you, the author, have written." Or "I like this slightly different theory a bit better than the one you employed." That type of separate opinion serves to clutter up the law and to deprive it of the more authoritative impact that it might otherwise have. I say that despite having written some dissents and some concurring opinions myself, but I felt on each occasion that I was faced with an exceptional situation where the circumstances justified taking that action.

Interestingly enough, in some countries—and I believe France is one of them—there are no dissenting opinions. As an appellate justice, once you have

---

[2] B. E. Witkin, *Manual on Appellate Court Opinions*, pp. 217–219 (West Pub. Co., St. Paul, 1977).

lost the vote with your colleagues, you suffer in silence and the opinion comes out as the opinion of the court. I'm not saying that I necessarily favor this approach. There have been some very notable dissenting opinions, on the U.S. Supreme Court in particular, where the dissenting view has served to illustrate the weaknesses in the majority's position and has ultimately carried the day in a future case. I previously mentioned writing a concurring opinion—actually, it was my very first opinion in the Supreme Court—in the case of *Rider v. County of San Diego,* which involved a tax issue. I had a very different approach to the question. That concurring opinion of mine ultimately was adopted by a majority of the court in the *Santa Clara County Local Transportation Authority* case as the view of the court on the tax question involved.

Having said that, I believe there are many concurring opinions that clutter up the appellate reports and clutter up the law in the sense of detracting from the guidance that might otherwise have been afforded to lower court judges, the bar, and the public. I find those opinions particularly disserving of the judicial process when they deprive the court of the ability to speak with the authority of a true majority, namely by depriving the author of having—in the case of the California Supreme Court—the votes of four or more of the seven justices on the court's opinion and by instead causing that opinion to be a plurality opinion reflecting fewer than four votes, accompanied by a separate concurring opinion with one or more votes.

I am happy to say—and tried to exert efforts as Chief Justice to this effect— that we have very much gotten away from plurality opinions on the California Supreme Court. If my recollection is correct, it's been years since we had a case that did not command at least four votes for the majority opinion. On occasion, we may be fractured with separate opinions, dissenting and concurring, but at least the reader can have the confidence of knowing that a majority of the justices of the court stands behind an opinion of the court. I would also say that the California Supreme Court has a much higher percentage of unanimous opinions than does the U.S. Supreme Court, and a much smaller percentage of split decisions decided by only a single vote.

Indeed, the U.S. Supreme Court has so often been known for those very split decisions, which gives one member a great amount of power in outcomes, does it not?

That certainly is the case. I will note, trying to be objective, that some of the commentators on the work of the California Supreme Court have described me—correctly or not—as often the swing vote on the court. Indeed that was true on several cases, but there are, as I said a moment ago, far, far fewer cases on the California Supreme Court that are decided by a single vote.

I know that I made a point, always—whether it was on the Court of Appeal or on the Supreme Court—of trying to accommodate the concerns of a justice who might basically be with me on the holding but who had a concern, let's say, with a particular paragraph or phrase or one theory. If I could accommodate that person by removing or modifying an offending portion of the opinion without detracting from the quality and force of the opinion, I would do so. I was not one who stopped counting at two on the Court of Appeal, or at four on the Supreme Court. I would go for that third vote in Division Four. On the high court if I had six votes, including my own, and I could somehow take care of the concern of the seventh individual on the court, I would make an effort to do so—not for reasons of personal pride or ego, but just because I feel that, to the extent the court—like, in other contexts, the judiciary as a whole—can speak with a single voice, the force of its pronouncements will be greater than when it is splintered. There are often very deep and good-faith differences of opinion that cannot and should not be buried under the cloak of unanimity, but very frequently there are differing concerns that can reasonably be accommodated. Often this can be done without detracting from the worth of the end product, while still performing the valuable function of what appellate justices are supposed to do, namely providing guidance to others rather than just venting their own spleen.

You were acting, perhaps, on a principle of guidance and also clarity as things to be sought?

Yes. Again, perhaps my training as an appellate lawyer led me to be concerned about that. I tried to be sensitive to nuances, to ambiguity, to lack of direction, to the practical impact on trial courts and practicing attorneys resulting from the pronouncements that come from on high.

Speaking now again of the Court of Appeal, you did start off saying that you had the luxury of composing a dissent from scratch on occasion. You made use of your staff attorneys, perhaps, more often on some of the other opinions. Other than choosing to write a formal dissent, what other avenues were open to you to resolve differences on this three-judge panel?

One never knew, really, which three justices of the four of us in the division were going to be sitting on a given case until shortly before oral argument, because the cases were assigned to us only several weeks in advance of argument. The ideal situation on a collegial court—by which I mean one that expresses itself through a body of participants—is to have the opportunity to interact on a personal level. There are appellate divisions where, unfortunately, by predisposition or differences in personality, the justices don't communicate that well or do communicate only formally through written memoranda.

I believe it is very constructive, both in terms of the quality of the end product and the efficient use of time, for a justice to be able to confer orally with one or more colleagues on the case. It may be a worthwhile exercise because the colleague has expressed some doubts. It may be before the author has even set pen to paper and wants to explore different possibilities with his or her colleagues to find out what might fly or what are the possible weak points in the approach being contemplated by the author. I recall situations—without any notice of subject matter—where one of us would feel quite free to knock at what was usually the open door of a colleague and say, "I'd like to talk to you about the *Smith* case, and this is what I'm thinking of doing. What do you think of this?" or "I see that you've expressed these concerns in the *Jones* case. What if we deal with it this way? Would that work?" These discussions could take place either before or after oral argument. I believe this was a very productive and enjoyable way of arriving at a constructive product to which all three participating justices could ascribe. Of course, so many of the cases before the Court of Appeal are routine and don't justify that kind of interruption of a colleague's time, but I never encountered a situation where my offer, or my colleague's offer, to discuss a case was rebuffed or viewed as unwelcome or unproductive.

These were clearly matters that the justices would take up directly with one another, rather than sending their staff attorneys out as emissaries?

That's correct. Sometimes there was a situation where resolution of what might be a knotty problem—and that's k-n-o-t-t-y and not the other kind of naughty [Laughter]—ultimately might require some research to see if there was another viable alternative, but at the Court of Appeal level the preferred course in our division was to just pop in and shoot the breeze and see if the matter potentially could be resolved that way.

At the Supreme Court level, justices had different approaches and proclivities in terms of whether they enjoyed informal discussions on legal issues or preferred instead to communicate more formally through written memos and/or through discussions and negotiations between their staff attorneys and the staff attorneys of another justice. But certainly at the Court of Appeal level, in our division where everyone was very outgoing and informal in his or her personal relationships—and of course you were dealing with only two colleagues on your case, as opposed to six—this seemed to be the best and most efficient way to facilitate arriving at a good decision and opinion.

I did want to ask about serving at the appellate level on a panel of three like that. That's a significant difference on the face of it from a panel of seven. What was the efficacy of that number on the Court of Appeal, in your opinion?

There are reasons why those who founded our system of government and our legal system picked a number greater than one, given the legal issues involved and the ramifications of the resolution of those issues. It was felt, presumably, that it was better to have more than one mind working on it and that there would be give and take in resolving these matters, even though it obviously would be more efficient to have only one person unilaterally pull a thumbs-up or thumbs-down on any case that was up on appeal. I think it's very worthwhile having a collegial body rather than a sole individual perform the function of judicial review. Some state high courts have only five members, ours of course has seven, and some have nine like the U.S. Supreme Court.

I don't know if you get more done with nine. The California Supreme Court produces far more opinions each year than the U.S. Supreme Court. The federal high court in recent years has been putting out 68 to 70, sometimes a bit more. The average for the California Supreme Court—when we're fully staffed and don't have a long-term vacancy—has been more like 112 to 115. We do that with seven justices, and we have automatic appeals, which consume a lot of time—that is, the death penalty appeals with thousands of pages of transcript and dozens of issues. We have to take all of those, unlike the U.S. Supreme Court that just occasionally will choose to take a capital case and limit itself to one or two issues.

I don't believe you are necessarily more productive with a number of justices greater than seven. That number seems perfect for California. There are some states, such as Washington State, that have nine members on their state Supreme Court. I also wonder whether you get more separate opinions on a case when nine justices participate. Of course, our court works year round. We don't have the luxury of meeting the first Monday in October and having all our cases done by the last day in June, and then having the summers off. I'd say that the California Supreme Court, with the number seven, is ideally constituted in terms of the workload it puts out.

One issue, perhaps tangentially related to the question that you just posed, Laura, is whether it is better to have a district of the Court of Appeal organized into permanent divisions or instead to pick three justices at random from a unitary appellate district to hear each case. California has been divided geographically into six appellate districts—actually, six Courts of Appeal totaling 105 justices. Although they are sometimes generically referred to as *the* Court of Appeal, each one of the six is a separate court. Three of the six appellate districts, including the Second District in Los Angeles, are divided into divisions, and the other three are not. The unitary or "no division approach" is followed in the federal circuit courts, including the Ninth Circuit, which comprises California and several other western states. This means that in that type of appellate court you have the luck of the draw as to which three judges will be selected to hear a given case. The Ninth Circuit does have a procedure under which, if a majority of the court agrees to grant *en banc* review, a larger number—which I believe comprises 11, but less than a majority—will hear the case *en banc*, superseding the opinion rendered by the three-judge panel.

I have come around to the view that I favor the nondivisional structure of the Third, Fifth, and Sixth Appellate Districts of the California Courts of Appeal—something established by the legislature and not by the courts' own choosing. That structure allows for more cross-fertilization, if you will. Appellate court divisions end up sometimes having the virtue of each justice knowing in advance the likely position of his or her colleague, but maybe excessively so. I believe some of these divisions evolve into something like a stale marriage. Some of the justices can even complete each other's lines before the sentence is over with. I think there's more stimulation in having to write for a larger entity on your own court—meaning the entire court, not just a division—having to anticipate other arguments, be confronted with challenges to one's reasoning and approach from a variety of colleagues and not just from two of your three division mates sitting with you on the case. That's how my thinking has evolved based on my observations and experience.

Yet you were sitting yourself in a large district with eight divisions overall?

Yes. It had seven then, and eight now. The contact with the justices in the other divisions was fairly minimal. Justices rarely discussed legal issues with someone outside their division. You'd have an administrative meeting of the whole district once in a while, but each division operated pretty much like a separate court. If an issue had been resolved by a division in the same district other than your own division, efforts were made to try to avoid a conflict in the law within the same district, but not always successfully. Under the principle of *stare decisis*, as interpreted by the California Supreme Court's opinion in the *Auto Equity* decision of many years ago, any decision of any division of any Court of Appeal is statewide law and is equally binding or persuasive not only on lower courts but on every other appellate court in the state, which doesn't mean they absolutely have to follow it, but it's not as if, because something comes from a different district, you can disregard it.

In a large district such as the Second District in Los Angeles, with so many different separate divisions, there comes to be a certain reputation that different divisions have.

That's definitely true. I believe there's a perception that if your case ends up in a particular division—and the assignment of cases to the divisions apparently is randomly made—your chances as a criminal defendant or as a plaintiff may be greater or lesser depending upon where you land. That's another reason why I favor the "no division" approach to the appellate districts. I say that, even knowing that I can't imagine a better and more enjoyable group of individuals than I was privileged to serve with in Division Four. But approaching the question from the standpoint of the overall judicial system, I believe the advantages of a "no division" district outweigh those of a district that is carved into divisions.

How do you suppose advocates viewed your division? What was the book on Division Four?

I believe we were viewed as kind of a mixed bag but middle of the road enough that advocates would not regard the result in our division as pre-ordained. We had a couple of individuals who were viewed as probably more sympathetic to the claims of criminal defendants than the other two, but I would say on the civil side the four justices probably were viewed as fairly similar in outlook. Some of the other divisions of the Second Appellate District were viewed as less flexible and more predictable in terms of outcomes than was Division Four.

It stands to reason that with divisions, reputations would develop among the participants out there in the world. I'm thinking about how interesting it must have been for you to participate in oral argument in particular, having been on the other side, as it were. I wonder what you might have learned or noted that you didn't expect, if anything, once you were on the bench side?

I certainly appreciated how important it is to let appellate counsel have their say. I don't mean to immunize them from vigorous questioning. But I found it rather disconcerting when I would see an attorney who was so eager to communicate his or her position on three stated points, let's say, and then be cut off and have counsel's allotted time run out with one interruption after another without having been able to address the issues. In fact, when I was in a position to have some control over the process after becoming Chief Justice, I would sometimes say to counsel, "Look, you've got two minutes left, and you never got to that other point or to that answer that you were trying to give. Although you only have two minutes left, I'd like you to address that."

As someone who had been an appellate advocate, I was sensitive to that situation. A lot of it, of course, depends upon the skill of the appellate advocate in trying to tap dance around different questions—and by tap dancing around I don't mean evading answering them but being able to answer the question and then move on to the points counsel wanted to make in his or her argument. As an advocate, however, you don't want to try to cover everything set forth in your brief in your allotted time of 30 minutes. That's foolish and doesn't get you anywhere.

I'd say there was generally a certain empathy for counsel but at the same time a real impatience with attorneys who wouldn't answer a question and had to be told, "I've asked for an answer." I saw some of my colleagues on the Supreme Court have to say, "Counsel, I've asked you that three times. I'm going to give you one more chance. What is the answer?"

Worse yet is counsel who is not being candid concerning something that's in the record, or about what a prior court opinion did or did not hold, and sometimes having to have his or her feet held to the fire to elicit an answer. It is far better for counsel to acknowledge the situation and, better yet, be the first to say, "I feel obliged to call the court's attention to some adverse evidence . . . " or "There's a legal argument or case authority against my position. Here is what it is, and let me try to demonstrate to your honors why it is distinguishable and why the present case should not come within the parameters of that holding." There usually are ways of dealing with impediments to one's position, but even if there are not, you don't want to impair your reputation as an appellate advocate by being less than candid.

Overall, what was the quality of the advocacy you were seeing in the intermediate Court of Appeal?

It varied quite a bit, and I would say maybe there was the beginning of a trend in those years, which has continued since then, for some attorneys to specialize in appellate practice. What you frequently saw in the appellate court was someone who might have been a real hot-shot as a trial lawyer but who had absolutely no skills as an appellate advocate. He or she might have been brilliant at destroying a witness on cross-examination but totally inept in making a reasoned, policy-driven argument before an appellate tribunal that was charged with the function of laying down a set of principles to guide lower courts, lawyers, and the public in future cases. Many trial lawyers did not—and to this day there are still some who do not—recognize the difference in the legal abilities required of an appellate advocate as opposed to a trial lawyer. Some make arguments to an appellate tribunal that would be more appropriately addressed to a jury. There are trial lawyers who want to argue their case before an appellate court out of a sense of pride, or want to impress their client or be retained by their client to handle the case on appeal, even though their qualifications are far inferior to what would be employed by an appellate specialist and diminish the chances of success for their client. I would amplify those observations when they're applied to an attorney arguing before a court of last resort such as the California Supreme Court or the U.S. Supreme Court. Conversely, by the way, some of the most brilliant appellate advocates are total duds when it comes to appearing in a trial court even in a simple matter, especially if it involves examining a witness.

The trend towards specialty in appellate advocacy is one that you support?

I certainly do. To analogize, I would say that someone who has a brain tumor or serious heart disease would choose ultimately not to rely solely on his or her general practitioner or family doctor.

That certainly makes the point, doesn't it? Thinking back on the Court of Appeal, what role did oral argument have in your decision-making process?

I will be candid and say that although it would occasionally affect how an issue was approached and maybe the theory upon which an issue was resolved, I cannot say that there were many cases where the oral argument actually flipped the case around from what we as a panel were prepared to do and was decisive in determining who ended up being the prevailing party. I won't say it never happened. I have seen it happen at the California Supreme Court and at the Court of Appeal, but it is clearly the rare exception. Nonetheless, I believe oral argument serves the valuable function of helping define the issues and providing a better idea of the full ramifications of a certain outcome if the point made by counsel is pushed to the extreme when tested by vigorous questioning. So oral argument can be important in terms of how an opinion is written, which can be as important as the way the issue is actually resolved in the case before the court, because how the opinion is written will often have great significance and perhaps even be dispositive as to how other cases are resolved in the future.

Also I liked the fact that, being in a somewhat ivory-towered environment as an appellate justice, oral argument does provide the only institutionalized direct contact with counsel. Otherwise we're interacting with counsel just through a cold record and the briefs, and in a noninstitutionalized way through bar association functions and committee work. I enjoyed having that face-to-face contact with counsel, seeing counsel spar between themselves and maybe with the court. I believe oral argument serves a useful function, and I would never want to see it eliminated. I think it sometimes doesn't serve as much of a purpose as it could and should, but that to me does not signify that it is without value.

Is there anything about the system that could make it have a more important role in the process or are you thinking mainly of how individual cases play out?

There is one appellate court that has a policy of issuing tentative opinions. Tentative rulings are often given by judges in trial courts, especially in law and motion, where these rulings will literally be posted on the door or sometimes communicated electronically the day before a hearing, indicating, "The court is inclined to rule in such-and-such manner." You can take your chances and take the position, "It's going my way. I'm not going to bother showing up." Or you can decide, "I'd better be there just to make sure that the other side doesn't show up and persuade the court otherwise." You can conclude, "The court's really wrong on this. I feel I have a good chance of persuading the court differently if I show up and argue vigorously." The court is giving you a sneak preview, if you will. Although this procedure is not uncommon at the trial court level, it's quite uncommon at the appellate level. The only court I know that does it on the appellate level in California is the Second Division of the Fourth Appellate District headquartered in Riverside, and they're very fond of that practice.

How did that practice start there, do you happen to know?

In recent years they decided it would be a worthwhile effort. I'm personally not that enamored with the practice. It puts counsel in the position of showing up before a panel and arguing that the justices are dead wrong on something, and you end up in a quarrel with the panel of justices deciding your case, instead of making your argument before a forum that is supposed to be truly open to persuasion. I'm not saying that they have their minds so set in favor of what they've put out that they would inevitably refuse to alter it. I have no idea how often they have ever actually changed a tentative opinion to a different result. I have heard that, based on the oral arguments, they occasionally change some language that had appeared in their tentative opinions. Just on an instinctive level I don't favor the idea. I authored an opinion for the Supreme Court, *People v. Pena,* holding that one aspect of the Division Two procedure violated the parties' constitutional right to oral argument.

Of course, each division is free to experiment and come up with a process that it believes will be most inclined to arrive at a fair and informed disposition. I commend the creativity of the Riverside division for coming up with this, and there are probably other things we could and should consider as well. Even though I personally don't favor this approach, that's not to say that appellate courts should not engage in such experimentation.

As you say, there could be improvements overall to the oral argument piece of the process that might make it more useful down the line?

Yes. One has to consider that, although the Supreme Court of California has what I call a high output of opinions—often in the 115-a-year range—we're dealing with thousands and thousands of opinions rendered by the Courts of Appeal. Those opinions, unlike Supreme Court opinions, are not required by law to be published in the official reports, which means that when they're not published, they don't serve as precedent for any future cases.

That's been a separate area of controversy, which we may discuss when we get to my years as chief, but I personally interceded on several occasions to defeat legislation that would have mandated that all decisions of the Courts of Appeal be published in the official reports. I believe constitutional issues of separation of powers would arise in the event the legislature were to act in that fashion, because the authority is explicitly given to the California Supreme Court to determine which appellate opinions shall be published.[3]

For a number of reasons, I don't believe it would be a good idea to publish all the Court of Appeal opinions, which often merely involve the application of settled law in affirming judgments in matters such as fender bender civil cases and joyriding criminal convictions. Publishing all these opinions would clutter up our appellate case reports to the point where we would have, instead of 10 percent, 100 percent published—multiplying by 10 the number of volumes, book shelving space, and reinforced concrete that would be supporting these volumes and making it still more difficult and time-consuming for judges and lawyers—even though they resort so often to electronic research today—to find the legal needle in the haystack when they're looking for dispositive precedential authority.

But as a very practical matter, you were beginning to experience that system on the Court of Appeal, the whole matter of publication, depublication, partial publication. How did you and your fellow justices think about that at that time, do you recall?

I recall that in our division—and I'm sure that was and remains generally the case—we were quite selective in deciding which opinions we would want to have published as precedent. Of course, when you'd done the necessary extra work in crafting an opinion that was destined for publication in the official reports—and make no mistake about it, opinions destined for publication received a lot more attention in terms of fine tuning and polishing and therefore took more time—you were inevitably disappointed when the Supreme Court ordered your opinion depublished and what you might have viewed as some of your finest efforts ended up on the cutting room floor, so to speak. [Laughter]

I'll confess that soon after I was appointed to the Supreme Court as an associate justice, one of the first things I did with one of my research attorneys who

---

[3] Cal. Const., art. VI, sec. 14.

had been with me at the Court of Appeal, was to inspect the—now accessible to us, previously inaccessible—internal memorandum of the Supreme Court central staff that had persuaded the justices of that court to depublish one of the opinions that I had worked on at the appellate court with this research attorney. We wondered, "What could they have found wrong or objectionable?" My recollection is that we learned there had been a paragraph toward the end of the Court of Appeal opinion that had contained some language that the Supreme Court thought might be confusing or misleading to lower courts and that, although not affecting the result reached by the opinion, might be troublesome in the effect it might have on future cases. That's what it's like to be on the receiving end on that question of depublication. [Laughter]

Let's talk more about the general matter of writing opinions on the Court of Appeal, both on your own and with your staff attorneys. What kind of general process did you follow?

I always made a point of giving my staff attorney free rein in terms of his or her research. I never purported to dictate a result to the research attorney by saying, "This is how the case is going to come out," or "I want the case to necessarily come out this way." My general instruction to each of the research attorneys was always, as a general matter, "Let the law take you where it leads you."

Having said that, if the law was quite uncertain or if there were different paths that the law had taken in this area—and there might, in fact, be a choice to be made—I would express myself on occasion by saying, "I'd like to go this way if we can, consistent with the law," or "I think this would be a more equitable result if the law permits it." Sometimes the law was so clear that I had to endorse a result that may not have been as fair as I would have thought appropriate, had the court been writing on an open question or a clean slate. But I always viewed my function as applying the law, and sometimes the objective of "doing justice" would come into conflict with applying well-established law. At the level of an intermediate Court of Appeal, you were bound to follow the precedent established by the California Supreme Court. You might decide a case differently from the way you would if it were an open question before the California Supreme Court.

You indicated how much you valued the work of your two staff attorneys, Mr. Wolff and Ms. Pope. As you would go through the process of working with them, to what extent did you consider angles or approaches that really differed from your own, as brought up by them?

I certainly did. There was a lot of give and take, and I found myself arriving at determinations, let alone discussions, of legal issues that I might not have been predisposed to, because of the input from my two research attorneys. By the same token, the give and take went both ways, and I sometimes would receive a very fine product, but it would be apparent from that product that there were avenues for going the other way as well. I would ask the research attorney, "Please write it up the other way and see if we can make a credible case for resolving the case in that manner." Then I would have two products and would decide, first of all, which one I found more persuasive, and then on occasion I would have my two judicial colleagues weigh in as to which was the more convincing resolution of the case. I would see which one would carry the day.

Can you give an idea of your overall caseload on the Court of Appeal, the nature of the kinds of things you were seeing and how Justice Woods assigned those?

She allocated the caseload in a very fair and equitable manner, and I never felt she assigned cases with a result in mind or favored any one of us with more interesting or more complex cases. I felt I had a very wide range of exposure to different legal issues.

We generally received cases about five weeks before a tentative oral argument date. There was a heavy caseload, and we were expected to circulate our draft in time for it to be examined by the other two members of the panel and for them to be able to prepare for oral argument. If there was a case that was particularly complex or troublesome, we had the option of asking that it be taken off the next month's tentative calendar. But that was clearly the exception.

I remember one case like that was *Moore v. Regents of the University of California*, a civil case in which it was alleged that UCLA improperly appropriated to itself the properties of a patient's blood in order to develop and patent, from this highly unusual blood type, a cure for various diseases. There were issues of whether these substances constituted property and whether the patient had given an informed consent to the university's use of his blood. I personally prepared a dissenting opinion in the case, and the California Supreme Court granted review. That, too, is a way in which someone's fine work can end up on the cutting room floor, because once review is granted, except in the very unusual situation of the Supreme Court specifically ordering otherwise, that causes the intermediate court's opinion, even though originally ordered for publication, not to be published in the bound volumes of the official reports, although it can still be found in the unofficial publication, *Cal Reporter*. I had written a very extensive dissent in the *Moore* case, and the California Supreme Court ended up going my way, so I wasn't unhappy the court took up the case—even though that relegated my dissent to the status of an unpublished opinion.

But as you say, for most cases the given schedule was pretty quick, in terms of the need to get started, circulate your drafts, and be ready for oral argument some five weeks hence?

Yes. There were thousands and thousands of Court of Appeal opinions put out every year, and currently only about 10 percent of them are ordered by the Court of Appeal to be published, a slight increase from 8 percent previously. The California Supreme Court, as we'll discuss later perhaps, has the authority to order depublished any case ordered published by the Court of Appeal. Getting ahead of ourselves, as Chief Justice I appointed my colleague, Justice Kathryn Werdegar, to head a committee that delved into the rates of publication and depublication and the factors that went into those determinations, trying to improve the process. The committee's revisions to the standards governing publication probably were responsible for the slight increase in the publication rate. They certainly clarified the factors that an appellate court should and should not consider in deciding whether or not to order its opinion published in the official reports.

How well has that worked out, other than the increase in publication? Has it served its purpose?

I believe it has. It was a very worthwhile effort.

You said you had a heavy caseload on the Court of Appeal. Knowing you were asked to resolve a range of issues, what kinds of things were you seeing?

There was a very broad range of every kind of issue you can imagine—from wrongful termination to construction defect cases, all sorts of tort cases, invasion of privacy, First Amendment issues, the whole panoply of everything that arose in the Superior Court of Los Angeles. I say Los Angeles because cases from the other superior courts within the jurisdiction of the Second Appellate District, cases arising in the counties of Ventura, Santa Barbara, and San Luis Obispo, are resolved in Division Six of the Second District located in Ventura. So every case appealed from the Los Angeles Superior Court, which is the largest trial court in the nation and perhaps in the world, with more than 400 judges plus dozens of subordinate judicial officers—commissioners and referees—came to the Second Appellate District. This provided the justices with a broad exposure to almost every aspect of the law, including cutting-edge issues such as the one presented in the *Moore* case I just mentioned. The variety of cases presented new opportunities to learn about the law in some areas in which I had not had much occasion to weigh in, and the opportunity to write an opinion on those issues.

You mentioned to me ahead of time a very few specific opinions you wrote on that court that you might like to touch on. The first of those that you called out was DiDonato v. Santini *in 1991.*

I was pleased to be able to write an opinion in that case, which dealt with an area of the law that had evolved in the criminal field but that was not the subject of much civil appellate jurisprudence. Can an attorney employ the right to peremptorily disqualify a prospective juror from the panel in a way that focuses on a specific identifiable group, where you're really, in effect, depriving the other side of a cross-section of the community? Although the U.S. Supreme Court and the California Supreme Court had spoken out in cases involving race-based exclusion of jurors in the criminal law area, very little had come down in the area of civil law and certainly not with regard to whether or not women constituted an identifiable class for purposes of the rule prohibiting that discriminatory practice.

This particular decision, *DiDonato*, involved a business dispute related to a family law matter, a suit brought by a woman seeking damages from her former husband. The holding of the opinion I authored for the court was that a party to a civil lawsuit cannot use peremptory challenges to exclude women from the jury panel on the basis of gender. I enjoyed authoring this opinion on what was a novel issue in the California courts and certainly was the first of many decisions that I authored later on, primarily on the Supreme Court, recognizing women's rights and addressing discrimination based on female gender.

To what extent did you recognize that this would be a pretty significant extension of existing "cognizable classes?"

I don't know to what extent I truly reflected on that at the time, perhaps because of the constant ebb and flow of cases into the appellate court and the speed at which one dealt with the tasks of digesting the briefs, conducting independent research, reading the record, circulating a memorandum, having oral argument, and coming out with the opinion within the requisite 90 days. I probably appreciated the significance of the opinion more in the aftermath of the positive reaction to it and to other related cases I worked on later.

Is it fair to say, though, that it was a pretty big deal?

I guess it was, but I pretty much took my cases in stride. Although the opinion was well received, I don't know that there was an enormous reaction to it. Again, it was a matter of, here's an issue—to me it seemed easy in the sense that there were clearly established principles. The only question was, do these principles extend to this situation involving the excusal of women jurors in a civil case? Certainly the discriminatory use of peremptory challenges against cognizable classes was an established principle. It's the application or extension of it in a different area that was most noteworthy.

Here was one of my cases for the next month's calendar. I had to resolve it, out it went, and the next ones were awaiting me—not quite the same as being in the criminal division of the trial court with your next two or three cases waiting outside in the hallway, but nonetheless being cognizant of the push of the case flow, having the opportunity, the luxury, to reflect but not to luxuriate either on the particular case of the moment without moving on to the others that you had to do. During my four years on the Court of Appeal I wrote more than 400 majority opinions, and about 37 of them are published in the official reports.

Say a bit more about how that opinion was received and perhaps the effect it had on the actual formation of juries.

I understand that the effect of the opinion was to curtail the use of peremptory challenges in this discriminatory manner in family-law related cases. That's what I heard later, maybe at an educational program. It certainly tied in with the growing interest I had in dealing with the question of bias in the judicial system.

After Chief Justice Lucas appointed me to the Judicial Council, while I was a Court of Appeal justice, I dealt with such issues—specifically as chair of a committee of the council that had to determine how to implement some 60 to 70 recommendations that came out of a lengthy study on gender bias in the justice system. This was one of several things that got me interested in and sensitized to women's issues, at least to the extent that the California Women Lawyers Association and the National Association of Women Judges bestowed some awards on me, the latter subsequently persuading me to become a member of their organization. [Laughter]

Let's move on to another opinion in People v. Simmons.

That case also was characterized as recognizing the interests of women in the context of a criminal prosecution of a male defendant for the offense of rape. The holding in the *Simmons* case was that evidence establishing that the victim had previously engaged in consensual sexual conduct with the defendant, or with one of the defendants, was not by itself sufficient to require that the jury be instructed that prior consent to sexual intercourse with the perpetrator would be a defense against the charge of rape. That was an issue that arose in the context of the trial court having refused the defendant's request that the jury be instructed that the defense of a reasonable belief as to the consent of the victim should be considered in light of the fact that there had been prior consensual sexual contact between the defendant and the rape victim. This opinion was viewed as significant from the standpoint of victims' rights advocates as well as women's groups and prosecutors.

How common was it at the trial level for that very sort of matter to come into play?

I don't know, but intuitively I believe it probably arose somewhat frequently. There could very well be situations of consensual sexual relations between parties who were on good terms and then the relationship souring and the male imposing his sexual will upon the woman who previously was agreeable to having sexual relations but who no longer was.

This tied in with later work that you did on the Supreme Court in related matters of civil rights, so it was certainly an issue you got to see carried forward in some interesting ways. We'll get into that in more detail, but these civil rights "classes" being recognized is something that takes shape over time, doesn't it?

It certainly does. The development of the law in the area of gender equality helped instill an interest and involvement on my part in this whole field, both in cases in which I authored the opinion and others where I was just a participant as a concurring justice, as well as in administrative actions I later took as Chief Justice.

While we're talking about this subject, it may be relevant to mention that the Second District Court of Appeal included in its ranks some justices who were truly pioneers in the area of women's rights in the legal and judicial professions, and with whom I was certainly privileged to serve. Those included Justice Mildred Lillie, who was ultimately to become presiding justice in one of the divisions, and Presiding Justice Joan Dempsey Klein, whom I mentioned previously. She and Presiding Justice Vaino Spencer were founding members of the National Association of Women Judges and of California Women Lawyers. Along with my own presiding justice, Arleigh Woods, they were all leaders in these areas.

Last among your specific written opinions—perhaps last and least, in this case—you mentioned to me a case called Silver v. Gold. *[Laughter] I'm laughing already.*

Oh, yes. I think I mentioned it in the context of there often being the opportunity for judicial humor. This is an impulse that is usually best to resist, especially knowing that one has a captive audience as a judge, certainly as a trial judge. But having said that, I could not resist such an impulse upon being assigned to write an opinion for the Court of Appeal, published as *Silver v. Gold.*

My opening sentence reads, "Despite its title, the case before us does not involve the relative merits of precious metals in the commodities market"—then a footnote reference to *Plough v. Fields*, a Ninth Circuit opinion—"but instead whether an unsuccessful attempt to disqualify an attorney from further representation of a party to a civil suit may form the basis for an independent action for abuse of process and malicious prosecution." You can see that certainly the underlying issues were not as frivolous as my opening sentence, but the caption of the case presented an irresistible temptation.

It sounds as if you dug up Plough v. Fields and found it irresistible as well? [Laughter]

Yes, and having two colleagues on the case, Justice McCloskey and Justice Goertzen, who both enjoyed fine senses of humor, they didn't give me any grief about putting this in the opinion. [Laughter]

Back to the broad picture. How did you like the appellate work?

I very much enjoyed the writing, because there were very few occasions when, as a trial judge, I thought it would be appropriate as opposed to presumptuous to write an opinion. I certainly thought it appropriate in the denial of the motion to dismiss the Hillside Strangler case. I mentioned I had written the opinion on some rather novel issues involving prosecutions of nursing homes in the municipal court as well as on a few—probably not more than three or four—other occasions. Writing now was everyday fare, and I enjoyed wordsmithing—and still do—very much. I also enjoyed doing my own research in addition to that provided by the appellate staff attorneys and appreciated the flexibility of the hours, allowing me to do as much work as I wanted to away from the court in the evenings or on trips. I could take my work with me. It was a wonderful change of pace.

It was good every few years to have a change in my official responsibilities—after my time in the attorney general's office of about seven years, five years on the municipal court, and then a few years in the criminal division of the superior court followed by a few years in a civil assignment, and then four years on the Court of Appeal.

You had experienced elections on the municipal court and the superior court, but you did also have a single retention election at the Court of Appeal level in November 1990, in which you were confirmed by 64 percent of the voters, along with Justices Goertzen and Epstein, who had similar percentages. What is there to say about that process of retention as you viewed it at that time?

I have pondered for some time, and especially as Chief Justice and on the national level when I was president of the Conference of Chief Justices, the merits of different forms of judicial selection. I concluded that the systems in most of the other states are inferior to that of California. I favor the retention process that we have in California when it's accompanied by proper information being supplied to the public to enable them to exercise their right of franchise in an informed manner.

The figure that you mention of 64 percent approval illustrates what was average. In fact, some years the average was 57 percent for justices on the ballot. Like my situation in the 1990 retention election and that of other justices—that year and other years—not a single issue or controversy was raised about any decision that any of us had made or as to our qualifications to hold office, and yet there was automatically a third or more of the population that would vote against a justice of the Court of Appeal or the Supreme Court.

Why? I think there was an anti-incumbent feeling. We did notice that people with certain names would receive several percentages higher or lower. For instance, there was a justice on the Second District Court of Appeal with the all-American name Jack Armstrong, who always got a few extra points. There were people with unusual foreign names who did decidedly poorer, one going down to defeat—not in a retention election, but as a trial court judge. That appeared to be the main issue when someone with a very all-American name, but almost no legal experience, ran against her.

One of the things that I worked on as Chief Justice—and again, getting perhaps ahead of myself, but it's somewhat inseparable from the question you asked—was appointing a Commission for Impartial Courts, chaired by my colleague, Justice Ming Chin, to explore, among other things, whether there were ways of improving the judicial election process. By the way, it was generally believed that Justice Chin, like Justice Armand Arabian, received a few percentages lower in the vote because of their names.

I believe the judicial election process works relatively well when the public is provided with sufficient information to assist them in exercising their right to vote. Otherwise the voter's reaction often is, "I don't know anything about this judge. Why should I be expected to vote in favor of a new twelve-year term for him?," leading the voter to mark the ballot "no" or to leave it blank. The odd name or other irrelevant factors can come into play even more when there's a dearth of information relating to qualifications and experience. A couple years ago I succeeded, with the cooperation of California Secretary of State Debra Bowen, in persuading the legislature to enact a statute requiring that biographical data for Supreme Court justices be included in the voters' pamphlet, since that is a statewide judicial office. This has resulted, I believe, in greater and more informed voter participation in those judicial retention elections. Approval ratings increase when voters can conclude with some confidence, "This person went to a decent law school. This person has relevant experience in private practice, along with some years of public service. This is what the person has done in his or her career." As opposed to being expected to accept an unknown, with basically no information on the candidate.

Back in 1990, what steps did you and your colleagues take before the election, if any?

In some years, and I don't believe it occurred yet at that election, the appellate justices got together, formed a committee, contributed about two hundred dollars each to it, and purchased some ads urging that the listed justices should be retained. There were visits to editorial boards of newspapers because I believe the public, given the dearth of information about these appellate justices whom they were supposed to retain or reject, would often look to newspaper editorials.

I know when I went around the state in later years as Chief Justice, I said to editorial boards, "You don't want to leave it just up to chance or to the whim of the voters. You should take a position—not that your recommendation will invariably be followed, but most of the time it will be. You endorse for virtually every office from president down to dog catcher, yet you leave judges twisting in the wind. You have an obligation to provide some guidance, and if there's a bad apple urge a 'no' vote, but don't just leave the judicial spots blank when you endorse on everything else." I believe that many if not most of the newspapers, due not just to my efforts but also to those of other justices, decided to take positions on those retention elections. They already were doing so in contested superior court and municipal court races, but not yet all of them were doing so in the retention elections.

How do you summarize the Court of Appeal years and the place of that in your career?

It was a position I was very happy to have. I thought I'd probably end up finishing my days on the bench there, but it turned out to be a transitional experience on the way to the Supreme Court. It was a time for reflection and the enjoyment of research and writing. My work gave me an overview of legal issues and of the judicial process as well, which I thought was quite valuable. Those were also the years when, due to the flexibility of my schedule, I was able to run marathons, train for them properly, and still do my work at hours that I chose.

I take it the effect on your family life also was positive?

It certainly was. Our three sons had much more of a chance to see me during those years.

Thinking back, I wonder what makes a successful Court of Appeal justice? What are the ideal qualities at that level?

There has to be a real love of the law, of legal research and writing, of reflection, and the willingness to forego experiencing the ebb and flow of humanity that you see in a trial court. Frankly, I know a couple of individuals who strove mightily to be elevated to the Court of Appeal and, once there, they were going stir crazy, poking their heads into the hallways looking for someone to come by. They didn't really enjoy the work and certainly not the relative isolation. Again, an illustration of the old proverb, "Beware of what you so earnestly strive for." [Laughter] I think that, without a doubt, they wished they were back on the trial bench.

Those justices who came straight to the Court of Appeal without being trial judges first didn't have the adjustment that the rest of you did, but they also didn't have the benefit of knowing that trial work. How did you come to view trial experience as an important qualification?

I don't believe lack of trial experience should be a disqualifier, but I feel having experience as a trial judge or at least as a trial lawyer adds something very valuable to the background of anyone who serves on an appellate bench—having a real understanding of what did go on in the trial court that may not be fully apparent from the record, having, even more importantly perhaps, a real understanding of the actual effect and ramifications in the trial court of the written appellate opinion that one is authoring or participating in. As an appellate judge, you don't just decide the dispute between the opposing parties. Your function is to establish precedent and rules for guidance in future cases to assist lower courts and lawyers and the public. If you haven't been there, it's not as likely that you'll be able to do as effective a job. You might still do a terrific job without prior trial experience, but my point is that you probably would do even better if you had previously served at the trial court level. I would make that comment even with regard to some of our high court jurists whom I would classify and others would classify as absolutely brilliant—that however brilliant they were, they would have been even more effective as a reviewing judge had they had that experience.

As a deputy attorney general arguing before the California Supreme Court and the U.S. Supreme Court, I was convinced, on occasion, that there was a justice—or more than one, perhaps, on a given occasion—who did not really understand the goings on in a trial court, who had to have it explained and still didn't fully grasp the realities, and who would have been more insightful if he had had that kind of prior experience.

Thank you for reflecting on that and on your Court of Appeal years. Anything to add?

On a personal level—since we've paralleled our discussion of my professional life with my personal life—I had an interesting experience as a victim of crime myself while I was serving on the Court of Appeal, apart from the occasional death threats that I received during various stages of my judicial career.

It happened that Barbara and I were returning from the Music Center in downtown Los Angeles one night, having been to the symphony. It was our habit to enter our home from the garage. On this particular occasion I didn't follow that practice, because there was another couple who had joined us at the symphony. I recall they both had arrived at our house separately, and one of them had left a car and needed to return one of the permits required in order to park on our street. So I let Barbara off in front of the house to wait for them.

I pulled into the garage, and before I could get the garage door down, two individuals who turned out to be members of a notorious gang forced me onto the garage floor and demanded my possessions. I felt the tip of a hand gun tapped against my skull a few times and was told, "Do you have any money in the house? Do you have any jewelry in the house? Do you have a safe? If you're lying, we're going to kill you." One of the individuals was in the alleyway, and I never got a good look at him. The other one I did, and I convinced him my watch and my wallet were all there was and that I had nothing of value inside the house. I made a quick calculation that it would be advisable to fib about not having a safe and about not having more valuables, despite the threat concerning lying, because I did not want them in the house with my wife and two of our three sons.

I don't know whether it was because of the judicial identification they saw when they took my wallet as I lay on the floor of the garage or something else, but after being told not to move, eventually I didn't hear them around anymore. I waited as long as I could get myself to wait, fearing that I might get my head blown off if I looked to see if they were still there. But I was concerned about Barbara's and the boys' presence inside the house and managed to turn around slowly and see they were gone. When I entered the house, I found out that Barbara and the boys were unaware of what had happened and were fine.

I summoned the police, of course, and the next day the chief of police—whom I knew—called me about the case. No fingerprints or other identifying evidence had been retrieved. He assigned the two top detectives from the notorious Menendez Brothers murder case to the investigation of our home invasion. What ensued was truly fine police work. The officers asked me to very carefully repeat the exact words that had been spoken to me about having any money, jewelry, or a safe in the house, and killing me if I lied. Of course without telling me what they were doing, they later went through the police reports in every jurisdiction in Los Angeles County of home invasions that had taken place in the last month and found one police report of a crime that had occurred in the San Fernando Valley in which the identical language had been used. A person already was in custody on that offense, and they placed his picture in a photo lineup and asked if I could identify anyone. I did identify the individual involved in the valley crime and said, "I'm about 95 percent sure, but if I could hear his voice I'd know for sure."

When I then attended an in-person lineup, I could have identified him with my eyes closed. His voice was so cold and specific and recognizable. This person had been apprehended and was in custody because he had entered a house while committing a similar offense and had brutalized the woman of the household. Because of the combined evidence in my case and the other case, he eventually entered into a plea agreement and received a very long sentence.

Not all such stories end with a happy ending, but I have to tell you about the silver lining to all of this. A few days after the incident, I received a telephone call fairly early in the morning before I had left for the Court of Appeal. One of the court clerks told me that someone had shown up with my judicial identification and had felt it was important enough to make a trip to the court to return the ID. I said, "Would you please ask him to stay until I get in? I'd like to thank him and also find out where he found it. That might be of interest to the officers who are investigating the crime." At that point they hadn't apprehended anyone connected with my robbery.

I ended up speaking to this individual, at first through my very broken Spanish, but then with the assistance of a bilingual member of the clerk's office. He gave me information about when and where he had found the ID. I said to him, "I want to give you a reward. It's just extraordinary that you would take the trouble to come all the way up here." Because he lived at least 10 or 12 miles from where the Court of Appeal was located. He declined anything, and I kept insisting. Finally he said, "Well," and he opened his wallet. "I tell you what I would take from you is—I've been out of work for about a month, and I spent my last couple of dollars on the bus fare to come up and return this."

Needless to say, my heart melted. I then and there called up one of my neighbors whom I knew owned a business that had a warehouse, and said to him, "You know the story of my home invasion of a few days ago," and explained what this Good Samaritan had done. I said, "Do you have any position open, by any chance?" He said, "Ask him if he's strong." This fellow responded, "*Soy fuerte*. I'm strong." My friend said, "Tell him he has a job at my warehouse. All he has to do is show up tomorrow with your business card."

He started crying and said, "Oh, what a good man you are." I said, "Are you kidding? You're the one who's a good man. Imagine, to take the trouble with your last couple dollars to return my identification." The end of the story is that I learned this man and later a relative of his, a brother-in-law or a cousin, both ended up working at the warehouse and turned out to be outstanding employees.

Where did he find your identification?

It was on a street corner in the Watts area. It certainly was nice to see the story end that way.

But there's nothing like being a crime victim yourself to bring it all home. What effect did that have on your view of such things?

No conscious effect. My attitudes toward criminal behavior and the causes of it and appropriate punishments had probably been well formed before this incident. Had I been someone with no prior exposure to the world of criminal law, it might well have had a major effect. Although the robbery was a rather startling experience at the time, I hadn't given it much thought until our conversations caused me to reminisce. This incident took place in 1990, a year before my elevation to the Supreme Court.

Thank you for telling me that, and I'm relieved to hear it didn't end badly. In fact, it ended very well with that silver lining.

It certainly did.

###

Chapter 8

Associate Justice of the California Supreme Court
August 16, 2011

Before we talk about your time on the California Supreme Court, you mentioned there was some earlier possibility that you might consider becoming a federal judge. How did all that come up?

As I indicated at one point in our discussions, I had been under consideration for appointment to the California Court of Appeal, and there had been a few occasions when others ultimately obtained the appointment. Because I did not know whether I would ever receive an appointment to the state appellate court, I applied for appointment to the U.S. Court of Appeals for the Ninth Circuit, that being the circuit that encompasses several western states, including California, and is the intermediate court between the U.S. district courts and the U.S. Supreme Court. I did so because I was eager by that point in my judicial career— having spent 15 years as a trial judge—to move on to appellate work as a judge. I more or less hedged my bets by applying on the federal side as well as the state side.

There was substantial support, I learned, in the U.S. Department of Justice for my appointment to the Ninth Circuit. The department was familiar with the work I had done as a deputy attorney general and as a trial judge. In fact, I was asked back to Washington, D.C., for a round of interviews, which I underwent on separate occasions in 1985 and 1986. My preference remained to stay in the state court system if I could be appointed to the California Court of Appeal, but of course I didn't know if that would happen. At the same time, having given serious thought to applying to the federal appellate bench, I was concerned that by pursuing dual applications to the federal and state appellate courts simultaneously, I could appear to be somewhat opportunistic and in fact impair my chances of appointment to either bench. With that concern in mind, I consulted Malcolm Lucas. I knew then-U.S. District Court Judge Lucas from both of us serving on Senator Pete Wilson's judicial qualification committee. I made an appointment to see him and asked—knowing of his close ties to the state appointing authority, namely Governor Deukmejian and the governor's advisors—whether it would be inappropriate for me to pursue both possibilities of federal and state appellate court positions simultaneously. His advice to me was that it would not be inappropriate, so long as I did not accept a state appointment to the California Court of Appeal, if offered, and then shortly thereafter leave the state appellate bench for a federal appointment, if that were to be offered. I took that advice to heart.

The offer of a position on the state Court of Appeal did come first, from Governor Deukmejian. In fact, when I had my interview with the governor's appointments secretary, Marvin Baxter—of course, we later became colleagues on the California Supreme Court—he brought up the subject and asked me to verify that if I were to receive an appointment to the state Court of Appeal, I would stay in that position even if an appointment to the federal Ninth Circuit were to be offered to me. I said, "I have no qualms about that." I had no hesitation. I made that commitment to him and shortly thereafter was appointed to the California Court of Appeal. As I said, my preference was to receive a state court appointment.

Why?

I had grown up professionally in the state courts. I had a certain affinity and affection for the state court system—perhaps bred out of familiarity with that system. The bulk of my career had been spent in the state court system. Basically I was a state court lawyer. I don't know of any better way of putting it. I just felt most comfortable with that system. But I was eager enough to try my hand at being an appellate court judge that I would have gone to the federal appellate court if that were to turn out to be the only avenue open to me for advancement and work as an appellate judge.

What about the differences in the two systems, as you perceived them then? What was your calculation there?

Of course, one of the things you and I discussed concerning the two different types of structure in our California Courts of Appeal is that in the Second Appellate District—unlike the federal Ninth Circuit—you're in a division with the same three out of four individuals on every case for the rest of your time on the court. In the Ninth Circuit you're matched up in different panels of three, randomly selected from the 29 active judges plus the senior judges who serve on the court. I like that idea of a different makeup of the panel, of the constant intellectual exchange. I'm not sure that I had formed the views that I'm stating right now as strongly as I hold them today, but I believe that was one attraction of the Ninth Circuit. On the other hand, I can't say that the accounts I had from Ninth Circuit judges of leaving Sunday evenings to fly off to distant locations to hear cases in that vast circuit—which comprises nine states and some Pacific territories—were particularly enticing. I actually didn't find the heavy diet of immigration cases and administrative law cases in the federal courts to be as attractive to me as the mix of cases in the state court system. But in any event, I was fortunate in not having to weigh those considerations very carefully, because the first offer of an appointment was to the California Court of Appeal, on July 23, 1987.

Interestingly enough, it was only a few months after my confirmation hearing for the state appellate court that I was, in fact, offered an appointment to the Ninth Circuit, to fill the vacancy created by the appointment of Anthony Kennedy to the U.S. Supreme Court. To the obvious surprise of the U.S. Department of Justice personnel who phoned me, I turned down the appointment. I noted that I had made the commitment that if I were to be offered an appointment first to the state appellate court, I would accept that appointment and stay there. It was suggested to me that perhaps I could ask to be relieved of that commitment. I said asking to be relieved of the commitment would, in my view, be the same as not honoring the commitment, and that I was not going to make that request. Of course, this was not a difficult decision for me to make, because my preference was, in any event, to serve on the state Court of Appeal.

I would mention as an interesting footnote that in recent years we've had distinguished jurists leave the federal bench to join the state bench. Of course, Malcolm Lucas himself was a prime example, leaving the position of U.S. District Court judge to become an associate justice of the California Supreme Court before later becoming Chief Justice. And Justice Carlos Moreno left the U.S. District Court to become an associate justice of the California Supreme Court. There are also two distinguished U.S. district court judges who left the federal bench to become justices of the state intermediate appellate court, Nora Manella, who had served as U.S. Attorney for the Central District before going on the U.S. District Court for that district and then left to join the California Second District Court of Appeal; and also Martin Jenkins, who left the U.S. District Court for the Northern District of California, headquartered in the San Francisco Bay Area, to join the California First District Court of Appeal. They left lifetime appointments on the federal bench, all four of them, to join the state bench, despite the need to face a retention election every 12 years.

As an aside, I'm curious about other judges you had come up through the system with. Do you have an idea how colleagues who wished to be elevated were proceeding in these matters and how much interest there was in federal judgeships as opposed to state?

There were some superior court judges who were interested in an appointment to the U.S. District Court, either because of the perceived prestige of being on the federal bench, the lifetime appointment, or the interest they had in the jurisprudence of the federal bench—or perhaps because they wanted to advance in the judicial ranks while continuing to serve on a trial court rather than doing appellate work.

You mentioned serving as a member on Pete Wilson's committee when he was a U.S. senator. I gather you later came to chair that committee as well. Perhaps you could talk about how that transpired and about the committee's work?

Pete Wilson was the mayor of San Diego and ran for the U.S. Senate in 1982 against Jerry Brown. Some mutual acquaintances of Pete Wilson and myself introduced us in light of our common interest in criminal justice matters. After he assumed office as a U.S. senator, he appointed me to his judicial qualification advisory committee. Initially I was a member and I later came to chair the committee. That committee had the responsibility of making recommendations and advising the senator on all appointments to the United States District Court in the Central District, which comprised Los Angeles and some of the adjacent counties, as well as the positions of United States Attorney and United States Marshal.

It probably should be explained, for those who aren't entirely familiar with the process, that although those appointments are formally made by the president of the United States, the way the process has evolved historically is that when one or both of the U.S. senators from a state are of the same political party as the president, the U.S. senator or senators of that same political party advise the president concerning the appointment, and that this advice really amounts to a de facto appointment authority, subject, I assume, to presidential veto if there were to be someone totally unacceptable to the White House for some reason or other. But aside from that, it's the U.S. senator—or senators, if there are two of the same party as the president—who as a practical matter makes the appointment of federal district court judges, the U.S. attorney, and the U.S. marshal. In contrast, the appointments to the appellate federal circuit courts have basically been appointments made by the U.S. Department of Justice, with a certain role, usually subsidiary, played by the White House.

Each of the four federal judicial districts in California had its own judicial selection committee. Those comprised the Northern District headquartered in

San Francisco, the Eastern District in Sacramento, the Central District in Los Angeles, and the Southern District in San Diego. Overseeing the entire process statewide was John Davies, who was a distinguished lawyer, longtime confidant, advisor, and personal friend of Pete Wilson from San Diego. Ultimately, when Senator Wilson became Governor Wilson, John Davies assumed the position of judicial appointments secretary. These federal judicial advisory committees are very important, because the appointing authority relies heavily on their recommendations. It's rare for an appointment to be made without the nominee receiving at least a qualified rating from the advisory committee. In fact, none of the candidates whom we rated "not qualified" ever ended up being appointed to the bench or as U.S. attorney or U.S. marshal, and usually the ratings of those appointed were higher than "qualified."

Were those the only two choices on this particular committee, qualified or not qualified?

No. Apart from "not qualified," there were ratings of "qualified," "well qualified," and "exceptionally well qualified." We would sometimes qualify our own qualification by adding a minus or a plus after the EWQ, WQ, or Q. It was a very detailed process that involved examining the legal career of the individual, inquiring as to community and professional reputation, and reading any of the applicant's opinions or other scholarly work. Ultimately the candidate would be interviewed by John Davies.

I should mention—as a tribute, really, to the process that exists on both the federal and state levels, in California anyway—that these committees were bipartisan and truly focused on merit selection. I prepared a report for Senator Wilson on his record of appointments to the U.S. District Court, not only in the Central District, where I was chair, but statewide on all of his judicial nominations. Senator Wilson and his advisors were very pleased with the quality of the appointments, which were well received in the press—the headline in a *Los Angeles Times* story on his appointments was "Excellence on the federal bench"— and also with the commendation he received for diversifying the appointments to the federal bench, not only in terms of gender but also in terms of race and ethnicity. Our committee recommended and Senator Wilson successfully urged the appointment of the first Chinese-American to serve on the federal bench in Los Angeles as well as the first judge of Armenian extraction to serve on the federal bench anywhere in the United States.

Aside from you and later-Justice Lucas, who was serving on that committee for Senator Pete Wilson?

We had some judges who served and also some attorneys in private practice from both political parties. The federal judges were Malcolm Lucas, Cynthia Hall, and William Keller, and among the attorneys were John Argue, Thomas Malcolm, and Bruce Hochman, who was a prominent tax attorney and an active Democrat. Also serving on the committee were John Arguelles, who had retired from the California Supreme Court, and Sheldon Sloan, who was in private practice but had served as a state trial judge.

How did you come to chair the committee?

I don't really know except that John Davies asked me to chair it at some point. It was something I took very seriously, because there were persons serving on the committee who were far more experienced than I was and at least a generation ahead of me. I probably got more out of this commitment than I contributed. There were definite insights that I gained into the qualities that make someone a good judge, and into the whole process by which judicial selections are made.

What are those qualities, generally speaking?

Certainly, you start out with the premise of the highest moral character, but in terms of legal abilities, we really focused very closely on experience as a state trial court judge or trial attorney. The committee felt that was a definite plus in terms of anyone being considered for appointment to the federal trial bench. We also looked to the scholarly qualities of the individual and examined his or her writings. The committee also cared very much about temperament, because there were all sorts of brilliant people out there who lacked a judicial temperament, especially considering how they might act once they were given that authority and donned a black robe. Would they or would they not be tyrants? I say this a bit tongue in cheek, but perhaps that was a concern even more so with regard to an appointment to the federal court than to the state court.

Lifetime appointments and all?

Exactly. These were real concerns. Hopefully the appointee also would be able to come to decisions that were thoughtful but that would be made within a reasonable period of time as well. These were all vital qualities. We made a point of considering not only the applications that came to us from persons who were self-nominated or nominated by others, but we actually affirmatively went out and sought candidates for consideration for appointment to the bench—individuals who perhaps were concerned that if their name were out there floating indefinitely it would impair their law practice *vis-à-vis* their clients, or who were concerned that perhaps they wouldn't be rated as favorably as we thought they would be. In any event, the committee actually recruited people to put their names in, and some of those persons were appointed to the federal bench. It was a very worthwhile process in terms of the learning experience for me and also, frankly, just from a parochial point of view it put me in touch with some very influential people. I believe the committee's work was of great benefit and credit to then-Senator Wilson in terms of enabling him to make diverse selections from among the finest members of the bar and the state bench for appointment to the U.S. District Court and the U.S. Attorney's office.

When you prepared this report showing his record of judges appointed, you mentioned learning that there had been quite a noticeable diversity in his appointments, both by gender and by ethnicity. At that time, in the 1980s, how did the committee think about such things?

It was a more controversial notion then than it is today in terms of having that be a consideration. I don't mean to imply in any way that quality was being sacrificed in the interest of diversity, but certainly if there were equally qualified candidates, the opportunity to diversify the bench was something that was relevant to Senator Wilson. For example, Judge Ronald Lew, the Chinese-American appointed, was the son of immigrants to this country. I believe the thought was—with our very diverse population in California, which now has no ethnic majority group—that the opportunity for people to see minorities on the bench, perhaps someone from their own ethnic background who is well qualified, sends a message of inclusiveness in our system of justice. That message is essential to the judicial system's earning the confidence and respect that it needs and deserves from the public it serves.

As you say, one result of serving in this capacity was putting you in touch with Senator Wilson and others, later Governor Wilson. What came next in terms of your own advancement from the Court of Appeal? If you would, start with your own thinking about elevation after that.

Chairing the judicial qualification committee helped me develop close personal relationships with Senator Wilson, John Davies, and other staff members in Washington and ultimately with those who went to Sacramento as well. I also established a relationship with Malcolm Lucas.

When Senator Wilson was elected governor in 1990, I was asked whether I would want to serve on the state judicial selection committee, and I declined. I did so, very frankly, with the idea in mind that I might have a chance at being appointed to the California Supreme Court. I felt it would be inadvisable and perhaps awkward for me to be serving on an advisory committee to Governor Wilson and then be evaluated by that committee, even if I were, of course, to recuse myself. I just indicated I thought it would better if I were not to serve on the committee.

How early had your own thinking included the possibility of the California Supreme Court? How far back did that go in your mind?

It's very difficult for me to put a time reference on all of this, as someone who really hadn't known why he was going to law school. [Laughter] One step in my life always seemed to lead somewhat naturally to the next stage. My going to law school got me interested in constitutional law. I had the idea of public service from my interest in the Foreign Service, so it became natural for me to consider going to work in the attorney general's office, and that led to an appointment to the bench. After serving on the municipal court, I wanted to try my hand in superior court with more challenging litigation in both the civil and criminal areas. Then, having had my time there, my long-standing interest in appellate practice remained, so of course it seemed natural to aspire to a career on the state Court of Appeal.

In terms of interest in the California Supreme Court, that was a court before which I had argued 11 cases as a deputy attorney general. I was familiar with the work of the court. It offered the possibility of deciding legal issues of statewide significance, as opposed to cases where there was an appeal merely as a matter of right. So that was a challenging prospect. Of course, having established a relationship with the appointing authority, now-Governor Wilson, an opportunity existed that wouldn't just be pie in the sky but one that I thought was realistic. He was familiar with my career and with the work I had done in the judicial selection process, and we had developed a warm friendship, so it seemed to be something that I could reasonably contemplate. What happened was that I did not formally apply. It was my view that an appointment to the California Supreme Court was one that would seek out the candidate rather than the candidate going after or applying for the position. When Justice Allen Broussard announced that he planned to retire, I was contacted by John Davies and was asked to submit an application for appointment to the California Supreme Court, which of course I did.

What did you think upon hearing from Mr. Davies at this particular time?

It certainly was very, very exciting. Even though I had been asked to submit my name, it was hard to imagine that the appointment would actually transpire. But the process went rather swiftly—I don't have the exact timeline in mind—and easily, much more so than my appointments to the superior court and the California Court of Appeal. The easiest appointments ended up being, oddly enough, those that bookend my judicial career, the appointment to the municipal court and the appointments to the Supreme Court as associate justice and then later as Chief Justice.

It is swift by any measure, at least on paper, because Justice Broussard retired in the month of August 1991 and you started your new position in the month of September.

Yes. Although Justice Broussard gave a few weeks' notice in advance of his formal retirement, it certainly happened quickly, because in that time frame I had to be evaluated by the State Bar's JNE commission and then go through whatever the governor's office does by way of background check.

What occasion did you have to meet with Governor Wilson himself?

In terms of the appointment process, I wasn't interviewed by him as such, nor by any member of his staff. I believe he felt he knew me well enough to appoint me. He asked me to fly up to Sacramento for the announcement of my appointment. That was really the process, in terms of Governor Wilson himself.

But as you say, you had known him for some time by then, quite some years really.

Yes, I'd known him and John Davies and Bob White, who was his chief of staff.

How do you characterize Governor Wilson on a personal level?

Principled, highly oriented to public policy, very direct, and very attuned to detail, and of course these perceptions were amplified when I had occasion to meet with him after he appointed me Chief Justice. Representing the judicial branch, I then had to negotiate with him and argue for more funding for the branch and in favor of policy changes, some of which he favored, some of which he didn't. It was very interesting undergoing that metamorphosis in our relationship. The friendship that had developed certainly continued but there was this formalized aspect to it where, although it certainly wasn't in any way adversarial, it acquired a professional dimension in addition to the personal relationship that we continued to have. I was doing my job focused on representing the interests of the judicial branch and the public interest in our system of justice, while he was properly concerned with a wide range of policy considerations in his role as governor and steward of the state's fiscal welfare. I had to go up there and fight for dollars for the judiciary while others were doing the same for education, transportation, the prison system, welfare, and everything else. I was one more official out there seeking public funds, and I don't say that in any negative way. It was the governor's job to have that broad perspective on all the needs of the state and of the public. I had the more parochial focus upon the system of justice and the people who work in it and the services that the justice system would be able to provide to the public.

I'm wondering about Governor Wilson's personal style in these matters. You say he was direct and oriented to detail. To what extent did he do negotiating and things like that himself?

Oh, he did negotiate himself, and he was very tough and specific in wanting to be informed of the dollar amounts and consequences of alternative actions, to engage in cost-benefits analysis, and all of that. He was very hands on in his discussions with me.

Thank you. I will look forward to talking more about your work with him. As we were saying, back in 1991 you were selected to join the California Supreme Court as an associate justice to replace Justice Broussard. Describe, if you would, your own preparation for the whole confirmation process.

The confirmation process for my appointment—as the 107th justice in the history of the court—went quite smoothly and was uneventful. I have a more detailed recollection of the confirmation hearing for my appointment as Chief Justice five years later than I do concerning what transpired for my appointment as associate justice. Immediately after the hearing, which took place on September 3, 1991 in Los Angeles, Governor Wilson administered my oath of office in the courtroom of the Supreme Court.

Coming up in a few days was the court's September oral argument calendar in San Francisco. There was a lot to do to get ready for my new position, specifically to prepare for the cases that I would soon be hearing, by absorbing the internal memoranda prepared by the justices and their staffs relating to the September cases and the briefs that counsel had written, and to basically relocate to San Francisco. This was quite a disruption in our lives, although a happy one, and of course a disruption in terms of our close proximity to our three sons and our parents, who would come to our home every Tuesday for a family dinner. And Barbara had had an interior design business in Los Angeles with her business partner Nancy Jacobson for 27 years that she reluctantly gave up when we moved to San Francisco and it became too challenging to maintain it from up here.

You mention that Barbara gave up her design business in Los Angeles. I can well imagine there were a great many personal considerations. How did you and she go about sorting this out?

Barbara always has been very gracious and generous with her time and energy, and she viewed this as a new challenge, a new opportunity for her as well as me, and not just a sacrifice that she was making for me, which it certainly was. She had training in art history at USC and UCLA and had been active at the L.A. County Museum of Art, so she—soon after we got up here—enrolled in a two-year docent training program for the Fine Arts Museums of San Francisco, the de Young and the Legion of Honor. She became an active participant in that program. What I truly appreciated was that, although I was going to have all sorts of professional involvements and establish new professional relationships up here, Barbara was coming to a city where she literally didn't know anyone. The Wilsons went out of their way to welcome us to Northern California. The first lady, Gayle Wilson, had a project to refurbish the Leland Stanford House in Sacramento. She felt there should be a proper reception venue for official visitors to Sacramento, especially given the circumstance that California is one of the few states without a true governor's mansion. Gayle Wilson wanted to promote interest in this project and invited about 12 to 15 very prominent women active in Northern California civic affairs and philanthropic work to Sacramento in conjunction with the project. She asked Barbara to join them and suggested that one of them give Barbara a ride up to Sacramento. From these contacts, Barbara and I ended up developing quite a few friendships that we still have to this day. Everyone was very hospitable and welcoming. We would also be invited to dinner at the governor's Sacramento residence. As a result of her conversations with the Wilsons on the subject of the arts, Barbara was appointed by the governor to the California Arts Council. Governor Davis reappointed her, and she served three years as its chair.

I remember a funny story involving B. E. Witkin, or "Bernie" Witkin, who of course was considered—and still is today, after his death—the guru of California jurisprudence. He had, I believe, a true liking for Barbara. At a reception soon after we arrived in San Francisco, I remember his telling her, "It's very fortunate that the Supreme Court is located just two blocks from the opera, the symphony, and the ballet. You should take advantage of all these cultural offerings." Then he said, "I really recommend the opera." Barbara asked Witkin, "Which opera is your favorite?" He replied, "My favorite is *Tough Times* by Joe Green." Barbara said, "I've never heard of that opera." Witkin explained, "*La Forza del Destino*, Giuseppe Verdi." [Laughter] That was his little gag on Barbara. But we did take advantage of having these and other cultural institutions a mere few minutes' walk from the court. Barbara—if I was working late and we didn't have time to grab a bite—would bring a sandwich to my chambers and then we'd walk over to one of those venues. This was the kind of welcoming advice that we had from all sorts of quarters, whether it was the justices, or staff, or people we met up here, such as Bernie and Alba Witkin, and it certainly helped us make the transition to our new life.

After such a big transition, I'm sure you appreciated that very much indeed. You mentioned your three sons—partly in connection with the decision to keep your longtime home in Los Angeles—but perhaps you could catch me up on each of

them and what they were doing. We talked a little about the eldest, Eric, but not
so much about the other two.

I'll finish with Eric and then mention our other two sons as well. After
graduating from Georgetown as an undergraduate and from its law school and
serving as a White House intern in the Office of Presidential Personnel, Eric
spent a year in San Francisco from the fall of 1993 to the fall of 1994 clerking
for a U.S. District Court Judge, Lowell Jensen. After that, from 1994 to 1997, he
was an associate in the litigation section of the San Francisco office of Skadden
Arps. During that time, Eric lived just about two to three blocks from us. When
he went to Sacramento to see me deliver one of my State of the Judiciary addresses to a joint session of the legislature, Dan Kolkey, the governor's legal
affairs secretary and later a justice of the Court of Appeal, met Eric and they
talked. After meeting with Governor Wilson, Eric was offered a position as deputy legal affairs secretary. He accepted and moved to Sacramento. Then when
Wilson left office, Eric accepted an offer to become deputy counsel to the U.S.
Senate Committee on the Judiciary. As I mentioned before, those were positions
that made him a useful addition to the various judicial selection committees that
he later served on. Subsequently, when he was being considered for an opening
as chief counsel, the top position to the committee, he had to determine whether
he really wanted to become a Washington fixture. He decided he did not, and he
came back to California and joined a law firm, located in Century City in Los
Angeles, that ultimately was expanded to include him as a name partner and is
now known as Browne George Ross. That's where he is today, handling a variety of business litigation and other matters. Eric has also been admitted to the
New York bar and the District of Columbia bar.

Our middle son, Andrew, has Barbara's great talent in the field of art and
art history. Andrew went to Bard College in the state of New York, where he
double-majored in literature and film. He did very well and then went on to earn
his master's degree at the Art Center College of Design in Pasadena. He has the
artistic bent and temperament to want to do things that lead him from one project to another, always exhibiting great creativity. He has had exhibits of his
photography in Los Angeles, San Francisco, Chicago, New York, and abroad.
Andrew has a wide range of interests, activities, and talents.

Our youngest son, Christopher, attended Emory University for a couple
years and then finished at USC. After living a short time in San Francisco, he
returned to Los Angeles and graduated from Pepperdine Law School. He is involved in the business side of the entertainment industry. Chris has developed a
specialty in dealing with literary properties and has worked closely with a number of authors in developing some of their works into various projects. He has
always excelled in sports and still plays in a softball league. His wife Rebecca
began her career in education through Teach for America and taught in South

Central Los Angeles for three years. She founded The Firm for Good, an executive search and consulting firm that specializes in recruiting for nonprofits and schools and also cofounded The City School, a charter middle school in Los Angeles. At the same time she and Chris are actively involved in raising two wonderful and very active little girls, Charlotte and Maya, who are now just about to turn five and three. Being involved in their upbringing is an experience quite different for Barbara and me from raising our three sons, and one that needless to say we very much enjoy.

Those are our immediate family members. I've talked previously of my sister Rita, an artist, who is married to a professor, now retired, Philip Daughtry, who taught English but also is a published poet and author. She has an art restoration business and also maintains her creative pursuits, mainly in sculpture. Barbara has a brother, Michael Schneiderman, who is very enterprising and has been involved in sales over the years and now his specialty has turned toward fixing up and renting out houses. His wife Ana Maria was born in Argentina, and she is a Spanish-language interpreter for the Los Angeles Superior Court. They have two talented daughters, Jennifer and Marissa. That pretty much rounds out the current members of the extended family, which also includes cousins and other relatives in Denmark and South America.

Thank you so much for talking about each of them. Maybe I could ask you more about your parents, whom we last mentioned when you were a trial judge in the Los Angeles area in connection with their visits to your courts?

My own parents, needless to say, were quite overwhelmed by my appointment to the California Supreme Court. They took the opportunity to see me on the bench. Happily, given the fact that it's a court with seven members on the bench, nothing as dramatic or colorful occurred during those visits to the Supreme Court as took place during some of the adventures that I discussed with you on the occasion of family visits to the municipal and superior courts. Of course, they were very happy and proud, especially as immigrants to this country, to see that our system allowed someone to rise to the top of the judiciary whose parents had come over from Europe with no family background in the law. It pleased me tremendously that, in addition to attending the hearing confirming my appointment as an associate justice, five years later my father, at age 92, was able to come up to San Francisco to attend the hearing confirming my appointment as Chief Justice, as did my mother at age 79 and Barbara's mother at age 83. My dad lived to 101, my mother to 89, and Barbara's mother to 93. I also had a very close relationship with Barbara's father, Benjamin Schneiderman, a medical doctor who had active service in World War II and passed away several years ago, as well as with her mother, Marja, who was a native of Denmark and a person with a very quick wit and a wonderful sense of humor right up to the very end. She left a legacy of storytelling, jokes, and quips that the whole family has kept alive.

Those were pretty much the transitional aspects for me and my family of my joining the Supreme Court—having the fairly routine confirmation hearing in Los Angeles, relocating to San Francisco, and then of course beginning some very intense on-the-job training and experiences as a new associate justice on the high court. I shortly was thrown into the midst of everything—right from the first weekly court conference to the first oral argument.

Perhaps you would be kind enough to talk about each of your colleagues when you first arrived. Perhaps you want to start with Chief Justice Lucas, since you knew him already?

He was very welcoming and immediately made me aware of what was expected, in terms of there being a number of case assignments that I was inheriting from Justice Broussard and some very heady matters on the next week's oral argument calendar. Justice Stanley Mosk was the most senior of the associate justices. Of course, you and I had occasion to discuss Justice Mosk and how he gave me my first job out of law school when he was attorney general. Justice Mosk sent me a handwritten letter dated September 4, 1991, that read in part: "My only advice for what it is worth—based on 27 years on this court—is to be your own self, totally independent. Although ours is a collegial group, do not walk in lock-step with others and you will earn the recognition you deserve." Next in seniority was Justice Edward Panelli, whom I had known on and off in various venues. Justice Joyce Kennard, likewise, I had known from the Court of Appeal for the Second Appellate District. Justice Marvin Baxter I knew somewhat, certainly as appointments secretary to Governor Deukmejian. Going on, there was Justice Armand Arabian, whom I knew from the municipal court, the superior court, and the Court of Appeal. These were all individuals whom—to varying degrees—I already knew when I arrived in San Francisco to join the court. I think the fact that I did know them, that we had some sort of personal relationship, caused our working relationship to start off right from the beginning as a very informal and sometimes humor-laden relationship.

Do you want to expand on that?

I think there's no better place to start with than my very first conference with the court. To explain, for those who may not be familiar with the practice, the California Supreme Court, with a couple of exceptions during the year, including some for the holiday season, meets every Wednesday when the court is not hearing oral argument that particular week. The purpose of the meeting, which is called a "petition conference," is to vote on any number of petitions seeking review, habeas corpus petitions, and petitions seeking extraordinary writ relief—prohibition, mandamus, et cetera—and on various motions. In addition to those meetings, once a month the petition conference is followed by an administrative conference of the court. At that conference we're joined by the clerk/administrator of the court. At the petition conference it's only the seven justices. No one else is present.

We vote at these petition conferences on as many as 300 to 400 petitions, most of which are petitions seeking review. The court is assisted by the very able efforts of what are now three central staffs: the civil central staff, the criminal central staff, and the capital central staff. The central staffs prepare memoranda summarizing the positions taken in the petitions and any opposition filed to them, and providing a very thorough analysis of the petition and a recommended disposition. What's significant in a decision by the court to grant review is not whether the Court of Appeal decided the case correctly, because with thousands and thousands of appellate opinions rendered every year—and there being only seven of us to write opinions in approximately 112 to 115 cases a year—we could not possibly take up every case that we think might have been wrongly decided. So in considering whether to grant review, we look for cases in which there is a question of broad statewide importance on a significant issue of law and/or a situation in which our intermediate Courts of Appeal have rendered conflicting decisions on the same issue of law in different cases. There are other alternatives, which I won't go into right now, to an outright grant or denial of review. We go through the cases, which are divided into an A list and a B list. The B list is a nondiscussion agenda, or "consent agenda," which can be elevated to the A list for discussion at the request of any one justice. But if there is no such request, we usually deny review without any discussion. The A list involves dozens of cases, individually discussed and voted upon by each justice in order of seniority. Unlike the U.S. Supreme Court, which has the junior members speak first, we go around the table in order of seniority among the associate justices, with the newest or least senior justice speaking next to last, followed by the Chief Justice, who then can in certain situations cast the deciding vote. Another distinction between the two courts is that on the California Supreme Court, it takes the votes of four or more of the justices to grant review, but on the U.S. Supreme Court, only four votes—one less than a majority of the court—is required.

I explain this somewhat elaborate procedure not only because of its historical interest in terms of the operations of the court, but also because it lays the groundwork for my welcome to the court and what I say, with a smile on my face, was an instance of hazing the new member of the court. On a prior occasion, Chief Justice Lucas had been presented with a full, elaborate, and colorful Native American headdress, with very lengthy feathers and other wrappings and pendants. One of the justices, I later learned, was assigned to distract me, and Lucas proceeded to don this headgear, which I had not noticed being present in the chief's chambers. They all were waiting for me to notice this and be shocked and make some inquiry, but I was so buried in the pile of petitions and in what I viewed, incorrectly I suppose, as the solemnity of the occasion, that I didn't look up. I had my face buried in my paperwork. Panelli had been assigned to take photographs of this event, and there are some very comical pictures that I have stashed away somewhere that show Baxter, totally cracking up but hiding behind a petition so he wouldn't be observed by me, and me carrying on while Lucas is busy going through the petitions. [Laughter] Ultimately, of course, I did look up and to my shock noticed that Chief Justice Lucas was attired in the paraphernalia of a different kind of chief than I would have expected to be reflected in his title of Chief Justice of California. Apparently, no other justice of our court before or after ever received this style of initiation, and I'm sure they perpetrated this gag only because I was personally known to each of them. It was done in very good humor to give me a unique welcome to the California Supreme Court with this very amusing practical joke.

There is another type of welcome I would characterize as a much milder form of hazing that is fairly routine to most new justices in recent history, even preceding my joining the court. It involves the following: the California Supreme Court, as we may have discussed, has three regular courtrooms—aside from the special sessions that we hold around the state that we'll discuss later. The headquarters, of course, are in San Francisco. There's a courtroom in Los Angeles, and there's one in Sacramento. Of all of them, the Sacramento courtroom is my favorite. It goes back to the early part of the twentieth century and is decorated with beautiful purple velvet drapery, ornate chandeliers, a lot of polished woodwork on the bench and around the walls, and a very ornate ceiling that is comprised of numerous identical geometric designs that basically form a diamond shape. There are dozens of these patterns throughout the ceiling of this magnificent courtroom. A rosette decorates each corner of each of these geometric shapes. For some reason or other, one of the diamond patterns—which are otherwise identical—is missing one rosette among the dozens and dozens on the ceiling. I don't know whether this reflects an omission that was unintentional on behalf of the craftsmen or instead echoes back to the medieval practice of always leaving at least one minor imperfection in a work of art so that one does not presuppose to infringe upon the perfection of divine creation. I don't know for what reason, but one rosette is missing.

What happened to me, and what has happened to other justices joining the court, is that I was told shortly before our first Sacramento session—which was two months after I joined the court—that a rosette was missing from the ceiling and that a test of the acuity of the new justice was whether he or she could locate where a rosette was missing. Of course, while still paying attention to the oral arguments going on that first morning of the session, my gaze constantly wandered to the ceiling in what turned out to be an unsuccessful attempt to locate the missing rosette. I wonder whether people in the audience who observe the spectacle of a new justice trying to locate the site of the missing rosette on the ceiling conclude that the novice jurist is lost in deep philosophical rumination or is seeking divine guidance. In any event, it's not uncommon for the new justice to be focused very much on the ceiling—and quite unfairly, because the seating arrangement on the bench reflects alternate seating in order of seniority, with the seventh member of the court seated to the far left of the Chief Justice. It happens that, when one occupies that seat, his or her view of the site of the missing rosette is blocked by one of the hanging chandeliers. Trying to find it is a somewhat futile exercise unless you're so keen on doing so that you guess that perhaps moving your seat around on the bench would provide you with a more expansive view. I'm afraid I failed the test and only later was laughingly informed that I really wasn't in a position to locate the missing rosette. [Laughter]

But I don't want to put everything in a frivolous light. There was a lot of preparation that a new justice had to do upon joining the court, even more so with oral argument just a week away—and even more so than usual with a very significant case on the calendar, the case of *Legislature v. Eu*, involving challenges to the term-limits initiative enacted by the voters. Not only was the constitutionality of term limits at stake, but also a provision of the initiative that reduced the budget of the legislature by 38 percent—perhaps on the somewhat naïve theory that this would encourage legislators to get rid of their political staff and focus primarily on hiring policy aides to assist them in their work. It became quite evident that the initiative did not succeed in achieving this apparent objective. Ultimately, for various reasons you and I probably will get into later, term limits ended up being a bad idea, in my view. In any event, it was not the court's responsibility to assess the wisdom of the initiative, nor our responsibility to decide whether term limits did or did not serve a valid or commendable purpose, but rather just to determine whether there was anything in the federal or state constitution that precluded the voters from enacting this particular measure. It was quite a learning process participating in the resolution of that case and acquiring a couple very valuable lessons in the process.

The initiative itself, Proposition 140 on term limits, had been passed by voters in November 1990, just the previous fall, winning 52 percent of the vote—a majority but not an enormous majority. Knowing you were ruling on a very particular matter before you, how did the court discuss the will of the people of California in this matter?

Our court's jurisprudence reflects, in statements made in our opinions, a strong recognition of the need to allow the public to carry out its will through the constitutionally authorized initiative process. This doesn't mean, obviously, that we forego our responsibility to pass upon the validity of measures enacted by the initiative process through an exercise of the people's will. We have invalidated measures directly enacted by the people, just as we have invalidated measures when enacted by the legislature. When we invalidate such measures it's because we have determined that there is a provision in the state or federal constitution that requires us to do so in the course of performing our responsibility to uphold the constitution, as we promise to do when we take our oath of office. This may be an appropriate occasion to make the observation that when the court engages in such action, invalidating an initiative measure, we are regularly accused of flouting the people's will. My answer to that is that we are not elected on a political basis, as are individuals elected to executive or legislative office. We are elected to perform our duty, which is to apply and uphold the law. The highest expression of the people's will is what they have enacted in their own state constitution and, on the federal level, in the federal constitution. This highest expression of their will includes the limitations that they themselves willingly have imposed upon their own ability to legislate—whether through their elected representatives or directly through the initiative process. When a court invalidates a measure that has been adopted by popular vote, that court is basically just honoring the people's will, the highest expression of their will, by enforcing the constitutional limitations that they have previously enacted. This point is well illustrated in the trilogy of marriage cases that we'll get to later in our discussions. If the people of California disagree with the court's interpretation of their constitution, they are empowered to amend the state constitution. It's easy—some would say all too easy—to amend the Constitution of California, unlike the very laborious process involved in amending the federal constitution, which generally involves a two-thirds vote in each house of Congress with ratification by three-fourths of the state legislatures. The people on occasion have exercised that power to amend the state constitution in response to a judicial decision, as they did with Proposition 8 regarding the right of same-sex marriage.

That is a rather lengthy answer to the question you posed, but the fact that the people have enacted a measure is something that is given considerable weight by the California Supreme Court—to the extent that if there's any way that the people's intent can be carried out without violating the constitution, the court will go to some lengths to try to do so. But by the same token it will not disregard its obligation to uphold the Constitution of California and the Constitution of the United States.

These principles do come into play time and time again during your service on the court. Back to term limits, how did the oral argument play out?

The oral argument was very engaging, as I recall it. It's quite commendable that when momentous issues like this come up to the California Supreme Court for decision, pitting one branch of government against another, the institutions involved usually take great pains to select from among the most accomplished of appellate practitioners, whether in-house or outside, to argue their positions.

Certainly, once the decision of our court came down, it caused quite an impact, in the long term, over the functioning of California government. When we get into what I view as the somewhat dysfunctional nature of California state government today, I would chalk some of that up to term limits. But aside from the long-term repercussions, there were two lessons I learned as a brand-new justice from the term-limits case—lessons that proved valuable to me when I later assumed my duties as Chief Justice. The first of these lessons learned is that legislators view many court decisions, especially those of the Supreme Court of California—and certainly those decisions of our court that directly involve the legislature—through a political prism. Legislators are political animals, even the good-government types, and therefore many of them seemed to view the action taken by the court in upholding the term-limits initiative as something motivated by political considerations, perhaps because most of what legislators do is motivated by political considerations. I don't use the word "political" in a totally negative way. They view themselves as responsive to the popular will. They're trying to give the people what they think the people want or what they think might be best for the people. The other two branches of government are so very different that way from the courts, where it is not our responsibility to do what's popular, or to further what might be good policy in our personal view, but to apply the law. It's mainly in a narrow range of cases where policy has not been determined by the executive or legislative branches that the question of what is good policy or not comes into being in rendering a judicial decision. Our function is basically to uphold the law, as we determine it to be— which sometimes is a difficult task, especially in the case of initiative measures—whether we believe it's a good law or a bad law.

Because so many legislators view everything politically, when a decision directly impacts them and does so in a negative way, their immediate reaction, even among some of the most experienced of them—and that was before term limits had had its real effects, so you had people who were more experienced instead of rotating in and out—was to view the decision as something that would merit retribution on their part, or, as they put it more succinctly, "payback." Shortly after the term-limits decision came down in October 1991—in an opinion authored by Chief Justice Lucas that I joined—the justices were in Sacramento for our November oral argument session. At a reception honoring the court, I was standing next to Chief Justice Lucas. A member of the legislative leadership came up to Lucas and—this is close to verbatim—said to him, "After what you guys just did to us, we would look like a bunch of wimps if we didn't do anything to you." He had in mind not only term limits, but also the 38 percent reduction in the legislature's budget that was part of the term-limits initiative as well as the elimination of future legislative retirement benefits. This legislator proudly announced that the pertinent committee in his house of the legislature had just cut the budget of the Supreme Court of California by, you guessed it, 38 percent, not coincidentally. [Laughter]

There was great concern that the Supreme Court, with that kind of a cut, might very well have been rendered incapable of performing our constitutionally mandated function of overseeing the cases that come up by the thousands and of rendering informed opinions on the cases we accepted for review. After a while, especially because this reduction in our budget got through one of the houses of the legislature, we began to explore what is termed the "inherent powers" of a court, an issue that, oddly enough, the presiding judge had asked me to research when I was a municipal court judge—because the L.A. Municipal Court was then facing the question whether it could continue to operate and perform its functions in the face of cuts imposed on its budget by the county. Now at the Supreme Court level, I updated my research to explore what were a court's inherent powers under that doctrine, be it the Supreme Court or a local court. The inherent powers doctrine basically holds that if the deprivation of financial and/or other resources is of such a degree that the particular court would be rendered incapable of performing its constitutionally mandated functions, that court under appropriate circumstances has the inherent authority to order the state treasurer—or in the case of a local court, perhaps the county auditor at that earlier time—to disburse sufficient funds to enable the court to continue its operations. We started to explore this possibility, and it was discussed in the legal press. Guess what the next move was? A proposed constitutional amendment was introduced in the legislature to deprive courts of their inherent power to take such action. That advanced in one house of the legislature, but in any event, happily, the 38 percent reduction in the court's budget and the proposed constitutional amendment did not make it through the legislature. The effort to pursue those two measures ultimately was dropped, but I would say without being overly dramatic that the Supreme Court was definitely headed into a constitutional crisis as a direct result of rendering its ruling upholding the voters' enactment of legislative term limits.

The second lesson I learned from the term-limits case was this. It's something that probably is apparent outside the courtroom and outside the law in everyday experience; I'm referring to the truism that sometimes it's not what you say, but how you say it that counts most. It became quite apparent that what particularly incensed the legislators was not just the court's action in upholding the term-limits initiative, even with its budgetary reduction provision, but some of the language that was employed in the court's opinion. This language was viewed—accurately or not, fairly or unfairly—as reflecting clear delight on the part of the court in clipping the wings of legislators and in arriving at the result that it did. I'm referring in particular to language in the court's opinion that spoke of "an entrenched, dynastic legislative bureaucracy."

"An entrenched, dynastic legislative bureaucracy," as in protecting against such a thing.

Yes. I think this language was very much responsible for the reaction that the Supreme Court—and I would say the court system of the state as a whole— incurred in the wake of the court's just having tried to do its job in determining the constitutionality of the term-limits initiative. This was damage that persisted for years, and I had to work quite hard—initially as Chief Justice Lucas' emissary in meetings with legislators, and later as Chief Justice in my own right—to overcome this reaction and to establish the kind of respectful, trusting personal relationship upon which so much depends in dealings among legislators and between legislators and the other branches of government.

Certainly, building a better relationship with the legislature turned out to be a very important task. Yet at the same time, neither I nor any other member of our court would ever determine his or her position on a legal issue that was before the court out of a desire to please or to avoid offending the legislature. The result arrived at in a case would not be, and is never, affected by such a consideration, but the language employed by the court can, I believe, appropriately take that consideration into account, without detracting from the forcefulness or integrity of the opinion. If the court's decision hopefully can be phrased in a diplomatic way, a lot of unnecessary grief can be avoided, especially if there's a reasoned explanation of why the court is compelled by the law to take the action it is taking. This explanation often can be as important as the result itself. That is a reason why, when I became Chief Justice, I made a point of very frequently assigning to myself the writing of the court's opinion in cases that involved disputes between two or three branches of government, whether it was the legislature and the courts, or the executive and the courts, or sometimes among all three branches. Because as Chief Justice of the state I had to devote so much time and effort to establishing good working relationships with the other two branches—both to secure adequate funding for the court system as a whole, not just the Supreme Court, but also to promote the judiciary's policy initiatives for access to justice and other objectives—I certainly didn't want one ill-chosen adjective or adverb to torpedo all of our good efforts.

You've stated very well that the three branches of government are very different in their prisms, if you will, but also in their actual processes. The way they get serious work done is very different, particularly in the legislative branch.

It is very different, and oddly enough, although we always speak as if there exists unqualifiedly a separation of powers among the three branches of government, I had occasion to note in the court's opinion in *Superior Court v. County of Mendocino* that this separation does not preclude the branches from having a codependent or interdependent relationship. Governors appoint judges. Judges rule on executive actions and legislative actions. The legislature provides funding for the courts to operate. There is this interplay, this interdependence, a system of checks and balances. The doctrine of separation of powers basically amounts to the principle that one branch should not interfere with the basic functions of the others. Of course, there are a number of cases—some of which I had occasion to write on—that involve a certain intrusion, if you will. The question always is, "Does the intrusion rise to the level of a violation of separation of powers?"

An illustration is the *Obrien* State Bar case. The State Bar is an arm of the judiciary under article VI of the constitution, and yet the legislature recently gave itself authority to appoint some of the members of the State Bar Court. When does such an intrusion rise to the level of unconstitutionality? We held it did not in that case, because of the predominant role of the Supreme Court in the appointment process. The same conclusion was reached in the *Marine Forest* case, which involved the legislature's specifying that it had the authority to appoint some of the members of the Coastal Commission, who otherwise would be considered gubernatorial appointees. The legislature, in the first version of the enactment, reserved the authority to remove at will its appointees to the Coastal Commission, and as proceedings commenced in the lower courts, the legislature—wising up and realizing this might be unconstitutional—amended the Coastal Commission Act to provide that members would be appointed for fixed terms and could not be removed at will, only for malfeasance. These two opinions, which I authored for the court, illustrate that there are many permutations to consider in determining the constitutionally authorized functions of each of the branches of government and each one's permissible intrusions on the functions of the other two branches.

Or perhaps a flip side, when it's not clear which branch should handle or resolve a certain thing. Just to finish about term limits, this was the start, of course, of a nationwide move in that direction. There were just two other states putting term limits into effect the same year as California did, in 1990. But then there was quite a move to expand this idea and have it take hold in other states. It has taken on a life of its own as a concept—at the local level, state level, and through some attempts to bring it to congressional representation.

That's true. It was pointed out to me by some of my colleagues at the Conference of Chief Justices—which is the name of an organization that meets twice a year—that everything seems to start in California, the good, the bad, the ugly, the in-between. [Laughter] Many reforms, as well as some of the fiscal crises and so many different things, do seem to originate here first—whether for better or for worse. Certainly California was very much at the forefront of the term-limits movement—not the very first in terms of a major state taking this step, but our state's action led to the success of such efforts in some other jurisdictions.

One irony is that then-Assembly Speaker Willie Brown was said to be a particular target of the term-limits movement here in California, and he, of course, saw the handwriting on the wall, as it were, and ran for mayor of San Francisco and was actually out before he would have been termed out.

Yes, I came to know Willie Brown because, although he left office after serving 15 years as Speaker of the Assembly before I became chief, I had been asked by my predecessor to go to Sacramento and meet with him.

I probably should mention at this point that, following very close upon the term-limits case, was the legislative reapportionment case that we decided in 1992, *Wilson v. Eu.* The California Supreme Court faced the unusual situation there of being asked by voters to intervene in a deadlock between the governor and the legislature on the issue of legislative redistricting. The law requires that state legislative and congressional districts be reapportioned every 10 years to reflect the latest census count. When Governor Wilson and the legislature could not agree on a reapportionment plan, a lawsuit was filed that our court took up directly, because the dispute had to be resolved quickly before the next election. The claim was that, because of population shifts, such a disparity had developed among the residents served by one assembly district as compared to another—and the same with regard to state senate and congressional districts—that those persons residing in newly highly populated districts basically had their vote count 50 percent less than that of someone from a district with a much smaller population. It became imperative to do something about this disparity in voting rights. But our court entered this dispute with the greatest of reluctance, because reapportionment traditionally has been a quintessentially political function—although maybe it shouldn't be, and maybe it won't be so much with the new citizens' commission in charge of reapportionment.

In the famous cases of *Baker v. Carr* and *Reynolds v. Sims*, which formulated the constitutional standard of "one person, one vote," the U.S. Supreme Court got into this "political thicket," as Justice Felix Frankfurter had described it in an earlier opinion. Similarly, our court couldn't properly escape the judicial responsibility of doing something about the situation confronting it, so we granted review but with the clear indication in our order and in subsequent orders that we hoped the governor and the legislature would get together on this, and as soon as they did, the court would bow out of the dispute. We didn't feel we belonged in this, but in the absence of any other remedy for the voters, we would perform our function and resolve the dispute.

We appointed three highly respected retired jurists to serve as special masters on reapportionment, who held hearings, took evidence, and did an exceptional job. They were former Fifth Appellate District Presiding Justice George Brown and former Superior Court Judges Ray Galceran and Thomas Kongsgaard. I saw the computers they used, even though in those days computers were rather rudimentary, which enabled the masters to focus on each district and literally move the lines around to see what that would do in terms of equalizing population, preserving the rights of racial and ethnic minorities, and not dividing up communities. They could zoom in on a district in quite incredible detail. I remember seeing some dots in San Diego Bay and being told, "These are the military voters who are on ships there." It was like going into a war room, going down to see where they were working, trying to balance all these competing considerations in coming up with fair districts. The masters came up with a plan, which we circulated and then let the attorneys argue. I remember the arguments went on and on. We allocated a lot of extra time. There were even individual legislators who were allowed to argue matters pertaining to their own district. If memory serves me correctly, Senator Ken Maddy from Fresno got up and argued about his particular district and why the proposed lines should be altered in some manner or other. We made some adjustments and came out with a final plan. The plan was praised on a bipartisan level as extremely fair to both major political parties and to everyone involved, and it served as the basic plan for the coming decade, until of course population shifts caused the districting to again get out of whack. This was another fascinating case to hear so very soon after joining the court. Reapportionment has remained a matter of interest to me to this day as a voter, in terms of having districts that are fair and that don't cause the two parties to send to Sacramento and perhaps to Washington, D.C. only the more extreme wings of their respective parties. I believe moderation suffers when reapportionment fails to make proper adjustments for shifts in population.

Of course, there have been incredible tales about the contribution to modern art that's been made by the drawing of some of these districts—I mean things that just boggle the imagination with creative gerrymandering. I still remember a story, from many years before I was a judge, involving Assembly Speaker Jesse Unruh. He took great interest and delight in having a personal hand in the drawing of legislative districts. I'm sure that the way they were drawn helped enhance his own authority. The account that I recall reading somewhere was as follows. At a news conference, Unruh unveiled a map of the assembly districts in Los Angeles County. To fully appreciate the story, you have to have a basic understanding of the geography of Los Angeles County. Of course, to the west is the large Santa Monica Bay that stretches for 30 or more miles. To the north of that are Malibu and Zuma, which at least then were considered Republican areas. To the south end of this crescent is the Palos Verdes peninsula, also a Republican area. What Unruh had cleverly done was to place the Malibu/Zuma area into the same district with the Palos Verdes area 30 miles away, in order to bunch all the Republicans into one district so that they wouldn't dilute the Democratic strength in other parts of Los Angeles County. At this news conference one of the reporters asked, "Mr. Speaker, with all due respect, isn't there a legal requirement that all parts of a legislative district be contiguous? You've clearly violated that, haven't you?" Unruh replied, "No, not at all. They are contiguous—at low tide." [Laughter] He had drawn a narrow strip through the surf line to connect these disparate areas 30 miles away to achieve this political objective. That to me is the classic but humorous gerrymander story illustrating the need for a more neutral process that, hopefully, we'll have now with the new citizens' commission. The voters should elect their legislators instead of the legislators selecting their voters.

The challenge to term limits and the matter of reapportionment were exciting cases. There were others, as an associate justice, that were less awesome. I know that Chief Justice Lucas, who usually was not the justice who engaged in the most questioning, often would save up something for the end that went to the heart of the matter. And sometimes he just enjoyed making an observation to lighten up the oral argument. One of my favorite moments of oral argument as an associate justice was the *Nahrstedt* case. Mrs. Nahrstedt kept three cats in her condominium unit. The CC&Rs [covenants, conditions, and restrictions] provided that no animals were allowed in any unit. It was obviously a question of balancing the rights of the condo owners' association and its members with the rights of Mrs. Nahrstedt—and perhaps those of the cats to the extent the cats had any rights. [Laughter] One member of the court, during the course of the arguments, asked one of the attorneys whether he was familiar with a certain statute. The lawyer responded that he was not, and the justice expressed surprise, although this was something that hadn't been briefed. I certainly didn't know about this statute, nor did the other justices appear to. This justice proceeds to read aloud this code section, a provision creating a special rule for seeing-eye dogs. The justice doesn't leave this alone, but follows it up with another question or two. Obviously counsel is using up his allotted time trying to respond to this line of questions. Chief Justice Lucas then interjects the following question. "Counsel, is there anything in the record whatsoever that might suggest that any one of Mrs. Nahrstedt's cats was a seeing-eye cat?" [Laughter] The entire courtroom erupted in laughter, with one exception, the associate justice who was asking the questions. That put an end to that line of questioning. It was a nice illustration of Chief Justice Lucas' ability to exert control, when appropriate, over the courtroom, and of his very keen wit.

There's probably one other thing, in terms of my initiation as a new justice, that merits mention if you'd like to go into that now, and that was the execution of Robert Alton Harris. I suppose one of the rites of passage—if one wants to call it that—for a new justice of the California Supreme Court is the rather grim sequence of events involving the court's role in an execution and the hours leading up to it. There had not been an execution in California for 15 years until this event, which took place April 21, 1992. There was a series of state and federal decisions that had reviewed and delayed the execution of the defendant over many years—a series of appeals, writs, and stay applications in his case, *People v. Harris*, as well as proceedings in other cases that had raised challenges to the imposition of the death penalty. Harris and his codefendant had abducted two teenaged boys in San Diego and shot them to death as they pleaded for their lives. Harris proceeded to consume the half-eaten hamburgers that the dead boys had been eating. Then he and his crime companion went off to use the boys' car to commit a robbery. The two defendants ended up being arrested by a police officer who was the father of one of the victims. Finally, after all these delays, Harris' execution was set for 12:01 a.m. on April 21. It was assumed that the legal proceedings had concluded on the preceding day.

Because this may be of interest in terms of the proceedings of the California Supreme Court, I should mention why executions are set at 12:01 a.m. California has a somewhat involved statutory procedure requiring that before an actual death sentence is carried out, a noticed hearing in superior court must be set before the sentencing judge, who then actually fixes the execution date, no less than 30 days and no more than 60 days hence.[1] The order issued by the sentencing judge is actually called a death warrant and is effective for 24 hours—only for the specific day in question. Consequently, the time for the execution is set

---

[1] Penal Code sections 1193, 1227; Calif. Rules of Court, rule 4.315.

by the warden for 12:01 a.m.—once he or she receives the date—to allow, if you will, the maximum window of opportunity, 23 hours and 59 minutes, to comply with the death warrant. If the execution were to be delayed beyond that day, the case would have to go back to the superior court for a hearing to set a new date.

After a 15-year moratorium on executions in California—while a variety of constitutional issues were being resolved by the U.S. Supreme Court, other federal courts, and our court—the time and date for the Harris execution was set. However, four individual federal judges proceeded, in sequence, to issue stays in Harris' case that night in the period leading up to the scheduled 12:01 a.m. execution and in the hours that followed. As each stay order was issued, the U.S. Supreme Court vacated the action taken by the lower federal court, and a new hour was set for the execution to take place that same night.

As this highly unusual sequence of events was taking place in the federal courts, the justices of the California Supreme Court were following their customary practice. While all this activity was transpiring on the federal side, the seven justices of our court, in accordance with the court's long-established policy, assembled in the Chief Justice's chambers, along with a few staff attorneys—usually persons who were tracking the particular case. We gathered, always, in order to remain immediately accessible in the event our court would be called to rule upon any last-minute stay application filed in the California Supreme Court. To facilitate this eventuality, in case there was a filing, the execution chamber in San Quentin Prison—which I had inspected years earlier in conjunction with my work as a deputy attorney general dealing with challenges to the death penalty—was equipped with three telephone lines—one to the governor in the event he chose to act on a last-minute application for a reprieve, a second line to our court, and a third line available for communication with the federal courts or other persons.

As this succession of stays was issued and in turn vacated by the U.S. Supreme Court, which apparently was having its own concurrent all-night vigil—perhaps not at the court itself but at least telephonically and/or electronically—it got to be rather late. At about 3:00 a.m. or so, Justice Mosk began to look at his watch repeatedly. Noticing this, Chief Justice Lucas—mindful that Justice Mosk was just a few months short of his eightieth birthday and might be experiencing some fatigue—inquired whether Mosk would prefer to go home and remain on call pending other developments in the Harris execution. Justice Mosk replied, "No. My only concern is that it has become far too late for me to cancel the tennis game that I've scheduled for early this morning." [Laughter]

To continue with the sequence of that night's events, when a federal judge issued a fourth stay that night, the U.S. Supreme Court finally had enough. It issued its final order in the *Harris* case, which stated, "No further stay of Harris' execution shall be entered by the federal courts except upon order of this court," meaning that before any federal judge in the United States could deign to consider issuing any further stay order in the case, the lower court would have to obtain advance permission from the U.S. Supreme Court to do so. This action by the U.S. Supreme Court enabled the warden to be able to finally issue an order that the execution be carried out, which he did. At 6:07 a.m. our court, through the open phone line that had been hooked up between the execution chamber and the Chief Justice's chambers, received the inquiry from the associate warden over the hotline that was customary during the course of such a night's events. This was always the language that the associate warden would direct to our court as we were seated around the Chief Justice's conference table. "Is there any matter now pending before the California Supreme Court that would prevent the execution from going forward?" Then, again following our customary routine, the clerk of our court glanced at the Chief Justice and then at the other assembled justices, and upon receiving a negative nod of the head from each of us, responded to the associate warden with the word "no." The associate warden soon came on the line again and proceeded to give us all—for some reason or other, and I don't quite know why—a running account over the phone line of each event in the execution protocol as it took place. I remember being informed, "Intravenous connection made to the left arm. Intravenous connection made to the right arm. Saline solution has begun to flow. Now the first chemical," such-and-such, "has been injected into the IV. Now the second chemical has been injected," and so forth. Then, after what seemed like a very lengthy period but I believe in Harris' case was only 14 minutes—during which not a single word was uttered by anyone in the Chief Justice's chambers—the silence was perforated by the associate warden's words, "Flat line," which indicated the medical personnel had verified that the EKG showed no more heartbeat and that the execution of Robert Alton Harris had been carried out at 6:21 a.m. When that was done, we all got up, went our separate ways, and quietly left to go home and get a bit of sleep as it was getting light outside after a very long night—all of us, that is, except Justice Mosk. Mosk decided that because he'd been unable to cancel his tennis game, he might as well proceed directly to the California Tennis Club and play his game, which he did.

The execution of Robert Alton Harris, among the various ones that I experienced, was by far the most dramatic in many respects, given the fact that it came after a lengthy moratorium, the interplay between the lower federal judiciary and the U.S. Supreme Court, and of course the late hour, capped off by Justice Mosk's remarkable resilience.

What do you suppose prompted Chief Justice Rehnquist, on the U.S. Supreme Court side, to make that order—no further stays without prior permission? Where was this headed?

I have to assume that the legal bases for the lower court orders that had come to the high court's attention—because the California attorney general's office, of course, filed a petition with the U.S. Supreme Court as each one of these stay orders came down—were viewed by the U.S. Supreme Court, to put it mildly, as lacking in merit, if not constituting a form of judicial insubordination. I suppose the U.S. Supreme Court concluded that the execution should go forward because the legal process had been exhausted and had not been unfair to the defendant. I have not heard any other explanation. I never learned what went on in the minds of the high court justices, what their attitude was toward the federal judges who had intervened. But four times turned out to be enough for the justices of the U.S. Supreme Court. It wasn't just Chief Justice Rehnquist. The whole court was participating, as far as I heard, in this all-night round of judicial orders.

Had they had occasion to take a step like that before on any other case, do you know, or since then?

I have never heard of any case before or since then that involved this ping pong of countermanded orders from coast to coast or from anywhere else in the United States.

What more can you tell me about how Chief Justice Lucas managed this process at your end? This, as you say, was a brand-new duty to the court as it existed at that time.

The atmosphere was very solemn, even though I don't think any of us had any real doubts about whether Mr. Harris deserved the death penalty. Or at least let me put it this way. If one could accept the death penalty, I believe each of the justices felt that Mr. Harris was a prime candidate or contender for it. Justice Mosk was against the death penalty, but he did—when he thought all of the proper procedures had been followed—vote to uphold death sentences. He did not seek to intervene here or to issue a stay or have the court issue a stay. I believe all the members of our court acted very professionally. Each justice had been furnished with a notebook prepared by the clerk containing contact information for each of the justices and tracking attorneys and clerks in case of unexpected absences or early departures, and also for various federal courts and prosecutorial and defense offices. There were persons in the clerk's office who specialized in handling capital cases, including Mary Jameson, a very able person in charge of the unit involved in receiving transcripts, communicating with the attorney general and defense counsel during the course of automatic appeals and writ proceedings, and then setting up the liaison that was involved on execution nights.

To what extent did you talk about it among yourselves after the fact, having gone through such a thing together?

I think it weighed on each of us, just the momentousness of the occasion. Even with regard to the least sympathetic defendant, it was a moment when human life was being extinguished after a lot of due process, but still, nonetheless, the state putting someone to death. No one took it lightly, even those who were firmly convinced that this was one of the most outrageous crimes that had come before us, although I soon learned there would be many to rival it, unfortunately.

As the first one in such a long time, what did this represent as you went on into the other related matters?

It became part and parcel of the many-faceted duties and responsibilities of the California Supreme Court. Of course, when I became Chief Justice I had to realize that, although there wasn't that much added responsibility in terms of presiding over this type of late-night conference, it still added a bit more solemnity to it for me, knowing this was a function that I was presiding over, that I had a responsibility for, and that I had to, with a nod of my head, communicate the go-ahead to the clerk, who in turn verbalized it to the associate warden at the other end of the line in the execution chamber that I could visualize from having been there.

Thank you for your account of that process, including the interplay with the U.S. Supreme Court and the whole federal side of it. It is a fascinating look behind the scenes.

I would like to add briefly that Chief Justice Lucas shared with me certain experiences in court administration that helped me learn some of the responsibilities that would ultimately become mine as Chief Justice and to receive some valuable training in those matters. In 1988, he had appointed me to chair an advisory committee to the Judicial Council charged with reform of voir dire—jury selection—and subsequently appointed me as a Court of Appeal member of the Judicial Council. After my elevation to the Supreme Court, he again appointed me to the council, where I chaired its executive committee as well as the committee charged with implementing the recommendations—of which there were between 60 and 70—of the gender bias committee that had conducted a lengthy study pertinent to all aspects of the justice system. Chief Justice Lucas also gave me the responsibility of looking into ways of reducing unnecessary delay and otherwise improving the processing of death penalty cases. I was asked to meet with the defense community and try to improve the procedures followed by the court and by our partners in the justice system—the public and private defense entities and the attorney general's office. That, of course, was something that I continued to work on once I became chief.

Additionally, Chief Justice Lucas had me going up to Sacramento to meet with legislators as a member of the Judicial Council. It was considered appropriate for me to meet on behalf of the Judicial Council with the leadership of the two houses of the legislature.

I think all of these experiences helped prepare me for the rather remarkable set of duties that fall upon anyone who assumes the position of Chief Justice, because the position is not merely Chief Justice of the California Supreme Court—which in itself is a substantial responsibility—but Chief Justice of California—of the judicial branch—which entails basically being CEO of a medium-sized entity with a budget that approached $4 billion, has almost 20,000 employees and about 1,700 authorized judicial positions—close to twice the size of the federal Article III judiciary nationwide—plus a few hundred subordinate judicial officer positions. All of that, when it did descend upon me, was made more comprehensible and perhaps a bit more doable by reason of Chief Justice Lucas having entrusted me with these responsibilities.

You've just mentioned half a dozen or so special assignments he gave you. Why do you think he was singling you out for these?

I don't know, of course, but he had become aware of my earlier duties on the lower courts, which had included some administrative responsibilities. He may also have engaged in the assumption that, because I was Governor Wilson's first appointment to the California Supreme Court and had a personal relationship with the governor, which was apparent from our mutual work on Wilson's judicial qualification committee, I would be the person most likely to be appointed to assume the duties of Chief Justice once the day came that Chief Justice Lucas would decide to retire. None of this was ever expressed to me directly. I can only speculate.

What was your own thinking about such a change, may I ask?

I enjoyed the challenges of trying to improve the judicial system. I had acquired some administrative experience from my previous assignments as supervising judge of the criminal division of the municipal court and of the West Los Angeles branch of that court, supervising judge of the criminal division of the superior court, and president of the California Judges Association. I also had learned from the various responsibilities given to me by Chief Justice Lucas. I thought I could do a decent job in that position. I had, as I have to this day, a great affection for the judicial branch and hoped to be able to contribute something, which is not in any way to suggest any deficiency on the part of any of my predecessors, because I believe that every person who comes to the position of Chief Justice builds upon the accomplishments of his or her predecessors and that it is always possible to add to those achievements, as I expect my successors to add to my own accomplishments.

Chief Justice Arthur Vanderbilt of New Jersey once said that judicial reform is no sport for the short-winded. I would add to that the runner's perspective and say that court reform is very much like a marathon without a finish line. [Laughter] The work is never done, and I know that my very able successor, Chief Justice Tani Cantil-Sakauye, will build upon the work of her predecessors. I'm sure that her successor—many, many years down the road—because Tani is only 51 years of age—ultimately will build in turn upon her accomplishments. That's what's so fascinating as I look back upon the service of my predecessors as Chief Justice, and how so many of them have added something worthwhile in the ongoing effort to improve our judicial system.

Modern judicial history in terms of the position of Chief Justice probably begins with the tenure of Chief Justice Phil Gibson, who served in that position from 1940, the year I was born, to 1964, the year I graduated from law school, and engaged in efforts to make sense out of a myriad of court levels and jurisdictions. He wrote an article in the *State Bar Journal*, I believe in the 1940s, in which he basically challenged any practicing attorney to identify the eight types of court that he described as then existing below the level of the superior court—there were two types of municipal courts, two types of police courts, city courts, city justices' courts, and two types of township courts, class A and B. He said there were very few lawyers who could identify the respective jurisdiction of each type of court. He was a great advocate for reform of California's court structure.[2] Of course, Gibson was followed by Chief Justice Roger Traynor, whose jurisprudence demonstrated a brilliance probably unequaled not only in the history of the California Supreme Court but among all state high court justices. Exceptional role models exist. Chief Justice Donald Wright was concerned with efficiency and making the judicial system work better than it was. As a deputy attorney general, I had the privilege of appearing before both Chief Justice Traynor and Chief Justice Wright. Chief Justice Bird had deeply felt concerns about access to justice and tried to improve the system in that regard. She also instituted the study on gender bias in the justice system. Chief Justice Lucas initiated projects to reduce court delay and to better coordinate the work of the existing municipal and superior courts. He instituted the study of improvements in the jury voir dire process and other aspects of jury reform. And he put in mo-

---

[2] Phil Gibson, "Reorganization of Our Inferior Courts," 24 *State Bar J.* 382, 384–385 (1949).

tion efforts to bring about some of the structural reforms that ultimately came to fruition under my tenure.

Each of the modern-day Chief Justices of California has been able to contribute something positive to the improvement of our system of justice—and that's one of the beauties and strengths of California's judicial system.

###

Chapter 9

Becoming Chief Justice of California
August 25, 2011

Chief Justice George, let's return to the subject of your years as an associate justice of the California Supreme Court, 1991 through 1996. Let me take you back to a couple of things about the very beginning. I don't think we had a chance to talk about your actual physical set up, your chambers vis-à-vis the chambers of your colleagues, and how those interactions took place.

When I joined the Supreme Court as an associate justice, the court was temporarily housed in leased quarters located at Marathon Plaza, because of the damage caused by the 1989 Loma Prieta earthquake. There was, in fact, a ten-year absence of the California Supreme Court and the First District Court of Appeal from the historic quarters that they had occupied since 1923 in Civic Center Plaza in downtown San Francisco. I was assigned the chambers of my predecessor, Justice Allen Broussard. Actually the building had been done up nicely in terms of transforming a commercial structure into premises that were suitable for the California Supreme Court. I found the courtroom quite appropriate and dignified. Our being there was not really a sacrifice except for the inconvenience of the court having to move. The Loma Prieta earthquake, from everything I was told, wrought such immediate and severe damage to the court's Civic Center quarters that, except for one brief visit to retrieve personal effects, no one was allowed back in until the renovation of the building was completed 10 years later. By then I was chief, so I was able to plan and participate in the move back.

We touched on your colleagues when you first joined the Supreme Court, Chief Justice Lucas and Justices Mosk, Panelli, Kennard, Arabian, and Baxter. How

257

do you compare this panel of individuals to the experience of serving with the much smaller panel on the Court of Appeal?

It was fortunate that I had some personal acquaintance or friendship with virtually all of the members of the court, so I felt that they were very receptive and, in any event, by nature very collegial individuals. But of course it's a very substantial adjustment to know that, instead of writing for two other justices and needing only one of them to concur in what one was putting out as a draft appellate opinion, you had six other persons you were also writing for—and that you needed, including your own vote, four votes to be able to carry a majority. That's not just a question of degree. It truly alters the process quite substantially in terms of having to take into account different views and maybe write in a more general fashion—or possibly in a narrower fashion—in order to be able to obtain the concurrence of a majority of the court.

We'll talk about specific opinions later on, but as a general matter you mentioned that these other justices had a range of preferences in terms of communicating with colleagues, some liking discussion, others preferring a more formal memo or perhaps working through their own research attorneys. What kind of atmosphere did you see in terms of the communication patterns?

There was a lot of flexibility in the approaches available. Also, the court was not on any kind of rigid turnaround schedule the way I had found to exist— perhaps as a matter of necessity—at the Court of Appeal level. There you were usually assigned a case only five weeks before the date contemplated for oral argument, although if the case turned out to be unusually complex, you could have it taken off the tentative calendar.

When a case was accepted for review by the Supreme Court and assigned to a chambers, the justice was really free to spend as much time on it as he or she wanted, within the bounds of reason. Many months could go by if that's what you thought was needed to prepare an analysis and disposition that would command a majority, or if that's what was required by the demands of one's workload. As Chief Justice, I always had a concern that a case I had assigned to a chambers could more or less disappear into a black hole and be overlooked. In fact, once in a while there were cases that were worked on for two or maybe even three years before they were able to secure a tentative majority and then be set for oral argument. Once oral argument took place, of course, the California Constitution required that the court file its opinion within 90 days, although in years past that had been disputed, and the Supreme Court had felt it didn't have to adhere to the 90-day rule. But the court certainly had made clear its adherence to the rule by the time I joined the court.

Occasionally, after becoming chief, I would consult a list indicating when cases had been fully briefed. If an inordinate amount of time had gone by, I'd inquire as to the status of the case. Sometimes after a couple of unsuccessful efforts at a calendar memorandum, the assigned chambers still was having difficulty coming up with something that would carry the day with the other justices and further delay could not be avoided. Some cases, due to the nature of the underlying dispute, clearly merited priority. In any event some cases might languish. The Chief Justice—whether it was Chief Justice Lucas or later myself—occasionally had to give a gentle prod to the chambers suggesting that a particular case should not be neglected.

What sort of style did Chief Justice Lucas display in these matters?

He was always the quintessential gentleman and certainly fostered an aura of collegiality among the members of the court. His suggestions always appeared to be constructive. He wasn't acting as if he were the boss of any of the justices. Certainly one has to keep in mind—as Chief Justice Lucas did, and as I also tried to when I became chief—that one may be Chief Justice of California, one may be Chief Justice of the California Supreme Court, but you are basically just one of seven votes. Unlike the situation in some states, the Chief Justice of our state handles his or her one-seventh share of the caseload and in many contexts can ensure best practices only by way of example and cajoling and reminding.

What about Chief Justice Lucas as a jurist himself? He had been a federal judge. What influence do you think that may have had upon him, now that he was in the California judiciary once again?

He did not have any of the—how shall I say this without sweeping with too broad a brush?—imperious attitude about him that some, certainly not all, federal judges had, with the lifetime appointment having gone to one's head. Bear in mind, too, that he had been a judge of the L.A. Superior court, as you know, before joining the federal bench. I think this quality that occasionally affects a federal judge—sometimes including a negative attitude toward the state court system—is more apt to arise in someone who has never served on the state bench and then receives the lifetime appointment with the jurisdiction of a federal judge. Chief Justice Lucas always seemed quite mindful of how the state court system worked and the fact that, as you and I have discussed, in excess of 95 percent of the court cases heard in the United States are heard in state courts rather than federal courts.

I wonder also about differences between the federal system and the state system in terms of the caseload and the kinds of things that are more prominent. You mentioned last time you were thinking of seeking appointment on the federal Court of Appeals but you weren't particularly enthusiastic about a lot of immigration and administrative law-type cases, which one might see more of there. I wonder how differences in the system itself might have had an effect on Chief Justice Lucas, if at all?

I'm assuming—although it's not anything that Chief Justice Lucas and I discussed directly—that the great control that a federal judge has over his or her calendar would enhance the administrative focus and concern with efficiency of a person who has assumed the position of Chief Justice of the California Supreme Court and of the state of California. Given the nature, complexity, and volume of a federal district court caseload, even if you're concerned only with running your own courtroom, you have to have some administrative skills, unlike the situation in the superior court, where even with direct calendaring I don't think it's anywhere near the administrative or organizational challenge that it is on the federal court. There are many superior court judges who sit in departments that don't operate under a master calendar court, who are challenged with having to juggle heavy caseloads of different types of cases. Nevertheless, I believe service on a federal court is much more demanding in this regard and would necessitate a judge's having to engage in efficient supervision of his or her caseload.

Certainly valuable experiences to bring to this new role. You knew Chief Justice Lucas fairly well by then and all the other colleagues to some degree. Can you reflect on how your relationships with them might have changed in this new setting?

It is different, naturally, to be with one's fellow associate justices on an equal footing. There is always a certain amount of deference or forbearance shown to an associate justice of the Supreme Court, and of course even more so to the Chief Justice, but the persons who were associate justices and whom I knew in that capacity—even though I had known them in a prior life—were now basically equals. We had the same kind of work responsibilities and received the same pay, so there wasn't in any way a hierarchy. It was very nice to be accepted as working with them on equal terms. I believe the fact that I knew them before joining the court made it even easier to engage in that kind of constructive relationship.

Do you have any thoughts on how these individuals influenced each other?

I suppose there was a tendency, as there probably is on any court, for there to be certain influences—I wouldn't necessarily say blocs—but some justices tended to engage in more like-minded thinking, at least on certain issues or areas of the law. Although there were always surprises, one could make a reasonable guess at how the lineup might be on a given case, depending on the issue. It doesn't mean that the justices had irrevocably made up their minds on how to vote on a case at an early stage, but just that, all things being equal, it was more probable than not that they would end up in a certain corner, given their votes on other cases that were relevant to the issue now at hand.

That leads to the question of there being a center on the court, as it was consti-tuted then. That is perhaps more an outside view from the court watchers, but I wonder how you might have thought about that at the time?

I'm trying to determine in my mind whether there really was a center of the court under Chief Justice Lucas. I'm not convinced there was. There were different points of view, but I think it was more a question of Justice Mosk and Justice Kennard being more likely to be in a dissenting mode on certain types of matters but the rest of the justices, while not being in lockstep, tending to be more often in agreement than not.

As vacancies occurred and new justices joined the court, and as the court came to be constituted under my stewardship as chief, commentators and the legal press did begin to evaluate the court as perhaps having two basically equal factions—equal in number—with my vote occasionally being the swing vote. Of course, there were cases that were decided by a 4–3 vote, and some of those are vivid in my mind, such as *In re Marriage Cases*, where clearly I was the swing vote. It did occur on some other occasions as well, but I never kept tallies. Like all of my colleagues, I'm sure, I just approached each case on a case-by-case basis. I leave it to the commentators and the academics to discern trends of the court as a whole, or trends in voting blocs on the court. That's not really my interest or focus, and I never bothered to engage in that effort. Although I recognize there's a legitimate purpose in trying to characterize the justices in certain groupings, I believe this can be overdone.

When these trends or affinities emerge, they obviously do not reflect any personal affinity on behalf of a justice with one or more other justices. It's just a matter of certain justices tending to be more like minded in their thinking on particular issues. It just depends upon the issue. There may be some who will vote, more likely, together on criminal matters but who probably would not do so in some areas of civil law.

As you just alluded to, there was a great amount of turnover among the justices while Chief Justice Lucas was leading the court, so there weren't these long periods of stability among the membership. That could have been a difference as well. That leads me to touch on the next new member who joined after you did, Justice Kathryn Mickle Werdegar, to replace Justice Panelli. Can you say a few words about her and what she brought to the mix?

She brought an intimate knowledge of the California Supreme Court's operations, having served as a research attorney for Justice Panelli. She was someone who had an even longer relationship with Pete Wilson than I did, going back to when they were classmates in law school. There were some occasions when we, that is, Governor Wilson and his wife, the Werdegars, Barbara, and myself socialized together. She had extensive academic skills and experience, having been associate dean at the University of San Francisco School of Law and also having been quite an achiever in terms of her academic career. She was first in her law school class at the University of California, Berkeley—Boalt Hall School of Law, as it was then known. Then when her husband, Dr. David Werdegar, moved to Washington, D.C. she transferred to George Washington University School of Law and promptly displaced the person who had been first in his class there, assuming that position herself. She is obviously very bright and also very pleasant to work with.

Before we leave the subject of Justice Panelli, the press had sometimes mentioned him as a possible successor to Chief Justice Lucas, should that retirement have happened while Justice Panelli was still on the court. Was that notion evident among you at the time?

I never heard any discussion of that when Justice Panelli left the court in 1994, nor before. It was not known when in the future Chief Justice Lucas would retire, nor that I would succeed him when he did retire two years later. I certainly had no inkling of when Lucas would retire, so I doubt very much that the Chief Justice position could have been a factor in Justice Panelli's decision to retire when he did.

I only wondered if that was something that was being widely discussed. You talked last time about Chief Justice Lucas' series of special assignments to you while you were an associate justice, saying he took you into his confidence and that he was sending you out as—can I characterize it as something of an emissary, even?—to the legislature at an early stage. What was he hoping you could accomplish there in the legislature on his behalf?

I believe it was just a question of liaison with the legislature being one of the myriad duties of the Chief Justice and that, given the enormous responsibilities of the chief's position, I was glad to have the opportunity to be of some assistance in that area. Certainly, Chief Justice Lucas made his own visits to the state Capitol, but he also did ask me to go on occasion. In the course of doing so, I did acquire some very valuable information and insights as to how the legislative process worked, in addition to what I had learned from my time as president of the California Judges Association.

It also was natural, I suppose, for him to ask me to assist in coming up with legislative and other solutions to the backlog of capital cases, inasmuch as I had handled many death penalty cases before the California Supreme Court and a couple important ones before the U.S. Supreme Court as a deputy attorney general.

An observer of this flurry of activity might think Chief Justice Lucas was grooming you as his successor. What chance did you have to discuss such a possibility openly with him, if any?

We did not have discussions in which it was assumed that I would be his successor, and of course I would be mindful of how inappropriate that kind of inquiry would be if made on my behalf. As long as Chief Justice Lucas held his position he was entitled to, and did, exercise his full responsibilities. It was only the legal press that spoke of "grooming." I tried to put a halt to it by telling a member of the legal press—it was Scott Graham of *The Recorder* of San Francisco—that I had heard this so often lately, I was beginning to feel like a French poodle, something I did not relish despite my French heritage. Scott wrote in October of 1995 that he found this response politically artful.

But speaking of the press, certainly some of its members had been thinking of you as an heir apparent right from the time you first joined the court. It did seem to be out there as a notion—reading the accounts now, years later.

It may have been an assumption made just on the basis of my having been Governor Wilson's first appointment to the high court, and assuming if he picked me for the first appointment he would also have me in mind to assume the chief's position. On the other hand, I also had had—as we've discussed— some substantial administrative responsibilities, even in the attorney general's office but certainly on the municipal and superior courts and as president of the California Judges Association. That may have been a factor in the governor's believing that I had some of the experience and skills that would be relevant to performing the duties of Chief Justice of California.

Yes. As we've noted, being a good judge and being a good administrator are two quite different things.

I agree. Sometimes a person has one skill to a great degree but lacks the other skill.

Thank you for reflecting on that. I wonder what inkling you might have had that Chief Justice Lucas would choose to retire by mid-1996?

I came to be aware of it but certainly can say it was not something expressed to me in confidence. He must have made it known generally to the court as a whole that he would retire soon. That's my recollection. He announced his pending retirement at the annual meeting of the State Bar in the fall of 1995, and very soon after that he gave the date when his retirement would be effective, which was at the close of business April 30, 1996. This formally created the vacancy to which Governor Wilson appointed me on March 28, 1996 as the 27th Chief Justice of the state of California. My confirmation hearing was scheduled for May 1, presided over by the Acting Chief Justice, Stanley Mosk, whom Chief Justice Lucas had selected to serve as Acting Chief Justice and acting chair of the Commission on Judicial Appointments.

Yes, let's go back and develop that sequence of events. As you say, Chief Justice Lucas let the governor know that he would retire come the first of May. What was going on behind the scenes after that?

The governor, by law, must submit the name of any prospective judicial appointee—whether the appointment is to a trial court, the Court of Appeal, or the Supreme Court—to the State Bar's Commission on Judicial Nominees Evaluation. Given the March 22, 1996 date of the report of the JNE Commission evaluating my qualifications for the position of Chief Justice, I assume Chief Justice Lucas gave formal notice to the governor several weeks before that date that he would be retiring as of a certain date, namely April 30. The governor upon receiving that formal notice from him would then conduct his own review of the person or persons whose name he would send out to the JNE Commission soon enough to allow that body the time permitted under the law—it is a government code section, I believe section 12011.5—to conduct an evaluation and report back to the governor and ultimately to the Commission on Judicial Appointments.

The commission under the statute has as much as 90 days to conduct its evaluation. It needs several weeks, because the commissioners send out hundreds of questionnaires to judges and lawyers. They check references and conduct a comprehensive evaluation of the candidate's legal and judicial abilities and moral character. Then when all of those questionnaires are returned, they schedule a face-to-face interview of the candidate with two or three members of the JNE Commission, at which any perceived weaknesses or criticisms are discussed, in addition to the results of the questionnaires generally. Then, a few days after that interview, which completes the investigative process for the commission, it prepares a report and sends one version to the governor detailing the breakdown of the commission's vote on the rating of the candidate. A second version—which just gives the overall rating and evaluation but doesn't break down the vote into separate categories—goes to the Commission on Judicial Appointments and to the public file, in the event the governor chooses to appoint the candidate.

Maybe I'll just mention, the report you just touched on—March 22, 1996—that I'm holding in my hand suggests that 25 members of this investigating committee—in other words, in a unanimous vote, all 25—rated you "exceptionally well qualified." That strikes me as quite a stunning vote, to have all the members in agreement. As you say, we don't see a breakdown here. When did you learn this result yourself?

That's something that the candidate wouldn't normally learn in terms of how the individual votes went, but I was asked by Governor Wilson, on one day's notice, to come to his office at the state Capitol on March 28, 1996. It was not an interview, as such. He just told me that he was appointing me Chief Justice. In the course of that discussion he handed me the governor's copy of that report. Unlike the governor's copy, the public report just indicates either not qualified, qualified, well qualified, or exceptionally well qualified, without breaking down how many commissioners voted for each category of rating. But he said he wanted me to have his version of the report because he was quite pleased that his nominee received the rating of "extremely well qualified" unanimously.

I was wondering who else he considered if anyone. You learned then that you were the sole possibility?

Yes. I learned my name was the only one he had submitted to the State Bar for evaluation as Chief Justice.

This report is fascinating. It consists of a paragraph, "summary of reported strengths," and then goes on to a selection of comments that various of the 25 reviewers made. At the end of that, it says: "Quite simply, the candidate reflects one of those very occasional moments in time when the right person is in the right place to the great benefit of the judiciary and the public." What do you know of that comment?

That was something that was reiterated orally at the hearing by the chair of the commission, Rita Gunasekaran, and embellished upon by her. It was a very lovely, almost cosmic way of viewing the process—and a bit daunting to be viewed by her as being almost providentially placed in the position of heading California's judicial branch. I did feel I was up to the task but still, of course, was somewhat in awe of the many responsibilities that I would be assuming and that would, I learned fairly soon, basically triple my workload.

What else do you recall of your conversation with Governor Wilson? He said, "I'm appointing you. You're it."?

That was basically it. He mentioned that we would be having a press conference momentarily and that he was appointing Justice Janice Rogers Brown from the Third Appellate District to succeed me, to fill my position as an associate justice.

Barbara had come up to Sacramento with me, and she greeted the governor as well. Then the governor, Justice Brown, and I proceeded down the hallway of the Capitol to the press room. I still remember camera flashes going off right and left, with photographers more or less trotting backwards to keep getting shots of us, and then going into this fairly small and crowded press conference room, having Governor Wilson make the announcement of his two appointments, and then being asked to respond to questions from the press. I don't remember what the questions were. It was quite an overwhelming experience, even though I had come to see my appointment as being on its way. Once it actually occurred it was quite an intense event. The news conference was pleasant; I don't recall any hostile questions. I had dinner with Barbara in Sacramento that evening and headed back to San Francisco. I soon learned my confirmation hearing before the Commission on Judicial Appointments was set for May 1, 1996.

Between March 28 and May 1 there were increased communications between Chief Justice Lucas and myself. He turned over files and studies to me and went over some of the procedures. But otherwise my duties continued as an associate justice, working on the cases that had been assigned to me. Nothing else happened of great significance during the period preceding my confirmation hearing. The hearing was held in the afternoon, and my family came up from Los Angeles, including my then 91-year-old father and my 79-year-old mother, our three sons, and also my sister and my in-laws.

Before May 1 arrived, how were you thinking about this in these intervening weeks?

It truly was a mixture of great pleasure at the governor's having shown the confidence in my ability to run this gigantic—and in my view finest—judicial system in the world and at the same time, naturally, being a bit in awe of all the responsibilities I would be assuming.

How did your colleagues respond?

Everyone was very welcoming and expressed eagerness to cooperate in the transition. I never had the sense of anyone questioning or resenting my appointment as chief. In fact, what I did—and I'm getting ahead of myself here, but it does relate to your question—immediately after becoming chief on May 1, was to schedule individual meetings between myself and each justice and his or her staff in their respective staff conference rooms. I went to each chambers and invited input from each chambers—justice and staff—as to how things were operating, how they could be improved, what were the problems, what were things they thought had worked well.

Tell me more about May 1, 1996, and how the whole confirmation hearing and then your actual swearing-in proceeded.

Chief Justice Lucas, having retired effective the preceding day, could not, of course, preside over the Commission on Judicial Appointments, a duty that comes with the position of Chief Justice. He had appointed Justice Stanley Mosk as acting chair of the Commission on Judicial Appointments. The other two members of the commission were Attorney General Dan Lungren and the senior presiding justice among the six Courts of Appeal. That was Presiding Justice Robert Puglia of the Third Appellate District, which is headquartered in Sacramento. Those hearings—which I'll describe, since we haven't had much occasion to speak about the procedure—involved notice having been given to the public, by way of press release, of the location, date, and time set for the commission's hearing on the qualifications of the appointee and an invitation to the public to submit correspondence and/or personal testimony to the commission in support of or in opposition to the nominee.

Customarily, the testimony in support of the nominee comes from witnesses—usually three to five—selected by the appointee as persons familiar with his or her qualifications and experience. Then any persons who have asked to testify in opposition to the nominee—and anyone is entitled to do so as long as the testimony is focused not on the process but on the nominee's personal qualifications—can testify. The representative—usually, but not always, the chair—of the Commission on Judicial Nominees Evaluation of the State Bar then testifies, relating not only the rating but basically the matters contained in the one-page report summarizing the qualities of the appointee.

Finally, the appointee testifies. It's usually a brief statement that provides an opportunity to address any written or oral comments made by the witnesses, especially those who may have testified negatively about the appointee. Then the appointee is subject to questioning by members of the commission. Finally the commission takes a vote and only rarely retires to deliberate before voting. Usually the chair just inquires whether the other members of the commission are ready to vote and, if so, how do they vote. It's either to confirm or not to confirm. After a vote to confirm, the commission recesses for a very few minutes to complete the necessary paperwork for the secretary of state and the governor. Thereafter a person selected by the appointee usually joins the appointee on the bench for the administration of the oath of office, often with family members of the appointee present on the bench. In my case, Governor Wilson asked to swear me in, and of course I was pleased to have him do so.

Before we get to that, I should mention that there were several persons who were very concerned about the court's parental consent abortion opinion, which had recently come down but which was not yet final. In other words, the opinion was still subject to a pending petition for rehearing which the court would, as it turned out, grant at a later date, thereby vacating the opinion it had rendered upholding the parental consent requirement. The court ultimately issued a new opinion after a new oral argument, striking down the requirement as unconstitutional.

Several individuals showed up in opposition to my appointment, carrying large placards, including photographs depicting aborted fetuses. Some brought facsimile blood that they desired to sprinkle around, and distributed hostile messages that spoke in terms of murder and baby killing and so forth. I didn't learn until after the hearing about the physical exhibits they had brought, because the security personnel apparently had been instructed not to allow individuals to bring exhibits into the hearing room. These individuals were very heated in their comments and were quite explicit in stating, both in their testimony and in their remarks to the press after the hearing, that they would oust me from office at the next retention election, which would be in November of 1998, in the event rehearing were to be granted and I were to vote to invalidate the parental consent statutes. I obviously did not make any commitment or give any indication of how I would vote with regard to the pending petition for rehearing, nor how I would vote on the merits of the case should rehearing be granted.

The testimony of one witness compared me to Chief Justice Rose Bird. The only comment I made in response to this point was that the one thing that Chief Justice Bird and I had in common was that we would each be shocked to be compared to the other. [Laughter] I let it go at that. There was some aggressive questioning from Attorney General Lungren, but I believe my responses were polite but firm.

What was the attorney general interested in, mainly?

The name of the case was *American Academy of Pediatrics v. Lungren*, so of course he was the defendant and a supporter of the parental consent requirement. I wasn't going to get into the merits of the case in my testimony, obviously.

In response to what I believe I can fairly characterize as an attempt on behalf of the hostile witnesses to intimidate me, once I became Chief Justice and once the court granted rehearing—and I recall the new appointee, Justice Janice

Rogers Brown, also voted to grant rehearing—I made a point, for two reasons basically, of assigning the case to myself. One, I wanted to demonstrate that I would not allow myself or the court to be intimidated by the threat of political retaliation. Taking on for myself some of the more controversial cases was a course of action, by the way, that I ended up taking on other occasions as well. And the other reason, which also influenced me in some future case assignments, was that I felt as Chief Justice I should have the broad shoulders to bear the reaction that would follow the court's upcoming decision on a controversial case.

This then-recent decision by the court in American Academy of Pediatrics v. Lungren *ended up being a large part of the hearing. It sounds as if it was quite a presence in the proceeding, if not a factor in the vote ultimately. How common was it for justices on the verge of taking their positions or being elevated to face that kind of opposing presence from members of the public?*

Although the nature of this opposition was unusual, it's not all that unusual to have a witness testify in opposition. However, when that occurs it almost always involves a disgruntled litigant or an attorney who lost a case before that appointee—whether the appointee is a superior court judge up for confirmation to the Court of Appeal or a Court of Appeal justice up for confirmation to the Supreme Court. In fact, of the persons who testified against me on May 1, I recall that one may have been in that category of what I would characterize as a disgruntled litigant or lawyer, with the others being from the antichoice, anti-abortion group.

Given all that exciting activity, how did the whole thing turn out, in your view?

I thought then, as I still do today, that it is important and appropriate that the practices and rules of the Commission on Judicial Appointments permit a public hearing where individuals can voice their views. Hopefully, both from the comments of the commission members and the testimony contradicting the protesting witnesses, additional light is shed on what the qualifications may be of the appointee and what factors are relevant or irrelevant to the appointee's qualifications and to the commission's decision whether to confirm the appointment. The process does serve an educational purpose for those in attendance as well as for the public at large. I found myself, as chair of the commission during the years that followed, fine tuning the rules to provide additional notice or explanation to members of the public of what is or is not the purpose of the hearing, and of what is or is not permitted of witnesses who seek to appear before the Commission on Judicial Appointments.

There's nearly always an opportunity for further education about how the court system works. But it almost strikes me that it was a foreshadowing of the kind of situation you had to face many times in the subsequent years.

It was, and I believe there is much that is misunderstood by the public concerning the work of a judge or a justice and how and why judges and courts decide matters. That's something that I know we'll talk about later when we get to my very substantial concern—which expanded when I became Chief Justice and worked with Sandra Day O'Connor on a national level—related to enhancing public education about our legal and judicial process. A public hearing of this sort does serve this valuable function and was not an unpleasant experience.

Let's go forward to your oath of office and that part of the proceeding for the day.

The hearings are held in one of the three courtrooms of the Supreme Court. By the way, the hearing filled the San Francisco courtroom in Marathon Plaza and was also broadcast to an adjacent auditorium and various other rooms in the building. Governor Wilson did not consider it appropriate to sit through the hearing of the Commission on Judicial Appointments itself, but when the commission recessed to do its paperwork he went from his office in the building to the hearing room and joined me on the bench to administer the oath of office.

I was very pleased to have my family in attendance on the bench. Governor Wilson was first to address the assembled group. He had some nice things to say about me and took note of the fact that I had been appointed to four levels of court by four different governors of both major political parties. In response, in addition to of course expressing my gratitude to the governor for the confidence he had shown in entrusting me with these new responsibilities, I couldn't help but kid him for being the only governor to have followed up my judicial appointment with a second appointment. In the sequence that he had recited, none of these three previous governors had ever given me a second appointment. We all got a good laugh out of that. Afterwards there was a celebratory reception at the World Trade Center in the Ferry Building. I also was pleased—and in a way I like to view it as symbolic, but of course it was just fortuitous—that my appointment as Chief Justice of California was confirmed on May 1, which is Law Day.

My first full day actually on the job—in the traces as Chief Justice, May 2—featured presiding over the confirmation hearing for Justice Brown to assume the position of associate justice for the seat I had vacated to become Chief Justice, and presiding over the execution-night proceedings in the case of Keith Daniel Williams.

Maybe I could ask you more about the confirmation hearing for Justice Brown. She had worked directly with Governor Wilson for quite some time, having served as his legal affairs secretary, and had been on the California Court of Appeal, although for a relatively short time and having written a relatively small number of published opinions. There was this matter of the Commission on Judicial Nominees Evaluation assigning her the rating of "not qualified." How was that matter approached and addressed in the course of the confirmation hearing?

It was a very difficult situation to be faced with my first day on the job. Of course, I don't mean to suggest it was all about me. It wasn't about me; it was about Justice Brown and her appointment. I had read over her opinions and I'd read over the report of the attorney general, which by the way is always prepared to assist the members of the commission. Of course, I reviewed the JNE Commission report.

I don't think any doubt was raised about Justice Brown's ability in terms of being a fine lawyer, about her ability to engage in legal analysis. Her judicial skills in terms of craftsmanship were quite apparent, I believe. What disturbed the JNE Commission was some of the language that she used in her opinions that the commission thought called into question whether she possessed the judicial temperament that was desirable for a judge and perhaps especially so for a justice on a collegial body of several justices in terms of the ability to work well together.

I have generally given great weight to the recommendations of the JNE Commission and have enormous respect for the time, effort, and dedication that its members provide and the contribution to the administration of justice they make by vetting individuals who will serve for many, many years, at whatever level of court. Having said that, I did feel that if there was a doubt—and given the other, positive qualities that the JNE Commission report enumerated about Justice Brown and what I view as the very substantial discretion that a governor does have and should have in making judicial appointments—any doubt should be resolved in favor of the appointee. I would not say this if a question of moral character were involved, but here the question was one of judicial temperament, with the appointee clearly possessing the judicial and legal skills to perform her day-to-day working responsibilities. Although I was not at all dismissive of the JNE Commission's concerns, I was inclined to vote in favor of her confirmation and did so despite the rating of "not qualified."

She was someone who at the outset, although quite shy and maybe even withdrawn in temperament, did appear to be collegial. In fact, about seven or eight months after she assumed office, she wrote a lengthy piece in a legal newspaper tracking my activities during a one-week period, and observing:

"James Brown, . . . the hardest working man in show business, . . . sang and danced, a whirl of continuous motion, until he left the stage, drenched with sweat, two hours and three encores later. I never thought I would see his like again, but that was before I met California's new Chief Justice, the hardest working man in court business." That was a very generous piece, demonstrating her skills as a creative writer, and it concluded with a favorable comparison between me and the "Energizer Bunny."[1]

But it soon became apparent that she did not get along very well with her colleagues. I heard reports from other justices on our court who, although in basic agreement with her position on a case, found that she could be very unreceptive and less than pleasant when approached in her chambers with suggestions on how to improve her opinion or accommodate a concern. That reaction occurred in various contexts, and Justice Brown had a few fairly heated exchanges with her colleagues in the written material circulated by the justices. I learned that Justice Mosk had met with her in a helpful but futile attempt to persuade her to tone down the rhetoric in her opinions.

There was a case, *People v. Mar*, that involved the use of stun guns on criminal defendants as a security measure during the course of a trial. She disagreed with the justification I put forth in the court's opinion for requiring safeguards on the use of stun guns and how precautions had to be taken against accidental electrical discharges and the ensuing effect of such devices on a defendant's exercise of his or her right to testify. I cited some studies in law reviews supporting the view taken by the court, and she came back as the sole dissenter to say that it was shoddy work to rely on student products—which are a principal source of law review articles—and that the majority's reliance on such sources wasn't worthy of the California Supreme Court. I then modified the Court's opinion to quote a passage from one of Justice Brown's own recent opinions for the court in which, in a single footnote, she herself had cited, as persuasive authority from "numerous legal commentators," three student law review articles. [Laughter] That got a bit personal. She did remove from her dissenting opinion a disparaging reference directed at one of the sources cited in the majority opinion, a Texas law school, after I pointed out that U.S. Supreme Court Justice Antonin Scalia frequently lectured at that institution.

I'll mention one other case. Justice Brown authored for the court the *Hi-Voltage* opinion holding that a city's policy requiring project bidders to have a specified percentage of women and minority subcontractors violated the state constitution after the passage of Proposition 209. On this occasion I was a dis-

---

[1] Janice Rogers Brown, "Ronald George: The Hardest Working Man in Court Business" (*Los Angeles Metropolitan News Enterprise*, p. 4, January 13, 1997).

senter. I just could not go along with her majority opinion, even though I agreed that the result, upholding application of the initiative, was compelled by law. The reason I couldn't concur was that I felt her opinion for the court contained a lot of dictum—unnecessary and inappropriate language—questioning the motives of persons who favor affirmative action and misrepresenting the history of affirmative action in the United States. Had her opinion not contained those references, I certainly would have signed it. But I felt compelled to write a separate concurring and dissenting opinion—and you and I already have talked about how reluctant I was to write separate opinions. She ended up having only three other justices with her. The others wouldn't sign her majority opinion even though they agreed with the result it reached.

When Justice Brown ultimately left our court, having been viewed initially as a possible direct appointment by President George W. Bush to the U.S. Supreme Court but confirmation to that position having become quite unlikely, she accepted a presidential appointment to the U.S. Court of Appeals for the District of Columbia Circuit. Based upon what I read in the press, the matters that troubled some members of the U.S. Senate, which in 2005 narrowly confirmed that appointment, included speeches she had given that were viewed by them as quite extreme and injudicious. There were senators who also held this view concerning some of her judicial opinions, with specific reference to the *Hi-Voltage* case that we just talked about.

Once Justice Brown was confirmed early in the month of June 2005, she indicated she would formally leave our court at the end of that month. We all expected she would be attending the next two or three weekly petition conferences. At a court petition conference held early in the month, nothing was said by her relating to her departure, despite the usual opportunity that I afforded for the justices to chat about personal matters and exchange news and so forth at the beginning of the conference. However, when we had completed our business at the end of the conference—and were all picking up our papers, standing up to start leaving the room—she announced, "I guess this is my last conference, so I won't be seeing any of you anymore." I recall that Justice Werdegar expressed astonishment—I think we were all somewhat surprised at that rather brief and brusque farewell—and responded, "Janice, you've been with us nine years, haven't you?" The response was either, "Yes," or "I guess so."

That was her departure, and at her request, no formal events were planned. She was the only colleague with whom I served on the Supreme Court whose relationship with the other members of the court could not accurately be characterized as truly collegial.

What's the lesson in all this?

One lesson certainly has to be that, among the qualities that have to be considered by the appointing power, is the collegiality of an appointee. I don't mean just whether the person is friendly or not, because we all have different personalities. A very integral part of a person's responsibilities—affecting his or her ability to do the job of an appellate justice—involves the ability and willingness to interact well with colleagues, to take suggestions and criticisms in tow, to work together to achieve the best possible product for the court as an institution. One can be absolutely brilliant, but if he or she lacks that ability to work in a collegial manner, in a cooperative sense, with the other members of the court—whether it's a three-justice panel or a seven-justice panel or a nine-justice panel—that's a serious deficiency.

I heard several stories as a member and president of the Conference of Chief Justices reflecting terribly acrimonious relationships among high court justices, posing far more severe difficulties than what I just illustrated here on the California Supreme Court. Some jurists are locked in the judicial equivalent of a bad marriage for many, many years, compelled to work together in a close environment. I've been told of instances of justices who literally do not speak to each other in the elevator. They would not exchange a "Good morning," won't greet each other's staffs, and include nasty personal barbs in their written opinions or utter them on the bench to or about each other. I think what's to be learned is that there are many qualities that go into making a good appointment to an appellate court but that the ability to work constructively together is probably as important as all the other qualities.

Thank you. I'd like to talk a great deal more about your other colleagues in due time, but perhaps for the moment we'll return to some of your first activities in this larger role as Chief Justice. Your first address to a joint session of the legislature to deliver the State of the Judiciary address occurred only a couple weeks after your swearing-in on Law Day of 1996. Could you turn to that for a moment and describe what happened on that day?

I was asked on fairly short notice—although I don't recall precisely when—to deliver a State of the Judiciary address to a joint session of the legislature, meaning that the state Senate and the state Assembly assemble in joint session in the Assembly chamber and the regular business of the houses is adjourned. The session is presided over jointly by the President pro Tempore of the Senate and the Speaker of the Assembly, from the dais. This is similar to the protocol followed for the State of the State, when the governor gives his address. The seven members of our court assemble at the rear of the chamber. The presiding officers of the joint session name an escort committee, usually I believe half a dozen legislators, from both houses, who would escort me down the center aisle to the dais and the associate justices to the front of the chamber. After some introductory remarks by the President pro Tem and the Speaker, I am given the floor.

One year, as I slowly made my way forward, greeting individual legislators in the process, Speaker Herb Wesson, a legislator from South Los Angeles, exuberantly proclaimed from the dais: "I'm going to say something I've always wanted to—'Here come da judge!'"

One of the Speakers of the Assembly in a subsequent year—I believe it was Fabian Núñez—made the observation, "You know, the Chief Justice is the only person we let lobby us from the floor of the legislature." [Laughter] That's true in a way. The content of the speech was always entirely up to me, although I received considerable assistance from my principal attorney, Beth Jay, and other staff in crafting my message. My colleagues all attended, and so did some other state constitutional officers.

As I prepared to deliver this inaugural address, I spontaneously came up with an idea that I would include in my remarks—an idea that ended up having far-reaching benefits for my tenure as Chief Justice. Although I had had 15 years' experience as a trial court judge, in view of my new responsibilities as Chief Justice of the third branch of government presiding over a judicial system with about 20,000 court employees—although it really wasn't a "system" at that point—I felt it would be worthwhile for me to visit the courts in all of California's 58 counties, in addition to the six appellate districts. I made a commitment during the speech to do that. On later occasions I made the observation that perhaps this was a commitment that I should have been committed for making, because it turned out to be quite an arduous task. [Laughter]

Bill Vickrey, whom Chief Justice Lucas had selected as administrative director of the courts in April 1992, accompanied me on this series of visits. On occasion there might be an additional staff member from the Administrative Office of the Courts. I know that Kiri Torre went on several of the visits. My objective was to get an up-to-date idea of what the situation and the current problems were in the various courts around the state.

My experience had been for the most part limited to my home county, Los Angeles County, which obviously is atypical in its size—although through educational programs and heading the California Judges Association I had some exposure to the situations in other counties. I wanted to have an in-depth view of the problems and possible solutions existing in the various counties so that I could better exercise my new responsibilities in being the Chief Justice of the entire state as opposed to just being Chief Justice of the Supreme Court.

Had anything like this been done before, to your knowledge?

I have been told that it had not. I wanted to follow through on my strong commitment to ensure that the judicial branch operated—and was treated—as a co-equal and independent branch of government. I already knew from my visits to Sacramento that there were many legislators who would ask questions like, "The judges—which department do they work for?" and, "Can't the governor remove you folks if we don't like your decisions?" and so forth. There really was a need for us to be recognized as a co-equal, independent branch of government.

Not only did you pledge to visit every one of the 58 counties, you pledged to do it in a year's time. How did you organize yourself to carry this out?

It was quite difficult. Our judiciary soon would consist of about 1,700 judges plus a few hundred court commissioners and referees. I met with a very large number of them and visited courts in each and every county, as well as the appellate courts. I felt my responsibilities were analogous to those of a corporate CEO and decided to engage in the "walking around" style of management.

Ours was recognized as the largest judiciary in the United States, and probably in the entire world if you qualify it by saying "law trained," because there are some third-world countries where they have lay judges. In fact, California previously had lay judges in its justice courts. These justices of the peace were not required to be trained as lawyers. In some small towns, you had the local barber or grocer doing double duty as the justice of the peace and potentially being influenced in his or her judicial decisions by the need to secure sufficient revenue for the local coffers by imposing large enough fines. The California Supreme Court, in the *Gordon* decision rendered in the 1970s, held that it was a denial of due process to require a person to come before a tribunal, on a matter involving a possible jail sentence, that was presided over by someone who was not an attorney.

In any event, there was a vast number of superior court judges, municipal court judges, and justice court judges to meet with. One thing that made it particularly difficult—when you ask how did I cope—was that I did not reduce my caseload. I continued to write my one-seventh share of the opinions rendered by the court. In some states the Chief Justice has a reduced caseload or basically no caseload at all. I used to grimace when I'd hear some of my fellow chiefs at the Conference of Chief Justices say, "I'm having a tough time with my 40 judges." That would be like one branch of one of our larger California trial courts.

Tending to my "day job" while embarking upon this journey made it difficult but did cause me to enhance whatever skills I had in multitasking. I completed the trilogy of modes of travel when I traveled to Fresno by train, so I can truly say that I worked on my opinions in trains, planes, and automobiles. [Laughter] I learned not to get carsick, even on curvy mountain roads. I do want to stress I was never at the wheel! The Supreme Court marshal or a California Highway Patrol officer would do the driving while I worked. The marshal, Harry Kinney, drove me during most of my travels and did a fine job. You'll hear more about him when I describe some of the individual visits. When the marshal's position was abolished, I was very pleased to have CHP officer Terry Tracy be the person in charge of driving me and providing security in the later years of my tenure as Chief Justice. There was actually a fourth mode of travel. When I visited the Native American tribal courts—there were two reservations with their own Native American judicial systems, the Hoopa and the Yurok nations—the Yurok took me up the Klamath River to their facility on a rather fast boat.

My goal was to have a current idea of the situation in the various courts and to be able to assist in providing possible solutions to their problems. I ended up serving as a sort of an informal clearinghouse in some ways, because I might be in one county and hear of a particular problem and be asked for advice on how to resolve it and then be able to say, "Last week I was in such-and-such county, and they had a similar problem. This is what they're doing about it. Why don't you call up their presiding judge?" It really was a process of cross-fertilization, if you will, which I believe tells volumes about the lack of cohesiveness of the branch at that time and the problems of dealing with 220 separate fiefdoms— separate justice courts, municipal courts, and superior courts—and the lack of adequate technology, which aggravated that lack of communication. I ended up informally—just depending upon what I happened to have heard, seen, and remembered—exchanging bits of information from one county to another.

I should say, before we get further into the visits, that each county was required by the constitution to have at least one superior court judge and one municipal or justice court judge. That was the constitutional minimum. Some of these very unpopulated counties—and there were about a dozen of them that had the constitutional minimum of only two judges—were small in land mass, and others were vast in land mass but still had a very small population. In some of these counties, there seemed to be very little communication with the outside world. This is in contrast to Los Angeles, which had one superior court with hundreds of judges, 24 municipal courts—including the Los Angeles Municipal Court, which had 64 judges on its own—and one justice court, on Catalina Island. You can imagine the tremendous variety across the state—between rural and urban counties, mountainous and desert, coastal and inland, highly populated and sparsely populated, and in their respective working conditions, problems, and facilities.

As for those small counties whose caseload did not justify even two judges working there full time, I would exercise my authority as Chief Justice—one of the powers is the power of assignment—to assign those judges to ride circuit and hear cases in different counties that had a need for more judicial personnel.

If a district had more than 40,000 population, it would be a municipal court district. If less, it would be a justice court district.

I note from your schedule that you started your visits in your home territory of Los Angeles and then went on from there. Given your familiarity with Los Angeles and, as you say, its vast size, how did you approach the job of making this kind of visit there?

The first visit of several visits that I made to Los Angeles took place about a week before I began my actual road trip. I flew down there. I met with the executive committee of the superior court, of which I had been an ex officio member many years before in my capacity as supervising judge of the criminal division, to learn about their concerns. I also met the same day with those justices of the Second District Court of Appeal who served in Los Angeles, meeting separately at a later date with the justices who served in Division Six, which covers Ventura, Santa Barbara, and San Luis Obispo Counties.

Once I announced I was going to make these visits, the courts seemed quite receptive and eager to have me come. I don't want to convey the impression that everyone thought the visits were a great idea right from the start. There were some—including a legislative staffer and Peter Belton, a longtime Supreme Court staff attorney—who told me later that they had initially considered my promise to visit the courts in all the counties as somewhat of a gimmick or publicity stunt. They admitted thinking that not much would come of the idea, but later becoming very supportive converts for the visits and for the court reform measures that clearly grew out of those visits.

The visits involved meeting not only with the presiding judge and the executive committee, but with all the judges of the court who were available. I also would meet as many of the court staff as I could. I would see whatever they all wanted to show me—in addition to courtrooms, jury rooms, and chambers, I'd be shown the custody lockup, the filing areas, and the counters where the clerks were dispensing services to the public.

In some places the county law library, which usually was not in the same structure as the courthouse, would be included because there was more and more of a trend for these libraries to be used not so much by the lawyers, but by the growing segment of courtroom litigants who lacked legal representation and were trying to use computers—which were coming into greater use then—as well as law books to try to research the legal issues in their own cases. Often county and city personnel wanted to meet with me about the court facilities, which were then owned and—using the term loosely in some contexts—"managed" and operated by the counties. In some counties, even the county seat had a tiny population. But both in small counties and large counties, these officials were very hospitable and yet quite candid in expressing and showing me what their problems were, which often involved the inadequacy of the county-owned physical facilities themselves.

After you started out in Los Angeles County you were doing this one or two days of most weeks—not every single week—but throughout that one year period from August of 1996 through August of 1997 you were regularly going on these visits. Not all were far-flung, but what effect did this have on the rest of your life? You mentioned working on court opinions on the road, but you were also leaving home and family every week. How did you set that up?

It was very disruptive, although my travel companions, Bill Vickrey and the marshal, seemed to view the arrangement as basically a chambers on wheels. Although I didn't have a portable fax machine or iPhone at that time, I was receiving phone calls and messages indicating that something should be faxed to me, and where would I be later that day? It was a constant diet of working on opinions and administrative matters, and phone calls to and from my staff and the A.O.C. staff. That made for a very busy schedule.

You mentioned that you occasionally invited your wife to go along?

Actually, it wasn't occasionally. It was just once. It was when the first actual road trip was going to get underway. She had said, "I think I'll go with you on these trips and visit the various county arts councils," because she was then serving as a member of the California Arts Council. I said, "The first one is going to be August 16," 1996. She asked, "Where you going?" I said, "In Marin County, I'm having a breakfast meeting with the judges and then a courthouse tour. By midday I'll be at the Solano County courts, and I'll have dinner and an evening meeting with the judges in Napa County." She was somewhat aghast and said, "Have a wonderful time. I think I'll opt out after all." [Laughter]

I never asked her again. But she did something quite wonderful that actually ended up taking her as long as my one-year tour of the various counties. Feeling a bit guilty at not accompanying me, Barbara proposed assembling a collection of historic county courthouse photographs, one from each county, to commemorate my visits, for display on the walls outside the Judicial Council boardroom. After the justices of the Supreme Court saw this photographic collection, they asked that the same pictures be displayed in the hallway outside the fifth-floor chambers. These photographs were published by the California Supreme Court Historical Society in 2000 in a small book called *California Court Houses*. They're lovely photographs, and each is accompanied by a few lines describing the particular courthouse and the year construction was completed, often with an amusing anecdote concerning the facility. This was a wonderful contribution to the Supreme Court and Judicial Council buildings and served to memorialize some of the history of California's judicial branch.

I can't stress enough how symbolic the visits were. Arrangements had to be made in advance, naturally. I didn't just drop in unannounced. There was a lot of excitement on behalf of not only the judges but the staff, and in the preparations they went through to arrange appropriate and informative meetings and inspections of facilities. It turned out to be much more significant and meaningful to them than I ever could have imagined.

I was amused that in some of the smaller counties, and I believe Tehama was one, the local sheriff—certainly not at our request—would dispatch uniformed personnel in marked vehicles to the county line to escort us to the county seat, complete with flashing lights. There was one county, Plumas, whose county seat was Quincy, where the community—unbeknownst to us—had organized a little parade. We were driven in a Conestoga wagon down the main street. It was very touching how eager they were for these visits to go well and how appreciative they were. Judges told me time after time that this was the first occasion in the history of their county that any justice of the Supreme Court—Chief Justice or associate justice—had ever made an official visit. They were very eager to be viewed as part of the judicial branch and not just be left to grapple on their own with the problems of caseload, inadequate facilities, and understaffing. They appreciated being recognized as a participating part of a statewide branch, rather than merely toiling away in isolation as one of these 220 separate fiefdoms that constituted our assemblage of independent trial courts.

These visits to appellate courts, trial courts, and tribal courts took a year to complete—from August 1996 to August 1997—and almost 13,000 miles of travel, mainly by automobile.

This tour was a vitally important learning experience for me that had a great bearing upon my ability to carry out my duties as Chief Justice, as I perceived those duties to be. Eventually I came to realize how fundamental the visits were to the structural reforms I was able to propose or support that altered the whole landscape of the judicial branch. Virtually everything I saw and heard during these visits ended up having a practical and utilitarian function, in terms of bringing about some later benefit. My observations played a great role in shaping what became my basic vision of creating a true judicial branch—one not just in name or theory, but in fact, function, and reality. The forms of transportation were varied, but the benefits were quite uniform.

What more can you tell me about those tribal courts and what their own particular issues were at the time?

One of the problems was the uncertainty generated by the overlapping jurisdiction of the state courts, the tribal courts, and the federal courts. In Humboldt County, we were pleased to see joint use of the courthouse by both the regular state court system and the tribal court. There are issues—some of which arise under the Indian Child Welfare Act and other legislation—that are truly unique to the Native American population.

In your visits to some of these outlying counties, many of which had not seen a Supreme Court justice before, what kinds of specific situations did you encounter in court facilities, chambers, jurors, all those day-to-day matters of trial courts? What did you see that might have surprised you?

Certainly the age of some of these facilities and their total inadequacy to meet modern needs was striking to me. My experience had been mainly with courthouses in Los Angeles County, many of which were behemoths with dozens and dozens of courtrooms. On my visits to rural areas, I was shown court buildings that had been built in the 1850s and in some instances were one-courtroom structures.

In fact, the Mariposa County courthouse is a beautiful historic court building that was woefully inadequate to serve the needs of the public, even in that small county. It's the oldest still-operating courthouse in the United States west of the Mississippi River and was built in 1854. It had no jury deliberation room, so when it was time for the jury to deliberate, everyone except the jurors left the courtroom and they sat in the jury box until they came to a verdict. I recall seeing a large black pot-bellied stove right in the middle of the courtroom, blocking one's view of much of the proceedings. [Laughter] There was a lot of cold weather in that area, so that's what they needed. Needless to say, the structure is on the national historic register. It was built out of hand-hewn lumber.

That's one illustration, and the photos displayed in the court building—replicated in the book published by the historical society—convey so much of this better than my words can. Speaking of Barbara's book of courthouse photographs, it includes a wonderful introduction authored in her capacity as chair of the Supreme Court Art Selection Committee. The introduction includes the following statement: "The great British Prime Minister Winston Churchill observed that 'We shape our buildings, thereafter they shape us.' So it is with the historic courthouses of California."

True to Churchill's idea, you arrived when the courthouses were shaping the people rather than the other way around. What kinds of innovations were people resorting to in the face of these facilities "challenges," shall we say?

People resorted to self-help. The times were reflected not only in the structures themselves, but in some of the recordkeeping. I was amazed to see shelves in the clerk's office of some of the oldest courthouse facilities holding tattered leather-bound registers that contained handwritten docket entries of decisions resolving Gold Rush-era mining claims, marital disputes, and criminal offenses, often reflecting the rough-and-tumble behavior of that era.

Such behavior extended to the justices of the California Supreme Court. The Court had a very colorful history in its early years. Some of these justices were hard drinking and violent men. David Terry, who served as Chief Justice from 1857 to 1859, killed U.S. Senator David Broderick in a duel. Terry always carried a bowie knife. He made a threat against U.S. Supreme Court Justice Stephen Field in a public place and was himself shot to death by a U.S. marshal assigned to protect Justice Field.

As an illustration of the speedy justice of the times, we have in the Supreme Court fifth floor corridors an etching that depicts the following scene. In the vigilante time around the Gold Rush era, a man was apprehended for breaking and entering a building in downtown San Francisco one night. No one was killed, let alone injured, but a safe was taken. On the same night the man was apprehended, a jury was assembled, he had what was called a "trial," was convicted, and then was hanged—all on the same night. These were very different times. Law and order vigilance committees were commonplace, and the text on the etching concludes with inquiry being made of the defendant after he was sentenced: "Do you have any requests?" His response was, "Yes, I should like to have a brandy and a cigar," which were furnished to him, and then he was promptly hanged. These incidents illustrate the kind of justice that characterized the courts of the time, from the Supreme Court level down to the local courts.

Outside a courthouse that I visited in the county seat of Sierra County, Downieville, a gallows that had been constructed immediately adjacent to the courthouse was still on display, although it hadn't been used since 1885 because the responsibility for executions had been transferred to the state prison system at San Quentin.

The Sierra County visit was interesting in its own right because of an interview I had with a member of the local press, the *Sierra Booster*. The reporter who interviewed me, Hal Wright, was also the editor and publisher of the paper and quite an extraordinary man. He was in his early nineties, born the same year as my father, and claimed to be the oldest licensed pilot in the United States and a distant relative of the Wright brothers. What I found most intriguing was that he was also the delivery man for the newspaper. Known locally as the "flying paperboy," he would pilot his single-engine plane alone over the various reaches of his county, parts of which were totally inaccessible in the winter snows, leaning out of the cockpit of his plane to drop the newspaper onto or fairly near the front porch of the farm or ranch of his subscribers. [Laughter] He was a very crusty fellow, asked pertinent questions, and added another colorful aspect to my visit to this county.

One of the areas of major concern for judges and court staff—and they frequently expressed this to me—were the grossly inadequate facilities for prospective jurors who were summoned to the local courthouse. One has to keep in mind, this was before the institution of the reform that we accomplished later in my tenure as Chief Justice of "one day or one trial" jury service. Under the new system, unless a prospective juror is sent to a courtroom that first day of being summoned to the courthouse, his or her jury duty for the year has been completed and the juror is discharged. In contrast, at the time of my courthouse visits in 1996 and 1997, jurors were summoned for what was then customarily a two-week tour of duty. In some counties it was a question of very inadequate facilities—such as an insufficient number of seats in the jury assembly room, or a leaky ceiling with pails gathering water to be avoided by the seated jurors. Amazingly enough, there were counties where there were absolutely no facilities for jurors. In some courthouses, jurors waiting to be summoned to a courtroom would sit in a hallway day after day with barely room for people to walk by, mingling with persons out on bail charged with sometimes serious criminal offenses; rival gang members; victims of crime; witnesses; family members—all in the same crowded corridor. At one courthouse, I actually saw jurors on the sidewalk holding umbrellas, standing in the rain waiting to be summoned to a courtroom, because there was no jury assembly room or space for them in the hallways. At another courthouse, prospective jurors were seated for days on end on the concrete steps of a stairwell waiting to be summoned. I observed prisoners being brought down in shackles from an upper floor, as the seated jurors were told to scoot over to the side to make way for the prisoners, who were being brought to a lower floor.

I suppose the most remote county of all was Alpine County. I was told at the time—and I don't think its population is much more than this now—that only 1,150 people resided in the entire county. Aside even from its small size and population, this county was extremely isolated, because it was perched over the crest of the Sierra Nevada and did not extend to the main thoroughfare east of the mountains, Highway 395. One of the legal newspapers, the *Los Angeles Daily Journal*, chose to follow me on that particular court visit to do a story. A CHP officer was driving me that day at a pretty fast clip, and I still remember the sight and sound of the *Daily Journal* vehicle—with reporter, photographer, and squealing tires—trying to keep up as we made our way through Carson Pass to the county seat, which was Markleeville. It was late May, but there still were snowdrifts in the 8,500-foot pass, which was closed in winter.

I inquired with the court officials about the crime rate in the county, being such an isolated and pristine location, and was told that the last major crime had been a break-in committed at the courthouse. I expressed interest, and they informed me that it involved a large bear breaking through the plate glass at the entrance to the court building, proceeding down to the sheriff's substation in the basement, leaving "a big dump," and then departing. They said that was their last major crime. [Laughter] I believe that the judge with whom I spoke said there were only three lawyers in the entire county. There were all sorts of things they didn't have there, that we take for granted. At least at that time—I don't know if it's still the case—any Alpine County student attending high school had to be bussed over to the State of Nevada. That was the nearest available facility.

Was it Alpine County or was it another one that I read about that was in such dire financial straits, that what little judiciary they had was threatened?

Yes, this happened in early 1997. The two-judge Alpine County court system was the first to report—given the substantial economic decline that was occurring then in the State of California—that it was in dire financial shape, and that in fact it had only $8 in its bank account. Their courts had a payroll to meet in the next couple days and needed assistance. The Administrative Office of the Courts arranged to have one of its staff travel to Sacramento, where the Alpine courts had their bank account, because there was no local bank. It was a small enough amount that the A.O.C. was able to lend some money so that the local courts would not default.

This was a story that soon was repeated in one county after another as economic times got worse, and not just in the small counties. By the spring, courts in major counties—some of our largest metropolitan counties—were in dire shape and were in danger of closing. This in turn illustrated not only the need—but provided the impetus—for me to persuade the legislature to agree to take over the responsibility for the funding of our trial courts from the counties, to shift that responsibility to the state, because courts were in danger of going belly up. I had to go twice to the legislature during my first year as Chief Justice to obtain emergency bailout money, so obviously we needed a more permanent solution. Alpine started it off, but eventually it got to Los Angeles and many other counties where the courts needed emergency bailout funds.

We may get to this in more detail, but that was a major court funding bill that you managed to pull off only a short time after completing this tour of the year's length. How did you do that?

I had always found in my communications with the governor and the legislature—and I made ample use of this in my State of the Judiciary addresses—that a story was usually worth a thousand words of explanation, a variation on the theme of a picture being worth a thousand words. I would salt my addresses to the legislature with numerous illustrations and stories. You probably have acquired the impression already from our various sessions that I like to share stories. I think they can be illustrative as well as entertaining and alleviate the flow of pure information. I thought that telling stories of hardships imposed—not just upon court staff and judges but upon the public, who have a right to expect the proper dispensation of justice from their courts—served to emphasize a very important subject. I felt, and feel to this day, that the dispensation of justice is one of the most important functions of government. If we can't do it in a fair, efficient, and accessible manner in safe and secure courthouses, then we're really failing in a very basic function of government. These illustrations, such as the ones I'm giving you now and a couple more that I'll share with you in a moment, graphically conveyed the situation to the legislature.

I also encouraged legislators to visit their local courts. Sometimes attending a crowded criminal arraignment calendar, seeing a heated family-law dispute resolved, or observing the difficulty of getting through a morning's complex set of law-and-motion matters would be worth more than any description I could give them. I encouraged judges to invite their local legislators—in their off time from their regular legislative sessions—to come down and see the conditions prevailing at the local courthouse. That often really made the difference. I'd also have local judges go up to the Capitol and speak to legislators—focusing on the representatives from their own districts—often in conjunction with my annual State of the Judiciary address.

When we could persuade a legislator to actually see what was happening in his or her own district and the experience of the local public engaged in trying to obtain services at the courthouse, as well as the difficult and sometimes unsafe conditions under which the legislator's constituent court employees were working, it served to provide strong motivation to take some action.

My own visits sometimes served a similar function. In a visit to Imperial County, to El Centro, I was told by a local deputy sheriff that they were very pleased for my visit for a number of reasons. It was pointed out to me, "Look, they just finished touching up the paint job on the outside of the courthouse, and the lawn is being mowed. We've been asking for this for years, but it was the occasion of the Chief Justice's visit that got the county board of supervisors to agree to that." One of the court personnel there told Harry Kinney, the marshal—and I don't mean any disrespect by repeating this story, but I find it amusing—that somehow our appearance was akin to a papal visit in terms of engendering interest, excitement, and refurbishing. There were many positive effects, and I know in Imperial they said, "Please come back again soon. We need to have our courthouse taken care of." [Laughter]

A quite ancient courthouse was still in use in Bridgeport, in Mono County. The judge who greeted me, one of the two in the county, insisted I see a panoramic view of the Sierra Nevada that one could observe only from the bell tower of this 1880 structure. Although in his seventies, he took me up a rickety set of wooden steps to the belfry, where a vast portion of the Sierra range was visible.

Another interesting story of a small county involved an earlier visit to Modoc County. It was hosted by Judge Bob Barclay, whom I mentioned in our previous discussions as a fellow executive board member of the California Judges Association. He insisted that I stay at his home in Alturas. I learned only the next day that he and Mrs. Barclay had relinquished their bedroom to me, the only one in the house, and had moved to the den for the occasion of my visit. Their hospitality was quite endearing. Judge Barclay arranged a fairly high-altitude run—knowing of my penchant for running—with the local county public defender. I believe we ran at above 5,000 feet elevation. Due to the fast pace kept by my running mate, and my not wanting to fall behind, this run certainly put my stamina to the test. Speaking of runs arranged during court visits, a more leisurely run was organized by a Riverside County superior court judge, Doug Miller, now a justice of the Court of Appeal, through the desert at dawn before we all assembled for a breakfast meeting.

Some of these visits—aside from showing hardship in terms of the facilities and the conditions under which court staff were operating—were truly inspirational. I can't think of a better illustration of how judges truly extended themselves to provide services to the public under the most daunting circumstances, than was provided by my visit to the Huntington Park Courthouse in southeast Los Angeles County. The judges in this small court facility had somehow managed to cobble together a much-needed additional courtroom. I believe they requisitioned space from a utility closet, a public hallway, perhaps in part from a restroom, and created an area to use as a courtroom, which they desperately needed to serve the very high caseload there. There was no money to furnish it, however. A local court commissioner, Gilbert Lopez, now a superior court judge, was an expert wood craftsman. Out of his own home workshop he managed to construct the judge's bench, jury box, and counsel table. This facility, which was proudly shown to me, was able to operate as a full-fledged courtroom thanks to his very special efforts.

Another illustration of making do with what one has, was provided by a visit I made to a one-judge courthouse in a rural area in San Luis Obispo County, Paso Robles, that had been the scene of an attempted hostage-taking. The judge who showed me around had been involved in that incident earlier in his tenure.

At the end of the tour of this clearly deficient structure, I was ushered into his courtroom and observed stacks of bound volumes of reported judicial decisions piled around the bench. I commented to him about how very impressed I was to find such an apparent scholar in these parts. The judge quickly dispelled the impression conveyed by the presence of these large books, informing me that the tomes served as a substitute for the metal shield that was needed to provide security, because the county had been unable to provide adequate protection for the bench officer serving in that courtroom. I did respond sympathetically that at least I was somewhat relieved to see he was employing federal casebooks for that purpose rather than bound reports of the California Supreme Court's decisions. [Laughter]

There were serious security problems in many court facilities. In some buildings prisoners were ushered through inner hallways to bring them into a courtroom, walking right by the open door of a judge's chambers or by a jury deliberation room. You and I have already discussed security incidents where judges, jurors, or others have been killed or wounded because of these unsafe conditions.

The ingenuity of small-county judges sometimes took a whimsical turn. One of them told me that when a visiting big-city lawyer would become a bit too pompous and condescending in the courtroom, the judge would signal the bailiff to substitute the "special" (that is, defective) chair at counsel table during the next recess. Its use would inevitably subject the seated lawyer to a backflip, much to the delight of the jurors and spectators.

Getting to another one of the positive success stories, I found Ventura County to be a true leader in something that soon became a priority of mine— providing more user-friendly and accessible justice to the public, whom the local court staff viewed as the "consumers" of our court system. Walking through the Ventura courthouse, I was struck by the fact that the court administrator, who was then Sheila Gonzales—her name is now Sheila Gonzales Calabro, and she retired this year as southern regional director of the A.O.C.—had instituted what I guess can best be called a customer satisfaction service at the courthouse. A couple of banners proclaimed, "We're here to serve you." Nearby tables were staffed by court employees eager to accept suggestions, answer questions, and give advice and instructions—not only to unrepresented litigants, but to attorneys, witnesses, jurors, and visitors. The Ventura court even had a mobile van that went into the hinterland of the county, providing a mini courtroom on wheels to serve people who might have difficulty coming down to the county seat for court services.

Again, this is another example of judges and court executives creatively extending themselves to the utmost degree to provide service to the public. It's a model that inspired many of our efforts at the Judicial Council and the Administrative Office of the Courts level to provide accessible justice in countless ways. I'm sure we'll talk about those efforts.

It's nice to hear of the examples you were seeing of ideas that could be used elsewhere to great effect. These were quite creative.

Yes, they really were. I also visited each of the six Courts of Appeal in the course of these visits to the trial courts and the two tribal courts. My last two days in the statewide tour took place on August 7 and 8, 1997, and included the Hoopa and Yurok tribal courts, in addition to the municipal and superior courts of Humboldt and Del Norte Counties.

It would probably be appropriate for me to note at this point the somewhat dramatic conclusion of my court visits. Friends with vacation property on the shore of Lake Tahoe had extended a standing invitation to me to visit them at the conclusion of my tour of the 58 counties. When the last of these visits was completed in Del Norte on Friday afternoon, August 8, I asked Harry Kinney, the court marshal, to drop me off at Tahoe, where Barbara had driven to join me that night as houseguests. As a celebration of the completion of my court visits, our hosts offered to take me waterskiing behind their speedboat the next morning. I accepted, imprudently as it turned out, exhausted as I was by all the driving of the preceding few days. I also chose to indulge my preference for using a single ski.

How much water skiing had you done up to that point?

I actually had done a fair amount. Running and water skiing were the only sports in which I had achieved some medium level of competence. In fact, when I was a child and visited southern France in conjunction with the two years I spent at the International School of Geneva, Switzerland, I was sort of a ringer for the local *club ski nautique* or water skiing team and participated in competitions we had with Italy in my age classification. I had learned to ski on a single ski and preferred that in mastering the slalom course.

You probably know that it takes a lot more power to get someone up in a water start on a single ski in terms of the larger volume of water that has to be displaced by the ski, than when you're taking off with two skis supporting you. What transpired was that—and I say this while accepting full responsibility for everything that ensued—there were far too many passengers in the boat, certainly for that altitude, which was over 6,000 feet at Lake Tahoe, at least for a single-ski take-off. I made about three or four attempts to do a water start but never managed to get above the level of the lake, so I resolved that I would instead attempt a takeoff with two skis and then drop one. This would be far easier.

Even that was not an easy takeoff, but I did get up. Once I was up on the surface, the boat planed and moved quite quickly at what felt like full throttle. A combination of very choppy water due to the wind, and my failure—perhaps due to fatigue—to realize that I should have loosened the binding more than I did, on the ski I intended to drop, caused the front tip of that ski to submerge itself while I was zipping along at quite a fast clip. The result was somewhat disastrous. I actually felt my left femur snap at the entrance to the hip socket. Down I went, and was left in the water awaiting the return of the ski boat, whose occupants were unaware of my plight and understandably made their first priority the retrieval of the ski that had come off in this mishap. [Laughter]

When the boat returned for me, it was too painful for me to move my lower torso, but I managed with my arms to raise myself to the side of the boat and ultimately be brought by ambulance to the hospital in Truckee. After waiting a few hours for another patient's true emergency to be dealt with, I was told that I did have a fracture of the femur at the entrance to the hip and would have to undergo surgery. I said to the surgeon, "Are you prepared to do that here?" He said, "We could bring you down to Reno or Sacramento." I said, "Just tell me two things, Doctor. Where did you go to med school?" And, "How any times have you done this before?" He'd gone to med school at UC Davis, I believe, and told me he had done this type of metal implant surgery 50 or 60 times. I said, "Fine. You can give me the morphine now, and let's get it done with." [Laughter] I had the surgery, which has left me today with a several-inch steel orthotic device in my left hip but with absolutely no side effects except that once in a while it sets off a sensitive airport screening device and alarms the TSA. [Laughter] I was discharged from the hospital the following morning, once the anesthesia had worn off, and I enjoyed the rest of my visit, Sunday and Monday, with my hosts—although, of course, I was somewhat immobilized.

Then the question of getting back to San Francisco arose. I wanted to demonstrate that there would not be any lingering incapacity on my part required by a lengthy convalescence and therefore was eager to return in time to preside over the court's Wednesday petition conference. The marshal, Harry Kinney, viewed this as another challenge that he would rise to. He secured a law enforcement van, which was necessary to accommodate my full-length plaster cast, and equipped the rear of the vehicle with numerous large overstuffed pillows to cushion me during the four-to-five-hour drive back to San Francisco. Like most law-enforcement types, Harry was prepared to affix a code name to this logistical exercise and told me that the plan acquired the moniker "Operation Pasha" because of the pillow furbishments.

When I did show up for conference, my fellow justices—having previously learned of my accident—appeared to be taken somewhat by surprise by my presence at the conference table. During the weeks that followed, I continued to honor various speaking commitments that I had made around the state. Even though my formal set of visits to the 58 counties had been completed, there were other appearances I had to make and, although on crutches, I managed to travel around.

There was even a cartoon—and this brings us around to the subject of trial court funding—that appeared in *The Recorder* portraying me airborne in the course of my water skiing accident, with a very recognizable Governor Pete Wilson at the controls of the speedboat, making a sharp turn and derailing my plans for trial court state funding legislation that I was pursuing at the time. [Laughter] That was a bit cruel, but I still got a laugh out of it.

What did this do to your running career?

Fortunately, with the assistance of physical therapy, I made a remarkably rapid and complete recovery from this injury. The extent of my recovery was most graphically illustrated by the fact that about five months after the accident, in January of 1998, there was a California judicial administration conference that was held in Monterey. Before the formal sessions got underway, a race was held at dawn, and I won first place. I thought being able to do that so soon after this accident was a testimonial to the fine medical care and physical therapy I had received, and also to the benefit of being in decent shape and being as persistent in my efforts at recovery as I was trying to be in many other efforts.

All in all my recovery was almost as speedy as Pete Wilson's conversion to state trial court funding. He ultimately signed that legislation. The bill was passed by the legislature while I was at the State Bar convention, still recuperating on crutches, in September 1997 in San Diego, about to give a version of my State of the Judiciary address to the State Bar conference of delegates. This was very exciting, last-minute news. It was one of those occasions when the clocks in the legislative chambers had been deliberately stopped because the Senate and the Assembly were compelled by a constitutional provision to conclude their sessions by that date at midnight.

The passage of our bill during this all-night session of the legislature caused me to totally rewrite the speech. My principal attorney, Beth Jay, was with me, and we changed the language to indicate that state trial court funding had been achieved and how significant it would be for all sorts of reforms that would be relevant to the judiciary, to the bar, and to the public served by the courts. Then, after I dictated to her the changes in the speech as she typed them on her laptop, she had to run around that Saturday morning to find a printer that would connect with her laptop. I received the speech, literally still warm in my hands out of the printer, just moments before I was to deliver it. This was a very dramatic conclusion to my efforts to obtain state trial court funding.

Once the legislature passed on the funding, how tough a sell was Governor Wilson, in fact?

We had meetings, and naturally there has always been a fairly automatic tendency by many legislators, many governors, and many persons in the Department of Finance, to say, "Let's try to shove as much of the funding burden as we can onto the counties," and, "Why do we want to have the state assume something more?" That certainly was the trend and was something we had to overcome. On the other hand, there was increasing recognition of the plight of the counties and the need to provide them with some sort of fiscal relief. One of the winning arguments was that there existed in theory—but needed to exist in fact—a true and independent third branch of government. I committed that there would be accountability to Sacramento if funding were provided by the state and that we would be in a position to know how and where it was being disbursed. Under the existing system, there had been no way of knowing how, and how much, the individual counties were funding their municipal and superior courts and what sweetheart deals existed between judges and county boards of supervisors. I knew there certainly were some of those arrangements.

I believe that Governor Wilson was sold on state trial court funding on the basis of fiscal responsibility and the overall benefit to the state and to the judicial branch.

Back to the State Bar meeting for a moment; how did they receive this news, hot off the press quite literally, about the trial court funding?

I remember that there was visible jubilation. People stood up and clapped and yelled. The timing was very dramatic, because although the bill was something that clearly was of the most direct benefit to the judiciary, it also benefited the bar in ways I had tried to make clear as I had lobbied for this measure with bar associations and legislators in the preceding months. The delegates seemed genuinely proud and overjoyed at the news and viewed it as their own victory and not just one for the judiciary. This community of interest was something I tried very hard to achieve on many occasions, and I believe successfully. I enjoyed a wonderful partnership with the State Bar during my tenure. Its leadership was extremely supportive when we were advancing reforms of either a structural or procedural nature. They also were very supportive of judicial independence and adequate court funding, and were resistant to cuts in court services that would affect them and their clients. Of course, on this occasion, I told them, "You are the very first persons to know this outside the Capitol building." They were thrilled to be included in this recognition and celebration of something that they had helped us achieve.

This victory certainly wasn't all my own doing, nor just the Judicial Council's and the A.O.C.'s. It was a real collaborative effort with the bar and county government, too. I want to stress the vital role played by CSAC, the California State Association of Counties. Naturally, CSAC viewed this as an important county relief measure. It was a question of marshaling various constituents. I found, as a general matter on countless subjects, that to the extent—through liaison meetings with different groups, whether part of the judiciary, the bar, or other organizations—we could get together behind a proposal, the force of our input to the legislature and the governor was much, much more than just the sum of the parts. That was certainly true in getting the bar, the counties, the sheriffs, and others on board to support state funding for the trial courts and the other efforts we were promoting.

With all those parties speaking with one voice, someone's got to listen, in a sense. It was a dramatic end to your tour around California, with the hip business, but it's fascinating how it played out, as it happened, in tandem with substantial results from that trip. What else did you learn and capitalize upon from those county visits?

It was, as I indicated, something that started out as a learning opportunity for me, to better enable me to perform my responsibilities as Chief Justice of the state, but it soon evolved into a plan for much-needed structural reforms. Aside from fostering a feeling of inclusiveness—in making judges and, equally important, the court staff feel like part of a greater statewide effort to improve the system of justice for the public we serve—the court visits truly did lead to specific reforms. Of course, the main ones structurally were first, the switch from county-based funding to state funding of our trial courts; second, the unification of superior, municipal, and justice courts into one level of trial court; and third, the transfer of ownership of the courthouses in California from the counties to the state under judicial branch management.

Let me say a word about unification, reflecting on the conditions that I observed during these visits. Very frequently, the courthouses were shared by the superior court and the municipal or justice court. I would find at one end of the courthouse a civil filing window for municipal court, at the other end a filing window for superior court civil matters, and the same duplication for criminal. I also saw duplicate jury pools and jury commissioners; duplicate interpreter services; duplicate purchasing of supplies; municipal court judges who, despite diligent attention to their duties, might be going home at two o'clock because they had finished their caseload of misdemeanors that were ready for trial that day or their preliminary hearings, while their colleagues at the other end of the building in superior court were overloaded with last-day cases facing potential dismissal. It became apparent to me that a merger or unification of the two levels of court—two levels but three courts, with the justice courts—would be highly desirable in terms of saving taxpayer dollars but also in having some of those savings employed not only to increase the efficiency and speed of court proceedings but also to improve and extend certain services to the public, thereby expanding their access to justice in ways that had not been available and perhaps not affordable before. Trial court unification—the merger of 220 separate superior, municipal, and justice courts into a single level of trial court—was achieved by our convincing the legislature to place before the voters an amendment to the California Constitution. The measure was approved by a two-thirds vote at the June 1998 election, becoming the second of our three basic structural reforms.

There was also the question of what to do with the status of court employees, who were county employees. After I appointed a commission to study the matter, a new status was arrived at. They weren't going to remain county employees. They weren't going to become state employees. The category, court employees, was established. That was part of the whole realignment.

Then ultimately, what took a few years to fully materialize, was the third of the three major structural reforms, the transfer of the approximately 530 court buildings and facilities from county ownership and maintenance— "maintenance" in quotation marks, in some instances—to state ownership under judicial branch management. This was one of the largest real estate transactions that had occurred anywhere in the United States, involving about 19 million square feet.

In the aftermath of this legislation, I persuaded the legislature and the governor, even though the state was then in difficult economic times, to authorize the issuance of $5 billion in courthouse construction bonds, which would be supported by revenue to be generated by the courts through new and increased fines, fees, and forfeitures. The bond issue therefore would not negatively impact the state's beleaguered general fund. Of course, the judicial branch needed these resources to enable us to take care of those courthouses, now that they were ours, and to replace and augment existing facilities. We prioritized among these hundreds of courthouses, doing more or less a triage. There were some facilities, roughly around 60, that were basically unsafe—even putting aside security issues. Some had asbestos or mold problems that were health endangering, and others might pancake even in a moderate earthquake. There were others with defects that were not as severe, and still others that just needed expansion.

A whole program was developed for refurbishment and, in some instances, demolition and replacement of the state's newly acquired court facilities.

Those were the basic structural changes in the judicial system that I would ascribe to these court visits. Of course, a host of other reforms, which we'll talk about in another session, were made possible by the structural reforms that gave us the resources and the means to perform the courts' mission of preserving and enhancing the public's access to justice. There are all sorts of improvements such as jury reform, specialized courts, assistance to unrepresented litigants, and other services that would not, in my opinion, have been feasible had we not structurally created a true judicial branch.

As you say, many of these came to fruition quite a bit later. It took you a long time to put them through. But it is fascinating to trace how many of them do come out of this first year and your relatively unplanned announcement that you would go to every part of the state. Is there anything you would have done differently, looking back?

I don't think so. There was no grand plan or strategy. With the able assistance of Bill Vickrey and the A.O.C. staff, I planned a schedule for the court visits. It was somewhat ad hoc, based in part on when people were ready to receive us, combining various visits geographically, and trying to meet my other commitments and responsibilities—fitting the visits in—because I was also flying back east twice a year for the Conference of Chief Justices and occasionally for other meetings. It all had to be coordinated.

These visits brought home to judges throughout the state the idea that I was their Chief Justice as well. I wasn't concerned only with the Supreme Court, and wasn't just a guy coming up from Los Angeles who would be focused only on the L.A. scene or on the largest courts; I cared just as much about those tiny courts serving counties that had just a few thousand inhabitants and only two judges. There were some judges in Los Angeles who, I believe, never ended up fully appreciating the circumstance that—as I viewed my responsibility—I had to act as Chief Justice of California, Chief Justice for all the users of the court system in the state, and that I couldn't show any particular "loyalty" as they may have viewed it, or preference, for my alma mater, Los Angeles. I had just as much responsibility for each court in the state—small or large, rural or urban—as I did for my own home county.

###

Chapter 10

Administering California's Judicial Branch of Government
September 8, 2011

Let's return today to 1996, when you first became Chief Justice of California. We talked about your first-year travels to the 58 counties in California, but let's return to the beginning. I'd like you to start off by saying a few words about your overall approach to your new role as Chief Justice.

I found, perhaps not consciously, that I was approaching some things differently, even in the area of decision making, than I had as an associate justice. There is something about having the responsibility of presiding over the court— even speaking only of its opinion-rendering responsibilities—that causes one, or at least caused me, to feel more of an institutional responsibility as opposed to just writing for myself. Although obviously when I was assigned a case and was writing as an associate justice, I was attempting to garner a majority of the court to adopt my views. Nonetheless, there still was a difference once I became chief. Although prior to becoming chief it was never a matter for me—or, I believe, for most justices on any appellate court of our state—of just venting one's own spleen, you did tend to think more of advancing your position, as opposed to speaking for the court as an institution. But I certainly assumed the latter function once I became chief. That included assigning certain types of cases to myself, as we discussed earlier, where the broad shoulders of whoever was chief should be employed to deflect the controversy and perhaps the conflict with other branches of government that might emanate from a decision. So that's a different way I had of looking at things, certainly in that context, than I had before as an associate justice.

To what extent did this surprise you?

It just seemed to gravitate naturally from my administrative role as Chief Justice of the branch. In the latter capacity it very soon became apparent to me how important it was to develop cooperative relationships with the other two branches—which might necessitate being diplomatic, even in the language employed in an opinion—although the desire to be diplomatic would never affect the result to be reached. The need became more apparent, in assigning a case to another justice or in writing the case myself, to take into account the circumstance that the interests of the entire judicial branch might be affected by the manner in which an opinion was worded. This perspective on my part just seemed to evolve naturally, but I always kept the two functions very much separate and apart when I'd go to Sacramento. Nevertheless, I occasionally encountered an unawareness or desire on the part of legislators to overlook the distinction between the Chief Justice as decision maker and the Chief Justice as administrator and leader of the branch. That distinction was not always as obvious to others as it should have been or, if obvious, it was sometimes ignored by those legislators whom I had to stop from discussing pending cases.

What priorities did you have at the outset?

I always viewed my first and foremost function as being a decision maker, as one of the seven justices on the high court. I thought that was the essence of my responsibilities as a member of the Supreme Court of California. It also happened to be what I most enjoyed. I can't say that my trips to Sacramento were the favorite part of my duties, although many of those visits were very pleasant and I developed some excellent relationships with persons in the other two branches. I certainly would have to say that one of the most gratifying and satisfying aspects of my tenure as Chief Justice—and of my entire professional career—was achieving the rather monumental and historic structural reforms to the judicial branch that you and I have discussed. Those often resulted from battles that were initially lost in one or more legislative sessions, only to squeak through the next session by a hair or come down to the last minutes of a legislative session. That certainly was illustrated by the passage of the Trial Court Funding Act of 1997. It was an overwhelmingly exuberant feeling of satisfaction to get that through after overcoming many obstacles.

Having said that, the day-to-day tasks that I most enjoyed were working on opinions—reviewing drafts of my colleagues, making suggestions, and especially working on my own opinions—working with a very, very qualified legal staff to craft opinions that would provide future guidance to appellate courts, trial courts, the bar, and the public. Another among the most enjoyable activities was presiding over the court's weekly conference, because that involved the warm relationships that had developed among the seven of us, as colleagues and ultimately good friends.

I'd like to return to your colleagues momentarily. May I ask, though, what sort of advice or transitional discussion did you have from Chief Justice Lucas?

There was very little that was actually formalized. What Chief Justice Lucas did was confer on me certain responsibilities in designated areas. Those include some things that we have already talked about during our discussion of my years as an associate justice, whether having the lead responsibility for coming up with some ideas to expedite the court's handling of capital cases, serving on the Judicial Council, having the opportunity to go to Sacramento to confer with the other two branches—but not in any way, of course, superseding Chief Justice Lucas' role in those areas. I benefited greatly from this important type of training or orientation. There were studies he turned over to me at the end, from his files. Of course, there was a certain continuity provided by his excellent staff, some of whom I asked to join my chambers. These staff members assisted me quite a bit in picking up the responsibilities that he had carried as Chief Justice.

Perhaps we'll talk for a few minutes about the research attorneys who worked on your own staff. I know you mentioned before you had brought a couple with you from the Court of Appeal, so those two had been with you already for a few years on the California Supreme Court. I'm speaking of Greg Wolff and Darien Pope. But from among those on Chief Justice Lucas' staff?

There were some very fine individuals. Chief Justice Lucas had a principal attorney—that was the formal designation—Beth Jay, whom I've previously mentioned and who had special responsibilities in serving as liaison to the criminal defense entities that were part of the formalized structure: the Office of the State Public Defender, the California Appellate Project, and then ultimately the Habeas Corpus Resource Center that we helped establish. She also served as the Chief Justice's liaison to the State Bar and to the Commission on Judicial Performance, and advisor on Judicial Council matters. It was very helpful to have her on my staff. She also assisted Lucas in speech writing, and I retained her in that capacity as well.

My own head of chambers as an associate justice, Hal Cohen, came with me to head the chief's chambers and in that capacity held the position of supervising attorney for the entire staff attorney component of the California Supreme Court. That was a major responsibility. Hal was an incredible resource and was universally respected on the court for his many talents. He had been the second-ranking student in his first-year class at Harvard Law School and had come out to clerk for one year in 1969. After I had assumed the chief's duties, we ended up celebrating Hal's thirtieth year at the California Supreme Court. When he ultimately retired because he wanted to pursue, at least part time, some other interests, he agreed to continue working in the capacity of a retired annuitant, more or less half time. Freed of his administrative responsibilities, he continued to provide excellent legal work as a staff attorney working on major cases with me and serving as an institutional memory for the court. He could remember what and when and by whom various things transpired over the course of his decades on the court. I'm pleased to say that my successor has retained Hal Cohen in that capacity. With half-time responsibilities—even aside from the brilliant qualitative nature of his work—he's as productive quantitatively as most staff members charged with full-time duties.

There were two other individuals who, along with Beth Jay, my principal attorney, and Hal Cohen, were part of what I would call the administrative component of my staff—although they worked on opinions as well. Jake Dear initially assisted Hal in some of the internal administrative responsibilities as a member of the chief's staff. Then Jake succeeded Hal, becoming head of chambers and therefore head of the Supreme Court attorney staff. Jake has truly exceptional research skills, especially when it comes to uncovering historical authority from earlier decades and centuries.

Once Jake assumed his full administrative responsibilities, Alice Collins very effectively assumed the duties of assistant supervising attorney, including recruiting and supervising the one or two law school student externs who would volunteer to work in our chambers each semester. Both Jake and Alice continued to do excellent work on the court's opinions. Those are the persons with whom I worked who were supervising members of my chambers' legal staff. Jake and Alice, like Beth, I had retained from Chief Justice Lucas' staff.

I also took with me other staff members with whom I had worked as an associate justice: Mary Wilcox came with me and then ultimately left the court; David Miller worked for me when I was an associate justice and Chief Justice, and then ultimately went on to our criminal central staff. With me for a while was Dennis Maio, who came from Justice Mosk's staff after the justice passed away. Dennis ultimately left for private practice. Ron Elsberry served on my staff for a while and ultimately chose to leave the court. Melissa Johnson joined my staff on a part-time basis. She had worked with the Administrative Office of the Courts. Sara Spero and Neil Gupta joined me from the court's central staffs. Two individuals joined my staff from the private sector, Inna Katsen and Emmalena Quesada. We've already mentioned Greg Wolff, who left my staff to become head of chambers for Justice Carlos Moreno, and Darien Pope, who moved on to central staff. The chief's chambers carries eight research attorney positions, some of which, as was the case with me, can be part time so that at various points I had nine individuals rather than eight working in that capacity.

I want to stress that a vital component in managing the workload of the various chambers were the judicial assistants. The Chief Justice has two executive assistants and the associate justices each have one. Luckily, I started off as chief with Janet Ellenberg, who came with me from my position as an associate justice with substantial prior experience with Justice Broussard and the A.O.C., and who was joined by Gale Tunnell, who had worked with Chief Lucas and previously at the court and at the A.O.C. Ultimately both Janet and Gale retired after many years of excellent service. Kate Lucchio and AhMoi Kim replaced them after receiving valuable training from their predecessors, and did an excellent job in carrying out their unique responsibilities in the Chief Justice's chambers. Those duties are very complex, because the assistants are not only scheduling secretaries; they field a wide variety of calls and requests and perform legal secretaries' work as well as other duties, some of which involve the Commission on Judicial Appointments. Apart from listing these tasks, I can't even begin to describe the complexity of the work involved in the preparation and circulation of legal memoranda of all sorts at the Supreme Court—calendar memoranda, opinions, memos, various analyses, and administrative material. The judicial assistants are kept very, very busy.

I never in my life as a lower court judge imagined that I could keep one executive assistant or personal secretary busy. I came to learn that as Chief Justice I had too much work even for two. I'm afraid I ran them ragged on certain weeks, and we ended up getting some additional assistance, whether it was from Janet or Gale coming in to help after they retired or from someone from the clerk's office, because there was such an enormous amount of varied work requiring specialized training and self-developed expertise. But we all worked very harmoniously, even under the most trying of circumstances.

One of the things that we've talked about and will probably talk about some more is the degree of collegiality among the justices. I always made a point of instructing both the legal and the executive-assistant component of my own staff that there are a lot of very bright, maybe even brilliant, individuals available to work at the Supreme Court. However, equally important—taking the brilliance and dedication as a prerequisite—was that they possess excellent skills in terms of being able to work well with each other as part of our staff and, just as importantly, with the members of other staffs at the Supreme Court, whether it was the staffs in the chambers of the other justices, the three central staffs, the clerk's office, the reporter of decision's office, or the judicial library. These were all vital components of the Supreme Court's structure, and I expected everyone to work well with each other and show a cooperative and constructive attitude toward suggestions or even criticisms that might come their way. I was always proud of my staff for adhering to those standards, as did—with just a couple of rare exceptions here and there—the various staffs of the other components of the court. Being able to work in a fully collegial atmosphere was essential to the functioning of the court, and especially so under the difficult circumstances that arose from the complexity and difficulty of the issues and matters that occasionally came up against deadlines. Although I did not conduct regular meetings of my entire chambers staff, all of us enjoyed going out to lunch to celebrate each staff member's birthday.

How did you go about setting the tone for this yourself? What was your style of interacting with your own staff?

I met with them one on one and usually would give them no direction at the outset in terms of how I wanted a case to be written up. I would have it quite understood that their responsibility was to have the court be guided only by where the law would take us on a case. Sometimes there were opportunities to go one way or the other, because the statutory or case law was fluid and there were important policy considerations on both sides of an issue. Then I might express a preference saying, "If we can, in an intellectually honest way, proceed along this route, x rather than y would be my preference. But again, let the law take us where it must." I did tell staff that I wanted them to always be collegial in drafting the formal written responses that I would circulate to material coming out of other chambers—and in their oral interactions with other chambers, even if they didn't feel that another staff member was treating them as politely as they should. They were not to respond negatively in kind, nor take pride of authorship to the point where criticism would be resented or where one would stop trying to accommodate—not stopping to count at four votes, but aiming for seven if possible, through accommodation.

I also took the initial step when I became Chief Justice—among the various outreach efforts that we'll talk about with officeholders and organizations outside the court system—of scheduling a meeting with each of the six other chambers and also with each of the central staffs, indicating to them what my objectives were as Chief Justice, but just as importantly my interest in hearing from them what their concerns might be concerning the operation of the court, things they thought could be done better, along with proposed solutions to existing problems. These meetings were important to me in formulating some of the policies and attitudes that I adopted as I assumed my duties as Chief Justice. I believe they also were helpful in establishing an atmosphere of trust and goodwill among individual chambers and with the chief's chambers, and in trying to instill the idea of teamwork on behalf of the court as opposed to seven separate law offices, which is what the arrangement ends up being in some courts.

You say part of those meetings was to articulate your objectives as chief. What were you emphasizing about your own objectives at that time?

I wanted to see how we could continue the efforts to modernize and expedite the exchange of views and ultimately the production of opinions for the court, maintaining the high quality that the court was known for but also attempting to reduce unnecessary delay. Chief Justice Lucas had instituted some important procedures that included monitoring the status of cases so they didn't just disappear into a dark hole. These included a series of lists designated by the color of the paper on which they appeared: the salmon sheet, which showed the status of cases actually under submission, that is, cases in which oral argument had occurred—which with only a rare exception is the occasion at which a case is taken under submission. Of course, that's important to monitor because of the 90-day rule, so that the production of majority and minority opinions occurs at a suitable pace to provide for an exchange of views but also adhering to the court's obligation to file its opinions on time, as required by the constitution. Then the blue list describing all cases in which a calendar memorandum—which is basically our court's term for a draft opinion or bench memorandum—has circulated, and the status of the preliminary responses due from the other six justices. Then the yellow list, which includes all the cases in which review has been granted but a calendar memo has not yet circulated. There are some other lists here and there that keep track of capital habeas corpus petitions and related motions and applications, but those three lists were the most important improvements that my predecessor instituted in tracking the case flow of the court. I tinkered with those lists, trying to further improve them, but basically they remained an innovation instituted by Chief Justice Lucas.

When you were having these initial meetings with your judicial colleagues and their staffs and with the various central staffs, what were you trying to accomplish, broadly?

I wanted to establish open lines of communication, so that the members of the various staffs, whether they were chambers staff or central staff, would feel encouraged to communicate to me and to my staff what might not be working as well as it should be, and any suggestions to improve the system. I believed conversely that this approach also would make these staffs even more receptive to what would come out of the chief's chambers in terms of changes of procedures. The objectives in setting up these meetings were qualitative in terms of improving work product, but they also were aimed at efficiency—at having things move faster without rushing them in any way, while never sacrificing quality for quantity or speed. I also set up occasional working groups to deal with particular problems at the court, and would have each justice designate one member of his or her staff to join that group so that we could come to a solution, sometimes in an informal way instead of having overly formalized approaches.

What did you learn from these meetings, from these various colleagues and staff members? What were their hopes for you and for the court?

There's an exceptional esprit de corps among the staff attorneys and also among the judicial assistants. Attorneys who work for the Supreme Court—and the same is true to a large degree of those who work for the Courts of Appeal— are persons who have chosen to forgo the much higher compensation that, with their high qualifications, they could expect to receive in the private sector. They've done that for a variety of reasons. I'd say first and foremost is the intellectual and general personal satisfaction of working at the highest court of the state on issues of paramount legal and social significance. I believe many of these persons are also very pleased not to have to deal with managing partners and clients and not to be concerned with billable hours, but I would say that first and foremost is the satisfaction of working in an atmosphere of constructive collaboration on highly significant matters. Most would be earning much more in the private sector. They receive no public recognition for what they're working on. No one knows that they worked on such-and-such major decision, so they labor out of dedication with the only credit and recognition coming from the justices and the other staff of the Supreme Court along with their own sense of personal satisfaction. It takes a very special breed of individual to do that. I believe it is about as noble a calling as one could imagine in the legal profession.

What do you recall of what they might have communicated with you when you first became chief in the way of ideas or suggestions, changes, what should stay the same?

A lot of it was fairly technical in terms of court processes. Some of the changes that ended up being made have become routine and are now taken for granted as part of the current operating procedures of the court, but they were important to them and important to me at the time. On the other hand, some of the other outreach efforts that I made, particularly with the press and with lawyer organizations, resulted in much more graphic changes.

Maybe even before we set the stage for those dealings with the outside world, as it were, perhaps we could return to the subject of the transition from Chief Justice Lucas in that he had his staff prepare for you a list of the Chief Justice's responsibilities. This runs to about a page and a half, and I wonder if we can take a look at this and lay out the whole realm that you were now responsible for?

Seeing the list enumerating the specific duties of the Chief Justice— prepared for me by Lucas' staff, I believe by principal attorney Beth Jay—was somewhat daunting, even though I had a pretty good idea about the breadth and complexity of the Chief Justice's duties. The various categories totaled up to be about two dozen areas of responsibility, and some of those had many subparts, so it was a bit overwhelming to see them laid out like that. Before actually going through these responsibilities, it might be good to note, first of all, the fact that the Chief Justice occupies several different roles and that various responsibilities reflect one role or another. There is a widespread lack of information, and I might call it confusion—even within the judicial branch—about the different roles of the person who serves as Chief Justice and the capacity in which he or she may be taking a particular action or exercising a particular responsibility.

First of all, of course, is the role of being a decision maker, one of seven justices and only one. There is the numerical reality that in deciding a case the Chief Justice's vote is no greater than that of any of his or her colleagues, obviously. Nonetheless, there is something qualitatively if not quantitatively different about the Chief Justice's role as decision maker. When I attended the opening of the new quarters of the Court of Appeal for the Fifth Appellate District in Fresno, I noted the plaque dedicating the courtroom to that court's former presiding justice, George Brown. It reads: "To be presiding justice . . . is unique and different from being an associate justice. It is true that it is only one seat, is only one vote, and only one signature, but it is always the seat in the center, the last vote, and the final signature." Although the role of the Chief Justice in the decision making of the California Supreme Court is reflected in only a single vote, he or she has a second role of being the presiding justice of the court, which is manifested in several ways. In presiding over the oral argument, he or she may have an impact upon the conduct of the arguments and ultimately upon the justices' post-oral-argument vote on the case, which takes place at a conference presided over by the chief immediately after each half-day session of oral argument. These functions may have a bearing on the resolution of the case.

The chief's function in assigning cases is another very significant responsibility as the court's presiding justice. That generally takes place within a day or two of review being granted, although obviously the assignment of the case is tentative. It's subject to the assigned justice being able to muster a majority of the court for his or her point of view. If that majority doesn't materialize, the Chief Justice reassigns the case. As I mentioned before, once in a while reassignment of a case occurs even after oral argument has taken place, when the assigned justice loses the majority and is unwilling or unable to accommodate the new majority and has to relinquish the case. When the Chief Justice assigns it to another justice under those circumstances, it's a very busy time indeed, with the 90-day clock running. But the chief's role in making the initial—and usually final—assignment of the case can be of crucial significance, because the odds favor the justice who has first crack at the case. Unlike the practice on the U.S. Supreme Court, where the Chief Justice assigns the case only if the chief is in the majority and otherwise the senior associate justice in the majority assigns the case, on the California Supreme Court the Chief Justice assigns the case in all situations, unless of course he or she happens to be recused from participation in the case. Also significant, in addition to presiding at oral argument, is the chief's function of presiding at the weekly petition conference—where the decision is made whether to grant review—as well as at the court's monthly administrative conference, reflecting the chief's leading role in establishing internal operating procedures for the court and proposing formal rule and policy changes.

A third role is acting as Chief Justice of California. Article VI of the California Constitution, the article that deals with the judicial branch of government, speaks in section two of the Supreme Court consisting of, in these words, "the Chief Justice of California and six associate justices." This phrase expressly recognizes that the Chief Justice has a major role apart from presiding over the court on which he or she sits, namely being head of the co-equal, independent third branch of government. That role frequently is overlooked at the state level just as it is at the federal level. We frequently see references to the Chief Justice of the U.S. Supreme Court, whereas his title is Chief Justice of the United States, just as the position of the state counterpart is sometimes referred to incompletely as Chief Justice of the California Supreme Court rather than its full and accurate title, Chief Justice of California.

How well is that distinction understood among the rest of us?

Not very well, I'm afraid. The press more often than not gets it wrong in that matter of nomenclature. I'm not saying it's of vital importance, but it's not fully understood. It probably does cause some confusion among the reading public, or the listening public in terms of the electronic media, because people probably wonder, "Why is the Chief Justice of the Supreme Court setting forth some rule or policy that relates to trial courts?" The answer is that the Chief Justice is doing so not in his or her capacity as Chief Justice of the California Supreme Court but instead in the capacity of Chief Justice of the State of California, head of the judicial branch of government, which of course extends to and through each of our 58 counties. To that extent, nomenclature is important, because use of an inaccurate or incomplete term probably helps foster the confusion and already-deficient understanding of most of our citizenry concerning our judicial branch and its role in our state government.

A theme we will return to time and again, no doubt.

Then, moving on to a fourth role of the Chief Justice, he or she serves as chair of the Judicial Council of California. That body was created by our California Constitution in 1926 in the sixth article, which deals with the judicial branch. I think it's important—in order to lay the groundwork for some of our later discussions—that I mention that in section 6 of article VI, the Judicial Council is given the responsibility for the statewide administration of our court system. That doesn't mean there are no matters relegated to local court administration—there are and there should be. But as to matters that are properly the subject of statewide court administration, those come within the authority of the Judicial Council. Some judges around the state are, in many instances, either unaware of or reluctant to recognize the authority of the Judicial Council, which may be a reflection of the fact that, although this body has been in existence for 85 years, only in recent years has it more fully assumed the exercise of the powers that the people of the state gave it and set forth in the constitution.

The constitution provides that the Judicial Council consists of the Chief Justice and various other judges at all levels. All of the judicial appointments to the council are made by the Chief Justice for specified terms; also four members of the State Bar are appointed to the council by the State Bar Board of Governors; and two members are appointed by the legislature, one from each house. Article VI specifies that the council has the authority to appoint the Administrative Director of the Courts, who performs such functions as are delegated by the council and the Chief Justice.

Significantly, the constitution provides:

> To improve the administration of justice the Council shall survey judicial business and make recommendations to the courts, make recommendations annually to the Governor and Legislature, adopt rules for court administration, practice and procedure, and perform other functions prescribed by statute. The rules adopted shall not be inconsistent with statute. The Chief Justice shall seek to expedite judicial business and to equalize the work of judges. The Chief Justice may provide for the assignment of any judge to another court but only with the judge's consent if the court is of lower jurisdiction. A retired judge who consents may be assigned to any court.

And then finally, "Judges shall report to the Council as the Chief Justice directs concerning the condition of judicial business in their courts. They shall cooperate with the Council and hold court as assigned." It's remarkable how many judges are unaware of the scope of the authority of the Judicial Council. They sometimes knowingly, sometimes unknowingly, insinuate that the council is exercising authority that it lacks, when in fact that authority is rather explicit. Chairing the Judicial Council obviously is a very important role for the Chief Justice.

One of the sentences I read provides: "The Chief Justice may provide for the assignment of any judge to another court." Now, when the Chief Justice does that, he or she is not acting as head of the Judicial Council and is not acting on a subject that requires action by the Judicial Council as a whole. Nor is the assignment function exercised as Chief Justice of the Supreme Court. It is exercised unilaterally, in the role of Chief Justice of California, as overseer of the judicial branch. Adding to the confusion is the circumstance that the assigned judges program has for administrative convenience been placed within the Administrative Office of the Courts. Although the A.O.C. as a general matter serves as staff to the Judicial Council, the assignments unit itself does not serve as staff to the council. Even though it is part of the A.O.C., it serves and operates, in effect, and for logistical purposes, as part of the Chief Justice's personal staff, even though that unit has been placed for supervisory purposes within the A.O.C. structure. Its function, however, is to assist the Chief Justice in exercising his or her own unilateral assignment power. This administrative structure is necessitated by the fact that we have more than 400 retired judges serving in the assigned judges program in addition to active judges serving by assignment in a county other than their own county. These assignments involve a tremendous amount of paperwork and telephone communication with the local courts and the assigned judges. The Chief Justice and his or her own personal chambers staff would be overwhelmed if these tasks had to be performed without the valuable assistance and expertise of the assignment unit.

Among the other capacities or roles in which the Chief Justice serves is as chair of the Commission on Judicial Appointments. Starting my first full day on the job, I presided for the first time over one of these hearings, as we talked about last time, with the confirmation hearing for Supreme Court Associate Justice Janice Rogers Brown on May 2, 1996, and extending through several hearings conducted during my last several weeks in office that included the confirmation hearing for my successor, Chief Justice Tani Cantil-Sakauye. I mentioned, in conjunction with your question at an earlier session concerning my own confirmation hearing as Chief Justice, that Justice Stanley Mosk served as acting chair of the Commission on Judicial Appointments at the hearing because of the fact that Chief Justice Lucas had left office, and therefore, of course, Chief Justice Lucas no longer could exercise the authority as chair of that commission. Why was it different with regard to the confirmation of my successor? The reason is that I chose not to retire before the expiration of my term. The constitution provides that if a justice of the Supreme Court, whether it's the Chief Justice or an associate justice—and the same provision applies to justices of our Courts of Appeal—does not file papers to stand for reelection by August 15, the governor shall nominate a person who, after evaluation by the State

Bar's Commission on Judicial Nominees Evaluation, has to undergo a Commission on Judicial Appointments hearing and then stand for confirmation before the voters at the next November election. If confirmed, the nominee takes office only on the Monday following January 1, upon the expiration of his or her predecessor's term of office. My term of office, like the term of the governor who appointed my successor, expired at midnight on January 2, but the confirmation hearing held under the procedures I just described took place while I still was Chief Justice and chair of the Commission on Judicial Appointments.

Another matter of minor confusion is that there are certain actions that are taken by the Supreme Court as a whole and not by the Chief Justice. Although I had hundreds of occasions to make appointments to the Judicial Council and to various Judicial Council advisory committees and task forces, appointments to the Commission on Judicial Performance, the constitutional entity that's charged with the discipline of judges, are made not by the Chief Justice but by the Supreme Court as a whole. Very frequently there was misinformation in the press about an appointment to the Commission on Judicial Performance having been made by the Chief Justice or by the Judicial Council or by the chair of the Judicial Council. It was none of those. That was an appointment made by the Supreme Court. This just illustrates the complexity of the various and sometimes overlapping roles of the Chief Justice.

In your time how did the court as a whole go about settling upon those appointments?

They would be taken up, generally, at one of our administrative conferences. I described the weekly petition conference at which the court would decide in which cases to grant review. Usually the third Wednesday of each month the petition conference is followed by an administrative conference, and matters such as an appointment to the Commission on Judicial Performance would be brought up at such a conference. Often there were formalized rules or policies that the court as a whole would adopt at the administrative conferences. There were other internal policies and procedures that the Chief Justice himself or herself would have authority to promulgate unilaterally, although depending upon what was involved and whether it was something of a purely technical nature or was more substantive, the Chief Justice might consult the other justices and discuss the matter before acting. There were many things that involved minutiae that the other justices would not be interested in and, of course, all of these changes would be placed in the court's "Internal Policy Documents"—a truly internal compilation to be distinguished from the published "Internal Operating Practices and Procedures"—that were available to guide the justices, the chambers and central staffs, and the clerk's office.

But on the Commission on Judicial Performance, in terms of names to nominate, people to consider, where did those come from?

Any justice might propose a name, and I often would circulate a memo inquiring, "How about so-and-so? A bio is attached. Please, if you have some other possible suggestions, circulate them within a couple of days before our next administrative conference." Sometimes names would come up informally. A judge might say, "I know there's going to be a vacancy, and how about so-and-so?" Then the paperwork would circulate. Very often there was only a single candidate considered by the court, but there was always the opportunity for any justice to put any name out for consideration. The same thing was true for appointments to various court committees, whether it was the Supreme Court's ethics committee or some other. The appointment decision often was arrived at informally and sometimes just by consensus.

You did have a lot of appointing power in different areas, either on your own or, as you say here, by the court as a whole. What kinds of skills or qualifications might you be looking for, for example, on the judicial performance commission?

It was very important to have someone on that commission who had a true working understanding of the operation of our courts, of the high standards that are expected of a judge, but by the same token who had a practical understanding of the sometimes difficult conditions under which a trial judge would be called upon to exercise his or her responsibilities. Commission members were not engaged in an academic exercise. To stand in judgment on a judge, they had to have a real understanding of the system, of the day-to-day routines and responsibilities of a trial judge, but also of the challenges facing an individual judge, often under trying circumstances. So those were important considerations, especially given the circumstance that the constitution provides for the Supreme Court to appoint only three judges to the commission, who serve with two lawyer members appointed by the State Bar, and six nonjudge, nonlawyer members appointed by the governor and the legislature.

In other appointments, such as those to the Judicial Council, I was very concerned that, first of all, the individual being considered for appointment have significant administrative talent and experience because, after all, the council is in a sense an administrative agency in addition to being a policy-setting body. It also was important for me to have individuals who would be willing to heed the advice that I always would give them when I would call them up personally and indicate I was appointing them to the Judicial Council, namely, "You do not exercise your duties as a member of the Judicial Council in a representative fashion, by being concerned with how a majority of the colleagues on your particular court would want you to vote." We have the California Judges Association, which very ably exercises a representative function. As a former president of that organization I have great respect for the role that's played by that body. But that is different from the governmental function of the Judicial Council. I don't want a council member to report back that 13 judges on his or her court favor a particular measure and that 11 judges oppose it. I would tell appointees to the council, "Your constituency is the entire judicial branch and, beyond that, the public interest as a whole."

That's why I always resisted moves to make the Judicial Council—and this was somewhat of a loaded term, I believe—a "more democratic" body. Selection as a member of the Judicial Council is not, and should not be, a beauty contest or popularity contest. The council was designed to be a constitutional body that would be composed of individuals who have the talent and willingness to exercise judicial administrative authority in a competent and fair manner. When there was a move in the California Judges Association to have the constitution amended to provide for an elected Judicial Council, I resisted this strongly, feeling it would be the death knell for a truly well-functioning Judicial Council.

At one of the annual meetings of the California Judges Association, where I would engage in a Q&A session, I made a point of saying, with regard to the idea of an elected Judicial Council that was the topic of some discussion there, that if CJA were to endorse that concept, I would view such action as a declaration of war on the council. My comment shocked many people, because I was known for being diplomatic in my various communications with our justice system partners and with others. But contrary to the view of some who thought the remark must have been an inadvertent slip of the tongue or a heated outburst, it was made with considerable forethought, and it accomplished exactly what I intended. CJA's consideration of that proposal came to a halt.

What I already had done—totally on my own and well before any of this discussion of an elected Judicial Council had occurred—was to voluntarily relinquish what was the Chief Justice's unlimited and sole authority, under the constitutional language that I earlier referred to, to make these appointments to the Judicial Council. I created authority in the Judicial Council's executive committee—authority that ultimately was encompassed in the rules of the Judicial Council—to evaluate potential appointees to the Judicial Council, whether individuals who were self-nominated, or nominated by others, or perhaps recruited by the executive committee of the Judicial Council, and for the executive committee to submit to me three names for each vacant position on the Judicial Council and on the numerous Judicial Council advisory committees and task forces. I committed myself to pick the appointee from among the three candidates put forth by the executive committee for each position. At the same time, I urged that our rules embody the goal of diversity on the Judicial Council and on the committees and task forces—not only administrative experience, but geographic diversity, large and small counties, urban and rural, reflecting various aspects of the state's diverse judicial system. That extended also to gender and race and ethnicity as well—no specific formula, but just to consider those factors in the mix of potential candidates for appointment.

The executive committee would take these considerations into account in passing on to me the three nominees for each appointment. In turn, in my selection from among the nominees, I also took these considerations into account, so that we would have people who, first and foremost, were administratively qualified to exercise their duties but who additionally came from a mix of the state's judiciary and its population. That to me is a much more appropriate standard for choosing persons to participate in the administration of our judicial branch than having a popularity contest—electing a judge perhaps just because he or she achieved a degree of notoriety as the result of making some colorful pronouncement or presiding over a celebrity trial.

Popularity, without regard to administrative skills, had until recently replaced seniority in many courts as the sole standard by which presiding judges were elected by their colleagues on the trial courts. I'm happy to say—not solely because there now are rules of court adopted by the council that recommend taking into account administrative qualifications—that even on their own, judges in their local courts began to realize that it wasn't a good idea to have a judge move up to the important position of presiding judge just according to seniority. We had an illustration of that when you and I discussed my time on the L.A. Municipal Court and the tenure of Presiding Judge Joe Grillo. Happily, at least in more recent years, judges have been wise enough in many—and maybe most—instances to look for leadership qualities that the particular judge has exercised in the last few years, maybe on the court's executive committee or on statewide committees, in deciding who would be a good person to entrust as presiding judge for the next year or possibly two years, often following one or two years as assistant presiding judge.

Speaking of administrative experience, although most presiding judges come and go after serving at most a year or two in that position after a year or two as assistant presiding judge, we have very talented court executive officers who spend a lifetime career being trained and working their way up the ranks in the profession of court administration. Our presiding judges, even on courts that have hundreds of judges and thousands of employees, often have little or no formal administrative career training. For this reason—although to the chagrin of some judges not serving on the Judicial Council—I always included court executive officers in my appointments to the council and, where possible, on advisory committees and task forces.

Why did you delegate part of your authority to the Judicial Council executive committee when you could have engendered a change of standards some other way?

I really did both in the sense that I first encouraged a change in the standards, but I thought it would be very good in terms of inclusiveness and a sense of participation if this change wasn't viewed as just a unilateral fiat. So I wanted to have the standards formalized in the Judicial Council rules. Very frankly, some appointments by prior Chief Justices had been viewed as attempts to just secure the vote of a yes man on the council or as a favor, which could make the appointment process look arbitrary and diminish the stature of the council.

Some of the latter concerns also affected my views about the exercise of the Chief Justice's power when it came to assigning lower court judges to sit as justices pro tem of the Supreme Court during a vacancy or to substitute for a justice who was recused or absent due to illness. The constitution places no limits or guidelines on the chief's assignment power. Chief Justice Bird occasionally would appoint a municipal court judge to sit as a justice pro tem on the California Supreme Court. It may have appeared, and it may have been intended by her, as a democratization of the assignment process. But when Court of Appeal justices were passed over and municipal court judges with no appellate experience were put on the Supreme Court, it could not help but convey the impression that the individual was cherry-picked, either as a favor or reward to that person or perhaps with a particular result in the case in mind. Chief Justice Lucas modified that procedure substantially and was appointing, I believe, only presiding justices of the Courts of Appeal to sit as a justice pro tem on the California Supreme Court. What I did, to get away completely from the still lingering perception that such appointments might be result-oriented, was to adopt a policy now formalized by our court.

Before describing that policy, I need to point out that occasionally there would be a need for an unanticipated appointment that would arise at the last minute. I remember once Justice Mosk became ill with the flu when we had a Sacramento oral argument session. Chief Justice Lucas had the clerk circulate word that if stipulations were not forthcoming—from counsel on the cases set on that day's calendar—specifying that Justice Mosk could participate in deciding the case despite his absence, Lucas would find someone in the court building who would be available to serve last-minute, and it would be Presiding Justice Robert Puglia. Somehow the stipulations, which had been slow in coming, materialized immediately.[1] [Laughter] The policy that I'm about to describe to you that I adopted is subject, with modification, to also being applied in that last-minute situation.

Under that policy, I directed the clerk's office to prepare a list of all of the state's 105 Court of Appeal presiding justices and associate justices in alphabetical order, excluding those who had served less than one year on the appellate court. When a vacancy arose in the composition of the California Supreme Court for whatever reason, the clerk would go down that list alphabetically and notify the next appellate justice of his or her imminent appointment to serve on the case. I wouldn't even know whose name would appear on the assignment order until it was presented to me for signature. It would be the next name alphabetically. If that justice were unavailable due to his or her own oral argument schedule or recusal or being on vacation, that justice would be bypassed and the next time there was a need for a justice pro tem the clerk would automatically go back to that person, and he or she would be the next appointment if available. In the event of a last-minute need to appoint a justice pro tem to our court, the clerk was directed to select the next available justice on the list from those sitting in the immediate geographical area where the Supreme Court is holding oral argument.

How well did the policy work?

It worked very, very well. I say that, even though—and on a couple occasions I could predict this from the nature of the case—as a result of my policy, I occasionally ended up on the losing side of a 4–3 case. But I thought, more important than anything else was having the perception in the judicial and legal community and with the public that a substitute justice had not been selected with a result in mind, that it was a perfectly impartial, blind selection of who would comprise the seventh member of the court.

As an aside, what do other states do about the matter of pro tem justices at the highest levels?

That's not anything I'm actually aware of. This policy just seemed to be the best thing to follow here. I can answer with reference to the U.S. Supreme Court. They have no such procedure, so if a justice is recused and they have a 4–4 split, the opinion rendered by that court generally consists of a one-sentence

---

[1] Cal. Const., article VI, sec. 2, provides: "Concurrence of 4 judges present at the argument is necessary for a judgment." It is customary for an absent justice who participates in the case by stipulation of counsel to listen to the audiotape of the oral argument.

order stating that the judgment rendered by the lower court is affirmed by an equally divided court—a decision with no precedential effect.

I should mention that multiple recusals on our court came to be more and more of a problem. It just didn't do to appoint several pro tems to serve together on a single case. I felt that if it went to three pro tems, even, it looked rather bad. Ultimately, we had what I viewed as a real embarrassment to the court. There were four of my colleagues who owned stock in companies—not the same company, but it was somewhat of a perfect storm where recusals occurred for different reasons in the same case. Of course, it's not totally unexpected. You can have cases involving the pharmaceutical industry, let's say, as an example, or the energy industry, where several companies are involved, or the banking industry. In the case in question, the conflict-of-interest situation had evolved and became apparent to the justices only after the court had had the case under review for some time. The court ended up concluding that it really had no choice but to dismiss review of the case. This generated some substantial—and I can't say totally undeserved—negative reaction from the legal press and even the general-circulation press, because the plaintiffs' rights ended up being subordinated to the need of the court to come up with a majority of sitting justices on a case, which the court was unable to do. I don't believe, despite the protests of some persons, that we should have kept the case. The ruling that the court would have rendered wouldn't have had any kind of meaningful precedential value, because with a majority of the court consisting of temporary justices, one would never know how a majority of the sitting justices would have ruled. Frankly, this can be the situation with even one pro tem or two pro tems serving when the court is closely divided, but to a certain extent that is unavoidable.

The justices each, by state law, are required to file statements of economic interests in which they list their stock holdings and other investments. Beyond that, I had the justices update their ownership lists of securities, showing new acquisitions and divestitures of stock. Although none of them knew what their colleagues owned unless they were discussing it informally, I told them I was going to access these documents—which were a matter of public record, so anyone had a right to see them, let alone myself—and would periodically circulate among the justices a list of securities in which more than one justice held ownership, alerting the justices whose holdings would thus bring about multiple recusals in a case.

I tried to apply peer pressure to my colleagues to avoid overlapping investments. This was successful in greatly reducing the number of stocks in which more than one justice owned shares, but did not totally eliminate such conflicts. I found it totally unacceptable when we had three justices owning the same stock. I made a point of selling stock where I comprised a third member of a group of justices owning stock in the same company. I got so sick and tired of feeling, "Here I am causing a recusal," that I finally decided to just get out of the stock market. This turned out to be to my benefit, because the timing was right as the stock market was falling. I wish I had done it a few months earlier. Then I would have been a financial genius. [Laughter]

I could guess, but why were the recusals becoming more and more of a problem, as you put it?

It might have just been the types of cases that we were taking up that involve multiple parties, but I think also, and I'm just guessing here, it may have reflected the realities of current corporate life, where more and more companies were acquiring other companies. Various entities, much to the surprise of the judicial stockholder, turned out to be a parent company or a subsidiary involved in an activity that was totally unrelated. You might have a manufacturing company that owned a motion picture studio—which was literally an example from the early 1990s involving Gulf & Western and Paramount Pictures. There were constant sales of subsidiaries, and it became very difficult to know which company might be a parent or, on the other hand, a subsidiary of another company, with mergers, acquisitions, de-acquisitions. I'm guessing somewhat, but I believe this situation aggravated what was already a difficult problem. We tried to ameliorate the situation by adopting a requirement that each party provide the court with a list of its parent company and subsidiaries within 15 days of a grant of review. Resort to a blind trust would not cure the problem, because all judges are required by statute to keep themselves informed of their financial holdings.[2]

I should mention another role, if you will, of the Chief Justice. That involves the Administrative Presiding Justices Committee, a committee of appellate court justices that ultimately became incorporated into the array of Judicial Council advisory committees and task forces but had existed independently. That committee is chaired by the Chief Justice, and its other members are the administrative presiding justices of the six Courts of Appeal in California. As we discussed earlier, the state is divided geographically into six separate districts. A couple of the districts have subunits geographically, but there are six administrative presiding justices. The Chief Justice more or less sits with the six dukes of the realm, although now there's a duchess involved, too—the Fourth Appellate District's APJ. [Laughter] It is a body that directs and coordinates the functioning of the appellate courts—which are six autonomous courts—on matters that merit statewide coordination.

Now, just to harken back to something that we discussed earlier in another context, three of our six Courts of Appeal are constituted by law into divisions.

---

[2] Cal. Code Civ. Proc., sec. 170.1(a)(3)(C).

In those courts, I would select one of the presiding justices, from among what were sometimes several, to serve as the administrative presiding justice. There's no provision in the state constitution for that position. That's a position that was created by the Judicial Council. In the First Appellate District, headquartered in San Francisco, the Second Appellate District, headquartered in Los Angeles, and the Fourth Appellate District, headquartered in San Diego, I selected individuals whom I felt would have the best administrative qualifications to serve as APJ, or administrative presiding justice. In the other three appellate districts, the third in Sacramento, the fifth in Fresno, and the sixth in San Jose, there was no choice to be made. Each of those is a unitary appellate court with no divisions, so automatically of course the sole presiding justice became the administrative presiding justice.

The Chief Justice guides the discussions and determinations of the APJ Committee. It is only an advisory committee, and I had to remind its members on a couple of occasions over the years that their vote was a purely advisory recommendation and that, as Chief Justice, I had the responsibility of doing what I determined was best for the appellate courts in certain matters, even though I took their advice seriously. It was a rare occasion that I proceeded contrary to their advice, and basically the committee functioned not only by vote but usually through consensus. The APJs accomplished many admirable things.

What kinds of work did you take up?

One thing, which I think is a wonderful example of constructive action, was when there was a controversy about instituting mandatory judicial education. Many trial judges were resisting the proposal for a reason that I'm not very sympathetic to, and that I believe cast them in a bad light with the public. They didn't want anyone telling them what they obviously—in my view—should do, and that is to keep themselves abreast of developments in the case and statutory law and various other policy developments, like other professionals. Due to their strong opposition and the whole to-do that ensued, the Judicial Council ended up making judicial education advisory. The council certainly was very supportive of it but did not impose mandatory requirements to the extent that there would be dereliction of duty or disciplinary consequences for not complying with what were the recommended number of hours of study in the subject matters covered. The administrative presiding justices of the Courts of Appeal, to their great credit—and it was Justice Arthur Scotland from the Third Appellate District who took the lead—said, "Why don't we set a good example, whether they follow it or not? Why don't we make judicial education mandatory for appellate justices, even if it's not mandatory for trial judges?"

The other APJs responded that they would like to consult with their colleagues and get back with an answer in the next couple weeks. They did, and there was overwhelming support for the proposal. The APJs said, "We'll do it if the Supreme Court will do it." So I asked my colleagues, and they unanimously agreed to do it. Judicial education became mandatory for Supreme Court justices and mandatory for Court of Appeal justices, but voluntary and only recommended for trial judges under rules that became effective in 2007.

I wonder if you could, in a general way, give me an idea—among these many areas, how was your time divided?

It was hard to generalize, because I regarded always, first and foremost, my primary responsibility as being to work on the opinions, whether they were my opinions or opinions for the court prepared by my colleagues that I would be signing onto or not signing onto. Sometimes the press of other business would relegate that primary function of working on opinions to the dining room table late at night or to planes, trains, and automobiles when I was on the road doing court visits or traveling to speaking engagements. I learned to concentrate and work on opinions in a variety of circumstances where I fortunately could turn off the distractions or travel without getting car sick and carry on with that aspect of my responsibilities. I otherwise never would have been able to perform this aspect of my duties.

Having said that, it's very difficult to generalize, because I couldn't ever count on a day without a great number of interruptions, some of them telephonic and others lengthy, sometimes involving a sudden crisis necessitating a dash up to the state Capitol. I'd have to attend unscheduled meetings, in addition to the scheduled liaison meetings that we'll talk about. All I can say is that there were days and evenings that were totally consumed with legislative and executive branch matters and occasional rare days when I could devote the entire day to working on case-related matters.

Those liaison meetings that we'll talk about were very time consuming. They were usually scheduled for two to two and a half hours, often took longer than that, and required preparation time. I believe they proved to be extremely worthwhile. There also were regular meetings with legislators and the governor and the Department of Finance that were not crisis meetings. I sometimes would have as many as a dozen half-hour meetings in a single day back to back at the Capitol. I don't feel I ever had to neglect my decision-making responsibilities, only to postpone them sometimes. As I have stressed, I always felt the cases were my foremost responsibility, and wanted to feel confident that I had been able to give them my best effort—even if it occasionally might take me longer to get to them because of having to tend to other responsibilities.

Let's turn again to the list prepared by Chief Justice Lucas. We can compare and contrast it, perhaps, with your own list. [Laughter] First of all, tell me under what circumstances and when, if you remember, did you receive this?

This list, as I said before, was somewhat daunting. It probably was given to me after my appointment was announced and before my confirmation hearing. I associate Beth Jay, Chief Justice Lucas' principal attorney and mine, with the preparation of the list. There were some responsibilities enumerated on that list that were surprises, that I didn't even know existed.

In addition to some responsibilities that you and I have already discussed, the list includes some related to the California Constitution Revision Commission, and to the Commission on Judicial Performance, which we've discussed somewhat, a body with the responsibility of disciplining judges and of approving judicial disability retirements, and whose decisions we would take up on discretionary review. One of the changes that I helped institute in the latter portion of my tenure as Chief Justice was having the opinions of the Commission on Judicial Performance published in the official case reports of the California Supreme Court in order to provide notice to judges of rulings by the CJP and therefore guidance as to what was or was not proper judicial conduct.

There is another area we haven't talked about, judicial emergencies. This is a term of art that is based on a statute authorizing the Chief Justice, in his or her capacity as chair of the Judicial Council, to issue a judicial emergency order when necessary. Under this authority, the Chief Justice can direct the affected court to hold sessions anywhere within the county, regardless of venue; to transfer civil cases to a court in an adjacent county; and to extend the time periods in criminal matters.[3] I had many occasions to exercise this power, due mainly to fires, earthquakes, floods, and occasionally mass protest arrests.

Something else occurred that didn't technically fall within the emergency provisions but that is somewhat analogous. Riverside County experienced tremendous growth, and in fact a few years ago its increase in population was larger than that of any other county in the entire United States over the preceding few years. Due to that circumstance and a chronic shortage of judges—despite my efforts, which were partially but not fully successful, in obtaining new judgeships for Riverside and many other counties—the court was starting to dismiss criminal cases, and civil trials had come to a total halt. There were some factors in addition to the population growth that contributed to the situation in Riverside. Frankly, I don't think the local court was maximizing the procedures that might've been available to them to expedite settlements and improve efficiency generally. And the D.A. had a very hard-nosed policy about dispositions.

---

[3] Cal. Gov. Code, sec. 68115.

But for whatever reasons, they got terribly behind. Serious criminal cases were being dismissed. There is the authority to refile in most situations, but you can't keep doing that indefinitely. In civil matters, litigants were being totally deprived of their access to justice, because under the law criminal cases get priority.

I remember receiving a pathetic letter from an elderly gentleman who said it had taken him years for his case to be set for trial. Then once he got on the civil trial docket, he was told that due to the chronic overload of criminal cases his case had been taken off calendar. Then the following year it got placed back on, and now it had just been taken off again, and he didn't know if he would live long enough to ever see his case go to trial. This was just one of many terrible illustrations of the situation in Riverside County.

In the spirit of our all being part of one large court family or community—a spirit that I think inhabits the vast majority of judges, court executive officers, and staff—I appointed a task force and called for judges to volunteer to go down to Riverside on assignment to assist the court in handling its caseload. The response was overwhelmingly positive, although there were a few judges whose position basically was along the lines, "We have our own court to contend with. This is not our problem." To me, such a reaction would be like Shasta County saying, "It's our water, and we're turning off the spigot and not sending it down over the Tehachapis to L.A." [Laughter]

More than a couple dozen judges participated in the program, led by Justice Richard Huffman of the Fourth District Court of Appeal, Judge Richard Couzens of the Placer County Superior Court, and Judge David Wesley of the Los Angeles Superior Court. Judge Wesley participated despite strong pressure from his presiding judge not to do so. The L.A. court, by the way, was a frequent beneficiary of the assigned judges program and was one of nine courts that had requested and received assistance from a 23-judge relief team that I had previously dispatched, in January of 1997, to assist with the backlog resulting from the three strikes law. Either ignorant of or indifferent to the Chief Justice's constitutional authority to assign judges to other courts without first obtaining permission from the local courts, Presiding Judge Stephen Czuleger sent an e-mail message (with a copy to the A.O.C.) to Judge Wesley—one of more than 400 judges on the Los Angeles Superior Court—informing him that Czuleger "would not authorize your assignment to Riverside County."

Judge Wesley and the other judges from around the state ended up going down to Riverside and remaining for weeks at a time to try criminal cases. Judge Couzens, being from a fairly remote area, was getting up at three or three-thirty in the morning to get down to the Sacramento airport and fly down Monday morning in time to do an eight-thirty calendar call. These judges were truly heroic. We also managed to use an abandoned facility, the elementary Hawthorne School, as a civil courthouse—which was permissible under the law because the facility could not accommodate criminal cases. Restoring the trial of civil cases earned the enormous gratitude of the community. This is an illustration of the system working together to deal with a crisis and having a real sense of a statewide court community.

When it was all over with, I recognized the judges participating in the program with a special ceremony. All of us at that ceremony were incredulous when the judges thanked me for giving them this opportunity to serve the local community and help out their fellow judges.

Your power to assign judges to different areas, different levels of court—how else did you use that?

There were numerous situations where a court was understaffed because of a chronic lack of sufficient judicial positions authorized by the legislature. There were times when a governor just hadn't filled vacancies, and if that's a two-judge court it can amount to a crisis. If it's a large court it isn't, but if it's a large court and there are 10 or 12 vacancies it is a crisis. Sometimes there was a long-term illness that kept a judge from performing his or her duties, yet the position wasn't open to be filled by the governor. Sometimes it was a vacation, and that would be, if we could, covered by our normal assignment policies. There were a couple of rural judges—I remember one, Carlos Baker—who served in every single one of the 58 counties by assignment, truly like the roving jurists of medieval England, riding circuit.

In some cases a whole court was recused, perhaps because a judge or member of a judge's family was somehow involved in the litigation. There were other cases where there was a change of venue because the case couldn't be tried in the community, due to excessive pretrial publicity. Sometimes I would assign a judge from the original county to move with the case to another county, to which the case was transferred. On some occasions, I would get personally involved in the selection of a judge for a very high-publicity case—unlike my role in the assignments to our California Supreme Court, where we resorted to the alphabetical list—because the ability to handle a very lengthy high-publicity case with a lot of press presence is something that not every judge is ready, willing, and able to do.

What did you look for?

A judge who was able to keep firm control over the proceedings and deal with a substantial press presence in an evenhanded way, not catering slavishly to the press, and not on the other hand having some visceral reaction against the presence of the press. Someone who could move the proceedings in an efficient way, because these cases usually were lengthy and had dozens of witnesses. Someone who might have to be willing to leave his or her home county for substantial periods of time and live out of a motel four or five nights a week and then commute back home over the weekend. Persons who had a lot of experience with difficult criminal law issues.

Sometimes there were civil cases that were "coordinated" proceedings. One of the Chief Justice's responsibilities is to coordinate cases, in the technical sense of the word, as follows. For example, a series of civil actions might be filed against the manufacturer of a particular consumer product, perhaps in San Francisco, Fresno, Los Angeles, and San Diego. The Chief Justice has the authority to refer a coordination petition, if one is filed by a party, to a judge for a recommendation—but it's still the Chief Justice's decision—whether to coordinate or combine these lawsuits into a single proceeding and then to select a particular court and judge to try the case. These proceedings can be extremely lengthy and involve a lot of complex law and motion rulings.

Aside from the ad hoc assignment of judges or justices to the courts under the chief's assignment power, the constitution also specifically gives the Chief Justice the responsibility of naming, and specifically assigning, judges in each superior court to the appellate division of that superior court.

One of the things that began to trouble me in making these hundreds of assignment orders was that, despite the very worthwhile and hard-working contributions made by the many judges who served in the assigned judges program, there were occasional abuses. I learned that some judges would divide their professional time between sitting in a public courthouse, handling jury trials, let's say, and then doing private judging on their own and abusing the system in the sense of handing out their private business cards to lawyers as prospective clients, if you will, or sometimes making arrangements over the phone or otherwise for their private arbitrations or private judging while they were in the courthouse, using court facilities for that purpose. The most egregious example of dual loyalties that came to my attention involved a rather lengthy San Francisco trial that had been assigned down to Los Angeles due to some circumstance that I don't recall right now. The San Francisco attorneys had to rent hotel rooms Monday through Friday, and perhaps some office space, in Los Angeles. Midweek the judge announced in this public courtroom, to counsel and to the jurors, that the case would be in recess for the rest of the week because the judge would be attending to his private judging responsibilities. The jurors and the San Francisco attorneys had to pack up their things and await the judge's resumption of his assigned judge's duties several days hence.

How did you learn about it?

If I recall correctly, it was Fritz Ohlrich, the clerk/court administrator of the Supreme Court—who was formerly the clerk of the Los Angeles Municipal Court—who heard of it and told me. These various abuses, as I would term them, caused me to institute a policy, which was criticized by many of the persons who were engaged simultaneously in both private judging and public judging by assignment. That policy was, "You can do one or the other for the year, but you cannot do both. You pick it. It doesn't mean it's a forever decision. If you decide that you don't like private judging and you want to come back to the public fold, that's fine, or vice versa. But for that year you choose one or the other." It was predicted that this new policy would cause a great drop-off in the number of judges who would agree to participate in our assigned judges program, but this turned out not to be the case. We lost a small number at first, but then the number in the program grew substantially and became larger than it ever was.

The new policy removed the perception of a conflict of interest and of a misuse of public resources. I have some editorials from 2003—one from the *Sacramento Bee*: "Ronald George's line: judges must choose private or public." Another one: "Life's tough, your honors," from the *Los Angeles Times*. Then *U.S.A Today*, "Rent-a-judges forced out of California courts; arbiters asked to choose between public bench or private for-hire cases." The press coverage was all extremely favorable, and we survived this mini-crisis in the judges assignment program.

What hesitation did you have to just force them to choose?

The only hesitation was that some persons who were sympathetic to the concerns that I voiced were still very fearful that we would decimate the assigned judges program and not be able to carry on. Every day I had about 150 retired judges assigned to help with the caseload around the state. I felt, number one, that this calamity probably would not occur, and number two, even if it did, we had to make this change. We couldn't have a system that was viewed as basically conflict-ridden and inappropriately using public resources, and—if we had to reduce the size of the program—that was a price we had to pay.

For the Judicial Council, you spoke about what you were looking for. Can you give me an idea of how many appointments you had to be considering at a given time to keep that body flowing along?

The appointments were for three-year terms, and persons could be reappointed for a second term of three years. A third of the council was up for appointment at a time, and persons were not automatically or always given a second term, but very frequently they were. Service on the Judicial Council is a great burden on its members. I have great admiration for them and for the people who serve on the advisory committees—where members often manifest their administrative capabilities and then are considered first and foremost among possible candidates for appointment to the Judicial Council itself. Council members receive large binders containing materials for each of the eight meetings held every year. There's a lot of preparation required, and usually it's a two-day meeting, the first day often being an issues meeting where we have an educational session or engage in discussions about personnel matters, legislative strategy, or litigation strategy—because sometimes the court system is subject to litigation, either as a plaintiff or as a defendant.

The council's decisions are made only at the open business meetings held on the second day at which, by the way, the public is allowed to speak on certain subjects the first half hour of the meeting. These meetings are always presided over by the Chief Justice and broadcast live on a closed circuit available to all courts. The council has internal committees that contribute greatly to council decisions on budgetary and policy matters and legislative proposals—which can be proposals initiated by the Judicial Council or instead by others, where we might take a support or an oppose position.

Given the changes you've instituted in the appointment process involving the executive committee and so on, what changes did you note over time in the functioning of that resulting body?

I noted a lot of changes from the time I first served on the Judicial Council as a Court of Appeal justice. Without any disrespect intended, when I look back at the meetings at that time and the composition of the council, it occasionally appeared to me as somewhat akin to a view of the Soviet presidium—a couple dozen middle-aged white guys all saying, "Da!" [Laughter] Over the years, I saw a real change in the council's composition—physically apparent but also just in the different backgrounds of the members—as well as a lot more discussion and debate. Much of that takes place in the internal committee meetings but it also occurs at meetings of the full council.

People sometimes criticize the council for so frequently being unanimous in its votes, but often that unanimity reflects the circumstance that major differences have been debated and worked out in one of the council's internal committees. The council is divided into four committees: Executive and Planning, Policy Coordination and Liaison—which deals with legislation, Rules and Projects, and Litigation Management. Still there often would be robust debate among council members, frequently reaching a consensus, so the process is, in my view, to be commended and not criticized. Members did not feel that they had to slavishly adhere to the Chief Justice's position. In fact, it was only on the rarest of occasions that I made my own views known. I normally would not voice them. There were a few times over the years when I felt that there were serious consequences in terms of the public perception of what we were contemplating doing or that bore upon our relationship with the legislature or the governor, where I would state—obviously never in the way of a command—my views of what the preferred course of action might be. I would not vote unless there was a tie. On a close vote we'd have a roll call, and then Bill Vickrey, our Administrative Director of the Courts, who served as secretary to the council, would announce the tally. If there was a tie, those present often would be somewhat atwitter: "The chief gets to vote on this, and we'll find out how he feels." [Laughter]

Of course, the Judicial Council conducted substantial deliberations on budget matters. This was a major responsibility when you consider that, until the recent cuts in the judicial branch budget, it was basically at the $4 billion level. I sometimes felt like the CEO of a medium-sized corporation, having responsibility, with the assistance of a great many other persons, over a budget of that dimension. I want to stress that, contrary to some judges' lack of information or occasionally the deliberate disinformation spread by others, these budgetary decisions are not made by A.O.C. bureaucrats, as they would view them, but by the Judicial Council after significant input from a committee of the presiding judges of the superior courts from all over the state. Those presiding judges are, of course, democratically elected by the judges of their own court. But the P.J.s do their best to consider the needs not only of their own court but of their fellow courts and of the judicial system and the public as a whole. Also taken into account is the position taken by the court executive officers, who meet and consider the views of all the trial courts in the state. And a trial court budget working group of trial court judges and court executive officers is appointed annually to provide advice on trial court budget issues.

You commented earlier that the Judicial Council in general was more fully covering all of its duties and responsibilities and areas of interest as outlined in the constitution than it had in the past. To what do you owe that change?

Some of this came about naturally as the Judicial Council evolved, and the A.O.C. along with it, from an entity that was focused—not necessarily inappropriately at that time—on the needs of what was then perceived to be the statewide system, namely the Supreme Court and the Courts of Appeal. The 220 separate fiefdoms that comprised justice courts, municipal courts, and superior courts were not truly part of the statewide administration of justice. I remember as a trial judge, maybe once or twice a year opening up my mail and finding a

report of a study done by the A.O.C. on interpreter services, or a statistical report on how many cases in various categories had been filed around the state.
But there was virtually nothing that affected the day-to-day operations of the
trial courts. Once we achieved the first and basic structural reform on the road to
creating what would truly be a statewide judicial branch and administrative
structure—namely the Trial Court Funding Act of 1997, during my first year as
Chief Justice—this, almost by definition, transformed the Judicial Council and
the A.O.C. into entities that were concerned, probably foremost, with the operation of our trial courts. This made for a very different Judicial Council and Administrative Office of the Courts and was the first big step in creating what
would be a judicial branch in reality and function and not merely in theory or
name. The council members were involved in totally different responsibilities
than before.

*As an aside on the members brought in by the State Bar and by the legislature,
what could they add to the mix of this body as a whole?*

Despite the occasional concern voiced about separation of powers by reason
of the legislature appointing two of the council members, given the very small
percentage of seats that they hold on the council I don't believe there's any validity to that concern. It's somewhat akin to a much greater legislative intrusion
on the judicial function that occurred when the legislature decided to get involved in the State Bar Court. I mentioned previously to you a decision I wrote
in the *Obrien* case that upheld this legislative involvement against the separation-of-powers argument. There was a far greater representation, if you will, of
legislators' appointees in that body than there is in the council, whose membership significantly is prescribed by the constitution, not by statute.

I believe the council has benefited greatly from the participation of its legislator members. Sometimes they give the other members a reality check. Admittedly the scheduling of our meetings often conflicts with their legislative functions, but they receive the materials and do attend when they can. We've had
some rather impassioned presentations by legislators such as Mike Feuer, who
recently chaired the Assembly Judiciary Committee, and Dave Jones, a former
chair. Also by Joe Dunn, who was a senator and is another strong supporter of
the courts. All three of them made it very, very clear to us—and I think most of
us knew this already, but it was important to hear it from these legislators—that
for the judiciary to have any impact in protecting its position as a truly independent branch of government and to further its general objectives, it had to
speak with one voice. That necessitated engaging in discussion on various matters with our judicial partners, the California Judges Association and with individual courts who may have had objections, and then attempting to resolve those
differences in-house.

If we went back to the days that existed when I became Chief Justice, where you'd more or less have the Judicial Council going up to the Capitol with one point of view and the California Judges Association with another, and the Los Angeles court with its own agenda, and then a few other courts or individual judges who would show up as free spirits, we would be told, as we were then— pretty much in these words: "We don't have to listen to any of you guys if you can't make up your mind. We'll just do what we want." That message was reiterated by legislators, such as the individuals I've just mentioned, in stressing the urgency of not reverting—in the face of new problems and new issues—to that earlier era when we were not respected as an independent voice. These legislator members of the council gave us very valuable advice, and sometimes they've given us instruction on how best to get something accomplished, and other times they've carried the ball for us. That's been very helpful.

The State Bar appointees do not present a separation-of-powers issue because, contrary to what some people believe or don't know, the State Bar is a public corporation that is part of the judicial branch. It is established as a quasi-governmental entity by section 9 of article VI, the judicial article of the constitution. So it does make sense for the State Bar to have representation on the Judicial Council. Although I call it representation, I stress to them too, "You're not to just advocate the bar's interests. We want your perspective—and it's very valuable, the perspective of practicing attorneys—but we want you to consider what is best for the justice system, including the judiciary and the bar and the public interest." They adhere to that standard and perform a very valuable function, just as court executive officers do, in providing information and perspective on things that judges, however experienced, might not be as effective in recognizing or in promoting. I'm very glad that we have those members of the State Bar on the council. They tend to be individuals who have excelled in the profession. I encouraged the State Bar Board of Governors over the years to appoint lawyers—again, not through a popularity contest—who have truly distinguished themselves in the bar on administration-of-justice issues. Consequently, we've had some former State Bar presidents who have served on the Judicial Council and have made valuable contributions to its work.

I'm sure we'll come back to the Judicial Council, but perhaps we'll briefly finish with this list of responsibilities as provided by your predecessor.

The Administrative Office of the Courts is included in the list of the Chief Justice's duties. Fortunately, the day-to-day supervision of that office was the responsibility of the Administrative Director and his chief deputy, Bill Vickrey and Ron Overholt, both of whom tirelessly served that office with total dedication to the interests of the judicial branch and the public. I would meet from time to time not only with Vickrey and Overholt but with some of the division chiefs who supervise various sections of the operations, and occasionally with the whole staff on some occasion or other.

This is probably a good time to observe that it's very easy to throw potshots at the A.O.C. as an overgrown bureaucracy, pointing out that it used to employ 200 individuals and now it's at about 900. But what this ignores is the parallel growth of the statewide administration of justice itself, which as I noted a couple minutes ago grew from having virtually no contact with the trial courts to now encompassing the whole statewide structure, trial and appellate. Tremendous new duties were thrust upon the A.O.C. by law—especially by the legislature's passage of the Trial Court Funding Act, and then through trial court unification and the court employees act, which made court employees "court employees" as such and no longer county employees, nor state employees, and by countless other obligations imposed upon the A.O.C. by the other two branches of government—often without the provision of any funding to carry out the new tasks.

The trial court facilities act alone, transferring the ownership and management of California's 530 courthouse facilities—with the obligation to repair and replace and construct courthouses—from the counties to the state under judicial branch management necessitated adding more than 200 positions to the A.O.C., not counting the related human resources obligations and office of general counsel obligations imposed on the A.O.C. I remember being in Sacramento discussing the possibility of transferring these trial court facilities, and learning that the governor had asked his staff, "If we undertook these responsibilities ourselves as part of the executive branch, how many people would it take to assume the obligation from the counties of owning and managing these 530 court facilities?" I heard that the Department of General Services said it would need about 2,000 additional employees. The A.O.C. agreed to assume this obligation and predicted it would be able to do so with 200-some additional employees. The A.O.C. did take over this responsibility but this required adding these 200 persons to its ranks.

Look at all the new obligations imposed by law—occasionally over our objection—upon the Administrative Office of the Courts, as the staff arm of the Judicial Council, to carry out operations mandated by the state legislature and to take over functions previously performed by the counties or by the local courts. To me it's shocking that the Administrative Office of the Courts has been able to do its job and not expand more than it has. In fact, on a workload basis, on a population-served basis, we have a smaller A.O.C. than Arizona's, proportionally. We have a smaller A.O.C. than the federal A.O.C., even though California's judiciary is much larger than that of the entire United States court system. Many of the criticisms leveled at the A.O.C., for what it has done and is doing, are very unfair, inaccurate, or uninformed.

Have there been instances in which things could have been better managed? I would say yes, and the area of technology is one—the case management system or CCMS. Technology problems seem to frequently befall government agencies. I'm sure you and I will discuss CCMS in greater detail at a later session.

Another subject on this list of the Chief Justice's responsibilities is oversight of the State Bar Court. I've already mentioned how the State Bar itself is basically an arm of the judiciary. Beyond that, the Supreme Court in recent years has exercised substantial supervision over the State Bar Court. We were seeing many instances where disciplined attorneys were not being dealt with as directly, as meaningfully as they should have been—being given a slap on the wrist when they had committed crimes of moral turpitude and when the protection of the public demanded more than that. Twice a year I would sign very lengthy lists admitting many hundreds of new attorneys to practice and to join what I believe we mentioned is now more than 200,000 lawyers in practice in California. It is understandable that the State Bar disciplinary system feels overwhelmed.

There was a case in which the justices all agreed that an applicant to the bar, who claimed to be rehabilitated after serving a prison term for bludgeoning and stabbing his sister to death, wasn't ready to be admitted to the legal profession. One day right about the time our court acted to deny the State Bar Court's recommondation that he be admitted to practice,[4] I was finishing my morning run at Crissy Field here in San Francisco along the bay, and someone comes running up to me panting, and says, "Boy, you're really fast, your honor. I've been trying to catch up with you. I want to talk to about my case." It was this fellow who had killed his sister. So needless to say, I had to interrupt and tell him that any conversation would be highly inappropriate. [Laughter]

Next on the list of the Chief Justice's duties is a lengthy set of responsibilities involved in presiding over the operations of the Supreme Court that for the most part you and I have already covered. There are additional responsibilities involving the three central staffs, the judicial library, the judicial college, the contract providing for publication of the court's opinions, the court's budget, supervision of the clerk/court administrator, promulgating internal practices and procedures, and acting on stay applications. Another item on the list was the public information office of the Administrative Office of the Courts. I had many dealings with this office that we'll probably cover separately when we discuss

---

[4] In re Gossage (2000) 23 Cal.4th 1080.

the several ways in which I tried to engage in an overall outreach program, which included efforts specifically directed at enhancing press coverage of the court and of the judicial branch—facilitating relations with the press by attempting to accommodate their needs and, hopefully, securing some benefits for the judicial system at the same time.

I'll conclude just by noting that there are several national responsibilities with which the Chief Justice is involved, as if all of this weren't enough. [Laughter] These activities include serving as a member of what's called the Conference of Chief Justices, the permanent organization of Chief Justices, where I was active and made presentations on budgetary and policy matters and lectured at educational programs as well. I served as the president of the organization for one year. When one is president of the Conference of Chief Justices, one also automatically serves as chair of the board of directors of the National Center for State Courts, which engages in policy initiatives and studies for the state courts and provides staff for the chiefs and for a number of other judicial organizations, including the American Judges Association, which is a trial judges group, as well as for the association of presiding justices of our intermediate Courts of Appeal, and a few other national judicial organizations. The Conference of Chief Justices meets twice a year in all sorts of places. I recall meetings from South Dakota to Puerto Rico and from Maine down to Alabama. I hosted the Conference of Chiefs one year in San Francisco, which was a major undertaking greatly assisted by Barbara. Marcia Taylor, an attorney with our Administrative Office of the Courts, provided me with outstanding assistance in carrying out my various responsibilities with the conference and the National Center.

I also served on two committees of the Judicial Conference of the United States. That body is, in some ways, the equivalent of the Judicial Council of California for court administration on the federal level, although frankly it has much less authority or at least exercises much less authority than our Judicial Council of California does. The Judicial Conference is chaired by the Chief Justice of the United States. Chief Justice William Rehnquist appointed me to the conference's Committee on Federal-State Jurisdiction, whose work focuses on the substantial interplay between the federal and state court systems and their many areas of common interest. Chief Justice John Roberts appointed me to serve on the Committee on Rules of Practice and Procedure, which is responsible for promulgating rules for the operation of the federal courts. While I'm talking about joint federal-state activities, I'll mention that there are various national conferences, attended by both federal and state judges, that I participated in. For example, one was held on issues of diversity and race and ethnic bias in the court system.

Another area of very close cooperation between the state and federal systems is the California State-Federal Judicial Council, of which I served as co-chair. California is one of the states that has one of those councils—not every state does—and it's a state where the council is particularly active. Half of the members are appointed by the Chief Justice of California and half by the Chief Judge of the Ninth Circuit. This council has committees that deal with various areas where there is an overlap or a need for coordination, such as jury reform, tribal courts, death penalty proceedings, judicial education and public information, and pro per litigation. We have been able to learn a lot from each other and sometimes bring about improvements in both of our respective systems. It's a very worthwhile endeavor. The council meets only twice a year, but there can be joint educational programs and committee meetings in between.

I even had some international responsibilities as Chief Justice. One of the other joint activities with my federal colleagues was the Anglo-American Legal Exchange, to which Chief Justice Rehnquist appointed two members of the U.S. Supreme Court, Justice Anthony Kennedy and Justice Clarence Thomas, plus two other federal judges, Chief Judge Deanell Tacha of the U.S. Court of Appeals for the Tenth Circuit, former U.S. District Court Judge Sam Pointer from Alabama, and myself as the only state judge, along with five lawyers from the American College of Trial Lawyers, to comprise a delegation to meet with our British counterparts. There was a lot of scholarly work that went into preparing papers and discussion points with our counterparts. We went to England and Scotland and worked very hard during the day. Some of our counterparts had glorious titles, of course: the Lord High Chancellor, the Lord Chief Justice, and the Master of the Rolls.

Spouses were encouraged to come, and we had terrific social events in the evening—our hosts really went out of their way. I know when Barbara was surprised to be introduced to the Master of the Rolls, I said to her aside, "Wait until you meet the Master of the Bentleys!" [Laughter] Bad joke, but we had a lot of good humor in our interchanges.

The following year, it was the American delegation's responsibility to host the meeting in the United States. These respective meetings took place in 1999 and 2000. With all of the elaborate events held at wonderful, ancient British facilities, we wondered how we could try to equal that. Justice Kennedy was up to the task in emulating the lavish hospitality we had been shown. He managed to secure the use of Mount Vernon after hours for just our small group. We were served a dinner that Martha Washington apparently had served to diplomats back in her time, on the veranda overlooking the Potomac. Our British guests were suitably impressed.

What was on that menu?

Being somewhat of a foodie, I should recall this better, but it has been a number of years. It may have been a game bird, a crab dish, some fairly exotic vegetables that we don't see much of today, and some sort of pudding.

But I shouldn't really stress the social side of these visits to the exclusion of the topics that we discussed. It's interesting that even the mother country that gave us our legal and judicial system found there were things to learn from its American offspring. The British legal system followed a practice, on appeal, of a barrister coming into the appellate courtroom armed with heavy tomes, and the oral arguments would go on for hours and hours. As the barrister would get from one point to another, he or she would resort to opening up these case books and reading opinions at length from them and then moving on to another book. The American participants in the exchange program suggested, "Why don't you use written briefs?" That's something that came out of an earlier Anglo-American Legal Exchange. More recently, a Supreme Court of Britain has been established in lieu of the Law Lords serving as the court of last resort. There are other areas where the British and American participants have shared their experience in trying to deal effectively with problems we share. These discussions were very intellectual and robust, replete with citations to legal authority. I believe all of the participants found them very beneficial.

There are a couple other international involvements I'll mention briefly. In the year 2000 I was asked by the government of the Republic of Mexico to head a judicial delegation to visit that country to share with the Mexican judiciary our experience where it differed from theirs—such as having jury trials in certain proceedings where Mexico did not have them, and instituting a system of expedited procedures where warranted. Of course, we also discussed the difficult process of extradition, which did not always function smoothly, especially when California authorities were seeking the death penalty and this decision conflicted with the Mexican policy against the death penalty, necessitating that a commitment be made on the part of California not to seek the death penalty, in order for Mexico to agree to extradite the suspect.

I ended up turning down invitations to participate in judicial presentations in Egypt, Canada, and China when it became apparent that my schedule no longer permitted me to continue making official visits abroad.

One other thing I would mention about the international aspects of my duties is that the State Department and some other entities occasionally would bring foreign delegations of jurists to the California Supreme Court and other courts to expose them to the American system of justice. One of the encounters that made quite an impression on me was a visit from the country of Yemen.

This was before the events of September 11, 2001. The delegation for the most part, as I recall, appeared in their tribal robes, and I was speaking through a translator to the Yemeni Chief Justice.

By coincidence we were having oral argument that day, and the delegation had sat in on one of our cases. I delayed the court's noon-hour opinion conference for half an hour after the session so that I could greet the delegation. I remember asking them a few questions more or less just to be polite—how they were selected for appointment to their positions, whether Yemen had jury trials, which I was fairly sure they didn't, and how did they like hearing oral argument? The Chief Justice said, "We were incredibly moved and impressed by this oral argument."

I thought, "This is too strange to let pass." It happened to have been an unusually dull case, at least from my perspective. It involved, I believe, which statute of limitations should apply when the State of California was being sued for certain alleged wrongful conduct. I couldn't resist asking the Chief Justice, "Tell me, what was it that so fascinated you?" I learned a great deal from his answer to my question. He said, "You cannot imagine what it means to us to see the spectacle of the government having to stand up in court and defend itself like any ordinary litigant. That's a concept totally unheard of to us, and it's so remarkable." He was obviously quite favorably impressed with this aspect of our system. What this incident taught me is that there are certain things we may take for granted that mean a lot to someone in an emerging democracy, and that we should make a greater effort to instill a sense of awareness and appreciation—in our own adult and student community—of the rights and responsibilities that we have as citizens and the importance of our independent system of justice.

On a final note, I would add that, in decorating my chambers, Barbara—about whose contributions to the art and architecture of the building we'll talk later—made a point of saying, "You should have some important artwork in your chambers, given the flow of international and national visitors that you know you're going to be having, something that reflects California."

Through some connections she had at the Oakland Museum of California, which has one of the most outstanding collections of California landscape art, she arranged for us to go to the museum and be permitted to select a suitable oil painting to be taken out on loan. Once I was there, I said, "How about two?" A number of paintings, from a part of the museum's collection that was in storage, were spread out in the basement. I felt like a kid in a candy store. One was a William Keith, who was a very noted artist. I finally got them up to four California landscape paintings, and we managed to have these beautiful nineteenth-century works installed at the court. I suggested that my successor renew the request, which she has done. This artwork lends an aura of California history that is very much appreciated by all who visit the Chief Justice's chambers.

That gets us to the end of this lengthy list of the Chief Justice's responsibilities, with a few digressions along the way.

###

Chapter 11

Presiding over the High Court
September 12, 2011

I thought we might talk more today about your judicial colleagues on the California Supreme Court after you became Chief Justice. You touched upon the fact that you had initial meetings with each chambers, with the justice and the justice's staff. What else do you recall about that initial series of meetings and what specific topics were of interest or concern to your colleagues and their staffs?

A lot of the discussions amounted to expressions of willingness on my part to be receptive to suggestions that might be forthcoming at a later date. It was important to open a two-way communication between myself as chief and the justices—as well as with the staffs themselves—and to encourage the staffs to communicate with me directly or certainly with my staff. It wasn't a question of just continuing the status quo, but instead of my being receptive to suggestions for changes in the court's procedures. With that in mind, I made a point of almost always keeping the door to my chambers open. There were improvements that came out of these discussions. I can't think of monumental changes but I know over the months following these meetings various suggestions were made. Some might be considered of a very minor or technical nature, but they were all part of oiling the machinery of our court operations, making us better able to communicate and to perform our tasks more efficiently.

You mentioned your efforts to set a particular tone with your own staff and to urge them to be as collegial and cooperative as possible with all of their col-

leagues. What was the value of setting that tone personally with these other staff members? What were you trying to do there?

First of all, of course, it's more pleasant for anyone in any kind of setting to be able to work with colleagues in a constructive atmosphere, rather than in an environment where there are personal differences that aren't dealt with in a constructive and friendly way. Beyond that, I believe that the actual work product of a collegial body, such as the California Supreme Court, is enhanced if the participants realize that they are encouraged to make constructive suggestions and, in turn, that they should be receptive when others make constructive suggestions. This is so much more productive than following the attitude of "My way or the highway," or "Since I have the votes, so what?," or "I know best. It's my case." That negative attitude didn't exist on my staff, and to the minimal extent it existed elsewhere I wanted to try to further diminish it by emphasizing the teamwork involved in the Supreme Court's operations and the fact that we all should do our very best to put out the finest product that we were capable of—considering other views, while not necessarily always adopting them, but being willing to listen to them.

Of course, any change in leadership at the top is a matter of concern to everyone, and it takes some time getting used to. How do you think those initial efforts paid off?

I believe these efforts did pay off, even though most persons probably viewed the transition as unsettling, because we're all usually comfortable with the status quo, and any change can be disruptive. On the other hand an opportunity was presented to make changes and advances. I would say though that, even aside from the advent of a new chief, there is something about a change in the composition of a Supreme Court—just the change in one position, even if the incoming justice does not have a philosophy or approach markedly different from his or her predecessor—that changes in a perhaps inchoate way the dynamics, the chemistry, the atmosphere at the court. It's hard to describe—at least for me—or to quantify, but if you take one of the seven parts and change it, even with what might be a like-minded part, it's a different court.

That change filters all the way throughout the organization?

It does. I have felt and observed this both when I sat on the Court of Appeal and on the state Supreme Court, in the changes in judicial personnel that I observed.

What example would you give of that, if any, from any point in your career?

It's something intangible. You feel it around the conference table, and I believe it affects the decision-making process, even without a drastic change in philosophy. Even without a change in personnel, when one person would be absent from the weekly petition conference—depending on who that was—there would be an intangible alteration in the dynamics and the atmosphere.

I'm thinking of when the court sits for oral argument or other purposes, a new justice means that everyone but the chief may change chairs, so quite literally there is a shakeup, isn't there, of a physical sort?

Yes, that's true on the bench, because the traditional mode of seating is that the person who is senior among the associate justices sits to the chief's immediate right on the bench, and the person next in seniority sits to the chief's immediate left, and then it goes back to the right side, back and forth, until the most junior justice occupies the seat on the far left of the chief. Around the conference table—where of course the justices discussed the petitions at the Wednesday conference, conducted the monthly administrative conferences, and convened following each half-day of oral argument—the seating starts at the chief's left.

The chief is seated at the head of the court's historic conference table, and the order of seniority goes around the table so that on the left side of the table are the three most senior associate justices in immediate order of seniority. Then on the other side of the table are the three least senior associate justices, so that the junior justice sits immediately to the right of the Chief Justice. I have heard of justices from prior years—before I joined the court—noting that although they had served on the court for a number of years, because of the relative stability in the membership of the court they never "got to the other side of the table." They never made it around the bend to the senior side of the table to the chief's left and inevitably ended up advancing, if they did, only on the right side of the table. [Laughter]

These are all arcane traditions and practices. There isn't any secret handshake on the court, but these things seem only a step or two removed from such quaint customs.

You did have some new judicial colleagues since you had first joined the court as an associate. We've had a chance already to talk about Justice Werdegar and Justice Brown; however, we haven't spoken yet of Justice Ming Chin, who preceded your elevation by only a few months as a new member of this court. Could you say a few words about him, please?

He had a very fine and wide ranging career. He distinguished himself in
military service in Vietnam. He was a deputy D.A. in the Alameda County district attorney's office and then went into private practice, where he had a very
notable career with a well-established East Bay law firm and then served on the
trial bench before being appointed to the First District Court of Appeal.

*How did you think about him as one of the newest members of this group, in
terms of how he might generally think through issues, either civil issues or certain views of criminal cases? Any particular way to characterize him?*

He had a lot of real-life experience in the law, both in his civil and his criminal practice, which was very helpful. I think that's worth a lot. Not that everyone has to come to the high court with that kind of experience, but it's very
helpful to have some individuals on the court with this kind of day-to-day experience in civil and criminal trial practice. Justice Chin also developed along the
way quite a knowledge and expertise in technology and science. I put that to
good use in having him chair our technology committee and help develop our
case management system and speak, as he did on occasion, at conferences on
science and the law, although he certainly didn't confine himself to that. He also
took on the chairmanship of the Commission for Impartial Courts that I established to deal with the problem of judicial independence as affected by judicial
elections, campaign ethics, public information, and related matters.

*Maybe we can speak a bit more about your colleagues in talking about the
Wednesday petition conferences—first of all, a description of what went on there
every week.*

The justices would meet to consider petitions at 9:15 every Wednesday
morning, except during weeks when we had oral argument and with a couple of
other exceptions during the year. On the third Wednesday of the month the petition conference would be followed by an administrative conference at which the
justices would discuss changes in internal policies, operating procedures, rules,
personnel matters and related questions, appointments the court might be called
upon to make, and various internal improvements. The petition conference was
the main occasion for the seven of us to be together in person, in addition to our
oral argument sessions. I eventually got around to having the windows double
paned, because every time a truck or bus would start up, the conversation would
have to come to a halt. We'd be drowned out.

It would probably be most helpful if I approach the task of describing the
weekly petition conference by proceeding in chronological order, in terms of
what went on. Justices would show up in my chambers as early as 9:00 a.m. I

would encourage everyone to feel free to chat. We didn't have to get down to business right away. These informal conversations touched on current events, things in our personal lives, sometimes subjects that were just scuttlebutt that some of us had heard about. The conversation sometimes went on for half an hour, rarely more than that, and sometimes less.

Then when the discussion seemed to be dying out on those unofficial topics, I would start the official business of the conference. We would vote on sometimes more than 400 petitions seeking review in our court. The petitions were organized into an A list and a B list. The B list was basically the equivalent of a consent agenda or nondiscussion list. Any one justice could have a case transferred from the B list to the A list, turning it into a discussion matter. This meant we would have the opportunity to address the merits of granting review before voting on the petition. First, I'd inquire whether there were any votes to grant matters that were on the B list or recusals to note on matters that were on that list. The reason such matters were given priority was that a clerk would be waiting in my outer chambers to obtain my copy of the B list with the notations I had placed on that list reflecting a grant vote or a recusal to be noted in the court's order, on behalf of any justice, as to a B list matter.

As a practical matter, how often did a justice ask that a B list case be brought forth?

It was unusual but it certainly happened from time to time. Sometimes that request would be made before the actual conference, but it was never too late to elevate a B list matter to the A list. The reason I would be eager to have the B list taken care of immediately was that a clerk from the calendar coordinator's office—which serviced the justices, recorded their votes, and monitored internal aspects of the court's operations—would record the justices' votes on these orders, which then would be given to other parts of the clerk's office to disseminate to the press and the public over the counter and on the court's website. It was important to turn over the B list matters right away to the clerks so they could start preparing orders that reflected grant votes and recusals on the numerous B list matters, because that was something the justices could determine very quickly but took the clerks a fair amount of time, whereas the smaller number of cases involving A list votes would require discussion, which could be lengthy. So this process gave the clerks a head start. The calendar coordinator's office would also take note of when I had set cases on the forthcoming oral argument calendar, and how we voted on the A list matters—which I'll get to momentarily. It also would take note of recusals.

How were the A and B lists prepared?

Generally, memos on the B list (and most A list matters) were prepared by the central staffs, who would do a workup on the case, and determine whether, in the staff member's view, the matter should be placed on the B list or on the A list. That listing determination was one with which the justices almost always agreed. But occasionally one or more justices would differ in terms of the perceived significance of the case and it would be elevated to the A list, which didn't mean it would necessarily be granted but it would be something deemed worthy of discussion.

The central staffs did a remarkable job in sorting out these hundreds of petitions and writing cogent memos, usually just a few pages long but sometimes 20 or more pages, in which they summarized the facts and the legal issues on which review or some other relief was sought, and then made a recommendation which—as I'll mention in a moment or two—is not limited to grant or deny. The standard under our rules for granting review had little if anything to do with whether the decision of the Court of Appeal from which review was being sought was correct or incorrect. The basic criteria for our court in deciding whether to grant review in the face of the up to 10,000 petitions a year we received—considering there'd be only seven of us, who could write opinions in only 110 to 115 cases, of which some were capital automatic appeals—had to be something other than whether the case appeared to have been rightly or wrongly decided. As reflected in the rules, the standard for granting review is whether the case presents an issue of statewide substantial importance and/or whether there is a conflict in the reported decisional law on the subject—whether the Courts of Appeal had come to different conclusions on a question of law in separate cases. Sometimes one, sometimes both, criteria were met. Most often neither one was.

Some of the B list petitions involved petitions seeking review that never should have been filed by an attorney. They were frankly just a waste of the attorney's and the client's time and resources and of the court's. There were some things you could file a hundred times and the chance would still be zero that there would ever be a grant or even a single vote to grant review. You can file a petition that says the evidence was insufficient to convict the juvenile of joyriding or that the judgment against someone in a fender bender civil case was not based on sufficient evidence, and that's never going to get granted. It's not something that should be part of anyone's practice of law, to litter up the docket with such matters.

Have such filings become more commonplace, or do you have any way of gauging the changes over time?

I don't know that they've increased. I think there were always frivolous petitions. When I was a deputy attorney general, I sometimes marveled at the filing of a petition seeking review after a judgment of the Court of Appeal in a no-merit appeal. There always seem to be some that fall into that category.

There's one rarely occurring event that nonetheless is part of the picture. We referred to it informally as a "rescue mission"—which might be a situation where, strictly speaking, the case didn't meet the standard for review of being necessary "to secure uniformity of decision or to settle an important question of law,"[1] but there was such an injustice or aberration from the normal operation of the justice system that the case cried out for redress. I really don't think that you'd see the court reach out to more than one or two in a year, and I'd say there were many years in which no rescue missions were undertaken. But I want to indicate in the interest of candor that, despite what I said about the standard for granting review, these rare exceptions would occur.

Our basic function in granting review was to focus on cases with widespread ramifications. In that situation, the filing of an amicus curiae brief could sometimes cast light on the potential significance of an issue. If a petition is filed by a party urging that the case presents a substantial issue—but added to that showing are one or more briefs of amici curiae showing that, from the standpoint of, let's say, a given industry or trade group or employee group, many more individuals and entities would be affected by the decision than just the named parties in the lawsuit—that might very well make the difference in persuading the court that the issue presented by the petition is in fact a substantial one and therefore merits review. We obviously had no limit on the number of cases in which we would grant review each week. Some weeks there were several, and other weeks there were none.

Before voting on the A list cases, we would go through what I previously described as the salmon sheet—named for the color of paper on which it was printed. I'd call each case on this list just to note its status, with the 90 days running on those cases—because they all were under submission and had been argued—and I sometimes would prod or inquire as to a justice's signature that was still to be forthcoming, whether to the majority opinion or to a dissent, just to make sure we wouldn't be too close to the constitutional 90-day deadline for rendering the court's decision.[2]

I instituted, with the court's consent, a rule that a dissent had to be circulated no later than the eightieth day, because it just wasn't fair for the author of a

---

[1] California Rules of Court, rule 8.500.

[2] Art. VI, sec. 19, provides: "A judge of a court of record may not receive the salary for the judicial office held by the judge while any cause before the judge remains pending and undetermined for 90 days after it has been submitted for decision."

majority opinion to receive a dissenting opinion on the eighty-eighth or eighty-ninth day and then have almost no opportunity to make responsive changes. Under the new rule, if the dissent is circulated after the eightieth day, it would not be filed with the majority opinion. It would be filed during the period in which the court retains jurisdiction to act on a petition for rehearing. During that period, the majority would have the time, the occasion, and the right to modify the court's opinion. I had one or two occasions where I was just about to have to invoke the 80-day rule, but I never had to. The mere existence of the rule took care of the problem by providing any dissenter with an incentive not to wait that late to circulate a separate opinion.

I don't believe any dissenter purposefully ever tried to sandbag the author of a majority opinion. It was just that on occasion, with the press of business and the difficulty posed by a particular case, the aspirational goal of putting out the dissent several days before the filing deadline just didn't materialize. Because of some complaints from authors of majority opinions that they were being put in an unfair situation, we instituted this rule. There were occasions when the majority opinion had circulated very late and it was understood that it would not be unfair to let the dissent be relieved from compliance with the strict 80-day deadline. When this happened, it was done with the express or implicit agreement of the author of the majority opinion. Or let's say the majority opinion had been timely circulated but some very substantial changes had been made after it had circulated. Then it was understood that the dissent would either come out or be modified beyond the eightieth day, so that always provided an informal safety valve as well.

The next item of business after that was the blue list, which chronicled all of the cases in which a calendar memo—which, as we've discussed, is more or less a draft opinion or bench memo—had circulated. After the briefs came in, the assigned justice would prepare and circulate a calendar memo to his or her colleagues. Under our practices, ideally within 15 days of that circulating, the six other justices were to circulate a "P.R." or preliminary response indicating anything from checking off a box, "I concur," to one saying "I concur with reservations," setting those forth, or "I disagree" or "I will dissent," sometimes relating dissenting views at great length in several pages of single-spaced typewritten comments. Then, when those responses would all be in, the author of the majority calendar memo would have the opportunity to put out a responsive memorandum—often called a "yellow memo," again by the color of the paper it was on—indicating how he or she would or would not accommodate the various reservations or suggestions. Sometimes one or more wholly new revised calendar memos would be circulated, inviting a new round of P.R.s.

It was only when four or more of the justices were pointed in basically the same direction that I would inquire whether the justices were ready to calendar the case for oral argument. We didn't wait for the last of the P.R.s to come in, necessarily. Sometimes there would be a straggler or two that would take some time to come in. But I would always inquire whether any of the not-yet-responding justices who had not circulated a P.R. would object if the case were to be set for oral argument. If there were no objections, and of course if the author of the tentative majority opinion was agreeable, I would set the case for oral argument, usually on the next calendar scheduled for several weeks hence. That could always be altered, but what I would do is, approximately four weeks before an oral argument session, I would verify which cases had been marked as ready to be set for oral argument. That would be the last opportunity to change the schedule by taking something off or adding something else.

Then I would make up the oral argument calendar, taking some pains, always, to schedule the cases in some kind of appropriate order. To provide counsel with close to a month's notice, the clerk would send out the calendar immediately, with a letter that called their attention to various procedures related to oral argument. I tried to mix it up so that one justice wouldn't have a bunch of his or her cases in a row for oral argument, because one usually would prepare for oral argument even more intensely on one's own cases. I tried to alternate somewhat between civil and criminal cases, but I would leave death penalty cases for the end of the calendar as the last and/or next to last cases in the afternoon. Counsel on those cases were given the opportunity to request 45 minutes per side instead of the usual 30 minutes, and it seemed right not to have other lawyers have to wait through a death penalty argument before their own case would be heard. I usually set cases that were of the most interest to the public or the press as the first or second of the morning arguments.

All of the counsel on the three morning cases would have to be in the courtroom for the 9:00 call of the calendar. In fact, they were supposed to be there at 8:30, at which time our able clerk/court administrator, Fritz Ohlrich, would in his avuncular fashion provide a very warm and helpful introduction for counsel before the court convened on the bench. He would explain the procedures and the dos and don'ts, which was especially beneficial for those who had never appeared before our court—how to stand and move the microphone and raise the movable lectern, and how to address the justices—hopefully as "your honor" or by name following the word "Justice," as opposed to "you guys," which we did hear once or twice and which prompted Justice Joyce Kennard to inquire, "Does that include me too?" [Laughter] There are all sorts of things that one might inappropriately take for granted, but Fritz put most of them to rest.

As a practical matter, how far ahead were you scheduling the oral arguments?

One month before. Of course we had sessions in Los Angeles four times a year, in Sacramento twice a year, and in San Francisco, our headquarters, four times a year. But we would often—and we'll get into the special sessions later on—substitute one of the away sessions for one of the arguments in our traditional three venues.

While we're talking about the routine of setting cases for oral argument, I'll mention a minor reform I instituted in our procedures. There were cases, especially those that might involve, for example, a wide range of participants in a case with industry-wide ramifications, where there was a great desire on behalf of various counsel to participate in the argument, whether it was because counsel felt he or she had something special to contribute to the decision-making process or just in order to be on record as a participant in the oral argument of a significant case. The reason I mention this is, the court increasingly was receiving requests for allocation of time from each side—which we would basically leave to the attorneys. They could seek to cede part of their allotted 30 minutes to *amicus curiae* and also could divide the time up among counsel of record. We were receiving more and more requests to give two minutes to Attorney A and three minutes to Attorney B, and another two minutes to Attorney C. It got very disruptive, and the attorneys who were allocated that minor role—and who had, perhaps, requested it and obtained it—barely had time to clear their throat before they had to sit down. It was a waste of time. If they were asked a question, the question would often consume at least half their time. [Laughter] A new rule was instituted at my suggestion that a party could not parse out the time allotted to its side in less than ten-minute increments, with the exception that counsel could reserve less than 10 minutes for his or her rebuttal. But we abolished the practice of having—which we actually had had in a few instances—several "two-minute wonders" up there, whose presentations were disruptive and not very helpful to the court. That was one minor reform we made in our oral argument practices.

Getting back to the order of proceedings in the weekly conference, when we were done with the blue list, I would call the A list. By the way, occasionally a case would be put over from the A list conference of one Wednesday to a future conference, but usually that would be done before the conference when a justice felt he or she needed more time to consider the case. Sometimes that time was used by the justice to write a memo supplementing the central staff memo—either in support of the original memo's proposed disposition or to propose an alternative. The central staffs did quite an amazing job of determining and explaining in their memos how and when, and how often, the issue before the court in that petition had come up in the past, and how the justices had voted previously on that issue. I'd see memos noting, for example, "This issue came up in 1988, when Justice Mosk voted to grant review in the such-and-such case." The central staffs maintained a record of how often an issue came up and what interest had been expressed in it, in what context, by various justices, all of which lent some context to the question of how important or wide-ranging was the issue in terms of whether it was a recurring one meriting review.

How long were those lists, as a general matter?

The A list usually comprised, I would say, 30 to 50 of the matters on the conference calendar, but it could be less, it could be more. I would call each case, and then in most instances we would just go around the table and hear from the six associate justices in descending order of seniority. Frequently, there was no discussion. On some of the most momentous cases, it was obvious that review was warranted, and there was no need to say anything further, regardless of our respective views concerning the merits of the substantive issues presented. Each justice would just give his or her vote. As Chief Justice, I would cast the final vote. Sometimes there was a lot of discussion, which often had very little to do with how earth-shattering the case was or was not. There might be a genuine debate about how important the issue was for purposes of whether we should grant review or not, or whether there truly was a conflict or wasn't a conflict with some other case, thus bearing upon whether review should be granted. If a justice had written a supplemental memo, I would call upon that justice first, out of the order of seniority.

How often did that happen?

It did happen from time to time. One thing I changed was that it used to be that if you wrote a supplemental memo, you were pretty much guaranteed that the case would be assigned to you. I noticed in the past that justices would sometimes write a supplemental memo that really didn't add much, just saying, "Yes, I agree with the memo written by central staff, and I think we should grant review for such-and-such reason." I made it very clear—I believe I did so even in my initial round of visits with the various chambers—that the writing of a supplemental memo that did not really play a role in the court's decision to grant review would not result in the case being automatically assigned to that chambers, and also that I did not welcome justices or their staff attorneys, as had sometimes been the case in the past, lobbying to be assigned a particular case. I said, "That's not going to play any part in my assignment policies." If there had been a case, whether it was on the A list from the start or maybe even a B list case that had been elevated to the A list, where a justice had taken the position that, contrary to the central staff recommendation of a denial, this was a case that really should be granted, I would automatically assign the case to that justice if it were granted, as opposed to the situation of a justice only having written a pro forma supplemental memo supporting the position taken by the central staff memo. I didn't want intrigue and game playing, and that was understood. No one seemed to have any problem with that.

When we granted review, I would always, that day or within a day or two, assign the case to one of my colleagues or to myself. There were different factors involved in that assignment process. As a general matter, I tried to keep the workload fairly even in terms of cases in which review had been granted. The capital cases were assigned automatically through the clerk's office on a rotational basis, regardless of length or complexity, on the theory that the cases would eventually even themselves out in the long term. Beyond general numerical equality, I tried to make sure that no justice became, perhaps unwittingly, the expert on tax law or condemnation or something else that they might not relish a full diet of, but also that each chambers was assigned a mix of cases generally, among civil cases, and a mix between civil and criminal cases.

Is there anything to be said for the idea that it would be beneficial to have experts in certain areas?

We all had to prepare our position on these cases, but if the issue was something fairly exotic, I might be tempted to give, let's say, a DNA case to Justice Chin, but not to have him necessarily do all of the DNA cases. A justice's expertise would come into play through his or her input into the case, regardless of who was the author of the court's opinion. Under our court's practice, only a justice who voted to grant review is eligible for the original assignment of the case, so this narrows the field. Unlike the procedure followed at the U.S. Supreme Court, the Chief Justice of California makes the assignment whether or not he or she is among the justices who voted to grant review. Something that has not received attention, I believe, is how an opinion can be authored on our court by a justice who is not shown in the order granting review to be among those who voted to grant review. This generally is a tip-off that the case had to be reassigned because the original, tentative author was unable to muster a majority.

Aside from these fairly objective criteria, there was another aspect to my case assignment process that was more art than science. This involved making a reasoned guess whether the assigned justice would be able to garner a majority of the court in favor of his or her ultimate opinion. It would be undesirable and dilatory to assign a case to a justice who would be unlikely to obtain the votes of at least three of his or her colleagues to join the author in the end, and for me then to have to reassign the case—having to reinvent the wheel by reassigning another justice to analyze the briefs and the record almost from scratch and circulate a new draft, resulting in another round of P.R. responses from the justices. Certainly the scenario that I just described did occur on occasion. Once in a great while—and then it was very disruptive—it happened after oral argument, when the 90-day clock was running, that the tentative author was no longer able or willing to accommodate the position of a majority of the justices, but that was very, very rare.

In assigning a case, I sometimes would look at prior decisions of the court in terms of how particular justices had voted in other cases in that area of the law to help me guess whether a particular justice would be likely to garner a majority if assigned the new case. One tool that I possessed in making an informed assignment of a case was heeding the views expressed by the justices around the conference table as they voted to grant review. To come up with a scenario, let's say that four or more justices voted in favor of granting review, which is a sufficient number under our court's procedures. In the U.S. Supreme Court one less than a majority, or four out of nine, can grant review, although I think they're pretty wary about doing that because the four wouldn't necessarily feel very confident about how the case would come out. But anyway, they have that authority.

Under the scenario that I've posed of several justices on our court voting to grant review, let's say all of those voting to grant review felt there was a conflict in the decisional law. However, all but one of these justices stated that the First District Court of Appeal's decision was correct in their view, while the remaining justice thought the Second District got it right and the First District erred.

Of course, the justices are sufficiently open-minded that they're not going to finalize their views on the case at the time they vote to grant review. They're going to study the briefs, the internal paperwork that circulates among the justices by way of draft opinions, and the P.R.s. They'll consider the oral arguments. But there probably is a substantial chance that the justices in the majority—who felt, in the scenario I just related, that in the conflict of decisions the First District Court of Appeal was correct—are going to prevail. If I were to assign the case to the lone justice who voted to grant review but felt the First District was wrong, that assigned justice might very well circulate a work product that would not command a majority. Then it would be up to him or her to decide whether to change the views expressed in the tentative opinion and instead accommodate the majority—which, in all sorts of contexts, can happen, of course, but often doesn't. When the latter situation occurs, and the assigned justice declines to accommodate the majority, a lot of time and effort has been expended unproductively in the sense that another justice and staff need to start almost from scratch. That's where there was a bit of an art involved, trying to assign the case to someone who I had a sense—either based on the discussion around the conference table or based upon his or her own predilections as reflected by votes in other cases—would be likely to recommend a decision in the case that would command a majority of the court.

You mentioned that, although you didn't view them as voting blocs necessarily, there were certain justices who tended to be more like-minded on particular areas of the law. With this panel as it existed at this time, how did you think about those groupings in terms of the individuals? You mentioned before that Justices Mosk and Kennard might be more like-minded in some areas. What about the rest?

There were certain groupings on certain issues, but I can't think of any two justices who would never part ways on a case. To generalize, you could say there were some justices who were more likely, for example, to find that error in a criminal case was nonprejudicial. You had other justices who might be more inclined than others to weigh individual rights more heavily than the rights of a public or private entity that was on the other side of the case. These are only gross generalizations, because I had seen all sorts of breaks in predictable patterns. One illustration is my dissent in a case, *People v. Ayala*, in which Justice Mosk wrote an opinion for a majority of the court upholding a death penalty conviction, and I voted to reverse.

As you make clear, you're talking about looking for remarks about a particular case and then making your artful decision on that basis. It is substantial power in your hands, however, and I wonder if you can compare the way you exercised the power of assignment with the methods of your predecessor, having served as an associate under him?

I cannot speak authoritatively to this, but the understanding was—on my part and I believe on the part of my colleagues—that my predecessor, Chief Justice Lucas, relied heavily upon his chief of staff in making the assignments. Perhaps there were exceptions to that on some very special cases where Chief Lucas made the assignment himself. I can't vouch for this, but my understanding was that his chief of staff assigned the cases and that justices and staff would go to this staff member and make requests to be assigned certain cases. That's one of the reasons I instituted the policy that I alluded to just a few moments ago.

My approach was to personally make the assignments, to perform a lot of these seemingly ministerial functions myself rather than delegate them to my chief of staff.

To what extent did you consult your staff members about this, if at all?

Once in a while—but not most of the time—I would ask my chief of staff, "Who do you think, given the lay of the land here, would be a good candidate for assignment of this case?" I might be told, "Maybe one of these two chambers would be best." As you point out, it's a very substantial power on behalf of the chief. Although it doesn't mean, obviously, that the person to whom you assign the case is going to be able to garner a majority, the justice who has the first crack at the case has a better than even chance of being able to prevail than if he or she comes in later as a dissenter trying to peel people off of what's a presumptive majority opinion. I will candidly admit that my own views of how a case should come out—which, like the views of my colleagues, I'm sure, were always tentative views subject to being changed by the briefing, the exchange among the justices, and the oral argument—played a role in my decision whom to assign the case to, whether it would be to one of the six associate justices, and if so to which one, or to myself. It is a substantial authority, one that probably isn't given as much attention as it deserves.

How did your methods in this change over the course of the whole time you were chief, if at all?

I believe my appreciation of the significance of the role I had in deciding which chambers would be assigned the case was something that evolved and that I began to realize more and more was a very important matter. I ended up often spending a lot of time, even agonizing, over where a case should be assigned.

How did you think about the matter of productivity and output by the seven of you?

It was something I was concerned with, never to the point of wanting to sacrifice quality for quantity, but I felt we had to, first of all, try to be as efficient as possible in getting cases out once we granted review. We had this other list, the yellow list that I didn't go through regularly at conference but I always had it there, and it chronicled the listed cases and their progress or lack of progress since review had been granted. Those were the cases in which a calendar memo had not yet circulated. There was a perception, and once in a great while it was accurate, that cases fell into a black hole once review was granted. The outside world never knew why a case might take so long to be set for oral argument. They just saw a date when review was granted and eventually a date when it was set for oral argument. The briefing might have just been concluded or maybe it was concluded months or a year before, and they were wondering, "Why hasn't the case been set for argument?"

Sometimes it hadn't been set for argument because no justice could command a majority. When I came onto the court I was assigned a major case on assumption of risk, *Knight v. Jewett*. It seemed the court was just waiting for a new justice to join the court and tackle it, because a couple justices had had a go at it and the case had not been in a position to be set for oral argument. I approached it a bit differently and managed to get something out that we were able to put out as a plurality opinion. The outside world has no idea whether there have been numerous drafts put out by the author of a tentative majority, what the responses have been, what changes and accommodations have been attempted, successfully or unsuccessfully, no idea whether the case has been reassigned— taken from one justice and given to another justice to start from scratch.

Often there are very good and legitimate reasons why the court seems to have taken forever to put out its opinion. On the other hand, there is the occasional case where the opinion comes out unusually soon—and it might be that the case had been assigned to a justice who had just finished up with another opinion, the briefing came in quickly on the new case and was given to a research attorney who had just cleared his desk, the opinion got out right away, and the legal newspapers write: "The court really pushed this case. It's obvious that for some reason or other they wanted to get their opinion out right away." It may have been totally fortuitous. I would get a big chuckle out of such speculation. On the other hand, when there is great delay there may be all sorts of other speculation. Sometimes it's, "The court has totally forgotten about this case. Isn't this terrible?" The court may have been doing tons of work on the case but been unable to get a majority on board and get the case ready to set for oral argument.

But once in a great while a case does languish in a chambers where the justice is occupied with a number of other weighty matters. Perhaps the attorney on the staff who was given the case to work up—and may have been given that particular case because this attorney has done a lot of work in that area of the law and is the logical choice to work on it—was up to his eyebrows getting some other cases out and just doesn't get around to it. No justice forgets about a case, but there may be certain situations where the Chief Justice has to, as I did occasionally, prod and say, "Look, we've actually gotten a couple of letters inquiring what's happening on the such-and-such case. We granted review two years ago and no one has heard anything." In some situations, the attorneys for the parties receive letters from the clerk requesting supplemental briefing, and they know something is up, that the court needs additional assistance.

What form would a prod like that take from you and in what setting?

I might bring it up at conference, or, much more likely so as not to put the justice in an embarrassing situation, I would just send a memo to the justice with a copy to his or her chief of staff saying, "This case has been on the yellow list showing we granted review two years ago. What's your estimate when you'll get something out?" or "We've received some inquiry or some complaint, and I need to be in a position to know what the situation is." As Chief Justice, you have to be kind of a gatekeeper just to make sure these things don't disappear. Once in a while I would receive an explanation that, for example, the assigned chambers was waiting for our court or the U.S. Supreme Court to act on some other case that was related in some way. Other times I would be told, "Thanks for reminding us; we'll really push this case ahead." Occasionally, the court—either at the time review was granted or after granting review—will put out an order to counsel stating either that briefing is deferred or the setting of oral argument is deferred or submission of the case is deferred pending the U.S. Supreme Court's decision in *A v. B* so that our court would have the benefit of the high court's opinion.

In addition to granting review and denying review, the court has many other tools at its disposal in performing its constitutional obligation to establish precedent and settle the law. One procedure is the "grant and hold." If the court has granted review on a case and then one or more other cases come up that seek to have the benefit of the court's review in the lead case, the court can and usually will grant review but, in its order granting review, will note that it is deferring briefing in the case and that the case is being held until final disposition in the lead case of *X v. Y*, which is the initial matter in which we granted review. Then when the opinion in the lead case comes out and becomes final—after the period for acting on a petition for rehearing or a request to modify the opinion has expired or been acted upon—the court will in the "grant and hold" case—and sometimes there are dozens of grant and hold cases involving some major issue—issue an order stating that the case of such-and-such having been granted and held, it is hereby transferred back to the Court of Appeal for redetermination in light of the lead case of *X v. Y*. Sometimes, however, the Court of Appeal's decision in the grant and hold case is entirely consistent with what we ended up determining we would do in the lead case. In that instance, we issue an order that doesn't burden the Court of Appeal with having to conduct further proceedings when they, in effect, got it right the first time. Our order in that situation instead will simply state that review is dismissed, and the opinion of the Court of Appeal stands.

If that opinion happened to be among the roughly 10 percent of the Court of Appeal opinions that the appellate court has ordered published—that is, to appear in the bound volumes and serve as precedent—the case remains unpublished, because our act of granting review, even on a grant and hold, has the effect of ordering that the Court of Appeal opinion not be published in the bound volumes and not serve as precedent. Even though the Court of Appeal ends up being viewed as having correctly resolved the case—after languishing before our court for several months in this limbo situation, or maybe even a year or two—its opinion does not then reappear as precedent as a published opinion except when, once in a great while, we specifically order that the Court of Appeal's opinion in the grant-and-hold case be republished in the official reports. But usually we don't take that action.

The reason for that might be—?

The reason we would republish it? If we conclude one of two things, I suppose: first, it might be that the grant-and-hold case serves to further flush out, perhaps in a slightly different context, the ramifications of the rule that we are establishing in the lead case and would be a useful addition to the jurisprudence of the state; or second—and I've seen this happen from time to time—the lead case decided by our Supreme Court decides to rely in part upon the authority and reasoning of that grant-and-hold case, which had been taken off the books by our order granting review. For us to say, "Yes, and as the Court of Appeal said in such-and-such case," we need to have a published opinion. So we would order it republished, if you will, so that we're not violating the cardinal rule of citing a nonpublished opinion. This gets almost metaphysical. [Laughter]

Yes it does. This whole matter of publication, which we touched on before, is very much of interest because California's system is rather complex in this way. Let's talk about this whole feature of appellate work in California.

Certainly, but why don't I first just add one other method we employ that is closely related to the grant and hold and then go on to answer your question. Another alternative to simply granting or denying review is the "grant and transfer," which is somewhat akin to the grant-and-hold process that I just described except that we do not hold the case. We grant review in this situation and transfer the case forthwith, in the same written order, back to the Court of Appeal. This type of disposition occurs in one of two instances.

One might be in the situation similar to the grant and hold where there already has been—instead of there being in the future—a decision by either the California Supreme Court or perhaps the U.S. Supreme Court that would be fairly dispositive of this new case, and the Court of Appeal didn't have the benefit of it because our decision or the U.S. Supreme Court's decision came down after the decision of California's Court of Appeal was issued. What we do then is grant review and transfer the case forthwith back to the Court of Appeal with directions to redetermine the cause in light of our ruling in *X v. Y* or in light of the U.S. Supreme Court's decision in *A v. B*. The second situation in which we might do a "grant and transfer" is where a Court of Appeal has received a petition for extraordinary relief, usually a petition for writ of mandamus or prohibition, and that court—quite understandably in view of the thousands of such petitions for discretionary review that it receives every year—has denied the requested relief summarily, as it usually does, in a one-sentence order stating, "The petition for such-and-such relief is denied."

The California Supreme Court may have a different view of the significance of the issue posed by the petition, especially in light of our overall perspective on a statewide level, where we do get thousands of petitions and have a record showing, over the years, how frequently a particular issue has come before us. With the benefit of a central staff memo, we may feel that this issue merits full review and shouldn't just be denied in a one-sentence order, even though the appellate court's action on the petition is purely discretionary. In that situation our court concludes the petition should not be denied summarily and that a full cause should be made of it, with full briefing on the merits, oral argument, and a written opinion from the appellate court. The word "cause" in that context has a different connotation than its use in the vernacular. A matter is a "cause" when it has been filed and heard in a trial court and there has been an appeal that reaches an appellate court. But if a petition seeking discretionary review by way of a writ is filed, that is not a cause unless and until the court in question issues what is called an "alternative writ" or an "order to show cause" and then orders briefing, usually followed by oral argument, and then issues a written opinion. That opinion subsequently issued by the Court of Appeal, may ultimately itself be— and very often is—the subject of a petition for review in our court.

What we're saying when we grant and transfer in this situation is, basically, "This is important enough that we want an appellate court to look at it on the merits," because when a Court of Appeal or even a trial court denies a petition for a writ that's seeking discretionary intervention by the court, the court can deny relief, can deny the petition, for many kinds of reasons. It may be that the

appellate court doesn't feel the issue is all that important. The court isn't necessarily saying there's no merit in the particular petition. Or it may feel that there's
been too much delay in coming to the appellate court, or there could be all sorts
of other procedural reasons that cause a court to conclude that it is not going to
intervene. It may not be a decision involving the merits. In fact, very often it's
not a decision on the merits. What our court is saying when it issues a grant and
transfer order under the circumstances I've just described is, "We at the Supreme Court have made a determination that this is important enough that we
want you, the Court of Appeal, to determine this petition on the merits, not necessarily in favor of the petitioner but to conduct a review on the merits," resulting in a decision that is then subject to our possible review.

This reminds me to note that once in a while we grant review on our own
motion when the parties have not sought review. We don't do that frequently,
but sometimes it may be sufficiently apparent that this is a matter of statewide
importance or that there is a conflict in the decisional law and that a particular
case provides a suitable vehicle for the Supreme Court to perform its function of
resolving the issue of law. Our central staff or perhaps an individual justice will
take note of the case and write a memo, and we may grant review on our own
motion.

I'm ready to move on to the question that you posed to me about publication and depublication of opinions. The constitution of the State of California
gives the Supreme Court the responsibility of determining which appellate opinions are to be published.[3] By rule, all of the California Supreme Court opinions
are published, both in "review granted" cases and in death penalty cases. The
court has developed practices, reflected in the rules of court circulated by the
Judicial Council, for determining how and when it should be decided whether to
publish a Court of Appeal opinion. More than 10,000 Court of Appeal opinions
are filed each year. The Court of Appeal was publishing about 8 percent of
them, but this has increased to about 10 percent.

Before I get to the subject of appellate justices deciding which opinions are
to be published and which are not, and the Supreme Court's role in reviewing
those determinations, let me indicate that there are some persons—it's almost a
kind of movement, if there can be a movement about anything as unexciting as
what gets published in the bound case reports—pushing to have all Court of
Appeal opinions published. Some federal courts have gone in that direction.

I feel very strongly that universal publication would be a bad practice. First
of all, it would mean there would have to be 10 times as many Court of Appeal

---

[3] Cal. Const., art. VI, sec. 14, provides in part: "The legislature shall provide for the
prompt publication of such opinions of the Supreme Court and courts of appeal as the
Supreme Court deems appropriate."

opinions that the appellate justices and their staffs, trial judges, and lawyers would have to ferret out in deciding what is the law. To have every civil case involving every slip and fall or fender bender, and to have every criminal case affirming a conviction for joyriding or theft or you name it, every drug case, cluttering up the official reports would, in my estimation, make it somewhat akin to finding the needle in the haystack when you had serious research to do. I realize that much of the research is done electronically, but you still would greatly compound the task of researching the applicable law. You also have these acres and acres of law books that you need to have in judges' chambers, in county law libraries, and in lawyers' offices. I know it sounds like the old refrain from *The Music Man* about "trouble in River City," but take the number of published opinions and multiply them from 10 percent to 100 percent publication, and you'd have great expense for those who need the hard volumes, which are in fact needed and will always be needed, whatever the advances in electronic publication. You need the office space or courthouse floor space for those volumes. You need the shelving. You actually need the steel reinforcement in the structure, or else my library there in my fifth floor chambers at the California Supreme Court would have ended up on the first floor. Universal publication would have a lot of consequences, including the time and energy devoted by government lawyers and private lawyers to researching 10 times as many opinions for no legitimate purpose. The cost of all of this has to be borne by someone, and it would be the taxpayers and the lawyers' clients.

Some persons felt that somehow an effort was being made to hide the development of the law through nonpublication and depublication. I suppose there are always going to be conspiracy theorists in any walk of life. I came to an accommodation to address this concern. I consulted the Reporter of Decisions, who told me—and they were always a helpful office, as I indicated before— "You know, in addition to putting out all these unpublished opinions the way we do at the clerk's counter, we could also release them on the judicial branch website for a period of 90 days." Anyone sitting at home or in a law office then can look and read this vast body of not really new law that's coming out, and then these unpublished opinions will vanish off the website and into cyberspace after 90 days, although you could always have the Reporter of Decisions retrieve them in hard copy if you needed them. That way everyone would know there's no vast conspiracy.

There actually have been three brothers who have had a lifetime obsession with trying to have all the Court of Appeal opinions published. One of them practically tackled me at the State Bar convention, trying to plead his cause, but my security intervened. I believe Justice Werdegar was giving a speech in Marin County that was disrupted by one of the brothers, who had to be forcibly ejected.

They feel passionately about this arcane issue. One of them has run for attorney general and for other offices on the platform of having all Court of Appeal opinions published—not an issue likely to kindle a great fire in the hearts of our electorate. [Laughter]

It is something that some people feel very strongly about. They go to Sacramento and, I guess, hang out long enough in the outer office of a legislator, so that on occasion I would get a letter from a legislator—that looked as if it had been prepared by one of the three brothers—that would go on at great length. It was usually about the same letter. Then I would write back or, if I happened to be in Sacramento, drop in and have a personal chat with the senator or assembly member who had sent the letter. After hearing my explanation, the legislator every time would drop his or her proposal to require universal publication. This happened in several legislative sessions.

Aside from the merits, I'm glad that such legislation always has been dropped, because it might spawn a much more interesting legal issue, namely a constitutional conflict—whether the legislature has the authority to require publication of all Court of Appeal opinions, when the constitution expressly reserves that right in the California Supreme Court. I believe that would pose a very serious constitutional problem over a minor issue. [Laughter] By the way, the California Supreme Court now depublishes an extremely small number of the thousands of Court of Appeal opinions. The depublications have fallen from more than 100 in some years in the late 1980s and early 1990s to less than a couple dozen in recent years and as low as four in one recent year.

It's the old separation of powers again. Are the folks seeking publication of all appellate opinions also pursuing this in the federal appellate level?

Yes, there is such a movement, but I'm not sure they're actually the same individuals. There may be different factors that would provide more justification for publication in the federal arena, where there are far fewer opinions. The deleterious effect of full publication might be less in the federal system, and the benefits greater. I don't know; I'm just raising that as a possibility. But I think it would be a terrible idea in California.

As another accommodation, I appointed a committee, which my colleague Justice Werdegar graciously agreed to chair, that studied the differences in publication rates among the Courts of Appeal and recommended some changes in the standards that guide those courts in determining whether to order an opinion published. The appellate justices participating in the particular case make that decision in the first instance, whether to order an opinion of theirs published, at the time they issue the opinion. Justice Werdegar's committee was very constructive and helpful. What they properly did was to outline factors that should guide an intermediate appellate court in determining whether or not to order an opinion in a particular case published and to list certain factors that should not be considered—for instance, protecting a trial judge or an attorney mentioned in the opinion from embarrassment should not be considered. In effect, I believe the Werdegar committee caused there to be created a presumption in favor of publication—not that this means most cases should be published, but that you should look more for a reason why an opinion shouldn't be published rather than just saying it has to be an extraordinary situation in order to justify publication. Probably as a result of the committee's report and recommendations, the percentage of published opinions has gone up by at least 2 percent, maybe more than that.

Some people felt it was, per se, arbitrary that certain Court of Appeal divisions published at a higher rate than others. But even there, subtle differences in caseload exist that would justify variations. The Sixth District Court of Appeal includes Silicon Valley, so a higher percentage of the cases involve complex civil litigation and therefore issues that might justify publication. The same is true to a large degree of the Fourth Appellate District, Division Three, which is headquartered in Orange County. One can't adopt the cookie-cutter approach of saying, "Because the Sixth District in San Jose publishes more than the Fifth District in Fresno, it shows something's wrong and capricious." That's not the case, and also there are always going to be differences that arise just because of the viewpoints and approaches of the various justices who happen to be serving on a court at a given moment in time.

The Supreme Court, by the way, also has the power to order an opinion published when it was not deemed worthy of publication by the Court of Appeal. Most of the time when our court does that, and it's not very frequently, it's when the Court of Appeal itself has had a change of heart. Why would they do that? The Court of Appeal, handling such a large workload, recognizes that, although they have pride in all their work, if they're going to certify an opinion for publication then they'll do that extra polishing and maybe cite some additional authority. If it's not going to be published—although this doesn't at all affect the result or basic rationale of an opinion—they may not give it that extra effort. They can't do that extra polish for every one of their thousands of opinions. They don't have the resources to do that. By the way, the Court of Appeal has the authority to order that only portions of an opinion be published, but the Supreme Court never orders partial publication or partial depublication of an appellate court opinion.

Once in a while, after the Court of Appeal's opinion is filed, the court receives a request from one or both sides in the case or from third parties who will say, "This is really important, and it does add to the law. We need the guidance provided by this opinion, and having it as citable precedent will avoid a lot of future litigation." It sometimes is too late for the appellate justices to change their mind about publishing their opinion. They may have lost jurisdiction; the time for them to act on it may have expired, but our court may still have jurisdiction. The Court of Appeal in that situation may communicate to us: "We would publish this opinion, but we no longer have jurisdiction. We request that the Supreme Court order our opinion published." Our court gives great weight to those requests. And it is extremely rare for our court to ever order a Court of Appeal opinion published at the request of one of the parties or of third parties when the appellate court has not joined in asking us to do so.

How does that resolve, though, with the overall duty to develop areas of the law?

It's a balancing of various factors. We may just feel as a matter of professional courtesy that if the authors of the opinion don't feel it is up to snuff qualitatively, we should defer to that. It has been very rare that we have not heeded their wishes concerning a request to publish a previously unpublished opinion. Perhaps we're providing more professional courtesy than we should. I don't know. Depublishing an opinion is sort of a misnomer, as the opinion appears in physical form in the paperback advance sheets but will not appear in the official hardbound reports if we order it "not for publication," thereby rendering the opinion uncitable as precedent.

When we depublish, we often are influenced by the views of third parties, whether it's an industry group or an employee group or a public interest group that may have pointed out to us the deleterious, misleading, or confusing effect of the appellate ruling. The views of those same entities or individuals also can be a factor motivating us to find the issue sufficiently significant to warrant granting review instead of ordering depublication. Sometimes persons or organizations petitioning our court will pursue both avenues simultaneously—asking for review to be granted but, if not granted, then depublication.

Occasionally, on our own and faced only with a petition seeking review, we will conclude that the case does not warrant granting review, but the points made in the petition seeking review are such that they would justify our ordering the opinion not for publication, even though there wasn't a specific request to depublish. Sometimes there's no filing of any sort with us, and just as we might, in the rare situation, grant review on our own motion, we might on our own instead order the opinion depublished.

How important is this phrase "not available as precedent" in this whole matter of publishing and depublishing?

It is very important, because it is considered quite improper and contrary to the rules for an attorney, in a brief or at oral argument, to cite a case that has not been ordered published. For purposes of consideration by a court—whether it's a trial court, a Court of Appeal, or our court—an unpublished opinion is the equivalent of a case that was never decided, with one important exception: when it is law of the case—established in that very same case—or related to the particular litigation, then you can cite it as a prior proceeding in the case that is now before the court. But you can't otherwise, in any California court, cite an unpublished opinion without getting slapped down by the court.

It's easy to see why there's a certain shroud of mystery around this whole aspect of the court's work.

It's almost metaphysical to think that something that appeared in written form is now depublished, just vanishes into some sort of stratospheric oblivion without being citable as precedent.

What else does the public need to know to have a better understanding of why it's done this way, other than the difficulty of dealing with the other 90 percent of the opinions if they were all published?

I suppose one could come up with this simple analogy: being a motorist and, instead of having a couple of signs on the highway directing you, "Slow to 30 around the turn," and "Stop sign ahead," having to confront 10 or 12 signs at once during your vehicular journey, by analogy to your journey through the law.

The sheer volume of legal cases in California is certainly a big factor. How did our system of publication and depublication get the way it is today?

The Supreme Court has exercised that authority since the early 1960s, when the sheer volume of opinions, resulting from the explosion in population and litigation, began to overwhelm the courts and the practice of law. There was no intermediate Court of Appeal until 1904, when the First, Second, and Third Districts were established to replace the commissioner positions at the Supreme Court. The Supreme Court would put out a volume—a very thin one, at that—of its decisions every year, starting with 1850, the first year of statehood. They were very short opinions, as well, so you didn't have the problem of being inundated in a sea of paper, in a constant snowstorm of jurisprudence the way we do now.

What are other states doing in this area, if anything?

I'm not certain, but I know they don't have a system as large as we do. There aren't any absolute truths here. Despite the arguments I've raised against 100 percent publication, if we had a system that was as small as so many of our states, the adverse effects of publishing everything would be much less severe than they are in our state. California is unique in many ways.

Is there any feature of our publication procedures that you feel still needs a bit of tinkering or outright change?

I think Justice Werdegar's committee performed a very valuable function. I'm not saying that its report takes care of the issue forever. I believe it will probably be a good idea, let's just say every 10 years or so, to take another look at the issue and see how the practices of the intermediate Courts of Appeal are working out, and to consult knowledgeable individuals and organizations like the California Academy of Appellate Lawyers to see how they feel about it and whether some fine-tuning or major overhaul would then be in order. I do find it unlikely that any change in circumstances would cause me to become a convert and favor publication of each and every opinion issued among the thousands and thousands of appeals that are determined as a matter of right in our state's intermediate Courts of Appeal.

The California Supreme Court's opinions are very different, because by definition we select those matters that involve issues of statewide importance and conflict in the law. There's no question but that anything we do is by its nature significant, although sometimes to a narrower segment of the popular or legal community than others. Publication of all intermediate appellate court opinions also would greatly expand and complicate the Supreme Court's obligation to monitor and resolve conflicts among the published, precedent-setting decisions of the six Courts of Appeal. Bear in mind there is a right of appeal of every minor, inconsequential case to the intermediate Court of Appeal. I suppose there is nothing that is totally inconsequential to the parties involved, but in terms of importance to the law, to the development of legal principles, many cases are totally inconsequential. Some individuals have even questioned whether that right of appeal itself should be limited. I'm not calling for that, but at least I'm calling for not spending the time and resources, with the consequent diversion, of publishing every decision that reviews a relatively inconsequential trial court ruling.

The reform you did institute to place the unpublished decisions in an electronic form available to the public, to all users, for 90 days—what response did you get to that change, and how much difference did it make?

I believe it more or less did hush the conspiracy theorists, because it is difficult to rationally make an accusation of trying to hide something from the public when it is being put out on the Internet. But this doesn't satisfy all of those people. It's a real matter of dogma for some of them. This electronic availability is useful to many persons, including lawyers who, even though they can't cite the unpublished opinions they find on the web, may be able to get an idea how the justices about to hear the case have ruled in similar situations. Yet, not only are the attorneys barred from being able to cite such unpublished opinions, but the Court of Appeal justices in that division aren't in any way bound to decide the same way as they did in their prior unpublished opinion. Nevertheless reading these prior decisions might give a lawyer some comfort and insight into what was previously decided by the justices in whose court the attorney is about to appear.

We've gone through the process of the Wednesday petition conferences. What might we need to add to our earlier discussions about the administrative conferences taking place monthly?

There is a broad range of administrative matters that can come before the court. Some of them involve rule making and internal procedures. For example, one thing you and I have already discussed is the manner in which I changed the policy on the assignment of justices pro tem to serve on the California Supreme Court. That eventually was adopted as a court policy at one of the administrative conferences.

Another administrative matter involves establishing a rotating list of acting Chief Justices. Even though I was always available, even on some of my exotic vacations—with the one exception of my first trip to Antarctica—there are certain things that require the immediate attention of the Chief Justice, such as issuing a stay or some other order. A rotational list of acting Chief Justices was put out once a year, starting of course with Justice Kennard as the senior associate justice, who would serve for three months as acting Chief Justice, followed by the next in line, Justice Baxter, and so forth. By the way, if the particular acting chief were not available for a particular action, the duty would automatically devolve upon the next justice in line until the clerk found someone who could act upon the particular matter. If I had to miss the court's weekly petition conference, the designated acting Chief Justice would preside.

I tended to be very much hands on even when I was away. I would receive FedEx packages and faxes and calls on my cell phone. I remember having a 45-minute conversation with three of my staff attorneys while I was in the Sahara Desert in Morocco, with perfect reception. I would lose the signal when I went the five minutes between my San Francisco home and the court's headquarters, but somehow that call from faraway was loud and clear. [Laughter] So much of the court's work could be done on the road, as I indicated in discussing the visits to the 58 counties—the car literally became a movable office. But there were some instances where you needed an acting chief.

What was your thinking in remaining so hands-on, even when you were away?

I'd like to think it was something other than being a control freak. [Laughter] I thought that because I had the responsibility for various things, there should be a certain continuity and consistency. Better to be given the opportunity to act on a matter than later find out something was done that I wouldn't have done or would like to undo. That was true with regard to my role as chair of the Judicial Council as well. I tried to exercise these various responsibilities wherever I was. Your reference to "hands-on" reminds me that I rejected suggestions I authorize the use of my facsimile signature on the frequent occasions when I was presented with hundreds of orders at a time to sign. My thinking was that to many persons the court system appears to be impersonal, and that it was important to directly lay hand to paper on all the original orders, leaving the facsimile signature for the copies.

This brings me to a fun, small change in our processes that relates to what we were talking about, being out-of-state. The California Supreme Court had an antiquated policy providing that once any justice went outside the state boundaries, he or she was divested of all authority—no longer could act on a matter, could not okay a change to an opinion, could not vote on a petition for review, and so forth. It was very disruptive, because my colleagues and I often would attend speaking engagements or conferences, and the minute we stepped across the state line we could not, under our prior case authority, continue to participate in a case. This could cause a delay in issuing an order, perhaps because there wasn't a sufficient number of justices available, or an opinion.

This is different from what happens with regard to the governor. The constitution expressly states that once the governor leaves the state, he or she has no authority to act and the lieutenant governor is empowered to exercise the full authority of the governor's office. Once in a while there was some mischief between those officials, created by that provision. I remember many years ago when Lieutenant Governor Mike Curb contemplated making some judicial appointments in Governor Jerry Brown's absence. Instead of filling dozens of trial court vacancies—which he could have successfully done provided the appointees would have immediately accepted the appointment and taken the oath of office—Curb chose to make one appointment to the Court of Appeal. That was the very kind of appointment that could be undone, because it was subject to confirmation by the Commission on Judicial Appointments and the governor was able to withdraw the appointment before the commission could confirm it. The appellate jurisprudence related to this incident, which involved Justice Armand Arabian, is set forth in the *In re Governorship* case.

The situation is different with regard to the California Supreme Court and its justices. Whatever difficulties or disabilities ensued from a justice's absence from the state, those were strictly self-inflicted wounds that the court had brought upon itself through its own decisions in cases it had ruled upon. It was rather absurd, because you could be in a populous area on the Nevada shore of Lake Tahoe and be deemed unable to carry out your judicial responsibilities. Yet if someone could reach you by shortwave radio at the top of Mount Whitney or in the middle of the Mojave Desert, you were inside California and there was no legal impediment to your acting, even though it would be pretty tough to get a piece of paper to you. [Laughter]

I decided that this was causing unnecessary disruption in our proceedings. Although I don't favor, generally, the use of the word "test case," I did decide we needed one to alter this procedure. The case the court employed was *People v. Billa*, a criminal case in which the court was unanimous—and a case of not above-average significance. At the very end of the opinion, in a footnoted reference to the justices listed as concurring in the court's decision, it was noted that I had communicated my concurrence by facsimile from out of state, where I was presiding over the Conference of Chief Justices. The opinion observed that although the early cases disallowing a justice's actions on a case while temporarily out of state "may have reflected the vagaries and unreliability of the communication systems of the time, modern methods of communication have rendered such concerns obsolete."

This is an illustration of the court's sometimes getting bogged down in old practices, just because they remained in existence, when the rationale had long since vanished and we needed to find ways of conducting the court's business more expeditiously.

I'm admiring some of the turns of phrase in that very much. Why was this the proper venue for making the change?

This case provided an ideal vehicle for instituting this change in the court's procedures. First of all, my vote wasn't going to make any difference—the opinion was unanimous—and the case wasn't monumental in terms of the significance of our jurisprudence. Second, there was such an obviously substantial and justifiable reason for the absence of the justice in question, namely myself, presiding over the Conference of Chief Justices, as opposed to: "Because Chief Justice George was lounging on the beach at Waikiki he couldn't be there to sign the opinion." [Laughter] Perhaps the most significant thing that came out of the case was not the resolution of the issues related to the criminal offense, but rather the ultimate footnote in the case dealing with the powers of justices of the Supreme Court.

Speaking of internal improvements, what else did you want to mention in terms of things you might have brought before the monthly administrative conferences with your colleagues?

One of those matters certainly was holding outreach sessions of the California Supreme Court. That's something that I am particularly proud of in terms of my legacy. The court, as I mentioned, with the rarest of exceptions, always stuck to its three traditional venues for oral argument, our San Francisco headquarters, Sacramento, and Los Angeles. The choice of those locations in turn has a bit of interesting history behind it that might be worth mentioning.

When California's first constitution was promulgated right before California became a state in 1850, there was no firm siting of the state capital. In fact, the capital moved around the state for some time. There were a number of cities and towns—San Jose, Vallejo, and Benicia—that served as the capital before Sacramento. Our second and current constitution was promulgated in 1878–1879, pursuant to a constitutional convention. That constitution permanently established Sacramento as the state capital, although legislation had specified since 1854 that the capital was Sacramento. The governor and the legislature were located in that city, and there was a move to require the California Supreme Court to situate itself in Sacramento as well. In fact, the court had previously met there. Right in Old Town Sacramento the Supreme Court's courtroom is still preserved as part of the state park system, on the second floor of the B. F. Hastings building, which had housed the Wells Fargo Co. and served as the national western terminus of the Pony Express. The bench accommodated three justices, which was then the composition of the court—later expanded over the years from three to five, and ultimately to the present number of seven justices.

When the 150th anniversary of the California Supreme Court occurred in 2000, the court decided at my suggestion to hold its session in the original Sacramento courtroom that had been used by our court from 1855 to 1859. These commemorative proceedings are set forth as an appendix, with a photograph, in volume 22 of the Cal 4th Official Reports. Side tables were used to expand the original three-justice bench to accommodate the seven current members of the court. Having sat in that courtroom in the 1850s, the court later returned to San Francisco. It even went down to San Jose for a while. The justices were not particularly eager to be required to permanently situate the court in Sacramento. What I'm about to recount to you, I found hard to believe until I called for a copy of the actual debates of the 1878–1879 constitutional convention. These debates included discussions on the question of the proper site for the California Supreme Court. The justices and their supporters were very eager that the court should be able to situate itself where it wanted to, which quite obviously was San Francisco. There were all sorts of aspersions made about the quality of life in Sacramento.

None of them true, of course.

None of them true now, perhaps, but some of them true then. [Laughter] Of course, the city was subject to frequent flooding when the river would go over the levees. There was one member of the convention who said that—and this is almost the exact language, as I recall—"A vulture flying over Sacramento would be likely to fall dead in its tracks." Another reference was made to the quality of the water in Sacramento being undrinkable, another to the wine available in Sacramento being adulterated, and another reference—reflecting, again, the frontier days in the aftermath of the gold rush era—to the quality of the local whiskey being quite inferior. There was also something that today would be characterized as a sexist reference to the quality of the female companionship available in Sacramento being quite inferior to that available in San Francisco. [Laughter] I don't know which one, or which combination, of these arguments carried the day, but the ultimate compromise was that the court would be able to situate itself wherever it darn well pleased, which obviously was San Francisco, provided it would hold sessions twice a year in Sacramento and four times a year in Los Angeles. That is the traditional practice that has prevailed to this day since the late 1800s, subject to the special sessions that the court holds elsewhere.

The legislature at some point passed a statute that required justices of the Supreme Court to reside in Sacramento. You may recall the famous case of *People v. Chessman* involving Caryl Chessman, who had the moniker the Red Light Bandit. He was one of the last individuals in California to receive the death penalty for a crime that did not result in the death of the victim, although he terrorized and sexually assaulted women. He became his own jailhouse lawyer, and a pretty good one, even though he had no formal training in the law. In one of his appeals to the California Supreme Court, he raised the following issue. He said that the justices of the California Supreme Court lacked jurisdiction to review the judgment sentencing him to death because they had not complied with the statute requiring them to reside in Sacramento. In its opinion, the court acknowledged that Chessman was correct concerning what the statute said. The court held, however, that the statute was unconstitutional because it purported to add to the qualifications required for holding the office of Justice of the Supreme Court. These qualifications are limited to those set forth in the constitution, and any statutory attempt to prescribe additional qualifications was therefore invalid. Chessman was executed several months later. His claim was one more episode in the history of the California Supreme Court's locations over the years.

The oral arguments held in the court's original Sacramento courtroom were just one of many special sessions of the California Supreme Court held during my tenure as Chief Justice. I would like to explain the origin of those sessions.

Had something like this been done before?

Special sessions of the court had been conducted in Monterey's Colton Hall, including one held in 1959 commemorating the 110th anniversary of the adoption of California's first constitution in 1849 at the convention held in that hall.[4] There have been a couple other special sessions in the past, but not on a regular basis, and prior special sessions were essentially commemorative in nature rather than an attempt to conduct outreach to the community.

What I wanted to do was extend in a different way the outreach that I had undertaken in making my visits to the 58 counties. I did that in several ways. First of all, at my suggestion the Judicial Council established the practice of having a group of council members go to outlying counties and follow up, in the aftermath of my visits, on what was being done to implement changes and how to address local problems. Those visits continue to this day and have been very constructive, causing the local judges, lawyers, court staff, and community at large to feel that they're part of a statewide effort and not just battling ahead on their own.

Preceding the actual outreach sessions, I started off my first year as Chief Justice by holding some commemorative sessions of the California Supreme Court in honor of notable figures, usually justices of the court, who had recently passed away. The session would consist of some prepared remarks made by var-

---

[4] Monterey did not meet the official criterion as a capital of the State of California, because the legislature never met in that city.

ious individuals called upon to address the court, and then some remarks by myself as well, all of which would appear in the bound official reports of the opinions of our court, usually accompanied by a photograph of the deceased individual. The outreach session proceedings likewise appeared in the bound volumes of our decisions, accompanied by photographs of the court in special session or of the student participants. I believe the first special session over which I presided—and these all appear in different volumes of the California Official Reports—was in Volume 13 in 1996, my first year as Chief Justice. If you look at these volumes you'll see along the spine of some of the books, in addition to the number of the volume, a small strip along the leather binding that indicates, for example, in this instance, "In re Memoriam B. E. Witkin," honoring our preeminent scholar of California law, Bernard Witkin, who wrote upwards of 30 volumes of law explaining and defining the law of California. The court held a special session in 1999 to commemorate the rededication of our Supreme Court's San Francisco courtroom after we moved back to our historic headquarters on McAllister Street following a ten-year absence due to the renovation necessitated by the Loma Prieta earthquake. I thought it would be appropriate when Justice Stanley Mosk attained the historic record of service in number of years on the California Supreme Court to have a special recognition. On December 26, 1999, Justice Mosk surpassed Justice John Shenk with 35 years' service on our court. His service on the California Supreme Court began in 1964, soon after he hired me to work in the California attorney general's office.

Additional special session proceedings held by the court are reported in other volumes of the Official Reports, memorializing recently deceased members of the California Supreme Court—Chief Justice Rose Bird and Justices Otto Kaus, Frank Newman, Allen Broussard, Ray Sullivan, Frank Richardson, Stanley Mosk, Marcus Kaufman, and David Eagleson, as well as Brian Clearwater, a member of the court's clerical staff who served as calendar coordinator. The court also commemorated the legislature's renaming of the Library and Courts Building, where our court holds its Sacramento sessions, in honor of Justice Mosk.

I also commemorated, from the bench, the 20-year anniversaries of Justice Kennard's and Justice Baxter's service on our court, and Justice Kennard surprised me at a court session with some remarks on behalf of my colleagues on the court, honoring my 10-year anniversary as Chief Justice.

As an aside, given his long tenure, what kind of position did Justice Mosk hold among this group by the time you became chief? How did you all think about and evaluate him?

Everyone showed him great respect. Some of the members of the court disagreed very strongly with him on some legal issues, but always politely. He would sometimes peck out these pithy dissents on his typewriter, which is still on display, with other Mosk and Witkin paraphernalia, in the court library. He was certainly the institutional memory of the court. He could tell you when and why something happened decades before any of us were on the court. He had a very sharp sense of humor. I remember his once noting publicly that he and I resided two blocks from each other in San Francisco, a "stone's throw away—and sometimes I felt like throwing one at Chief Justice George."

I think we all grew to have a warm affection for him. Of course, he had a great political sense, having run for and served as Attorney General of California. He had a fine way of expressing himself and composed some very amusing turns of phrase. Many years before I joined the court, he wrote a wonderful concurring opinion that explained his about-face, his change of position on an issue, contradicting an earlier position he had taken. The opinion collected all sorts of memorable quotations from literature and legal opinions in which persons had had to explain their 180-degree change of view. He invoked those to justify his own. I believe the case was titled *Smith v. Anderson*. He concluded with the observation that wisdom comes seldom enough that we should not reject it merely because it comes late.

You were describing the commemorative sessions and saying that you did one for him upon his reaching 35 years.

Yes, 35 years. I also vividly remember the very shocking and difficult day, June 19, 2001, that I learned of Justice Mosk's death at the age of 88. CHP officer Terry Tracy, who was in charge of my security and of driving me to Sacramento and other places, had gone to pick up Justice Mosk and saw an ambulance at the location of the residence. He learned that Justice Mosk had died. Justice Mosk had postponed over and over and over again the decision of whether or not to retire. I have it on good authority that he finally decided he would retire and that he had planned to put his letter to Governor Davis, announcing his retirement, in the mail the very day he passed away. I had the sad task of coming to court and asking his judicial secretary to convene a meeting of his staff. No one else at the court knew yet, other than Terry Tracy. Of course, they were all wondering why would I convene them for a meeting—even though I had previously held a liaison meeting with them. Then I had to break the news to them that he had passed away. Of course they were shocked. There were some immediate things to be done. I ultimately, by the way, took on a member of his staff, Dennis Maio, to join my staff. But there was the question of what to do with the cases assigned to him that had been argued and submitted. Some of the justices had suggested having to schedule the cases for new oral arguments or vacate submission.

There were seven of these cases among those assigned to him. I suggested that each of the remaining five associate justices take over one of the cases, that I take two, and that the court get the opinions out within the 90-day period without having to vacate submission and defer them. We did that. Of course, the outside world never knew which of those cases originally were Stanley Mosk majority opinions in the making. His passing certainly was a real loss to all of us, and I particularly felt that way, having told you his story of the five stages of our professional relationship over 37 years. For me, that was the real passing of an era, having worked under him, with him, or together with him since 1964.

As a judicial colleague, how do you evaluate his legacy?

He made very valuable contributions to the law in many areas. I respect him very much for the fact that, although he and I differed on the subject of the death penalty, he would still vote to affirm some of the death penalty judgments that came before him despite his personal opposition and not let his own views prevail over what he thought the law required of him as a justice of the California Supreme Court.

The volume that contained Justice Mosk's memoriam also contained what might be viewed as the first of the true outreach sessions that I helped institute involving the court's traveling to Orange County to celebrate the 100th anniversary of the old Orange County courthouse and of the Orange County Bar Association. That was an event of great interest to the community—not just the legal and judicial community but the community at large. They took great pride in this wonderful old building and were very pleased that our court held a session there. That special session gave rise to the court's making special sessions a regular event and devoting ourselves to one of these outreach sessions each and every year. Some of my colleagues were skeptical or doubtful at first about doing this, but I think after the very next one all of them seemed to be total converts.

The following outreach session instituted what became a very important component of these annual visits, namely direct involvement of the student population. I give a lot of credit for that to recently retired Fifth Appellate District Presiding Justice James Ardaiz in organizing our visit to Fresno in 2002. By the way, it was particularly festive for the whole court to travel to Fresno on the train. We were greeted on the station platform by the mayor and other local officials and the press, of course, who made quite a big to-do out of our visit. Justice Ardaiz, in conjunction with the local educational community, did a lot of planning—and this became more or less the template for future visits—where the superintendent of schools and the school principals would be involved in planning a curriculum for the student activities in preparation for our visit. They would receive materials and be instructed on the court system generally, and on the operations and procedures of the California Supreme Court. An 11-minute film prepared by the A.O.C.—"Inside the Supreme Court"—was shown to the students and other spectators right before the special session began, showing the court at conference and on the bench, along with instructive remarks by the clerk and others. The students also were provided with summaries of the cases on that session's oral argument calendar, explaining the legal issues. These were prepared by our staff attorneys in a neutral way, obviously not indicating any leanings on behalf of the court, but focusing on what the issues were that caused us to grant review. The students also were given a little talk before we took the bench. An effort was made to bring them—sometimes it was hundreds of students—in and out of the courtroom in between cases or sometimes during a case without being disruptive, so that as many as possible would be able to see the court in action. There were also many others, hundreds more, who had the opportunity to see the oral arguments on television through a direct link very generously provided by the California Channel at its own expense as a public service. There were judges and lawyers who volunteered to be mentors in the classrooms, who would watch the televised oral arguments with the students and explain anything that the students wanted to discuss. I called this electronically expanding the walls of both the classroom and the courtroom.

What became a very exciting feature for them—and it started with this first Fresno session—was the school officials' selection of students to walk up to the lectern and ask questions of the court. While the lawyers in these cases were nervously waiting to argue the first case, they had to sit back and watch the students come up one by one, with great poise, to ask questions of the justices in the presence of lawyers and justices and the public and—probably most terrifying of all—in front of their fellow students. [Laughter] They did it with remarkable ease. There is always a photograph in the appendix to the Cal 4th volume of the court's opinions that memorializes our special session. One of my favorite photos shows a beaming young woman from a Fresno area high school, as she—with obvious confidence—addresses her question to one of the justices. On either side of her you see the attorneys waiting to argue the first case, a very important one. I believe it was *In re Rosenkrantz*, dealing with the governor's authority to reverse decisions of the parole board on life-term inmates. First came a half hour of these student questions, which were part of the televised program. The California Channel, to its further credit, rebroadcast the various sessions several times around the entire state. The broadcasts served to educate not just the students but their parents and the community at large. When you consider the rather disturbing lack of familiarity that so much of our adult population has concerning the operation of our government generally and our judicial system in particular, this really served a very important purpose.

You seem very enthusiastic in describing these experiences. What kind of response and feedback did you get from the educational institutions in question?

First of all, the schools should be very much credited, because they put a lot of effort into this program—from the superintendents all the way down to the teachers. They were very enthusiastic. I received dozens of letters from principals, teachers, students, and their parents, saying how in some instances this had actually been a life altering experience and how students were now more aware of their rights and responsibilities as citizens. Some were even inspired to want to go to law school. I would relate in my remarks at these special sessions any personal connections that current or former justices of the California Supreme Court had to the local community. I'd also sometimes remark at the session that the court looked forward to the students' reaping the benefits of this program, that we hoped the participants found it as worthwhile as we did, and that perhaps someday some of the students would be participating themselves as lawyers in oral arguments before this court or be occupying seats on the bench.

Each of the seven of us became very enthused about the program. It became an annual tradition. It was always, "Okay, where are we going this year?" Various courts or counties would actually volunteer to host our court. I'd get lobbied, "Can you get the court to come down here?" In addition to the sites I've mentioned, the California Supreme Court held special oral argument sessions in San Jose, San Diego, Redding, Santa Barbara, Santa Rosa, Riverside, and Berkeley.

Some of these visits occurred in small communities, with students and teachers being bused hundreds of miles to and from the outlying region. The program wasn't necessarily confined to one county. It might be a multicounty effort bringing students to the site of the special session. I don't want to mention which visit involved the following episode, because I don't want to put any area of the state in an embarrassing position. One of the participating half-dozen high schools in the region was located in an economically disadvantaged area. It was a major hardship for some of the students to participate, for their parents to make basic provisions for their court visit. We learned after the fact that the principal of the school, out of his own pocket, had bought new shirts for the boys so that they could come to the court session and look presentable and not be inferior in their attire to the students from other high schools.

Some of the justices made a little contribution out of their pockets to the principal when they found out about this, which was only afterwards. I heard that one of the buses from another school broke down, and those students never got to our court session.

Why was this kind of outreach, to students in particular, so important to you?

I thought that's really where our greatest hope is. Children are our future, as I've said in the context of access to justice issues, which is why we have the A.O.C.'s Center for Families, Children, and the Courts trying to do more for children involved in our court system. If we don't imbue them with a sense of the importance of our system of government, we really fail at a very basic level. So to me that was very, very important. I think morally we have an obligation to instill this awareness in our young people, but we should do so for pragmatic reasons as well. I believe these outreach sessions are one of the most admirable things we are doing as a court.

Even the regular three locations in which the court sits—that's a continuing effort built into the system to be present in all parts of the state.

Yes, because we are a statewide court. We're not just that group of jurists up there in San Francisco. However, I don't want our court to take full credit for outreach efforts, to the exclusion of other courts in California. There are intermediate appellate courts that are doing that now too. The Third Appellate District, located in Sacramento, encompasses an enormous number of counties—about two dozen in its domain—and is making a point of trying to hold sessions in all of them. They're well on their way to achieving that. Some trial courts, including the Los Angeles Superior Court, have held trials in school auditoriums, and these sessions can be an excellent teaching tool.

Since we've been talking about venues for oral argument, may we spend a few minutes talking about that part of the process and how you presided over it as Chief Justice?

On our court's return visit to Fresno in 2010, the local press took student involvement another step forward by providing training to students who had given thought to becoming journalists. During the noon hour between our morning and afternoon sessions—squeezed in between our deliberations on the cases—I was asked to conduct a press conference with the students at which they would ask me questions on camera. This press conference was covered by the local television stations and focused on the local sessions of the California Supreme Court as well as the court's work generally and the legal system.

What were they interested in, do you recall?

In addition to questions concerning decision making and how and why we take up certain cases, they asked why it takes so long to render death penalty decisions. They had questions about what happens when your personal feelings come in conflict with what the law requires, and what causes a judge to recuse oneself from participating in a case.

It's a great question from any member of the public, something we've probably all wondered about.

Yes. They asked very informed questions. They were well trained by their journalist mentors and conducted themselves in a very fine way. It made for a busy day, doing that during the noon hour, but I thought that was a very nice element they added.

After having visits from you during your first year as chief, all these various counties, several of them were seeing you again. This time you had all your colleagues along. You said your colleagues became converts to this program. What do you think switched them over?

I would think more than anything else was the enthusiasm of the students, their active role in posing questions, and their appearing quite interested in the proceedings—which we knew from the accounts we received in subsequent correspondence. We felt that this experience of the students could very well have a positive impact on their lives. I think that that this—more than anything else— was what made us quite enthusiastic about the worth of the outreach program. We also saw the press coverage and the comments that the students made to local reporters.

What benefits accrue to the justices by getting out there in the real world for a time?

I think that's important. It reminds us of something we should certainly not forget in any instance, that we're not up there in an ivory tower dealing with problems in the abstract, but making decisions that, for the parties if not always for us, are the most important decisions conceivable and that have a lot of practical impact on the day-to-day lives of individuals and institutions. Of course, most judges make an effort to be aware of that, but this practical consequence of the decisions we render certainly was reinforced in our minds by seeing real-world people come in and out of the courtroom rather than just the usual parade of dark-suited lawyers.

###

Chapter 12

Justice System Partners
September 27, 2011

We talked some about the initial liaison meetings that you held with various parties upon becoming Chief Justice. Let's return to that and perhaps start by recapping the kinds of meetings you initiated within the Supreme Court and the judicial branch.

My desire initially, upon becoming Chief Justice, was to establish a good working relationship with various components of the California Supreme Court and of the Administrative Office of the Courts, which of course serves as the staff to the Judicial Council. I wanted this to be a two-way street, where I could be informed of various problems or matters that could be the subject of improvement. At the same time, I indicated I would welcome their suggestions in tackling those problems and wanted to keep the channels of communication open. I already mentioned in our discussions that I scheduled a meeting with each justice and his or her chambers staff. Of course, as new justices came on later, I had a different kind of meeting with them to initiate them or orient them to the work of the court. I did that with Justice Moreno and Justice Corrigan and then with my successor, Chief Justice-designate Tani Cantil-Sakauye. I went over some of the things that you and I discussed in terms of the court's internal processes, usually taking the new justice out to lunch.

In addition to these meetings with the justices and their staff, I met with each of the central staffs. At that time we had only a civil central staff and a criminal central staff. The creation of a capital central staff was one of my objectives. We did manage to get funding for it and to create it in 2002. I had a meeting with the clerk's office. I also met with the Reporter of Decisions' office, which performs the very valuable function of technical and stylistic review of opinions of the California Supreme Court even before they are filed at the clerk's office in slip opinion form. It also conducts later reviews at the advance-sheet stage of publication and again before the opinions are published in the bound volumes. They also review the Court of Appeal decisions before they are published in the bound volumes. Also I met with the staff of the library that serves both the Supreme Court and the First District Court of Appeal.

My meetings also extended to the various divisions of the Administrative Office of the Courts. I periodically had meetings with these divisions or their directors and also spoke at the all-A.O.C. meeting—where the whole component of hundreds of staff members got together once a year. But the first round of meetings were orientation sessions to help me learn what each division was doing and to communicate with them. Although I won't mention them all, these divisions and units included the Office of the General Counsel, the Office of Governmental Affairs, which is located in Sacramento, the Trial Court Administrative Services Division, the Human Resources Division, the Finance Division, the Center for Families, Children, and the Courts, CJER—the educational division of the A.O.C., the Appellate and Trial Court Judicial Services Division, the Information Services Division—which is basically technology, and the Office of Court Construction and Management.

What kind of general impressions did you come away with from this series of meetings within the A.O.C.?

My impressions were that the divisions of the A.O.C. are led by and composed of extremely dedicated individuals who toil very, very hard with limited resources and whose primary objective is to serve the courts of the state and the public. I believe they're underappreciated by the judges in the state as a whole. Now, that's a generalization, but I think that many persons do not fully understand the types of things that are being done by these individuals at the A.O.C. and how much the work of the trial courts is facilitated by what is being done by the A.O.C. staff in providing resources, expertise, and assistance of all sorts. There are also three regional offices that we set up for the San Francisco bay and coastal area, a second one in Sacramento for the interior part of the state, and a third one located at Burbank in Los Angeles County, servicing the Southern California counties. Those regional entities have permitted judges to have direct dealings with experts in, let's say, human resources, or in resolving legal questions and defending lawsuits through the Office of the General Counsel, or judicial education, and so forth, without having to travel to San Francisco or otherwise deal with the overall statewide entity. I made a point of visiting those regional offices periodically and believe they have served a very important function.

I did continue my visits to courts around the state during my entire tenure as Chief Justice after that year-long set of initial visits was over, but obviously not on the same systematic basis. These subsequent visits occasionally involved groundbreaking ceremonies for new or refurbished courthouses or ribbon-cutting dedications of those facilities once they were completed, and I accumulated quite a collection of inscribed ceremonial hardhats and shovels that were given to me. I also attended some ceremonies commemorating the transfer of courthouses from county ownership to state ownership and judicial branch management.

We also were building some very fine facilities at the appellate level authorized before passage of the Trial Court Facilities Act. I spoke at groundbreaking and dedication ceremonies for the Fifth District Court of Appeal in Fresno and for the Fourth District Court of Appeal, Division Three, in Santa Ana. Some visits during the initial journey to the 58 counties produced very noticeable improvements in local courthouse facilities. When I visited the juvenile facilities in Fresno and San Bernardino Counties, I was horrified at how terrible they were, with teenagers being confined there under conditions that included vermin and unclean quarters and the kids having to sleep on the floor because there wasn't even enough space or bedding for them. I ended up describing those two juvenile facilities as the worst I had seen in the whole state, and the press picked that up. I believe my observations helped shame the county boards of supervisors in those two counties into doing something about these conditions, because the counties were still responsible at that time for the facilities. Both of those counties were very grateful, or at least the judges were, for my negative comments and invited me there both for the groundbreaking and the dedication of new facilities. These new state-of-the-art juvenile structures became models for the rest of the state. Some good certainly came from that criticism.

The outreach efforts also included some special courthouse dedications. There was a greatly respected judge, Richard Arnason, who had served on the bench in Contra Costa County since 1963. It was a pleasure, having known him for many years and having assigned him as a retired judge to some high-profile cases, to be able to participate with him in dedicating the Richard Arnason Courthouse in his county.

A rather special facility, a community court, exists in Orange County— dedicated to military veterans and the homeless who have problems that involve petty crime but also socio-economic, quality-of-life issues, that are all tied in to their being repeat offenders on minor transgressions in the criminal justice system. The judicial officers and staff working at that facility make a real effort to provide these veterans with job training and mental and physical health counseling. The D.A., the public defender, and social services all work collaboratively and have offices in the court building. Judge Wendy Lindley presided there and helped set up the program. Here too, my showing up was an outreach effort designed to show that the Judicial Council is supportive of these excellent efforts.

I guess I should mention finally in this area of special visits, in terms of liaison, that I was asked by several courts to preside at unification ceremonies when the municipal court judges were sworn in as judges of the superior court.

There was also a quirky situation in El Dorado County, where all of their judges—I believe there were six of them—due to the schedule of retirements and elections just happened to be taking office for new terms at the same time. They said, "Wouldn't it be great if we got the Chief Justice to come swear in the whole court?" So, at the request of the presiding judge, Suzanne Kingsbury, a valued member of the Judicial Council, I traveled to El Dorado County for that purpose.

There were many other judicial branch entities that regularly asked me to participate in one event or another. Every year I was part of an excellent orientation program organized by the Judicial Council for judges newly taking office or elevated to a higher level of court. That would encompass a week's worth of educational programs at the A.O.C. headquarters and include a half-hour visit to my chambers, where I would explain to them what went on at that historic Supreme Court conference table—the various actions that the court takes at Wednesday petition conferences, post oral argument conferences, and administrative conferences. Then I would conclude by describing some of the responsibilities I have as chair of the Judicial Council and as Chief Justice of the state and encourage them, when they were settled in their new assignments, to volunteer to be among the hundreds of judges who serve as members of the advisory committees to the Judicial Council and its task forces, pointing out to them also that it was from the ranks of those who labored in the vineyard, so to speak, in those assignments that I chose individuals from among those nominated by the council's executive committee for membership on the Judicial Council. Those were good meetings, with an opportunity for them to ask questions, and they would always conclude by having a group photograph taken with me, which they started to ask for and then we just made it routine.

There's also, of course, the new judges' college, which as I mentioned is traditionally held on the Berkeley campus of the University of California each summer. I would give some welcoming remarks and answer questions from the new judges and judicial faculty.

There were other events that related to the judicial branch. We recognized the 100th anniversary of the creation of the Courts of Appeal. Originally there were only three, but all six appellate courts were eager to celebrate. I participated at their request in a special court session that featured a bench of seven justices—each of the administrative presiding justices of the six Courts of Appeal, and myself as the presiding justice. Some commemorative remarks were made that I believe are published in the bound volumes of the decisions of the Courts of Appeal. Perhaps of special interest to you, we also launched an oral history legacy program of the Court of Appeal justices.

There were other court-related outreach efforts. I was very supportive of drug courts and attended a couple graduation ceremonies, which were truly heartwarming. I remember those in San Francisco and Alameda Counties, in particular. The judges would get off the bench to directly congratulate persons who had truly turned their lives around—because it was not just staying out of trouble; it was getting a job, keeping a job, in some cases reuniting with a family. There were hugs and congratulations and handshakes. I continued to follow up and support our trial courts in these efforts.

Another very heartwarming experience was participating in the L.A. Superior Court's "Adoption Saturday" program. What happens in that program in Los Angeles—and I believe in Sacramento and some other counties—is the culmination of weeks of paperwork and other efforts made by lawyers to facilitate adoptions where, in many instances, the prospective parents cannot afford to hire counsel. The attorneys prepare all the paperwork and make other arrangements that culminate in a Saturday court appearance, where the court formally acts on the adoption and makes it a legal reality. I was asked to the L.A. court to observe the process and perhaps preside over one adoption myself, and then to participate in a press conference about the program. It was a very different type of courtroom scene than any I had seen before, with balloons and teddy bears all over the courtroom and of course a very festive atmosphere. What was wonderful was that among the participants were name partners of major law firms who had done the paperwork and who were representing the families at these special hearings.

Instead of just doing one case, it was like getting into a bag of M&Ms. I couldn't stop once I started. [Laughter] Using my authority under the California Constitution to assign judges to different courts and levels, I had assigned myself to be a judge of the Los Angeles Superior Court for the day so that I would have jurisdiction to conduct these proceedings. I ended up doing 10 adoption cases instead of the one, and it was a very enjoyable experience. There was even one amusing quasi-adoption that one could call the eleventh one. When one of these adoptions had been completed, the father, somewhat sheepishly, said, "Our new son, Timmy, has one request. He wonders could you adopt the family dog—" who happened to be present, I believe—"into the family as well?" I did something that seemed a bit extrajudicial and incorporated Timmy's pet into the family unit. These were wonderful efforts that were created—and I want to give him full credit—by Judge Michael Nash, who's the supervising judge of the Ed Edelman Children's Court, which is named after a very fine former member of the Los Angeles County Board of Supervisors. Judge Nash, you may recall, is the Michael Nash who was one of the deputy attorneys general who prosecuted the Hillside Strangler case.

Could you say more about the specialized courts that have developed within our system? You're making a specific point about how interesting and educational it is to visit the drug court, to visit the adoption court. What's the role of these special courts, and how well are they working?

There's a national movement that, due in part to California's experience—although California can't take full credit—tries to deal with quality-of-life offenses that are particularly tied to social and economic problems, by addressing those problems and keeping the individual from just returning to a cycle of petty crime. I would also add to that mix, of course, the veterans' and homeless court I just mentioned. Generically they came to be known as collaborative justice courts in the sense that there was collaboration, not only between the courts and counsel, but also between the prosecution and the defense—who would not be purely adversarial in these courts, but frequently would work with each other and also with social services agencies and mental health professionals and others to try to turn the person's life around rather than just saying, "You did this, and you're going to get five days in jail," and then that person would be back in court again.

Now we have all sorts of specialized courts. Placer County even had a teen court where, by stipulation of the parties, the teen would admit his or her criminal infraction, and a jury of other teenagers would be impaneled to propose a solution and a punishment. I observed some of those proceedings in Placer County at the suggestion of Judge Richard Couzens. We also have domestic violence courts, which lend themselves to specialized counseling and other intervention designed to keep these problems from recurring and to deal with the situation holistically in terms of the family unit. The National Center for State Courts, which staffs the Conference of Chief Justices, has worked to encourage the chiefs to establish various types of those courts in their states. We had a committee of the Conference of Chiefs that I served on for many years dealing with collaborative justice courts, which they called "problem-solving courts."

Some of what has been instituted in California came about as a result of visits by myself and others to various states, where we learned from their experiences. For instance, we picked up some good ideas about jury reform and self-help centers from Arizona. Traveling to New York State, we learned about their experience with business courts. The concept of a business court sounded a bit elitist, so we created "complex-litigation courts." These courts handle complex cases that may be class actions or other matters instituted by plaintiffs and their counsel, and are not confined to disputes between or among various large business entities. Again, we benefited from New York's experience, but we took it a step further. Other states asked me at the Conference of Chief Justices for copies of the manual that we had developed under a committee chaired by Court of Appeal Justice Richard Aldrich, an exceptionally helpful treatise on handling all sorts of complex litigation matters through specialized procedures, resources, and training for judges and staff.

Another idea that germinated in New York was the Midtown Manhattan Court, which dealt with quality-of-life issues involving persons whose petty crimes were devaluing the surroundings in a given community and causing economic loss for the residents and merchants in the area. That example in turn influenced us in California in setting up specialized courts like veterans' and homeless courts, in particular. That's one of the great things about this process of cross-fertilization among the states. In a way it's a parallel to what I described in discussing with you my initial round of visits among the 58 counties, where I would pick up—in what was then a decentralized system—problems and success stories in one county and sometimes be asked about similar things in another county. I described my serving as an informal clearinghouse in trying to arrive at statewide best practices. The same thing that exists as a microcosm in California is present on a national level. The states borrow and learn from each other. That's one of the beauties of our federal system. U.S. Supreme Court Justice Louis Brandeis recognized that each of the states is free to operate as social laboratories. Similarly, the judicial systems of our 50 states are laboratories. They try certain things—some things work, some don't—and out of that develop best practices that are transportable to other jurisdictions, sometimes with adaptations to the needs of the state or local community. That's how so many judicial reforms have originated.

Speaking of complex-litigation courts, I made a point of visiting some very fine efforts set up in Los Angeles, Orange, and San Mateo Counties as complex-litigation facilities that saved tremendous time and expense for the court system and for the parties involved. At the other end of the spectrum from complex litigation is something that is actually called the Cow County Judges Association. It's an organization comprised of rural counties that are smaller in population, but not necessarily in geographical area. I attended their meetings occasionally in, obviously, out-of-the-way places and spoke to them and heard about their particular needs and responded to their questions. I don't know exactly how small a human population or how large a bovine population qualifies a county for membership in the Cow County Judges Association or if it's a question of the ratio between the two populations, but it is a group that meets regularly and engages in fruitful discussions. I also made a point of reaching out to the more than 400 retired judges who volunteer their time in our assigned judges program. They have special needs and interests, and I would address them periodically. I established a little news bulletin, containing a column by me, that went to them regularly. I also have spoken to a unit for retired judge members of the California Judges Association, dealing with their particular needs.

One of the very fine efforts of the Judicial Council, *vis-à-vis* the trial courts, are the annual recognitions for innovations achieved by trial and appellate courts in implementing a new service, or some better or more efficient way of providing a traditional service, that has benefited the court system and the public and that serves as a model for other courts to emulate as a best practice. Those are called the "Kleps Awards," named after California's first administrative director of the courts, Ralph Kleps, who served from the creation of the office in 1960 until 1977. What we did initially was have an awards ceremony at which the various innovations were verbally described, but—a picture being worth 1,000 words—we eventually substituted a video presentation that graphically depicted what the court had achieved. It might be a new process at the clerk's counter. It might be a better way of keeping court records or of expediting a process in the courtroom. Whatever it was, it was memorialized on film, played to the audience before whom the recognitions are given, and made available online and generally for any other court to emulate and possibly adapt to its own particular local needs.

What kinds of innovations were being recognized in this way?

Every kind of thing from Ventura's sending a mobile courtroom van into the hinterland, or simplifying forms, to changing procedures at clerks' counters and thereby saving a lot of time and record keeping, things of that sort. The A.O.C. keeps a record of these accomplishments, which are available for any other court to adopt and adapt.

I had many occasions to meet informally with some other entities that are not strictly part of the judiciary but that we interact with, sometimes addressing them more formally or administering an oath of office to their members. Among those entities is the Commission on Judicial Performance, the constitutional entity responsible for the discipline of judges and also for approving judicial disability retirements. Working with CJP, we have tried to improve the disciplinary procedures and ensure that they are consistent with due process, because judges sometimes complained in the past that the process was not as fair to them as it should be. I believe CJP currently has excellent procedures, very much improved from what they were many years ago. Also their opinions, as I mentioned before, are now published in the Official Reports of the California Supreme Court, available to provide guidance to judges and serve as precedent. Also I made an effort to have the California Supreme Court improve the quality of its appointments to vacancies on the Commission on Judicial Performance, to select not only persons who had expressed an interest but who truly had proved themselves knowledgeable and helpful in the area of judicial ethics and court administration and who exhibited, equally importantly, an understanding of the challenges that face the trial judge in an often-frenetic courtroom environment. In passing judgment on the judges, the commission members—instead of approaching complaints of judicial impropriety in the abstract—need to have some understanding and empathy for the circumstances under which the judge engaged in the challenged conduct. All of these are things that have improved the process.

There's also another body that we've referred to in our discussions, an entity of the State Bar called the JNE Commission, which is an acronym for the Commission on Judicial Nominees Evaluation established by section 12011.5 of the Government Code. I would meet with them every year and administer their oath of office. The statute requires that before a governor can finalize a trial or appellate court appointment, he or she must submit the candidate's name for evaluation by the JNE Commission so that the governor, although not bound by it, will have the benefit of the commission's evaluation. The commission is very diligent in sending out what is often hundreds of questionnaires, undertaking background investigations, and then conducting an interview with the candidate. That process has been vastly improved too in terms of due process to the nominee. There were some transgressions in its early years that truly were not consistent with due process. But now it's generally considered a very fair process, and the people who serve on that commission—like the members of the Commission on Judicial Performance—do so at great personal sacrifice, lugging large binders for meetings around the state, putting in many, many hours in addition to their regular day jobs.

You have mentioned before how thorough that process is. What was the nature of the earlier transgressions?

I heard stories that—given the sources—I take to be true, of candidates being evaluated by a commission member who was an active campaign supporter of the electoral opponent of the nominee. I also know that in its early days, the interviewing commissioners would not always give notice of negative information that they had acquired through their investigation or through the questionnaires, and would totally surprise the nominee who, if given notice, might have had a better chance at the interview of refuting the accusation. Other objections were made in terms of lack of due process, but those are two examples. Now it's a very fair process, and I think they have eliminated most of the deficiencies, although I had, in recent years, a couple occasions to point out some deficiencies in their procedure. One was not giving adequate weight in their questionnaire to government service, specifically legislative service, because the commission had not updated its questionnaires to reflect the revised standards adopted by legislation. The other was not giving sufficient weight to someone's appellate experience as an attorney when that person was up for an appellate appointment, and just focusing on the fact that the person had average but not exceptional trial court experience. In one instance a person was being appointed to an appellate position and had exceptionally broad experience as an appellate lawyer, which was given insufficient weight in my view. There's always some fine-tuning that can improve the process.

The State Bar Court also has asked me to meet with them from time to time, and to administer the oath of office. Our court has tried to help them improve their procedures, because the California Supreme Court reviews their work. For a while our court felt that the State Bar Court and the State Bar prosecutor were being too lenient with lawyers who were subject to discipline for serious transgressions. We made our concerns known and pointed out some improvements that could be made in existing procedures.

There were many other groups that I would try to maintain liaison with— statewide bar groups, including of course the State Bar itself, local bars, ethnic minority bars, legal services groups. Many of these events were occasions to help the group confer awards and once in a while for me to receive one of their awards, to address them, or to speak with them informally.

Before we leave the State Bar, may I ask upon becoming Chief Justice how did you think about that entity as a whole and what sort of relations you wanted to engender there?

I always viewed the State Bar as one of our primary partners. In some ways I suppose you could say we were joined at the hip by the constitution, which—I believe it is article VI, section 9—created the State Bar as a public corporation in the judicial article of the state constitution. They represent, of course, the major consumers of judicial services, on behalf of their clients. I believe that, as officers of the court, as they've always been called, they have at least a moral obligation to support adequate funding, resources, and facilities for the courts and to support the courts' efforts to preserve judicial independence. I have therefore always viewed the members of the State Bar as a natural constituency, and have delivered a second State of the Judiciary address to them at the State Bar convention every year, paralleling my address to a joint session of the legislature. Both the State Bar leadership and the conference of delegates have been excellent partners and very good about recognizing the need to preserve and protect the independence of the judiciary. That concept of independence, I want to make clear, does not mean unaccountability. It recognizes a certain interdependency among the three branches of government, but with the judiciary standing on its own as a separate co-equal branch of government.

We can finish with the other entities, perhaps, and return to the State Bar for a fuller discussion.

I had many different contacts with the State Bar that we'll talk about, including speaking to or with their various units, such as the litigation section, and will later discuss what attending the State Bar convention was like. Every year I had a series of liaison meetings in my chambers with various entities that were, I believe, pleased to be consulted and to discuss their interests and concerns and in turn help the judicial branch when they could do so consistently with their own objectives. To hold those meetings also in the inner sanctum of the court was meaningful to them, I believe. In addition to the State Bar, one of our very best and most supportive partners was CSAC, the California State Association of Counties. That is the organization that is comprised of members of the board of supervisors of each of the 58 counties. We worked very closely with CSAC on all of our structural reforms, starting with trial court funding. That was a classic instance of where we had a total mutuality of interest, because the counties were in dire straits at the time, as they very much remain today, and the state's assumption of this funding responsibility provided a great measure of fiscal relief to the county governments. Although the counties were very happy to see what they viewed as county relief coming down the pike, the courts were pleased to no longer be dependent upon the irregular and unequal funding provided by the various counties, determined by which county the individual court happened to be in and depending upon whether the particular county was willing and able to devote adequate resources to the funding of its trial courts in the face of competing demands for other services—whether they were health services or law enforcement or libraries or parks. The funding received by a trial court also appeared to depend upon whether whoever happened to be on the county board of supervisors that year had a good or a poor relationship with whoever happened to be the presiding judge of the local court. We worked closely with CSAC on this reform. They were very pleased with the outcome and were a great beneficiary.

Your predecessors as chief may not have had much occasion to interact with the individual counties in the way that you did, owing to the work towards unifying and state funding and so on. To what extent were you forging brand-new relationships with CSAC and the supervisors and some of these county entities?

I think I was, in many instances. I had met some of the supervisors when I made visits to their counties. Then some of them ended up being officers of the CSAC organization, and we followed up with them or else had the benefit of their input into the organization. I think this was new territory, basically, as was a lot of this interaction with other entities. I'm sure that there were some who thought these initiatives were, perhaps, overly assertive on the part of the judiciary or the Chief Justice in particular. However, the judicial branch lacks the same resources available to others for lobbying in Sacramento—for want of a better word. Lawyers and business entities and unions can and do contribute financially to the political campaigns of legislators and state officeholders in the executive branch. But judges are severely restricted in their ability to contribute or to engage in political activity. There also exists a certain affinity between the politicians who are elected to the county boards of supervisors and their political colleagues who are serving in the state legislature, some of whom used to be county supervisors. But when the judges go to the Capitol, all they can do is plead "good government" and invoke the interest of the public that is served by the judiciary. So it was very important to forge this alliance with the county supervisors.

I should note that, on a couple of occasions, I ended up helping to formalize a most personal partnership between two justice system partners of ours. CSAC's executive director, Steve Szalay was very helpful to us. He strongly supported our efforts to win passage of the trial court funding reform. We also were working on this measure with Governor Wilson's deputy director of finance, Diane Cummins, who later became a fiscal adviser to John Burton, President pro Tem of the Senate. These two justice system partners, Steve Szalay and Diane Cummins, got to know each other through working on our issues, and eventually became partners themselves. I was asked to officiate at their wedding, which I did. [Laughter] This gave new meaning to the concept of justice system partners. There was another similar instance. I appointed Kathleen O'Leary—who then was on the Orange County Superior Court and now is presiding justice of the Fourth Appellate District, Division Three—to a committee dealing with access to justice issues. I also appointed to that same committee Ken Babcock, an attorney from Orange County who was very much involved in legal services in that county. On one occasion the committee had a meeting in San Diego, and the two of them decided they would travel to the meeting together by train—although they dispute to this day whose idea this was. It turned out that the two of them shared a four-hour roundtrip commute on the train between Orange County and San Diego and back, and ended up getting married. I've been credited with facilitating that union between justice system partners.

Getting on to the more traditional type of judicial system partner, there were liaison meetings in my chambers with the attorney general and his top staff, as well as the California District Attorneys Association, which is the association of the elected D.A.s themselves, not the rank and file. Another group we would meet with regularly was the Consumer Attorneys of California, the plaintiffs' bar, who have tremendous influence in Sacramento. They have been among the very most supportive of our justice system partners. At the drop of a hat they would call or even fly up to Sacramento on our behalf in times of crisis. They have an excellent staff led by Nancy Drabble and worked with us on a broad range of issues. We also had very good relations and support from the California Defense Counsel, the civil bar, and their outstanding legislative representative, Mike Belote, who also is the legislative representative of another major partner, the California Judges Association. I had many scheduled meetings with CJA, but whenever a problem arose that couldn't be resolved by picking up the phone, the president of CJA, sometimes accompanied by other officers, would come over and we would chat. I would address the California Judges Association when it met concurrently with the bar convention. The association would ask me to engage in what they called a fireside chat. Three armchairs would be placed on the stage, and I would have two interrogators, judges from the association, putting questions to me submitted by the membership. The Judicial Council also maintained a good dialogue with CJA—in part through my appointment of CJA leaders to the council—and worked very well together with the organization, especially through the close collaboration of our respective legislative units in Sacramento. Other groups I would meet with included the criminal trial defense bar—the California Public Defenders Association together with the California Attorneys for Criminal Justice.

What were the foremost concerns of those defense-related groups?

Some of it involved timelines for filing habeas corpus petitions under the federal act. I'd say their primary concern was being provided with sufficient resources to defend persons convicted of capital offenses. Chief Justice Lucas had given me some responsibility in this area to help bring up the hourly pay of the private lawyers doing this work, which was about $60 an hour when I joined the court. I ultimately helped get it up to $145 an hour. The amount of automatically allowable habeas corpus expenses was expanded greatly from about $3,000 to $20,000. We also discussed efforts to recruit more lawyers to undertake defense work. Most of these concerns were generally shared by all three official defense entities, which are first of all the Office of the State Public Defender that—unlike the California Public Defenders Association—is comprised of lawyers handling appeals. Oddly enough, the state P.D.'s office was established by the legislature as part of the executive branch, whereas the second of the three defense entities, the Habeas Corpus Resource Center, was established under the judicial branch and the judicial budget. Third, there's the California Appellate Project, which receives funds from various sources, including some private fundraising.

I also had productive meetings with the County Counsels Association. Another group that I would meet with regularly was the California State Sheriffs Association, which is an organization of principals, the elected sheriffs themselves and not the deputies or assistants. The Judicial Council tried to work with the sheriffs to resolve our differences. We frankly did have differences concerning the budget for security, which is the largest and fastest-growing part of the judicial branch budget. There were a lot of disparities in terms of the types of service provided to the courts, and the cost of those services charged to the courts by the various sheriffs around the state. Sometimes there were misunderstandings that we had to deal with in order to try to coordinate our position so we wouldn't be at loggerheads with the sheriffs. They were very powerful politically, being elected officials and political animals themselves. They had a lot of clout with the executive and legislative branches, and we tried to have their support whenever possible.

You had a personal interest and also experience with security matters in our court system. What did you do to convince them that you shared the basic concern? What was your message to them? '

It was just to highlight what they already knew, that there were real security problems. They showed me photographs of what was uncovered in one day of screening at a major Los Angeles County courthouse, a whole arsenal of weaponry. The disputes were really about the need to provide adequate funding for the sheriffs' court security budgets. We spoke of having to pay benefits and retirement costs for their deputy sheriffs who provided perimeter security, transportation, and bailiff services for the court. In some instances, senior deputies were assigned to courthouse duties as a reward, when the job could have been done as well by deputies who were in a lower salary range.

There also were problems of courthouse design that went back many years, to a time when judges in many counties weren't consulted on courthouse construction. You had court facilities with a multitude of entrances to the building, necessitating a lot of perimeter security, and then perhaps not enough personnel to staff the individual courtrooms with adequate security. In some locations the funding was inadequate to purchase the required screening devices. In others, the equipment had been purchased but the funding was inadequate to man the equipment. We came to an understanding that some functions could be performed by private security firms under the supervision of sheriffs so that the courts wouldn't have to pay for sheriffs—who had had to qualify by meeting peace officer training standards—to perform some of the more menial functions, such as monitoring screening devices at the courthouse entrances, that perhaps could be done as well by others under their supervision.

There have been proposals to make the provision of court security more competitive and to allow trial courts to bid out individually for court security services not only to the sheriff, but also to a marshal, a chief of police, a private entity, or the California Highway Patrol. The sheriffs do point out that they have charge and custody of the prisoners and that courthouse operations would be less coordinated if they had to hand prisoners over to another law enforcement entity at the courthouse. I'm not convinced that this is a real concern, because it did not pose a problem between the Marshal's Office and the Sheriff's Office when I served on the L.A. Municipal Court. I do know that something has to be done about the escalating costs that have been built into the system—whether or not the sheriffs could be charging less than they do. Of course, we're taking security concerns into account in our new court construction projects, consulting judges and court executives, to avoid the situation existing in some facilities where chains of prisoners or individual inmates are brought through crowded public hallways or inner hallways where they go right by judges' chambers and jury deliberation rooms. The system is not working right, mainly due to inadequate funding provided by the legislature, resulting in violent and sometimes fatal incidents inside courthouses that are supposed to be sanctuaries for the resolution of disputes rather than crime scenes in their own right. This situation is one more aspect of the inadequacy of the funding being provided for the courts. A $40 per case security fee was enacted, but that still isn't taking care of it.

The problem is aggravated by the fact that each local court does its own negotiation with the local sheriff on the details of the contract that provides for the sheriff to furnish court security. In effect, the leadership of the superior court is bargaining with their own colleagues, their uniformed associates at the local trial court level. It's not really the adversary role involved in normal contract negotiations. A parallel situation exists when it comes to the negotiation of court employee salaries and benefits, where judges are negotiating with their courtroom clerks and reporters. The negotiations between the sheriffs and the judges are complicated by the circumstance that both parties are elected officials. The sheriffs have been able through their negotiation position and their very effective lobbying in Sacramento to end up receiving very lucrative contracts and personal benefits. This has contributed to the judicial branch's security costs, doubling during the past decade to $500 million. These costs go up about 7 percent a year and constitute the largest item in the budget of the judicial branch. Something has to be done about this. The sheriffs feel they're not getting paid enough by the courts for their services, and the courts feel they're paying too much or at least that they don't have the funds to pay for adequate security or for what the sheriffs are charging. I don't know that the proposal for competitive bidding—which I think the Legislative Analyst's Office has endorsed—is going to go anywhere, because of the political clout of the sheriffs. This is one area where, even though the meetings I've had with the sheriffs were very friendly and enjoyable and both sides have tried to work together on joint problems, often successfully, it's sometimes been a rocky road with the sheriffs. I recognize that they have their own problems obtaining adequate funding for their operations from the counties. The sheriffs do an excellent job in providing court security, and our differences with them have been almost entirely about money.

Another group that I have met with regularly is the California Academy of Appellate Lawyers, a group I have great respect for. I previously mentioned that they have an annual weekend retreat, which I have attended some years, at which all sorts of appellate issues and improvements in the system are discussed.

Also as Chief Justice I served as chair of the board of directors of the California Supreme Court Historical Society, which of course is the entity that initiated this current oral history project, as well as the histories of several of my predecessors. It is a very committed group and has done a lot to preserve the history of the California Supreme Court and other courts. Some of its members have made enormous efforts to preserve historic memorabilia, publish various journals and periodicals, and conduct educational programs. I know there was a wonderful event that you were present at a few years ago, Laura, where copies of the oral histories of four of my colleagues were formally presented to each of them—Chief Justice Lucas, Justice Panelli, Justice Arguelles, and Justice Arabian. In fact, the event was rather amusing in one respect. I spoke and introduced Chief Justice Lucas, who began to give some remarks. Selma Smith, who for many years has done wonderful work for the society in the area of publications—she was admitted to the bar in 1943!—realized that everyone present might not stay to the end of the full program. She was eager to capture the moment, an historic one, of having 11 justices—seven current and four past—of the California Supreme Court all in one place. Concerned with losing this unique photo opportunity, she rushed over to me, whispered in my ear, and with apologies to Chief Justice Lucas, I interrupted his remarks and said: "There's only one person on the face of the globe who would be capable of simultaneously interrupting two Chief Justices, and it's our own Selma Smith. But she has pointed out the desirability of capturing this moment in a portrait of the 11 justices of the Supreme Court while we are all here." [Laughter] That photograph was taken and is proudly displayed in the hallways of the California Supreme Court.

We must credit you with getting all the sitting members of the court to attend after their day of oral argument in Los Angeles. What else would you like to see the California Supreme Court Historical Society take on?

I'd like to see it complete its forthcoming book on the history of the California Supreme Court, because there's no truly in-depth history of the court. That work is well underway. Various authors have taken responsibility for individual chapters. Perhaps the society could do more to generate interest outside the judicial and legal community in the work of the California Supreme Court and its historical development. I know at the U.S. Supreme Court there is a very large and active historical society that displays memorabilia and has more or less a permanent exhibit at the court of artifacts and matters of current interest regarding that court. Perhaps, given a topic that we've touched on a bit and I know we'll touch upon some more—the disconcerting lack of civics education and civic awareness in our country—it would be a useful function for the historical society, despite its name, to focus on future history as well, and current events, and to generate more awareness and hopefully interest in the workings of the California Supreme Court and our court system in California.

What other groups would you like to mention meeting with?

There were local bar associations and ethnic minority bar associations that I met with. Also, as Chief Justice, I served *ex officio* as a member of the American Law Institute, which does very fine work in codifying the law of the American jurisdictions. There were various legal and judicial groups that would meet in San Francisco, including periodically the American Bar Association and its sections and task forces, and I would often be asked to speak at those gatherings. I spoke to the National Association of Women Judges, the Pew Commission, and to conferences addressing the topic of children and their involvement in the judicial system. When numerous judicial associations such as the American Judges Association and the various associations of intermediate appellate court justices, court clerks, court executives, and law librarians would meet in California, I would address them. I would also meet every year with civics teachers who would come for a week's program at the A.O.C., stressing the concern I have about the level of civics education in our schools and how important it is in terms of understanding our judicial system.

There was a broad range of political and other views represented in the various groups that asked me to speak to them. To show no favoritism, I covered a wide spectrum here, so I met with various units of the Federalist Society, the Lincoln Club, Democratic and Republican groups, Crime Victims United, public employee groups and other labor unions. I spoke at the Rand Institute, CJAC— the Civil Justice Association of California, which was a tort-reform, business-oriented group, the Los Angeles Breakfast Club, the Los Angeles Town Hall, and the Commonwealth Club of San Francisco.

You mentioned earlier the Central Valley magazine, *Vox Pop Influentials.* They wanted a Central Valley angle for an article they were writing on me, based on the vacation property that Barbara and I owned a share of since 1972, in Three Rivers at the entrance to Sequoia National Park and Mineral King. It was a major part of our three sons' upbringing, fishing and swimming in the Kaweah River and hiking in the Sierra. My visits there also provided an occasion for philosophic discussions on the law with my friend Ron Olson, a prominent Los Angeles attorney who owns the adjacent property. These chats usually took place midstream in the river on a large rock, below a small waterfall that separates our properties. I accommodated the magazine with a favorite photograph that Barbara had taken of me diving into the very turbulent river adjoining our property during the spring runoff. Publication of the photo promptly elicited reader complaints that, dramatic as the shot was with my diving among rocks into treacherous whitewater generated by the snowmelt in the high country, it must have been PhotoShopped, and then other complaints that I was setting a poor example for the local kids. Every year there were accidents in the river. The magazine's readers had to be informed that this was water that I was very familiar with and that I knew every rock in the riverbed, since it was adjacent to my property.

One of my speaking engagements apparently was considered a true turning point in the history of one organization. I accepted the invitation of BALIF—which stands for Bay Area Lawyers for Individual Freedom, a group of gay men and lesbians who had formed this association as more or less a gay-rights bar association—to address their group. This was in 1997, many years before any of the same-sex marriage litigation began. They were pleased to hear from me that California was the first state to form a committee, to advise the Judicial Council, focused on studying sexual-orientation bias in the justice system. I believe they also were very appreciative of the fact that the Chief Justice and his wife would attend their meeting, as did Justice Werdegar. They told me afterwards that they viewed our attendance as a major development for their group.

There were other speaking engagements that ended up being a form of outreach although they had originated as commitments by the court even before I joined it, in conjunction with our oral argument sessions in Los Angeles and Sacramento. Justice Panelli was credited with getting the court committed to attend a dinner event of the Italian-American Lawyers every year in Los Angeles, and we kept up with it even after Justice Panelli left the court. Inevitably it was the same day that another group called Chancery, a group of distinguished downtown Los Angeles lawyers, would meet and honor the California Supreme

Court in conjunction with the court's presence for the October oral argument session. On a busy day of oral argument, I would run from the morning session, often having to postpone our post-oral-argument session to the end of the day, to attend Chancery with my colleagues and give some remarks, which I got into the habit of doing extemporaneously, but it was always some sort of a mini State of the Judiciary address. Then we would have an afternoon session of oral argument, followed by a post-argument conference on the morning and afternoon cases, and then dash off to the Italian-American Lawyers. That, I think, happened every single year while I was chief.

In conjunction with the court's June oral argument session, the Beverly Hills Bar Association gave a lunch honoring the justices, at which I would deliver another mini State of the Judiciary address. I enjoyed looking into the audience at that event and seeing our eldest son Eric and members of his law firm in attendance. In Sacramento, where the court held oral argument twice a year, we would annually have one event given in our honor by the Sacramento Barristers and another by the Women Lawyers Association, and I would provide extemporaneous remarks at each. In San Francisco, even though that was our home base, a similar event was held by the San Francisco Barristers. I also enjoyed being asked to participate in conferring awards on behalf of the San Francisco Bar Volunteers in Legal Services every year to individuals who had contributed exceptional pro bono service. It was gratifying to see the great variety of the services performed by these award recipients.

Most significantly, every year an extremely sad and moving event was held, called the California Peace Officers Memorial, honoring the officers, from local and state law enforcement agencies throughout the state of California, who had died in the line of duty the preceding year. Hundreds of uniformed officers from dozens of law enforcement agencies would drive their patrol cars and motorcycles from all parts of the state to attend and pay homage to their fallen colleagues. The events start off with a private ceremony in one of the large hearing rooms in the state Capitol, and each of the family members and some colleagues of the fallen officer would come up to the stage and shake hands with the governor, other executive and legislative branch leaders, and myself. When that ceremony was over, these officials would reassemble on the west steps of the Capitol and then walk from there to the Library and Courts Building, now named after Stanley Mosk, which is about a block distant. Lining our way on both sides of this route were several hundred police officers from numerous law enforcement agencies, forming a cordon several officers deep on each side. Then we would speak at the public ceremony that's held right outside the Library and Courts Building. It's a very emotional and heart-rending scene, especially because the surviving spouse, sometimes accompanied by minor children, sometimes babes in arms, walks up to the very poignant statue of a widow clutching her children that commemorates peace officers fallen in the line of duty, and places roses at the monument. A white dove is released, as that is done, for each officer. Sometimes there are quite a few—a double-digit number—of officers being honored that year. Bagpipe music is played, which brings additional tears, and then a 21-gun salute is fired at close range. It was a very moving ceremony, and I felt very honored to be asked to speak and participate and represent the judicial branch, along with the governor, the attorney general, and the legislative leadership.

As part of my effort to foster our agenda—whether it was policy issues or budget matters—I met with legal services groups, numerous editorial boards, chambers of commerce, business lawyer groups, family law centers, self-help centers, and public employee union representatives. Some of the local bar associations, such as the Beverly Hills Bar Association, were especially supportive of our funding needs and our policy initiatives and also were very protective against efforts to encroach on judicial independence. However, there were bar associations that, on occasion, received enormous pressure from the presiding judge of the superior court in their county. During visits by the presiding judge, sometimes even to law firms, lawyers were told to toe the line and endorse the position of the local court, which sometimes took a position very much at odds with statewide interests and, in my view, contrary to the public interest. Some attorneys shared with me their concern that, as local practitioners, they would suffer adverse consequences if they did not support the presiding judge's policies. Complicating the situation was the fact that some superior courts were managed better than others. Some were poorly managed or mismanaged.

By separately meeting with each side of the criminal bar—the D.A.s and defense counsel—or on the civil side with the plaintiffs' bar and the civil defense bar, I often realized that both sides were concerned about the same problems of court process. Hearing that, I would offer to form a working group to arrive at a solution mutually agreeable to both groups, with the third participant being representatives of the Judicial Council or the A.O.C. We followed this course for improvements to jury selection, ethics standards for private judging, improving discovery procedures, and some other issues—to everyone's enormous satisfaction. If we went to the legislature and said, we've got the plaintiffs' bar and the civil defense bar and the judiciary united—or the prosecution, the criminal defense bar, and the judiciary—and we all want this, the agreed-upon legislation would just sail through like a hot knife through butter.

Indeed, you mentioned being advised by legislators serving on the council that you needed to speak in a unified voice when going to Sacramento in order to get things done.

Apart from the benefit derived from the judiciary presenting a united front with our justice-system partners, yes, that was definitely a major concern. We were advised repeatedly that if the judiciary itself did not speak with one voice, we would get nowhere. In fact, if we were bickering that would be our downfall. We heard that message repeatedly from legislative leaders, some of whom addressed the Judicial Council to that very effect. I recall hearing Senator Joe Dunn, Assemblyman Phil Isenberg, Senator Bill Lockyer, Assemblyman Dave Jones, Senator Darrell Steinberg, Assemblyman Mike Feuer, and Senator Don Perata, among others, say that a unified approach was absolutely essential. We would receive this advice, but it had to be stressed time and time again, because otherwise the various judicial entities and factions would try to go their own way to satisfy their parochial concerns, even to the point of having individual courts pursue their own objectives by sending their own representatives to lobby in the state Capitol. I remember something disastrous that almost happened, many years before I became chief, when three or four municipal court judges went up to the Capitol to complain about their health benefits, and the legislature in response came very close to increasing the judges' contribution rate to their retirement system from 8 percent of salary to 11 percent for all judges in the state. It's an illustration of how some judges are politically naive and inept and can really bollix things up for the other 1,700 judges by pursuing their own agenda. This doesn't mean that everyone has to march in lockstep, but the important thing is to iron out the differences, work out a suitable compromise, and then go up there with one voice. Being chief advocate for the branch out of necessity, I found it much more difficult to do my job as Chief Justice when these elements—either for selfish reasons, or out of total naiveté about the workings of the legislative process—went off on their own.

Other groups I met with included visiting teachers with students from the grade school level through law school. After they observed a session of oral arguments, I would remain on the bench to chat with them or invite them to my chambers to discuss the process, without getting into the details of the cases, of course. I also had meetings with the Inns of Court, which involve law students and new lawyers in orientation into the legal profession by longtime practitioners, and with the Judicial Administration Fellows, who are placed into judicial branch internships. I went to undergraduate classes and to law schools and spoke not only at my alma mater, Stanford Law, but also Hastings, UC Berkeley—where for several years I was the guest lecturer at a political science class given by a former legislator—Santa Clara Law School, University of San Diego Law School, and delivered commencement addresses from time to time, sometimes receiving an honorary degree in the process—from the law schools at UCLA, USC, Southwestern, Pepperdine, and Loyola of Los Angeles.

Aside from giving a great number of interviews in person, I would make it a point to answer phone calls from the press or sometimes surprise reporters by dialing them back when they had left a message. I made myself accessible as an important way of communicating with the public through the press, making sure the reporters understood the issue at hand. On some of the TV or radio shows where they had call-ins or community forums, I would answer questions about the judicial process. I can think of at least a half dozen radio broadcasters in Los Angeles, San Francisco, and some other places who would encourage their listeners to call in with questions for me to respond to, as long as the audience was informed that I could not comment on current cases. I was even persuaded to be a guest on a South Central Los Angeles hip-hop radio station broadcasting from the Magic Johnson Theater, where there was a lot of action going on in between the questions, but people voiced down-to-earth concerns about the legal system that I attempted to address. I loved the introduction I received: "The chief is in the 'hood!"

The court also prepared a video that I believe I mentioned in conjunction with the special court sessions, "Inside the Supreme Court," that included interviews with the justices in their chambers and showed us not only on the bench but around the conference table. This video really gives people an idea of how the court works and was also shown in schools and community forums.

I taped remarks for juror orientation videos and wrote a little piece for some of the jury orientation booklets that were handed out—all a way of reaching the public.

The job "as you saw it" seems an important phrase here, because you are describing dozens of different kinds of groups. Certainly some of these appearances would be made by anyone serving as Chief Justice, but it seems to me you're demonstrating a hands-on and active outreach philosophy. What were you trying to do by appearing yourself, rather than sending some emissary?

I thought that showing up myself, as the person in charge, somehow conveyed a sense of the importance of the judicial system and what we were trying to do. Some of these activities may seem menial, but I think they had symbolic value—whether it was my showing up for jury duty or at the Administrative Office of the Courts' "bring your children to work day," which I always called the "sticky hands brigade," because I would shake hands with dozens of kids age three or four up through teenagers, have their picture taken with me in the courtroom of the Supreme Court, and tell them what important work their parents were doing for the court system. I believe it's very important for the person on top to show that there's a face behind that message and that it isn't just a bureaucracy, in order to motivate people to act for the welfare of our vital third branch of government.

You not only accepted a lot of invitations by various groups, but you initiated many of these liaison meetings. Did you ever say no?

There were occasionally conflicts in schedules, and then I had to deal with the fact that people would say, "Please prepare a videotape that can be shown at our meeting." I learned that doing that ended up being almost as much work, but I would usually do it. My family said I didn't say no often enough. [Laughter] At this point, I might question whether I should have arranged to have more spare time in my life, but everything seemed important and still does in retrospect, so it's very hard to say no. I enjoyed virtually all of my activities, although some more than others, but the problem was how these activities really added up cumulatively while one is also trying to work on opinions late at night or in the car or in the plane. However, it all really came together as part of my efforts to establish the judicial branch as an entity that would be better understood and respected as a co-equal branch of government, and to obtain the resources that the courts needed to carry out their duties to the public.

There are some more things I would like to add concerning my relations with the State Bar, which involved many kinds of contacts. One of the annual liaison meetings in my chambers was with the president and officers of the bar and their very able staff, including Judy Johnson, who did a great job as executive director. The Board of Governors of the State Bar always held an annual dinner honoring the California Supreme Court, which gave the justices an opportunity—with each justice seated at a different table—to converse with various members of the board and staff. I mentioned already my dealings with the State Bar Court judges. I would videotape remarks for some of their programs, such as the LAP, the Lawyers Alcoholism Program, in which we encouraged those lawyers who have substance abuse problems to seek counseling. In fact, we ended up encouraging judges who had substance abuse problems to get involved in parallel efforts.

The most intense contact with the State Bar was something that my staff ended up calling "hell week," reflecting the ordeal of the cumulative commitments that I had each year at the State Bar convention, although individually I enjoyed them each. The weeks approaching that event imposed frenetic scheduling duties upon my judicial assistants, who had a lot to do with coordinating my large number of appearances, and for staff—my principal attorney Beth Jay, and Peter Allen and James Carroll from the A.O.C.'s office of communications—who provided valuable assistance in helping me prepare my remarks for the multitude of speaking engagements that did not simply involve impromptu remarks. The annual meeting consisted of concurrent conferences of the State Bar of California, the California Judges Association, and occasionally CJAC, the California Judicial Administration Conference. These three conferences sometimes would be held in separate hotels in the same city, and I would be rushed back and forth from one event to the other. Anaheim, San Diego, Long Beach, and Monterey were the favored venues.

What usually started off these very busy four days would be a State Bar lunch on the Thursday, then the social highlight—and often the highlight in terms of speakers—would be the California Women Lawyers dinner, which was preceded by their reception. I frequently would be called upon to administer the oath of office to their officers. Then, I believe two years ago, I was told that I had been selected to be the first "nonwoman" keynote speaker. [Laughter] The next day, Friday morning at eight o'clock, was a meeting of the bench/bar coalition, a very helpful group of lawyers, judges, and court executives who would promote the Judicial Council's objectives on funding and policy matters by attending the State of the Judiciary address in the state Capitol and then fanning out to meet with key legislative leaders, as well as their own representatives in the legislature. The members of the coalition followed up during the year with visits in the local districts with their legislative representatives. That was a very important part of the Judicial Council's advocacy efforts. Meeting with the bench/bar coalition took up much of the morning. During the noon hour there was usually a luncheon hosted by the California Judges Association or the State Bar that I would attend. That afternoon began with a series of award ceremonies at which I was asked to present recognitions on behalf of the State Bar. One was the Public Lawyer of the Year Award, which they now very kindly have renamed the Ronald M. George Public Lawyer Award. I believe that around the state there now are six awards that bear my name. It's almost embarrassing and at the least a bit confusing. [Laughter] Later that afternoon came the pro bono awards, which were given to persons whose achievements were truly exceptional, in various categories of solo practitioner, small firm, large firm, corporate counsel, and young lawyer. It's a ceremony that I felt truly honored to participate in. I would also participate in conferring the Diversity Award upon a person who has taken action to help diversify the legal profession or the judiciary.

Every year, on Saturday morning, I would deliver a State of the Judiciary address at the annual meeting and swear in the president and officers of the State Bar, the conference of delegates, the Young Lawyers Association, and the California Judges Association. Added to all this were more receptions, awards, and meetings. I found my participation in these activities to be worthwhile on my part, given the excellent support the judiciary has received over the years from the bar. I have reciprocated and supported the bar on its dues legislation and other matters. Concluding, on Sunday morning, was something that the California Judges Association called "A Conversation with the Chief." That's where they had me on the dais in an armchair fielding questions put to me by two judges on behalf of the membership.

I've had about 12 scheduled speaking engagements in that four-day period, in addition to several others that are sometimes quite impromptu. I have to add one amusing item to this litany of speaking engagements. I remember one Saturday evening in Monterey I was fairly bushed after running around to different venues at various hotels. I finally was done with my duties and was already anticipating the Q&A session with the California Judges Association scheduled for the following morning. I undressed and was trying to get some sleep. There was so much conversation from down the hallway that I just couldn't get to sleep, so I figured, well, it's got to be a reception for lawyers or judges. If you can't fight them, maybe join them—I can't really go over and complain. I got dressed again, walked down the hallway, and saw that apparently it was not a judicial group. Someone said, "Oh, please, come on in," and ushered me into the hospitality suite. The sign said "CABL reception," so I thought, I guess they're having a cable television industry reception here. As soon as I entered I realized that, with the exception of myself, every single person in that rather large group was black. After a few seconds, I recognized some very prominent attorneys and heard the speaker, who was addressing them all from a small dais, turn to me and say, "We are so honored to have a visit by the Chief Justice to the California Association of Black Lawyers. Chief, please come up here and share your thoughts with us." [Laughter] I hadn't realized that "CABL" did not stand for cable TV but for one of the ethnic minority bar associations. I ended up having, at the end of that tiring day, one additional, totally unexpected speaking engagement. I did get back to sleep chuckling at the whole sequence of events and then had my CJA question-and-answer period the next morning.

You previously mentioned working well with the bar's executive director, Judy Johnson. How much difference did it make which individual was serving as president in a given year?

It seemed that every president came with a particular agenda, whether it was adequate funding for the bar, enhancing civility among members of the profession, or mandatory legal education. To some extent they achieved those purposes, but I thought it was unfortunate, as it is in so many organizations, that you're somewhat of a lame duck halfway through your twelve-month term, and it does cramp your ability to get everything done that you could and should be able to.

On other hand, it's a great personal sacrifice and a sacrifice to one's law firm to engage in the duties of president of a State Bar, let alone California's, which has more than 200,000 members. It might be unreasonable to assume one could do that for more than one year. Of course, perhaps some arrangement could be made where more of the duties would be shared with the president-elect in order to give the president of the State Bar additional time in which to accomplish his or her objectives. I always felt a bit sorry to hear the lofty objectives expressed by the incoming president after I swore him or her in, and see what would happen—both the expected and the unexpected—during the president's year in office. That's why, of course, a strong executive staff is very important, and I think the bar by and large has been very well served by very capable people on its staff.

I read that early in your Chief Justiceship you personally sent a letter to all the members of the State Bar, in 1996, urging them to take on or increase pro bono work. What was the genesis of that?

I did that because I was surprised to learn how few attorneys at that time were engaging in pro bono work. I thought that sending an individual letter to each member of the bar would encourage lawyers to volunteer for such activity and at the same time perhaps remove or lessen the pressure that, in some law firms, was exerted by partners on young associates not to do pro bono work, and not to deprive the firm of billable hours. I believe there was a begrudging acceptance of pro bono work in many law firms, in effect telling associates, "Well, you can do it if you want to, but we still expect those billable hours," or "Do it on your own time." That's why I mentioned to you, in discussing Adoption Saturday, how important it was to see name partners in major law firms stepping up to the plate and saying, "Look, I engage in pro bono work. We not only condone it, we encourage it." And that's the reason I sent the letter. I also sent a communication to all judges indicating that they should try to facilitate the vital and commendable efforts of lawyers to engage in pro bono work. It wasn't as if the judge himself or herself, of course, could go out there and represent a client, but knowing that lawyers were engaged in pro bono work, there were certain things that judges and staff could do to perhaps help expedite certain proceedings, or show an understanding with regard to those efforts, in terms of managing the court calendar and requests for continuance, and so forth.

These communications from me dovetailed with some of the efforts I participated in at the annual meeting of the State Bar to recognize individuals who have contributed exceptional pro bono work. There were similar events in which I participated in Alameda, Contra Costa, and Los Angeles Counties. I'll discuss some of these other efforts when you and I get to access-to-justice issues. There are many ways in which the position of Chief Justice can be a bully pulpit in terms of encouraging people to engage in positive behavior by giving recognition to it.

You were able to think consciously about that bully pulpit and how to use it?

Yes, I realized—just from the enormous appreciation expressed at the moment and in follow-up correspondence, sometimes way out of proportion to the minimal effort that I might have exerted—how important my just being there and saying a few words had been to an organization in achieving an objective that had been uphill until then.

We were talking about the State Bar. I wonder what changes you noticed in that very large body over the time you were chief?

I think much of the problem experienced by the bar was brought about by the fact that because the conference of delegates was an integral part of the State Bar, the bar was viewed as having taken positions on all sorts of controversial political, social, and even international issues addressed by resolutions adopted by the delegates that were not viewed as germane to the function of the State Bar, the legal profession, or the practice of law. In fact, there were cases, the *Keller* and *Brosterhous* opinions, holding that the State Bar, by using compulsory membership dues to engage in this function, had violated the First Amendment rights of its objecting members. The courts used the analogy of improper use of compulsory labor union dues. Because of some of these resolutions, there was a fair amount of animosity against the State Bar, some of which came from members of the bar itself who brought these lawsuits, and others from outside the bar, including persons in the legislature and in the executive branch. The State Bar ended up curtailing the scope or purview of these resolutions. Ultimately this was a major factor in the Conference of Delegates being split off as a separate entity, even though they continued to meet concurrently with the State Bar organization. I would meet separately with both organizations, addressing them briefly and swearing in their officers. By becoming a separate entity not funded by compulsory dues, the delegates preserved their right to adopt resolutions on any subject.

There also is increased recognition that the State Bar should do what it can with its membership to improve the image of lawyers, which is sometimes negative, and to increase civility between and among lawyers and between the bar and the bench.

Thank you. Moving on to the press, what was your personal view of media relations and how to approach it as Chief Justice?

I had received some advice when I became Chief Justice that it was not a good idea to speak to the press. "Don't ever forget that they are your enemy." I chose to disregard that advice. Following it can certainly become a self-fulfilling prophecy. I realized that, for better or worse, the press are the eyes and ears of the court in terms of the public's awareness of what goes on in the court system. If the public doesn't understand what the California Supreme Court—or the courts in general—are doing, they're probably not going to like what the courts are doing. In turn, a negative attitude of that sort from the public can come back to haunt the judicial system in many different ways.

Before I try to enumerate them, I just want to stress how important I feel public confidence in the court system is. I regard an independent court system, with sufficient resources to provide the public with fair and accessible justice, as the linchpin of our democratic system of government. Without that, I don't think we can truly function as a democracy the way the Founders of our nation and our state intended. It's very disheartening to me to see how little understanding there is of government in general, but of our judicial system in particular. It's very disconcerting to see how many people lack an adequate understanding of it and of their rights and responsibilities as citizens.

That brings me back to the importance of relations with the press. Of course, I tried to always approach things on a personal level, realizing that the members of the press are working men and women who are assigned the difficult task of understanding what is often highly complex decision making, sometimes having to grapple with obtuse verbiage in our opinions, and under very strict deadlines—which for the legal newspapers are even earlier, sometimes mid-afternoon. They are charged with understanding, digesting, and analyzing these opinions—as well as the broad policy and budget initiatives undertaken by the Judicial Council—in a manner that can be communicated and understood by the lay public. It was obvious to me that it was in my best interest to have input into this process. The press was going to write or broadcast a story with or without my input.

As long as one knows how to deal with the press, which I don't feel is that difficult—and I just mean trying not to make a fool of yourself and not speaking inappropriately—as long as you know how to deal fairly and candidly with the press, there is minimal risk, with 99 percent of the reporters, in speaking to them. There's going to be a story anyway, and I believe it's going to be a less informed story if it doesn't have your point of view in it. It may be that the reporter is under a misconception of fact or theory that can be readily dispelled by an informed source speaking to the press, so I always availed myself of that opportunity. I would dial them back myself if there was a message while I was away from court or on the bench. I would meet with new reporters on the beat. I would sometimes end up taking them out to lunch to explain the court's somewhat arcane processes. I found that most reporters are fair and will give you an opportunity to tell your side of the story, so I made a point of being accessible and candid. I think it served me and served the court system well. That doesn't mean that one avoids all negative stories or stories that one would prefer not be reported in a certain way, but I believe that the advantages of speaking to the press far outweigh any disadvantages. I established a Bench-Bar-Media Committee to try to more or less regularize or institutionalize this type of communication back and forth.

Among the reporters who were leaving their position with their employer, we managed to find positions for some of them in the Administrative Office of the Courts, which improved our ability to communicate with the media and to take advantage of these reporters' perspective on the court system. Some of them accepted those offers and are with us today, and there are others who found other employment, but they all appreciated the effort, including my showing up unexpectedly at a small farewell gathering for one reporter who had lost his position. The benefits of this policy of openness and accessibility were mutual to the press and to myself and the court system. Both the Judicial Council and the Supreme Court, as well as myself personally, were very well served during my time at the court by Peter Allen, James Carroll, and Philip Carrizosa at the A.O.C.'s Office of Communications, and by Lynn Holton, our very dedicated public information officer.

I annually gave a press holiday party in my chambers. It usually was attended by 20 to 25 newspaper reporters from the print media and the electronic media, as well as a few editors. We had various tasty fare for them. Some years, Barbara baked banana bread that they all liked. The only persons in attendance were the press, Lynn Holton and myself. Once we all sat down, following 30 or 40 minutes of standup conversation, I would give them a wrap-up of what I thought were major issues and accomplishments at the California Supreme Court, the Judicial Council, and the A.O.C. during the past year, and what might lie ahead. They were invited to ask me questions about anything I had discussed or about any other subject, and to voice concerns and suggestions they might have.

There were many beneficial ideas that came out of that annual event. For example, we regularized the filing times for our opinions so that the press would know that, absent some very unusual situation, opinions would always be filed at the clerk's counter and on the court's website at 10:00 a.m. to give them more time with the early deadlines for their stories. The press, as well as counsel, would receive at least one day's advance notice of which opinions were coming out and which cases were on the petition conference list for the upcoming Wednesday. We tried to never issue more than two unrelated opinions on a single day, unless there was also a death penalty case, when we might go to three opinions. We didn't want to burden the press with too much to digest in one sitting. Similarly, where possible I would schedule the oral arguments in the more newsworthy cases as part of the morning calendar to facilitate the press being able to write articles to meet that day's afternoon deadline. Of course, the advance notice of filing didn't indicate which way the opinion was going to come out, but it included the name and case number and the court's official summary of the issues. When we granted review of a case, we shortly came out with a summary of the issue or issues upon which the court had granted review. We'd use that same summary in giving them notice the day before the opinion came out, so they could—especially given their difficult deadlines—assemble the copies of the briefs and other filings that we made available to them, get up to speed on the issues and the parties' positions, schedule interviews with the attorneys, and go over the notes they had taken at oral argument, if they had chosen to attend, and be all ready to read the opinion from a copy off the clerk's counter, or electronically within 20 seconds of it being available at the counter, and schedule interviews with the lawyers who had argued the case and with potential commentators.

An improvement to the court's operations in the area of security resulted from one of my holiday parties for the press. Peter Blumberg, a reporter assigned to cover the court, had complained about having to go through security coming into the building and then, before entering the courtroom for oral argument, being screened again. I explained, "Very frankly, I don't think our security is that great at the entrance to the building. The seven justices are up there sitting in a row, so we have to have adequate security in the courtroom, given the heated feelings that people, whether connected with the case or not, might have." He took this as an invitation to buy a knapsack at a camping store, a coil of wire at a hardware store with some batteries and other things, and put the knapsack through the perimeter security at the entrance to the building. He passed through with flying colors, even though I kidded him about being very close to fitting the profile of a terrorist, with his scraggly beard, disheveled hair, and rather informal attire. This incident culminated in a lengthy article in the *Daily Journal* that benefited us by motivating us to take steps to ramp up our building security.

How did individual members of the press respond to this new approach of yours?

They seemed to really enjoy it and were very appreciative. I even received—which is unusual from the press—a couple of books as retirement gifts from them. I remember one was *The Education of Henry Adams*. I believe we built up a lot of mutual respect and very good personal relationships, much trust, and actual friendship. Sometimes reporters from the national press attended too—the *New York Times*, the *Wall Street Journal*, and *U.S.A Today* and some broadcast reporters from out of state.

What kinds of regular relationships were you able to develop with national press outlets?

I know that the *New York Times* wrote some editorials about the crisis in trial court funding in California that seemed to be motivated in part by conversations with me. I was quoted in some publications on the subject of the death penalty. The one and only time I ever made page 2 of the *New York Times'* "quote of the day" was in December 2004, in an excerpt from an interview I had done with Adam Liptak concerning the dysfunctionality of the death penalty in California. Without getting into that whole area, which I know will be a separate topic of conversation between you and me, I was quoted accurately as having said—in the body of the article—and now prominently quoted on page 2, "The leading cause of death on death row in California is old age." It's literally true, and it served to illustrate the point of the story.

The *New York Times* also published an op-ed piece that I co-authored on access-to-justice issues. The press has certainly been accommodating in giving the court system exposure to the public through their efforts. They also wrote very generous profiles of me and my efforts in the *San Francisco Chronicle*, the *Los Angeles Times*, and the *Sacramento Bee* and other publications. The *California Lawyer* asked me to join their editorial advisory board, which I agreed to do as a means of having input into stories that they write, whether about the judiciary or otherwise. I also had an op-ed piece in the *Los Angeles Times* and wrote a piece for the *San Francisco Chronicle*, at their request, on California's initiative process. This isn't strictly speaking press, but I also wrote some articles on issues of court administration, in the *NYU Law Review*, based upon the Brennan Lecture I delivered there, the *California Law Review* of the University of California, Berkeley School of Law, and the *Golden Gate University Law Review,* and a piece on the initiative process that appeared in the *Stanford Law Review.*

You mentioned the Bench-Bar-Media Committee, and I know you asked Justice Moreno to chair that. Can you say a bit more about the work of that group and what you think it accomplished?

One of the most important things this committee can do and is doing is to promote a better understanding, on both sides, of how the other side functions. I believe that judges need to be sensitized to the legitimate needs of the press, which I think almost all of those needs are. Of course, they would like more than they can have. I remember being kidded by one editor at my annual press party, "We sure would like an eighth seat at the court's conference table." [Laughter]

I think the press likewise needs to make sure that, at least in any decent-sized publication—and the same applies to the electronic media—the person assigned to cover a court receives some basic training on the function of the court system and understands the basis upon which judges and courts render decisions. It's very harmful to the public's understanding of our judicial system—which, as I said a moment ago, I consider so important—for the press to resort to a sports mentality in writing up the decision of a judge or a court, "Here's the winner. Who's the loser?" "Corporation won. Employee lost." "Criminal won. Public safety lost." It's not just about who won and who lost, so it's important that there be media workshops that instruct the press on the basics, and instruct judges on the basics too. That's why I hope we can further expand upon this effort. Judges don't decide cases in order to set a criminal free or to harm an employee. It's so vital that the story explain in a simple, short, and straightforward way, the basis for the court's ruling—how and why the court came to its decision. If crucial evidence is kept out, it may well be because of restraints that the people adopted through their passage of federal and state constitutional prohibitions against unreasonable searches and seizures. Government action may be restricted because of the First Amendment right of free speech or the Fifth Amendment provision that property not be taken "without just compensation."

The head of the California Newspaper Publishers Association and I met with the Chief Justice of Washington State, Gerry Alexander, to learn about that state's very fine bench-bar-media program. I adopted it as somewhat of a model in setting up our committee, again showing that the states and their judicial systems are all laboratories that can learn from each other. California has a lot to export, and we do. But there's a lot that California can learn and has learned from other states.

Even the foreign press has been interested in what we're doing in California. There was a very fine piece in a British publication, the *Economist*, about how California's governmental system works or doesn't work, including the court system. I have had direct inquiries occasionally from the British, French, German, and Mexican news media about the California courts.

I helped organize a statewide conference of court public information officers to assist in giving them better training in terms of what they properly can and should explain to the press and what is off limits. We still have problems—and we'll talk about this when we discuss my opinion in the *NBC Subsidiary* case—with the actions of trial courts that close their proceedings to the public when they should not. Both the U.S. Supreme Court and the California Supreme Court have made it clear that only truly exceptional circumstances justify closing court proceedings or sealing court files. When judges ignore this, it engenders a lot of ill will on behalf of the press, because they just cannot afford to retain a First Amendment lawyer to file a lawsuit every time a court improperly closes its doors even out of, perhaps, a well-motivated concern for the privacy of the parties. The basic principle recognized in the *NBC* opinion is that the constitutional right to open courts extends to civil proceedings as well as criminal. Adherence to this principle helps to ensure that the system is operating as it should be—fairly, presided over with competent jurists, and without undue influence or corruption.

At the time you issued that decision, the U.S. Supreme Court had been silent about the civil side, and you were establishing that open courts would apply in civil trials too. How did your decision affect what happened elsewhere in the civil arena?

It led to the Judicial Council adopting rules—at my suggestion—governing the sealing of court records as well, because depositions, exhibits, and other parts of the court record are also on occasion rendered confidential by court order. The decision, from what I heard, also had a lot of impact outside California. Perhaps as a result, I had a number of appearances and received some awards from various organizations, such as the California Newspaper Publishers Association, the California Society of Newspaper Editors, the First Amendment Coalition—I spoke before them two or three times—the Sacramento Press Club, and the Society of Professional Journalists. And we organized an event for the ethnic or minority media as well, focusing on their particular needs. I've always considered myself a firm proponent of access. There will be a couple of additional opinions that I'll mention later, relating to access to public records of employees' names and salaries, that reflect this overall view. With regard to the press, that probably covers it. I would just add as a final note that I guess my accessibility inspired the *Daily Journal* to send Katrina Dewey, who was then its Los Angeles editor, to include me in a piece on the daily lives of eight busy individuals. She followed me around for one day in 2003 from early morning to a speaking engagement late in the evening, and wrote that up.[1]

Did you wear her out?

I think I did. I remember her asking, "How are you ever going to get out of this particular gathering to meet the next one that you're due at five minutes ago?" I said, "The key is, avoid eye contact and walk fast." [Laughter]

---

[1] "An Insider's Look at the Lives of the Top 100," *Daily Journal* (October 27, 2003).

We're going to touch today also on relations with the other branches of state government.

When a major reform was achieved, dealing with the legislature was as gratifying as any professional experience I've ever had, implementing something I felt would benefit the judicial system and the public for decades to come. At other times, having to work with the legislature was absolutely the most frustrating and negative experience, in terms of human behavior and motivation, that I could imagine. It's been some of each, but for better or for worse, even though my favorite part of my responsibilities as Chief Justice of California was, as I said before, working on opinions, a major part was acting as chief advocate for the judicial branch in Sacramento.

I thought it was very important, coming into that position, for me to overcome the residue of resentment over our court's decision upholding the voters' term-limits initiative. I started coming up to Sacramento with that hanging over my head. On the other hand, there certainly was an olive branch extended in the invitation to deliver a State of the Judiciary address scheduled to take place on May 15, two weeks after I became Chief Justice. This was the first of what became 15 annual State of the Judiciary addresses I delivered to joint sessions of the California legislature.

I found there was a whole set of skills I needed to employ in performing that function. A preconceived notion existed—whether justified or not—that many judges were haughty and removed from the process of everyday life. It was important to counteract that expectation and still be a forceful advocate. At the same time, one had to be diplomatic and treat the legislators with a lot of respect and recognize that with legislators, by and large, their relationships—whether between one legislator and another or with an outsider such as myself—are largely personal. If you can learn to get along on that level it makes a big difference, even if you have different points of view. Sometimes the appropriate use of humor and informality would go a long way toward greasing the machinery of interbranch relationships. That's something I soon learned.

On the legislative side alone, you had a great many personal relationships to nurture. Even the leadership turned over so frequently, especially in the Assembly. How did you go about, with each new leader, establishing such a rapport?

That was a real challenge, and it shows a real down-side of term limits, because you were confronted with this turnover of members of the Assembly, who were limited to three two-year terms. Legislators in recent years came to the conclusion that it was better to put in a virtually inexperienced legislator as speaker—in order to have continuity in the leadership for five and half years—than to have a more experienced, seasoned speaker and have him or her depart in a year or in a few months. Until this practice of selecting a newly elected member as Speaker was adopted, it was almost Queen for a Day, as in the title of the old soap opera. Leaders occupied the speakership for a very short period of time and didn't have a chance to acquire the special skills that go into being an effective Speaker before being term-limited. Compounding this situation, for whatever reason—and I don't know if it's connected to term limits or to something else—there is an ever-decreasing number of lawyers who are serving as members of the legislature. Not that all lawyers are necessarily reasonable and fun to work with, but at least in terms of the concepts they deal with, lawyers are at least trained in working with laws. If you're going to be passing laws, this does help. Not that I would ever want to see the great majority of the legislature be lawyers. I think we need a good cross-section of the community serving in that body. But when you have such a dearth of lawyers, the legislative process suffers not only in the lawmaking function, but frankly in its basic understanding of the role of the judiciary as a co-equal branch of government. I remember when lawyers were competing to get on the Assembly Judiciary Committee or the Senate Judiciary Committee. Now there aren't enough lawyers to fill either one of those committees, so you have nonlawyers serving on them. I'm not saying a nonlawyer should never be appointed to either of those committees, but I think when you are filling those committees with nonlawyers just because you don't have enough lawyers, that's unfortunate.

This problem—in combination with the turnover due to term limits—causes legislators to be less effective, to have less authority, and for staff to be in a position of sometimes calling the shots. I want to stress, however, that there have been marvelous staff persons for whom I have great respect and whom I enjoyed working with. But you do have other staff who really march to the beat of their own drum and who feel quite free to pursue their own agenda. Some of them actually end up causing problems with legislation—even occasionally killing a bill—because of an unrelated dispute they may be having with another legislative staff member. This ends up subjugating the merits of the bill to personal rivalries. Sometimes it's a conflict between assembly staff and senate staff, not even involving different political parties. There are all sorts of complications, and those are the day-to-day ones.

Other complications occur that are quite insidious, when a staff person in a position of authority actually countermands legislative leadership that is weak or even cowardly, and staff either pushes through or stops a bill because of his or her own agenda or the staffer's alliances outside the legislative process. This phenomenon was especially prevalent among staff who themselves—or through a legislative member—were closely allied with the public employee unions, who have assumed the stranglehold position that was occupied 100 years ago in the legislature by the railroads as the most powerful lobbying force in the state Capitol until the advent of the initiative process brought the railroads under control. I've seen bills die in the last minute through the shenanigans of key staffers or union lobbyists invoking the other's authority as the legislative clock is ticking toward the constitutional deadline. There's an old adage in Sacramento, "That's the time when bad bills squeak through and good bills die." I learned after the fact of instances where a staffer who worked for a legislative leader, without having consulted with the leader, proceeded to an ongoing legislative committee hearing and authoritatively directed one or more legislators how to vote on the pending bill.

While we're talking about legislative staff, there are some incidents that illustrated for me the madcap, carnival, or playground atmosphere occasionally on display in the state Capitol building. One staffer, considered quite eccentric by his colleagues, served as an extreme example of someone who, for whatever reason, was never reined in. He would, on occasion, literally be running after me as I made my rounds through the hallways of the state Capitol, shouting my first name. "Ron! Ron! I want to talk to you about something," in a very loud voice while shoving food into his mouth, dropping it, and running around other persons blocking his way, eager to share some sort of political insight or bit of information or offer some advice that he thought was important. These weren't antagonistic encounters, but this fellow was quite a character. I was told by a knowledgeable source that on one occasion a female legislator was desperately trying to escape this staff member. I heard the incident described as, "like a coyote trying to gnaw its paw out of a trap." Anything to get away. She darted into the ladies' room and, believe it or not, he followed her in there, continuing his harangue while she was inside the stall attending to her business. [Laughter]

I'll share one more story involving an episode that had occurred shortly before one of my visits to the Capitol. The same staffer apparently was visibly upset at being double-crossed, as he viewed it, by someone who worked in the governor's office. The governor's assistant had acquired the moniker of "the tuna," apparently because of the shape of his corpulent physique. The "double-crossed" staffer whose antics I've been describing was standing in front of one of the capitol building's elevators. It momentarily opened and was jam-packed with other staffers and tourists and schoolchildren visiting the Capitol. Recognizing someone he knew in this crowded elevator, he shouted as the doors were closing, "I just got fucked by the tuna," to the total consternation of those in the elevator. [Laughter]

Although it was always a challenge to educate the other two branches of government concerning our respective roles with each other, sometimes the greatest challenge was dealing with our own folks in that regard. This difficulty is, I believe, causing the judiciary more harm than anything being done by the other two branches of government. It brings to mind the phrase "being one's own worst enemy." I'm very sorry to see my successor have to deal with the self-destructive behavior of some of these judges. Unfortunately such tendencies tend to come out more frequently when fiscal times are difficult and perhaps when there is a change of leadership in the judicial branch. Putting aside these periodic concerns, there are people who believe—as a great generalization—that perhaps because judges are steeped in precedent and have been taught to follow it, many of them are inherently resistant to change. Some judges have a parochial view of their reign over their own turf, over their own fiefdom, as such. Some therefore assume a very self-important attitude. This is something that has to be overcome. It was a subject that was frequently mentioned by legislators and their staff when I was in Sacramento. Many judges are jealous of their personal prerogatives and feel that their discretion should be without limits. I believe this phenomenon may provide part of the answer to your earlier question about why some judges resisted unification as strongly and as long as they did, being concerned with the trappings of office more than with the benefits that would be provided to the statewide administration of justice.

My view has been that the judicial branch, although independent, is really codependent. We are provided with our resources by the taxpaying public through their elected representatives in the legislature and by the governor. We therefore have to be accountable for these public funds. There was generally a lack of accountability when funding for the courts came from the counties. This was complicated by all sorts of sweetheart deals between counties and local courts involving links between the salaries of county supervisors and those of judges, judicial sign-offs on legislative block grants to counties, and the eligibility of judges for benefits conferred upon county supervisors. Under the former system of county funding of the trial courts, we never were able to find out exactly what monies were being received by those courts, what reserves they had, and what expenditures were made. It was sort of "scratch my back, I'll scratch yours," between counties and many of the local courts. That's something that had to be overcome. I believe it's far better for the Judicial Council and the statewide administration of justice to have oversight and to be responsible for ensuring accountability, rather than to have the legislative and executive branches be overly intrusive in trying to monitor what each court is doing. The latter course would cause far more interference in the affairs of local courts. But some judges have this nostalgic view of the "good old days"—which, as in so many other contexts, were often not all that good—as a time when they thought they could readily obtain everything they wanted from the counties, just for the asking. I would have to remind them of the 1976 episode, which I shared with you, of Presiding Judge Grillo not even being reimbursed for his travel expenses to Sacramento and choosing to march over to the L.A. County Hall of Administration across the civic center mall with his bailiff to arrest a county employee for contempt of court for following the orders of his county superiors. With the advent of state funding during my second year as Chief Justice, spending on the trial courts doubled from about $1.5 billion to about $3 billion during my last year in office.

All of these concerns helped formulate the initial philosophy that guided my visits to Sacramento. You asked about changes in the speakership of the Assembly. Whenever there was a change of speaker I would go up and have a meeting with him or her. I tried to stress that I was just at the head of the parade and that there was a whole branch of government that I was speaking for. My efforts were reinforced by members of the Judicial Council, the Bench Bar Coalition, and the A.O.C.'s Office of Governmental Affairs. Officials and staff in the legislative and executive branches were, for the most part, receptive once they really understood what our goals were, and once they developed a personal relationship with us and with our justice system partners. The counties, through CSAC, were particularly helpful in this regard, as were the consumer attorneys and the California Judges Association. When things went well, my experiences in Sacramento truly were very gratifying on a personal level.

The first such major experience, as I previously mentioned, was with the trial court funding bill and being able to announce its passage to the State Bar after the legislature had stopped the clock before the preceding midnight deadline. A second of these experiences involved Darrell Steinberg, before he became Senate President pro Tem, and at a time when he was chairing the Assembly Judiciary Committee. His committee had voted down what became the third of my priority structural reforms, the Trial Court Facilities Act. I believe there was concern about what the financial impact would be of the state's assuming the vast responsibility of taking over California's 530 courthouses.

I was out of state in Idaho when that happened. I learned of the action his committee had taken, and I called him back. I said, "Darrell, you can't imagine how much this means to me. So much is at stake. I implore you, please, is there anything that can be done about it?" I reiterated the arguments in favor of the bill. He reconvened the committee; they reversed their decision, and the bill went on to pass both houses of the legislature and was signed into law by Governor Davis. A copy of the bill, SB 1732, was sent to me by Governor Davis, with the following inscription dated September 30, 2002: "Chief—Congratulations on these landmark reforms of the judiciary! Now if you could just help me out with the executive and legislative branches—Gray." That was a moment—the second of three illustrations I'll give you—where I truly felt my advocacy had made a difference. It was personally very satisfying.

The third experience was in 2010, when the judicial branch was in totally dire straits, and we were begging the legislature to extend some fees that were about to sunset and to enact some new fees just to get us by. They asked, "Why should we do anything about our $200 million-plus cut in your budget if the governor isn't budging from the extra $100 million cut that he imposed on the courts?" I came to an understanding with the legislative leadership that, if I could get the governor to reverse his position on the $100 million cut, they would reverse their position on the $200 million cut. I don't know if they thought I was on a fool's errand or not, but I had a meeting with Governor Schwarzenegger and made a very strong pitch—to the point where I think some of my staff, and maybe some of his staff, raised their eyebrows at whether I was being overly assertive. Miraculously, the governor agreed to do just that and restored the $100 million to the judicial branch budget. The legislature then went on to give us the new fees and extend the existing fees that were to sunset. We ended up coming through that last year in fairly good shape. We were able to avoid reinstating the one-day-a-month court closures of the previous year, and to get through okay.

Every year brings new crises and new battles up there, at least in bad fiscal times. But those successes were very satisfying moments. It was extremely busy running up and down to Sacramento all the time. I was very well assisted in this way and many others by California Highway Patrol Officer Terry Tracy, who was assigned to my security and transportation. I would look up an hour and 15 minutes later, working on an opinion, and there I would be entering the subterranean garage under the Capitol. Then we'd be back in San Francisco after having a full day of meetings and stopping en route for dinner.

One such meal stop was amusing. I guess some people who knew a bit of my background assumed that because I was a runner, I was a real health buff. Terry and I stopped midway—I believe it was in Vacaville—at an In-and-Out Burger. The fellow behind the counter yelled out, "George. Double cheeseburger with bacon." To my embarrassment, another customer turned around and said, "You're busted!" [Laughter] He was a legislative staffer. Months later, I was asked to administer the attorney's oath to him when he passed the bar exam, and he presented me with a double cheeseburger with bacon as we stood on the floor of the Senate—which was not in session at the time.

Although there often was a certain amount of mirth, some of those days were exhausting. There were days when I had as many as 12 half-hour meetings back to back, with individual legislators, then, on a day in the following week, 12 more meetings. Sometimes I would be kept waiting, and I'd run late to the next meeting, so it was really like being in a squirrel cage. But it was so important to have those meetings.

I wanted to mention that there were also meetings with the executive branch. I had many meetings with Governor Pete Wilson. Dan Kolkey was his legal affairs secretary, and my son Eric was working for Dan as a deputy legal affairs secretary. John Davies was the judicial appointments secretary, although he advised the governor on a great many other legal and judicial issues. Bob White, the chief of staff, attended those meetings, as did Pat Clarey—people who were very friendly to me and to the judicial branch. Governor Gray Davis got us going with our court technology project. He couldn't believe that we had 70 different systems and various permutations of them, and he told us that we needed to pursue a statewide computer system. He was very convincing. He was ably assisted by Lynn Schenk, his chief of staff, and Burt Pines, his judicial appointments secretary, on a number of judicial branch issues. There were other people who served as judicial appointments secretary over the years and consulted me from time to time on pending appointments—Chuck Poochigian, Tim Flanagan, and most recently Sharon Majors-Lewis under Governor Schwarzenegger. Governor Schwarzenegger's chief of staff was Susan Kennedy. I had many productive meetings with her and other individuals in the administration and developed really fine personal relationships, both with the staff in the governor's office and the governors themselves.

Speaking with a broad brush, what did you learn about how to get things done in Sacramento?

I certainly tried to invoke the public interest and make it clear that—in contrast to most other groups that might be viewed as special interest groups—what I was asking for was not for the benefit of judges or even courts, strictly speaking. It was on behalf of the public and its access to fair, accessible, and efficient justice. Of course, governors would greet me in their office in recent years with stories that were bona fide: "We're cutting out healthcare to blind individuals, to children with terrible diseases, to old people with Alzheimer's. We don't have enough money for wheelchairs." It's very difficult to go up there and be in competition with those very legitimate needs. It was a struggle to always be the advocate for the public's interest in the justice system, because until that system involves an individual who's in court—on what may be the most important day in his or her life—people don't think much about the justice system. They do somewhat when they're involved in jury service, which is another matter we'll talk about and which is why I think jury reform is so important. But they normally don't really think about it, so it's not as tangible or immediate a concern as what people have in other areas, such as schools, parks, social services, and law enforcement. I had to convey to each governor the importance to the public of what we did, and be strong and at the same time respectful.

A couple more thoughts about the legislative process. I certainly felt the German chancellor, Otto von Bismarck, Count Bismarck, had it right when he proclaimed, "There are two things that people should not see being made. One is sausage, and the other is laws." The way hearings were held and conducted was often the antithesis of what one would expect by way of due process in a court. Sometimes, despite all the prescribed procedures about first and second readings of bills and ample notice, these steps were totally evaded at the end of the process, in the last hours. Bills could be "hijacked," which might mean that the Assembly would pass a bill on one subject, let's say regulating taking scampi out of season under the Fish and Game Code. The bill would get over to the Senate side, and someone would offer an amendment—if the bill wasn't thought much of, or wasn't likely to go anywhere—to delete all the language except the bill number. After being amended, it might suddenly resurface as a bill addressing some of the needs of the judicial branch.

Yes, the term "hijack." Let's take it in a completely different direction.

Yes. Another favorite term up there was "gut and amend," and the term gut is used as one uses it in the sense of cleaning fish. The same concept here. There might be no hearings on the bill—the innards could be removed, and the bill could reappear in a totally different form. One bill might be joined to another, posing a potential problem under the single-subject rule. I know that at different points, we saw our courthouse construction bill linked to the construction of a new east span for the Oakland Bay Bridge and to a recycling bill—subjects totally unrelated to our own, perhaps tied to each other for the sake of political convenience. I had to get used to this process, as well as the clock stopping at midnight to meet constitutional deadlines. It was very disconcerting at times because, although I've talked about some major legislative victories, we had occasions when things died just as the clock was running out, and we had to wait another year or two and start over to get a certain reform through.

Another thing I learned in this process was that it was much, much more advantageous for the judicial branch for there to be a very strong leader in the legislature, even if the two of you disagree on some subject involving the judiciary, than to have someone nominally in charge who might be the friendliest pushover and then end up not exerting any authority and have staff run circles around the leader. There were people in Sacramento, like Speaker Willie Brown—whom I dealt with as an associate justice when Chief Justice Lucas sent me up there—or Senator John Burton and Senator Don Perata who might not always agree with you, but they would look you in the eye, tell you what they would or would not commit to, and you could take it to the bank no matter what would happen. You wouldn't have any phony excuses or prevarication. They wouldn't allow staff to circumvent them, and they managed to get things done. That was something I learned to understand, appreciate, and respect.

We can return to the subject of the other branches because it's a very rich vein. Perhaps you could be thinking, before next time, about how you became a good lobbyist and what else you picked up about how to accomplish things in Sacramento.

Certainly. I'll just respond to that briefly by saying that Senator Burton and Governor Schwarzenegger each complimented me in a backhanded way on that very point. Governor Schwarzenegger said he was seeing me around his office more than he encountered some of his top aides. Although Senator Burton has been quoted as calling me "a damned good ambassador for the judiciary," he told me at one point that if I came up one more time during that legislative session, under the law I would have to register as a lobbyist. [Laughter] These are just acknowledgments of what you said, that I did end up becoming lobbyist-in-chief for California's judicial branch. [Laughter]

###

Chapter 13

Working with California Governors and the Legislature

October 3, 2011

We were talking last time about your work in Sacramento while you were Chief Justice and about the legislative process, including examples of your interactions and stories about staff members to the legislators. Let's talk more about that process and about legislators that you worked with personally.

I believe the legislature has been rendered less effective in recent years by a variety of factors. One is the effect of redistricting which, in many cases, has caused the legislative representatives to reflect the more extreme elements in their own political party rather than the center ground that is more geared toward compromise and achievement. Another factor, term limits, has made it more difficult for persons to acquire expertise in the legislative process and specifically in judicial branch issues—and thus has made legislators more dependent on staff and on fundraising—combined with the trend toward fewer and fewer lawyers serving in the legislature.

Finally, there is the impact of the initiative process, which in many instances has imposed spending mandates upon legislators, whether in worthwhile areas such as education and transportation or in other areas. The passage of initiative measures ties their hands, very much so, and therefore also indirectly affects funds available to the judicial branch. At the same time, restraints—some enacted by initiative—have been imposed on the ability of legislators to raise the revenue to pay for those very same spending mandates, leading to a kind of gridlock. Added to this mix is a constitutional provision that makes it very difficult to change a law once it is enacted by initiative. It's sort of a perfect storm between spending mandates, restrictions on revenue raising, and the near inability to change whatever one has done in these first two areas. Unless the initiative expressly reserves such power in the legislature, fixing something enacted by an initiative requires the approval of the voters. That generally entails additional delay and expense. This is so even if the proposed change would be basically consistent with what the electorate presumably had in mind in enacting the legislation.

These combined factors cause legislators to have less of a sense of responsibility on a long-term basis for the obligations they undertook when they were sent by the voters to Sacramento to run the state and take care of its problems. All of this in turn contributes to producing an environment in which legislative staff can run amok, engage in their own personal disputes or rivalries, and further their own agendas, sometimes in direct contradiction to what their bosses in the legislative leadership have wanted them to do or have promised others, including myself, that they would do. I believe this to be a very destructive process. There are some legislative staffers who are the finest professionals that I can imagine in any walk of life, but there are others who are not. This situation, unfortunately, serves to empower those who are up to their own mischief, and who can sometimes summon allies who are politically powerful outside the legislature to help them do their bidding.

As we get to the subject of individual legislators, an old maxim comes to mind that came from Tip O'Neill, a former Speaker of the U.S. House of Representatives. He said, "All politics is local." I certainly saw political considerations influence the attitudes of individual legislators—or even those of their whole caucus—toward the judicial branch because of something they were personally concerned with. I remember dealing with one state senator who found it impossible, on virtually every occasion I had to meet with him, not to bring up his own divorce proceedings and how he thought he'd gotten a raw deal at the hands of his wife and her attorneys and didn't feel the court system dealt with him fairly. This was not even in the course of discussing family law issues. We were talking dollars and cents, talking about every other kind of issue, and virtually every time it was an obsession with him. This legislator could not get off the topic of his own divorce. It seemed to pervade his attitude toward the courts. There was also a legislator I dealt with who had many constituents who owned yachts and who, despite the state's budgetary deficit, resisted efforts to close a loophole that permitted California residents to avoid California taxes on the sale of their vessels by temporarily mooring them in Oregon waters. It made a lot of sense to close this loophole, but apparently that was something he was unwilling to do. Another instance was a legislator's preoccupation with a citation that his wife had received as a motorist for making a rolling stop, and what he viewed as the excessive amount of the fine. He stated openly that this experience led him to oppose the surcharge on traffic and criminal penalties that we were desperately seeking in order to fund a $5 billion, revenue-based bond issue that would enable courthouse construction to proceed without impacting the state's beleaguered general fund. Having this revenue bond based on traffic fines and other criminal penalties was a necessity if it were to get through, which it ultimately did. Occasionally, a totally unrelated decision of the California Supreme Court or perhaps of a lower court—the Court of Appeal or even a trial court—would be on the mind of a legislator the day I would walk into his or her office. I'd have to hear about it, and the court ruling would be invoked—highly inappropriately—as a reason for not addressing the judicial branch's budgetary or policy needs that were to be the subject of our meeting.

What would be your method for trying to respond to something like that?

I would attempt to impress upon them that I came as a representative of the public's interest in our statewide system of justice and that it was totally inappropriate for us to discuss court decisions that were not yet final. Sometimes they'd even bring up cases and issues that were awaiting decision in our court. Even though our decisions aren't final until the time for acting on a petition for rehearing has passed, I would sometimes have to deal with a rather heated tirade against some not-yet-final decision that our court or some other court had rendered. Sometimes this occurred in person when I was meeting with them because, as I said previously, in the eyes of most legislators everything is viewed through a political prism. There seems to be a perception that if a court rules a certain way, it is trying either to assist the winning party or to damage the interests of the losing party, rather than the court just calling the case as it is compelled to do under applicable legal principles.

This all goes back to the early advice we discussed—that I received when I was sworn in as a municipal court judge—that every time a judge makes a decision, he or she makes a temporary friend and a permanent enemy. From time to time I had to recall that advice, especially during visits to Sacramento. I remember receiving an exceedingly angry call about 10 minutes after news of one of our rulings hit the air waves. The caller was a very powerful state legislative leader, who was absolutely livid at the court's order refusing to remove, from the ballot, an initiative measure that addressed the question of reapportionment. I also recall being approached at a social event by a very powerful member of Congress who expressed great annoyance at that same decision and said, "Okay, well, now you've just forced us to have to spend a lot of money to make sure the voters defeat this measure."[1]

Of course, these considerations were totally irrelevant to me and my colleagues. I don't think people understood that I and many, many other judges and justices have had occasion to vote to uphold measures that they thought were foolish or ill-advised legislation. Likewise, many of us have had occasion to render rulings that the judges truly hated to make, invalidating measures that they personally favored and would have—or perhaps did—vote for at the polls. But in light of the legal arguments made, those judges had to invalidate the measure before them. There were many illustrations of this phenomenon, including one that you and I covered in our discussions concerning my years as an associate justice on the Supreme Court—a decision that I did not author but that I joined in, upholding the term-limits initiative, *Legislature v. Eu.*

Another very graphic example came directly from the mouth of the chair of the Assembly Judiciary Committee, Mike Feuer, as quoted in an interview reported in the spring 2011 edition of the California Judges Association publication *The Bench.* The interviewer inquired about the impact of there being fewer and fewer attorneys in the legislature and whether that makes it difficult for the interviewee, as chair of the judiciary committee, to describe to his colleagues the importance of the justice system. Here's the response by Assemblyman Feuer: "Yes, it does. Here's what that means as a practical matter: When the [Senate Bill] 1407 debate was happening on the floor, again, the debate about whether there should be revenue bonds used to make our courts physically safer, no Republican voted for that bill in my house. The reason which they gave publicly was that they were dissatisfied with the Chief Justice's majority opinion in the *In re Marriage Cases* and because of that dissatisfaction, they were reluctant to do anything to benefit the court system. It's hard to know where to begin in critiquing that approach to lawmaking, to legislating. But at a minimum it displays a stunning lack of appreciation for what separation of powers means and an appalling apparent disbelief in judicial independence." That's out of the mouth of a member of the legislature's leadership. It's not just my surmise or rumor or scut-

---

[1] Our court granted review and set aside a lower court ruling that had removed Proposition 77 from the ballot, in order to enable us to determine whether the measure was valid despite the slight discrepancies that existed between the version submitted to the attorney general's office and the version circulated for signature. The initiative measure would have transferred from the legislature to a panel of retired state and federal judges the authority to draw districts for seats in the legislature and on the Board of Equalization, as well as in the U.S. House of Representatives. As predicted by the member of Congress, a lot of money was spent and the measure was defeated at the ballot. In an opinion I authored for the court, *Costa v. Superior Court,* we determined after the fact that the slight discrepancies in the versions of the measure did not render it invalid.

tlebutt. I find that quite illuminating, and I appreciate the fact that Assemblyman Feuer would speak so candidly on that issue.

By the way, the person who was carrying our courthouse construction bond measure as a key supporter for the Republican minority turned into a leading opponent because of the *In re Marriage Cases* decision I wrote for the court, so it wasn't just a few stray members. Although our bill ultimately passed, I nonetheless found that reaction very disturbing. There also had been reactions to the decision that I authored for the court in the *American Academy of Pediatrics v. Lungren* case involving parental consent to abortion, along with a threat from some legislators: "There's something we can do about you judges." I was told that when I made one of my visits to a legislator in the Capitol.

So those are some illustrations of political legislative reactions to nonpolitical judicial decisions. Other impediments to the judicial branch's legislative agenda arose from rivalries between or among legislators—political and nonpolitical rivalries, and sometimes turf battles in the same house or between the two houses of the legislature. On many occasions I saw bills defeated or deferred for reasons having nothing to do with their merits and had to wait an extra year or two to get them through because of obstacles such as these.

We spoke about your efforts with individual reporters and media outlets to assure an education—on the part of reporters and through them the public—about why a court makes a decision, that it isn't just winners and losers or a matter of political preferences. But here you're talking about the legislative branch. How do you think now, having gone through all this, about the education of legislators on these points and the solution to that great divide in thinking?

I don't want this to sound in any way condescending, but I wish there was a more formalized orientation program for new legislators. We do have a reception in conjunction with the State of the Judiciary address every year at which we can mingle. We have items out for display in the rotunda of the Capitol. I once was asked to actually make a presentation to new legislators and gave sort of a mini civics lesson on the respective roles of the legislature and the courts. In fact, there's a wonderful article written by Terry Friedman, who was an excellent legislator in the California Assembly and then became an excellent judge of the L.A. Superior Court and has since retired. He wrote a piece in the mid-1990s before he became president of the California Judges Association, discussing the differences between the role of a legislator and that of a judge.[2] In that article, he went through a whole litany of differences about how legislators may acquire

---

[2] "Why Can't We Just Get Along?—Judges and Legislators Play by Different Rules," Terry Friedman, *California Courts Commentary* (publication of the California Judges Association), November 1995.

information from any source, whether or not it is hearsay, and how everything is interrelated. A judge instead is confined to the record of things actually brought to court for his or her consideration of the case, subject to limitations on what he or she properly may consider. Personal ex parte contact with a legislator is not inappropriate or improper, whereas with a judge it certainly is. Political or popular influences are relevant to a legislator's decision making. They must not be considered by a judge, who also is not fully free to comment on judicial decisions he or she—or other judges—have arrived at. It's a wonderful piece, and I've just touched upon some of the highlights. Enacting legislation and interpreting it are two fundamentally different functions. It's as if legislators and judges lived on different planets. Judge Friedman's article should be required reading for every new legislator, and probably for every new judge as well. As I mentioned, I did address legislators at their invitation on one occasion as part of an orientation program. Perhaps a solution, in addition to reading materials such as Judge Friedman's article, would be to have some kind of presentation made by one or more judicial representatives right at the very beginning of each new legislator's term. Even though legislators will always be political animals, at least they should understand—and I'm not sure most of them do—the drastically different functions that we as judges perform in contrast to what they do as legislators.

Perhaps I could ask you about individuals serving in leadership positions. On the senate side, you had a series of people serving as President pro Tem while you were Chief Justice. Could I ask you to say a few words about each and how you might have worked with him? Bill Lockyer was President pro Tem at the time you became chief and also worked with you on legislation, both as a senator on the judiciary committee and as a leader. What sort of a guy was he?

Senator Lockyer had a great intellectual curiosity and still does. He reads voraciously, knows a lot about a lot of subjects, and gets right to the heart of things. He's very much of a political animal, but he does understand the role of the judiciary and was the co-author of our initial reform—state trial court funding—that basically enabled everything else that came down the pike to happen. This legislation bears his name and that of Assembly Member Phil Isenberg. The two of them worked very hard to pass the measure. Bill Lockyer also worked with us on unification of the trial courts. I had discussions with him about what it would take to get a constitutional amendment proposal through the legislature and accepted by the electorate. My view was that if he would make it a local option, we could get it through, rather than trying to mandate it overnight for everyone. That latter course, by the way, would have been much easier for me but was not politically feasible in my view. I knew it then, and I certainly knew it after the process was over, but I was convinced that if we made it a local option, we could ensure that every court ultimately would choose that option, so we worked together on that strategy. We worked together on other things, including jury reform. He was very helpful and knowledgeable.

John Burton was someone I found very easy to work with, although some persons didn't share that view. He appeared to have a gruff personality but really had a very big heart underneath it. People had the perception, which was probably fairly accurate, that John Burton couldn't say good morning to you without adding on a few four-letter expletives in the process. [Laughter] That was just the way he speaks, but he was very committed to the judicial branch and to the many causes he believed in. By the way, he had been hired as a deputy attorney general by Stanley Mosk, as I had been, and told me the story of showing up for his interview dressed in extremely casual attire, I believe in jeans and a t-shirt. A top aide to Mosk said, "We can't hire that guy, can we?" Mosk knew Burton's family and said, "I don't care if he comes in here wearing a swimsuit. He's hired." [Laughter] Burton kept up a longstanding friendship and affection for Justice Mosk and, when Mosk passed away, saw to it that the Library and Courts Building in Sacramento was named after Justice Mosk.

What was the key to working successfully with Senator Burton?

I believe it involved countering the perception, which perhaps he and many others in the Capitol shared, that each and every judge was haughty, self-important, and in effect unable to relate to the concerns of everyday people. I was always at my informal best when meeting with John Burton. I had meetings in his office and elsewhere. I remember having lunch with him at Delancey Street, the San Francisco drug rehabilitation facility where he often liked to eat. He was fun to deal with, and if he was not willing to abide by your position he would candidly tell you so. If he was with your position, you could count on this commitment without being concerned whether his staff would follow through or instead torpedo it.

I remember there was an amusing incident when I was going into his office with my delegation of Bill Vickrey, Ron Overholt, and a couple of other people from the A.O.C.'s Office of Governmental Affairs. Who should we pass while we're going in to lobby while another group lobbying Senator Burton was going out? The chair of the California Arts Council—my wife Barbara George—and her staffers. This greatly amused John Burton, and he proclaimed to both groups, "You know, I've just figured out a perfect way to fully fund the California Arts Council. You'll get every penny you ask for, even in this difficult year. I'm going to take it out of the judicial branch budget." [Laughter]

He also had some fun introducing me when Governor Davis gave his January 2000 State of the State address. It was almost as embarrassing as it would have been to receive a negative reference in the introduction. All the constitutional officers were present and received the customary pro forma introduction without any embellishments. The *Sacramento Bee* reported the pro Tem's remarks as follows: "Thank you Mr. Speaker, Governor Davis, honored guests, Chief Justice George—a great man and a great Chief Justice."[3] I was the only official who had any explanatory reference added to my name and title. Legislators from both houses and both political parties—in a rare display of bipartisan unity—burst into knowing laughter. The complimentary introduction I received illustrated once again how everything in Sacramento is viewed through a political prism. It reflected the decision I had rendered for the court a few weeks earlier in *Senate v. Jones*, which kept off the ballot an initiative measure that would have reduced legislative salaries at the same time as undertaking a reapportionment plan, because the court found the proposal to be in violation of the constitution's single-subject requirement.[4] This introduction caused me to laugh and probably turned my face a couple shades of red, but did not elicit any comment from me.

But I managed, in that same venue, to kid him a bit as well. It was customary for me to mention in my State of the Judiciary address various achievements of the judicial branch during the preceding year and some of the challenges that lay ahead. I was very proud of something that you and I will talk about, jury reform, and specifically the writing of new jury instructions in plain language. I announced that the California judiciary was very pleased to have received a national award, the Burton Award for Legal Achievement. This recognition encourages the use of plain language, and thus recognized California's new jury instructions. I interjected in my address: "I just want to reassure the members of the Senate and the Assembly that this award does not in any way reflect the plain language used by your President pro Tem. It's a different Burton involved in this award, and I can assure you it has nothing to do with the plain language this Burton uses." I did get unanimous uproarious laughter from both sides of the aisle and both houses, all of whose members were well aware of the colorful language always used by Burton, and—for the first time—I saw him blush. [Laughter]

I also recall that during one of my other State of the Judiciary addresses, I got into a bit of a coughing fit midway. He leaned forward on the dais where he and I were, along with the Speaker of the Assembly, and very kindly poured me a glass of water and passed it to me. So I announced to the legislature that I trusted this act signified that the President pro Tem would be carrying my water for the duration of the legislative session. There's always a time and place for a

---

[3] Capitol Alert, *Sacramento Bee* (January 10, 2000).
[4] Cal. Const., art. II, sec. 8(d).

little bit of humor, and I think that it sometimes—and, on this occasion, literally—helped lubricate the way in my political dealings at the Capitol.

Fun aside, what could you learn from someone like President pro Tem Burton?

I learned to respect his concerns involving the judicial branch, namely that it focus upon those who were underserved by government, and perhaps by the judiciary, and focus upon those aspects of our reforms that truly would help individuals who lacked the funds to hire counsel. My discussions with Senator Burton reinforced for me the importance of demonstrating how we were trying to make the judicial system more user friendly and not just focus on the large institutions. I think he appreciated our efforts, from everything he told me and others. He thought that the focus of the judiciary was much more balanced than he had viewed it in the past. We developed a very nice friendship. In fact, after I mentioned in my retirement statement that one of the things I was looking forward to doing was reading more books outside the law, he proceeded to walk over to the Supreme Court and deliver a book as a retirement gift, which was very nice of him.

Thank you for mentioning Senator Burton's interest in increasing accessibility to underserved individuals. Such things are often painted with a political brush as issues that belong to one party or another but never both. You're demonstrating instances where you were able to work together on joint areas of interest for the benefit of all. But it's hard not to bump up against political parties in the legislative setting. How did you learn to negotiate those waters?

When talking about issues, I attempted to show I had an understanding of the legislative process and the realities, especially in terms of what funding was available, and how what I was asking for was not something for judges, not something for the courts, but basically for the public interest and access to justice. I think my words and actions convinced most legislators of this premise—not that everyone agreed with me on absolutely everything. I'm sure there was no one who accepted my complete agenda. My own wife doesn't agree with all of the decisions I have rendered. But I believe there was a general acceptance that I was acting in good faith in my administrative capacity in trying to do what I thought was in the best public interest within the confines of the law and of the resources that were available.

I also want to mention Senator Don Perata as another wonderful pro Tem to work with. He seemed to relate to a lot of what we were doing from his background as a schoolteacher. He had a great interest in civics and the educational process. Like Senator Burton, Senator Perata was a person who—if he gave you his word—you could count on it. You didn't need a handshake. You didn't need anything in writing. You didn't have to worry about an aide running circles around him and doing his or her own thing. You could totally rely on it. He wouldn't countenance that kind of insubordination on his staff. Don Perata was very complimentary of the Administrative Office of the Courts, and I think it reflected very well on Senator Perata himself for asking for and receiving a more than one-hour briefing—I believe on two occasions—about the $5 billion courthouse construction bond measure. He really soaked up the details, and he described it as the best briefing he had ever received in his time in the legislature. He was totally well informed about the bill, was able to answer questions on it, and pushed it through. He asked me to participate as a co-presenter at a press conference on the legislation. It was really a team effort, and I knew that with that kind of preparation, background, and support, we were likely to get the bill through.

I want to touch on Senate President pro Tem Darrell Steinberg as well.

Yes. Senator Steinberg is someone who is truly a good-government type and who was very eager to support us. I mentioned in our last session that previously, as chair of the Assembly Judiciary Committee, he had revived our courthouse transfer bill after his committee had initially voted it down. It's something that over the years I've reminded him I was forever grateful for. He very much believes in the independence of the judiciary as a co-equal branch of government and was quite strong in supporting us in our funding efforts when we were facing very severe budget cuts in 2009 and 2010. I enjoyed my relationship with him very much. Just as a matter of interest, I'll indicate that he was very enthusiastic about the selection of my successor, as he was a classmate of now-Chief Justice Tani Cantil-Sakauye at UC Davis School of Law and knows her well.

You touched last time on the importance of strong leadership in these legislative bodies, and we've just been talking about some presidents pro Tem who were considered pretty strong leaders. Can you expand on why that is so important?

I think the party caucuses take direction in many matters—and certainly the judicial branch's needs are less political in the view of most legislators than many other matters—so that's the type of subject where direction and expression of commitment, on behalf of the speaker or the president pro Tem and the minority party leadership, can have great influence in guiding the legislative body to a result that will protect the public's interest in the functioning of a fair and accessible justice system. If it's just left to the sidelines to compete with special-interest legislation, the needs of the courts can easily be lost in the shuffle. I believe it is particularly important to have strong leaders who are aware of the importance of the role of all three branches of government and who also will not tolerate the shenanigans of those few staff members who subordinate their bosses' commitments to their own individual preferences or their desire to engage in paybacks, for whatever motive. I think one of the greatest curses any Chief Justice has to deal with is a weak and indecisive legislative leader who does not have control of staff and does not give sufficient direction to the party caucus.

It would amuse me to see that if I'd had a meeting with someone, whether it was the leader of one of the houses or just a member of a budget or policy committee, everyone else we'd encounter at the Capitol seemed to know it and what I'd been up to the last day or two. [Laughter] Just being there, being a known presence in the corridors, being greeted by legislators, being seen going in or out of someone's office, encountering legislative staffers, knowing them by name, running into lobbyists for various organizations, whether connected with the judicial branch's interests or totally unconnected, one became somewhat of a fixture in the state Capitol.

You said that Senator Burton joked that if you showed up any more often you'd have to register as a lobbyist yourself. How did you come to view that, frankly, lobbying role of yours, and what made you good at it as time went on?

Some persons who were familiar with my initial vocational aspirations, namely diplomatic service in the State Department, thought that whatever interest, training, or skills I might have acquired in that pursuit served me well in dealing with the executive and legislative branches. I believe it was simpler than that. As a political science student I believe I had a good understanding of what all three branches of government were supposed to be doing. Also, just from personal experience, I believe I had a pretty good sense of knowing that people like to be treated decently and candidly. If one went in and tried to deal with people in a receptive and respectful manner, and was as above-board as possible, not only was that the right thing to do, but from a selfish standpoint it was the best thing to do. You in turn would be treated better if you acted that way than if you came in as some imperious judge or justice. That always worked best—not coming in with an aura of the importance of one's position. Senate President pro Tem Don Perata, recalling his days as a high school history teacher, remarked that "Some judges believe history began the day they put on a black robe." Somewhat more directly, Assembly Speaker Fabian Núñez employed a vivid anatomical reference to describe the recently visiting presiding judge of the L.A. Superior Court.

Another legislative leader with whom I had a very enjoyable and productive relationship, although his speakership preceded my becoming chief, was Willie Brown. As you recall, when I was an associate justice Chief Justice Lucas had me visit the Capitol on various assignments for meetings with legislative leadership. Speaker Brown and I developed a friendship too, and he had me swear him in to his first term as mayor of San Francisco on the steps of City Hall. I occasionally cross paths with him in San Francisco. He always enjoys running into Barbara and, as a result, at some function or other, he gave me the best introduction I've probably had from anyone: "This is the Chief Justice of California, Ronald George," embellished with a few nice words. "And here is his lovely wife Barbara George, chair of the California Arts Council, and without her Ron George would still be on the municipal court hearing traffic ticket cases." [Laughter] I've enjoyed that tremendously, even more than Barbara did. I have quoted the introduction on other occasions, once or twice when Willie Brown was in the audience, and he would laughingly wave me off, saying, "Oh, no. Don't repeat that."

Knowing that Speaker Brown is himself a lawyer and was, as you say, a very longtime leader of the Assembly—a length of service we no longer have—what was the key to working well with him back in those early days when you were an associate justice?

It was basically explaining in a very clear-cut manner what we wanted, why we thought it would be in the interests of those concerned, and just being up front. You knew right away yes or no, and you could rely on it. You really could.

I've talked a lot about individuals who happen to be Democrats, and that's just because, as legislative leaders of the majority party during almost all of the time I served as chief, they were the ones most in a position to help us achieve what we were trying to implement for the judicial branch. But I don't want in any way to overlook some very fine Republican leadership that was of great assistance too. Senator Jim Brulte was an outstanding minority leader in the Senate. Senator Dick Ackerman also was very helpful to us on a number of matters. So were Chuck Poochigian, Dave Cox, Mike Villines, Bill Campbell, and Rod Pacheco. Bill Morrow took a leading role in the passage of some legislation to expedite the preparation of the record in death penalty appeals. There were some very fine people on both sides of the aisle with whom I was able to work. Speaking of legislative leadership, Curt Pringle, who served as Speaker for about one year, was another Republican who assisted us on some of our issues.

I wonder how you worked with the two judiciary committees directly.

I had special meetings with those members on occasion. In fact, I remember once Dave Jones, who was chairing the Assembly Judiciary Committee at the time and helped us on some important access-to-justice issues, organized a dinner meeting of that committee with me and other judicial branch representatives.

We worked closely with Senator Joe Dunn, who chaired the Senate Judiciary Committee and was a great exponent of an independent judiciary and of how important it was for us to speak with one voice. There were many other legislators who were very helpful. Senator Martha Escutia, who chaired Senate Judiciary after chairing Assembly Judiciary, was of great assistance to the judicial branch in achieving trial court unification, the transfer of California's courthouses from the counties to the state, and court interpreter and other access-to-justice issues. Bob Hertzberg was an outstanding Speaker who was a lawyer. He had a deep understanding of the role of the judiciary as a co-equal, independent branch of government. Speaker Antonio Villaraigosa and Speaker Fabian Núñez were quite helpful to us. Noreen Evans, Debra Bowen, Denise Ducheny, Ellen Corbett, Mark Leno, Sheila Kuehl were all legislators who provided great assistance to us. I visited with some of them in their districts. Although the legislators I mentioned were not the only ones who were helpful to us, and although I don't want to accentuate the negative, most of the others were not all that interested or informed on our issues. There also were some legislative staff members who had acquired great expertise on judicial branch issues. It really was a very fine partnership, by and large. It's just that it could have been and would have been even better and easier but for the fact that there is among many members of the legislature a certain disconnect in terms of the vital role played by the judiciary in protecting the fundamental interests of the public in fair and accessible justice.

Shall we turn to the executive branch? Governor Wilson, of course, brought you to the role of Chief Justice and was our governor until early 1999. Knowing you already had a long relationship with him, start off, if you would, talking about when and how you consulted with him back and forth once you became Chief Justice.

Once I was appointed to the high court by Governor Wilson and became for the most part a San Francisco resident, we were in regular contact. I had some contact with him even before I became chief in the sense of having meetings in the Capitol, as I did with the legislative leadership, at the behest of Chief Justice Lucas. We saw each other socially too, and Governor Wilson and his wife Gayle, sometimes accompanied by his chief of staff, Bob White, and John Davies, his judicial appointments secretary—who was a very close friend and advisor to the Wilsons and is sorely missed by so many people since his recent demise—would occasionally come to dinner at our apartment here in San Francisco, sometimes accompanied by John's wife Ann. It was an opportunity for candid discussions, never related to cases before the court, of course, but just to matters of public policy and the justice system occasionally, and all sorts of other things.

What were his primary interests in those areas?

He was concerned about delays in the civil justice system and how they impacted the economic climate of California. He also felt that the laws on the books should ensure that upon conviction persons deserving of punishment would receive speedy, certain, and substantial justice. We had discussions that sometimes went on rather late at night. Barbara and I couldn't believe that our guests still would make the trip back to Sacramento that night, although they were not behind the wheel themselves. I remember on more than one occasion Governor Wilson politely asking Barbara if she would mind if he, John Davies, and Bob White would smoke their cigars. I would join in for a puff or two just to be a convivial host. Barbara would say, "If you want to do that, you have to go out onto the balcony." She'd close the sliding door behind us, and we'd be out there in the cold and foggy night air of San Francisco as we continued our discussions in an outdoor environment while the apartment was kept a smoke-free zone for the women in the party. [Laughter] Those were fun discussions. Once in a while we got together in Sacramento at the governor's residence.

Interestingly enough, despite the personal relationship that went back a few years, Governor Wilson was no pushover. I certainly didn't get everything I wanted. I have to indicate that the question of state trial court funding was not one that he was enamored of. He was really a hard sell and had to be convinced of its merits before he would support it.

I think there were even reports that there was a stalemate between him and Senator Lockyer as the pro Tem. How was that resolved?

Yes. In many ways I was sort of the go-between. I was told by Senate President pro Tem Bill Lockyer on more than one occasion—not just on this issue, but on many others—"Look, Governor Wilson appointed you. The burden's on you. You go try to talk him into this."

As go-between, how did you convince Governor Wilson in the end?

I think the governor was understandably concerned about undertaking a commitment on behalf of the state at a time when the state was—as it so often is, on a cyclical basis—in difficult economic times. What really helped sell the idea of the state assuming the responsibility for funding the trial courts was that the counties were in terrible fiscal shape. I advanced the state trial court funding proposal in part as a means of relieving the counties of their very substantial financial obligations to the courts that competed with the difficult task the counties had in meeting the need for all sorts of other services, whether it was libraries, parks, law enforcement, or various social services. I think that was probably one of the larger selling points. It wasn't so much viewed as just conferring a

1. Business cards collected by Chief Justice George's father

2. At age 19 in Africa, while considering a career in the Foreign Service, with college classmate Don Emmerson and the prime minister of the British Cameroons and his cabinet, at Government House, 1959

3. Representing the State of California at the first of six oral arguments before the U.S. Supreme Court, 1969

4. As a Deputy Attorney General, reading the transcripts in Sirhan Sirhan's appeal from his conviction for the assassination of Senator Robert Kennedy, 1971

5. Taking the oath of office as a judge of the Los Angeles Superior Court, with Barbara and parents, sons, sister, and uncle, 1978

6. Attorneys in the Hillside Strangler trial (1981–1983) conferring at the bench with Los Angeles Superior Court Judge George: Roger Boren, Katherine Mader, Gerald Chaleff, and Michael Nash

7. A controversial dive into the Kaweah River, Three Rivers, California, 1980s

8. Trekking in Nepal at 10,000 feet, 1988

To Justice George and Eric George
With best wishes, R̶onald Reagan

9. Visiting President Ronald Reagan with son Eric George at the president's Los Angeles Office, 1990

10. Governor Pete Wilson after administering the oath of office to Chief Justice George, 1996

11. Court reform is like a marathon without a finish line. Photo taken at the San Francisco Marathon, June 23, 1991

12. Testing out the Indianapolis 500 Speedway at the Conference of Chief Justices, 1997

13. The California Supreme Court at its weekly petition conference in the chief's chambers, late 1990s: Justice Kathryn Werdegar, Justice Ming Chin, Justice Janice Brown, Chief Justice Ronald George, Justice Stanley Mosk, Justice Joyce Kennard, and Justice Marvin Baxter

14. The California Supreme Court in its Sacramento courtoom, late 2000s: Justice Carlos Moreno, Justice Joyce Kennard, Justice Kathryn Werdegar, Chief Justice Ronald George, Justice Ming Chin, Justice Marvin Baxter, and Justice Carol Corrigan (Sirlin Photographers)

15. Presiding over the Judicial Council in its boardroom, early 2000s

16. Signing resolution declaring November as Court Adoption Month, 2005

17. Taking off on a dawn run at a California Judicial Administration Conference pre-session event, January 1988 (five months after breaking a hip in a waterskiing accident)

18. After receiving the Rehnquist Award at a ceremony at the U.S. Supreme Court, with Barbara and sons Andrew, Eric, and Chris, 2002

19. Working on a Supreme Court opinion in Ketchum, Idaho, winter of 2002

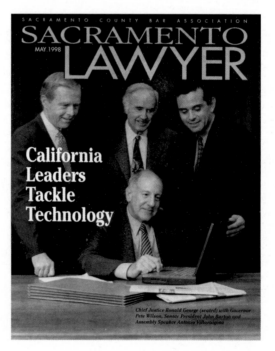

20. Cover of *Sacramento Lawyer* magazine, May 1998: Governor Pete Wilson, Senate President pro Tem John Burton, Assembly Speaker Antonio Villaraigosa, and Chief Justice Ronald George

21. Administering the oath of office to Governor Arnold Schwarzenegger, with Maria Shriver, 2003

22. With former Governors Gray Davis, Jerry Brown, George Deukmejian, and Pete Wilson, at the induction of Governor Schwarzenegger, 2003 (Photo: Governor's Office)

23. Chief Justice George with Speaker Willie Brown, Governor Gray Davis, Gayle Wilson, Speaker Antonio Villaraigosa, Governer Pete Wilson, and Governor Arnold Schwarzenegger on the dais at the latter's second inauguration, 2007 (Photo: Jim Wilson, *New York Times*)

24. Delivering the 2009 State of the Judiciary Address to a joint session of the California Legislature

ILLUSTRATION BY GEORGE RIEMANN/CONCEPT BY THE RECORDER

Ron – mend quickly and hang on: we'll get there! Best wishes, Pete

25. Temporary setbacks: a broken hip and Governor Pete Wilson's position on the proposal for state funding of the trial courts (*The Recorder*, 1997)

26. An editorial view of the Los Angeles court's occasional go-it-alone approach (*The Recorder*, 1999)

May 11, 2001

Ron— Thank you for your bold leadership and good counsel. Best, Gray

Palais de Justice

ELECTRICITY

GEORGE

DAVIS

State of the judiciary

27. Governor Gray Davis, although preoccupied with the energy crisis, approves legislation transferring ownership of California's courthouses from the counties to the state (*The Recorder,* 2001)

'WHEN YOU WAKE UP, YOU WILL GIVE US 50 NEW JUDGES. AND A RAISE.'

Speaker Núñez

28. Overcoming legislative resistance to the creation of new judicial positions and judicial pay raises (*The Recorder*, 2006)

29. Chief Justice's $5 billion courthouse construction bond proposal approved by the legislature and Governor Arnold Schwarzenegger (*The Recorder,* 2008)

'ALL RIGHT CHIEF, THE BALL'S IN YOUR COURT.'

30. San Francisco Mayor Gavin Newsom Brings Marriage Case to the California Supreme Court (*The Recorder*, 2004)

31. Governor Arnold Schwarzenegger with outgoing Chief Justice Ronald
George and incoming Chief Justice Tani Cantil-Sakauye, 2010 (Photo: Larissa
Gomez and Justin Short, Governor's Office)

32. Barbara and Ronald George at the San Francisco Civic Center State Office
Complex, renamed by executive order of Governor Schwarzenegger, December
2010 (Photo: William Porter)

benefit upon the courts or the public served by the courts, but a way of assisting the counties at their time of great financial difficulty. Because there was arguably more of a justification for having greater uniformity in the state's administration of justice than there might have been for some other needs, the courts turned out to be the preferred means, in the eyes of some, of conferring financial relief to the hard-strapped counties.

From there how did it go with Governor Wilson?

He also was not a great fan of my second proposal for structural reform, the unification of the trial courts, whose enactment as a constitutional amendment did not require direct involvement by the governor. I believe, from discussions with John Davies, that this was based primarily on the fact that Governor Wilson felt—as I believe almost any governor would feel—that a governor would prefer to have two chances to appoint individuals to judgeships, first at the municipal court level and then perhaps to confer further recognition on them by a second appointment to the superior court if they merited advancement. An appointment to the lower court served to test them out, to see how they did at the municipal court level, and also permitted the governor to appoint people with fewer years' and less extensive experience to the municipal court, because the constitution provided only a five-year threshold of experience for appointment to the municipal court and 10 years for a superior or a higher court. I believe that in terms of the number of appointments available to the governor and the types of individuals whom the governor might think of appointing, he wasn't all that enthusiastic about unification. I viewed combining the three types of trial court as highly desirable, even if there were going to be some bumps in the road, and even if some of the municipal court judges elevated to the superior court perhaps would not have merited elevation. I felt that although Governor Wilson's concerns were well taken, one had to look at the issue from a long-term standpoint.

In that regard, it was somewhat similar to having merged the osteopaths into the medical profession, and the state police into the California Highway Patrol. Some of the same arguments were made years earlier about whether these categories of individuals truly merited treatment as co-equal members of the larger, more well-established or more highly regarded professional group. Again, I think in all of these instances it was a question of taking the long-term view of the process, even with the inevitable difficulties that would have to be overcome. It proved to be that, with very few exceptions, the municipal court judges who were elevated acquitted themselves very well, and in some instances better than some of the superior court judges who had been appointed initially to that position. The bench was strengthened, and as a result we have much more efficient use of judicial and other resources and more services available to the pubic

in more locations because of unification. But there definitely was resistance that
had to be overcome.

I would say that in all respects, with Governor Wilson I had to justify every
dollar I was seeking. He was very much a hands-on kind of person, so although
he was very generous in his comments announcing my appointment as Chief
Justice and during my tenure, and when I announced my retirement, he wasn't
profligate in his allocation of state resources to the judicial branch just on the
basis of his appointee as chief having asked for them. Everything had to be justified. I'm not in any way being critical of him for that. On the contrary, I would
say that I admire the fact that he could adhere to his own principles without being persuaded by a personal relationship or favoritism in any way. It also was a
pleasure working with his staff—a very able chief of staff, Bob White, John
Davies and others in the appointments area, and Pat Clarey, among others. They
were a very good and strong team.

To what extent did they seek your advice on appointments?

They did from time to time, although as I mentioned I had declined to continue serving on his judicial selection advisory committee once he moved from
the U.S. Senate to the governorship.

*An interesting sidelight is that your eldest son Eric served Governor Wilson as a
deputy legal affairs secretary. I wonder if you can talk about his role with the
governor and how it might have intersected with your own interests.*

There was a need to determine whether I would have to recuse myself on
Supreme Court cases involving the governor's office. Dan Kolkey, the legal
affairs secretary, wrote a legal opinion letter concluding that would not be required. Eric stayed clear of working on anything that might possibly get involved even peripherally in litigation that would come to a lower court and
therefore potentially to the Supreme Court. Governor Wilson was always effusive in his praise of Eric's work, and thanked me so much for, in effect, bestowing my firstborn unto him. [Laughter] Eric developed a very close camaraderie
with Dan Kolkey and other persons who worked in that office, and he learned
quite a bit about government.

*Say a few words more, if you would, about financial matters in Governor Wil-
son's time and how you might have worked with him on behalf of the judiciary's
budget.*

My first year as Chief Justice, which of course occurred during Governor
Wilson's administration, was a year in which the state had a rather severe eco-

nomic decline. By April and May of 1997 we had courts in major metropolitan counties in dire straits, including Los Angeles. That, in turn, provided a real impetus for the Trial Court Funding Act to be passed. Although we were under a county-based funding system, I had to go twice to the legislature for emergency bailout funds just to keep courts from going under, from having to engage in massive layoffs or shutdowns or not be able to make payroll. It became apparent—and this was actually beneficial to our long-term efforts in a way—that we had such a severe crisis that the courts just could not continue to operate based on county funding, based upon whether a particular county had a good or a poor relationship through its board of supervisors with whoever was presiding judge of the local courts that year, or based upon whether the county was able and willing to fund the courts in the face of competing demands for other services. The current situation clearly was so untenable that it actually helped get this reform through. I learned, however, that despite publicly stating its support for this reform and others over the years, the judicial leadership of the Los Angeles Superior Court unsuccessfully lobbied in the state Capitol against state trial court funding and many of the other efforts of the Judicial Council. Much of this opposition was engineered by that court's highly manipulative court executive officer, who in my view did not serve the best interests of the court's judges or employees.

What else would you like to say about your work with Governor Wilson?

I was very grateful—and I remain very grateful to this day—for the opportunity he gave me to serve the judicial system and the public that we serve in this capacity. I had no idea how enormous a task it would be, but I suppose this can be viewed to a certain degree as self-inflicted punishment, because the position of Chief Justice of California is really whatever the incumbent makes it to be, as little or as much. A lot of these were new responsibilities, new tasks that I undertook that went beyond what I was, perhaps, obliged as a matter of law to perform by way of the duties of the office. It may seem at times that it's more work than can be crammed into a 24/7 schedule of every hour of every day, but it still is a job that has to be performed by one person only, even though it's the work of three, perhaps. It's a wonderful opportunity, and even on the most trying of days I don't think there was anything else that I would rather have been doing in any other position in any walk of life.

That's a very nice compliment of getting the chance to do that. You certainly were on shifting ground, however, with so many changes occurring around you. Let's move on to the next governor you worked with, Gray Davis, elected in the fall of 1998. What was your personal history with him, if any, before he took office?

Other than just meeting him very casually at receptions or so, I did not have any prior relationship with him. I viewed it—again, speaking in terms of job responsibilities—as my job to get along with whoever was governor and to try to further the interests of the judiciary with the assistance of any governor. I undertook that task with Gray Davis, and found it a true pleasure to work with him.

I remember that on the way to Sacramento to swear him into office, there was a figurative bump in the road. There had been a last-minute request that I should bring a Bible upon which Sharon Davis would have Gray Davis place his hand during the administration of the oath. In the rush of things, I forgot to bring a Bible. We had a bit of time to spare, so I sent Harry Kinney, the court's marshal, off to find one. He came back shortly thereafter with a grin like the Cheshire cat in *Alice in Wonderland*. He had gone to the state library and managed to check out, after substantial persuasion on his part, an historic Bible from the 1800s that several prior California governors had used and inscribed in taking their inaugural oath. It was one of the few books I've ever handled that literally had wormholes in it. [Laughter] He produced this Bible, and we went off to the swearing in.

Getting on to my relationship with Governor Davis, he was detail-oriented and, like Governor Wilson, a lawyer. He was very eager to promote the concept of complex litigation courts, which we had adapted from a New York model of business courts, as you and I discussed. He felt strongly that such courts would be important in terms of attracting economic growth to California, keeping business here, and having large disputes handled with expertise and expedition in our California court system. With great support from him, we established a pilot program of complex litigation courts, which now exist in several counties. I ended up visiting some of them personally—in Orange, Los Angeles, and San Mateo Counties—and being very favorably impressed with them. Governor Davis deserves a great deal of credit for that. That was one of his priorities, and he has mentioned these courts on various occasions and how important they are to him. He also was very supportive of our transfer of courthouses, through Senator Martha Escutia's bill, from county ownership and maintenance to state ownership under judicial branch management, and signed that legislation into law. In the area of technology, he urged us to embark upon a statewide case management system.

I worked closely with Governor Davis' judicial appointments secretary, Burt Pines, who also was called upon by Governor Davis to give advice on matters beyond judicial appointments and specifically on some of our judicial branch issues. I knew Burt Pines from when he was City Attorney of Los Angeles and I was on the trial bench. We kept up our relationship over the years. Burt

Pines has told me—and it was gratifying to hear it—that on several occasions he saw Governor Davis' views change as a result of meetings I had with the governor. He had seen Governor Davis go into a meeting holding a certain position and then, as a result of my personal advocacy at the meeting, the governor had adopted our position. Burt went on to serve as a very respected member of the Los Angeles bench.

What was the secret to convincing Governor Davis of something, whether you knew it was a change or not?

I believe he had a very pragmatic approach. He just wanted the details and the facts, and to show him it would work. I don't believe ideology ever played any part in those determinations. Barbara also developed a nice relationship with First Lady Sharon Davis. My relationship with Governor Davis actually continues in a capacity we'll discuss later, with the Think Long Committee for California.

I know that you had informally expressed to me an interest in any views I might have with regard to the gubernatorial recall election, and I don't know if this is an appropriate time where you'd like me to speak to that or not?

It's a perfect time.

I felt, and I feel today even more strongly, that recall—even though it is available under the constitution with the other progressive era reforms that came in, the initiative and the referendum—is not an appropriate tool except in the most exceptional situations. I can imagine an occurrence of gross malfeasance in office that involves corruption or a physical or mental incapacity to perform one's duties. But to recall an elected official merely because of buyer's remorse on the part of the electorate, or because of disagreement about a policy decision here or there, is a true mistake. I think the remedy in that situation should be confined to not reelecting that person—assuming the officeholder is not already barred from reelection by term limits. This was a second term for Governor Davis, and I truly believe it was a real misuse of the people's recall power to remove him from office. I voted against it. Without implying any criticism of Governor Schwarzenegger's performance in office, I believe that the history of our state has proved that California is not any better off for having gone through the recall process than it would have been, had we just waited for the next election and then elected a new governor at that time instead of displacing someone who was into his second term. I very frankly would opine that I consider Governor Davis to have been very much the victim of machinations by Enron and other energy companies that followed deregulation, having been blamed for things that he should not have been blamed for and that were mainly outside his control. He probably wasn't as smooth in dealing with some of the legislators—even though he had been an assemblyman himself—as he could have been, but I don't believe that relatively minor inadequacy substantially impaired his ability to govern the State of California or justified his removal from office.

As you say, he'd only just begun his second term, and there was no formal or informal charge of actual wrongdoing along the lines of malfeasance or something like that, so it really was an unusual set of circumstances—economic, with all of the energy concerns, but also just the political timing of it.

Yes, I believe that Governor Davis' situation illustrates a common syndrome—the person in charge, whether of a state or national government, a corporate entity, or some other organization, often gets blamed for an unfortunate turn of events largely outside his or her control. The public is not very forgiving of bad news and, in its search for a scapegoat, often blames the messenger. I don't think removing Gray Davis was a wise use of the recall authority that's conferred upon the public by the constitution. I'm not sure what anyone else in his position of governor could have done at that time given what was going on, from what I've read about Enron and the efforts of other energy companies to game the system to drive up the price that consumers had to pay for electricity.

What constitutional remedy would you like to see in California, if any?

I consider the constitutional remedies of initiative, referendum, and recall to be important additions to the public's rights, enacted as part of the progressive movement and the ensuing amendments to the California Constitution enacted in the early 1900s. I don't favor eliminating those rights, but perhaps the threshold qualifying requirements for invoking those rights should be raised. As with many other matters, such as the need to understand the function of the courts when exercising one's right to vote in judicial elections, there is a need to better educate the public about the particular responsibility involved—in this instance to achieve a better understanding, in terms of civics, about the job of governor and what can and cannot be done by the person occupying that office, and the proper exercise of the recall power. Ironically, the people's exercise of their own power of initiative has contributed to the frequent inability of the persons whom they elect to executive and legislative office to perform the basic functions of those offices.

Thank you for reflecting on that. That recall election of October 2003 swept Governor Arnold Schwarzenegger into office. I wonder, first of all, what you thought of that news when you first heard it. Do you remember?

I was quite surprised. Many people were predicting that Governor Davis was going to lose the recall election, and perhaps because of my belief that I didn't think a recall was merited I was blinded to the political danger that he faced. I didn't think a recall was impossible, but I just didn't think it was likely. But again, one of my responsibilities as Chief Justice was to get along with whoever held the office of governor, consistent with the responsibilities I had as a decision-making member of the Supreme Court and as the Chief Justice of the state. Shortly after the October 7, 2003 recall election that would remove Governor Davis from office, I communicated to Governor-elect Schwarzenegger that I was available during the transition period to provide any sort of orientation he might wish to have concerning the judicial branch and to meet with him if he wished to do so. He did want that, so we had a good session on October 22, 15 days after the recall election, at his suite in the Sacramento Hyatt. I made a presentation and responded to many questions from him.

A couple weeks later, he called me to ask for a favor. He said, "It may sound funny coming from someone who's a professional actor, but I would like to have a dress rehearsal for the inauguration. Would you come up to Sacramento a day early?" It was the Sunday before the Monday, November 16, 2003, inauguration, when Barbara and I went up to the governor's suite at the Hyatt for this purpose. When we arrived, his family was still en route to the Hyatt—his wife Maria, their children, and her parents, Sargent and Eunice Shriver. During this rehearsal, which was more or less directed by some advisor of Governor-elect Schwarzenegger's—a figure from the entertainment industry whose name I don't recall—Schwarzenegger asked Barbara if she would be a stand-in for Maria. She held a Hyatt Hotel magazine in place of the Bible, and the governor-elect went through the oath. I assured him—as I do every time I administer an oath or officiate at a wedding ceremony—that I will recite four or five words at a time for the participants to repeat and will treat them as if they're not very bright five-year-olds, and not to worry about getting an onslaught of lengthy verbiage from me. I also lack the self-confidence of Chief Justice John Roberts that would enable me to administer an oath by memory, so I always hold a small black leather-bound booklet containing the oath, which I inscribe to the office-holder to keep as a memento. Anyway, not surprisingly, Governor Schwarzenegger performed quite nicely in this new role for him. Shortly after I met the Shrivers at the Hyatt suite, an amusing incident occurred when Maria and the children arrived. As soon as he entered the room, the youngest son of the Schwarzeneggers, who I believe was about six years old, saw an enormous chocolate replica of the state Capitol building on the table and made a beeline for it, ready to scoop out a big piece of the dome, and was stopped by his mother at the last moment. This was my initial contact with the rest of the Schwarzenegger family.

The next day around midday was the actual inauguration. Barbara and I had spent the night at the Hyatt, and I took a morning run around the Capitol. There were large crowds already assembling, and I remember being recognized by a couple attorneys and being asked, "What are you doing out here?," and their taking my photograph. I had not seen fit to bring any identification with me, and when I returned to the Hyatt in running clothes, sweating quite a bit, I was almost denied admittance to go in and clean up in time to participate in the inauguration, until one of the security persons recognized me and vouched for me. [Laughter] But I guess there were serious security concerns, especially because the ceremony was being held on the west steps of the Capitol. I believe there was an advisement that maybe this wasn't a great idea from the standpoint of security, because there were going to be thousands and thousands of people on the Capitol Mall. But the governor and his advisors wanted to have it there, so he was advised by law enforcement to wear a bullet-proof vest. I, in turn, received advice that because I was going to be in close proximity to him when I administered the oath of office, I too should wear a bullet-proof vest.

Was that a first?

It was the first and only time I've ever worn a bullet-proof vest. I wish I had been wearing one when I was held up at gunpoint in my garage in 1990. [Laughter]

When we met the day before in his hotel suite, I tried to establish a direct personal relationship with the new governor. I spoke about how my parents, like him, had immigrated from Europe and were still alive and active, and how they'd been impressed that someone with Governor Schwarzenegger's background could come to this country as an immigrant and make his way up to the position of governor of our most populous state. He was interested in that. I gave him, as a little memento, a pin that had dual flags, the flag of the United States and the flag of California. He seemed happy to have that and pinned it onto his suit jacket. When I ran into the governor in the hotel lobby later that evening in the company of some of his friends who had travelled from Austria to attend the inauguration, he asked me to exchange a few words with them in German, which I did. The events of that day were the beginning of what developed into a very pleasant and productive personal relationship.

The next day something of interest occurred as we left the west steps of the Capitol after the otherwise uneventful inauguration. We were walking, escorted through the Capitol back to the governor's office, when he turned to me and said, "Well, the first thing I'm going to do when I get to my office is repeal that car tax," which was his expression and the popular expression describing the vehicle license fee. That much-disliked fee had become a major issue in his election campaign, and repealing it was a commitment he was eager to honor. Getting rid of the fee was a very popular political platform in California and some other states as well, even though I frankly consider it a rather progressive tax. If you own an old clunker you pay so much. If you own a Rolls or a Bentley you pay more. If you have five or six cars, you pay more for each one. But in any event, I think this was one more indication of people perhaps not wanting to pay their way—here in terms of the toll that vehicles impose upon our highway system and the need to pay for its maintenance. I had to reply to him, "Governor, with all due respect, it's the second thing you'll do. You first have to sign this oath that I just administered to you." So we got back to his office, sat down, and after signing the oath but literally before I could get out of my seat—because my business with him was done—he was motioning in the camera crews to record his repeal of the so-called car tax, which punched a hole of several billion dollars in California's state budget for each of several years to come. One could argue that this action, at the least, exacerbated California's difficult fiscal situation.

I had some initial meetings with Governor Schwarzenegger on the budget. It's customary for the Chief Justice—at least it has been with me—to meet in December with the governor, but naturally he was just coming on board, and there weren't terribly meaningful discussions that first year. My next real contact with him after Barbara and I attended the inaugural events was to invite him to address the Conference of Chief Justices in January 2004. I happened to be president of the conference that year. Everyone told me it was absolute folly to ever host the meeting at the same time you're president, because it's piling two difficult tasks upon each other. But I thought somehow that I would like to get this all done with and that it might be interesting to host a meeting while I was actually in charge of the organization. I asked him and to my surprise, given that he had so recently taken office, he agreed to address the Chief Justices from all the states and territories, who were to assemble in San Francisco for a several-day meeting. I knew he would be a big draw, of course, because the whole country was quite fascinated with the process of this recall election, let alone that the winner was an action-hero movie star. There were all sorts of negotiations with his staff, and I remember they decreed that in terms of the format for his address, which would be at the St. Francis Hotel on Union Square, the governor and I had to be alone on the stage together. We would both be standing in front of a drapery and that, ideally, there should be a potted tree—specifically a *ficus benjamina*—at either end. Those were the suggested props, and I said okay, that's fine.

Everything was all set up. Part of hosting a meeting of the Conference of Chief Justices involves arranging for social events in the evenings and on the weekend that precedes the meeting. There is a certain responsibility—placed upon the hosting Chief Justice and his or her spouse and the court administrator and staff—to plan some interesting and fun excursions. The days are filled with educational sessions and committee meetings, but each state somewhat tries to equal or outdo the others in terms of planned social activities. Barbara was in charge of planning the social events, beginning with a wonderful tour to the Napa Valley. It happened that we knew Gil and Beth Nickel, who owned Far Niente Winery. Barbara arranged a special tour there for the Chief Justices. On Saturday, while I was there and the chiefs and their spouses were enjoying themselves, my cell phone rang. I answered the call and—hearing what I believed to be a phony Austrian accent—I almost made some joke about it before realizing that it sounded like the man himself. Why would he be calling me? I feared the worst. Obviously he's canceling; this is terrible. No, that was not the purpose of his call. His words still ring in my ears. His heavily accented voice announced, "Mr. Chief Justice. You know I'm supposed to talk to your group of Chief Justices Monday morning." I said, "Yes, Governor. We look forward to your being there." He said, "Well, I have a speech written by my lawyers, and it's a bunch of crap. What should I do?" Those were his exact words. [Laughter] I said, "Governor, my suggestion is that you just forget about the script or any formal speech prepared by lawyers. Get up there, just speak from the heart, and share your experiences and your thoughts about the courts." He said, "All right."

Monday morning came; the governor showed up at the St. Francis, and we both walked out onto the stage together. There was loud applause, and he turned around to everyone and said, "I see you have a very popular Chief Justice." Of course he was yanking my chain. They were applauding him. He added, "Yes, he's so popular, we should make some movies together." Then he proceeded to give an excellent off-the-cuff speech. He said, "Let me tell you about my views of the justice system. I grew up as a youth in Austria. I learned in school about the rights and obligations given to you by your American Constitution, a model for the world. Next I came over to the United States as an immigrant. I had no money and was seeking employment as an actor or any other kind of job I could get." He continued, "When I studied to become a U.S. citizen, I had to learn about your Bill of Rights and government. As a struggling young actor seeking any kind of employment, I was helped out by lawyers. Then, as a successful businessman, the courts were always very fair to me. I have real faith in the American system of justice." Even the more cynical Chief Justices, especially those from the eastern states who wondered what was happening out here in California, [Laughter] were very impressed. They gave him a hearty standing ovation. His remarks, by the way, were followed by those of the mayor of San Francisco, Gavin Newsom, who gave excellent extemporaneous remarks as well. That was the next stage in my relationship with Governor Schwarzenegger.

As you'll see from our later encounters, we developed a very friendly, informal, and humor-filled relationship.

A newspaper article described a chance encounter I had with the governor a few months later in Sacramento: "Happening upon state Supreme Court Chief Justice Ronald George lunching at the Esquire Grill, Schwarzenegger placed his hands on George's shoulders and started massaging. 'You're looking really good. Are you working out?,' George said Schwarzenegger asked him. 'I said, I've got to be in shape in case I have to arm wrestle you over the budget.' He said, 'What do you mean? I'm giving you everything you asked for!'"[5]

I remember one year I had a follow-up meeting with him on budgetary matters. The meeting happened to fall on St. Patrick's Day. The custom was that I was ushered into his office, and he would come in a minute or two later. As I stood there waiting for him, he walked in attired in total St. Patrick's Day mode—the shiniest green alligator boots, a big green necktie, and so forth. As he proceeded to look me up and down, he said, "Mr. Chief Justice. Don't you know it's St. Patrick's Day?" I probably should not have been so fresh, but I couldn't resist it. It was a budget meeting. It was a time when large cuts were being made. So I said, "With all due respect, Mr. Governor, I have to tell you that I was afraid to bring anything with me even remotely resembling the color of money, out of fear that you'd take it away from me." [Laughter] That elicited a big belly laugh from him, and we got down to brass tacks.

I had a fair amount of success with him on budgetary matters. The other outstanding discussion we had took place in the fall of 2009. I went up there at a time when the economy was terrible. There was a pet project that I was eager to advance that no state had yet adopted. It was called Civil Gideon. The proposed legislation would provide, as a parallel in a limited category of civil proceedings, what the U.S. Supreme Court's landmark decision in *Gideon v. Wainwright* had conferred as a matter of constitutional right upon defendants charged with crime, namely the government's provision of counsel at no expense. The idea was not to provide counsel in every kind of civil case, such as a fender bender automobile collision, but only in that narrow category of cases where the issues were of such fundamental importance in terms of basic rights—custody of a child or perhaps eviction from the family residence—that the participation of counsel in the case might truly make a difference on a matter of great significance. I was urging that, just as a pilot project, the governor sign into law this bill that I had advocated very strongly for with its author, Assemblyman Dave Jones.

---

[5] *Orange County Register*, July 4, 2004.

Where did the idea come for this?

From the American Bar Association. Two of the most fervent supporters of the proposal in California were Assembly Members Mike Feuer and Dave Jones, persons who deeply believed that access to justice is furthered by the provision of counsel if a litigant cannot afford to hire an attorney. We've talked about pro bono efforts, self-help centers, and other means of assisting unrepresented litigants—greatly assisted by the creation of the Equal Access Fund in 1999—but there are some cases where I believe there has to be government-provided counsel if a litigant cannot afford to hire an attorney. For every case that legal services organizations are able to accept, there are half a dozen or more that they can't. That was the pitch I was making to Governor Schwarzenegger. In return, he gave me the speech I expected to receive. "You know we're having to slash health care for children who have fatal diseases and wheelchairs for Alzheimer's patients. Any program requiring new funds is dead on arrival here this year, however worthy it is. There's just no way. We're not authorizing anything new."

I reflected on this and thought, well, I'm going to be shameless. I resorted to the following—something I hadn't thought about until midway through our meeting. I said, "Governor, remember how your father-in-law, Sargent Shriver, whom I had the pleasure of meeting at your inauguration, made his name in Washington working on the War on Poverty and legal services for the poor? If you give me funds for this pilot program, I promise you it will be enacted as the Sargent Shriver Civil Counsel Act." This elicited an uproarious laugh. He turned to his chief of staff and, assuming a boxing stance, exclaimed, "What do I do with a Chief Justice like this? First I get a punch in the gut and then an upper cut. How do I deal with this?" Then he turned to his director of finance and said, "Well, could we come up with funds for this?" The director of finance, not terribly enthusiastically, said, "Yes, we could." There was no commitment, so I thought I'd just wait and see what happened, and yes, funds for the project ended up being included in the budget, and I persuaded the author of the bill to insert the Sargent Shriver title into the act. I'm very proud to say that the program is underway now, and in fact, just this year it's coming into being. Justice Earl Johnson, recently retired from the Second District Court of Appeal, was appointed by me to chair a committee to select counties for the project. Justice Johnson has taught and written on the subject of legal services and is currently writing a history of legal services in the United States. In fact, I received an award earlier this year from the Western Center on Law and Poverty bearing Justice Johnson's name. He, along with Justice James Lambden from the First District Court of Appeal, have been among the strongest supporters of legal services in California.

This all demonstrates the importance of personal relationships in Sacramento. That's why some of these personal interactions, although not always relating to substantive matters of great significance, all go toward building relationships that are so integral to getting things done in the state Capitol, whether it's with the executive or the legislative branch.

Naming the act after his father-in-law was certainly a deft touch, but what does that tell you about Governor Schwarzenegger?

I believe that even putting aside that maneuver on my part, he had a genuine empathy for persons who are in difficult financial straits. In his remarks to the Conference of Chief Justices, he alluded to his own past, reflecting the fact that he's not someone who came into the world with a silver spoon in his mouth. I believe that I gave him a good excuse or rationale for approving the legislation, although his heart was probably inclined in that direction.

We developed a very nice relationship. Barbara and I would see Governor Schwarzenegger on some social occasions. When my mother gave a party at the Peninsula Hotel in Beverly Hills to celebrate Barbara's and my fortieth wedding anniversary, Governor Schwarzenegger was in attendance. When I sent him an amusing birthday card, he wrote back that "most people probably wouldn't expect the Chief Justice of California to have a great sense of humor on top of all that legal knowledge . . . [as] one of the best judges in the world. . . ." And Barbara served on the California Arts Council with the Governor's sister-in-law, Malissa Feruzzi Shriver, and the two women have worked together on various projects.

He had married into a very prominent political family of Democrats. What indication or direct experience did you have with the influence of Maria Shriver on his views?

I'm certainly not privy to anything other than speculation. Maria Shriver asked Barbara to be a member of the Minerva Committee that was involved in her excellent annual governor's women's conference. This committee would recommend nominees to receive the Minerva Awards, which gave recognition to women of achievement. The conference was attended by 14,000 persons, predominantly women, and was held in Long Beach. The first lady, the governor, and an outstanding group of speakers—one year including the Dalai Lama—would address the audience.

The governor's wife never got involved in any of our issues directly, but the governor certainly was sympathetic. We had had terrible cuts to the judicial branch on top of the regular cuts that the legislature had imposed—a second round of cuts of $200 million more—and then the governor used his line-item veto authority to knock off another $100 million, not out of any animus toward the judicial branch but paralleling other cuts reflecting desperate attempts to just get through the fiscal year. I conferred with our people in the finance division of the A.O.C. and concluded that the judicial branch was in a situation that might not permit it to continue performing its core functions. It was that bad.

You'd already had the one-day-a-month court closings and were facing that and more, I take it?

Yes. As I mentioned at our last session, I went to the legislature and told them that they had to reverse the additional $200 million in cuts that they had imposed on us if court closures and employee layoffs were to be avoided. I wanted an extension of some court-imposed fees that were due to expire, to sunset, and some new fees to be imposed so that we wouldn't be calling for tapping the general fund, which was already tapped out. The legislative leadership responded that it could not justify doing that when the governor had cut our budget by an additional $100 million—but that if I could get him to reverse his cut, they would restore the $200 million. I don't think they expected that I'd be able to do it.

How did you do it?

I made a presentation to him that was—and I guess I don't have a better word for it than this—so assertive that my staff raised their eyebrows and seemed somewhat shocked. But I made an argument that probably was the equivalent in volume and tone that I might have made as a prosecutor to a jury. [Laughter] The governor listened quite attentively and did agree to reverse the $100 million cut that he had imposed. I took that back to the legislative side, and they were very surprised and pleased. When all was said and done, 2010 managed not to be that bad a year for us. We did not have to reinstitute court closures, and we got through okay.

What does that say about you, that you were willing to come on so strongly in this instance?

I was concerned that I might jeopardize the relationship that I had with Governor Schwarzenegger, but by the same token I felt that this concern had to be secondary to the concern I had about the judicial branch's ability to survive under the cuts that we were undergoing, and that I had to go ahead and make the pitch. The worst that could happen would be that I'd be kicked out of his office. [Laughter]

A calculated risk?

Yes. And it ended up being fine. But of course every year is a new crisis. The next year, 2011, was not on my watch, but my sympathies are out there for my successor and for whoever occupies that office in the future, being so dependent upon the judgment and goodwill of the other two branches of government and the cyclical fiscal situation of the state. It's a battle that has to be re-fought every year or at least every year in which there are bad economic times.

That positive relationship continued to the mutual end of our respective terms. He issued a proclamation[6] while I was on vacation in Antarctica the last two weeks of my term that—after many whereas-es—concludes by stating, "It is hereby ordered that the San Francisco Civic Center Complex comprising both the Hiram M. Johnson State Office Building and the Earl Warren Building shall be known as the Ronald M. George State Office Complex." The historic Earl Warren Building houses the Supreme Court and the First District Court of Appeal, and the Hiram Johnson Building houses the Administrative Office of the Courts and regional offices of the governor, various state constitutional officers and agencies, and state legislators representing San Francisco. I feel deeply honored and grateful, although the renaming of the buildings was in a sense somewhat ironic, because I had made it clear that I was quite opposed to Governor Schwarzenegger's proposed sale of several state office buildings—including the two in question—to private investors to help alleviate the state's fiscal crisis. A lawsuit, filed on a pro bono basis by attorney Joe Cotchett at the behest of the former president of the L.A. State Building Authority, Jerry Epstein, stopped the sale in the last few days of the Schwarzenegger administration.

When I walk by those buildings in Civic Center Plaza, it's quite a pleasure for Barbara and me—as it was for our three sons, who were up here several weeks ago—to see my name on the exterior and in the lobby areas of these magnificent structures. They occupy an entire square block, between McAllister Street and Golden Gate Avenue, and between Polk Street and Larkin Street.

I believe the official dedication is yet to come?

Yes, I believe something is planned toward the end of this month.

Congratulations. That is a very nice honor.

Thank you.

We've touched on the three individuals who served as governor while you were Chief Justice. But I know you also had some interactions with our new governor,

---

[6] Executive Order S-17-10, December 21, 2010.

who came in as you were going out, Governor Jerry Brown. Tell me about those, please.

Sure, and of course he's our old governor as well as our new governor. As old governor, he is one of the four governors who appointed me to one of the levels of the California bench, namely the L.A. Superior Court. Over the years, I have had occasion to run into him from time to time at various events, either official events or social encounters. He's always engaging to talk to, expressing interesting ideas. We had a more formalized relationship once he became attorney general because, as I mentioned earlier, among the series of annual liaison meetings I held in my chambers as Chief Justice was a meeting with the attorney general and his top staff. In the initial meetings with Attorney General Jerry Brown, he brought with him his wife Anne Gust, who is an attorney—as is the governor—and an exceptionally astute and pleasant person. I found it interesting to have Attorney General Brown indicate to me that she was there as an unpaid advisor, but that basically, in his words, she was "running the office." He had no reluctance to make that clear. I suspect that when she was absent from the meeting I had last year with Attorney General Brown, it was because she was running his political campaign. She had a very distinguished career working in a high administrative position at the business enterprise The Gap, whose founders—the Fisher family, friends of ours—gave glowing reports of her abilities. I also had interesting discussions with Attorney General Brown in his capacity as one of the three members of the Commission on Judicial Appointments. As you know, the commission has to pass upon every appointment or nomination to the Court of Appeal or the California Supreme Court. We would meet in the judicial robing room outside the Supreme Court courtroom, where the hearing takes place. There was an opportunity to engage in conversation before a hearing, after a hearing, and between multiple hearings. Attorney General Brown was always a very lively conversationalist and would bring up all sorts of legal and political questions, so I feel that I managed to establish some rapport with him and gain some insight into his manner of thinking.

Governor Jerry Brown and I made back-to-back presentations to the Think Long Committee for California earlier this year, he on California's budget crisis and I on the problems involved in the initiative process. In fact, last month I had a phone call from Governor Brown under rather amusing circumstances. I was performing my role as grandfather and taking our five-year-old and three-year-old granddaughters to the new dinosaur hall at the Museum of Natural History in downtown Los Angeles, an organization on whose advisory board I used to serve. With me were Barbara and our son Chris, the father of the two little girls, who was keeping them quiet by playing a video movie for them in the back of the vehicle. It was the film *Rio*, so there were a lot of squawking bird sounds in the background. My cell phone rang, and it was Governor Brown wanting my views on an issue. As we proceeded to have a telephone conversation that probably ended up being between 15 and 20 minutes long, I motioned to my son to turn off the video. He was shaking his head and whispered to me, "If you turn off that video there will be more squawking from the girls than there is squawking from the birds on the video." [Laughter] So we compromised with a slight diminution in volume. My conversation with the governor proceeded, with interjections of bird squawking throughout. [Laughter] So there's still some contact with the person occupying the governor's office, even though I have ceased to be a person occupying the office of Chief Justice.

I'm glad you mentioned the attorneys general. Of course, you also worked with Attorney General Brown's predecessors in that role, Bill Lockyer and Dan Lungren. Can you talk about each of those in that capacity?

There were some relations in terms of task forces that the judiciary formed or that were formed jointly by the attorney general's office and the judiciary, for example in the area of collection of funds, trying to improve recordkeeping involving convictions that entailed payment of restitution fines and other fines. I remember that Attorney General Lockyer convened a conference on domestic violence. One of the findings, which was disturbing to me as a judge, was that judges in our trial courts were not enforcing gun-possession restrictions in domestic violence orders and that there was a very high incidence of threatened or actual violence against spouses or partners or even children, emanating from possession of a firearm by the offending domestic violator. That was a lesson for us, and we took some steps to try to improve that situation. So there were certain joint efforts where—even though the attorney general was a partner with us and at the same time was an advocate before us—we could still meaningfully cooperate in the partnership aspects of our relationship.

As a former employee of the attorney general's office, how did you view the development of that whole operation over time?

I guess I have a bit of the attitude that I criticize in others, of looking back to the "good old days." The attorney general's office was a much smaller unit back then, and one could virtually luxuriate in the time and resources that were available to fully develop a brief and to prepare for oral argument in the high courts of California or the United States. In all fairness, the press of business due to California's enormous growth in population and the resulting growth in litigation has turned some of the practices that we followed into a luxury that probably can't be afforded anymore. I did reminisce a bit about my days in the attorney general's office when the A.G.'s office came to me and asked me to be videotaped for a history they were preparing on the office of the California attorney general. That office has undergone great changes, needless to say, but there

always is a different emphasis by different attorneys general on the various duties of the office—on consumer rights or constitutional rights or environmental
matters or on criminal prosecution.

*Is there anything that you'd like to add, in a general way, about the executive
branch and your interactions there?*

Probably not, except to note—as I did with regard to the legislative
branch—that there were some truly outstanding professionals in the Department
of Finance and in other units in the executive branch with whom we were
pleased to work and obtain the benefit of their expertise in formulating the policies and strategies and budgetary requests that helped us achieve our occasional
successes—which we might not have been able to accomplish but for their true
concern for the interests of the judicial branch apart from their primary obligation of serving the governor and the executive branch.

*You did manage to forge a lot of partnerships there. Do you think you were
mostly self-taught, or how did you learn to succeed in this very different arena?*

I think it really was self-taught, and trial and error, seeing what worked. But
again the underlying premise was to try to develop a personal relationship of
trust, an informality in the relationship, and a commitment to pick up the phone
and call each other if there was a problem that could be worked out instead of
running to the press with an accusation or just peremptorily denying something
that was requested. I think all of that really is, or should be, part of a common
sense approach to dealing with other individuals with whom one is professionally bound to interact.

*Other than the top leadership of the Administrative Office of the Courts, who
else within the judicial branch did you involve in your liaisons in Sacramento
with the executive and legislative branches?*

I only included A.O.C. personnel in my Sacramento meetings. I would usually—not always, but usually—be accompanied by Bill Vickrey, the Administrative Director of the Courts, very often by his chief deputy, Ron Overholt, almost always by the director of the Office of Governmental Affairs. That was a
succession of extremely dedicated and effective individuals, including Ray
LeBov, Kate Howard, and currently Curt Child. Curt Child helped us get
through all sorts of scrapes and achieve all sorts of successes in the recent, difficult years. I can't sing his praises too highly, but I don't want to focus just on
him. He has an outstanding staff, and I could mention about three or four of
them right off the top of my head who come to mind but if I did I'd probably be
leaving out some others who were equally deserving of mention, so let me just

say that there is no division in the Administrative Office of the Courts that works harder or more effectively than the Office of Governmental Affairs, which of course is located in Sacramento right across from the state Capitol. They can be in the Capitol building literally on a moment's notice, and they help organize members of our bench-bar coalition to come up in regular course to attend the State of the Judiciary address and then fan out to the offices of legislative leaders and of legislators whose constituents they are. Our staff in the Office of Governmental Affairs also arranges bench-bar events in local legislators' districts. They also are part of the vital effort of working with our justice system partners through setting up and attending the liaison meetings in the chief's chambers that I described in an earlier session with you, as well as coordinating strategy with these partners on a day-to-day basis in the halls of the Capitol—with counties, the consumer attorneys, the D.A.s' association, the criminal defense bar as well as the civil defense bar, the sheriffs, the business community, and others. They are a vital part of our efforts and of the success that we've achieved.

Who among your judicial colleagues at any level of the system did you call upon to aid your efforts in Sacramento?

To varying degrees, they were called upon to aid the efforts that were ongoing in Sacramento—not necessarily by going to Sacramento but through their participation in one group or another—or other efforts to improve the administration of justice and the operations of the judicial branch. Directly involved in our legislative efforts was Justice Marvin Baxter, whom I appointed to the Judicial Council and specifically appointed to head one of the four internal committees of the Judicial Council, the Policy Coordination and Liaison Committee. That committee passes upon legislative proposals, either those that we initiate or that other entities initiate—when we're called upon to take a position to support, oppose, or modify. That's a very important effort, analyzing and taking positions to present to the Judicial Council as a whole, in terms of what the council's position should be. Justice Carlos Moreno served at my request as head of the foster care commission, which involved representatives from the other branches of government, and was responsible in large measure for persuading the legislature to enact some vitally needed reforms in that area. Justice Chin has been involved in court technology and our information system, CCMS, and in that capacity has had some involvement with the legislature too. He also headed the Commission for Impartial Courts that studied and made dozens of recommendations in the areas of judicial selection, ethics, campaign financing, and public information and education. Additionally, he headed our efforts in the area of science and the law. Justice Kennard headed a committee that revised the appellate rules of procedure and practice. That was an enormous undertaking assisted by experts from the academic community and a broad array of lawyers and other judges. Justice Werdegar, in turn, headed up the library committee as well as a committee that looked into the whole area of publication and depublication of Court of Appeal opinions and revised the pertinent standards. And then finally, Justice Corrigan undertook something that we'll get to when we talk about jury reform—the very important, extensive, and long-lasting effort to write new jury instructions. I appointed her to this task when she was still on the Court of Appeal, but it continued into her years on the Supreme Court.

This is a brief description of some of the extracurricular assignments undertaken by the associate justices. I may be leaving out some of their contributions, but I wanted to convey the idea that each and every member of the California Supreme Court has been an active contributor to the welfare of the branch—to judicial and legal practice beyond the confines of engaging in day-to-day opinion writing and decision making and involvement in the court's own internal procedures.

But the main one haunting the halls up in the Capitol was Chief Justice George?

Yes, I'm afraid that's true, but heavily reinforced by these visits from Judicial Council members, bench-bar coalition members, and A.O.C. staff. A widely circulated newsletter on government and politics listed me in 2009 as one of the "top 100 political players in California."[7] I viewed my various titles—which we've gone over at different points—of chief of the court, chief of the branch, and so forth as also encompassing the title of chief lobbyist, and maybe I should add "chief cook and bottle washer." [Laughter]

###

---

[7] *Capitol Weekly*, April 16, 2009.

Chapter 14

The Judicial Council and the Administrative Office of the Courts

October 20, 2011

We agreed that we would start off today with a bit of discussion about the Judicial Council and, by extension, the Administrative Office of the Courts. Could you review, to get us started, the constitutional basis for the council itself and some of its authority and official functions?

California is one of many states that has a Judicial Council, but by no means do all states have one. In some states the Supreme Court of the state conducts the administrative responsibilities that are performed by a council. This, to me, would be extremely burdensome, at least in a state such as California with a large caseload and an enormous judicial branch. Recognizing the need for judicial administration—although that recognition had not truly extended to the trial court level—the legislature proposed to create a Judicial Council, headed by the Chief Justice, and the voters approved that in 1926 through an amendment to the California Constitution, which is now found in section 6 of the judicial article, article VI. However, it became apparent over the years that the resources possessed by the Judicial Council to undertake its responsibilities really consisted only of the expertise, goodwill, and energy of those persons actually serving on the council. There was no actual staff, except over the years a few attorneys here and there were assigned to assist the council. But basically the administrative structure of the Judicial Council consisted of the members of the council.

In 1960 there was a further amendment to the state constitution that created the position of Administrative Director of the Courts. The first person who served in that capacity was Ralph Kleps, whom you and I mentioned in the context of the Kleps Awards that recognize innovative achievements by trial and appellate courts around the state. Then, the following year, the Administrative Director of the Courts was officially provided with a staff, an office entitled the Administrative Office of the Courts. That was created by legislation rather than constitutional amendment. The council adopted a mission statement and refined it over the years. It amounts basically to setting direction and providing leadership for improving the quality of justice and advancing the consistent, independent, impartial, and accessible administration of justice.

As I mentioned earlier, the Chief Justice makes all 14 of the judicial appointments to the council, which are specified by the constitution to include judges and justices from the various levels of court for fixed terms. The State Bar Board of Governors appoints four lawyer members, and the legislature appoints two members, who traditionally have been the respective chairs of the Senate Judiciary Committee and the Assembly Judiciary Committee. That comprises the council, although additionally there have been nonvoting members. Over my tenure as Chief Justice, I relied very heavily upon court administrator nonvoting members. They don't vote when the full council is actually taking a formal vote, although they participate fully in the discussions. As a practical matter, a great deal of the council's work is done in its four internal committees, which I discussed with you at an earlier session. The nonvoting members of the council do vote in the internal committee on which they serve. That's basically the structure of the council, and in all of the reforms that we have mentioned and that we will discuss today the Judicial Council acted as either a major player or, in some instances, instigator of these structural changes under the leadership of its individual members.

We did touch on at least one of the internal committees in a prior discussion, and that was the executive committee and its role in aiding you in selecting appointees to the Judicial Council. But let's return to the work of that executive and planning committee as a separate entity and how it was staffed.

Justice Richard Huffman of the Fourth Appellate District is someone who dedicated a great amount of talent and energy in his service as chair of the executive committee. I had a lot of confidence in his work in that capacity and asked him to serve repeatedly beyond two terms. I told him that there was an exception that I had created to the Thirteenth Amendment to the U.S. Constitution and that there was in fact indentured servitude in his particular case. [Laughter] He very graciously agreed to continue his service in that capacity. In addition to setting the agenda for the council meetings, including which matters would be made part of the discussion agenda and which would be part of the consent agenda, he and his committee were very active in coming up with three potential candidates for every one of my appointments to the Judicial Council and to the numerous advisory committees and task forces. Sometimes those were persons who had submitted their own names. Sometimes they were nominated by other individuals. Sometimes the executive committee actually went out and recruited individuals to submit their names. But it was always those individuals who had excelled in court administration on their own courts or in their work on the Judicial Council advisory committees and task forces or in the California Judges Association who were given the most serious consideration for membership on the Judicial Council itself.

What sorts of planning matters did this committee get into, since planning is part of its official title?

The full Judicial Council, which customarily met for two to three days at a time, generally would convene on eight occasions during the year. This doesn't count the separate meetings of the internal committees themselves. One of those eight sessions a year was a planning meeting where we would review our strategic goals[1] and determine how our actions were serving to advance those goals and what additional action should be taken by the council to achieve those goals—more or less a look backwards and a look forward, as opposed to just grappling with a particular crisis or other immediate needs facing the council at a particular meeting. A planning session afforded an opportunity to take a long-term view of the role of the council and engage in strategic planning.

Moving on to the Policy Coordination and Liaison Committee—which we have talked about very briefly—what was the purview of that group and how did you work with it?

That group was also served by an individual whom I asked to stay on the council more or less in perpetuity, and that is my colleague on the Supreme Court, Justice Marvin Baxter, who had worked in the administration of Governor Deukmejian and had valuable insights into the Sacramento scene and into

---

[1] The first being "access, fairness, and diversity," the second, "an independent and accountable and co-equal branch of government," third, "the modernization of management and administration," fourth, "the quality of justice and service to the public," fifth, "education of judges and court personnel and professional development," and sixth, "technology."

the legislative process. The primary focus of that committee was monitoring and supporting legislation proposed by the Judicial Council and possibly taking a position on legislation proposed by others—supporting, opposing, or urging modification of pending bills. The committee monitored all sorts of legislative proposals, even if the council was not taking a position on them. That was a major task as well, and it involved working closely with the A.O.C.'s Office of Governmental Affairs located in Sacramento.

How often was it the position of that committee and therefore of the council that they should pursue a modification of a pending piece of legislation?

That would happen from time to time where we might agree in principle with the legislative proposal, but there were aspects of it that the council found objectionable. Just to give you an example, anything that might restrict the exercise of judicial discretion would pose a red flag to the Judicial Council. We might favor the overall goal of the legislation from the standpoint of policy, but oppose the way it was written in terms of the restriction it would impose upon the ability of judges to exercise their discretion. That problem usually could be worked out. Then we would go to a position of full support. We worked closely with our justice system partners to iron out problems that we saw in proposed legislation, enabling us to support things that they wanted that would be consistent with the interests of the judiciary and the public. We sought to instill an understanding by which our justice system partners would lend their support to our legislation, which frequently was the case and made all the difference whether our proposal succeeded or not. As I've said before, the impact of the support of the judiciary joined by, let's say, the support of both sides of the criminal bar, both sides of the civil bar, or the sheriff's or county government amounted to much more than the sum of the parts. We really could see things sail through when all or most of these justice system partners could get together and join forces.

We talked quite a bit about the very different lens through which legislators often view matters coming before them. How much of an issue was it in terms of educating about judicial discretion and helping people to understand what the judicial branch had to cope with there?

This was an important matter, because many legislators, aside from the fact that they weren't lawyers, were of course subject to term limits, which kept them from developing long-term expertise in judicial branch issues. Many of them had a tough time differentiating the judicial branch in their minds from the Department of Fish & Game and the Board of Cosmetology in terms of our being an independent, co-equal branch of government and not being subject to the same sort of micromanagement that they might feel was appropriate for a particular executive branch agency. This crucial distinction always was a key element in the process of reeducating the legislature, with its constant turnover in membership, about our unique role in the structure and functioning of state government. That doesn't mean that the judiciary considered itself unaccountable, although I think there are a few people on its fringe who think it should be. But we're receiving public funds provided by the taxpayers, and allocated by the executive and legislative branches. Therefore, there has to be accountability to those branches by the Judicial Council, which disseminates the funds. There also has to be accountability by the recipient trial courts—whose recommendations guide the Judicial Council's disbursements. By the same token, the individual courts need sufficient independence to employ those funds in a flexible manner, without being micromanaged by the Judicial Council. In turn, the council resists attempts by the executive and legislative branches to micromanage the judicial branch.

California, already for many decades, has had legislative involvement in judicial branch matters that exceeds what exists in many other states. By way of example, the legislature codified the rules of evidence in an Evidence Code that is a well-wrought document, but in many states the formulation of rules of evidence is something that is left to the judges alone, either as an administrative matter or through case law. I do feel that some sort of codification is required. Case law probably isn't adequate to afford sufficient guidance to trial lawyers and trial judges. But again, here it was done by the legislature. There has also been a fair amount of legislative intrusion in the Supreme Court's exercise of responsibility over the State Bar, where the legislature gets involved through legislative enactments and year-to-year detailed oversight of the State Bar's budget. Again, that's the type of thing that is better left to the judicial branch, since the bar is an arm of the judiciary. Also, rules of civil procedure are codified to a greater extent in California's Code of Civil Procedure than they are in some other states. Again, I'm not necessarily weighing in on whether that is excessive, because it's been this way for many years, but I just point out in terms of our relationship that there is a certain overlap in the functioning of the legislative and judicial branches in certain areas.

What is the positive side of having such close involvement by the legislature in judicial things, if any?

I believe the legislature, especially some of its more exceptional leaders who have truly understood the judicial branch, have made great contributions to our efforts at structural reform that never could have succeeded without legislative involvement. These changes required legislation or the placement of proposed constitutional amendments on the ballot. Working together with the legislature and various governors, some reforms were achieved that—even if the judiciary had had the authority to implement them unilaterally—probably would not have materialized, just due to bickering among judges. The switch to state trial court funding and the transfer of courthouse facilities of course could not have occurred without legislative and executive branch action. Unification of the trial courts is something that judges never would have done on their own, and did require a constitutional amendment proposed by the legislature and approved by the people. These are all matters in which the judicial branch has benefited greatly from legislative and executive branch involvement.

Returning to the Judicial Council's policy committee, you indicated how eager you were to have Justice Baxter chair it and to keep him on in that role. What was his approach to leading that important area?

He was very pragmatic and had a low-key approach to things. I believe he did his very best to see to it that the members of his committee approached things on a nonpolitical, nonpartisan, and nonparochial basis—not considering matters from the viewpoint of the interests of their own court but from the standpoint of the judiciary and the public it serves. I think his ability to know how things are done in Sacramento has served the committee and the full council very well.

The third major committee, Rules and Projects, didn't have a long-serving chair. That committee tended to have a rotating chairmanship, but that's not in any way to minimize its work, which was very important. Almost everything passed through the rules committee in some fashion or other, whether it was strictly speaking a rule or not, just in terms of its format, how it fit in with other guidelines and policies of the council. That committee often improved the language of various proposals.

Thinking back, were those three committees the right number and the right ones? How well did the whole committee system work?

I think the system worked very well, and the members put a lot of effort into their service on the committees, which met in between the formal Judicial Council meetings. I think some people on the outside, even judges, would remark about how often the Judicial Council acted without as much debate as they might have anticipated, or acted by unanimous vote. I believe those observations are somewhat exaggerated but, to the extent they are accurate, they fail to take account of the reality that very much of the determination of policy was made in the internal committees. Many differences were thrashed out and compromise positions were adopted, so that when something came before the full council, what might have been the source of very heated debate had been resolved and then was put forth as something that was palatable to a broad section and maybe the full membership of the council itself.

But such action at a later time might have appeared more of a rubber stamp or something that was decided behind the scenes? Is that the idea?

Yes, or somehow as action taken at the direction of the Chief Justice, which was an absurd idea, because I did not communicate my preferences to the internal committees. In fact, it was extremely rare that I communicated them to the full council even on major issues in which that body was engaged in debate. On a very few occasions there was a tie vote, and it was only then that I would cast a vote. Council members then learned for the very first time what my position was.

But as you say, hammering out areas of difference and difficult details at an earlier stage allows something to go forward with a lot of work done on it and is perhaps a different kind of management technique almost, in terms of when and where things should be worked out. I wonder, how can that be more understood by the outside world?

The council certainly is quite open in putting out material on its website and elsewhere and establishing internal rules that are a matter of public record in terms of how it functions. In some ways the council acts like a legislative body. The process I described to you is the way a legislative body often and perhaps ideally would work—working to resolve differences and arrive at a consensus instead of having just the group or party that has a majority—however slight it might be—cramming something down the throats of those in the minority. It's far better, I've always felt, to try to work out a consensus. That was also my philosophy in writing opinions as a justice of the court, and I believe it works very well at the legislative level as well, expanding that concept to include what the Judicial Council was engaged in, which was basically legislating in the manner of rulemaking and policymaking.

How did the members of the Judicial Council itself view this concept of consensus as a desirable goal?

I often found them very enthusiastic about having overcome great divisions in their ranks and having come forth with a fine product that, to the extent possible, took into account all the competing interests. By the way, council members weren't advancing their own personal agendas when they took positions. They received a lot of input from judges, court staff, and lawyers and always showed a lot of concern for the interests of the local courts and the public at large. Now, I'm distinguishing here the question of representing their own court. As I mentioned previously, members were told when I appointed them not to go back and take a headcount and find out that thirteen judges on their court favored a policy and 11 opposed it. But members were receptive to what the trial judges in our state as a whole did support and did not support, and they acted with those expressed concerns in mind in taking action as members of the council.

Returning to the Administrative Office of the Courts, I'd like you to reflect, if you would, on the structure there. It has these 10 or so different divisions now, and some of them we discussed in more detail, such as the Office of Governmental Affairs. But how do you see that structure functioning today, and how did it change during the course of your tenure as chief?

I mentioned before that until the advent of state trial court funding, the Judicial Council and its staff, the A.O.C., were viewed—I believe correctly—as having very little to do with the trial courts apart from an occasional study such as those relating to interpreters and court delay. Their focus was almost entirely on the Courts of Appeal and the Supreme Court. Once the source of funding was switched from the counties to the state and the Judicial Council became the channel through which public funds were disbursed to the trial courts, there was a need to greatly expand the Administrative Office of the Courts to perform duties that now were mandated by the legislature to be performed by the Judicial Council and the A.O.C. That involved everything from trial court services and human resources and finance to every other kind of function one might imagine, such as a role in training and qualifying interpreters.

Then, as more and more responsibilities were shifted to the statewide administration of justice and removed from the counties, as a form of county fiscal relief, various matters that had been mandatory functions of the counties were now mandatory functions of the A.O.C. That certainly was graphically illustrated by the transfer of the 530 court facilities to the management responsibility of the Judicial Council and the A.O.C. I think most of the occasional carping that one hears from people about the substantial growth in the size of the A.O.C. is a cheap shot reflecting either a deliberate or an uninformed disregard of the shift in responsibilities to the A.O.C. as mandated by the legislature. Functions formerly undertaken by the local courts and by the counties are now, by law, the obligation of the Judicial Council and the A.O.C.

We touched on the Court Case Management System, which already has a long history from its original conception. Can you expand on that as an example of a branchwide initiative that started small and replaced other systems but really involved a substantial commitment and a substantial new system for the future?

I remember both Governor Wilson and Governor Davis being very critical of the fact that we had to come in and ask for augmented funds to assist the local courts in meeting their technology needs by way of fixing one system or another one and trying to coordinate a few systems here and there. They both felt it was quite imperative that we move away from a judicial branch that had about 70 different technology systems, with another few dozen variations on those 70, and move to a modern statewide technological system to better serve the needs of the judiciary and those of the public. We also had to be capable of providing information to the governor's Department of Finance and to the legislature, both of which were being asked to supply public funds to keep our systems going. I was publicly referring to the judicial branch's information systems as an electronic Tower of Babel. Not only were they separate, but they could not even communicate with each other, and they suffered costly breakdowns. I mentioned to you the contrast of going into a private commercial establishment, such as a department store. If you wanted to find out if they had an item of apparel available in a certain size and color and they didn't have it at that particular outlet, they pressed a few buttons and could tell you that they had it in their store in Chicago or New York and you should get it a few days later. In seeking funds from the governor and the legislature, we didn't have the capacity to know the extent and nature of judicial branch expenditures for statewide planning purposes. I was asked how many third-strike cases we had pending in the state, and I had no way of knowing. There were no records kept in many of the counties reflecting the amount and use of county funds that had been provided to local court systems. In order for us to be accountable for the state funds that the judicial branch had sought and obtained, we had to have the ability to track our funding. An effective case management system also involved just knowing what cases might be related to each other. A graphic example would be having a husband and wife engaged in marital dissolution proceedings. There might also have been proceedings related to a domestic violence restraining order. You might have a juvenile delinquent in the family and a dependency matter involving another child. You might have the father involved in a criminal charge. Yet each of the courts handling those separate matters might be unaware of the others, even if it were in the same county.

There are enormous services that can be and are beginning to be performed by this system. A letter from the Presiding Judge of the Orange County Superior Court, Kim Dunning, that I received in October of last year recounted the positive and successful experience that her court, and the superior courts of San Diego, Ventura, and San Joaquin Counties have had with the development of the new case management system. I have received communications from court clerks and judges indicating to me that various tasks undertaken in their courts that previously took seven or eight hours were now being done in two or three hours. Lawyers can be made aware of where there might be cases related to the lawsuits they are pursuing—litigation in the same county or in other counties. The system would also help in coordinating their various court appearances when conflicts in scheduling arise. There are so many different ways in which this is a service that would very much benefit the bench, the bar, the public, and the other two branches of government as well.

It seems that inevitably there are problems with new technology systems. California, like many other jurisdictions, has had problems in that area over the years—such as the computer system for the Department of Motor Vehicles several years ago, which was a big scandal, and also one for child support as well. There does seem to be something about these systems, both in California and in other states, that evokes the modern-day equivalent of an ancient curse—May you have a technology project!—in terms of delays and cost-overruns arising from complications and unexpected problems. Part of the difficulty that we've had, at least in the perception of the growth of this effort, was that it started off without a business plan for an entire system. With the encouragement of persons in the executive and legislative branches, the project grew topsy turvy to cover a statewide system. Although the system was not managed as well as it could have been, critics—I believe unfairly—point out that it was originally a project of so many millions and now look how big it has grown. But it grew to be a totally different system. It's like saying, look how much the A.O.C. has grown. That agency originally was focused on a much narrower segment of tasks, and therefore now that legislation has vastly expanded the mission and responsibilities of the council and the A.O.C., they need far more personnel. They spend more money because they took over other functions from local courts and from the counties, so you're really dealing with a totally different subject matter. You can't just look at the technology system and fairly say, "How it's grown," or look at the A.O.C., "See how it's grown?" They are different creatures altogether from what they were in their initial inception and creation, charged with vastly expanded responsibilities.

What was your own role in overseeing this project and keeping it on track?

I personally am not well trained in technology, and have publicly described myself as "road kill on the information highway." [Laughter] My own role was basically speaking from the bully pulpit. I visited the Deloitte operation in Orange County that was the major contractor on the system. I saw the system in operation in its prototypes in the Orange County Superior Court. I was very favorably impressed, so I used my enthusiasm for it, my recognition of the need for it, as a talking point with our justice system partners and in my State of the Judiciary speeches and my advocacy meetings with various governors. Of course, I relied on the Administrative Office of the Courts, because it was their proper role to oversee it and not for me to try to micromanage it. We also had a technology committee chaired by Justice Chin overseeing the project.

Thank you for reviewing this comprehensive system for the state. Is there anything else you'd like to say about CCMS and how it is faring today?

I would like to point out one thing that isn't taken into account in assessing the costs of CCMS. The presently existing systems are very costly. There is a great expense just in the upkeep and repairs to the multitude of current systems that are constantly on the verge of crashing, and that do crash occasionally. So it isn't all new money going into this system; some of it represents a shift from the expense of maintenance and replacement costs for the present set of incompatible and antiquated systems. I would also point out that, for instance, the Sacramento court complained bitterly about the system not working. Against the advice of our tech people, that court had tried to perform certain functions on the prototype of the system that they had. When these attempts were unsuccessful, the court refused to give permission to the outside vendor to come in and fix it. So some of the complaints about CCMS really reflect self-inflicted wounds.

Unfortunately, the development of a single statewide information system for the judicial branch is at risk because of the severe budgetary cuts that again face the judicial branch this year. Those judges who welcome any chance to lessen their accountability to the statewide administration of justice have taken advantage of the state's fiscal crisis, and of insufficient oversight by the A.O.C. in its management of the planned statewide information system, to urge that it be abandoned. I hope, both for policy and budgetary reasons, that if the judicial branch is forced to abandon its single-system plan, it is able to salvage the work that has been done so far and use it to ensure that further development and deployment of information system technology for the judicial branch continue through separate systems that are mutually compatible with each other.

I'd like to bring up one other thing within the A.O.C., if I might, and that is the establishment of the Administration of Justice Fund. Can you say a few words about that, please?

This was the act of an extremely generous couple, Ralph and Shirley Shapiro, who have been long-standing friends of Barbara's and mine. The Shapiros always have had a great interest in our court system, and our travels together have afforded many opportunities to discuss my work as Chief Justice and the efforts being made to improve our judicial system. Perhaps in part because Mr. Shapiro is a graduate of UCLA Law School in addition to being a CPA and businessman—although he hasn't practiced law for many years—he was concerned about the fact that funds were not available for certain judicial branch functions such as bringing in lecturers, welcoming international and national visitors, and other special projects. In fact, he asked, "How are you doing some of these things?" and was shocked to learn that Bill Vickrey, Ron Overholt, and I were often just paying for certain things out of our own pockets that could not be the subject of public funds. It sometimes might just be providing condolence or get-well floral arrangements or wine at a reception.

Mr. Shapiro set up an Administration of Justice Fund, basically—in its formal statement of purpose—"to provide resources for special outreach activities, events, and programs that benefit and support the goals of the judicial branch and for which funding might not be readily available or for which the use of taxpayers' funds might be deemed inappropriate." Special authorizing legislation was enacted to permit use of the fund, which is monitored by the state controller as well as by the judicial branch.

The fund has sponsored a number of educational and research programs, including a Bill of Rights student art contest—part of our ongoing civics education effort. A very innovative project made possible by the fund was the artwork created by the Orange County schools for the new facility of the Court of Appeal in Santa Ana. The students studied opinions issued by the court and created various paintings illustrating cases that inspired them. Those paintings are now displayed in the court building and were provided free of charge to the court. While saving public money, the project also involved students in a very worthwhile learning activity. The fund also supported a California science and the law conference and the celebration I referred to previously of the hundredth anniversary of California's Courts of Appeal. The fund was used to facilitate an exhibit on the U.S. Supreme Court decision in the school desegregation case, *Brown v. Board of Education*, focusing both on the decision and its legacy. Also supported by the fund are continuing programs giving recognition to judicial branch leaders and employees for length of service or for particular achievements, such as the Kleps Awards and others. Our Shapiro Purpose of Justice Lecture, which is given annually in San Francisco, has had outstanding speakers. Kenneth Feinberg, the former special master for the September 11 victim compensation fund, discussed the role of the courts in those cases and the funding that's available. The Chief Justice of Arizona, Ruth McGregor, spoke about her state's approach to the sentencing and community corrections challenges facing the judicial branch. Justice Albie Sachs of the high court of South Africa addressed issues of constitutional justice in postapartheid South Africa. We also had a brilliant debate between Dean Kenneth Starr of Pepperdine School of Law on the conservative side versus Dean Erwin Chemerinsky of the UC Irvine School of Law on the liberal side, analyzing the impact of several recent decisions of the U.S. Supreme Court. The Administration of Justice Fund also has assisted the new judicial officer orientation program that I mentioned, involving about 10 one-week sessions for newly appointed judges or justices or commissioners who come to San Francisco for training in their new duties. The fund also has supported an A.O.C. courts forum where matters of particular interest to A.O.C. employees are addressed, as well as national and international outreach that has included a visit by a judicial delegation from the Republic of Mexico to California designed to facilitate that nation's interaction with American state courts and with our federal judicial system.

I could go on and on, but this wonderful fund has been augmented by donations not only from the Shapiros but also from other individuals as well. It has brought about a lot of innovation and improvement in the judicial system that would not have been possible were it not for the use of these private funds. Mr. and Mrs. Shapiro have never had any matter come before the California Supreme Court. Had they, of course, I would have recused myself. Although our friendship is what gave rise to their establishing and maintaining this fund, their generous donations have continued after my retirement. It has been a totally selfless gesture that they get nothing out of other than the satisfaction of doing something very worthwhile.

We can note that my institution, the Institute of Governmental Studies at UC Berkeley, has applied for and received some funding towards this oral history we are working on today from the Administration of Justice Fund. You've given a very good idea of the broad range of activities that have been made possible by this. What has it meant to you on a personal level?

It truly made my task so much easier. There were things that, of course, I could have tried to do out of my own pocket, but there certainly are very substantial limits on that. Many things just would not have been accomplished, and these wonderful programs for the most part would not have existed, without the support of the Shapiros. The Administration of Justice Fund is just one of their many charitable endeavors, and one that I'm personally extremely grateful for.

Over the years, almost annually, Barbara and I have taken some very exotic trips with the Shapiros and our mutual friends Robert and Milly Kayyem, for example spending a couple weeks exploring in a van, as we did in Iceland, taking a ship to Antarctica, going to Morocco and camping out in the Sahara, and trekking in Nepal.

As an aside, which of these places are your favorites?

Each new trip seems to become our favorite. Barbara and I have been to East Africa with these two couples, and to New Zealand, the Dalmatian Coast, Japan, you name it. Recent trips with the Shapiros included one to southern Africa with Charles and Miriam Vogel, both former justices of the California Court of Appeal and close friends. Barbara and I returned to Antarctica earlier this year with our eldest son Eric, expanding the trip to encompass the explorer Shackleton's journey to South Georgia and Elephant Islands.

The great benefit now, in retirement, is that I can travel without having a suitcase filled with legal briefs and administrative documents, and no cell phone ringing with news about some crisis in Sacramento. I told Bill Vickrey after my first visit to Antarctica that this turned out to be the only place where I managed to be out of range of his cell phone calls. I mentioned to you having a very lengthy conversation with my chambers staff while I was in the Sahara desert, in southern Morocco. [Laughter]

Let's move on to reviewing the major structural reforms to the judicial branch. Some of these we have certainly talked about on other occasions, but I wanted to run through the major ones as a group today, to talk not only about enactment of these various measures and what they entailed but also how you worked in a liaison capacity with the legislature and your various justice system partners, as you call them.

We might start with the Trial Court Funding Act of 1997. We have discussed this one a fair amount, but let's just review where that stood when you came on as Chief Justice and where it went from there.

There were efforts made in past years to try to change the system of funding the trial courts, but not to much avail. The priority that I came to give to providing funding for the trial courts through the state government, as opposed to reliance on county government, was very much the result of what I observed during my first year as Chief Justice, traveling around the state visiting each of the 58 counties and the six appellate districts. At the same time, 1996–97 happened to be a time of severe economic decline, as happens quite periodically in California—a year of real difficulty for state and local government. I had to twice go to the legislature my first year as Chief Justice to seek emergency bailout funding and soon came to the realization that this was no way to run a court system and that we needed a more stable and dependable system of funding. I also realized in the course of the various visits that there was a large disparity, a substantial inequality, in the amount of funding available to individual trial courts depending upon the ability and willingness of each county's board of supervisors to fund the trial courts in their particular county in the face of competing demands for county services, whether it was parks, law enforcement, recreation, health services, or social services. The funding also seemed to sometimes depend upon whether whoever was on the board of supervisors that year had a good or a poor relationship with whoever was presiding judge of a particular court. There were severe problems that existed for various courts as a result of years of chronic neglect in funding. Some courts were much better off than others. Some were better managed than others. But some simply had been denied resources, including adequate facilities, over the years.

To me, this was a matter of real concern, not just in terms of equity among courts but because of its impact upon each court's ability to provide accessible and fair justice to the public—which I consider one of the primary obligations and purposes of government, and one that should not vary from county to county depending upon the ability and willingness of the respective counties to provide adequate funding for their courts. Interestingly enough—the analogy just came to me—that was part of the rationale for the California Supreme Court's decision, well before my time on that court, in the *Serrano* case—holding that the right to education is so fundamental that the resources to fund it should not vary substantially from one school district to another depending upon the property tax revenue that might be available to the individual school district.

To me, state funding for the courts also was integral to creating a co-equal, independent branch of government—not just in name or theory, but in function and reality. Having a co-equal branch, independent but accountable, is not just an abstract end in its own right; it enables the court system to carry out its function of providing the public with accessible justice. State funding truly became my first and foremost priority in terms of long-term objectives, in addition to being the means to address the immediate crisis then confronting the courts. I mentioned in my State of the Judiciary address—and later drew up documents graphically illustrating—the fact that there was basically a timetable under which counties were facing court closures. By early March of 1997, I had 16 counties listed. By early April, an additional 23 counties faced court closures. It was like a rolling electrical blackout, if you will. By the time we got further into the year, I indicated—and this was written up by the vice chair of the Assembly Judiciary Committee, Assemblyman Bill Morrow, a Republican from Orange and San Diego Counties—that 51 of 58 counties would be in a crisis situation due to insufficient funding.

The shift to state funding became imperative. I believe many legislators were motivated—even though we didn't get it through the first time we tried—by the circumstance that it was also a means of providing county relief, because county governments in many instances were close to going belly up themselves. Some of the legislators, and I believe this was true of Governor Wilson too, to a large degree, ultimately backed our proposal because in the end it was providing several hundred million dollars of relief to the beleaguered counties. The legislation also, by the way, created about 40 new judgeships that were sorely needed. I was very pleased when this ultimately passed. I mentioned to you that I was able to announce it at the State Bar convention—the clock had been stopped before midnight to avoid the constitutional deadline, and the legislature had acted literally in the last hours and minutes of its session.

Governor Wilson ended up praising the bill. The President pro Tem of the Senate, Bill Lockyer, described it as the most meaningful reform of the California judicial system in this century. A member of the Republican leadership, Assembly Member Curt Pringle, said that the legislation "represents one of the legislature's most significant accomplishments of the session," that he considered it historic legislation designed to ensure that our justice system serves the people of California responsibly and fairly, and that the bill would help out the financial situation and the well-being of the entire state. This was truly monumental, and everything else that happened—some of which you and I will discuss by way of structural reforms—would not have been possible without this initial reform of trial court funding. Under this legislation, spending on our trial courts doubled from $1.5 billion in 1996–97 to $3 billion in 2009–10.

One of the loose ends that had previously blocked passage of the bill was the issue of the right of employees to collectively bargain on noneconomic working conditions and also what the status would be of employees of the superior and municipal courts, who had been county employees. Now the court system was going to be state financed. Would they remain as county employees? Would they become state employees? Would there be a new category of employee, trial court employees? It was this last course that was ultimately taken after study by the Judicial Council, its committees, and a task force appointed to make recommendations on the subject—recommendations that ultimately were adopted by the legislature.

How did the various parties line up on that matter initially?

There was a lot of infighting on the court employee issues, and it was a matter that, had it not been left to a later day, would have ended up killing the entire trial court funding proposal.

But by separating it and taking it up again later you managed to save them both, as it were?

Yes. We formed a task force and got together the counties, the employee groups of the local courts, and the A.O.C., and worked it all out. It was a major achievement and permitted state trial court funding to go forward, which in turn made everything else possible.

What was your own view of the best solution?

Definitely the one that was adopted. I believe it has worked out well, even though there are some details that could be improved.

Was that Governor Davis who actually signed that into law, or was it still Governor Wilson?

It was Governor Wilson who signed the state trial court funding bill. There was a one-year transition period in which to adjust to it. It was Governor Davis who signed into being the Trial Court Employment Protection Governance Act of 2000 as well as the courthouse facilities legislation.

We'll get to that in a moment, but as you say, the Trial Court Funding Act really set the stage for all the others. Chronologically, I guess the matter of unifying the trial courts came up next and was put before the voters in 1998. Where did that whole idea stand when you took over, and what approach did you take to moving it along?

Again, that was something that had been discussed for many years. I can't take credit for just coming up with the idea of merging our trial courts. As I mentioned before, one of my predecessors, Chief Justice Phil Gibson, had bemoaned the fact that several levels of trial court existed below the level of superior court and that any practicing attorney would be hard pressed to name, let alone define, the respective jurisdictions of each of those courts. Over the years, some of the courts mentioned by Gibson had gone by the wayside, but we still had justice of the peace positions in our justice courts, serving districts with less than 40,000 in population. So there remained three types of trial court—justice, municipal, and superior—at the time we moved forward with our unification proposal to have the legislature place a constitutional amendment on the June 1998 ballot for voter approval.

Part of the problem, too, was that there were various services that were provided only by the superior court at the county seat. You had some counties that were vast geographically but had a very small population, so a member of the public would have to drive to the county seat, maybe a few hours, to try to obtain, let's say, a domestic violence restraining order, only to be told, "Sorry, we only do those on Tuesdays. Come back next week." That type of judicial service normally wasn't available, let's say, in one of the four court locations around the county that served as municipal courts or justice courts. What I observed in the course of my visits was, to me, the absurdity, in a time of financial crisis, of having at one end of the courthouse a municipal court civil filing window and at the other a superior court civil filing window. It was the same for criminal filings, and separate interpreter services, separate jury commissioners, sometimes. Separate jury pools, separate purchasing of supplies. Seeing municipal court judges, no matter how diligent they were, perhaps going home in the afternoon at two o'clock because they had finished their day's calendar of preliminary hearings or misdemeanor trials and their superior court colleagues being up to their eyeballs in last-day criminal or civil cases facing dismissal. To me it didn't make sense to have this duplicative, overlapping set of court systems.

There was a lot of resistance among many judges to court unification. Some of it reflected, probably, a sincere belief that many of the municipal court judges were younger and less experienced, and weren't qualified to do superior court work. In some instances there may have been some truth in that. In others, it was absolutely not true. I was aware of some municipal court judges who were as competent if not more so than the judges serving on the superior court in the county. Some of the judges had genuine concerns about whether the court would be too large to be manageable. I was pleased that they proved this was not the case, by resolving their problems and establishing a workable system. I believe there also may have been some concern about assignments and who would be presiding over what type of cases, and at which courthouse. In any event all of that was overcome, and I was very glad to see them unify. Some of it was elitism, I believe—maybe the feeling that if you were going to be a superior court judge you had to be superior to something and you had to have a court—which actually was called an "inferior" court, reflecting inferior jurisdiction rather than a qualitative comparison—below you. I described some things to you about my own experience on the L.A. Municipal Court, the dining room in the main courthouse reserved for superior court judges. [Laughter] But in any event—just in terms of efficient use of the resources provided by the taxpayers, in terms of providing accessible justice and reducing delay in the proceedings, especially in courts that were underfunded—to me the only logical course was to eliminate this duplication among the levels of trial courts.

There were initial steps to permit cross-assignment of judges, using my authority as Chief Justice to assign municipal court judges to the superior court. There wasn't too much in the opposite direction—which would require the consent of a superior court judge to be assigned to the municipal or justice court—but such assignments did occur in some places. The only real solution was to unify the courts completely, and that would require a constitutional amendment. I had discussions with Senate President pro Tem Bill Lockyer, who was eager to have this done, and Phil Isenberg, the chief backer of the bill in the state Assembly, on how the resistance of some courts could be overcome. How could we get this through politically? My answer was that I thought we had to do it on a local-option basis to get the measure through the legislature. That approach, though necessary, made it a lot harder for me. It would have been very nice to have this done with just one stroke of the pen statewide, but that wasn't to be. Consequently, a constitutional amendment was proposed that would permit the judges of any given county to unify by separate favorable votes of the superior court judges and of the municipal court judges in that county. The positive vote of both levels of judges would be required for the county to become a county with a unified court. The voters approved the proposed constitutional amendment by about a two-thirds vote.

There were some counties in which the judges, municipal and superior, were totally on the same page and very eager to unify. Some actually voted to unify—they prided themselves on this—within hours of the results of the constitutional amendment being formally approved. There were others that also came along quickly, and basically about 50 of the 58 counties unified in short order. There were four counties—Monterey, Yuba, Merced, and Kings—in which court unification was delayed by provisions of the federal Voting Rights Act. Under that legislation, which of course was enacted to deal primarily with problems of racial discrimination in the electoral process that existed in the deep South of our nation, a certain percentage of minorities in the population and other circumstances would give rise to a presumption that any change in voting practices would have a negative impact on the voting rights of minority-group residents of the county and would not be permitted absent "pre-clearance" by the U.S. Department of Justice. Kings County was the last to unify, in 2001. The burden was imposed upon the counties and the courts involved—with assistance from the general counsel's office of the A.O.C.—to convince the Justice Department that there would be no discriminatory impact upon minorities, even if unintended, by virtue of moving to countywide superior court districts from municipal and justice court districts. Those local judicial districts comprised a part of the county in which a minority might have a greater proportionate role than it would have in a countywide election, thereby reducing the impact of minority voters. We were able to convince the Justice Department that clearance should be given, but it took a lot of documentation and time. The last two of these, Monterey and Kings, had me come down to swear them in.

There were also a couple of counties, Kern County and Los Angeles County, where the superior court judges just voted it down. The municipal court judges wanted it, but the superior court judges didn't. In fact, it was only on the third vote that the L.A. Superior Court judges approved unification, which occurred in 2000. To put it bluntly, using the old term, I had to use "carrots and sticks" to help bring it about. The third time was the charm. It was very gratifying in the end when the municipal court judges and their family members and guests were gathered in the Biltmore Bowl hotel facility in downtown Los Angeles, which was the venue selected by the superior court for the swearing-in because everyone couldn't fit into the largest courtroom. The court has done a great job in coordinating the municipal and superior court judges into what is the largest trial court in the world, with more than 430 judges plus commissioners and referees. I was called upon to swear them all in, which I also did in San Diego, Orange, Alameda, and San Francisco Counties. These were wonderful ceremonies—some of them massive in scale—and very joyous occasions for those involved.

Since Los Angeles was not only your own old stomping ground but also the largest of the county superior courts, how did you view the reticence to adopt this and what did you do directly about it?

I regretted their resistance and thought much of it reflected an elitist approach by superior court judges to municipal court judges. I believe there were some judges who had bona fide concerns, and others who were motivated by less lofty concerns. It had to be made clear that there would be disadvantages in terms of the funding to be provided if a court were not making the most efficient use of its available resources, including black-robed resources. [Laughter] By then the vast majority of the courts, or I should say of the judges in the various counties, had voted to unify. There was a reluctance, certainly, on the part of a couple courts for them to be standing alone as holdouts, I believe.

The appointment of new judges replacing retiring judges also helped take care of the problem. As with so many subjects, it gets to be somewhat of a generational thing, whether you're talking about court unification or technology, interracial marriages and perhaps gay marriages as well. As the older generation dies out, opposition seems to evaporate and the newer generation of the general population—or of the judiciary—isn't troubled by the same things that troubled their predecessors. In any event, it was a cause for great celebration to finally have that accomplished.

As we've also talked about, you did in time oversee the transfer of the court facilities in all the counties to state ownership.

Yes, that was the third of the three basic structural reforms. These three measures had a couple of—I guess one could call them—appendages. I would characterize the trial court employees act as an offshoot of state trial court funding. With regard to the transfer of court facilities, that was followed in a later year by a $5 billion revenue bond issue to enable the courts to restore and in some instances retrofit or replace existing court facilities. But once the first two basic reforms had taken place—the structural changes of the state taking over trial court funding, and the courts having unified into one level of trial court, one superior court in each of the 58 counties—it didn't really make sense for the counties, who were basically out of the court business, to maintain responsibility for owning and maintaining the 530 courthouse facilities in the state. In some instances I have to use the word "maintaining" in a very loose sense, because some of the buildings were quite unsafe and decrepit. There were courthouses that had issues of asbestos, mold, seismic safety, fire safety, plus design elements that posed security risks. It just didn't make sense for the counties to be saddled with all this valuable real estate requiring substantial expenditures for maintenance. Again, it was a matter of county relief. This legislation was put forth by Senator Martha Escutia. Governor Davis also deserves credit for supporting this legislation, as does Darrell Steinberg, then-Assembly Judiciary Committee chair.

After the passage of the courthouse transfer legislation, the transfer of each building had to be negotiated separately with the particular county. Some of the structures were multi-use facilities, and in a few instances it was difficult to find new quarters for the county board of supervisors. I attended a ceremony marking the first transfer, in Indio in Riverside County, with the chair of the county board of supervisors handing me the traditionally oversized key to this large, beautiful facility. Like some others, it was multi-use, also housing the board of supervisors and other offices of county government, which were in effect evicted from their quarters, although obviously with their consent, because the counties were great partners in this and all our other efforts. In some, where parts of the premises had been leased out, complicated negotiations took place. Some courthouses were historic buildings, built in the 1800s, that the county wanted to be able to preserve as museums or for other uses, but health and safety requirements made this a complicated arrangement. Attending the transfer of the 1854 Mariposa County courthouse, the oldest one still operating west of the Mississippi River, was another memorable event for me.

The person who provided the greatest assistance with the passage of the bond legislation, which came a few years later, was Senate President pro Tem Don Perata. At his request I joined him at a news conference to announce why we were seeking $5 billion worth of bonds. It was a revenue bond, not a general-obligation bond, so it didn't impact the state's beleaguered general fund. The bond issue was supported by new and extended filing fees and other special fees. I believe our efforts to obtain passage of this legislation also were assisted by Governor Davis' having appointed me to a commission called Building California for the Twenty-First Century, which helped raise the consciousness of people concerning the infrastructure needs of the state. I was the sole judicial representative, which gave me further motivation to share information about the plight of the judicial branch's physical infrastructure with the other branches of government, and how urgent were the judiciary's needs for courthouse expansion and improvement. Much of this could be analogized to the simple situation of a homeowner having a small leak in his or her roof. You let it go, and it turns out to be a very large leak and ends up damaging the interior. That was the condition of some of our courthouse facilities. We're making great progress with these courthouses. The A.O.C. did a sort of triage here, categorizing what was truly a life safety issue—what has to be retrofitted or replaced immediately—then what can wait until the next phase, and finally what is just an enhancement and least important.

Now there is a separate division at A.O.C. that oversees the court facilities and their renovation, when necessary?

Yes. That's the Office of Court Construction and Management.

That's all directly related to this unification of the courts, and transfer of facilities to the state, and to state funding of the court system?

Yes. That transfer of facilities has been described by others as the largest real estate transaction ever in the State of California, given the number of square feet involved and the value of the property.

You've been successful, as we've talked about, in the subsequent provision of funds to renovate those facilities and to manage them and to keep the courts open after the economic difficulties statewide of the last couple of years.

Yes, and in terms of new construction, too. What's so important about the judiciary having the management responsibility instead of the state, through the Department of General Services, is that judges and court administrators, of course, will have a much better awareness of the particular needs of the courthouse facility than someone who is just generally an expert in construction matters or even in the construction of government buildings—but not in the particular security needs of the courts. We've had, as I mentioned previously, people killed in courthouse facilities, places that are supposed to be a site for the dispensation of justice, a place providing security, and not a crime scene. I mentioned my own experiences with having a juror from my courtroom stabbed in a public restroom of the Criminal Courts Building, and visiting the main L.A. County Courthouse shortly after a family law litigant was fatally shot by her husband right outside a courtroom. A lot of our security problems would be lessened or eliminated by truly professional courthouse design, which we are now able to provide. You have facilities with insufficient or nonexistent perimeter screening at multiple entrances, and sometimes inadequate design of facilities to accommodate the movement of inmates from the lockup to the courtroom, going right by inner offices, judges' chambers, or jury rooms. All of these concerns are being addressed now by our professionals involved in courthouse design and construction. You won't see chains of prisoners or individual inmates brought through crowded public hallways in the courthouses that are being designed now.

This puts us into the broad area of other branchwide reforms that you've been able to oversee during your time as Chief Justice. What else would you like to see in the way of court security matters?

As I mentioned at one of our earlier sessions, I feel that, with all due respect to the fine job that the sheriffs do, there are many reasons why it would make sense for there to be—as there is in New York State, for example—a statewide system of court marshals, instead of the sheriffs exclusively being given the task of providing courthouse security. I had experience with the marshal system when I served on the L.A. Municipal Court. The marshal was an appointee of the judges and accordingly took orders, appropriately, from the judges, from the court. The sheriff in each county is an elected and therefore political figure who feels, with some justification, that he or she is an independent entity, and there's only so much that the court can direct them to do, given that they have their own independence from the court. What troubles some people is that the deputy sheriffs may be witnesses in a given trial. At the same time, the sheriff has charge of the jury that is determining the case, even more so when the jury is sequestered, and may be bringing the exhibits and the other evidence to the jurors during their deliberations and having charge of their notebooks. You might in the same trial have deputy sheriffs on the stand whose credibility was one of the issues at the trial—interrogating officers, or officers who had handled the evidence and were maintaining chain of custody, or officers who were investigators or on patrol and who were eyewitnesses to—or even participants in—confrontations with the defendant. There was this overlap, almost incestuous, between the role of a deputy sheriff as court officer and the role of other deputy sheriffs from the same office as "witnesses for the prosecution," if you will. There's just something a bit incestuous about all of that. In terms of the appearance of propriety, I believe everyone including the sheriffs would actually be better served by having a professional entity, a marshal's office, perform those functions, as is done in the federal courts.

New York State has professionals whose main function is courtroom duty, in contrast to the deputy sheriffs who, perhaps as a reward for long-time service on the street, sometimes conclude their career by being assigned to courtroom bailiff duty. Now, the sheriffs' position is that they're in charge of transporting prisoners, and that there is some difficulty or inefficiency in handing over their prisoners to the marshal who presumably would have charge of the lockup. To the extent that's truly a problem, I believe it could be minimized or eliminated. It was not a problem during my years on the L.A. Municipal Court. I favor the assignment of professional courtroom marshals rather than officers taken off the beat for a tour of duty in the courthouse—even though they are well-trained law enforcement professionals. New York State has a marshals' academy, and its graduates are trained to be court professionals, just as interpreters and court reporters are. I believe we should approach the selection of this type of court personnel the same way. That would take care of some of the problems I've observed and some of the perceptions that are created. I was unsuccessful at one of my early attempts at lobbying when, as an associate justice of the Supreme Court, I urged Governor Wilson not to sign the legislation that basically gave the sheriffs a monopoly on the provision of bailiff services. The sheriffs are a very political and powerful entity in the legislature, so they need to become convinced that their interests and everyone else's interests would be better served by the creation of a marshal's office, because that's probably not going to happen over their objection.

Similarly, the court reporters enjoy a virtual monopoly, with few exceptions, in preparing the verbatim record of court proceedings. Our efforts to reduce expenses to the courts and to litigants by switching to electronic record-ing—as some states have done—have been stymied by the political power of the court reporters and their allies, the other public employee unions.

You mentioned court interpreters a moment ago. Would you please review for me the changes you oversaw in that area throughout the judicial branch?

As I have discussed with you, one of the overriding concerns that I had in performing my duties as Chief Justice was with access to justice. That takes so many different forms. It involves court design as well. The A.O.C. produced an excellent film that other chief justices asked me for, called *Obstacle Courts*, showing what it's like to try to get around a courthouse, into a courtroom, into the witness box, and so forth if you are in a wheelchair. There is every kind of aspect to access to justice, and we'll discuss some others under that rubric, I'm sure, but one of the most basic aspects of access to justice is language access. If you can't even understand what's going on in court, you can't be viewed as hav-ing access.

We're having an earthquake.

I think we just had an earthquake. [Laughter] Which has come and gone.

I was amazed—and every time I recite the figure I'm shocked at it—that in any given year more than 100 languages are translated in our California courts, literally everything from A to Z, from Albanian to Zapotec. This reflects the rich cultural diversity of our state but also creates a problem of access and a need to provide adequate interpreter services. One of the things that I strongly supported was increasing the number of languages in which we would have interpreters available and certified as such, as professional interpreters. Many judges have had the experience of having someone appear before them as a party or a wit-ness accompanied by teenaged or even preteen offspring or nephew or niece who is doing his or her best to translate the court proceedings for the non-English-speaking person before the court. I have a lot of interest in our trying to increase, as we have been, the language accessibility provided by the courts. When we get to our self-help services I'll describe what we've done on our web-site that is available in different languages. But first and foremost we have to have it available in the courtroom.

Part of the problem is that one might have a three- or four-minute arraign-ment in some far northern county with no interpreter available and have to summon one at great expense to the local court, which gets billed for at least a half day and maybe a full day of service for something that was just a few minutes of interpretation, because the interpreter has to be paid for his or her travel time. We've been able in some situations to have telephonic interpretation. I believe AT&T has assisted in that effort, but we definitely have to do much more to provide such services. I'm quite attuned to the particular challenges posed by the need for courtroom language interpreters from having a sister-in-law from Argentina who is an interpreter for the L.A. Superior Court, Ana Maria Schneiderman. But it's all part of recognizing the fact that we are now a state with no ethnic-majority population, and are faced with the need to provide services for our diverse population.

That need also relates to the issue of diversity in judicial appointments and in the appointment of commissioners and referees by local courts. There is growing recognition of the worth of rendering the bench less monochromatic, if you will—not that there has to be or necessarily should be any proportional representation. But there should be some general recognition, I believe, of the state's population in our court system that in a broad way reflects our diversity, so as to help litigants and other people in general have a sense of confidence in the judicial system. With that in mind, I participated with the governor and the legislature in working on legislation to gather statistics on the racial and ethnic diversity and gender diversity in our court system in order to assist in the process of making judicial appointments and in the subordinate judicial officer appointments made by the trial courts. Some courts have even created special outreach programs to the ethnic bar associations, encouraging and telling them how to apply for appointment, and responding to their questions. Members of the governor's staff and of the A.O.C. have participated in such programs.

Judicial education programs are now being given on the subject of diversity. Instead of just having separate courses available at the judicial college on the need to consider race and ethnicity in certain contexts, that subject is woven as a theme into all sorts of substantive and procedural courses on the law taken by judges. Sometimes it involves monitoring the actions of court staff. Sometimes it just involves being sensitive to the fact that in some cultures certain behavior is intended or reflective of something quite different from what we might assume as Caucasians. One illustration that is often mentioned in the context of judicial education is that in some Asian cultures it is considered impolite to look one directly in the eye and that therefore, if a party or a witness with that ethnic background is avoiding direct eye contact or is looking at his or her shoes or at the floor, most likely it is not a reflection of evasiveness or lack of honesty. These considerations are all reflections of the multicultural society we have here in California.

These reforms to improve access to justice did take a lot of different faces. You mentioned the self-help centers a moment ago. Perhaps we can talk about those for a few minutes?

Certainly. It has become clear—and I view this as one of the great challenges facing us—that fewer and fewer persons are able to afford counsel. It's a matter of constitutional right, of course, to persons charged with criminal acts but it's not a matter of right in civil proceedings except in the rarest of situations. Yet very substantial rights, such as custody of children, division of marital property upon a divorce, landlord-tenant eviction, may be at issue and yet be handled in court by a litigant without the assistance of counsel. There are areas in California where 85 to 90 percent or more of the family law cases are resolved without the participation of an attorney. Again, here is another obstacle to access to justice. How can you vindicate your fundamental rights while navigating your own way through a complex set of legal procedures? I'm very proud that our Administrative Office of the Courts has taken the initiative to develop self-help centers, for which it is recognized nationally. It has a division called the Center for Families, Children, and the Courts headed by Diane Nunn. Among the many exceptional persons on her staff is Bonnie Hough, who has made a specialty and a national name for herself working to set up and improve self-help centers.

There are many ways of approaching the whole problem of access to justice. We talked about specialized courts, such as drug courts dealing with substance abuse; domestic violence courts; teen courts; even for the business community and the tort community, complex litigation courts; courts for veterans and the homeless. California took some inspiration from New York's efforts in its Midtown Manhattan Court, which involves defendants convicted of minor offenses performing community service work as part of their sentence. We discussed special programs for adoption, such as Adoption Saturday. The self-help centers are one more manifestation of the many ways we can provide access to justice. The number of such centers has increased from only one in 1997 to well over 100 and includes at least one in each county. Another innovative approach was Ventura's concept of the mobile van going off to the hinterland, while at the main courthouse banners and tables were set up offering help to unrepresented persons.

We've been able, especially in the Bay Area, San Diego, and Los Angeles, to enlist volunteers to help unrepresented litigants—a program called Justice Corps, which is related to Americorps. College student volunteers assist persons at self-help centers that are set up in the courthouse or at other locations. There's always a fine line between rendering assistance on how to fill out forms, and not engaging in the unauthorized practice of law. This is something that is always of concern to court clerks. Another approach in addressing the problem of unrepresented litigants has been to persuade attorneys to engage in pro bono work. I believe I mentioned to you that several years ago I sent out an individual letter to every lawyer in the state, 200,000+, urging them to engage in pro bono efforts. I was asked every year to confer the State Bar's pro bono awards at its annual meeting. There are other similar events that I traditionally participated in, the so-called CLAY awards, the magazine *California Lawyer*'s awards that include recognition for pro bono efforts, and the VLS, Volunteers in Legal Services, program of the San Francisco bar that recognizes individuals who have performed exceptional pro bono work.

One of the more innovative programs was one that I participated in on a couple of occasions with my colleagues across the street in the U.S. District Court courthouse, first with then-Northern District Chief Judge Marilyn Patel and later with Chief Judge Vaughn Walker. That involved the two of us holding a joint news conference at which leading law firms would sign a pledge to devote either 3 percent or 5 percent of their billable hours to pro bono work. The managing partners of major law firms would show up. The important thing was to not just have a firm begrudgingly allow its junior associates to do this kind of work, but to have even managing partners and other partners set an example by engaging in that work, and to have the junior lawyers, who of course would be concerned about their future prospects at the firm, receive credit against billable hours for the legal work they were doing in a pro bono capacity. It was wonderful to see senior partners step up and literally sign the pledge. By the way, as is the case with many other altruistic acts, pro bono work often turns out to be as much of a benefit to the lawyer donating it as to the recipient. There were countless lawyers who would tell me that they learned new skills and got involved in new areas of the law that they never would have encountered but for volunteering to do pro bono work. They said it first of all enhanced their skills in their regular area of practice but, perhaps even more importantly, made them feel they were true professionals and not just businessmen engaged in the business of law. They felt very gratified and enriched, and sometimes even very emotionally involved, from having helped persons in need—sometimes through class-action proceedings that benefited a broad range of people. In terms of volunteerism, this really involves lawyers giving back to the community. Again, it's one more way of trying to deal with the need for legal services where they are not provided as a matter of right.

In addition to the problem of clerks and volunteers having to avoid being engaged in the unauthorized practice of law, some of the attorneys felt there was some difficulty in their just dealing with what might be considered as one part of the case and then being viewed as having abandoned their client or not providing adequate legal representation for other parts of the case in the broader sense of that word. It involved a concept called the unbundling of legal services. I remember that one of the leaders in the access-to-justice area, Justice James Lambden from the First District Court of Appeal, in making a presentation to the Judicial Council, said, "This is rather absurd. I don't know how this term ever originated, because 'bundling' was the term used by the pilgrims in putting two young people together to assist in a potential courtship. The couple would be placed in the same bed but fully clothed with a board between them. What can this possibly have to do with legal services?" My reply was, "The one connection is that both things are about access." [Laughter] Perhaps one could view it that way but, in any event, successful efforts have been made to formally disengage a lawyer in those circumstances from the responsibility of having to represent clients throughout all of a case or controversy.

In addition to the regular kind of self-help center, there was one whose dedication I attended in Fresno that was the first to focus on the Spanish-speaking population of the Central Valley. Again, even the subject of legal services has some tie-in to the court visits I undertook during my first year as Chief Justice, because among the various community groups with whom I would meet were the county law librarians. I learned a lot from those visits. When I first became a lawyer, county law libraries were considered basically the exclusive domain and resource of lawyers and judges. But as more and more people came to represent themselves, law librarians were called upon to assist in providing services for pro pers, as we call them. That graduated into providing some electronic access to individuals who didn't have their own computers. The county law libraries have been funded by the counties, usually inadequately, and by court fees and donations as well. They have come to serve a very important function in providing self-help services.

I met a very impressive woman at a meeting of the Conference of Chief Justices. She was a nun of the Dominican order by the name of Sister Sharp. She made a presentation that very favorably impressed me with what she had accomplished in setting up self-help centers in Arizona. I invited her to come to address the California Judicial Council, and she shared her experience with us. I should mention that the self-help centers weren't totally adequate by themselves in terms of the access they provided to some people, so we set up a self-help website, which now gets millions of hits every year. It goes beyond just showing you how to fill out the proper forms. It may have a video about the court building itself, showing you how the proceedings typically are conducted in the courtroom. It may even have information such as how to locate the nearest domestic violence shelter if you're someone in urgent need of obtaining a restraining order. The online services are quite extensive. The website is available in its entirety in the Spanish language, and parts of it are available in various Asian languages as well. My fellow Chief Justices were very impressed with our website when Bonnie Hough and I made a presentation to them about it at one of our annual meetings, and many intended to emulate it. The Conference of Chief Justices now has an access and fairness committee that has received positive recognition.

I also set up what became known as the *Elkins* task force after an opinion I wrote for the court, *Elkins v. Superior Court*. The task force was charged with making recommendations for balancing the competing considerations confronting a family law judge faced with an unrepresented litigant and a heavy family law calendar. The work of the task force is still underway, but it's coming up with excellent recommendations that I expect will very much improve family law procedures and the courts' approach to unrepresented litigants. This was an area where—much as I said I kept my administrative duties quite segregated from my decision-making responsibilities—there was a confluence, in a way.

I guess while we're talking about areas where my decision-making and administrative duties coalesced, I might make a brief reference to a couple of cases in the criminal area, *People v. Engram* and *People v. Hajjaj*, which dealt with the consequences of the congestion in the Riverside County courts. Those were cases in which I authored opinions for the court noting that the rights of the criminal defendants had been impaired by reason of the ensuing delays. In those cases we held that the superior court was not required to employ its specialized civil departments to bring criminal cases to trial within the period prescribed by statute, and that if a criminal case was not brought to trial because of the unavailability of a judge or courtroom, this circumstance did not provide the "good cause" required for going beyond the speedy-trial provisions, and the case would have to be dismissed. In other words, it was the legislature's routine, systemic underfunding of the court system, and its failure to create a sufficient number of additional judgeships, and perhaps some other systemic factors, that caused the defendant not to be brought to trial in a timely fashion. Therefore, protection of the defendants' speedy-trial rights required that their cases be dismissed. *Hajjaj* was one of the last opinions I wrote, in November 2010, a month after *Engram*. In that case, we held that the fact there was a remote courtroom open at 4:15 p.m. at the other end of Riverside County—seventy-six miles away—did not mean that a court was "available" to try the defendant's case that day. He still could insist on his speedy-trial rights and obtain a dismissal. Again, in this situation, as in the family law proceedings at issue in *Elkins*, I authored opinions for the court that intersected with my administrative actions, here with the Riverside task force that I previously described to you, which employed judges I assigned from around the state to assist the local courts in handling their backlog of criminal and civil cases facing dismissal.

I don't know if you recall, but I wonder if the court agreed to hear and decide these cases for the very reason that they were bringing forth a larger systemic problem of the judiciary itself?

That certainly was on my mind, but I can't speak for my colleagues. Clearly, these cases all present various issues relating to providing access to justice in one way or another.

I don't know if you can generalize, but I wonder to what extent your colleagues shared your interest and commitment to these kinds of access issues?

Speaking to my own feelings, I believe over the years I became more and more sensitized to the problem, perhaps through exposure to cases that wended their way up to our court but also probably due to changes in the economic climate in California and the fact that fewer and fewer people were able to afford counsel in civil matters, even persons in the so-called middle class. I wouldn't be surprised if the thinking of some of my colleagues also evolved due to those circumstances. I know that several of the justices addressed access issues in their various speaking engagements.

I tried to talk up the issue whenever I could, whether it was through awards ceremonies, task forces and committees I appointed, or articles I wrote. I guess my evolving interest in access-to-justice issues probably began with Chief Justice Lucas' appointment of me to chair the committee to implement the recommendations of the gender bias committee. Its report included a broad spectrum of between 60 and 70 recommendations, which we triaged: what can be done immediately with changes in court practices and rules? What required legislation? What might require substantial funding? I believe that the important thing with studies of this type—and we have had many on various aspects of access and fairness—was not to end up having a document that merely gathers dust on the shelf the way so many reports do, but instead a plan that would actually include an implementation program and schedule. I ended up getting involved in establishing committees to deal with bias based on race and ethnicity, sexual orientation, and physical disabilities, and finally we just encapsulated everything under the rubric of an Access and Fairness Committee, which is what we have now instead of separate committees. That's what the Conference of Chief Justices also has done.

Did your own views actually change in any of these areas, or was it really just a matter of seeing more and more what needed to be done out in the judicial system?

My thinking probably evolved as I saw the practical ramifications of lack of counsel. It's one thing to recognize it as a problem in the abstract, but when you see it graphically illustrated in the context of particular situations or legal disputes it becomes even more telling. I guess at this point in my life I may be afforded the luxury of being able to quote myself. There was a large banner that was put up every year at the annual State Bar pro bono awards event that I was asked to participate in, and I think it really captures the whole situation rather succinctly: "If the motto 'and justice for all' becomes 'and justice for those who can afford it,' we threaten the very underpinnings of our social contract." I had made that statement in one of my State of the Judiciary speeches—I believe in 2001—and it became the motto for the annual awards ceremony on the banner that was displayed.

I wonder what else you would like to see happen in the future in this broad area of access to justice.

Of course it's evident that the problem is being attacked from many different directions. It may seem that there is a lack of coordination, which in some respects is true, but I believe a broad range of approaches and solutions will continue to be required. There won't be one catchall way of dealing with the problem. I would like to see the State Bar continue to do its part by encouraging lawyers to volunteer their time. I'd like to see judges encourage pro bono work, because there are things they can do not only to help unrepresented litigants, but also to facilitate and encourage pro bono work by expediting certain procedures so that lawyers feel they can volunteer their time without sitting around all day in court waiting to perform their pro bono work. Also, I would like to see the provision of adequate funding for self-help centers and, in some situations, for the direct provision of legal assistance as we have it under the Sargent Shriver Civil Counsel Act pilot program. I believe a multifaceted approach is probably what's necessary, so it really boils down to adequate funding and having a culture established among lawyers and judges where this kind of effort is encouraged.

One thing that can help is the type of program the L.A. Superior Court and some other courts have experimented with—defining a category of litigation that will receive expedited processing. Under such economic litigation projects, there are vastly simplified discovery proceedings, so that you don't have a lot of delay and added expense, and these cases are heard sooner. They also have time limits in terms of how long each side is given to present its case. Cases involving minor damages shouldn't get drawn into all of the convoluted legal process that we have when one corporation is suing another one.

Shall we turn to the matter of jury-related reforms in our judiciary? I know you worked on several major reforms there.

Jury reform was one of those matters that rose to the top in terms of my interest, again influenced substantially by the round of visits in my first year as Chief Justice. I described to you the inadequacy of some of the jury facilities and the fact that they were nonexistent in some situations—jurors seated in crowded hallways, on concrete stairwells, standing out in the rain under umbrellas. This aspect, of course, ultimately relates to our courthouse transfer and construction program, but there were other things that were less tangible than actual buildings.

When I became chief, California was tied, oddly enough, with New Jersey as the two states providing the lowest daily compensation for persons serving on jury duty, namely five dollars a day. I managed to work with legislators to triple that to 15 dollars a day, which is still woefully inadequate. I believe the amount paid in federal court was about 40 dollars at the time. I don't know if it has been raised since then. What California pays is quite inadequate, but at least jurors aren't out-of-pocket anymore for their lunch and parking.

One of the things that I think has worked out extremely well on many different levels—benefiting the jurors, the litigants and the lawyers, and the system and the public's perception of it—is our legislation that created the "one day or one trial" mode of jury selection. Under that system, although one might be on call for a couple of weeks, having to check by phone to see whether one's group is summoned to the courthouse for jury service the next day, if you actually are told to show up at the courthouse and you do show up, you have completed your service for the year and are excused at the end of that first day if you have not been sent out from the jury assembly room to a courtroom engaged in jury selection that day. This is important in many respects. First of all, it makes it difficult for persons who perhaps are active professionals to say they are too busy to sit around for two weeks in the jury assembly room waiting to see if they'll be called. No one is too busy to show up for one day, and I believe that persons who actually end up serving on a jury by and large feel that it was a very worthwhile experience. But those who were sitting around for two weeks never seeing the inside of a courtroom often were quite embittered and considered the jury system and maybe the whole court system inefficient and insensitive in wasting their time.

I believe there are important consequences that come from how we treat or mistreat our jurors. To the extent that we mistreat them, this comes back to haunt us in many ways. It may affect how they serve as a juror on a case, but in any event it may affect how they vote in elections involving ballot measures affecting funding for improvements in the judicial system. It may also affect how they vote on judicial candidates. There's usually a quarter or a third of the electorate who will vote "no" in a judicial retention election or against the incumbent judge even when no issue has been raised. To the extent they're not treated well, that circumstance may impact them. It may affect how they communicate with their legislators in terms of judicial branch funding and policy matters.

In addition to all of that, treating jurors correctly is just the right thing to do. I think it's very important. Another way the system benefits from the "one day or one trial" mode of jury selection is that you end up with a much broader cross-section of the community serving on juries. You don't have the professionals getting out of jury duty that easily, based upon their occupational commitments. Having a broad cross-section of the community is important in many respects. I think you get a jury that's better able to cope with resolving the issues, due to the breadth of experience and background. You also satisfy the constitutional requirement of a jury of your peers representative of the community.

However minor the case may be, it can be the most important thing in the life of one or more of the parties appearing before that jury. Jury service is vitally important from the perspective of our citizens and their sense of sense of civic duty, and it gives them—as another benefit—a better understanding of the workings of our justice system. So when our citizens are called upon to pass judgment outside the jury box, at the election booth or elsewhere, they have a better, more realistic understanding of how our court system operates than they would have, had their understanding been premised solely upon watching television and motion picture dramatizations, with all the lack of realism inherent in those depictions. Many jurors observe that they would want themselves or a family member or close friend to have their case tried by a jury representative of the community at large.

I would, from time to time, receive phone calls from federal judges or other persons asking, "I can't possibly show up for jury duty. Could you get me excused? The local court won't do it. The presiding judge won't." I would always say, "How can I intervene? It wouldn't be right. Besides, I show up myself." I have honored a jury summons each of the four times I received one during my tenure as Chief Justice, and once since I left the bench earlier this year. I know the court personnel in Los Angeles were very happy to say, "Look, the Chief Justice has shown up here. So has the Cardinal." They give some examples at the jurors' orientation so someone who thinks he or she is a big shot because that person is a lawyer or a physician or business executive can't as readily claim to be too important to spend time serving on a jury. I've been very glad to try to set that example. As Woody Allen has said, "Ninety percent of life is about showing up." [Laughter] Just showing up sets an example.

May I ask where the idea came from to make it one day or one trial?

The Judicial Council, including myself and the Administrative Office of the Courts, were privy to writings and recommendations of various jury studies that had taken place over the years. Particularly instructive was the report of the Blue Ribbon Commission on Jury System Improvement, appointed by Chief Justice Lucas, which issued its report during my first month as Chief Justice, recommending a host of jury reforms. Although "one day or one trial" was not my idea, it's one that I very enthusiastically adopted and promoted. That program, and increasing the compensation of jurors, were the first two big jury reforms, not counting the construction of jury facilities.

The third such reform is one I was very much involved in planning and promoting—perhaps in part because of my own prior experience involving my years on the L.A. Superior Court serving on the CALJIC committee writing jury instructions. This reform was preparing jury instructions in plain English as opposed to the customary legalese. The way jurors are instructed on the law is another facet of how we treat or mistreat our jurors. To shove convoluted legal concepts on them and then expect them to apply them in their deliberations causes a certain degree of resentment. When the instructions are unnecessarily complex and filled with legal jargon, this complicates the already difficult task facing jurors in performing their duty to apply the law after resolving factual discrepancies.

I believe the civil and criminal jury instructions were revised separately. Which of those was in greater need?

I would say that perhaps the criminal law instructions were most in need of revision, because some truly archaic terms that were traditional in the area of criminal law caused constant difficulty for jurors. Additionally, some of the grammar, syntax, and choice of language were truly Victorian in style. The L.A. Superior Court formed committees beginning in the late 1930s—one for civil, BAJI, and one for criminal, CALJIC—and began to publish pattern jury instructions designed to replace the practice of judges of just sharing their work product with each other. The goal was to have a more standardized approach to jury instructions, which was a very important and worthwhile objective. West Publishing Company took over the cost of publishing these instructions in bound form. The L.A. Superior Court received many thousands of dollars in royalties, which they were able to put to whatever use they wanted. Although the instructions in these books were a Los Angeles product, judges around California and elsewhere came to use them as standard jury instructions. I viewed this as having been a very worthwhile effort on behalf of the court. The problem was that these instructions had not been converted into user-friendly language. To me, updating their style became a vital part of the goal of jury reform.

These standard or pattern jury instructions devised by the CALJIC and BAJI committees were basically snippets of appellate court opinions—in other words writings or communications between appellate court justices and their colleagues on the trial bench, and to lawyers, concerning which legal principles were involved in the case and how those principles should be applied. The instructions were not designed to carry out their basic function as effective tools of communication between judges and lay jurors. I felt it was absolutely essential to attempt to change this situation. I appointed a task force, which had numerous meetings with the Los Angeles judges. What we wanted to do was convert or translate these archaically worded instructions into more up-to-date, user-friendly language. We proposed putting L.A. Superior Court judges from the BAJI and CALJIC committees onto our new committee and giving them a prominent role. But they resisted this. I believe some of them felt that these old instructions have served everyone well for many, many years. Who knows if they'll be deemed deficient by appellate justices and cause judgments to be reversed? But to some judges the resistance seemed more like a turf war.

Because some of our most distinguished appellate justices, trial judges, lawyers, and academics were serving on the Judicial Council advisory committee on jury instructions, I did not share the concern about appellate reversals. Perhaps once in a while one of the new instructions would not pass muster, but that happens occasionally with the old instructions and doesn't justify blind adherence to an antiquated past practice. Some of the opposition to our new approach came not only from the traditionalists who found comfort in embracing jury instructions that went back to the 1930s—although periodically updated—but also was based upon a concern about the royalties involved, about whether CALJIC and BAJI royalties would still flow to the L.A. Superior Court. I heard some expressions along those lines. Because we could not come to an agreement—and we certainly didn't want to have litigation between the L.A. Superior Court and the Judicial Council over copyright issues and other things—I ultimately concluded that we weren't going to be able to revise these pattern or form instructions and that on this matter, as on so many others, there would be continued resistance by local judges to any change. The best course of action was to engage in a totally new effort, to start from scratch to research and draft brand new instructions based upon the existing law, without reference to the long existing instructions.

This was a difficult task because, on the one hand, it was imperative to avoid having convoluted, confusing, impenetrable legalese, but it was equally important not to misstate the law by an improved change in style that brought about an unintended change in meaning in the eyes of an appellate court and thereby risk reversal. I appointed a very capable First Appellate District Court of Appeal justice who later became my colleague on the Supreme Court, Carol Corrigan, to head up this effort. She took the main responsibility for the criminal area, and the civil area was the main responsibility of now-retired Justice James Ward of the Fourth Appellate District. They started right from scratch. This was thought to be a one- to two-year effort originally, when we were talking about basically cosmetic changes in wording. I got teased by Justice Corrigan as this project extended into more and more years, that I had essentially pulled a bait-and-switch operation. I had gotten her to agree to a quick rewrite, and instead involved her in an eight-year project of researching case and statutory law and drafting original new instructions. Justice Corrigan took in stride, with her characteristically wonderful sense of humor, the fact that I had gotten her into a much grander project. The end result was much better for it and received great national recognition and praise, including my receiving, jointly with the committee itself, the Burton Award for Legal Achievement I alluded to earlier.

I do want to share with you my favorite example that I think illustrates everything about the benefits of the new jury instructions, nicely encapsulated. The BAJI and CALJIC instructions of the L.A. Superior Court contained—and still do—a basic instruction to the jurors intended to guide them in determining the credibility of a witness who claims not to remember certain material events, an instruction whose wording probably would not pass muster with any high school grammar teacher or newspaper editor, in view of its syntax and double negative. The instruction reads: "Innocent misrecollection is not uncommon." This stilted language is difficult for jurors to understand. The new Judicial Council civil instruction on the same subject is straightforward and much easier to understand: "People often forget things." Our new criminal instruction is similar.

Now, there's just so far that you can go, and there is an old Court of Appeal opinion [*People v. Halbert*] from, I believe, the 1920s that says any jury that can't understand certain terms wouldn't be able to understand an explanation of them either. Justice Baxter once regaled my colleagues and me at one of our petition conferences with a story from his days as a deputy D.A. in Fresno County, relating that a jury hung up in a murder case because they thought that in light of the jury instructions, the prosecution had clearly failed to present proof of an important item of evidence in the homicide, the murder weapons. No "mallets" had been produced. Well, it was "malice." They thought that "malice," when the judge read it, meant mallets, and because there was no evidence suggesting that the victim had been killed with a mallet, the jury hung up. [Laughter] That was from his own experience.

The end product achieved by our committee of judges and lawyers was greatly assisted by nonlawyer experts in the art of draftsmanship, and by public comment from the bench and the bar. These new instructions have been well received by judges and scholars. They have not caused a wave of reversals of trial court judgments. I have been told anecdotally by judges—this is not a scientific study—that the new instructions seem to have substantially reduced the number of questions posed by deliberating jurors that inquire: "We can't figure this out. What does this mean? Would you reinstruct us?" It probably also has reduced the number of hung juries where the jury hangs up because it just can't figure out what to do, perhaps because the complex jury instructions didn't give them the guidance they felt they needed.

By the way, the former L.A. Superior Court committees now operate as West Publishing Company committees that continue to publish the old instructions, which are used less frequently by trial judges than the new Judicial Council instructions.

I'll just briefly cover a couple other things involving jury reform. Local courts have been encouraged to undertake their own efforts to make jury service more enjoyable. An example of the innovations that occurred once we got going on jury reform included Stanislaus County's having a cappuccino cart come into the jury assembly room. Just little things like that can make a big difference. Some counties—I believe San Diego is one of them—would provide free public transportation to and from the courthouse, on the city's trolley cars, for jurors displaying their juror's identification badge. There was another county or two that did the same on their municipal bus lines. Some courts had arrangements with local business establishments to provide discounts for meals purchased by jurors while serving on jury duty.

I also sent a letter that went to 10,000 senior business executives in 2003 calling for the establishment of a roster of businesses that were paying employees their wages while they served on jury duty, because the only obligation imposed on a juror's employer under the law—it's found in the Labor Code—is for the employer not to discriminate against the employee by reason of his or her taking the time to engage in jury service. But there is no obligation by the employer to actually pay the employee's wages while on jury duty, so we encouraged businesses to do that nonetheless. I'm looking here at an *L.A. Times* editorial from 2003 that says: "The Chief Justice recently wrote 10,000 senior executives who don't pay their employees, asking them to weigh the importance of jury service to our democratic ideals against the relatively modest cost." The editorial then goes on to note that I had compiled an honor roll of companies that continue to compensate their employees during their jury service. At our urging, some bar associations, including Los Angeles, have been putting together a list of participating law firms that are following the same example set by these businesses, this being even more appropriate for legal professionals.

What kind of response did you get from the business community and from the legal community?

To the extent there was response, it was mainly favorable, although not entirely so. Some persons would talk about the cost to the business, complaining to me directly. I would say, "How would you like it if you or your business had a case that was of great importance to you and all you had was retired people, and kids just out of school who hadn't been able to get a job yet, serving on your jury? Wouldn't you want more of a cross-section of the population?" Some of them would get that point.

Additionally, we would declare a juror appreciation day. Some of us on a national level—I believe it was through the Conference of Chief Justices—proposed to the federal government that there be a postage stamp promoting jury duty, since the post office seems to honor just about everything else. This was done, and stamps were issued proclaiming appreciation for jury duty. There also are pamphlets and orientation videotapes for prospective jurors that include a message from me stressing the importance of jury duty. Again, sort of a bully pulpit approach.

What else would you like to see in the way of reforms to benefit the jurors' participation and experience?

We really need to increase their compensation. I believe that is fundamental. It's not all about money, but the compensation that is given to them does say something about how we value their time, and I think it's kind of insulting to give them a fraction of the minimum wage prescribed by law. Perhaps we can further improve the determination of when we need to summon in jurors who are on telephonic call. But by and large I believe the system is working well.

I consider trial by jury to be a vital part of our whole system of justice and democratic form of government. It's based upon having—unlike the situation in some other countries—a buffer between the state and the individual. One's fellow citizens are standing in judgment on your case. It isn't just the often massive power of the state facing a litigant, especially in a criminal matter, but rather having one's peers stand in judgment on whether the government has made its case or hasn't. Again, that may be something we take for granted but that we should cherish.

An entirely different area but one in which you did some reform throughout the judicial branch is the whole matter of private judging—judges who are partici- pating in our system but also, either simultaneously or after the fact, are in- volved in private judging. You did talk about putting in place a system where sitting judges could do either/or but not both during the same year. But let me ask you to give an overview of that area and what you worked on.

My feelings about private judging are somewhat mixed. The reality is that we need to have it as long as our public judicial system is not provided with adequate funding and resources, including a sufficient number of judgeships to handle the burgeoning caseload. California appears to be one of the most liti- gious areas in the United States, and our country in turn is far more litigious than most other nations, so public and private judging clearly are growth industries. I'm grateful for the contribution that persons involved in private judging have made to lessen the strain experienced by the court system in trying to deal with the existing caseload. That effort probably has reduced what would be even more delay in our public court system. I'm sorry there is such a need for this, however. In an ideal system we would not need to depend upon private judging. We might have private judging only in those small categories of cases where the litigants want to avoid public scrutiny and conduct the proceedings in secrecy to protect the privacy of those involved.

I've been a big exponent of opening up the court system, so naturally, in rulings I've made for the court and in administrative actions I've taken, I have struck down restrictions on public access to our public system of justice. My feelings are that we have to ensure public access subject to the narrowest of ex- ceptions. When privacy is terribly important, the litigants have to opt for private judging. Sometimes there are other reasons to choose private judging— occasionally, but certainly not always, the decision may be speedier in a private forum. You also may be able to handpick your decision maker.

But some problems do occur with private judging. One of them, you've al- ready noted, is a problem of potential conflict of interest, which I dealt with by not permitting persons to go back and forth by doing public and private judging simultaneously, public by assignment and private by arrangement. Another un- fortunate perception arises; people are led to believe there is a two-track system of justice, one that may be speedier, and where those who can afford it can pick their own decision maker. For those who can't, they wait in line and receive some sort of service that's inferior. I believe that, to a large extent, those perceptions are inaccurate, but I understand how they arise.

There are particular deficiencies that were very well expressed in an opinion rendered by Court of Appeal Justice Miriam Vogel from the Second Appellate District, who is now retired from the bench and engaged in private appellate practice. Shortly after I became Chief Justice, the opinion that she wrote in the case of *McMillan v. Superior Court* was the subject of requests to depublish. I had to be absent from the court's petition conference at an out-of-state meeting and did not anticipate that my colleagues would vote to depublish this opinion, because I thought it made some very insightful observations related to abuses that occur in the use of referees as well as private judging. Although no longer published in the official reports of the court of appeal, the opinion still can be found in the unofficial reports as *McMillan v. Superior Court* (1996) 57 Cal.Rptr.2d 674. There were private judges who formerly served at various levels of the state court system who petitioned the California Supreme Court to have Justice Vogel's opinion ordered not for publication in the official reports, meaning it would not be citable as precedent and would not appear in the bound volumes. Had I anticipated as a new Chief Justice—I didn't—that perhaps this opinion might be depublished, I would have had the matter put over to a later conference when I would be there to advocate for it.

But in any event—and I'll quote a few sentences here from her opinion— Justice Miriam Vogel addressed what she called "the problems inherent in the creation of a second separate judicial system." She noted: "For some time it has been apparent that our state court judges have been required to handle too many cases with too few resources. What this means of course is that the public purse strings remain tightly knotted while litigants are given the privilege of paying twice, first through taxation, then again through a user's fee disguised as a payment for a referee to handle discovery disputes so trial judges can try cases. What this also means is that our courts are experiencing the wholesale departure of judges from the public system to the greener pastures of private judging, where they can and do earn more money, receive more help, obtain better accommodations, and work as many or as few hours as they choose." She goes on, "We are aware that many lawyers believe some referees favor larger firms because they will be repeat customers, try to compromise to avoid angering either set of lawyers and losing a source of repeat business, improperly threaten adverse rulings if obviously excessive fees are questioned, and so on." She also points out that, through the L.A. Superior Court's reference procedure, a process was thrust upon unwilling participants who didn't even select private judging in the case and yet by court order were compelled to pay for it. She notes that "The judicial system is suffering from the competition among and the conduct by some private judges and mediators," and that "trial judges are not entitled to abdicate their judicial responsibility by simply rubberstamping whatever the referee does." She concludes: "Our concern is that we are too fast approaching when the law in its majestic equality will forbid the poor from using not only a private system restricted to the wealthy but also the public system theoretically available to all. Before it is too late we believe the legislature should re-examine the entire notion of involuntary references and either withdraw its approval of these references or at least impose some limitations on the process. To leave things as they are is to slam the courthouse doors in the face of the poor."

Justice Vogel was dealing with the involuntary submission of discovery matters to referees by judges who were often appointing their then-retired colleagues from the L.A. Superior Court bench as referees. But what she says is insightful beyond that, in terms of the concerns that some people have—and I share many of them—pertaining to the entire system of private judging. Again, the prevalence of that system reflects the inadequacy of the resources provided to our public justice system, which as I've mentioned to you I regard as one of the core functions of our government.

You mentioned that the Supreme Court had communications from those hoping the opinion would be depublished. What sort of response did the opinion get, aside from that?

I recall that it created a bit of a to-do. I believe that's why certain prominent members of the private judging corps petitioned to have the opinion ordered not for publication. I doubt that our court's action, depublishing Justice Vogel's opinion, would meet the later adopted standards that came out of Justice Werdegar's committee that I mentioned to you, prescribing that an opinion should not be depublished to protect the viewpoint or reputation of others.

She was calling on the legislature to step in here?

Yes. Interestingly enough, after studying the problems highlighted by Justice Vogel's opinion, the legislature did, at the behest of the Judicial Council, take action to bring about some reforms, and changes have been made to the Rules of Court. However, the legislature had a very difficult time passing a bill establishing standards of conduct and disclosure applicable to persons engaged in private dispute resolution, having been lobbied fiercely on the subject. They chose a device that I proposed to them on this occasion and on some later occasions as well. When they had difficulty coming up with a precise solution, they could pass a bill directing the Judicial Council to adopt rules on such-and-such a subject. This would get the legislature off the hook and would provide a more meaningful input through the Judicial Council's fact-gathering process for fine tuning rules that would approach the problem with judicial expertise and that would not be written in concrete to the degree that legislation would be. It's far easier of course to modify a rule of court than a bill signed into law. The California Constitution expressly, in its grant of authority to the Judicial Council over various matters, specifies that the council, in order to improve the administration of justice, shall survey judicial business, make recommendations to the courts, make recommendations to the governor and the legislature, and "adopt rules for court administration, practice and procedure, and perform other functions prescribed by statute." In effect, that last clause provides an open invitation and authority for the legislature to refer any appropriate matter to the Judicial Council for resolution through the council's rule-making authority or otherwise. There's another part of that same section of the constitution, article VI, section 6, that provides: "Judges shall report to the Council as the Chief Justice directs concerning the condition of judicial business in their courts. They shall cooperate with the Council and hold court as assigned." That provision has relevance to a later discussion you and I probably will have relating to the efforts of some judges to disengage themselves from what they view as state control and go their own way without being part of the statewide administration of justice. But the standards of conduct that the Judicial Council adopted—pursuant to this constitutional authority—for persons engaged in private dispute resolution have worked quite well and solved a problem that the legislature was unable to solve itself.

While we're discussing the general subject of ethics, I want to mention that the adoption of ethical standards for judges—which is another topic we might touch upon briefly—is a matter that the constitution entrusts to the Supreme Court, not the Judicial Council.[2] The court amended the provisions in the Code of Judicial Ethics that pertain to prohibited political activity to also apply those provisions to lawyer candidates for judicial office, and gave formal required approval to the State Bar's related changes to the rules of professional conduct, thereby making the pertinent canon in the code applicable to lawyer candidates for judicial office.

How tough a sell was that?

I don't think it was all that tough a sell. Obviously there must have been some lawyers who were displeased. There have been campaigns such as, "My

---

[2] Cal. Const., art. VI, sec. 18, subd. (m).

opponent, Judge So-and-So, has never sentenced a single person to state prison." Well, the opponent was a municipal court judge who could only sentence people on misdemeanors, which involve county jail sentences. [Laughter] That's an egregious example, but there were many others.

The Supreme Court also exercised its constitutional authority over judicial ethics to establish a committee charged with issuing opinions interpreting the Code of Judicial Ethics.[3] Judges also were provided with what amounts to malpractice insurance, at no cost to them, for their legal defense in proceedings that might be brought against them before the Commission on Judicial Performance, provided they have taken an ethics course. So ethics education basically became mandatory, unless a judge chooses to serve without the protection of the legal defense provided for disciplinary proceedings. Like almost every other judge in the state, I signed up for the ethics course, again to set an example. More recently, we've arranged for opinions of the Commission on Judicial Performance to be published in the Official Reports that contain the opinions of the California Supreme Court, so that the commission's opinions will be readily available to provide notice to judges and justices concerning what is permissible judicial behavior and what is not. Those are various things that we have done in recent years in the area of ethics.

What about the matter of ethics as it relates to private judging?

There have been complaints that private judges are not held to the same standards as judges who serve in our public courts as far as disclosure of potential conflicts of interest is concerned. Certainly California has very high standards as to what it requires of the judges who preside in its courts. Although the measures that you and I just discussed have brought about some major improvements as far as disclosures and potential conflicts of interest pertaining to private judges, there remains a rather troubling aspect that one can't really put one's finger on. This relates to the inevitable tendency of private judges to be influenced, perhaps subconsciously, by the repeat litigant—often an institutional litigant who appears before you—who you want to keep retaining you, and the possibility that certain categories of cases—if not decided favorably to that litigant—will not be coming your way in the future. The private judge, unlike the public judge, cannot totally disregard the impact of his or her decision making on the judge's pecuniary interest. I know that sounds harsh, but Justice Vogel was correct in pointing that out.

---

[3] Retired Judge David Rothman has devoted years to writing and updating his authoritative *California Judicial Conduct Handbook*, a treatise on judicial ethics.

I remember an old case from way back in law school—I think I did have occasion to cite it once or twice since then—that involved a public, not private, judge. I believe the case was *Tumey v. Ohio* in the U.S. Supreme Court, where the compensation of the local judge—and the funds available to his court—were determined by the amount generated by the fines that the judge would impose upon those litigants whom the judge found guilty. Obviously, if not a direct conflict of interest, there certainly was an appearance of a conflict. The U.S. Supreme Court found this to be a denial of due process. We don't tolerate such a conflict of interest in a public court. But isn't there something akin to that in the situation of the private judge who isn't directly receiving compensation the same way, but still may be receiving an overall financial benefit that may relate to the outcome of the disputes brought before that judge? At least there certainly can be that perception.

It's an interesting question, and as you say private judging is a fact of our system. We aren't taking care of all judging matters without it, so it's easy to see how all these kinds of complexities have developed. One that we mentioned and haven't talked about too much yet is the phenomenon of judges in our system who go into retirement and engage in private judging. They have often been longtime public servants at a limited income, and this is of course a natural way for them to continue their careers and make more money. What view do you take of all that?

I'm sympathetic to a judge feeling the need to augment his or her retirement income, especially those in what's called the Judge's Retirement System II. The law was changed to provide a substantially inferior retirement benefit for judges who first took judicial office after November 1994. Of course, it's up to each judge to determine what he or she may need or want as additional income. Private judging, like sitting by assignment after retiring, offers the stimulation of being active intellectually and resolving disputes to the benefit of the parties and the overburdened court system. I'm certainly not critical of judges wanting to go into private judging. I'm especially pleased that many retired judges, more than 400, have chosen instead to participate in the assigned judges' program, where they make very substantial contributions to our public judging system while supplementing their retirement benefits. But it may be that private judging needs to be subject to more of the rules and practices that govern retired judges who serve by assignment in our public courts, in order to avoid some of these potential or perceived conflicts of interest. I would like to see the need and demand for private judging lessened through the provision of adequate resources and judgeships to the public sector's judicial system, so that only exceptional circumstances—such as the need for confidentiality—would motivate litigants to opt for private judging.

What chance, if any, did you have to talk with Justice Vogel about her thoughts and her decision in this case?

I do remember hearing from her at one point how disappointed she was that her opinion had been ordered depublished. Without making much in the way of excuses, I did explain to her that I certainly would not have voted to take that action and that it was done in my absence from conference. I believe most Court of Appeal justices, including she, are fairly resigned to whatever action the California Supreme Court takes with regard to either a depublication order or a reversal of a judgment that they have rendered. Not that the Supreme Court is omniscient by any means, but it does have a different perspective. We have the benefit of a statewide, systemic perception of the issue involved in a case that probably goes beyond that of the authoring Court of Appeal justices just by reason of the circumstance that we consider about 10,000 petitions every year seeking review and other relief, and we're able to see how frequently an issue arises and, even more importantly, in how many and varied contexts the issue arises.

Something that understandably may have seemed quite clear and appropriate in the context of one case before the Court of Appeal may be viewed from a different perspective by the justices of the Supreme Court. I don't mean to imply that the Court of Appeal justices have blinders on when it comes to the practical results or the ramifications of their rulings for future cases and other litigants, but only that the Supreme Court, being the statewide court that has such a great amount and variety of litigation come up to its level, does of necessity acquire a broader perspective.

The big picture is different, shall we say?

Yes. It's a bigger picture.

I wonder if we might touch just briefly on the question of alternative dispute resolution of various kinds. What is the place of that in the overall system?

Of course, by and large, that is up to parties to arrange willingly. But a matter that's been of concern to me and to the court over the years is that often the agreement of parties to be bound by alternative dispute resolution may not be one that is entered into in a totally voluntary way. There have been decisions of our court—they were not authored by me, but I can remember a couple of them off the top of my head—that were significant in this area of the law. The *En-*

galla case and the *Armendariz* case expressed a concern that in many situations there exists something akin to what is usually termed a contract of adhesion, where there is such a disparity in bargaining power that there isn't a true opportunity on the part of one party to say, "No, I won't sign this agreement subjecting myself to mandatory arbitration." What do you do if you have a dispute with the phone company or perhaps with your healthcare provider or your stockbroker? You often are placed in the situation of having had to sign away your right to go to court in order to do business with one of these entities.

Those are good examples, because that kind of phrasing appears in all kinds of places, doesn't it?

Yes it does. Those opinions of our court are very interesting reading because they go through a litany of promises set forth in contractual language, sometimes promising speedier resolution—which is not always the case, in fact—or impartial and dispassionate resolution of the dispute. Note that it's one thing, perhaps, when you've got two big boys who enter into an agreement—General Motors decides that it's going to buy its steel from U.S. Steel. One party or the other doesn't live up to the agreement. They can agree to any means they want to resolve any dispute that may arise, whether it's dispute resolution by a private judge or arm wrestling. [Laughter] But when it comes to the consumer entering into that agreement with General Motors or another powerful entity, it is a very different matter. I do have a real concern about the inequality of bargaining power.

There's an opinion I wrote in the *Grafton* case, which held you can't be bound to a waiver of your right to jury trial in a predispute situation. It's one thing if you end up having a dispute with an entity and then decide that you are going to waive jury and the other side does too. But to agree even before a dispute arises that if you should have to go to court you won't have the right to jury trial is not permissible. That's another, slightly different aspect of the problem that you and I are discussing.

It's a matter of the balance of power in a lot of these situations.

Exactly right. The parties that have at least a rough equality of bargaining power or at least don't have a gross disparity in bargaining power, and where there's a true choice whether to do something other than sign on to compulsory arbitration, can agree to pretty much anything they want in my view. But otherwise, there has to be a certain fairness in the process.

How frequently did the court take on these kinds of matters?

We first began to take them on after the landmark *Moncharsh* decision authored by Chief Justice Lucas, establishing the rule that arbitration rulings resulting from a contractual agreement to arbitrate are not subject to judicial review for errors of fact or law, except in the most narrowly defined circumstances. It was thought by some that arbitration had pretty much been given free reign
by that decision. We later began to see cases, in which Supreme Court review
was being sought, showing that—in addition to the narrow exceptions recognized in *Moncharsh*—there was a need to ensure that before a party was held by
an agreement to engage in arbitration against its will, the agreement had been
entered into under circumstances that were fair.

*It's a large area that probably holds much more activity in the future. Did your
own views of that change over time?*

I initially was not as aware of the frequency of situations in which there was
a true disparity in bargaining power. Some of these cases that reached us certainly opened my eyes to that being a real problem. I believe our court rendered
some important decisions that somewhat leveled the playing field and no longer
left it a field on which David and Goliath do battle. [Laughter]

###

Chapter 15

Reforming the Judicial System
October 26, 2011

I thought we'd start today with a brief discussion of a few other reforms that you undertook while you were Chief Justice of California. I think the first of those had to do with rulemaking?

Yes. As we mentioned before, the Judicial Council has explicit rulemaking authority under article VI, section 6, of the California Constitution, specifically in the words of the constitution: the authority to "adopt rules for court administration, practice and procedure, and perform other functions prescribed by statute. The rules adopted shall not be inconsistent with statute."

The Judicial Council's enactment of statewide rules affecting court procedure and administration, among other subjects, is an area of considerable importance. In the annual liaison meetings I had with our various justice system partners, concerns were expressed that although we were one statewide court system now that we had achieved state trial court funding and unification, a wide array of practices, sometimes formalized in rules, continued to impede the effective practice of law from one jurisdiction to another and within various districts of a single superior court. That had been even more true before unification, when you had 25 separate courts in Los Angeles County—each one potentially with its own rules on certain matters that affected attorneys' practices. As a result of these concerns, the council, at my urging and that of others, began to exercise more and more of the constitutional rulemaking authority that it possessed but had not fully exercised in the past. We basically began to preempt more local rules by promulgating additional statewide rules in areas such as law and motion and discovery practice and adding to the rules in probate, so that attorneys would not face inconsistent requirements in their practice of law. Of course, there was resistance to this, I think in some instances just because there are judges who seem to oppose anything that's new. But this development was greeted with a lot of appreciation by the bar. Lawyers usually were not confining their practice to one district of a court or to a single court. For them, it was almost like having to pass through national borders with customs officials every few miles.

I had received numerous complaints about the Los Angeles Superior Court's so-called blueback rule. If you didn't have a sheet of blue paper between certain segments of the filing, your filing might be rejected. I heard from one bar leader that he'd gone to one of the district courts on the last day for filing and had had his pleading rejected because it didn't conform with the blueback rule. This rule became notorious and a major matter of contention.

Moreover, some judges just felt they should have full authority, full discretion, to do whatever they wanted in terms of establishing rules for their own courtroom apart from the courtwide rules. Some of their rules were quite parochial and in a way silly. These were called "local local" rules, meaning basically that individual judges posted their own rules on the door at the entrance to the courtroom. This caused real difficulties in terms of lawyers from around the state having to comport themselves in a very detailed manner consistent with the predilections of the individual judge who happened to be sitting in that courtroom. These "local local" rules in effect proclaimed: "In addition to any statewide rules, and apart from what the Los Angeles Superior Court as a whole might require by its rules, in Department X thou shalt do such-and-such if you want your papers accepted, or if you want to approach the bench or a witness, or if you want to offer an exhibit."

The Judicial Council attempted to develop best practices by learning what the different courts were doing and why they had a preference for doing things a certain way. Before statewide rules would be promulgated, we would study that input and then try to establish what was the best practice and modify it accordingly if necessary. This was one more facet of developing what truly became a statewide administration of justice, as opposed to a set of what was 220 fiefdoms of individual trial courts in California, each doing things its own way for historical or other reasons. This ties in a bit with what I said about jury instructions, trying to have something that was user-friendly—in that case for jurors and here user-friendly for attorneys or unrepresented litigants. I know that some of my former colleagues on the L.A. Superior Court had just assumed that because I was an alumnus of the L.A. court, I would automatically stand up for anything that the court was doing. I had to remind them that I considered myself the Chief

Justice for all the 58 counties and the courts and the public served by those courts, and it wasn't just a question of loyally adhering to what I had grown up with while serving as a judge in the Los Angeles courts.

In Los Angeles, but also elsewhere, how were these new rules received?

I think with some grumbling, but for the most part now I think they are just considered an everyday matter. But again, it was more the concept of change—and change coming from the statewide administration of justice, the Judicial Council—than the actual substance of the change that often caused the "ruffling of feathers," as I would put it.

What caused you to begin taking on this matter of making more uniform rules throughout the state?

Basically our justice system partners, the attorneys, were quite perplexed and burdened by this array of different rules from jurisdiction to jurisdiction. When plaintiffs' attorneys and the civil defense bar agreed there was a problem that needed to be fixed, that would catch my attention. It was at their behest that I considered this situation and agreed that there was a problem and that something should be done about it. Again, this was—like virtually all of my efforts—not something I did unilaterally but that I established working groups or committees or task forces to study, to come up with proposals and circulate them widely among the bench and bar for public comment, to modify the proposals in accordance with comment when that was necessary, once in a while to abandon the idea if it proved not to be worthwhile, but otherwise to go ahead, keeping in mind the statewide interest of the public.

Let's turn to something that may have been universally well received, and that was your efforts to establish new judgeships and also to raise judicial salaries in the state.

Part of the problem in terms of workload was the grossly inadequate number of judgeships. The process for creating new judgeships had been a highly political process in the past. There might or might not be a particular need for one or more additional judgeships, but often the determination whether to create them was governed by political factors such as who wanted them, who were the likely appointees, who was the governor who would be appointing them, and was the legislature of the same party as the governor? There often were trade-offs where a county that wanted more judgeships, presumably because there was a need for them, couldn't garner legislative support from other areas of the state to create those judgeships. In order to get those votes, the legislators from the county in need would say, "We'll give you an additional judgeship or two here as part of the package to entice you to vote for our judgeships." In some instances the legislative log-rolling process created judgeships that really weren't needed, at both the trial and the appellate levels.

One of the things that I was very grateful for—among the various efforts of judges, court administrators, and lawyers to improve the administration of justice in our state—was the work of the Judgeship Needs Task Force that conducted caseload-based surveys of exactly where there was a need to propose additional judgeships. For many years it seemed like an empty exercise, but eventually the group was listened to. The Judicial Council asked the National Center for State Courts, which serves as the staff for the Conference of Chief Justices, to conduct a neutral survey of the additional judicial positions needed by California. This was totally outside the political spectrum. They were experts brought in from out of state. The result was a recommendation that, at a bare minimum, California needed 350 additional judgeships. I used that study to come up with a proposal for 150 of the most-needed new judgeships and—to make it politically more feasible—broke it into three segments of 50 each. We persuaded the legislature and the governor to create the first batch of 50 judgeships and then finally to provide funding for them. We also were successful in obtaining passage of legislation that is allowing the conversion of 162 court commissioner positions to judgeships over a ten-year period. It took a lot of doing, but first of all the legislature agreed to our methodology—that a nonpolitical, judge-determined process would be used to determine where the new judgeships would go. What was significant and truly impressive was that the legislation allocated the judgeships by making specific cross-reference to the Judicial Council report indicating where the new judgeships were most needed.

We did manage to get the first 50 new judgeships. On the second phase, we obtained authorization for 50 more but then the economy went south and the funding was postponed year after year, so we're still in that process. Hopefully, the third batch of 50 will eventually be authorized and funded too. But by now, with the additional growth in population and litigation, that 150 figure—which was inadequate to begin with—is even less than what is needed today. To illustrate this point, I would refer to our discussion concerning the task force of judges that I assigned to go down to Riverside County to help handle its caseload. Although there were a couple of other factors that contributed to the crisis there, first and foremost was the growth in population—and therefore in litigation—in that county. I'm hopeful we can do more to create additional judgeships. It's not a question of trying to make things easier for the very hardworking judges who frequently work under next-to-impossible conditions, but rather of enabling the courts to perform their basic function of providing the public with access to justice. If there aren't enough judges to handle the caseload, there won't be an opportunity to have one's case heard, no matter how fair the judicial process is. I mentioned how the court had entirely stopped hearing civil cases in Riverside County, and that criminal cases were being dismissed.

It also became imperative to raise judicial salaries. That's another component of keeping enough qualified people on the bench without having them leave, not only for greener pastures, but in many cases telling me with teary eyes that they simply could no longer financially afford to stay on the bench. I had judges tell me that there was nothing they would rather be doing, but given their obligations to their family and the need to help their offspring through college, they just could not afford to live on a judge's salary. I undertook an effort to obtain higher judicial salaries in addition to the increases that are automatically provided by law. There's a section of the Government Code, I believe it's 68203, that provides a yearly increase to judges tied to the average salary adjustment provided to state employees. But I felt the judges had fallen enough behind that that they needed an extra boost on top of the automatic increases, so I went to Governor Davis and convinced him there should be a 17 percent judicial pay raise in addition to the annual increase. For political purposes, it was agreed that breaking it into two packages of 8.5 percent each would be most likely to succeed. The legislature and the governor approved the special 8.5 percent increase in the first round. Then there was a set of circumstances, including both the economic downturn and the recall of Governor Davis—which meant having a new governor who was not bound to the commitment made by Governor Davis—that caused the second half of the increase to fall through.

The inadequacy of judicial salaries is a national problem, and there have been recent reports about lawsuits filed by the judges in New York State because of this situation and finally a partial remedy enacted by that state's legislature after years of inaction. Federal judges many years ago instituted litigation, which reached the U.S. Supreme Court, challenging their compensation.[1] Even without the second 8.5 percent increase, California—when I last checked—was number one in the salaries paid to its judges, even though they still don't receive adequate compensation, especially given the cost of living here. Certainly, as I mentioned, the retirement system for more recently appointed judges provides a woefully inadequate retirement benefit, especially as compared to those earlier appointees in the first tier, such as myself. I engaged in a major effort every year to increase judicial salaries and retirement benefits. Even in bad fiscal years, I'd make a point of talking to the governor in question and pointing out that we

---

[1] United States v. Will (1980) 449 U.S. 200.

were losing very good judges—and failing to attract a diverse pool of applicants from both the private sector and the public sector in our diverse legal community—because of the fact that our retirement system, even more than our salary compensation, was inadequate. Overall, between the years 2000 and 2010 the salary of California's trial judges was increased by 45 percent—from about $122,000 to about $178,000. The higher salaries of appellate justices were similarly increased.

Whom did you work with in trying to increase judicial salaries?

The bar was very supportive, and I believe that the various governors and legislators began to understand this truly was a problem. Of course, some legislators would gripe that judges already were making much more than legislators. But judges were basically career individuals, whereas many legislators were not, especially under term limits. The legislators were not in a comparable situation, but we received no sympathy from them regarding our retirement benefits, given that the California Supreme Court's decision upholding term limits had totally eliminated future retirement benefits for all legislators.

This may be something that the media and the public don't readily have much context for. Once you won these salary increases, what kind of response did you get out there in the world?

There was gratitude from most of the judges, but like much of the gratitude that anyone in the public or private sectors receives, it is usually temporary and soon replaced with the attitude, "What have you done for me lately?" [Laughter] We made a strong case for higher judicial salaries that is illustrated by a story that appeared in the legal newspaper the *Daily Journal*. The headline read: "No Justice If the Chief Justice Earns Less Than a First-Year." The article states: "For himself Chief Justice Ron George is taking the situation with good humor," and quotes me as saying: "'It does put things in focus when one's own offspring two or three years out of law school can surpass one's salary as a Chief Justice. But that also has a comforting aspect when it is your *own* offspring.'"[2] [Laughter] Putting aside the higher salaries received by lawyers in the private sector, I indicated in the interview that I was particularly concerned about discrepancies within the public sector, where a deputy D.A., or deputy public defender, deputy county counsel, or deputy city attorney in a metropolitan area at the Grade 4 level routinely earns more than a judge. There's no legitimate justification for why a line deputy D.A. should make more than the judge before whom he or she

---

[2] *Daily Journal*, February 4, 2002.

is appearing. That discrepancy did have an effect on the ability to recruit and retain judges on the bench.

There were other disconcerting aspects of judicial compensation. The Los Angeles courts had sort of a sweetheart deal with the county board of supervisors where the board members' salaries were pegged to those of the superior court judges. Back in the old days, when there were block grants to counties for each judgeship, the judges had to give their consent to those grants. My understanding from the history of this process is that the judges gave their consent with the implicit understanding that they would in turn receive fringe benefits that the counties bestowed upon the county's own top executive officers. The judges and the supervisors both were receiving something of benefit that the other received, scratching each other's backs, so to speak. With the added benefits and funds provided by the county, totaling about $46,000, judges of the L.A. Superior Court were, and presumably still are, receiving more by way of overall compensation than the higher jurisdiction justices of the Court of Appeal in their own geographical area. Some judges maintained there was nothing wrong with that disparity or with the difference in compensation that resulted statewide among superior court judges, even though the constitution specifies that the legislature shall "prescribe" the compensation of judges.[3] That word has been interpreted over the years, in various contexts, as designating a non-delegable function, meaning that the legislature itself has to fix judicial salaries—which theoretically it was doing but, as a practical matter, was not doing in Los Angeles.

After a lawsuit was brought, the Court of Appeal in 2008 held in the *Sturgeon* case that the county benefits received by the Los Angeles judges were invalid for the reason I just mentioned. After the Court of Appeal issued its opinion, some judges in Los Angeles, and to a lesser extent in a couple of the other counties where the judges received substantial county-provided benefits, were furious at the Supreme Court and therefore, above all, at me for our court's not granting review in that case. Their reaction to this dilemma provided a good illustration of the naïveté and lack of awareness of some judges concerning the legislative process and the political realities involved in that process, and most disturbingly an unawareness of what was mandated by well-established constitutional and legal principles. Had our court taken up the case, I'm confident we would have been compelled by law to come to the same result reached by the Court of Appeal.

After we declined to grant review, the Los Angeles court—and local lawyers enlisted to support it—came running to me to ask that I lobby in Sacramento for a solution to restore their benefits through effective legislative authoriza-

---

[3] Cal. Const., art. VI, sec. 19.

tion. I devoted my energies and expended a lot of political capital in strenuously lobbying the legislature for the enactment of special, carefully crafted legislation providing authorization for the payment of these extra benefits by the counties to the judges because, with such legislative authorization, the benefits would pass muster under the constitution. Without specific legislative authorization they would not. Here the judges seemed to have no problem with my butting into matters of local practices and benefits. [Laughter]

The legislature held the purse strings?

Right, but it was fundamentally a legal question of complying with the constitution's mandate that the legislature "prescribe"—or specifically authorize—the additional compensation. Once the legislature said, in effect, "We prescribe that judges around the state shall receive *x* number of dollars, and we further prescribe that they may also receive additional benefits offered by their counties," it was performing its task under the law of prescribing the compensation to be received by judges. To get back to your earlier question, once the bill was signed into law—yes, there was effusive gratitude. When I visited the Los Angeles judges at their request, the presiding judge of the court, Charles (Tim) McCoy, presented me with a Louisville Slugger baseball bat signed by each member of the court's executive committee and the court's executive officer, inscribed "Home run, Chief!" But again, that was good for the day, and we soon moved on to other matters involving occasional disagreements.

Who were your allies in the legislature on this matter?

Some Los Angeles-based legislators, certainly, and I believe some lawyers who were in leadership positions and saw that it was important to me and the Judicial Council and to the local courts to try to remedy this problem. As you can imagine, the appellate court's decision had not prompted any outrage in the state Capitol. Nor was the press particularly supportive of our legislative rescue mission.

It's an interesting matter, though, to compare the salaries of judges with those of other public servants trained as lawyers. What do you think the structure should be, or what other improvements could be made for the salary structure at all levels of the state judiciary?

I believe a critical guiding principle is that we should be able to attract and retain the best and the brightest and do so from a wide-ranging diverse pool of applicants so that we don't only recruit to the bench middle-aged lawyers who have managed to accumulate a lot of money in their private practice and can afford, with what they've squirreled away, to make a financial sacrifice by going on the bench. We also want to have a segment of accomplished public lawyers, but we won't even have them if the public lawyers are receiving a higher salary or greater retirement benefits than the judges. One of my bosses in the attorney general's office, Bill James, was acknowledged to be one of the very, very top appellate lawyers in the state, and he turned down a judgeship because he could not afford, with his family of many children, to take the salary cut from being an assistant attorney general to being a judge.

Interestingly enough, some of the finest lawyers from racial and ethnic minority groups are earnestly sought after by private firms that are eager to diversify—whether that is because it's the right thing to do, or to attract a wider range of clientele. I was told by the ethnic bar associations that the best and the brightest of the racial and ethnic minorities were receiving salaries high enough that it made a career on the bench much more difficult for them to accept. The goal has to be to have a bench not appointed on a quota system by any means, but one that generally reflects a picture of what our society in California is like today, a judiciary that's not monochromatic or drawn only from a certain social or economic level of our society.

Another thing we managed to do for the most senior or eldest judges and justices—at the instigation of Justice Mosk and Justice Vaino Spencer, who were both in a position to offer political assistance—was persuade the legislature to remove the age cap on retirement benefits. It used to be that if you stayed on the bench past the age of 70—later on it was changed to starting a term after the age of 70—the retirement benefit was cut very substantially. That penalty provision was eliminated, so that was another success we had in the area of salaries and benefits. In the past, the California judiciary had lost some of its most distinguished members, such as Chief Justice Roger Traynor, because of this penalty imposed by the judges' retirement system. There was also a program to induce judges to stay on the bench after they reached their retirement eligibility age, in the form of an increased benefit they would receive once they ultimately did retire. Something would be added for each year they stayed beyond eligibility. Many judges were retiring the date they met the age and length-of-service qualifications for retirement. The rationale I conveyed to the legislature for this program and for the salary increases and the other benefits was this: if a judge retires, you're going to be paying an appreciable retirement benefit, especially for those who come within the original judges' retirement system. At the same time, you'll be paying the salary of the new judge appointed to replace the retiree. It really is in the interest of the executive and legislative branches to keep the experienced judge on the bench instead of bearing the dual burden of meeting the state's retirement obligation to the retiring judge and the salary obligation to a replacement judge. That was a major selling point.

As I mentioned before, the original judges' retirement system had gotten so out of whack that it was out of the question to fix it. We had proposed year after year that the legislature put some money into it to reduce the unfunded liability, and make some changes, but it didn't do so. The legislature fully funded all the other retirement systems but not the judges', so it ultimately concluded there was no alternative but to create a second tier—and basically second-class—group of judges and justices, who would receive a substantially inferior retirement benefit.

As an aside, what do you note about current practices for recruiting new judges to the bench in California?

The Judicial Council, and myself personally, have participated in efforts to dissolve some of the mystery that goes into the Byzantine process of applying for and being appointed to a judgeship. A substantial number of new judgeships were created in conjunction with the switch to state funding of the trial courts. We found that an obstacle to the creation of the further new judgeships that we ultimately obtained was the feeling of some legislators that there was not enough diversity in the judicial appointments being made. The actions we took were multiple. First of all, with regard to the hiring of subordinate judicial officers—commissioners and referees—which comes within the authority of the individual trial courts, we urged that the need for diversity be taken into account and that more of an effort be made to have the subordinate judicial officer appointments reflect the population in a general way. Second, we agreed to support legislation requiring that statistics be maintained of the racial and ethnic diversity of the persons applying for appointment to the bench and of those persons actually appointed to the bench by the governor. The new judgeships were created only after the governor agreed to have that go through. Then third, we participated in efforts with the governor's judicial appointments secretary to present programs and publications to the ethnic minority bar associations explaining how the application and appointment procedure works. Qualified members of the groups were urged to apply for judicial appointments.

Some people held the view that applying for a judicial appointment was somewhat of a club-ish procedure with a lot of inside maneuvering going on and that only persons who knew their way through the process would receive an appointment. It was felt that applicants from the minority population weren't aware of how to proceed effectively and therefore experienced greater difficulty in being appointed. I'm not sure whether that perception reflected reality or not, but the perception was important and therefore we participated with the other two branches of government and bar groups in taking steps to dissipate that perception and make the process more open.

How well have these measures helped the situation?

I believe they have helped and that governors have actually gone out of their way to recruit from the minority population.

I want to talk also today about your efforts to collect unpaid fees and fines.

This grew out of my involvement in the Conference of Chief Justices, which had undertaken studies that estimated there was nationally somewhere in the neighborhood of $5 billion of fines and forfeitures imposed by state courts that were going uncollected. The ensuing estimate, based on population and court structure, was that the California courts were owed about one-tenth, or half a billion dollars, of that uncollected revenue. Because of that, I appointed a task force to see how the courts' collection procedures could be improved and standardized. Different approaches were being followed around the state. In some counties the court would send a letter to the delinquent party basically saying, "You owe us this amount, and it would be nice if you showed up and paid it." There were other counties—I believe Sacramento was one—where a uniformed deputy sheriff would show up at the front door to announce, "You owe this amount. You should be forthcoming in paying it, or else there might be consequences."

This led to an effort to standardize and improve the procedures in California and also to obtain authority for the state Franchise Tax Board to withhold the overdue amounts from income tax refunds and other payments, as is done with child support. On a national level the Conference of Chief Justices undertook a similar effort, but the Internal Revenue Service, for reasons that seemed at best bureaucratic, resisted efforts to have state-court-owed funds withheld or retained in making tax refunds. Our California task force was quite successful in setting up a process that achieved some positive results. We had a collaborative court/county working group on enhanced collections that during the first year increased felony, misdemeanor, and infraction revenue from fines and assessments by about 27 percent over the preceding year. Agreements were entered into with private collection agencies under which, after a suitable amount of effort had been engaged in by the courts and counties, the delinquencies were turned over to collection agencies to keep a portion of what they were able to collect and transfer the balance to the county and the court. The courts throughout this process have been sensitive to the fact that of course not all of these amounts are collectible. Although there are persons who, of course, might be scofflaws and might not be located or be made to pay, there are others who simply can't afford the fine. For many years there has been a rule in California under a California Supreme Court decision that well preceded my time on the court—I think it's the *In re Antazo* decision—that held an indigent defendant can't be incarcerated for failure to pay a fine if in fact he or she lacks the ability to pay that fine. So we worked on dealing with that problem through a subcommittee that was appointed to recommend a revised and standardized system for fee waivers.

There's another reason to improve court collections, even aside from the fact that the courts are starved for sufficient revenue. Improved collections are thought to promote respect for the justice system and ensure that a variety of court orders are more consistently obeyed. I believe that any time you allow court orders and penalties to be ignored, you diminish the public's respect for our judicial system and for the rule of law. By doing so, you may foster disrespect and disregard of other court orders that have nothing to do with fines. If one can, with impunity, disregard a fine, then why abide by other conditions of probation, such as not using narcotics, arming oneself with a weapon, engaging in violent behavior toward one's spouse, or whatever the restriction might be. These joint efforts provide another good illustration of what can be achieved through a constructive collaboration among the courts, the counties, and the legislature.

We also succeeded in having legislation passed that in many instances allows persons who owe money to the courts to pay by credit card. It also authorized courts to use collection agencies. The collections legislation, like some of our other important bills, was carried by Senator Escutia and is another fine example of looking at an old problem and coming up with some worthwhile new solutions. We also came up with a plan to allow courts, like the counties, to charge fees for setting up installment payments and to charge interest on delinquent fees and fines.

Let's turn to the subject of cameras in the courtroom in California. I note that both of your most recent predecessors as chief were also interested in this. I read that Chief Justice Bird had, in her time, started with an experimental phase as early as 1980 that resulted in a rule change to allow cameras in the courtroom, effective in 1984. Chief Justice Lucas appointed a task force that worked with the Judicial Council and did a study of judicial discretion on the matter— approved, I gather, by the council just after you became Chief Justice in May 1996. Where did it go from the time you took over?

I tried to have the California Supreme Court set an example by its own actions—just as we did in terms of our general outreach effort, by holding special sessions of our court in various venues—allowing the televising of our proceedings basically whenever it was requested. I don't believe we turned down any timely requests by the media.

As a reaction to the O.J. Simpson trial, there was a lot of resistance to allowing television cameras in the courtroom, and of course there can be instances of abuse. If you look at the appendix to the U.S. Supreme Court's opinion in the *Billy Sol Estes* case, a photograph shows the trial courtroom inundated with cameras, wiring, and media personnel wearing insignia. The courtroom basically looks like a very busy TV studio. The standards established by the Judicial Council provide real limitations on the type of equipment, the movement of equipment and personnel, a prohibition on insignia that are apparent and distracting, and limitations on the noise level caused by operation of the equipment.[4] Of course, many problems can readily be dealt with by providing for pooling by various television stations through one designated representative. Our court had the broadcasting unit of the Administrative Office of the Courts operate the television cameras and feed the broadcast to the stations' television trucks parked outside the court building. There are many ways of televising court proceedings in an unobtrusive way.

So basically, with a lot of assistance and generous participation by the California Channel—which didn't make any money on this and might have lost money—that network would broadcast our proceedings as a public service whenever there was a request to do so and would rebroadcast them throughout the year. I used to joke that we could probably fund the entire budget of our court if we were to televise the oral arguments in all of our cases—and have the less interesting ones broadcast at midnight sponsored by the makers of Sominex or some other medication designed to deal with sleeping disorders, because hearing them would help people who had any difficulty in falling asleep. [Laughter] But we only televised those cases where there was a request, as well as the full proceedings conducted during the special outreach sessions that were meant to be educational.

The rules were revised and made televising discretionary. I myself felt it was very important to televise arguments when there was a request to do so. We'll probably discuss the subject of civics education in a forthcoming session, but I'll note briefly that the American public is quite uninformed about the operations of its court system, of how and why cases are decided by judges and by courts, more or less viewing things through the lens of a sporting event. Who

---

[4] Calif. Rules of Court, Rule 1.150.

was the winner? Who was the loser? There needs to be more of an understanding of the process and how a decision doesn't necessarily reflect a judge's or a court's personal views or a political, social, or economic agenda—but instead just the court's perception of what the law requires, regardless of the judge's own personal views. I think that the judicial process is vastly clarified for a viewing public that sees the interplay between counsel, the questioning, the answers, the basis in a trial court for the rulings made, why evidence is admitted or excluded, and so forth. I believe that the public's exposure to the process is extremely important as part of the growing effort to restore the civics education that seems so lacking in our public schools today.

That actually ties in with something that I have felt strongly about and that is reflected in some of the decisions I rendered for the court that we'll discuss soon, especially the *NBC Subsidiary* case, where our court held that the right to public judicial proceedings extends not only to criminal cases—where the U.S. Supreme Court had recognized it in the *Press-Enterprise* cases that arose out of Riverside County—but also to civil cases, subject to narrow exceptions.

There was a very thoughtful op-ed piece this month written by Kenneth Starr, the president of Baylor University and former federal appellate judge. The headline tells it all: "Open Up High Court to Cameras."[5] He urges that all U.S. Supreme Court proceedings be televised, even though there are justices who have very strongly resisted that. I believe Justice David Souter more or less used the words, "over my dead body." But I believe, as Ken Starr says, that the benefits of increased access and transparency are many. He says, "Democracy's first principles strongly support the people's right to know how their government works." I wish the high court would follow the example of the California Supreme Court. Ken Starr also bemoans what he calls "the apparent collapse of civic literacy in public schools." He raises the question: "If the justices won't open the courtroom doors to cameras—proxies for the public eye—of their own accord, then Congress has the capacity and the duty to take action."

This raises the very troublesome question of whether something as integral to the control of the courtroom as televising the proceedings—whether at the U.S. Supreme Court or at any other federal or state court—is so particularly within the inherent powers of the court as to be outside the purview of permissible regulation by the other two branches of government. I would not assume, as Ken Starr appears to, that Congress can exercise such authority without violating the constitutional principle of separation of powers and bringing about a confrontation between Congress and the high court. I certainly would have raised this issue had there ever been an attempt by the legislature and the executive to

---

[5] *New York Times*, October 2, 2011.

mandate televising the proceedings of the California courts, even though I favor allowing broadcasting as a matter policy. But happily, we've been fairly progressive on our own in opening up our courtrooms.

I do notice that my successor is faced with some opposition from trial judges to a proposal that would make it easier to get cameras into the courtrooms of the state court system here in California. The proposal was that cameras would be permitted upon request unless the judge gives specific reasons for disapproval, and that such action by a trial judge could be reviewed by a higher court. There was judicial resistance, based again on the question of statewide authority and of limiting the discretion of individual judges to run their own courtrooms. The committee that made the recent recommendation to facilitate broadcast coverage included judges, court staff, lawyers, and media representatives and was created by me in 2008 as a two-year project to address existing limits on the public's access to the courts. Because of the opposition expressed, the proposal to make those alterations in the current rules is not being pursued this year.

Backing up to the changes approved by the Judicial Council in 1996, how good a decision was it to retain judicial discretion?

I believe there should be judicial discretion, but it should be a reasoned exercise of discretion given the constitutional and statutory presumption in favor of open courtrooms and the public's need to know—to know as a practical matter through the press as the eyes and ears of the public. Most courtrooms don't seat more than two or three dozen persons, so it isn't just a question of everyone's having the right to travel down to the courthouse and see what's going on. You may not be able to get into the most publicized trials, the ones of greatest interest. I think it's important that judges exercise discretion in a manner whereby they at least give reasons for curtailing or eliminating the public's observation of the court proceedings through electronic media coverage. We limit judges' discretion in all sorts of matters. One analogous area I could give is the area of sentencing, where after decades' worth of experience with totally indeterminate sentencing we now have a compromise whereby a judge on almost any offense is faced with a punishment statute that prescribes the lower, middle, or upper term for the given offense. If the judge decides to impose a sentence of the middle term, he or she is not required to specify any reasons. But if the judge wishes to deviate below or above the middle term—to the lower or upper term, respectively—then he or she is required by law to give reasons, to give an explanation. In the absence of such reasons, the judge has committed reversible error. The same is true with respect to the judge's decision to impose consecutive sentences.

Why not require the same thing when the judge is curtailing the electronic opportunity of the public to observe something as vital as what's going on in the courtroom. As I pointed out in the *NBC Subsidiary* case, open proceedings are important not only for cases that might be of sensational or prurient interest, or some other interest inherent in the particular case involved, but also because the right of public access significantly affords a basis for the public to become aware of how their court system is operating. The demeanor of the judge—is justice being dispensed fairly and impartially and courteously and efficiently?— may bear upon whether he or she should be reelected or retained. It might bear upon whether favoritism of some sort, for whatever reason, appears to be shown to one party or one lawyer over another. So openness is something that I think our society has a great interest in. It's not much that we ask that a judge set forth his or her reasons for curtailing that—which may be bona fide reasons—and I believe that requiring a reasoned explanation makes more sense than just permitting a thumbs-up-thumbs-down approach with no explanation.

How much should we be looking to the First Amendment as a guide to developing the law in this area?

The decisions of the U.S. Supreme Court in the *Press-Enterprise* cases and other cases are based on First Amendment principles. *NBC Subsidiary* started out as a case purely involving issues arising under the First Amendment and article I, section 1, of the California Constitution. But research conducted by my assigned staff attorney uncovered a long-overlooked statute, enacted in the 1870s, that mandated—in the court's view—open proceedings in all cases, civil and criminal, subject to narrow exceptions.[6] We called this statute to counsel's attention and asked them to brief it. The court applied a maxim of jurisprudence providing that in construing a statute, a court undertakes to interpret it in a manner consistent with the dictates of applicable constitutional provisions. So in effect, our interpretation of the code section was infused with First Amendment principles, and our decision ended up being a combined statutory and constitutional ruling.

All states, I believe, allow cameras in the courtroom to some extent, but how might California's approach have differed?

I'm not fully familiar with the practice in other states, and I believe it would potentially vary quite a bit, from taking a couple of still shots when the court is not in session to fully televising, from beginning to end, all proceedings. But I

---

[6] Cal. Code Civ. Proc., sec. 124.

understand that, although it was preceded by some intimations in other rulings, our *NBC Subsidiary* opinion is considered the first case to firmly establish a right of public access—on behalf of the media and the public at large—to proceedings that are civil in nature, notwithstanding the fact that this principle was well established in criminal matters.

I realize there is something else that relates both to open courts and to salaries that I would like to mention. Because of budget cuts, the courts had to take a number of measures to try to conserve resources for court operations. With great regret—notwithstanding my commitment to keep courts open in every sense of the word, including operationally open—the courts, through the Judicial Council, with a lot of input from judges and court staff around the state in terms of what alternatives, if any, existed to meet an additional last-minute cut imposed on our operating budget, decided that we would close the courts one day a month. The related furlough of court employees caused some bad feeling—I even have an article with a photograph published in a legal newspaper showing a street protest outside my chambers, with a demonstrator wearing a Ron George mask and a judicial robe with Monopoly money coming out of the pockets of the robe, and carrying a placard that proclaimed, "Here we're being forced to work for less." Court closures were not something lightly undertaken, but we felt it was necessary to take uniform, statewide action to avoid far worse consequences. I asked judges statewide—at all levels, including the Supreme Court—to sign up for a voluntary waiver of their salary for one day per month to show their support for their employees and to demonstrate to the legislature, the governor, and the public that judges were doing their part to implement savings to get state government through the current fiscal crisis. I'm proud to say that more than 90 percent of the judges in California signed up to do that voluntarily, in the face of the constitutional protection they receive against any diminution of their salary during their current term of office.

Now, once the court closures no longer were necessary, there was some dispute as to what should happen with the funds accumulated from the salary-waiver savings. I think most courts appropriately employed the savings, although there were a couple courts that chose to put them into some special funds of their own for pet projects. But the main point I want to make is that I thought the vast majority of the judges in the state were quite noble in voluntarily choosing to forgo a day of salary for each of several months. All members of the California Supreme Court participated in that effort, as did almost all of the justices and judges of the Courts of Appeal and the trial courts.

How did you go about making this request?

There was a communication sent to all the judges just making the case for it, and I believe that the equity in proceeding in that manner was quite apparent to most judges. Some said no—as a matter of what they described as judicial independence and their own authority, they just weren't going to do it despite the substantial salary increases they had received over the past several years. Then—speaking again of our efforts to strive for openness in the judicial branch—there was resistance by some judges to making public the names of the judges who had agreed to join in the voluntary judicial pay cut, because this information would point out which judges had declined to participate and might be used by an election opponent. Everything had a bit of an edge to it, politically or otherwise.

It's fascinating how some of these issues are related in one way or another, as you say—elections and all these considerations cross over, don't they?

Yes. They truly do.

To finish up about cameras in the courtroom, may I ask if your own views changed at all over time?

I let cameras into the courtroom on several occasions as a trial judge, both from time to time in the Hillside Strangler case and in some other matters—including I believe the McMartin preschool case, when I was handling that in the master calendar court. There are always aspects of the proceedings that most any judge would not permit, such as televising jurors' faces. There's enough pressure on jurors as it is, without facilitating attempts to intimidate them. I believe that many people, and I share this sentiment, feel that the cause of cameras in the courtroom was set back by the way in which they were employed in and around the courtroom in which the O. J. Simpson case was tried. That proceeding certainly highlighted in my mind the need for a judge to maintain control of his or her courtroom, a necessity that extends beyond merely exercising control over the electronic media and the lawyers—who shouldn't be allowed to take over the courtroom—but also control over obstreperous witnesses, parties, and even spectators. A judge has to act courteously and dispassionately but also with firm control of the courtroom. Failure to do so engenders disrespect for the judicial system and the law. That's a lesson that was learned from the O. J. Simpson trial, maybe learned all too well, because that experience caused real apprehension among many trial judges about letting cameras into the courtroom. In somewhat of a non sequitur, it also led to the same reluctance on behalf of some appellate justices, where the negative consideration of potential intimidation of witnesses or jurors or others—by reason of the presence of cameras—just doesn't exist.

Some persons, even justices of the U.S. Supreme Court, have voiced a concern that lawyers—or even judicial colleagues on the same bench—might be tempted to showboat when cameras are broadcasting appellate oral arguments. Of course every group of judges on a multijudge court is going to be different, but I would say—based on my own observations—that I did not see any difference between the behavior, questioning, or attitude of my colleagues on the bench when cameras were present and when cameras were not present. Certainly we had some highly publicized proceedings involving abortion, gay rights, issues involving the governor and the legislature, and I didn't see any difference in the way our court proceedings were conducted, with or without televised proceedings.

Is there any difference in your mind in a high-profile case?

I suppose that there's more of a potential for someone to want to act out a bit or showboat, if you will, but as I said, I believe that's subject to judicial control. To the extent a minimal amount of negative performance ensues, the benefits outweigh the detriment in my view.

Shall we move on to our major topic for today, the administration of capital punishment in California?

Yes. That is certainly a subject that has been woven through most portions of my career—as you know from our discussions—as a deputy attorney general advocating in favor of upholding the death penalty in cases that I argued before the California and U.S. Supreme Courts in the late 1960s and the early 1970s; as a superior court judge, in many trials over which I presided in which the death penalty was sought; certainly as a member of the California Supreme Court deciding automatic appeals from judgments of death and ruling on habeas corpus petitions in such cases; and then finally as Chief Justice being engaged in efforts, both internally within the court as well as with our justice system partners and the other branches of government, to attempt to improve the efficiency and the fairness in handling capital cases.

Of course, in one of our earlier sessions you and I spoke about my early experience as an associate justice, within a few months of joining the Supreme Court, participating early in 1992 in execution-night proceedings of the court in the case of Robert Alton Harris. Then, again, my first full day on the job as Chief Justice, May 2, 1996 and into the very early hours of May 3, included presiding over our court's execution-night proceedings in the case of Keith Daniel Williams.[7] Earlier that day I had presided, also for the first time, as chair of the Commission on Judicial Appointments in the confirmation hearing for Justice Janice Rogers Brown as associate justice of the Supreme Court to fill the vacancy that was created by my elevation to the position of Chief Justice.

This was jumping in with both feet in any number of ways.

Yes. Unfortunately, Justice Brown—instead of being able to celebrate her appointment to our court with family and friends that evening, as planned—was obliged to participate in these execution-night proceedings.

I guess to get a handle on what I view as the problems and the potential solutions for the administration of capital punishment California, would you like me to give you a bit of an overview? Because I think that's integral to our discussion—an overview of how the system works or doesn't work, somewhat dysfunctionally, in terms of how the cases get to us.

Yes, please. How do death penalty cases come up to the California Supreme Court?

The California Constitution provides that after a judgment in any civil or criminal case is rendered in the superior court—except when the death penalty has been imposed—an appeal to the Court of Appeal is a matter of right, provided a timely notice of appeal is filed. Subsequently, the party that does not prevail in the Court of Appeal has the right to seek review in the California Supreme Court, but an appeal to our court is not a matter of right and in fact our court grants review in only roughly 2 percent of the cases in which review is sought in the Supreme Court. But when there is an appeal from a judgment of death—or even should there be no desire to appeal on the part of the defendant, there is what is called an automatic appeal and an appeal is deemed taken—that appeal bypasses the Court of Appeal and goes straight to the California Supreme Court, where the justices must hear it. It's not discretionary, and this is the only kind of appeal that the Supreme Court is obliged to entertain.

The process for the assignment of death penalty cases also differs from the process by which review-granted cases, civil and criminal, are assigned by the Chief Justice—a process that I described to you in one of our earlier sessions. Capital cases are assigned on a rotational basis by the office of the clerk, regard-

---

[7] This 1996 execution followed our court's 1988 affirmance of defendant's conviction for murders he committed in 1978. People v. Williams (1988) 44 Cal.3d 883; 751 P.2d 395.

less of length or complexity, on the theory that the law of averages will even things out and that it would be too difficult to try to engage in an evaluation of each individual capital case to somehow allocate them in a more equitable manner. There is, as I alluded to, a disparity in the length of transcripts. Transcripts average in the neighborhood of 10,000 pages per case, and we had some cases where there were 70,000 or 80,000 pages and even approaching 100,000 pages. You can imagine that a research attorney on a justice's staff can spend the better part of a year reading through such a transcript and researching what are often literally the dozens and dozens of legal issues in the case. There are a great number of issues raised by conscientious counsel who feel that with the life of his or her client at stake no stone can be left unturned, but also acting out of a concern that a court could deem counsel inadequate and to have denied the defendant his or her right under the constitution to effective legal representation if counsel has failed to raise each and every conceivable issue. Consequently, these cases with very unpleasant facts, to put it mildly, impose a great sense of obligation on the part of counsel to do a very thorough job, given what's at stake, in raising a multitude of issues that counsel feels should be researched and written up. Resolving them, in turn, places a tremendous burden on the court.

I also should mention that there are all sorts of procedures in the trial court, unique to capital cases, that lengthen and complicate the proceedings in some fashion or another and give rise to further claims in our court and in the federal courts on appeal and in habeas corpus proceedings. Decisions of our court and the U.S. Supreme Court require that in any type of case, the use of peremptory challenges to remove prospective jurors from the panel be exercised in a manner that does not exclude jurors based on impermissible factors such as race or gender. Additionally, in cases in which the prosecution is seeking the death penalty, jurors who voiced doubts about the death penalty—or, for that matter, about life imprisonment without possibility of parole—may not be excluded unless their views preclude them from considering either punishment under any circumstances relevant to the case before them. Until it was eliminated as part of a voter initiative, there used to be a rule—created by the California Supreme Court's *Hovey* decision—requiring that the examination of prospective jurors on the subject of their views concerning the death penalty take place in what was described by the court as a sequestered courtroom from which each and every other prospective juror had been excluded.[8]

Needless to say, depending upon the particular case, the former procedure could add weeks or months to the trial. In fact, when I was working on proposals

---

[8] Cal. Code Civ. Proc., sec. 223, adopted in 1990 as part of Proposition 115; Hovey v. Superior Court (1988) 44 Cal.3d 543; 749 P.2d 776.

to improve voir dire, or jury selection, on behalf of the California Judges Association, I was able, in testifying before state and congressional committees, to point to the most egregious example I was able to find—a case that was tried in the Palmdale-Lancaster area of Los Angeles County in which it took nine months to select a jury in a one-defendant capital case. I'm sure that the trial judge was attempting to comply with appellate court holdings, and that the attorneys on both sides felt confident they truly had performed wisely in picking the jury, to the benefit of their respective side. Guess what? After a lengthy trial the jury hung up, and the case had to be retried. Happily, individualized voir dire was eliminated by the initiative measure, but the whole process is illustrative of factors that can unduly prolong a death penalty trial.

Many of the other procedures uniquely applicable to capital cases really do enhance the fairness of the proceedings. There are separate guilt and penalty phases, and if one or more special circumstances are alleged and found to be true in addition to a finding of first-degree murder, the jury goes on to a second phase of the trial called the penalty phase, in which it is directed to consider additional evidence presented by both sides under guidelines—supplied by the trial court in its instructions—designed to assist the jury in choosing between the two alternate punishments of death or life in prison without the possibility of parole. There are different categories of evidence that come in at the penalty phase that would not be admissible at the guilt phase or at any normal noncapital criminal trial—specifically types of prior criminal behavior that otherwise would be excluded. And the defendant may introduce evidence in mitigation showing adverse influences in his or her early or later life, certain mental conditions that would fall short of insanity, and basically, in the words of the applicable statute, any mitigating or extenuating circumstance.[9] All the court proceedings are reported and transcribed, which also causes delay through additional hearings to settle the record.

Then, when we get to the review process, there is the automatic appeal that I mentioned. One or two attorneys are appointed to handle the automatic appeal. Unfortunately, because of the existing limitations on the compensation that our court is able to pay appointed counsel—that is, counsel other than the office of the state public defender, which cannot handle all of the caseload—there are years of additional delay in finding attorneys able and willing to accept appointment. The court established standards for appointment that I'll mention momentarily when we talk about steps to improve the process. I would receive a report on whether an attorney applicant met the standards, and I would personally approve or disapprove each appointment.

---

[9] Cal. Pen. Code, sec. 190.3.

Is that the same way that your predecessor had handled such matters, do you know?

I believe I made some changes in the procedure, but we always have had court staff do a thorough investigation of the qualifications of an attorney applicant who wanted to be placed on the list for appointment. That included looking at his or her prior written work, making an inquiry in the legal community concerning his or her qualifications, past experience that the court might have had with the attorney, and so forth. It was only if I was confident an attorney would meet the standards for being suitable for appointment, not just in terms of the minimum constitutional requirements but of doing a good job for his or her client and assisting the court as well, that I would approve the appointment. Had I not cared, and if the court had not cared about the quality of legal representation, we could have taken care of our appointments backlog lickety-split. I know from the Conference of Chief Justices there were instances in some states in which, at the trial court level, a judge calling his or her probate calendar would spot an attorney in the back row and say, "Counselor, I've got a death case going tomorrow. We're going to pay you $500. Be ready." I think one of those states later upped it to $1,000 a case, but was appointing people without expertise, without an opportunity to prepare, without the required resources. It would be very easy the way the courts in some areas of the United States appoint counsel, to avoid a good portion of the delay in reviewing these cases, but we had a tough time finding lawyers who would accept payment for what we were able to pay and at the same time would be competent in our view to handle those cases.

One of the most egregious things about the death penalty process in California—and something that I view as part of what I have publicly described as its dysfunctionality—is the fact that there is typically a three-year delay between the imposition of a death sentence in the trial court and the Supreme Court's appointment of an attorney to represent the defendant. Obviously, nothing happens in that three-year period, and it can be even longer than three years. To me, that's just unforgivable and casts the system, in fact the entire judiciary of the state, in disrepute in the eyes of the public. I managed, through some of the improvements in compensation that I'll mention momentarily, to reduce that delay somewhat. We were getting the number of capital defendants on appeal without counsel down from the 80 to 90 range to a lesser number that still was objectionable. One thing that we managed to be successful in doing was getting through some legislation vastly reducing the delay that ensued from the need to prepare a transcript of every trial court proceeding, however minor, in a capital case. Senator Bill Morrow worked on that with us. I communicated with trial judges, through written and verbal means, how vital it was as part of their duties to attend to settling the record, as it's called, at an early stage when things are still relatively fresh in the minds of the trial judge and the attorneys. There's a human tendency once a trial is over with—it's sort of like cleaning the crumbs off the table after the banquet—of wanting to go on to something else, so judges having a backlog of trials did not give high priority to scheduling these hearings to go over the transcript and make sure it was complete and accurate before it could be transmitted to the Supreme Court. Now there are timetables set up that require that various steps be taken within specified time limits.

Of course, after the one or two attorneys are appointed on appeal—it may be the office of the state public defender or private counsel, assisted by the California Appellate Project—they file lengthy briefs, usually following several extensions of time. Then the attorney general's office files a responsive brief, after many extensions obtained by that office. As long as counsel appear to be diligent, the court feels it must grant these extensions. I know that people get impatient with that, but the parties are under the same burden as the court is, with enormous transcripts and dozens of legal issues. Then oral argument is set, and we give counsel on each side 45 minutes instead of the usual 30 minutes.

Soon after the automatic appeal is heard, state habeas corpus proceedings may proceed. On rare occasions, the appeal and the habeas corpus proceedings will proceed concurrently. Usually, our court appoints separate counsel, one or two attorneys, to handle the habeas corpus proceedings. This task involves the use of substantial investigative funds to go beyond the transcript, beyond the record, and seek out new, additional evidence to present why the person's death judgment—or perhaps his or her conviction in its entirety—should be set aside. Because of the even greater difficulty in finding counsel willing and able to accept appointment in the habeas corpus proceedings, they often are delayed additionally.

I gather in the past it was sometimes the same attorney or attorneys doing the appeal and the habeas corpus. Can you comment on that, please?

Yes. One of the changes I made was to unlink the appointment of automatic appeal counsel and habeas corpus counsel. I did that after concluding that doing so would enable us to attract more attorneys to handle the automatic appeals, and therefore reduce the delay in handling these appeals. To me, the first review—namely the automatic appeal, which is the one that exists as a matter of right—was the one to be prioritized. To me, it was unconscionable to allow so much time to pass with nothing happening on a capital defendant's case. I observed—I suppose generally, from my career as a lawyer and as a judge and justice—that although criminal defense attorneys don't inevitably fall into two neat categories, it's pretty close. You have trial attorneys who are capable of undertaking the most vigorous defense of the defendant, making objections right and left, responding to the objections of others, cross-examining witnesses, making impassioned arguments to the jury. But put so many of these trial-attorney specialists before three justices of the Court of Appeal in even a garden-variety criminal case and they feel totally ill at ease and unable to respond effectively to questions from the bench and to make a logical, reasoned argument that is persuasive to an appellate justice. By the same token, there are attorneys who I know have appeared before the seven justices of the Supreme Court of California and even the nine justices of the U.S. Supreme Court, have fielded the questions with which they were bombarded—questions of minutiae in the record and of great policy and constitutional import—and yet are totally ill at ease appearing before a trial judge with one live witness in a habeas corpus proceeding. So I concluded that we would attract more attorneys for both types of proceedings if we didn't link the legal representation in a manner that required an attorney to undertake both the automatic appeal and the habeas corpus proceeding in order to receive an appointment. Now, there are obviously some attorneys who do a wonderfully credible job in both types of legal proceedings, but they are clearly the exception. Most will not feel as adept at both types of proceedings and will, for that reason, decline an appointment if required to accept both types of legal representation. The number of automatic appeals without counsel declined, I believe, in large part because of the unlinking of the two proceedings as well as the increase in compensation. We didn't do as well in reducing the backlog of unrepresented habeas corpus petitioners.

You were able to attract more attorneys on the automatic appeal portion, but not so much so on the habeas proceedings?

Yes. I should mention that both the automatic appeal decisions and the habeas corpus rulings of the California Supreme Court are, of course, subject to certiorari review in the U.S. Supreme Court. That review is still not the end of the game, because then another phase begins where the condemned inmate—which is a term used for someone under sentence of death—seeks the appointment of counsel in federal court to file a habeas corpus proceeding in the U.S. District Court, whose ruling inevitably is appealed to the Ninth Circuit U.S. Court of Appeals. The ruling of that court in turn is subject to a certiorari petition in the U.S. Supreme Court. I want to make it clear that by no means is all of the delay that encumbers the review of capital cases in California the result of action or inaction by the California state courts. On the contrary, a very sizable portion of it emanates from the federal courts. As we discussed earlier, the *Harris* case was a prime illustration of that. A succession of federal habeas corpus petitions was heard by the U.S. District Court and the Ninth Circuit U.S. Court of Appeals over a period of several years. Then there was a series of stay interventions by federal judges, which culminated in what was basically an all-night judicial ping-pong match between the U.S. Supreme Court and the Ninth Circuit that I described. Shortly before the execution took place at approximately 6:00 a.m., the high court issued an order providing that "No further stays . . . shall be entered . . . except upon order of this court."[10] This gives you an overview of what can transpire in capital cases through the two-track system of judicial review.

Once the judicial proceedings have concluded, clemency may be sought from the governor. There's an odd provision of law that blurs the line between executive and judicial functions by providing that a governor "may not grant a pardon or commutation to a person twice convicted of a felony except on recommendation of the Supreme Court, 4 judges concurring."[11] On a couple occasions during my tenure as chief, the court was called upon to perform this function. There sometimes is also a further last round of habeas corpus filings in the California Supreme Court as the execution date approaches.

Pursuant to the statutory procedure that I mentioned to you in discussing the Harris execution, the trial court on several weeks' notice schedules a hearing to set the execution date and issues what is termed a death warrant. That is an order that the defendant be executed—which always is scheduled to take place at San Quentin Prison—and is effective for 24 hours only, for one day. Therefore, in order to provide what I would describe, for want of a better phrase, as the maximum "window of opportunity" to carry out the execution, it is customarily set by the warden, in consultation with the California Department of Justice, at 12:01 a.m. to provide a 23-hour-and-59-minute opportunity to comply with the death warrant, notwithstanding delays that may be caused by short-lived stays issued by one court or another or other delays in the procedures that may unexpectedly occur. If the execution is not carried out on the specified date, the trial court is obliged by law to schedule a hearing to set a new date for the execution.

Now, having described all of these proceedings, I'm sure it comes as no surprise that death penalty cases often are literally million-dollar cases when you consider all the expenses in the trial court, on appeal, on habeas corpus, in various courts, including the compensation of multiple defense attorneys, investigators, and experts, plus the expenses of the attorney general and of the defense

---

[10] Vasquez v. Harris (1992) 503 U.S. 1000; Gomez v. United States District Court (1992) 503 U.S. 653; Harris v. Vasquez (9th Cir. 1990) 949 F.2d 1497.

[11] Cal. Const. art. V, sec. 8.

entities that assist the counsel who represent the defendant. The delay that occurs in carrying out or, as the case may be, setting aside the judgment of death rendered by the trial court currently averages about 25 years from death judgment to an execution that's carried out. As I mentioned previously, the only time I ever made the *New York Times'* page two quote of the day was with my observation, which was literally true, that the leading cause of death on death row in California is old age. I believe that generally suicides ranked as the number two cause, with other causes vying for third place with the occasional execution.

In my view, this protracted and dysfunctional process places the administration of justice and all of the courts, state and federal, and government as a whole, in a very bad light. California, in 1977, in the wake of U.S. Supreme Court decisions—some of which we've discussed in conjunction with the cases I argued before the high court, plus the *Gregg* decision in 1976—reinstated its death penalty procedures in a permissible fashion, passing muster under U.S. Supreme Court jurisprudence. Since then California has accumulated more than 720 individuals on death row, more than a dozen of them women, but there have been only thirteen executions in this 34-year period, while several dozen death row inmates have died of old age or various infirmities. There have been no executions in California since early in 2006, because of orders from the federal courts finding the manner of administration of lethal gas and the training of prison personnel to be deficient, and staying the carrying out of further executions. I believe legitimate questions have been raised concerning the effect of the delay in carrying out death sentences and about how much has been spent on the death penalty without executions taking place.

In today's *San Francisco Chronicle* there's an article that indicates that billions of dollars have been spent on capital punishment in California since the procedures were reinstated in 1977 and that the thirteen executions that have taken place since that year have, if you divide up the total spent, cost the taxpayers upwards of $300 million for each execution. I have no way of knowing whether those are accurate figures, but they're being used by the proponents of an initiative that will be on the ballot next year proposing to substitute life imprisonment without possibility of parole for the death penalty. I have read that large sums have been spent on death row inmates for geriatric medical care and, in some instances, even for organ transplants.

This drive to put such an initiative on the ballot directly follows attempts in the legislature that were stymied over the summer to put a similar proposal forward to voters. What's your take on the fluctuations in public opinion about the use of the death penalty?

I believe Californians have a very mixed attitude about the death penalty. A recent poll shows somewhat of a decline in public support for the death penalty, although it still is overwhelmingly favored. Of course the responses vary a bit when you ask people about the alternative of life without any real possibility of parole. But there still seems to be a lot of support for the death penalty. Although Californians may want to keep the death penalty on the books, they don't appear to want to have it carried out in great numbers at the pace they do in Texas, for instance, which has had almost 500 executions in the same 34-year period in which California has had 13. Maybe that's why, when I went to Sacramento in an attempt to obtain some improvements in California's dysfunctional death penalty process, I had minimal success in my conversations with legislators from both major political parties. I found it rather ironic that the law-and-order folks, the real conservatives who were criticizing the courts for the slow pace at which the death penalty was being carried out—and I can understand and sympathize to a large degree with their frustration—were totally unwilling to appropriate any funds for the kind of reforms that I felt would truly expedite the process and eliminate much of the delay. The more liberal elements of the legislature had no problem with a 25-year delay in implementing a death sentence. They probably just wished it took 40 or 50 years to carry it out, in the absence of a total abolition. So you had this perfect storm of individuals lacking any incentive to change the system and actually feeling their respective interests were being served by maintaining the status quo. My thought was that, apart from some other reforms that we proposed and that I'll discuss with you, just raising the fees to be paid to appointed counsel to a level where they would equal or be competitive with what the federal courts pay their appointed counsel in capital cases would go a long way toward at least eliminating the unconscionable three-year or greater portion of the delay in which nothing happens in an automatic appeal in California due to the lack of appointed counsel in the case.

How big was the discrepancy in what the state was paying and what the federal courts were paying?

It was a two-figure difference in terms of hourly rate. The total was not an amount that should have made a difference to the legislature, given the overall cost of the death penalty process. It would have been a very minimal increment in the cost of administering a death penalty system in California.

But it would have had symbolic value as well?

It would have had symbolic value in assisting our court in recruiting appointed counsel, although I'm sure in the eyes of some legislators it was a question of, "Why should we reward these attorneys who are defending some of our most heinous criminals?" But if you want to have a death penalty you have to pay for it, just as you do for all the other services that Californians seem to want to continue having and not sacrificing in this time of economic decline. At the same time, Californians seem not to want to pay the increased taxes required in order to continue receiving these various things.

Even those defendants have rights that the system is duty bound to uphold, as far as trial and further processes in death cases.

Yes. The federal and state constitutions compel the courts to uphold those rights. As I said a moment ago, had I been willing to approve the appointment of any and all applicants to represent the individuals on death row at the lower level of compensation that existed, we could have found lawyers to do so. It wouldn't have been right. It wouldn't have afforded the constitutionally guaranteed right to effective representation by counsel, and I believe it probably would have cost the state even more in the long run, because there would be more reversals of judgments of death for ineffective counsel by either the state courts or the federal courts. But that's the long-term view that not everyone was taking.

You said you didn't get where you wanted to go in Sacramento in this matter. But how did you try to make the case, both to those who favored the death penalty and those who opposed it?

I indicated to both sides in the legislative debate that I thought it was unconscionable and dysfunctional to have a system that dragged on that long. I certainly did not favor, and I don't generally favor, strict and arbitrary timelines. But having said that, it makes sense to take the position that within five years, more or less, we should know whether a death judgment is valid and should be carried out or, if it is not, the case should be remanded back to the trial court for a new trial. It's not fair to the system and, perhaps most importantly, it's not fair to the victims of the crime and specifically to their surviving family members, to give them no closure, to have these cases drag on for decades. It's not fair to the prosecution, in the event of a reversal or a habeas corpus petition being granted years later, to have to go back and scrounge up long-lost witnesses who may or may not still be available and have a firm recollection of the events of many years before. I suppose in a way it's not fair to the defendant, even though his or her life has been prolonged, to be in that state of uncertainty. In fact, some defense counsel have raised claims in federal and state court that the inordinate delay in carrying out a sentence of death that has been imposed constitutes cruel and unusual punishment in its own right, even though the defense in large part has helped bring about the delay. I tried to make that point to both sides in the legislature. I mentioned to opponents of the death penalty the perception of some that it wasn't fair to defendants or to the loved ones of defendants. To the law and order folks, I mentioned that we had a death penalty only in name and theory and that it would make more sense to pay for a system that worked than to have this go on and on and be unfair to the families of victims. They listened, they heard, but we were only partially successful with our proposals to adequately fund the adjudication of death penalty appeals and habeas corpus proceedings. I'll mention a few things that did bear fruit and that I think somewhat ameliorated the situation.

I mentioned to you in a previous discussion that Chief Justice Lucas had entrusted me with some responsibilities in the area of trying to reduce the delay in the Supreme Court's handling of death penalty cases. The rate of hourly compensation was $60 when I started on that effort. Ultimately, when I was chief, we managed with authorization from the legislature to have it raised to $145 an hour. Fixed fees, an alternative to hourly fees, were raised accordingly. Habeas corpus proceedings involve going outside the trial court record that was reviewed on the automatic appeal and raising new factual and legal issues. The investigative expenses automatically allowable for those proceedings, without requiring prior court authorization, were increased from $3,000 to $25,000. Additionally, certain costs became separately reimbursable so they would not be charged against the amount of these allowable expenses.

The Habeas Corpus Resource Center was established as a very worthwhile innovation to provide expert legal representation in habeas corpus matters and also to assist attorneys in private practice who accepted appointment in such proceedings. The center also performs the additional function of collecting briefs and expert testimony for use in future habeas corpus proceedings, providing a bank of very helpful material for the defense. I should add, by the way, that the Habeas Corpus Resource Center, oddly enough, was made part of the judicial branch and therefore part of the judicial budget. The Office of the State Public Defender that handles the automatic appeals is part of the executive branch, for some reason or other.

I always ended up being an advocate for these defense entities during my various lobbying trips to Sacramento. I would say, "This is a three-legged stool, and if you don't provide enough funds for the attorney general, as well as the defense entities and the courts, you're not going to move capital cases."

How did the Habeas Corpus Resource Center come into being, vis-à-vis the state public defender's office?

It was thought that it was better to separate the two functions of representation in automatic appeals and in habeas corpus proceedings, even in the public sphere. I know the public defender's office wasn't entirely happy with that. They wanted to do some habeas, and I think some of the habeas center's lawyers wanted to expand into appeals, but each office had more than enough to do in performing its allotted function.

By the way, most public and private defense counsel were very grateful for these reforms in the area of compensation. I was sent a publication that came out after I retired called *California Appellate News*, published by the appellate defense counsel. They had a nice article that went through some of the measures I've just mentioned and said I had left a legacy of commitment to court-appointed counsel.

We also obtained legislative authorization for a capital central staff, the third of our central staffs after the criminal and civil central staffs. That, of course, provided great assistance to the justices and their attorney staffs. As I said, the capital central staff was created with a legislative appropriation. The rationale for establishing it was, in part, that there were a lot of motions and applications that would come up in the course of an automatic appeal that might relate either to the appeal or to the parallel habeas corpus matters. A chambers attorney and justice would be busy working on other matters and might have to go back to that transcript of ten or twenty thousand pages or more and ferret through the record to be able to act on such a motion or application and then go back to the other case at hand. This could happen repeatedly over a period of months or years, and there wasn't always consistency among chambers in how certain matters would be presented to the rest of the court for action. We developed real expertise among capital central staff in handling these motions and applications. After a while this new staff also undertook the preparation of calendar memos, or draft opinions, in capital cases—work product that is always assiduously reviewed, of course, by judicial chambers staff and the justice who is assigned to author the opinion. This was another improvement that has helped expedite capital matters.

It does sound valuable. How did you think to separate out capital matters on a central staff?

I felt that we had to develop a corps of experts in dealing with those issues. The issues are so unique to capital jurisprudence that just assigning them to staff with experience in the general area of criminal law and having a single central staff handle both the regular criminal caseload and the capital caseload would not be efficient.

I should point out that the capital caseload probably consumes 20 to 25 percent of the court's time and effort and that, to the extent the court is occupied with that vital function, it is kept from performing its basic function of deciding substantial questions of statewide importance and resolving conflicts in the civil and noncapital criminal areas of the law. Although capital cases literally present life-and-death issues for both the victim and the defendant, it is a very rare capital case that contributes anything to the jurisprudence of our state outside the narrow confines of death penalty law, which largely involves procedural law unique to death penalty cases.

A limited value in the legal issues found in those cases?

Yes. I wrote majority opinions during my tenure on the court in 56 capital cases and, I believe, separate opinions in five additional capital cases. I can think of only one of these cases where the law that was developed in the opinion truly had a substantial significance to the jurisprudence outside the area of death penalty law. Most of it was just narrowly of interest to the capital defense bar and the prosecution.

What was the nature of that one significant legal development?

The case was *People v. Zapien.* It resolved some issues related to multiple hearsay evidence and therefore actually made a contribution not only to criminal law in an area having nothing to do with capital offenses, but also to civil jurisprudence, because of the discussion of the hearsay rule in the context of prior inconsistent statements by a witness. There were other issues, of course, involved in other death penalty cases that didn't relate to capital jurisprudence, but in terms of something I would view as a truly substantial contribution to the law, it occurs only rarely in death penalty cases. They divert the court from performing its basic function of overseeing the development of the civil and criminal law of our state.

There was a proposal strongly backed by Justice Mosk that was embodied in proposed Senate Constitutional Amendment 31. It would have created new positions on the California Supreme Court to make it a court of 15 justices, with seven justices hearing civil cases and seven other justices comprising a separate court of criminal appeals, which is the system that exists in Texas and Oklahoma—and only in those two states. The chief justice could preside on both courts.

I know from my exposure to that concept at the Conference of Chiefs that it's not one that—at least in my opinion and in the opinion of most others—works well. I believe such a system would be cumbersome and bureaucratic, would have muddled the development of the law, and would not have served California well, so I'm glad the proposal went nowhere.

What occasion, if any, did you have to discuss these general ideas with Justice Mosk?

He went off on his own basically and proposed it and had an ally in Senator Quentin Kopp. When he mentioned it at a petition conference I certainly had no hesitation in telling him why I didn't think it was a good idea. I don't believe any of our colleagues supported it either. But it never came to be a point of heated disagreement between the two of us. He favored it, and I communicated my opposition to it in Sacramento.

One beneficial process, although less tangible, that assisted our efforts to expedite the capital case log were the meetings that I held and that my principal attorney, Beth Jay, held with the various criminal defense entities, the private bar—the California Attorneys for Criminal Justice—the local or county public defenders, and the three official defense entities—the office of the state public defender, the California Appellate Project, and the Habeas Corpus Resource Center. I also met annually during the last several years with a group of superior court clerks, described as the death penalty clerks, whose responsibility was to make sure that the exhibits and transcripts in the automatic appeals were accurately and fully completed and transmitted to the California Supreme Court. The purpose of these clerks coming to the Supreme Court for an educational program was to have our staff impress upon them how vital their task was and how, when on occasion it wasn't done properly—if the clerks just out of frustration threw everything into a box without indexing and collating the transcripts—they'd have to have it all sent back to them, and how vital it was that they receive specialized training and adhere to it. The clerks appreciated the program and my involvement in it.

They were able to learn a lot from you about the consequences of their own handling. I wonder about the reverse. What did you learn from them about what was going on in the trenches that you may not have known before, if anything?

I did know, from my own visits, about the often-terrible facilities that were provided to the superior court clerks for the storage of exhibits, and that you had flooding and rats running around these dungeon-like basement areas where every kind of court exhibits from documents to weapons and narcotics to bloodstained clothing were kept. The clerks also noted that court reporters—who might have handled a five-minute continuance proceeding—retired and went off to Arizona or Hawaii and couldn't be located to complete a missing portion of the transcript. Of course, if they died or became ill, someone else had to be brought in to try to read their notes, which in the case of official reporting is not always an easy thing to do, because it's done on somewhat of a phonetic basis. Some of those things I knew from my own experience as a trial judge. Others I didn't, or didn't know the degree to which it was a problem. But my pep talk was really just the icing on the cake. They had a several-day training session here where they worked with Mary Jameson, who was head of our clerk's office unit dealing with capital cases and does an excellent job in handling the interaction between the trial courts and the Supreme Court on these matters.

Those various efforts helped somewhat in improving the court's processing of capital cases. The major proposal I came up with ultimately was endorsed by our court and by the California Commission on the Fair Administration of Justice, a commission established by the legislature and chaired by former Attorney General John Van de Kamp. The commission's executive director was Professor Gerald Uelmen of Santa Clara University School of Law, who has written extensively on the death penalty and on the work of the California Supreme Court, and is quite an expert on both. The commission—conditioned on the necessary funding being made available—endorsed the proposal that I'm about to describe to you. It would allow the California Supreme Court to transfer a certain number of automatic capital appeals—and we proposed 30 a year—to the intermediate Courts of Appeal.

These would be cases that would not involve novel issues. So many of the legal questions in capital cases have been settled by the decisions of the U.S. Supreme Court and the California Supreme Court, but counsel feel duty bound—especially at the risk of their legal representation being deemed constitutionally ineffective—to raise these boilerplate issues over and over again, hoping that some court on some occasion is going to take interest in one of them. Most of the capital cases involve the application of settled principles of law to the individual circumstances of the case then before the court. Transferring 30 of those cases each year to the six Courts of Appeal would be appropriate. After all, these courts handle special circumstances first-degree murder appeals, including those that started off as capital cases and that concluded ultimately with a verdict and judgment of life without possibility of parole. So the justices and their staff already have the expertise to write opinions on most of the issues arising in these cases. There was a cost element, too, however. We felt an obligation in making this proposal to provide the appellate courts with additional staff attorneys to assist them in handling the transferred capital cases. Of course, the funds weren't available during the difficult fiscal times currently facing the state. That's the principal reason why, for now, we did not go forward with our proposal, although again I still suspect that there are some who don't want the process to move any faster and others who don't want to spend the relatively modest funds for staff to help make the process move faster.

There would be a certain amount of oversight engaged in by the California Supreme Court under this proposal, but not to the degree where it would add to the overall delay by providing duplicity of review. Such review by our court after a decision rendered by the court of appeal would be designed to ensure that the Supreme Court of California had examined the case and felt comfortable with the decision rendered by the Court of Appeal. Our court would file an order indicating its approval—not writing an opinion but just noting its approval of the decision. If the Supreme Court wanted to grant review, it could grant review on just one issue instead of on all the dozens of issues usually presented. The basis for review in our court would be expanded uniquely for capital cases beyond the traditional two questions: number one, is there a substantial question of statewide importance?; number two, is there a conflict in the law that needs to be resolved? It would be expanded to cover a third area that normally is not something the California Supreme Court would look at, namely, is there just an ordinary error? It could be a finding by the Court of Appeal that, yes, there was error but it wasn't prejudicial. Or yes, there was error and it was prejudicial, so the prosecution might want to seek review. The proposal would thereby provide an added level of assurance that there was adequate oversight of those capital cases and yet would burden the Court of Appeal with only, as I figured it, each of the 105 justices writing an opinion in a death penalty case about once every three years. So to me, it made a lot of sense because currently, under the constitution, the California Supreme Court has authority to transfer any kind of civil or noncapital criminal case to the Court of Appeal, with the sole exception of capital cases—where the constitution provides that an appeal must be taken directly to the California Supreme Court. I believe this is a good proposal and hope the legislature gives it additional consideration as a proposed constitutional amendment in the future when the state's fiscal situation improves.

There's another proposal that I favored and that has been endorsed by the California Supreme Court and the California State-Federal Judicial Council, a separate body from the California Judicial Council. The proposal is that when a federal court is prepared to appoint habeas corpus counsel to review a California death penalty conviction, that court would appoint habeas counsel to handle both the state habeas and the federal habeas proceedings. Such a process would avoid the further delay and expense involved in having the defendant's legal representation shift from trial counsel to automatic appeal counsel to state habeas counsel and then to a fourth set of players on the defense side—federal habeas counsel. It's among various proposals that the cochair of the California State-Federal Judicial Council, Senior Ninth Circuit Judge Arthur Alarcon, has endorsed. He has written very thoughtfully and constructively, from his perspective as a federal judge and former state judge, about the problems that exist in California's handling of capital cases and the problems that the federal court system has in reviewing the rulings of state courts in capital proceedings. There's a lot of discussion and effort going on to improve the system for handling capital cases. However, such proposals almost always require additional funding, which seems, of course, to be elusive.

The second proposal you mentioned—the one endorsed by the California State-Federal Judicial Council—where did that idea arise, and was it limited to liaison with California?

I believe it was limited to California. It arose in the context of our council, co-chaired by Judge Alarcon and myself and composed half of federal trial and appellate judges from California and half of California judges at the Supreme Court, Court of Appeal, and superior court level. The council also has a habeas corpus committee that was chaired by Judge Joan Weber of the San Diego Superior Court, who was very active in this and other efforts to coordinate the actions of federal and state courts in capital litigation. I also brought up this proposal when I went to Washington, D.C. with tin cup in hand, attempting to obtain money for various state court projects and to demonstrate a federal nexus to those projects in order to justify spending federal money on them—and that included our information system, our technology. We felt there was a rationale for the FBI and Homeland Security being able to obtain information and faster access to it from our state system, and vice versa. I also invoked the delay in capital cases. There are ramifications for the federal courts that emanate from state death penalty litigation, just as there are from state court technology. People who commit state crimes often commit federal crimes as well, and cross state lines in the process. The federal courts also have an interest in proceeding with their review of these capital cases at an earlier date. Having joint counsel to represent the defendant both in federal and state court would facilitate this. The proposal was that Congress appropriate funds—which would save our state some money too—for the appointment of habeas counsel to concurrently undertake both federal court and state court representation, especially because the federal courts often remand the habeas corpus proceedings to state court for exhaustion of available state court remedies before proceeding in federal court. The other thing I want to mention about the discussion of dual federal and state habeas corpus representation is that there were several objectives: financial efficiency, reducing delay, and also actually enhancing the quality of legal representation in capital litigation. There was always an overriding concern with ensuring that the proceedings were as fair as possible at the trial and appellate and habeas levels. I think those are objectives, in all of the proceedings, that all of us had in mind.

Again, was this being proposed just for California, growing out of this California State-Federal Judicial Council and knowing that California's situation is quite different from most other states?

My discussions with Senator Dianne Feinstein were centered on California—a limited focus that could be rationalized, I suppose, as a pilot project. But the logic of it would certainly extend as well to other jurisdictions that have capital punishment, although I think, due to the number of people on death row in California, the size of our state, its caseload, and the amount of delay, such an effort could be particularly beneficial in California.

What view did Senator Feinstein take?

She certainly listened politely. I don't believe she took any action to advance the proposal in any tangible way. I don't know if she's still giving consideration to it. The main focus of our discussions was on getting funds generally, including for technology. I know that Judge Alarcon, who has a personal relationship with the senator, was going to try to pursue the death penalty proposal with her directly, so I hope something comes of it.

Judge Alarcon has been an active voice in all this for some time and indeed co-authored the recent study talking about the great expense that California has borne in trying to carry out the death penalty as it was intended. How do your views of the big picture line up with his?

I'm sympathetic. I think he's made a very thoughtful contribution to the study of California's handling of death penalty cases. There were some points on which I didn't agree with him entirely. He gave me the courtesy of an advance copy of his study, and I made a few suggestions for changes in some factual descriptions of what took place at the California Supreme Court in these matters. I think it's very important that we have the benefit of a whole mix of ideas from well-informed individuals who are constructive and don't just have a one-sided stake in the process. I'm not dismissive of those persons who are partisans on this issue, but I think it's very helpful when persons such as Judge

Alarcon and John Van de Kamp and his commission weigh in without a particular ax to grind. Their interest basically is just in good government.

Going back to the first proposal, the one endorsed by Mr. Van de Kamp's commission, I gather you testified before that commission and that was your first public airing of the idea in some detail. How was it received there?

There was a lot of interest. I limited my personal appearances before legislative and legislatively-created bodies, but this was one where I was pleased to share my views and to have the commission basically support them. I believe the reaction of the Courts of Appeal was fairly positive, as long as they would be provided the additional resources they would need. They did not want to feel that their work product, qualitatively or quantitatively, in noncapital criminal and civil cases would suffer by reason of their undertaking this additional responsibility, but I believe most of them saw the logic in the proposal. It doesn't make sense to have these dozens of capital cases every year funneled to seven persons at the apex of the court system in California who have all these other substantial responsibilities, when the 105 Court of Appeal justices, in my view, are equally qualified to help shoulder this task.

The proposal, as you've just described it to me, was quite detailed—thirty cases a year and other specific aspects. I wonder if you can describe the process of coming up with, first of all, the idea, but then working out those details. Whom did you consult?

There was a lot of study undertaken by my staff in the chief's chambers before this was even floated. We were scratching our heads trying to come up with some way to deal with this problem—given the fact that we weren't going to receive an enormous increment to our court's resources, monetary or otherwise. We were posing the question, "How else can we deal with this? What are the procedural problems that could and should be overcome to facilitate the fair and orderly disposition of these cases?" This proposal benefited from a fair amount of discussion among various members of the court and the staff of the various chambers before it saw the light of day.

You described the reception you got among the Court of Appeal justices. When and how did they first learn about this idea?

My recollection is that I brought it up to them during one of the meetings of the Administrative Presiding Justices Committee. I had previously worked with them on other matters, such as the adoption of minimum standards of performance for appointed counsel and compensation levels for counsel. This was something we were doing at the Supreme Court level, raising the minimum qualifications for appointed counsel, so they understood what we were trying to do and were basically sympathetic.

Of course, while my colleagues and I were tinkering with possible changes in the procedures involved in the processing of capital cases in our court, we were faced with a constant barrage of substantive and procedural legal issues raised in the automatic appeals and the related habeas corpus proceedings filed in our court. Being immersed in the day-to-day functioning or dysfunctioning of the system undoubtedly had some effect upon my own continuing perception of capital punishment, in terms of how it's administered in California and the justification for it.

Yes. It may be that your own view of it evolved some over time as a result of these different factors.

It has. Of course, there are so many arguments that are made concerning the death penalty. Some persons believe that basically it's a question of morality and that capital punishment is indefensible. There are arguments made that capital punishment—the state's taking of a life under any circumstances as a form of punishment, no matter how fair the procedures—is unconstitutional. I personally don't share those views, although I respect them. I view it as my function to apply the law as the people have enacted it at the voting booth or through their elected representatives, except when there's a specific constitutional or legal impediment to doing so. I've written 56 opinions for the court in capital cases, setting aside the death penalty in seven of them. There was even a case, *People v. Ayala*, where Justice Mosk—despite his personal opposition to the death penalty—wrote an affirmance of a death judgment and I wrote a dissent, in which Justice Kennard joined. A majority of our court in that case found harmless the circumstance that defense counsel had been excluded from a portion of the proceedings that examined the views of prospective jurors concerning the death penalty. I concluded that the exclusion of the defense from those proceedings was prejudicial and necessitated reversal of the judgment of conviction in its entirety and a remand for a new trial. Although I'm certainly open to finding the presence of error in capital proceedings and finding such error to be prejudicial, I'm of the view that if there is to be a death penalty—which in my view is a question for the people of our state to decide directly or through their elected representatives—that form of punishment is administered in California in basically as fair a manner as it can be administered, and as fairly as it is anywhere in the United States.

Interestingly enough, there has been a historical cycle in capital punishment laws, as there was with regard to sentencing in noncapital offenses. I believe we discussed how there was strictly determinate sentencing and then, as a penological reform intended to take into account the individuality of the offender, we went to an indeterminate reform whereby the parole authorities would set a particular term in light of the defendant's past and his or her prospects. Subsequently, this came to be thought of as unfair in giving insufficient guidance or hope to an offender concerning a release date, so we in California then went to a three-tiered set of punishments for most offenses, lower, middle, and upper, with findings having to be made to justify deviating from the middle term. In many ways, there has been a parallel evolution in capital jurisprudence, because in England about a couple centuries ago, there were specific crimes that inevitably were punished by the death penalty, without any deviation. That certainly was thought to be harsh, and what happened as capital punishment evolved in the United States, was that in jurisdictions having the death penalty, the jury was given discretion to decide between death and life. This was thought to be humane in enabling the jury to consider the individual factors attending the defendant and his or her crime and background. But that in turn came to be viewed as harsh and unfair, because it was thought that the jury was able to impose a death verdict for any reason, legitimate or spurious, or for no reason. Such reasons conceivably could include the racial background of the defendant or anything else that we would deem objectionable or irrelevant.

Too much discretion?

Exactly, too much discretion. Of course, I got into some of those frays in my role as a deputy attorney general in the *McGautha* case that we discussed at one of our early sessions, in which I represented the State of California before the U.S. Supreme Court. I prevailed on the theory that the absence of strict guidelines to assist the jury in making its determination between the alternate punishments of death and life imprisonment did not deprive capital defendants of due process of law. But then, in the *Aikens/Furman* line of cases, I had to basically defend the system against a new line of attack, namely that the absence of those standards, even if not a deprivation of due process under *McGautha*, constituted cruel and unusual punishment under the Eighth Amendment of the federal constitution.

When the U.S. Supreme Court came down with its ruling in *Furman*—because as we talked about, *Aikens*, although the lead case, had been rendered moot by the California Supreme Court's decision in *People v. Anderson*—there were only two justices, Justices Brennan and Marshall, who found that the death penalty was per se cruel and unusual punishment under any and all circumstances. Their view was rejected by the high court in a subsequent case, *Gregg v. Georgia*, which sanctioned a procedure that steered a middle course between the impermissible extremes of a mandatory death penalty and a procedure permitting standardless discretion in the imposition of the death penalty. The remaining justices of the high court, to the extent one can cobble together some kind of holding and guidance from its multiple individual opinions, only concluded that the death penalty was cruel and unusual punishment as applied in *Furman* and in the other two cases that followed *Aikens*. The opinion for the court in *Furman* was just a one-page per curiam opinion that ended up holding that the imposition of the death penalty in those cases constituted cruel and unusual punishment in violation of the constitution. Each of the nine justices wrote separately, filing his or her own concurrence or dissent. None of them was able to gather more than three other justices to support them, so there's no controlling opinion rendered by a majority of the court. In contrast, a majority of the California Supreme Court, in *People v. Anderson*, held the death penalty was per se cruel *or* unusual punishment under any and all circumstances. "Or" was the operative word in the state constitution as opposed to "and" under the federal constitution, in the majority's view. Therefore, in California, the death penalty was outlawed under any and all circumstances until the initiative passed in November 1972, an effort that I worked on as a deputy attorney general with Governor Deukmejian, then-Senator Deukmejian, before my appointment to the bench.

In considering the fairness of the death penalty as it is administered in California, I relied—both in arguing *McGautha* before the high court and in formulating my own personal views—on the circumstance that special procedures exist under California law governing the penalty phase of a capital case that render the procedure as constitutionally permissible and fair to both the defense and the prosecution as would be any formalized procedure that might be imposed by the U.S. Supreme Court. I'll go through these quickly. The jury, by statute and standard instructions given by the trial judge, is conferred evenhanded discretion in choosing between the two available punishments of death and life imprisonment without the possibility of parole. You don't have a presumption one way or the other the way you did in some states. All competent and relevant evidence permitting the jury to judge the accused, and not merely the crime, is admissible on the issue whether the defendant is to live. Broad leeway is given to counsel in arguing to the jury which punishment is appropriate in light of the evidence, so long as the jury does not consider extraneous matters and is not restricted in its consideration of proper factors. There's a special, stringent rule of prejudicial error, making any substantial error per se cause for reversal. There is multifaceted review of every jury verdict that imposes the death penalty. First of all, the trial judge has not only the power but the duty to evaluate the punishment imposed by the jury and can reduce a death penalty verdict to life imprisonment. Then the California Supreme Court engages in both automatic appellate review and habeas corpus review of the judgment and of the punishment imposed, followed by federal court habeas review. Finally the governor reviews each capital case, having the authority—which has been frequently exercised in past years—to grant a pardon or commutation. So these are all things that—in my view today, and as I argued about 40 years ago before the U.S. Supreme Court—help render California's death penalty procedures fair as well as constitutional.

The question, of course, is always raised, "Isn't there a burden to demonstrate a justification for the death penalty?" The briefing that I undertook in the U.S. Supreme Court in *McGautha* and *Aikens* convinced me then and convinces me today that there are legitimate grounds for having the death penalty. Although it is controversial, I believe in the theory of deterrence. The death penalty obviously doesn't deter all murders, but there are documented instances in which someone's life has been saved because the criminal was deterred when he or she readily could have killed the victim and been unlikely to be apprehended. I rely on legal authority and data, cited in the briefs I filed, describing incidents in which a criminal sets out to commit a robbery or burglary and deliberately chooses not to bring a firearm, or brings a toy firearm, or brings a real firearm and doesn't bring ammunition, or has a loaded gun and doesn't use it. It might involve a victim who is the lonely liquor store clerk late at night, or a pursuing police officer on whom the criminal has the draw. There have been instances where, basically in these words, the apprehended suspect says, referring to the execution chamber, "I thought of that little green room. I didn't want to press the trigger," or "I didn't want to bring a loaded firearm."

But I think the crucial problem regarding the justification of deterrence is that arguably there is little or no deterrent when it's known that there is a 25-year delay in carrying out the punishment. Not to reduce it overly simplistically, but if one were to tell one's child that, "In a couple of years I'm going to reduce your allowance or give you a spanking," it probably wouldn't have anywhere near the effect of imposing that punishment more immediately. Again, I don't favor lickety-split justice but I think, as I said a moment ago, that within about five years we should be able to determine whether a death penalty judgment should be upheld or not. The decades of delay make the death penalty, the court system, and government in general look dysfunctional and somewhat ridiculous—like something akin to Charles Dickens' depiction of the Chancery Court in his novel *Bleak House*.

Another argument that is used to justify the death penalty is incapacitation, that it precludes a criminal from harming, perhaps killing, someone else. One might ask, "Wouldn't life imprisonment accomplish that?" But there are many instances of prisoners—some of them life-term inmates, who by the way are generally considered to be the most dangerous of the inmate population—killing guards, civilian prison workers, and fellow inmates. There also have been instances of defendants who escaped or were paroled, sometimes after their sentence was commuted to life with parole, and who then went out and killed again. There is a case I handled as a deputy attorney general, *People v. Nye*, that illustrates the point of incapacitation. After obtaining reversal of his death penalty judgment, the defendant was retried and again received the death penalty, which was affirmed by the California Supreme Court. After his sentence was reduced to life imprisonment in the wake of the *Anderson* decision invalidating the death penalty in California, the defendant was released on parole—only to commit another murder. The case of *People v. Wein* provides a similar example. An additional rationale for the death penalty was invoked by Justice Potter Stewart in his concurring opinion in *Furman*, expressing the view that retribution served a legitimate function for society in this sense. Without weighing in on this, I am just pointing out that there are various justifications for the death penalty that have been recognized.

To the extent my views have evolved, I would say the following. Initially, of course, I was acting as an advocate, and I always felt that the State of California was entitled to the most vigorous advocacy I was able to provide, as long as it takes place in a fair and ethical manner, just as the most heinous criminal is entitled to effective legal representation under the Sixth Amendment to the federal constitution. But I do believe there are some concerns about the death penalty that are more legitimate than others. Interestingly enough, Justice Stewart, in one of those nine separate opinions in the *Furman* case, stated the following view: "These death sentences are cruel and unusual in the same way that being struck by lightning is cruel and unusual." Then he observes that the petitioners were among "a capriciously selected, random handful among people similarly situated." He says, "I simply conclude that the Eighth and Fourteenth Amendments cannot tolerate the infliction of a sentence of death under legal systems that permit this unique penalty to be so wantonly and freakishly imposed." In other words, Justice Stewart viewed the death penalty as freakish, like being hit by lightning. That's an interesting argument. I'm not saying I'm convinced by it, but it does give one pause.

You have, first of all, the circumstance that each state is free to decide for itself whether or not to have capital punishment. But of course that's a traditional matter, the definition of crime and the definition of permissible punishment being determined, under our federal system, by each state, subject to federal constitutional limitations. So there always will be variations in punishments meted out in our individual states. The question is, to what degree is that justifiable or not? Then, going beyond the matter of federalism, it is clear that—within a state—enormous variables exist. For instance, not only is capital punishment never imposed in modern times in San Francisco, but candidates for district attorney campaign on pledges never to seek the death penalty in any case. In contrast, the same type of crime that might not cause the D.A. to allege a special circumstance—the prerequisite to seeking the death penalty—in Los Angeles County, might readily incur one across the county line in neighboring Orange or Kern or Riverside County. You could have the exact same crime, let's say a straightforward street robbery homicide, result in the seeking of the death penalty in one part of the state and not in the other, among various defendants with similar past histories and records. This, to me, raises some troubling issues. I'm not saying I find this necessarily rises to the level of a constitutional infirmity, but it may raise policy concerns about the manner in which the death penalty is administered in California.

One specific area that troubles me in terms of the development of the law are the cases relating to victim-impact evidence. The U.S. Supreme Court had held in the late 1980s, in the *Booth* and *Gathers* cases, that the prosecution was not entitled to present evidence of the impact of the victim's death on his or her family, friends, and other loved ones. But a couple years later, in 1991, in *Payne v. Tennessee*, the high court overruled its own decisions of just a few years earlier and held that victim-impact evidence now is admissible with few, if any, clear limitations. Although the *Payne* decision contains some cautionary language, it has given rise to prosecutors' routinely presenting to jurors videos depicting the life of the homicide victim, from infancy through college graduations and marriage ceremonies, sometimes accompanied by rather emotional music. Aside from that being troublesome to me in its own right—and I've had to author some opinions for the court in this area—I'm concerned by two things.

First of all, the U.S. Supreme Court was very quick to overrule its own recent precedent. Second, I not only feel that changing the law in this manner is somewhat disturbing, but that the manner in which judicial decisions uphold the admission of this type of evidence aggravates the already existing disparities in the imposition of the death penalty. Putting aside the geographical variations in charging policies that I mentioned a moment ago, victim-impact evidence can bring about total disparities in the punishment meted out to otherwise identically situated offenders in the same local jurisdiction. A criminal goes up to someone on the street, attempts to rob him, and shoots him to death. The victim in criminal A's case is a well-respected community leader and family man, and the jury is presented with all this victim-impact evidence from witnesses that, without exaggeration, often literally elicits tears from those in the courtroom. Then you've got criminal "B," who commits the identical crime against another victim. This victim happens to be homeless, has no friends or family members to be contacted to come to court and testify. I believe that the jury can't help but be more inclined to impose the death penalty in defendant A's case than it would be in the case of defendant B. The prosecutor presumably wouldn't bother presenting victim-impact evidence if that were not true. Why should imposition of the death penalty hinge upon such factors? So this, to me, is a troublesome area of the law and leads me to a final point that I'll make on the subject of the death penalty.

My ultimate concern is that we're expending a tremendous amount of effort and expense to impose death sentences and send people to death row under circumstances that almost totally undermine the deterrent effect of the death penalty. A person sentenced to death knows that he or she in effect is being given a life-without-parole sentence, because the odds are that he or she is going to die of old age behind bars. Is it worth it to maintain this fictitious system and have only thirteen persons be executed in the last 34 years since the restoration of the death penalty in 1977, the last in 2006—and currently maintain about 720 prisoners on death row—at tremendous cost, at a time when we're severely cutting funds for education, public safety, parks, and social services? If the death penalty were truly being enforced, I would have no problem with its being imposed and carried out. But on a cost-benefits basis, I find it difficult to justify the negative impact that it has on the state in terms of financial cost—and disrespect for the criminal justice system—when only a minuscule percentage of the death sentences imposed are actually being carried out and the legislature doesn't seem to want to provide the funds to fix the system. Basically, my attitude is—fix it, or get rid of it if you're not willing to fix it. I wonder, as a matter of policy, not of law, what justifies continuing with the charade that the death penalty has become? That is the evolution of my thinking on a pragmatic basis—as a voter, not as a judge ruling on these matters. I may have mentioned, when we were talking about the collaborative justice courts that deal with drug problems and quality-of-life issues, that it has been said we've tried being tough on crime but that we also have to be smart on crime. I believe this applies equally to the subject of the death penalty. The state's difficult fiscal situation may account for why public polls and commentators show some reduction in the public's support for the death penalty, because although it's on the books, it's extremely expensive from the outset of trial proceedings to the final review, and yet it isn't being carried out. If it were being administered fairly and properly and efficiently it would be one thing, but with a 25-year delay, you're losing most of the justification of deterrence. It ends up being a life sentence anyway.

I'd say most people, even those who support capital punishment, don't want to have executions set lickety-split the way they do in Texas. There are problems with the type of review and the jurisprudence that you have there and in some other states, sometimes leading to wrongful convictions. The U.S. Supreme Court has had to intervene in several cases where the Texas courts permitted the introduction of expert psychologist testimony and argument to the jury indicating that blacks as a race are more likely to pose a future danger to society than members of other races. That was used by the prosecutor as the justification for why the defendants in those cases should receive the death penalty—because of their race, life imprisonment wouldn't adequately protect society given this propensity to violence.[12] That's not the type of jurisprudence that we would ever tolerate in California or that we would want to see employed in expediting the process here. We could, however, speed up the process and still be fair to defendants, to the prosecution, and to victims' families and benefit the court system, but again I don't know that there's the popular will, at least in the legislature, to allocate the funds required to do this. If there isn't the will to do so, why bother having the death penalty? I guess that concludes my thoughts on this subject. Unless the other two branches of government want to raise the fees that we pay to defense counsel and appropriate the funds needed to undertake the other reforms proposed to expedite the process, I'd say it doesn't seem worth it on a cost-benefits basis to continue with the present system. It's an empty and costly exercise in formalistic ritual to say that we have the death penalty when in fact we don't.

As you mentioned, you have publicly called the current system dysfunctional. What do you see ahead if things continue the way they are, given the strains that capital punishment puts on our judiciary?

I can see the question being put to the voting public in some fashion or another, either through arguments made in the press or through an initiative, basically posing the question, "Would you rather have x millions of dollars put into your school system or into your local law enforcement, or would you instead rather have that money used to house inmates on death row who, under the odds, will never be executed but will die of old age—considering all the expense that precedes their being charged and convicted, and their cases reviewed, before they conclude their 25-year wait for old age to resolve the matter?" I understand it costs more to house an inmate on death row than it does to send a person to one of the finest private universities in the nation. At a time when the State of

---

[12] See, e.g., Buck v. Thaler (2011) 565 U.S. ___ , 132 S.Ct. 32 (dissenting opinion of Sotomayor, J., on denial of certiorari); Saldano v. Texas (2000) 530 U.S. 1212.

California is spending more on its prison system each year than on its system of higher education, the current situation poses some very troublesome questions for the people of our state.

If nothing changes, how much worse will it get?

Most years two or three dozen new death verdicts rendered by juries in the State of California further augment the population on death row at San Quentin Prison. Maybe some of those juries render these verdicts partially out of a sense that the defendant never will be actually executed. I don't know. That's just a possibility. But I think it's a matter of public knowledge—and public criticism—that so few executions take place, and that it takes the courts so long to review capital judgments. I suppose we'll keep adding to the ranks of the 720 individuals on death row. I believe the state, at great expense, is building another death row to house all these people, the vast majority of whom will never be executed. Any solution to this conundrum, as with so many things, will depend upon public awareness of the ramifications involved and of the choices being made—and upon that awareness being communicated to the people's elected representatives in the executive and legislative branches. Again, fix it or get rid of it. The public has to resolve the question where it wants to allocate the very limited resources available to our state and local governments.

Given that the Commission on the Fair Administration of Justice and you and your colleagues and others have put so much effort into suggesting ways that the system could be revised, what is the best way to proceed with trying to effect some of those changes, given the current political and financial climate?

An initiative may qualify for the November 2012 ballot proposing—on various grounds, including the expenses involved in capital punishment—that life imprisonment without possibility of parole be substituted for the death penalty. Perhaps those persons who support the death penalty will conclude that if California is to have a cost-effective death penalty, we should enact the transfer proposal that would enable the California Supreme Court to send cases down to the Courts of Appeal to eliminate years of delay, that provision should be made for the same counsel to represent capital defendants in federal and state court habeas corpus proceedings, and that some money should be thrown in to provide additional compensation for lawyers who undertake the difficult task of representing persons on death row. This last step need not be taken on the rationale of being charitable toward the defense bar, although I think they're performing a very noble calling—but just as a means of reducing the time it takes to find lawyers who are both willing and able to do this work. John Adams, the second president of the United States, was commended for undertaking the defense of British soldiers who were charged with murder. He viewed that as a high calling for a lawyer, and we should properly recognize and reward people who undertake such tasks. But for those proponents of the death penalty who disagree with this premise, they still could decide that these measures will expedite the process and therefore that putting some more money into the system is justified even if it increases the compensation of defense counsel and requires hiring additional staff attorneys for the Courts of Appeal. I suppose this would be the flipside of the argument advanced by opponents of capital punishment that a cost-benefits analysis favors a total abolition of the death penalty.

Now that you're retired, what level of involvement in these matters do you expect to pursue?

I don't plan to make any kind of crusade out of my position. I probably won't be speaking publicly about the issue. My views eventually will be out there in this oral history for people to consider if they wish. I do think that the system we have now is intolerable, both from the standpoint of someone who favors the death penalty and someone who opposes it—and even for anyone who is just concerned about our government's being, and appearing to be, dysfunctional. I believe that the current state of capital punishment in California undermines our values in ways that go beyond the question of the death penalty and the functioning of the court system.

###

Oral Argument and Judicial Opinions
November 2, 2011

Chief Justice George, I thought we might start off today talking about oral argument. Could you start with a bit of overall background about the purpose of that part of the process in our appellate system?

Oral argument is something that I personally welcomed in the sense that so much of the process of a reviewing court is rather impersonal, focused solely on paper. It is, of course, the kind of direct contact with counsel that one has regularly as a trial judge but not as an appellate justice. It also serves the actual substantive benefit of helping the court resolve the issues, even though they usually have been laboriously briefed for months beforehand.

The California Supreme Court sets the case for argument usually four weeks in advance and at a point when at least a majority of the court, four or more of the seven justices, are headed in the same direction. This doesn't necessarily mean they all agree on the precise parameters of the forthcoming opinion, but basically they do agree on the resolution of the case. The California Constitution requires all courts to render a decision within 90 days of a case being submitted, and submission takes place in our court at the time of oral argument—except for the very rare instance where the court wants additional briefing or has to vacate submission due to some extraordinary development.[1] It just

---

[1] A judge or justice of any California court may not receive his or her salary while any case remains pending for 90 days after it is submitted for decision. Cal. Const., art. VI, sec. 19.

would not do to await oral argument and only then start scrambling to get seven people committed in writing to precise positions with the 90-day clock running. Our court, unlike the U.S. Supreme Court, does not have the luxury of hearing cases the first week of October and waiting until the last day of June to render our decisions. This 90-day time limit is what governs the setting of oral argument. If there is a disagreeing justice or a nonresponding justice who has a strong objection to the case being set for oral argument even though four or more justices are agreed that it should be set, normally the setting of the case for oral argument would be deferred, although certainly there's no veto authority on the part of individual justices.

As the date of oral argument approaches, frequently the authoring justice—the justice tentatively assigned by the Chief Justice to write the opinion—will circulate what's called a yellow memo responding to the preliminary responses that his or her six colleagues have circulated, indicating how the authoring justice intends to deal with the suggestions or criticisms set forth in the preliminary responses. This memorandum circulated by the author also may bring his or her colleagues up to date on any later developments in the case or in the law that might have occurred since the calendar memo, or draft opinion, circulated months earlier.

Of course, we've already discussed that the California Supreme Court has three traditional venues—San Francisco, where its headquarters are located, Sacramento, and Los Angeles. We also hold special sessions around the state once a year under our current practice. The setting of the case at a particular geographical site usually has nothing to do with where the case arose or was tried, and usually nothing to do with any other factor. It's normally just a function of when the case is ready to be set at the next calendar. Having said that, there were some exceptional situations where we took into account the intense local public interest in terms of where we set the case. The *In re Marriage Cases*, for instance, fell into that category. Given the San Francisco origin of the legal dispute concerning same-sex marriage and the intense level of public interest there, it made sense to set the case at one of the court's San Francisco sessions. With the special sessions, we have tried to take into account their location in the sense that there might be some cases that arose out of the geographical area where the session is being held and that therefore would be of greater interest to the student and general population whom we include in our outreach efforts. For instance, when we met in Fresno we were able to have some Central Valley cases with local agriculture issues placed on that oral argument calendar as well as some other issues that were of particular interest to students, such as privacy questions in the use of cellphones.

Are you mainly making these decisions of location yourself, or what is that process?

It's something that I would propose to my colleagues, or one of them might suggest, "This would be a good case for Fresno, involving as it does an issue of water allocation for agriculture," let's say. So those are some general logistical considerations.

Since you inquired about the purpose of oral argument, I would say, first of all, that argument in the Court of Appeal can be as vigorous and extensive as it is before the California Supreme Court. But in some instances argument before the justices of the intermediate appellate court may extend only a few minutes, just providing an opportunity for counsel to respond to any questions the justices may have. In the California Supreme Court it's unusual for counsel not to use up their entire time, which is 30 minutes per side and which may be divided between counsel of record and perhaps include argument by amicus curiae. As I mentioned before, it's 45 minutes per side in automatic death penalty appeals.

Candor regarding the facts in the record and the existing law is absolutely essential. It is far better to call the court's attention to something that is adverse to your position and attempt to distinguish it, than to have opposing counsel—or, worse yet, the court—confront you with it and think that as an "officer of the court" you may be hiding something.

Among the many articles that have been written giving advice to counsel concerning oral argument is an excellent one written recently by Jerry Falk, a noted San Francisco appellate specialist, on arguing before the California Supreme Court.[2] He explains what leads up to oral argument and makes a couple of points that I'll just quote directly and certainly endorse. He says: "It's a conversation, not an oration." I would add that we have had counsel who have tried to go on and on with their rhetoric and on a rare occasion inappropriately have mildly objected when the court has interrupted their speech. The whole point of oral argument is that it's supposed to be a dialogue. Mr. Falk suggests keeping in mind the overall objective of the California Supreme Court in writing an opinion—why it granted review in the case—and thinking beyond the bounds of the dispute between the parties. His advice is also to: "Listen to the question. Don't praise or editorialize about the question, and don't put off answering." This advice reminds me of a couple of stories concerning Chief Justice Earl Warren and oral argument. There's a famous instance of an advocate being asked a question by Chief Justice Warren—I remember hearing about it when I went back there to argue—and the attorney responding, "I'm not there yet. I'll

---

[2] "Preparing for Argument in the California Supreme Court," Jerome B. Falk, Jr., *California Litigation*, Vol. 24, No. 2 (2011).

get to that later." The attorney was told, "You're there now, counsel." [Laughter] I think that's important to keep in mind. On another occasion, a probing question by Chief Justice Warren was met with counsel's observation, "That's a good question Your Honor!" Warren's response to counsel was, "Well, *I* thought so!"

Getting back to Mr. Falk's article, he also writes: "If at first you don't succeed, try something else." In other words, don't keep beating a dead horse if it looks as if you're not getting anywhere. Again, this relates to some of the earlier advice: "Keep your nose out of your notes." Don't read a speech. If you have to write one out, do so but try to memorize it and consult a bit of an outline to make sure you haven't missed any points, but don't read. That's just repeating what could have or should have been in your brief. Sometimes you are sort of damned if you do, damned if you don't. If it's in the brief, why are you arguing it? And if it isn't in the brief, why are you coming up with a new point? [Laughter] In any event, expect to have your speech interrupted by questions.

Another matter—I don't believe it's covered directly in the article—is that you may be asked a question on something that you were planning to reach as perhaps your third point, and you're on the second point. How should you handle this? I mentioned to you previously that I found that an effective tool was seizing upon the question as entrée to discuss that third point then and there. Then weave your way back to where you wanted to be, because otherwise you can find yourself not covering the ground that you need to before your time is up. So those are general suggestions that may be helpful to counsel who are arguing.

It can be advantageous, in a case with broad ramifications, to cede a portion of one's allotted time for oral argument to amicus curiae, even though it does come out of your own time; we don't give additional time for AC argument. The crucial role of amicus curiae can be, first of all, in urging that review be granted in the first place, convincing the court that this is not just a narrow dispute between the parties in question—as important as that dispute may be to them—but that there are broad ramifications to an industry, to an employee group, to society at large that merit the California Supreme Court's selection of the case for review among the 1 or 2 percent of the cases in which review is granted, because it involves a question of substantial statewide importance and/or a need to resolve a conflict in the law. Second, once review has been granted, the filing of amicus curiae briefs addressing the merits of the legal contentions can be very helpful to the party being supported, and to the court as well.

However, in many cases the court was troubled, as was I in particular, by the fact that each side in the case might allocate segments of its allotted 30 minutes of argument not only among the attorneys representing multiple parties, but also to a multitude of amici curiae. I had the impression that some attorneys simply desired to be on record as a participant in the argument in this about-to-be-important decision. Some wanted their 15 minutes of fame, as Andy Warhol might have put it—which actually were closer to 15 seconds of fame, in a succession of two-minute oral arguments. [Laughter] In some cases it was almost ludicrous. There was an article in one of the legal newspapers headlined, "Too Many Counsel Spoil the Argument, Judges Say." It noted that on the calendar no fewer than 14 attorneys strode to the podium over the course of two cases argued the morning of April 9, 1997, meaning that they had an average of about seven and a half minutes per attorney. The article quotes me as having said, "The court will now have the experience of three consecutive two-minute rebuttal arguments. Out of an abundance of charity, we won't keep track of the time it takes to clear your throats."[3] Ultimately, I proposed to the court, and we adopted, a rule specifying that, aside from an attorney being allowed to reserve a short amount of time for rebuttal, no argument of less than 10 minutes would be permitted—so that the court would not have to endure a series of little snippets of oral argument, which really don't end up being useful.

We also adopted a rule paralleling one followed by the U.S. Supreme Court that requires each party to disclose any support given by the party to an amicus curiae. Until a few years ago a party could finance or even ghostwrite amicus curiae briefs for the very purpose I mentioned—namely to show widespread interest and application and relevance of a ruling that the court might render, when this might just be conjured up by a party. I think we needed to know which were the decoy missiles and which was the real one, so under our formal rules, like those of the U.S. Supreme Court, there must be disclosure by counsel of any party support for an amicus curiae brief.

How did the legal community respond to that change?

I never heard any fuss about it. I think, if anything, anyone would have been embarrassed to protest, because even without a rule it's pretty apparent that's not proper behavior. So I doubt that anyone felt inclined to say, "We don't like that. That's not fair." The attitude was probably more like, "We would never do that, so of course we have no objection to that rule."

Even experienced attorneys can get a bit flummoxed by the experience of appearing before the California Supreme Court—perhaps because we're the highest court in this jurisdiction, or the fact that there are seven of us ready to fire away with questions. In any event, this trepidation has given rise to a couple

---

[3] *The Recorder*, April 22, 1997.

of amusing incidents. One of them involved the president of the Consumer Attorneys of California, a highly respected and experienced lawyer named Sharon Arkin, with whom I had had many meetings, accompanied by her colleagues from that organization. She had appeared before our court on prior occasions. At one oral argument, she blanked out on my name while responding to one of my questions. Then, after pausing, she ended up calling me Justice Baxter followed by "Judge," and then, as she put it in a news story that appeared in one of the legal newspapers, "… in my blonde, Valley Girl way, I said, 'Oh, my God.' The whole courtroom cracked up."[4] This can happen, and I teased her about it after it was written up in the newspaper. But it just illustrates that anyone, even a fine, highly experienced attorney, can have this equivalent of writer's block—I guess, oral-argument block. [Laughter] Justice Sandra Day O'Connor told me that on a couple occasions she witnessed attorneys faint as they were summoned to the podium to argue their case before the high court.

I'll mention one other pitfall that arises out of our sometimes confusing rotation among multiple venues. There were two occasions, memorialized in one of the legal newspapers, on which an attorney appeared for oral argument in the wrong city—promptly on time, but in the wrong part of California. [Laughter] In a story headlined, "800 Miles Later, a 30-Minute Supreme Court Argument," the reporter wrote that when the attorney finally arrived, "he looked as if he had been beaten up." He was a total mess and his clothing was all askew. He had come from a town 10 miles south of the Oregon border, had driven to San Francisco instead of Sacramento for the 1:30 p.m. oral argument session, and finally showed up in Sacramento later that afternoon.

What became of him in that case?

The article indicates that the marshal told him after his breathless and embarrassed apology that late as he was, he had better go to the restroom and clean himself up. The article indicates that I remarked from the bench that if it was any consolation, he wasn't the first lawyer that year to travel halfway across the state only to arrive at the wrong courtroom. That distinction went to another lawyer who, in June, had flown up to San Francisco from Orange County one morning, only to discover that the justices were sitting in Los Angeles. [Laughter] I put his case over to the afternoon calendar, and he flew back to Southern California in time to make his argument. The article continued, "Rubbing it in a little, George told the attorney he had the unusual distinction of visiting two of the court's three courtrooms on the same day," pointing out to the attorney that

---

[4] *The Recorder*, April 19, 2005.

the location of the argument is printed in large bold letters on the top of the calendar that was sent to him. The reporter asked if I was prepared to have the court punish lawyers who inadvertently arrive at the wrong city, and I said no. "The embarrassment is probably sufficient self-inflicted punishment."[5]

Speaking generally about oral arguments, I've already mentioned that we televise them basically whenever we've been asked to. Also, all of the special sessions are televised. By the way, we have an overflow auditorium in San Francisco and sometimes in other venues where those who can't find seating inside the courtroom are allowed to see it on a large screen. It's also televised into the chambers, so that the staff attorneys can observe. When we had the *In re Marriage Cases*—the court certainly didn't arrange this but the city and county government of San Francisco did—a gigantic screen was set up in the middle of Civic Center Plaza to enable the throngs outside to see the arguments.

As for why justices will ask questions—some more than others—frequently, of course, it's simply to obtain more factual information from the record. Despite the examination of the transcripts undertaken by the justices and staff, the needed information may not have been uncovered, or its relevance may not be fully apparent. Sometimes the justices' questions relate to the applicable law and perhaps to legal authority that counsel have not cited in their briefs. On occasion, the purpose of a question from the bench is basically just to push counsel's position to the extreme, to reveal what the logical consequences would be of the position taken by counsel. In that context it is important to keep in mind that the reason the court took the particular case is probably not just to narrowly resolve the dispute between the parties but to establish a principle, a rule, a precedent to guide other courts, the bar, and segments of society in future situations. Consequently, the position taken by counsel has to be examined in light of its ramifications for individuals and institutions in contexts well beyond what's involved in the case at hand. That can be an important purpose of oral argument.

What's a good example of an issue area where the oral argument would serve that purpose well?

The court might be faced, let's say, with an employment dispute where an employee was wrongfully discharged in his or her view. The court might well be persuaded, however, that recognizing the claim in a certain context might prove unworkable in the sense of hampering not just the company but business in general in a way that might end up being adverse to the overall interest of employ-

---

[5] *The Recorder*, November 13, 2001.

ees. Recognizing the claim might also conflict with state and federal statutes outside the employment sphere.

The fascination of the law, especially at the level at which it reaches the California Supreme Court, is that frequently there is a clash of competing legal principles, even constitutional principles. Such a conflict can be the subject of probing questions from the justices. One good example is illustrated by the opinion I wrote for the court in the case of *Aguilar v. Avis Rent-a-Car*, where you had a hostile workplace environment caused by the company's tolerance of a supervisor who made a practice of directing racial epithets to lower-grade employees and creating an atmosphere in which there was a constant element of racial bias infused in the atmosphere of the place of employment. One might recognize this immediately as a hostile workplace environment, but on the other side there was a claim that free speech rights were implicated. The issue was raised whether a First Amendment right exists to use a racial epithet in addressing subordinate employees. In the opinion I wrote for the court, I rejected that claim and resolved the issue in favor of the right to be free of a hostile work environment, although serious First Amendment issues had been raised. This case illustrates how equally viable legal and constitutional principles can clash with each other, calling upon a court to try to resolve the conflict and decide which principles should prevail in a given situation. Our court's decision was by a four-to-three vote.

Another purpose in a justice's promulgating a question may be to make a point with a colleague further down the bench, more or less implicitly communicating, "Look at this." Or, "I told you so."

You're communicating with one another, in other words?

Yes, and perhaps the attorney, whether sensing it or not, is playing the role of a ping-pong ball in that dialogue between two or more justices. Sometimes it's difficult for the justices to get a question in, too. There have been situations where all seven of us are firing questions away at an attorney, and one or more of the justices may ask a series of lengthy, related questions. Another justice may end up not having had the chance to ask a question and may say, "I'll reserve my question for the next attorney or for rebuttal." Sometimes justices will defer to each other once they both start talking at the same time. Sometimes they won't, and it's whoever continues speaking or speaks loudest who ends up being able to pose the question and obtain an answer. There is no protocol in terms of who goes first or who cedes to another; it is not based on seniority or anything else. Sometimes it's more or less just a situation of jumping in there, and seeing who can get his or her licks in.

In your role as Chief Justice, the person in charge of these proceedings overall, was there any difference for you in finding cause to intervene with other justices?

No, I would never intercede. The only thing I would do is perhaps—and this would usually be at the end of the argument—if there was a question that had been asked and the attorney just hadn't had the chance to answer it because time ran out and maybe there was another question that intervened, I might say, "Counsel, your time is up but you may provide—or we would be interested in—your response to Justice So-and-so's question." On some occasions, the time would run out while a lengthy question was being posed to an attorney, so at the conclusion of that question, before it could be answered, I would say, "Counsel, your time has expired but you may respond to the pending question by Justice So-and-so," so that both the attorney and the justice would know that this wasn't carte blanche to go on and on, but by the same token the attorney wouldn't unfairly be denied the opportunity to respond to a question where the time had run out in the middle of the question. These were some of the traffic-directing functions that I had, in addition to keeping track of time even though counsel are supposed to do that themselves. They're never supposed to ask the court how much time they have left, but they would often run over in their attempt to get as much time as they could. I have always admired counsel who could adroitly answer the questions, cover all of his or her points, and then inform the court, "We submit unless there are further questions," and do that without being told, "Your time is up."

After the argument is concluded, the last words on the case are usually the Chief Justice's pronouncement, "The matter stands submitted." Again, in very unusual situations we might then, or after the case is submitted, call for additional briefing while the 90 days is running. We might wish to await an important decision from the U.S. Supreme Court and then welcome additional briefing on that opinion. We have the authority to vacate submission, obtain additional briefing, and then resubmit the matter. Sometimes we might vacate submission because we are aware there's a ruling pending. Knowing that the U.S. Supreme Court heard argument in the spring, and that the court is expected to come down with its decision before the end of its term in June, we might just defer submitting the matter at the time of oral argument. But in, I'm sure, 99 percent of the cases, submission occurs at the conclusion of the oral argument.

Then we go into postargument conference. We sit around the chief's conference table and go over the three morning cases during the noon hour, and at the end of the day we go over the three afternoon cases. Once in a while due to a noon engagement, we confer on a full calendar of all six cases at the end of the day. The discussion does not start off in the order that takes place in resolving petitions at the weekly conference—the order of seniority among the associate justices, followed by the chief—but instead starts off with the tentative author of the majority opinion presenting the case, indicating any reaction to particular arguments that came up, perhaps for the first time, at oral argument or to the manner in which they were made, and indicating how the oral argument will or will not affect the drafting of the opinion in final form. After that, if a dissenting calendar memorandum was circulated before oral argument, which rarely occurs, I would call upon the dissenter to speak next. Then the remaining justices, without regard to whether their preliminary responses voiced agreement or disagreement with the majority calendar memorandum, speak and vote in order of seniority, with the chief going last.

This does not happen often, but once in a great while I saw the oral argument, despite all of the briefing, despite all of the preparation by the justices, flip things around 180 degrees, and the losing party ends up being the winning party. Then the question arises whether the tentative author is or is not willing to accommodate the new majority among the seven justices. As I said before, when the author is unwilling to make that accommodation, I had to reassign the case to another justice, who would in some instances start pretty much from scratch with the 90-day clock running, because a change in the justices' positions would rarely provide legal cause to vacate submission. Then a new work product emerges from the newly assigned author. This doesn't happen often after oral argument, although frequently how the opinion is written on one or more issues is affected by the oral argument, even if it doesn't change the bottom-line result. The opinion's analysis clearly can be altered.

You talked on another occasion about how, generally, oral argument doesn't change your own views, although it can, but that it serves a useful function. Can you reflect on how your colleagues viewed oral argument? Were there any significant differences in its role in the process for them than for you?

I don't think there was a fundamental difference among the justices. I believe we all approached the function of oral argument pretty much the same way. Candidly, some of the justices enjoy oral argument more than others. On occasion—depending upon the issues and upon the presentation of counsel—it can be dull, although I've always found that a truly fine appellate advocate could make oral argument quite enjoyable on even the dullest of issues. There were others who, in even the most exciting disputes, could render oral argument quite tedious and soporific. An advocate should keep in mind that the court on a given day of oral argument—which may be one of three or four days of consecutive oral argument—might be hearing within a six-or-seven-hour session, half a dozen cases with issues ranging from insurance law to tort law to civil rights to employment discrimination to a dispute between two branches of government to a death penalty case. In a single day there can be a multitude of issues spanning a wide spectrum of the law, and the justices are constantly switching gears. The justices, with the assistance of staff attorneys, do a lot of preparation before oral argument, so counsel should approach argument in that context and with the realization that, although oral argument is the big moment for counsel and for the parties in the given case, it is only one part of the continuum. The best use of oral argument is to pique the justices' interest in the issues, to address their concerns, and to stress what's most significant—highlighting what might be of the greatest benefit to one's client in terms of using the 30 minutes in the most profitable way—and not just to rehash one's position by reciting or summarizing what's already in the briefs.

You've used the phrase "firing questions" a couple of times. What's the value of, in some cases, being a very active questioner?

In some cases it can be very important for the justices to perform the function of exploring the ramifications of counsel's position, instead of merely letting counsel keep reiterating the injustice that his or her client might suffer if the client doesn't prevail in the matter at hand. It is important to keep counsel focused on the way many other people and institutions, and society in general, are going to be affected by how the court rules in the particular case before them. Justice Baxter is well known for being quite effective in posing hypothetical situations, saying, "All right. But what if such-and-such would happen?" Once in a while counsel would be foolish enough to say, "But that's not our case here." And of course Justice Baxter, or whoever the questioner might be, would say, "We recognize that, but our decision is going to affect people and institutions beyond your client." Sometimes a hypothetical question would be very illuminating in terms of pushing the application of counsel's position to its full parameters and focusing counsel's argument on the court's function of laying down broad, generally applicable rules and principles.

Was that the sort of thing the justices might discuss in chambers ahead of time?

Normally not, if you are referring to questions the justices might pose at oral argument. I think that as each of us engaged in our individual preparation for oral argument—rereading the internal exchanges, the calendar memo, and the preliminary responses to it and any responsive memoranda, and looking over portions of the record and the briefs—at least on my behalf, certain questions would come to mind that I'd jot down, a few points that I wanted to explore at oral argument. But just as frequently, it would be something that counsel said or that one of my colleagues said or asked that would prompt my interest or my curiosity in posing a particular question in order to follow up on a line of questioning that others had instigated. I believe that, for the most part, oral argument is a very spontaneous, unscripted process for the justices in terms of their role.

To what extent did your own approach to it change over time, if at all?

I suppose I grew to appreciate more and more the fact that, whether I would be writing for the majority or one of my colleagues would be undertaking that task, we were really coming up with rules to govern the conduct of others. I became focused on that, as opposed to being constricted to the equities between the parties themselves. I believe that is something, the longer one is on the court, that one becomes aware of and sensitized to.

Once a draft opinion had circulated following the post-oral-argument conference, discussions among the justices might continue. One or more chambers might believe that a point made at postargument conference wasn't adequately addressed in the way the opinion was actually fashioned, or that new concerns or issues had arisen, or that further research had uncovered additional points that should be addressed. Through written memoranda and often through direct oral contact among the justices' staff attorneys, many exchanges could ensue, back and forth. In fact, in very complex situations there might be a conference with several and maybe all of the chambers being represented by staff, trying to work out some language that would accommodate these conflicting concerns. Sometimes very substantial changes in the draft opinion emanated from exchanges like that, and on some occasions just one or two words were deemed objectionable and would be readily changed by the author. Every change, however minor, necessitated circulating a written notice and each justice's filing of a pink sheet in which one had to okay the change if one had already signed off on the opinion, even if it was changing a word like "substantially" to "appreciably." A justice joined in an opinion by signing the original, which was kept in the calendar secretary's office. If you had signed and one or two words were changed, you'd nevertheless have to give your okay that your signature was still in effect. Otherwise, the opinion could not be filed. More extensive changes to the opinion might require resignature. So in some cases a tremendous amount of discourse took place, back and forth, formal and informal, in the process of finalizing a written opinion, between the time of oral argument and the actual filing of the opinion.

We've talked about your process in your own chambers for writing opinions, to some extent, but as a prelude to discussing particular cases I wonder if you might describe how you would assign cases to the research attorneys on your own staff and the kinds of considerations you might have in making those choices.

I tried—just as I did in making assignments among the seven chambers—to ensure that there was some variety in the assignments and that someone didn't get stuck with all the tax cases or all the insurance cases. However interesting those cases can be on occasion, most persons would not want them as a steady diet. But I also recognized—and this is somewhat in conflict with what I just said—that there were staff attorneys who had particular expertise in some areas and that sometimes the case was important enough that I just didn't want to forgo that expertise. On occasion, in that situation I would assign the case to someone with less expertise but have the other attorney with the expertise review it and give input into the draft, so I would be able to accommodate both of these concerns.

That amounts to a bit of a mentoring system, in some sense.

Yes. In fact, as I mentioned previously, that's something that I did back in the Court of Appeal, where I had only two research attorneys but I made sure that every work product I received, at least substantial work product, draft opinions, had been reviewed by the second attorney before I would receive it for my review, so I would have the benefit of that second look. I instituted in my Supreme Court chambers what we called a buddy system—where one staff attorney, not necessarily on a continuing basis but usually on a case-by-case basis, would have a buddy reviewer. The other attorney reviewing the particular work product wasn't necessarily someone with greater seniority on the staff, sometimes it was lesser, but was someone who would review the memorandum and make suggestions. I always believe that another set of eyes generally improves any product. That worked very well. I should mention that, depending upon the case, there might be interaction between me and the assigned staff attorney during the course of the preparation of the calendar memorandum, the responsive memos, or the ultimate opinion, instead of deferring my review until I received a completed draft. When I would assign the case—and I always made the decision personally as to which staff member would receive which case to work up—I would normally not give any direction. I might give a description of what the issue was, and "Such-and-such is particularly interesting," or whatever, but the understanding always was—and I think I made it explicit when someone was new to the staff—that the law should take him or her where it would, and that's what was important and not starting off with a result and then tailoring the work product to come up with that result.

What freedom did you feel to communicate to a staff attorney the possible concerns of other justices that you might already be aware of?

I might do so, certainly if I was aware of particular concerns, either because of what had been expressed about the case at the time we granted review or just based on the past predilections of the justice in other cases. I would share these concerns and communicate to staff that those were matters that we had to take into account in trying to obtain a majority of four or more justices. I might confer with the assigned attorney and certainly invited the assigned attorney to request a meeting, once his or her research got to a certain point where there was more than one route that it could take. The attorney might be eager to learn my views as to which seemed to be the more plausible way of resolving the case. Occasionally, it was pretty much an equal choice where one could go. The law hadn't been sufficiently established in other contexts as to suggest a particular result in the case before us, and perhaps there were good policy arguments that could be made on both sides. This presented me with an opportunity to weigh in as to what the preferable outcome might be from the standpoint of legal policy if that could be done in an intellectually honest way, with faithfulness to the law.

But often the most important thing was just to provide certainty for lower courts, lawyers, and the public—in particular, for example, an industry group. Sometimes all they cared about, or what they cared most about, was having a result one way or the other so that they would know how to comport themselves, how to conduct their business practices. That's why excessive delay is so harmful to the judicial process and to the manner in which the court system may be perceived. Given the inconvenience and the expense that a party or an industry or other group may incur by reason of a lengthy delay in resolving a legal question, the strong preference literally is sometimes to obtain any ruling, even if one loses, rather than be in limbo for another couple of years. That's a consideration that the courts always have to be mindful of.

You talked before about, if there is a choice in the way to go, there's the old maxim of constitutional law that one should avoid casting a constitutional basis for a ruling in doubt. How do you view that maxim of avoiding the constitutional issue where possible?

It is one of the maxims of jurisprudence that a case should be decided on nonconstitutional grounds rather than reaching out for the broader constitutional basis. This approach was most notably put forth by U.S. Supreme Court Justice

Louis Brandeis in his opinion in the *Ashwander* case. Sometimes there comes into play the maxim that if a statute is susceptible of more than one construction, the construction that will preserve the statute, that will uphold its constitutionality, should be adopted by the court, rather than another construction that would invalidate the statute. The approach that will uphold the statute occasionally may involve a more expansive interpretation of the statute, a broader interpretation than what might be gleaned from the statute's wording, or a narrower approach, but such an approach is deemed preferable to not engaging in that effort and thereby having to declare the statute unconstitutional. Courts occasionally are criticized for going beyond their proper function by, in effect, rewriting legislation to make the statute apply in a broader or maybe a narrower fashion in the court's effort to uphold the statute's constitutionality. However, it seems to me that it is far less intrusive for a court to engage in that function, in terms of forgoing judicial restraint and violating the separation-of-powers doctrine, than it would be to invalidate the entire legislative enactment. It may be far preferable to put a judicial gloss on what the legislature did and hopefully intended to do, rather than just say they didn't get it quite right and therefore their work product is thrown out and they can go back and try again.

You had occasion to confront that very situation.

Yes, I certainly did on many occasions. You and I spoke about the opinion I wrote for the court in the *NBC Subsidiary* case. My staff attorney, in conducting his own independent research, came across a statute enacted in the 1870s—not cited in the attorneys' briefs—and we had the clerk's office bring it to the attention of counsel for supplemental briefing. The statute, which provided for open courtrooms, established a statutory policy that made it unnecessary to reach the First Amendment issue or its state constitutional counterpart. Our opinion infused the statute with constitutional dimensions by construing it in a manner consistent with First Amendment principles. The process I just described also illustrates what a truly engaging intellectual exercise it always was to work with staff. I found my staff attorneys highly capable in terms of their research abilities, their incisive legal analysis, and their wordsmithing. There was a lot of give-and-take, and crafting opinions was clearly a partnership effort between myself and my staff that I truly enjoyed. As I've already indicated, working on my own opinions and having input into the opinions written for the court by other justices was by far my favorite part of the many responsibilities I had as Chief Justice, along with presiding over the weekly petition conferences.

The individuals I had on my staff over the years were very capable attorneys. They also needed to have diplomatic skills, because they were not working only for me—in the sense that their work product had to gain the support of at least four members of the court. They sometimes had to engage in discussions and negotiations with the other chambers, which I encouraged them to do even if we had four votes. I've previously mentioned to you that I did not stop counting once I had a majority of the court express agreement with my position. If I had six votes and I could acquire a seventh vote perhaps by modifying an offending paragraph to satisfy one of my colleagues, I would engage in that effort because, to the extent the court could speak with one voice, its rulings would be accepted as having greater force and would provide greater certainty to guide lower courts, lawyers, and the public than if it reflected a smattering of views scattered over the official reports of the court's written opinions.

We might begin talking about some of your specific opinions. Is there anything more, though, to add about the general process you employed?

I'll just make a couple of observations. Obviously, some cases were of far greater interest to the public than others. I would sometimes make a point of including in the opinion of the court, usually at the outset, a summary of what the issues were and how the court was resolving them—in as close to lay language as possible—as part of my civics effort to foster public understanding of the courts. My purpose in doing this was to provide the public and the press with something that a person not trained in the law could grasp and understand concerning what the court had decided and how it arrived at its decision, instead of launching right away into some of the legalese that confounds most laypersons. I think that approach to opinion writing can be particularly helpful in cases of great interest to the public. Also, perhaps at the risk of not entertaining the reader with as much colorful language as might be welcomed in terms of pleasure reading, I tried to stay away from flamboyant language and usually, but not always, resisted the temptation to impose humor on my captive audience.

Then, just as a general consideration, there was always a debate among justices on various appellate courts including our own, and a lot of scholarly writing on the subject, concerning the proper use of footnotes. I know there are competing considerations. What is more disruptive, having a string of legal citations in the text and maybe even in the middle of a sentence, or instead using footnotes? One writer described footnotes as stalagmites poking up from the bottom of the page. I think it was Noel Coward who likened the distraction of footnotes to having to go downstairs to answer the doorbell while you're making love. [Laughter] There's an ongoing debate about the use of footnotes in judicial opinions, and there are things to be said on both sides.

What is your own view?

I find footnotes to be preferable, although someone else likened reading a heavily footnoted passage to trying to play a fugue on the organ while having to keep your attention both on the keyboard and on the pedals at the same time. But I think all things considered it's more disruptive if the text is interrupted with a lot of parenthetical citations, so I tended to lean more in the direction of favoring footnotes and certainly not banishing them entirely as some jurists have sworn to do.

What are your thoughts about the overall length of opinions?

The California Supreme Court has been both praised and condemned for the length of its opinions. The style of opinions certainly evolved over the years. Originally, the court's role was viewed as primarily resolving the dispute between the parties. There's a classic opinion in the *Robinson* case that reflects the jusrisprudence of an earlier era. It's a case in the fifth volume of the California Supreme Court's reports, from the year 1855, and sets the stage for my answer to your question. I will read the opinion in its entirety to you, not omitting a single word. "Heydenfeldt, J., delivered the opinion of the court. Murray, C. J., concurred. The court below erred in giving the third, fourth, and fifth instructions. If the defendants were at fault in leaving an uncovered hole in the sidewalk of a public street, the intoxication of the plaintiff cannot excuse such gross negligence. A drunken man is as much entitled to a safe street as a sober one and much more in need of it. The judgment is reversed and the cause remanded." That is the entirety of the opinion.

That communicates a number of things about another era, doesn't it?

It certainly does. However, on the negative side, truly, is an opinion, *People v. Hall*, in the preceding volume, Volume 4 of the first series, which dealt with the question of whether a person of Chinese extraction could testify as a witness against a Caucasian defendant in a criminal prosecution. The court, in a rather expansive interpretation of the Civil Practice Act, which precluded Native Americans and African-Americans from being allowed to testify as witnesses, in effect held—with all sorts of terrible aspersions against the Chinese and their culture and history—that they were basically as inferior as the other, specified minority groups and therefore the court would expand the statute to also disqualify Chinese witnesses. As a result, the court reversed the defendant Hall's murder conviction because a Chinese witness had been allowed to testify against him. There are vignettes from the early jurisprudence of the state that are amusing and others, like the *Hall* case, that of course are to be condemned as racist. That *Robinson* opinion involving safe sidewalks was an extreme example of brevity, with a bit of mid-nineteenth-century wisdom. The *Hall* opinion fortunately was superseded by 20th century opinions that led commentators to place the California Supreme Court in the vanguard among the protectors of civil liberties.

The opinions tended to expand in length over the years, and I can't help but say that one contributing factor—even in the years that I've been a judge—was the advent of word processing equipment. I remember as a young deputy attorney general having some changes I wanted to make to a brief, approaching one of the secretaries who were assisting the deputies attorney general, and being asked, "You mean you want me to do this all over again?" It might be just changing two or three words, but she usually couldn't make the correction right then and there and had to re-do the entire page in original and carbon copies. Over the years, the technology advanced to the point where you could take long passages out of other material and electronically insert them, in addition to making changes that you were going to make in your own text. It became all too easy to engraft large segments of quoted material into legal briefs and judicial opinions.

That's the negative side of the trend to lengthy opinions from the California Supreme Court. The positive side is that the court's opinions are designed not only to resolve the dispute between the parties in the case, but also to provide guidance to persons and institutions beyond those involved in the particular litigation—to establish guidelines and precedents for many different situations and to provide a true rationale for the court's decision, how and why the court arrived at its conclusion. Added to this consideration is a provision in the current California Constitution that pertains to the writing of appellate opinions. Section 14 of article VI specifies: "Decisions of the Supreme Court and Courts of Appeal that determine causes shall be in writing with reasons stated." This provision was not part of the original constitution adopted in 1849. Decisions have been rendered interpreting the requirement that sufficient reasons be given in an appellate opinion. It can't just read, "We decide this, *x, y, and z*." The court has to set forth a reasoning process in its written opinion for the result it reached. That's a factor in the length of our court's opinions. Even though there are some decisions that are, perhaps, longer than they should be, I weigh in on the side of a longer, more thoroughly explicated decision. I believe that one of the important reasons that decisions of the California Supreme Court are followed more than the decisions of any other state high court is the fact that our opinions do explain; they do set forth the reasoning for the result that's reached and the ramifications of the particular decision. They discuss pertinent authority at some length, often including authority in other state and federal jurisdictions, providing a survey, if you will. I realize that our opinions are not supposed to be law review articles, but by the same token they're not supposed to be just a thumbs-up or thumbs-down fiat either. I'm pleased that we give as thorough an explanation as we do in our rulings.

We have discussed some considerations involved in the opinion writing process. I'll just briefly mention again that when a hot-button issue was involved—and examples would be abortion, gay rights and disputes among the three branches of government—I frequently would assign the case to myself. I would do so partly because of my view that the Chief Justice should have the broad shoulders to withstand the strong reaction or backlash that might ensue from a ruling on a controversial issue, and also because of the substantial role that I had to play as Chief Justice in dealing with the other branches of government. I felt it was important that opinions involving disputes between or among two or three branches of government be couched in as diplomatic and reasonable a tone as possible—basically that whatever the result, it be communicated in a diplomatic fashion, given the need for the judiciary to work with the legislature and the governor. These considerations would never affect the result reached in an opinion I was writing for the court, but it might affect the choice of wording. You and I spoke quite a bit earlier in our discussions about the damage that ensued from our court's ruling upholding the term-limits initiative—not even so much from the result, but rather from the tone in the wording of the opinion.

Having all of this in mind, I thought it best that certain cases come out of the chief's chambers. I kept in mind the words of the L.A. Municipal Court presiding judge who had sworn me in, Alan Campbell, who advised me that every time I would make a decision I would make a temporary friend and a permanent enemy but—knowing that—I should forget it and go out and do my job. So, although these considerations never affected the result in any case, sometimes it was best if things came out of the chief's chambers.

I don't know if you want me to mention the quantitative aspects before we get to the substance of the opinions?

Sure. Let's take a broad look at your body of work, shall we?

Of course, on the trial court I had the experience of writing only a few lengthy rulings that might be termed memoranda of opinion, on the municipal court for instance dealing with the complex nursing home prosecutions I mentioned previously. Then, for example, on the superior court in making rulings on the Hillside Strangler case, particularly the memorandum of opinion in denying the prosecutor's motion to dismiss. My prior experience as a deputy attorney general writing briefs in the U.S. and California Supreme Courts also helped prepare me for the opinion-writing tasks of an appellate justice. On the Court of Appeal—according to an estimate I read somewhere in the press, and I have no reason to doubt it—I authored about 400 majority opinions during the approximately four years I was there. The reason that this is an approximation is that, as we discussed earlier, opinions of the Courts of Appeal are published in the official reports only when ordered published by the court, subject to possible depublication by the Supreme Court of California. I wrote, I believe, about 37 majority opinions that were published in the official reports, along with a few concurring or dissenting opinions.

Given that the 400 is an estimate, that sounds like a pretty high output in four years' time.

I don't know that it was any higher than most of the justices. Most of those opinions were short, and some were memorandum opinions. They had to meet the test of what I just stated a moment ago of giving reasons—but sometimes they were pretty close to the edge in meeting this requirement. Some were written up by central staff when they were basically no-merit appeals, but an appeal to the Court of Appeal is a matter of right. So that number of opinions probably was quite average.

Then, on the California Supreme Court—where all opinions are published in the bound volumes, which of course signifies that they can and will be cited as precedent unlike unpublished opinions—I authored 281 opinions for the court and 53 separate opinions, including concurring, dissenting, or concurring and dissenting. When I left office, the staff assembled and categorized my opinions into 21 areas of the law. I know that you and I, mercifully for the recipients of this oral history, will not discuss the holdings of all of the opinions or even opinions in all of the categories. But just to delineate the areas in which I did write majority opinions for the Supreme Court, they encompassed, as the staff categorized them: appellate procedure, capital cases, civil procedure, civil rights, constitutional law, contracts, corporations, criminal law, criminal procedure, elections, employment and workers' compensation, evidence, family law, government and administrative law, insurance, interbranch relations and the scope of authority of the branches, arbitration and the private practice of law, real property, tax law, torts, and public utilities. I mention these 21 areas just to illustrate the breadth of the work of the California Supreme Court. Others could carve out different categories in the caseload, but it does give you an idea of the breadth of the work done by our high court in resolving various issues.

By the way, I was pleased that shortly after I left office, the publisher of the official reports, Lexis Nexis, very kindly presented me with a six-volume leather bound set of all the opinions that I had authored for the court and a one-volume set of the published opinions that I'd written for the Court of Appeal. I should mention that those six volumes of California Supreme Court opinions were culled from 50 bound volumes of the official reports. My very first opinion upon joining the California Supreme Court as an associate justice appeared in Volume 1, page 1, of the fourth series of the California Reports in the *Rider* case. It was actually a concurring opinion. Those opinions over the 19 years extend from 1 Cal.4th through 50 Cal.4th, covering the years 1991 to 2010. That's the quantitative as opposed to qualitative or substantive review of the opinions I authored for the California Supreme Court.

Since I mentioned separate opinions, this might be a good time to make an observation about separate opinions. As I indicated, I wrote my own number of separate opinions, 53 over the 19 years that I was on the court. But the subject of separate opinions is one about which there has been a difference of opinion among members of the California Supreme Court over the years in terms of the advisability or wisdom of writing separately, especially in a concurring opinion. With a dissenting opinion, if you have a disagreement with the court's decision that causes you to be unable to concur in the result, you certainly shouldn't just subjugate your feelings and "go along to get along." On the other hand, having once dissented on a point of law the better view, I believe, is that having noted your dissent, you don't keep dissenting every year ad infinitum each time the issue arises in a new case. Not everyone ascribes to that view, but the recognized authority on California law, the late Bernard Witkin, in his treatise on writing appellate opinions, indicates that the better position is to state your disagreement and then, under the compulsion of *stare decisis* and majority rule, move on and accept the majority holding for future cases, until such time as a change of circumstances may lead the court to reconsider that holding.

Of course, writing separately as a dissenter—and this also applies to a concurring opinion—can serve a couple of functions. First of all, if you believe something's basically wrong with the majority opinion, you should feel obliged to set that forth. Doing so might also serve the purpose of carrying the day in a future case. There are U.S. Supreme Court justices from past eras who have noted this rationale for writing separately and stated they hoped the injustice they thought had been perpetrated by the majority of the court would eventually be righted by the court changing its course in time. Of course, you have notable cases like the *Dred Scott* decision or the antecedents to *Brown v. Board of Education* that graphically illustrate this point. Actually, I was pleased that the view I put forth in my concurring opinion in the *Rider* case of what I thought was a

Chapter 16

better way of dealing with a tax question was later adopted by a majority of the court in a subsequent case.[6] So aside from venting one's spleen, a utilitarian function can be served by writing separately. Another example, which I believe we covered fairly thoroughly, was the *Hi-Voltage* case upholding Proposition 209, where I felt I could not in good conscience go along with the majority opinion's negative characterization of the history and motives of the proponents of affirmative action. Two other justices likewise were unable to go along with the majority's view.

Those are some of the considerations affecting a justice's decision whether to write separately. There have been justices, though, who—on various courts, and frankly, I think occasionally on the California Supreme Court as well—have just decided to write separately on a particular issue, instead of basically saying, "I'll hold my nose and sign the opinion, even though it isn't written as well as I would have done it." Sometimes a justice, aside from engaging in the minimal vice of only venting one's spleen, will deprive the court of a majority of four votes because he or she—while basically agreeing with the author—feels compelled to engage in a slightly different treatment to satisfy his or her own preferences, and thereby precludes the court's opinion from having the force and authoritative guiding effect that it would have had as a majority opinion, as opposed to a plurality opinion.

One occasional practice that I consider to border on the bizarre has been for a justice to author a separate opinion concurring in the majority opinion that he or she has authored for the court.[7] I had occasion once, in a discussion with Bernie Witkin on that subject, to ask him, "Isn't this the jurisprudential equivalent of playing with oneself?" [Laughter] With his characteristic guffaw, he endorsed my view. As a pragmatic matter too, writing a separate opinion concurring in your own opinion for the court serves mainly to highlight the fact that you've put something out there that the rest of the court refused to go along with. Wouldn't silence have been more consistent with one's goal of furthering one's views, better leaving the separate approach not discussed and available for another day when perhaps there might be more votes to adopt it? That's my take on this type of separate opinion.

There we are, perhaps, at the point of discussing the substance of various opinions.

---

[6] Santa Clara County Local Transportation Authority v. Guardino (1995) 11 Cal.4th 220; 902 P.2d 225.
[7] Justice Mosk set forth a rationale for doing so, in Hawkins v. Superior Court (1978) 22 Cal.3d 584; 586 P.2d 916.

We've worked ahead of time to select together a number of cases to talk about in particular areas of the law. Perhaps we'll dive into those, and you'll feel free to comment on your earlier statement that sometimes how an opinion is written is as important as the opinion itself, the outcome itself.

Let's start off with a couple of specific opinions you wrote in the area of tort law. We touched on another occasion, very briefly, on the case Knight v. Jewett, *which came early on in your career as an associate justice in 1992. You mentioned that more than one other justice had approached this opinion and hadn't managed to command a majority. Perhaps you can tell me the story of this case from the beginning, as you know it.*

I had a limited exposure to what had gone on before I came onto the court, but I understood that more than one justice had tried to take on this difficult area, which involves something that is known as the doctrine of implied assumption of risk. Even after I did tackle it and we had an opinion out there, it was an area that continued to challenge the court over future years. I ended up writing some opinions in this area, and other justices did too. What was basically involved in *Knight v. Jewett* was a game of touch football. The plaintiff was knocked over, and the defendant stepped on her finger, causing her some injury. The question posed by the case was to what extent, when you engage in informal sports activity of this sort, are you assuming the risk of injury that might result from the negligence of another participant? I'm talking about ordinary negligence here. One assumes and anticipates that everyone on the two teams isn't necessarily going to follow all the rules of the sport and behave perfectly on the field. On the other hand, there may be certain reckless conduct or gross negligence that goes beyond the conduct one would expect from a participant, and that one would not anticipate, and that therefore might give rise to a legal claim against the offending party. That's what this case involved, and I managed to write an opinion that Chief Justice Lucas and Justice Arabian joined. There were separate opinions by three other justices who concurred in different parts of the opinion I wrote for the court. So there was a majority holding but not one that was endorsed by the same four or more justices.

Interestingly enough, over the years there were other opinions that came to the court applying these concepts in the *Knight* case in the context of various sporting activities and different degrees of negligence. I'm not listing these in chronological order, but *Parsons v. Crown Disposal Co.* was another opinion I authored. This case involved horseback riding, specifically riding a horse in the vicinity of where machinery was operated, in this case a loud garbage truck. In light of the skittish nature of horses, the issue arose concerning the extent to which there was a duty of care that was breached—and what should have been anticipated by the rider of the horse, the plaintiff, who was thrown from the horse and injured when it was spooked by the sound of the loading mechanism. Then there were a couple of opinions I authored involving public swimming pool activity, *Kahn v. Eastside Union High School District* and *City of Santa Barbara v. Superior Court*. The latter case involved whether there could be a release of liability for future gross negligence in the context of recreational swimming for developmentally disabled children. These questions involving the doctrine of implied assumption of risk came up in many different contexts, but they all arose out of the holding in the touch football case, *Knight v. Jewett*. I know that the court, in additional opinions that I did not author, had to resolve similar questions that arose in the contexts of other sports, including skiing.

What did you do differently from your colleagues to manage to get an opinion out in this case? Do you recall?

I recall that there was a lot of negotiation that went on among the chambers until we could come up with an opinion that at least three justices would join and then have other justices sign on to different parts of the three-justice opinion. It took a fair amount of effort to do that, and we didn't resolve all questions for all time, because as issues in this area of the law came up in future years we found ourselves in difficulty again.

Why is this larger area of comparative negligence so tricky?

Of course there are a lot of competing social concerns, but one might say that about other areas of tort law as well. The area of comparative negligence has a great variety of different aspects and factual situations in which these competing social interests and legal theories can present themselves. Maybe it's a perfect storm of all of those elements. There's also a lot of academic literature in this area of the law, and I'm not sure if that has helped or complicated the process, but I found this to be one of the most contentious areas of jurisprudence in my experience on the court.

I wonder, as a young associate justice, newly joined at this time, what did you take away from the experience of hammering out this opinion and this result?

It certainly taught me, if not the wisdom, at least the necessity of negotiating, trying to craft something that would bridge differences and lead the justices of a collegial court to as much common ground as possible under the circumstances.

We might take a look at the case Peterson v. Superior Court, *which you authored in 1995.*

This was one of those rare instances where we overruled prior case authority decided by the California Supreme Court. The case involved the issue whether the doctrine of strict liability—that is, liability regardless of fault and imposed only by operation of law—should be imposed on a hotel proprietor or a residential landlord for injuries that were caused by some defect in the premises that was not the fault of the landlord or proprietor. Because the defect exists, should the landlord or owner be liable in a court of law for the resulting damages? The argument in favor of strict liability was premised on the implied warranty of habitability that binds a landlord—a warranty guaranteeing that whatever premises he or she rents out are basically habitable. Does this warranty cover defects not caused by the landlord and even those that the landlord was unaware of, or is it limited to ensuring that the traditional needs of a tenant for things like heat and water are met? Here the court, in a unanimous opinion that I authored, did hold that the landlord should not be subject to liability for defects that were not his or her fault. The *Peterson* case involved a hotel premises and an injury that arose out of a slip and fall in a defective bathtub.

You said it was rare to overturn one of the Supreme Court's own precedents. Put that in context for this opinion.

This was a situation in which the court—with all six of my colleagues joining me—just felt that the rationale for application of the doctrine of strict liability did not apply. There are certain situations in which it should and does apply. An example would be the manufacture of power tools, where the item is totally under the control and design of the manufacturer. There may be defects that would not be apparent to the consumer. But that rationale really didn't apply here.

What life did this principle have beyond the rendering of the opinion, if any?

I don't recall the issue cropping up again in our court, or the extent to which it arose in the courts of other states that might have had occasion to cite our opinion. But despite my general belief that we should adhere to precedent and not overrule it lightly, this was a situation where I concluded we should not adhere to wrongly decided precedent.

Let's move into some of your opinions in the area of criminal law. Shall we start with People v. Cahill, *which you authored as an associate justice in 1993?*

That case was an interesting one in that there was thought to be a generally applicable rule requiring reversal of a criminal conviction if a confession was erroneously admitted into evidence. I distinguish between a confession—which is an admission by the defendant of all the basic elements of a crime and would be sufficient to establish his or her guilt if corroborated by other evidence—and a defendant's admission, which would just be a statement damaging to his or her case, but wouldn't cover all of the elements of the charged offense. The prosecution would still need to prove one or more other elements of the offense by additional evidence. The rule requiring automatic reversal was thought to apply regardless of the quantity or strength of the other evidence admitted at the trial. *Cahill* recognized, or if you will created, an exception in a situation where there were multiple confessions. In that situation, it appeared quite reasonable to conclude that whatever special weight would be given by the jury to a confession submitted into evidence because of its significance in coming from the mouth of the suspect, if there was a properly admitted confession in addition to the erroneously admitted confession, such error shouldn't bring about the somewhat draconian result of causing the entire trial and conviction to be thrown out when there was an admissible confession and corroboration of that confession. That was a groundbreaking new precedent in the criminal law, and one that engendered very vigorous dissents by Justices Mosk and Kennard. But the court held that under those circumstances we could properly find the error harmless beyond a reasonable doubt, which is the highest standard of review, and affirm the murder conviction and sentence of life imprisonment without possibility of parole.

What reverberations did you note later on?

I know there were some commentaries claiming this decision countenanced the coercion of involuntary statements from defendants, but actually in fact it was not a question of coercion or involuntariness in the true sense of the word. It was just a failure to give a sufficient advisement and obtain a sufficient waiver of rights, which to me is distinguishable from using a stomach pump or physical or psychological means to obtain evidence by overcoming the will of the suspect. I'm not saying that we should encourage shoddy police practices of not obtaining the waiver of rights required by law, but to reverse the conviction and send it back for a new trial when there was other clearly competent evidence—including a properly admitted confession—to sustain a conviction didn't seem to make sense to me or to a majority of the court.

We also might look at the criminal case People v. Ewoldt, *which also crosses over with matters of interbranch relations and so on. What was significant about this one?*

The court was faced with one of the ramifications of another Proposition 8—not the one that dealt with gay marriage but the so-called criminal justice initiative of 1982—that provided in part that relevant evidence is not to be excluded in a criminal proceeding. The question arose whether certain sections of the Evidence Code were still operable in light of that enactment. In particular, section 1101 provided that evidence of uncharged offenses is admissible to show a common scheme or plan, although that statute recognized there were limitations on the admission of evidence of uncharged offenses. The court held this section of the Evidence Code is still valid in the face of Proposition 8. Section 1101 indicated, in specifying the categories in which evidence involving uncharged offenses would be admissible, that evidence of character to prove conduct on a specified occasion was inadmissible. That prohibition remains in effect despite the passage of Proposition 8, which our court found not to have repealed section 1101 by its broad command that relevant evidence is not to be excluded in any criminal proceeding.

I'm just recalling that you had had occasion to consider this whole question of prior-conduct evidence in some of your trial work going back quite a ways.

Yes, and that's something that continues to confound trial judges in certain situations—whether there is enough relevance to show a common scheme or motive or intent, or is the evidence of past misconduct just being offered to show the defendant's bad character, which in turn would not be permissible. It's an area that still causes appellate courts difficulty in its application, including our own court. These issues continue to arise, sometimes as subsidiary issues in the large caseload of capital cases that we have.

You are being asked to draw lines in difficult territory at times?

Yes, and in territory that is dependent upon minor factual nuances that might differentiate one case from another. What is basically a common scheme or plan? What characteristic makes an uncharged offense similar to a charged offense? Does it have to bear a unique signature or is a general similarity sufficient? There are some situations that are remarkable in how much of a copycat pattern they provide. On the other hand, you have attempts made at trial to demonstrate a similarity between a charged offense and an uncharged offense that really don't illustrate much in the way of parallel conduct. After all, how many ways are there that you can hold up someone on the street? Now, if you're wearing a particular kind of bandanna, and maybe an unusual phrase or firearm is used, maybe you're wearing sunglasses and it's nighttime—that could be fairly unique. But the law both pre- and post-Proposition 8 does not permit the admission of evidence of another holdup bearing only everyday similarities to the charged offense. That wouldn't meet the test.

This is perhaps an area where your experience as a trial judge might have been helpful to you?

Yes, I think so. It really helps if one can view these issues not just as abstractions but in the light of real day-to-day experience as it comes to the courtroom.

This had come up as an initiative?

Yes, Proposition 8 had come up as an initiative encompassing the Victims' Bill of Rights, safe schools, all sorts of issues.

There was that added aspect of ruling on a matter that came up to the court in that fashion?

Yes. Part of the initiative had been invalidated by an opinion rendered by the California Supreme Court before I joined the court—a provision that would have mandated our state courts to interpret basically all of the rights that a person charged with a crime might possess under the state constitution identically to the interpretation that the U.S. Supreme Court would give to the comparable rights in the federal constitution. The California Supreme Court found this provision to be an impermissible attempt to *revise* the state constitution by means of an initiative, as opposed to a permissible amendment of the constitution proposed by the legislature,[8] because this provision in Proposition 8 would have restricted the judiciary's interpretation of a whole panoply of rights set forth in the state constitution. However, an initiative provision that attempted to do something similar but confined itself to Fourth Amendment search and seizure protections was upheld by the California Supreme Court and to this date does provide that in interpreting those protections, the state courts must view the state

---

[8] Raven v. Deukmejian (1990) 52 Cal.3d 336; 801 P.2d 1077; Cal. Const. art. XVIII, secs. 1, 3.

constitution as conferring the same rights as those conferred by the Fourth Amendment as interpreted by the federal courts.[9]

That's an important point, isn't it, to clarify. Thank you. People v. Banks, *which I gather centered on a sobriety checkpoint?*

Yes, this was an interesting situation in which our court had to interpret a U.S. Supreme Court decision that had upheld sobriety checkpoints. There was language in the federal high court opinion that may or may not have suggested, depending upon one's view, that the presence of advance publicity was a pre-requisite to the validity of a sobriety checkpoint. Our court, over the dissenting votes of two justices—an interesting combination, Justices Mosk and Panelli— held in an opinion I authored that a properly conducted sobriety checkpoint was constitutionally valid notwithstanding the absence of advance publicity. Shortly after this decision came down I was driving through the Gold Country with Barbara and our sons and was amused to point out to them the unannounced sobriety checkpoint we encountered as a result of the recent ruling.

As you say, that's an interesting combination of dissenters. Do you recall where they differed with you?

Basically I think they differed in interpreting what the U.S. Supreme Court's opinion had held. There's an old maxim of jurisprudence, cited in the majority opinion, that states that cases are not authority for propositions not considered. You can't just look to a case that has certain factual elements and conclude, "Because in the case of *x* such and such were the facts, this means they are part of its holding on the legal issues, and the holding will be considered applicable only if those facts exist in the case to which that holding is being applied." I believe that was basically the point of contention between the majority and the dissent in the *Banks* case—different interpretations of the U.S. Supreme Court opinion on the subject of sobriety checkpoints.

Another interesting issue that arose in a criminal case was presented in the opinion I authored for the court in the *Williams* case, in which our court rejected the theory of jury nullification. That theory would allow jurors to act in a basically lawless fashion by following their own personal views concerning the justness of the applicable law. Condoning such an approach could in a given case inure either to the advantage or the detriment of a criminal defendant or a party to a civil suit.

---

[9] In re Lance W. (1985) 37 Cal.3d 873; 694 P.2d 744.

Moving into family law, if you're ready, we have another case in which the Court of Appeal was reversed, I believe, in In re Marriage of Simpson. *This goes back to 1992.*

Yes. This involved the important question in family law matters of calculating support, both spousal and child support, in the context of a spouse's earning capacity. The opinion I authored for the court held that the trial court was not restricted to considering only the actual earnings of the husband at the time of trial but could consider his earning capacity. At first glance one might wonder, why consider the fact that he could have been earning more? There was evidence in the case suggesting that the husband, who had had a very vigorous work routine during the marriage and had devoted an exceptionally high number of hours to his employment, had voluntarily reduced his work regimen and in fact had done so unjustifiably for the express purpose of lowering his income so as to negatively affect his ability to provide support for his ex-wife and his child. Our opinion, in reversing the judgment of the Court of Appeal, held that the trial court had not abused its discretion in considering the husband's earning capacity as opposed to his actual earnings. The standard was basically that of an objectively reasonable work regimen. A court would not require someone to seek to engage in an extraordinary work regimen, but that's what the husband originally had voluntarily done, before then putting himself in a situation where he didn't have an objectively reasonable work regimen but rather an unreasonably meager work regimen motivated by the rather negative objective I mentioned.

Child support is an interesting area of family law. I wonder how this result could go forth and have a larger life beyond this particular case?

I suspect, although I don't have anything other than my own conjecture, that this issue arises from time to time in family law matters—in terms of trying to ascertain what would be a reasonable work regimen in computing that vital amount of support, as opposed to just having it be a matter totally within the discretion and control of the higher wage earning spouse.

It's certainly an interesting twist on the question. Other cases in the area of family law?

There are a couple of other opinions I authored that may be of particular interest. One was the Barry Bonds case, *In re Marriage of Bonds*. The Court of Appeal had held that the premarital agreement was subject to strict scrutiny because Mr. Bonds' wife was viewed as less sophisticated concerning the negotiations and did not have independent counsel, nor had she waived counsel in entering into the premarital agreement. The opinion, which was unanimous, held that the trial court had acted properly in concluding that Bonds' wife had voluntarily entered into the agreement. She had the opportunity to consult with counsel and was told that she could, but chose not to do so. All of the circumstances relating to the negotiations suggested she had acted voluntarily and that the courts should not, in the area of premarital-agreement negotiations, import all of the considerations that govern the area of commercial contracts, where you have the concept of contracts of adhesion based upon unequal bargaining power—concepts that you and I discussed recently with regard to cases such as *Engalla* and *Armendariz*. We discussed those cases in the context, I believe, of private judging—but those considerations, applicable to commercial transactions, were deemed not to apply in the *Bonds* case.

Do you recall why the court took this case?

To put it perhaps in oversimplified language, the Court of Appeal's decision came close to enunciating a *Miranda*-like right to have counsel present—in the absence of a waiver of that right—in this area of premarital agreements. I believe the court was eager to shy away from importing such concepts into family law from the criminal law.

Given the well-known person involved in this case, what sort of response did your decision get?

Perhaps it obtained more attention in the general press than it might otherwise have, but certainly it was just as vital a matter of concern to the family law attorneys as if it had been Joe Six-pack with a more modest income and support level at stake.

There is, since you ask about other family law matters, one that I would be eager to say a couple of things about and that I consider among the opinions I'm most proud of. That was the case of *Elkins v. Superior Court,* that I previously mentioned in conjunction with a task force that I established to focus on access-to-justice issues in the area of family law. The case involved a local court rule and scheduling order providing that in marital dissolution trials, parties had to present their case by means of written declarations—truly restricting their basic right to offer oral testimony, which of course can be far more convincing. The parties also were required to lay a somewhat difficult procedural foundation, in advance of the proceeding itself, in order to present exhibit evidence. Our court, recognizing that the basic right of due process possessed by all litigants involves having their day in court, held that the restrictions imposed by the court denied that right and were inconsistent with statutory provisions as well. The procedural requirements disapproved by our court's opinion were not mean-spirited or selectively applied to Mr. Elkins, who nonetheless was severely restricted in the presentation of his case as the husband representing himself in these proceedings. The court-imposed restrictions had been adopted as a matter of policy, reflecting the court's view that the rights of self-represented litigants had to be balanced against the heavy caseload of the court in family law matters—where frequently one or both of the litigants were unrepresented by counsel. Such cases substantially delayed the family court's handling of its calendar to the detriment not just of the court but of the litigants in trailing matters who were waiting to have their cases heard with or without counsel. Despite the legitimacy of these concerns, my opinion for the court reached the conclusion that the local practices were an abuse of discretion because the sanction for not complying with them was to exclude the bulk of the husband's evidence as a result of his failure to file the declarations that were required in advance, in order to establish the admissibility of his evidence at trial. Our court considered the sanction disproportionate as well as inconsistent with the general policy that courts must follow of deciding cases on their merits and, where possible, not on the basis of procedural obstacles.

One of the aspects that was interesting about the opinion was—as I mentioned earlier—a rare confluence of my decision-making responsibilities and my administrative responsibilities as Chief Justice and chair of the Judicial Council. A footnote at the very end of the court's opinion in *Elkins* referred the general question of balancing the rights of unrepresented litigants with the need for efficient operation of our family courts to the Judicial Council for study and report, including the promulgation of new rules of court.[10]

There was no problem in delivering this communication. I put on my hat as chair of the Judicial Council and appointed a task force that has done exceptional work, chaired by Second Appellate District Court of Appeal Justice Laurie Zelon, in holding hearings and coming up with proposals for policies and rules

---

[10] "We recommend to the Judicial Council that it establish a task force, including representatives of the family law bench and bar and the Judicial Council Advisory Committee on Families and the Courts, to study and propose measures to assist trial courts in achieving efficiency and fairness in marital dissolution proceedings and to ensure access to justice for litigants, many of whom are self-represented. Such a task force might wish to consider proposals for adoption of new rules of court establishing statewide rules of practice and procedure for fair and expeditious proceedings in family law, from the initiation of an action to post-judgment motions. Special care might be taken to accommodate self-represented litigants. Proposed rules could be written in a manner easy for laypersons to follow, be economical to comply with, and ensure that a litigant be afforded satisfactory opportunity to present his or her case to the court."

that will have an enormous impact in the area of family law, even though this is still a work in progress. We've never had so many people ask to serve on any Judicial Council committee or task force—several dozen volunteered. Some persons, including the former State Bar president Howard Miller in introducing me at my last annual meeting of the State Bar, have stated their view that this judicial opinion is the most important decision I have rendered as a judge in any field and that it will have a great impact in the area of family law. The court's decision and the Judicial Council's study and recommendations have been very meaningful to the family law bar and have caused me to be recognized with various awards.

You say you are at least as proud or more proud of this decision than any other?

Without making it number one, I would put it among the top three or four opinions I have authored for the court in terms of its significance and the personal satisfaction it has brought me.

I don't know if you want to tip your hand now or if you want to identify the others as we go along?

I'll be glad to mention them now. They would be *Warfield v. Peninsula Golf & Country Club*, establishing gender equality in the context of right to membership in various types of organizations that come within the rule of that case—public accommodation entities. Also, in the area of family law, in addition to *Elkins* I clearly would include the *In re Marriage Cases* involving the right to same-sex marriage, which I'm sure we'll discuss at some length. Fourth is the case of *NBC Subsidiary v. Superior Court*, which—as we discussed in the context of relations with the press—clearly established the right to open court proceedings in civil cases. The U.S. Supreme Court precedents in the *Press-Enterprise* cases and other decisions had established that right in the context of criminal proceedings, but it had not been fully recognized in the civil context until my decision for the court in the *NBC* case. Various media groups have indicated to me, by way of certain recognitions and awards, that they consider this to be a landmark decision, not only in California but nationally. I would put these cases foremost among those that have given me the greatest satisfaction in terms of their practical impact—which, aside from my fascination with the legal issues involved, is something that adds another element or layer of professional satisfaction. These decisions are not merely exercises in legal abstraction, but have direct and deep consequences for individuals and society at large. I am deeply indebted to the staff attorneys who worked with me on those opinions—

Hal Cohen on *Warfield* and the *In re Marriage Cases*, Jake Dear on the *NBC Subsidiary* case, and Alice Collins on the *Elkins* case.

That certainly ties in with the views you've expressed of the judiciary's responsibility to the citizens. I note that these cases were across a variety of areas. Is there anything you want to add about Elkins *and the effect of that over time?*

Only to say that the ramifications of *Elkins*, through the resulting task force, will be further augmented over time. When we discuss ultimate challenges that might face the judicial branch in the future, I will certainly count, among the top three or four challenges, the increasing problem that will be presented in California and elsewhere from the circumstance that more and more litigants, not only in the family law area but in civil matters generally where there is no constitutional right to counsel, have great difficulty vindicating their rights by reason of their inability to afford counsel. In some cases, it just isn't economical— even if the litigants could come up with the funds by mortgaging the house or going into bankruptcy—to hire counsel as an option, given the cost of legal services compared to the amount in controversy, even though that amount may be significant. It just may not pay to go to court, even if you are confident you will prevail. Sometimes the cost of legal services will eclipse the amount at stake. That's why I mentioned the possibility of encouraging, as the courts have experimented with on occasion, an economic litigation program with drastically simplified procedures, perhaps, a stage between small claims and general civil litigation. Otherwise we're going to be, in effect, denying practical access on the part of so many individuals to our court system, even though they're paying for it as taxpayers.

How can we think about the number or percentage of people who might be facing this sort of issue? How big is the problem?

I can speak with some specificity about the area of family law where, in some parts of our state, 85 to 90 percent of the cases have no lawyer on either side in a family law dispute. It's somewhat similar in some other areas such as landlord-tenant and domestic violence restraining order proceedings.

Who else is interested in this idea of having a stage between small claims and general civil litigation, with simplified proceedings?

There has been discussion of it in some of the bar publications. I know that Presiding Justice Norman Epstein, of whom I spoke previously, was involved in a Los Angeles Superior Court economic litigation project. I'd like to see more of that, even in an era of declining resources available to the courts. There's a parallel decline in the resources available to people in the community and therefore—and perhaps ironically—there is an even greater need to provide legal services. Yet we're cutting back on all of these things, and unfortunately there are officeholders with funding responsibilities who consider such special court programs to be frills. I instead view them increasingly as necessities and vital services to be provided by the court system.

What about opinions you authored in the area of—as you've described it—election law, interbranch relations, government law—a triad of related areas?

This is a field that I somewhat focused on in the opinions assigned to myself, again due to its sensitivity involving potential invalidation of actions taken by the electorate, the legislature, and the governor—with many opportunities to annoy many people in this particular domain of the law. [Laughter] Focusing first, as you did, on the matter of elections, there was an opinion I wrote for the court, *Senate v. Jones*, that dealt with what was Proposition 24, titled the Let the Voters Decide Act of 2000.

A wonderful title, I might add. [Laughter]

Yes, one to instill, I suppose, hesitation in the resolve of any timid judge or justice ruling upon it. But, notwithstanding its title, four justices joined my opinion removing Proposition 24 from the ballot and the ballot pamphlet. Taking its place was, in large block letters, the message: "Removed from the ballot by order of . . . ." I don't recall whether it said, "court action" or "the Supreme Court." But it was made quite clear to the electorate that judicial intervention had kept them from being able to vote on this measure. We took this action because the initiative ran afoul of the single-subject requirement of article II, section 8 of the California Constitution that, in our view, precluded combining a transfer of the power of reapportionment from the legislature to the Supreme Court, with a reduction in the compensation of state legislators and other officers in the same initiative proposal.

Both hot button issues on their own, much less together.

Exactly. The purpose of the single-subject rule is to prevent what is commonly called logrolling, where voters are presented with a very troublesome dilemma, almost a Sophie's Choice, if you will. They could like one aspect of this, perhaps the reapportionment, and hate the salary aspects or vice versa. They would have to decide, "Do I hate one proposal more than I love the other

one? How am I going to vote?" Under the single-subject rule, the voter is entitled to the choice of voting for one or the other or both or neither, but not having
to link his or her vote on one proposal to a vote on another. We held that permitting such an initiative measure to appear on the ballot would create voter confusion, obfuscate the intent of the voter, and violate the constitutional provision
limiting initiative measures to a single subject. Single-subject-rule violations are
among those rare instances where, in ruling on an initiative, the court generally
feels it needs to act before the voters act, because after a positive vote by the
electorate it would be impossible for the court to ascertain whether the voters
would have independently approved each of the separate subjects in the initiative. When there are other types of challenges to an initiative measure, the
court's preference generally is not to interfere with the electoral process, to let
the voters go ahead and vote and, if it does pass—and of course it may not—
then see if there are infirmities in the measure and, if there are, whether a remedy exists to deal with those infirmities. But a violation of the single-subject rule
is almost unique in the sense that it's not susceptible to being dealt with—to
being corrected, after the fact—because if it passes the court will never know
how many voters may have been strongly against one of the two or more provisions but made this difficult choice, this draconian choice of which one to reluctantly support in order to further the one they favored.

The way for proponents of a measure to avoid this problem is to concurrently gather signatures and otherwise qualify two or more initiative measures,
which minimizes any additional cost to them. But often proponents deliberately
choose to further their multiple objectives by engaging in logrolling so as to
maximize their chances of having the voters approve each of the separate
measures through a single initiative.

This is probably a good time for me to make a point that I have had to make
occasionally in press interviews or public meetings. How can the court justify
thwarting the people's will, either by keeping something off the ballot or by
invalidating it after it passes? My answer is simple and straightforward: in taking such action the court is not thwarting the people's will; the court is upholding and honoring the ultimate expression of the people's will, the constitution
that they themselves enacted, in this instance by promulgating the single-subject
rule. It's the people who imposed upon themselves—upon their ability to enact
laws—the limitation that they may not do so if the questions contained in an
initiative measure violate their own single-subject rule. I believe that most ra-
tional individuals, when given this type of explanation, retreat from the angry
accusation that the court is somehow setting itself up as a super legislature. We
didn't invent the single-subject rule; it was adopted by the electorate. We didn't
invent any of these other constraints that cause us with, believe me, the greatest

reluctance, to get into confrontations with the other two branches and enter what Justice Felix Frankfurter once called the "political thicket."[11] The court is compelled by the constitution to intervene in what in some ways are political questions, and is duty bound to resolve the constitutional issues that then confront it.

But there it is again, this widespread notion that the court is itself taking a position.

I've had occasion during my 38 years on the bench to invalidate laws that I personally thought were good policy and, maybe on occasion, that I even voted for on the ballot, and on the other hand to sustain laws that I thought were silly or dumb, because there was no legal obstacle to the enactment of those laws. This subject is related to another that you and I have discussed, the civics education that we truly need in order to maintain our judicial system—the how and the why of judges making decisions totally apart from what their personal and political or social or economic preferences might be. When we get to the three marriage cases I'll point out a passage that reflects one more attempt on my part to reinforce this lesson by providing an explanation for the series of rulings by our court.

Your constitutional duty to explain?

Yes, we discussed the requirement in the California Constitution that an appellate court provide decisions "in writing with reasons stated." But in some situations, it is advisable for the court to go beyond that minimum requirement and provide a more complete explanation of its ruling.

There are opinions that I authored in other cases involving elections or interbranch issues that I might allude to briefly, subject to further questions from you. A cousin of the single-subject requirement for initiatives and for enactments by the legislature is the requirement that each constitutional amendment proposed by the legislature for the voters' consideration be submitted in a manner that it can be voted on separately. In *Californians for an Open Primary v. McPherson*, I wrote an opinion for the court holding that the subjects of primary elections and state bond obligations were insufficiently related to be submitted to the voters in a single proposed constitutional amendment.

The *Costa* decision involved discrepancies between the version of an initiative measure that was submitted to the attorney general's office for title summary and the version that was circulated on petitions for signature by registered voters to qualify the measure for placement on the ballot. I concluded for the

---

[11] Colegrove v. Green (1946) 328 U.S. 556.

court that the discrepancies were inadvertent and didn't mislead the public or otherwise undermine any of the provisions governing initiatives.

How hard is it to make that kind of a distinction, in your mind?

It might be difficult in some situations, but it was pretty clear that the differences in this case were very minor. The proponents had different versions of the initiative floating around, and it appeared they inadvertently submitted the wrong one—another instance of sloppy procedures being followed in the process of qualifying a matter as an initiative.

Without going into detail, there were two separate concurring and dissenting opinions by your colleagues in Costa. My larger point is, how much could the court as a body come to agreement on these kinds of things that are so loaded politically but also so challenging to navigate?

If I recall correctly, the differences of views among the justices were not so much about whether the discrepancies really could be misleading or how substantial those discrepancies in wording were, but rather—and I don't say this in a pejorative way—whether the justice was a purist and took the view that whatever the wording is in one format, it has to be totally identical in the other format, even if the difference in wording could not possibly lead to a difference in meaning. I don't find that an unreasonable position, but I did find it a position I didn't agree with, especially given the court's traditional deference to the people's right to engage in lawmaking through the initiative process. My thought was that unless those discrepancies would truly have a potential bearing on the people's informed exercise of that right, the discrepancies should not cause the people to forfeit their right to vote on this measure.

How did your colleagues view that traditional deference?

I think we all tried to honor it, but the proof is in the pudding when that deference comes up against a specific irregularity in the proceeding and then one has to decide how important it is to honor the strict letter of the requirement—in this instance, of identical wording—in the face of otherwise depriving the people of the right to vote on a measure that had qualified for the ballot.

It's sort of a matter of harmless error?

Yes, very much so. That's really what it is.

There was another opinion, *Bramberg v. Jones*, that I wrote for a unanimous court involving an initiative measure, Proposition 225, that conflicted with a provision in the U.S. Constitution, not the state constitution. As we viewed it, this initiative measure instructed and indirectly attempted to coerce federal and state legislators to propose and support a congressional term-limits amendment to the U.S. Constitution. Because article V of the federal constitution vests exclusively in Congress and state legislatures the power to propose and ratify constitutional amendments and doesn't contemplate a state's allowing its electorate to do that indirectly, we found that the initiative measure basically was a usurpation of authority that resided in Congress, and in state legislators as part of the ratification process.

I also authored the opinion in the *Independent Energy Producers* case which dealt with whether the initiative power allowed the voters to confer additional authority on the Public Utilities Commission, which itself is a constitutional entity. We answered this question in the negative. Interestingly, this case illustrates a secondary point. The initiative ended up being defeated at the polls, but the case was an example of our court's occasionally writing an opinion in a case that had become moot. The court is especially inclined to do so when the issue might evade future judicial review in another case. Here, the issue arose in a short time interval in the electoral process where there was not much of an opportunity for the court to review the matter. In these circumstances, we retained the case to nonetheless provide guidance for future elections, even though the case was technically moot because the measure had been defeated by the voters.

There are other election decisions that I wrote. I'll just mention a couple briefly, and then there's one that I want to discuss at slightly greater length. One of the two meriting brief mention is *Vargas v. City of Salinas*, which discussed the extent to which a municipality could expend public funds to send communications to the voters regarding a ballot measure, without crossing the threshold of becoming an advocate and improperly expending public funds in that effort. In this instance we found that these expenditures did not involve improper campaign materials or activities. They were purely informational.

That strikes me as a distinction that might be hard to make in some particular instances.

Yes, definitely. Again, there is the worthy objective of having the voters better informed, but some people didn't want that information out there and used the argument of improper expenditure of public funds for political purposes to try to keep the voters from getting the facts. The election basically involved questions of municipal expenditures and a utilities tax imposed by the city.

The other election case I would mention briefly that led to the one I'll talk about at somewhat greater length, is *Amwest Surety Insurance Co. v. Wilson* and then *People v. Kelly.* In the *Amwest* case, I wrote an opinion for the court holding that the legislature exceeded its authority in amending Proposition 103. That was an initiative measure that regulated certain types of insurance and imposed a rollback in premiums. This particular initiative measure specifically reserved power in the legislature to enact measures in furtherance of the purposes of the initiative. The question here was, had the legislature properly amended the statute enacted by the initiative or had it instead altered the initiative rather than clarified it? Had the legislature therefore not furthered the purposes of Proposition 103 and perhaps abrogated its purposes? We came to the conclusion that the legislature had done the latter and therefore its enactment was invalid.

One of the points that I make occasionally in noting the difficulties brought about by the initiative process is reflected in the *Kelly* case that I just mentioned, because the opinion in that case illustrates one of the three prongs of what I view as the perfect storm that contributes to the dysfunctionality of California government, at least in times of economic difficulty. First, we have the initiative measures that mandate expenditures for various things, such as education and transportation. Second, we have the initiative measures that make it very difficult, if not impossible, to raise the revenue to carry out those very same mandates, let alone to operate our state government. Then, here's the third prong. We have a provision in the state constitution, article II, section 10, that provides: The legislature "may amend or repeal an initiative statute by another statute that becomes effective only when approved by the electors unless the initiative statute permits amendment or repeal without their approval." So unless the initiative says expressly, "It's all right for the legislature to fix this or change it," the legislature can't do that—even if the intended change would be consistent with the overall objective of the people in enacting the initiative. Instead, you have to wait until the next election to try to fix it by qualifying and passing a new initiative or obtaining the electorate's approval of a statute proposed by the legislature. This constitutional provision severely limits the legislature's ability to deal with changes in circumstances that occur subsequent to the passage of an initiative, or to remedy defects that might inadvertently have been written into the initiative.

The unanimous opinion I authored for the court in the *Kelly* case, with some regret on my behalf, shows how this constitutional provision contributes to the paralysis of the legislative process once a measure has been enacted into law through the initiative process. The *Kelly* case, for me, is the quintessential illustration of the difficulty caused by this constitutional provision. What was before the court was the medical marijuana initiative called the Compassionate Use Act of 1996 that authorized the possession and cultivation of marijuana by persons who were qualified patients or primary caregivers, of course premised upon some medical need. The voter initiative authorized possession or cultivation of a quantity of marijuana reasonably related to the patient's current medical needs. It soon became apparent, if it wasn't before—and I am somewhat jesting here— that what was viewed as a reasonable amount in Orange County, which might be one joint, might differ very much from a reasonable amount in Mendocino County, where it might mean a large truckload. [Laughter] So the legislature tried to deal constructively with what was an obvious problem, acting with the best of objectives. Persons using and cultivating marijuana for medicinal purposes are entitled to some guidance so that they don't run afoul of the law. So are law enforcement officers, so that they are able to enforce the law as the voters intended, without transgressing the rights of medical marijuana patients and their caregivers, or failing to pursue their enforcement obligations because of the uncertainty in what qualifies as a reasonable quantity under the initiative.

The legislature quantified what is a reasonable amount by defining it as eight ounces of dried marijuana or a specified number of plants. But my colleagues and I had to invalidate as unconstitutional the statute that the legislature passed in its attempt to define what is reasonable, because the legislation "burdened a defense" provided under the initiative, thereby amending it. Legislative attempts to amend an initiative measure, unless specifically authorized by the particular initiative, violate the constitutional provision requiring that such changes be submitted to the electorate for its approval. Way beyond its importance in the context of compassionate medical use of marijuana—and I don't denigrate the importance of that subject—this case illustrates one of the follies of the role occupied by the initiative process, and the consequences of that role in the lawmaking process of California government. This aspect of the initiative process, along with initiative measures imposing spending mandates and restrictions on raising the revenue to pay for those spending mandates, in combination with term limits and the gerrymandering of legislative districts, have served to greatly reduce the ability of the legislature to perform its constitutional role in an effective manner.

There are certainly many aspects to this whole situation that are major issue areas in and of themselves. The fact that the legislature cannot remedy the defects in an initiative in some cases has been much discussed and the question has been raised, should there be some change in the process to allow those defects to be addressed at an earlier stage?

This question certainly has been raised, and I suppose at a later point in our discussions when we get into my service on the Think Long Committee for California we might discuss what changes in the initiative process itself might be advisable. I'm not in favor of eliminating that process, but I do believe it causes more problems in California—not just by reason of what is illustrated by the *Kelly* case, but for other reasons as well that I'll detail later—than it does elsewhere in the United States among the roughly two dozen states that permit initiative measures.

But in Kelly, you were compelled to go the way you did, even with regret?

Yes. It's an illustration of having to render a decision that went totally against the grain for me and, I suspect, for many if not all of my colleagues, who were unanimous in concurring in the *Kelly* opinion.

You mentioned, in the general rubric of this area of the law, "interbranch relations and separation of powers." If you wish I can just briefly, subject to further detail being elicited by your questions, go through some of those. There were several opinions that I authored in the area of separation of powers.[12] These cases illustrate the numerous contexts in which the interplay among our three branches of government can arise. When we talk about separation of powers, the term is not strictly accurate in the sense of a true and full separation, because there is a mutual dependence or interdependence of relations among the three branches. It is more accurate to refer to our federal and state systems as characterized by checks and balances. Look at the judicial branch, for instance. We pride ourselves on our independence, although we are accountable, obviously, to the voters. We are dependent in various ways upon the executive and legislative branches. The executive appoints judges, and in the federal system those appointments are subject to legislative confirmation. The legislature and the executive provide the funding for the operation of the judicial branch. We in turn, despite the shared responsibility entrusted to the legislature and the governor in their lawmaking capacity, have the authority and obligation to interpret—and in appropriate instances invalidate—the legislation enacted by those two branches of government.

There is a separation of powers, but these powers are not totally separate. This circumstance is recognized in some of the language that I included in my unanimous opinion for the court in *Superior Court v. County of Mendocino*,

---

[12] Article III, section 3, of the California Constitution provides: "The powers of State government are legislative, executive, and judicial. Persons charged with the exercise of one power may not exercise either of the others except as permitted by this Constitution."

where the legislature enacted a statute declaring that trial courts shall not be in session on unpaid furlough days agreed upon by any county and its employees. The case raised the issue whether this degree of legislative and executive intrusion in the operations of trial courts violated the inherent powers of the judiciary. Our opinion held this was not the degree of involvement that would intrude upon the courts' constitutional functions or violate the principle of separation of powers. Yet one could imagine a more extensive attempt by the legislature and the governor along similar lines that would reach the point at which it would constitute a violation.

There was the case of *In re Attorney Discipline System*, involving a political stalemate over the governor's veto of the State Bar dues bill passed by the legislature. California was left without a functioning State Bar. As I've noted earlier in our conversations, the State Bar is recognized as a public corporation under article VI, the judicial article of the state constitution, and operates as an arm of the Supreme Court. Added to that is the circumstance that the State Bar has as one of its primary functions the admission of attorneys to practice and the discipline and possible removal of attorneys from practice. As a matter of public protection—consumer protection if you will—our court felt it could not assume a hands-off position in this dispute between Governor Wilson and the legislature once a lawsuit was filed. We had to step in and did so with the greatest reluctance, making it very clear in preliminary orders that, as I would now put it in the vernacular, "The minute you folks in the executive and legislative branches come to an agreement on this, we're out of here. We'll dismiss this lawsuit." [Laughter]

How did this disagreement arise? What was going on behind the scenes?

I believe that much of the governor's displeasure with the State Bar involved the fact that the bar was taking some actions that the governor did not consider to be appropriate within the purview of the bar's responsibilities. The bar's Conference of Delegates was adopting resolutions that dealt with international issues and social issues that arguably had little if anything to do with the practice of law. The State Bar, of course, is a compulsory membership organization. It's not voluntary like the Bar of San Francisco or the Los Angeles County Bar Association. You have to be a member of the State Bar in order to practice law in this state, so there were legitimate issues that had reached the U.S. Supreme Court and the California Supreme Court in the *Keller* and *Brosterhaus* decisions, holding that it is a violation of a lawyer's First Amendment rights to have his or her compulsory dues—and this built upon some of the labor-union-representation cases—used for political and other purposes that the lawyer might disagree with.

We talked about how the State Bar ultimately separated out those kinds of issue endorsements to solve that problem.

That's correct, and that really did go a long way toward resolving the dispute.

What do you make of Governor Wilson's position with regard to their disciplinary powers?

I can see the point he was trying to make, but I was concerned—certainly as a justice of the court confronted with complaints from the public—that as a matter of public protection, the court had to impose dues and take other measures to the extent necessary to maintain the system for admitting lawyers to practice and disciplining them when necessary. I see an analogy to the U.S. Supreme Court's decision in *Baker v. Carr*, in which the high court concluded, out of necessity, that it had to resolve the legal dispute over reapportionment because there was no available legislative remedy to ensure protection of the public's rights—despite, as I mentioned earlier today, Justice Frankfurter's warning in a previous case that the court would be entering the "political thicket." In the State Bar case, the California Supreme Court unenthusiastically entered the political thicket, having concluded that judicial intervention was required in order to protect the public from unqualified or unscrupulous persons being involved in the practice of law.

Consequently, without jumping in and taking over the entire State Bar operation or levying the full amount of dues, the unanimous opinion I authored for the court relied upon our inherent authority over the practice of law, over the State Bar, to impose a proportional dues payment obligation on each attorney that was tailored to provide sufficiently for only the admissions and disciplinary functions, and to keep the rudimentary functions of the bar and its offices open without funding the full panoply of bar services. The court's action was greatly facilitated by its appointment of Elwood Lui—a noted attorney and former Court of Appeal justice and former president of the California Judges Association—as special master for the court. Again, this was an instance in which the court—not in any way overreaching or wanting to extend its authority—with the greatest of reluctance undertook a role because it felt it was compelled by law to do so. This was another one of those cases illustrating a fascinating interplay among all three branches of government.

Another interbranch conflict arose in the context of the State Bar, and specifically the State Bar Court, after the legislature passed and the governor signed a bill that provided for these two branches of government to make some of the appointments to the hearing department of the State Bar Court. The question arose whether the legislation conferring this authority intruded upon the judiciary's role and violated the separation-of-powers clause of the constitution, because of the circumstance that I previously mentioned of the State Bar being an arm of the court system. The opinion that I authored for the court in this case, *Obrien v. Jones*, upheld the legislation because of provisions involving the Supreme Court in screening and evaluating applicants for appointment to the State Bar Court—even those applicants to be appointed by the other two branches of government—and the fact that the court continued to appoint all three judges to the review department of the State Bar Court and retained ultimate authority over attorney discipline. All of that led the court to conclude that this legislation did not defeat or materially impair the Supreme Court's authority or violate the separation-of-powers provision. Even though the legislation did somewhat intrude on the court's authority, it did not do so to the degree of being unconstitutional.

Another State Bar matter arose in *Warden v. State Bar*, involving a legal action against the bar challenging the constitutionality of the mandatory continuing education program for lawyers on the ground that, in providing exemptions for elected officials and retired judges, the program violated equal protection principles. My opinion for the court upheld the regulation.

What about mandatory continuing education—the policy matter of having such a requirement in general?

I think it's essential to require attorneys to keep abreast of new developments in the law, just as it is for medical doctors to be apprised of new techniques and new research. However, I did find some aspects of the continuing education program to be a bit silly in terms of what qualifies as education. If you looked at the list of the courses, some of them didn't quite encompass basket weaving but did get somewhat close—reading the legal newspapers and such. I do believe that the concept, as opposed to some of the outer fringes of the program, have served a very worthwhile purpose. Certainly we wouldn't want to have lawyers out practicing law who are ossified in their thinking based on what the law was when they graduated from law school many years ago. Being aware of how the law has evolved since my own graduation from law school in 1964, and knowing that there are persons practicing law who are considerably older than I am at my present age of 71, I feel that it is very important for lawyers as well as judges to engage in continuing legal education. The point is made that lawyers or most lawyers will engage in it on their own. My feeling about that is that the ones who engage in it voluntarily are really not the subject of this legislation. It's the lawyers who won't do so voluntarily who most need the mandate.

There are a couple of additional cases that I'll mention in the area of inter-branch disputes where I have authored the court's opinion. One was the *Manduley* case, involving "The Gang Violence and Juvenile Crime Prevention Initiative," Proposition 21, which granted D.A.s discretion to file specified charges against minors directly in adult criminal court without any judicial determination that the minor is unfit to be tried as a juvenile. The primary question presented was whether the legislation improperly infringed upon the judicial discretion that otherwise existed in making that determination and therefore violated the separation-of-powers doctrine. The opinion held that the legislation did not, and also that the initiative did not violate the equal protection or due process guarantees or the single-subject rule.

A very interesting separation-of-powers issue arose in an opinion I authored for the court in *Marine Forest Society v. California Coastal Commission*. This decision involved the question whether the fact that the legislature itself could appoint members of the Coastal Commission rendered the coastal act and the Coastal Commission unconstitutional. The court found that the degree of legislative involvement in the appointment process did not render the act unconstitutional. What was interesting was that, after the Court of Appeal's opinion held the act to be in violation of the separation-of-powers clause of the constitution but before our court could complete our review of that opinion, the legislature enacted and the governor signed an urgency measure amending the act so that the legislature no longer had the authority to just willy-nilly remove its appointees from the Coastal Commission the way the legislature sometimes does with its own internal committees when a member has cast a vote that the Speaker or the President pro Tem doesn't like. Our court reviewed the coastal act and the coastal commission's composition in the context of that amendment. In light of the current wording of the act, we found there was no violation of the separation-of-powers clause in having this degree of legislative involvement in the type of enforcement agency in question.

I'll bet you heard from a lot of people on that one.

Yes, and it was amazing in a way because the Coastal Commission had been around for many years since it was created by a 1972 initiative measure and a 1976 legislative enactment, yet this attack was brought so many years later.

There was also a series of decisions I wrote in the area of interbranch relations that are probably too complex to warrant detailed discussion here, involving the extent of the governor's role in the budget process. One was *White v. Davis*, where the question was whether the right of state employees to their compensation could be suspended during a budget impasse existing prior to the final enactment of the applicable appropriation. We upheld the withholding of such payments, even though they would ultimately be payable once there was a budget, under the employees' right of contract. Then there was *St. John's Well Child & Family Center v. Schwarzenegger*, which held that the governor's line-item authority to blue pencil or reduce certain appropriations applied to items of appropriation that had already been altered by the legislature, a very technical ruling; and the companion case, *Professional Engineers v. Schwarzenegger*, where the court upheld the governor's authority to institute a mandatory furlough of represented state employees—although we came to this conclusion because the legislature had in effect, by its other actions, ratified what the governor had done, by that body passing certain appropriations reflecting the savings anticipated from a work furlough. Our opinion was a mixed victory for each of the other two branches of government.

The final area I would allude to here in terms of interbranch relationships was a series of opinions I wrote involving the authority of the governor and the parole board to prevent the release on parole of persons who were serving life terms of imprisonment. There is a relatively new constitutional provision, article V, section 8, that gives the governor the authority to review the parole board's decisions and to thus preclude the parole authority's release of a prisoner. It's a complex area because what these decisions hold, considering them together, is that it's not an unbridled authority, the way the governor's power of clemency and pardon appears to be, subject to the Supreme Court's role regarding twice-convicted felons, which I described to you. There are certain limitations on the governor's exercise of discretion in the matter of parole. There must be—and this is a term of art—"some evidence" to justify the governor's reversal of the parole board's order of release. The governor customarily prepares a written statement reciting the evidence. The governor and the parole board must, when finding a person unsuitable for parole, premise that finding not merely upon the gravity of the underlying offense on which that conviction is based, but must focus instead upon the future dangerousness of the individual, and specifically upon evidence or indications demonstrating such future dangerousness.

This matter of "some evidence" is challenging, though?

It certainly is, and it's not a situation where the court would normally get involved in weighing that type of evidence. But the opinions I have authored—and some of the others that have come down from the Court of Appeal and our court—have established the principle that there has to be something of substance before the governor or the parole board. The court doesn't weigh this evidence and conclude, "This counts a lot more than something else," but rather approaches the question with the proviso that there has to be some evidence that is prospectively relevant to future dangerousness and not merely the nature of the crime, however terrible the crime was. Under the law that has been enacted by the other two branches of government, eligibility for parole is contemplated and specified by law for all persons convicted of second or first degree murder—except for the situation of first degree murder with special circumstances, where the law specifies life imprisonment without the possibility of parole unless the judgment imposes the death penalty. When the other branches specify the punishment of life without parole for a category of offenses so serious that the offender never should be considered for parole, the courts must—and do—uphold it. In fact, that is the premise in the legislative scheme that provides for special circumstances. When the prosecutor, in the exercise of his or her discretion, alleges along with a charge of murder in the first degree a special circumstance, the jury's finding that the special circumstance has been proved brings about a second phase of the trial in which the jury is called upon to decide between the punishments of death and life imprisonment without possibility of parole, provided the prosecutor chooses to seek the death penalty. The prosecutor may be content to just leave it as life without possibility of parole without proceeding with the second phase of the trial. Or the jury may decide, after the second phase, to impose the lesser punishment. In either of those situations, there's no second-guessing, by the courts, of a governor's or parole board's decision to parole a life-term prisoner, because the prisoner cannot be considered for release on parole. But in all other situations—where the punishment is, let's say under the three-strikes law, 25 to life—the law contemplates that the prisoner will serve a life term *with* the possibility of parole. Therefore, the decisions of the California Supreme Court hold that one cannot automatically, as a parole board or as a governor, preclude any consideration of the possibility of parole. The possibility of parole has to be considered, and if there's some evidence supporting the decision to deny parole, that decision is not going to be second-guessed by a court. But parole can't be denied based just on the nature of the crime, because that would amount to life without possibility of parole, which is a punishment reserved only for cases in which one or more special circumstances are alleged and proved. Referring to these decisions collectively, without getting into the particular aspects of each of them, the opinions that I wrote for the court include *In re Rosenkrantz, In re Lawrence* and its companion case *In re Shaputis*, and finally *In re Prather.*

Here is another area of the law where we see this configuration of moving parts—almost like a kaleidoscope—in which the three branches of government with all of their vast authority come into conflict, almost like a collision of planets. The legislature has prescribed punishments for the various categories of murder, the executive enforces those enactments and exercises its authority over parole, and courts are called upon to define the authority of the other two branches and to resolve the conflicts that arise between them in exercising their respective authority, consistent with the separate—but somewhat interdependent—powers of the three branches. Added to this mix is the active role of the electorate in enacting some of the provisions in this area of the law.

A kaleidoscope is a great image. Where did your colleagues come down on this matter of the governor's parole review authority? How contentious an issue was that within the court?

In some cases it was contentious. In *Rosenkrantz*, the initial case holding that the courts have the authority and responsibility to review the governor's exercise of his parole authority, there were concurring and dissenting opinions, although I had four justices on my majority opinion, one of whom, by the way, was a pro Tem because of a disqualification on our court. The *Lawrence* opinion, holding that the governor lacked "some evidence" upon which to conclude that the petitioner's release on parole would represent an unreasonable risk of danger to the community, was a four-to-three decision. Obviously, it's an area where there's been substantial disagreement among the justices of our court, although some of the opinions in this area, like *Prather*, were unanimous. Any time you get involved in the relationship among the three branches of government there is the potential for very strongly held views, because this area of the law lies at the very heart of the judicial process, involving the courts' appropriate deference to the other two branches of government and the expectation that they in turn will show proper deference to the judicial branch and its functions— a hope that is not always realized.

My last question on this area is what response you got from the governors in these cases, realizing they weren't all decided at the same time—any particular feedback?

None. However, as the result of some of the cases we discussed involving other areas of the law, I received some very inappropriate communications from persons in the executive and legislative branches.[13] In one instance, a legislative leader picked up the phone less than 10 minutes after a court order was posted on the web and was made available at the clerk's counter—leading me to assume that he had not had the opportunity to fully and carefully reflect upon the action taken by the court. He was quite angry. That same order prompted a congressional leader to express great displeasure to me.[14]

I always declined to get involved in any debate with legislative or executive officials over the Supreme Court's opinions, on two grounds. First of all, the case was still pending until such time as the period had expired for acting on any petition for rehearing that might be filed. Second, the decisions that my colleagues and I rendered were not designed to reflect our personal views but rather our understanding of the law. That was our obligation as set forth in our oath of office—to apply and uphold the law, including the constitution—and not merely do what might be viewed as reflecting the popular will or the current political view held by the legislature or the governor. Again, this is a repetitive lesson in civics that always seems to have to be retold in Sacramento.

---

[13] For example, my opinion for the court in the parental consent case involving abortion rights prompted legislative threats to the judicial branch budget and an allusion to my upcoming 1998 retention election as Chief Justice. There was also a heated phone call to me by a member of the governor's senior executive staff regarding a Supreme Court ruling that had declined to review a lower court decision imposing substantial liability on the state's general fund. Our court's decision preserving judicial discretion in sentencing matters in the wake of the Three Strikes Initiative brought about an angry tirade against the justices of the court from an elected statewide officeholder. The *In re Marriages* decision resulted in a number of legislators withdrawing their support for the bill that authorized the issuance of courthouse construction bonds. On occasion, state legislators would angrily—but mistakenly—blame the California Supreme Court for rulings handed down by "that San Francisco court," the U.S. Court of Appeals for the Ninth Circuit.

[14] As reflected in my opinion for the court in *Costa v. Superior Court*, we reversed orders of the lower courts and issued an order in August of 2005 restoring to the November 2005 special election ballot an initiative measure that would have shifted from the legislature to a panel of retired state and federal judges the function of reapportioning congressional and state legislative districts. The measure was defeated at that election, but we nonetheless issued an opinion setting forth the reasons for our action, in order to provide guidance in future situations.

Chapter 17

The Marriage Cases and Other Noteworthy Opinions
November 9, 2011

We left off last week talking about some of the opinions you authored on the California Supreme Court, both as associate justice and as Chief Justice. We're going to start today with a few that don't fit readily into a category of cases but that are worth talking about for their larger implications for the development of California law.

You wrote the opinion in 2004 in People v. Pena, *a criminal procedure case that had implications for the judicial branch in a larger sense. Would you talk about the importance of that case?*

Pena, which I mentioned in one of our early discussions, dealt with an important aspect of the appellate process, specifically the constitutional right to present oral argument on appeal. In an effort to be innovative, one of the divisions of our six Courts of Appeal, Division Two of the Fourth Appellate District, instituted a procedure that is followed from time to time at the trial court level but not often at the appellate court level, namely preparing and disseminating a tentative opinion or indicated ruling, accompanied by a suggestion that counsel waive oral argument. The opinion I wrote for our court found that certain aspects of this procedure infringed upon the defendant's right to oral argument. The notices sent to counsel included a statement by the appellate court that it had already determined that oral argument would not aid the court in its determination of the issues in the particular case and had further determined that the tentative opinion, which had been made available to counsel, should serve as the final opinion from the court. The oral argument waiver notice also had an admonition that if counsel were—and I would interject the words "so bold" as my words, not the appellate court's—to request oral argument notwithstanding this communication from the Court of Appeal, counsel was not to repeat arguments already made in counsel's brief, and that if counsel violated this admonition, sanctions may be imposed on counsel. The appellate court's procedure obviously could have a chilling effect upon counsel's exercise of his or her right to participate in oral argument and also ran counter to another principle that is recognized by most appellate courts in most situations, namely, one is not free to make an argument for the first time orally that had not been raised previously in the written briefs. Our court directed the Court of Appeal to refrain from using this type of waiver notice in the future. This didn't mean the appellate court couldn't issue tentative opinions, but it couldn't accompany it with this kind of heavy-handed oral argument waiver notice.

Had you ever seen such a waiver before?

No, I had not. In rendering this decision, our court exercised its authority—apart from its ability and duty to rule on the merits of various claims, based on constitutional or statutory authority or case law authority—to employ what is described as its inherent supervisory authority over the lower courts, to direct the appellate court almost as a quasi-administrative matter to refrain from employing that type of waiver notice in future cases.

How was the decision received by that Court of Appeal?

They modified their practice. I believe they thought it had been quite fine before, and I picked up a bit of grumbling, but what they basically wanted to do was issue tentative opinions, something they're entitled to do and are continuing to do, but without the somewhat coercive accompaniment of this particular type of oral argument waiver notice.

There's another decision that comes to mind in conjunction with our discussion of appellate process, an opinion I wrote for the court in a case called *People v. Kelly*—a different *Kelly* case from the one I mentioned that involved the medical marijuana initiative. In this *Kelly* case, our court concluded that the Court of Appeal's opinion did not satisfy the constitutional requirement in article VI, section 14, of a decision in writing with reasons stated. The Court of Appeal's opinion did not describe the defendant's contentions or why there was no merit in the defendant's contentions. It merely indicated that the appellate court had reviewed the entire record and had found no arguable issues. This raises a point that I think will be relevant in the discussions you and I will have regarding California's jurisprudence and why our decisions are followed by other jurisdictions to such a large degree—namely that our state's constitution imposes an obligation on an appellate court to set forth its reasoning in its opinion, which in turn makes our opinions more likely to be followed and cited and persuasive to other jurisdictions, rather than the conclusory type of treatment that is given in a memorandum opinion.

To your knowledge, how common was it to see an opinion that did not give reasons at all or gave insufficient reasons to meet the constitutional requirement? Is there any way to generalize?

There are some opinions in the Courts of Appeal that are prepared by central staff that are basically viewed as rulings on no-merit appeals. In those cases it's tempting not to go through the exercise of delineating the particular contentions and indicating why they're without merit. Certainly a full treatment isn't necessary, but it should be possible to write one of those no-merit appeal opinions in two or three pages and still give the parties—sometimes a criminal defendant who has chosen to represent himself or herself—the satisfaction of knowing that the court has at least identified and confronted the claims that are being made. I believe that frequently my colleagues and I would see opinions that came pretty close to the line in terms of not stating reasons but perhaps were just barely enough to meet the test. It's probably unusual to have one that so clearly fails to even go through the motions of reciting and considering the individual claims made by the appellant. It's something that I think arises most frequently, when it does arise, in the context of criminal appeals, especially those that are no-merit appeals.

Let's take up this case Bronco Wine Company et al. v. Jolly, *which you authored in 2004, the so-called wine labeling case.*

I truly enjoyed working on this case for a number of reasons. The case was handled by some excellent attorneys on both sides, and it involved the question of whether one could label wine with a "Napa" designation when in fact the grapes had been grown in the Central Valley and then trucked up to the Napa Valley for bottling. This was one of those cases where, contrary to my usual practice, I said to the staff attorney to whom I assigned the case, "Although we always want to let the law take us wherever it does on any given case, if there are options here I certainly find this conduct offensive, as a matter of policy, and would very much prefer not to permit it."

What was your thinking behind this, in truth-in-labeling terms? Or what line of reasoning made you so eager to reach that result?

Aside from my affinity for truth in labeling, here you had some very strong equities supporting the Napa Valley growers and their stake in being able to have only those wines involving grapes grown in Napa marketed as Napa wine. The land in Napa is much more expensive, and Napa Valley wines have a certain cachet and reputation that are known worldwide. To have someone in effect deceive consumers with wine that generally is not of the quality of Napa wine and is less expensive to produce is in my view against public policy. Even though there was some labeling that referred to Lodi, California, many California or out-of-state consumers, either buying wine at a retail establishment or at a restaurant, wouldn't necessarily know that Lodi was located in the Central Valley when the bottle proclaims, in much larger letters, "Napa" on the label. The brand names included the designations "Napa" and "Rutherford," a region within Napa County, although those brand names were used exclusively to sell wines made from grapes outside Napa County. When I asked the question at oral argument, "Doesn't your client's labeling of its wine "Napa Ridge" reflect an attempt to deceive? Why didn't you just call it Lodi Ridge?" I got some sort of half-baked answer about the word "Napa" just having a nicer ring to it.

But the interesting part of the case involved the history of wine labeling. Even though we normally don't, as justices, identify the staff attorney who assists us on a particular case, I can't resist mentioning that I chose Jake Dear to work on this case for two reasons. First, he's very much a legal historian in terms of his enjoyment and ability to go back decades and more to the origins of a legal doctrine or principle. Second, he's very much a wine connoisseur himself, so I figured he would ferret things out and have the best chance of finding the applicable law. Sure enough, Jake's independent research went back to the nineteenth-century labeling provisions of federal law. A basic principle in the law is that normally, if there is both federal and state regulation in an area, the federal regulations will preempt or supersede the state regulations, especially when interstate commerce is involved to some degree. However, Jake's research uncovered that, although there had been federal regulation of the subject of wine labeling, it was of a type that specifically delegated to and relied upon the states regulating this field. It was an expression of deference on the part of the federal regulatory authorities. Jake came up with two to three dozen authorities, cases and regulations that had not been cited in the lawyers' briefs. We had the clerk send out a letter to counsel calling the attention of both sides to those authorities, inviting them to file supplemental briefs and to be prepared to respond to questions at oral argument related to those authorities. Here is an instance typifying the high quality of Supreme Court staff attorneys. Jake's independent research had uncovered legal authority that experienced counsel had not found, and it was possible to come up with a result under state law that I thought was quite fair and appropriate, notwithstanding the fact that federal law existed in that area. The difference between the federal law and the state law was that the federal law grandfathered in winemaking enterprises that existed before certain regulations went into effect. The offending wine grower here had purchased some wine bottling facilities in existence in Napa before the cutoff date, so he claimed that he was immune from the state regulations because under the federal law he could do what he did, due to his having acquired these pre-existing facilities. It was a rather technical type of legal issue but with some very basic everyday principles involved—namely consumer rights and truth in advertising, protecting not only consumers but also the legitimate interests of Napa winegrowers.

I note this was a unanimous decision of the court.

Yes it was. This case was also significant in expressing a concept—somewhat technical in terms of our discussion today—of there being a "presumption against preemption." This means that a court should not assume, just because there are regulations in both the federal and state sphere, that the federal regulations would necessarily supersede the state regulations, even though the federal often do. Here it was clear that the federal act was intended to supplement but not supplant the long-standing state regulation of labeling in the wine industry.

Did that presumption against preemption have greater significance?

Bronco has been cited from time to time in totally different contexts for that proposition of law.

We also want to take a look at your opinion in County of Santa Clara v. Superior Court.

This was an interesting case. There are many local entities—municipal and county, and regional governmental districts—that bring public-nuisance-abatement actions against private individuals and organizations for engaging in environmental pollution or other harmful conduct. The local governmental entities as a general matter, and probably even more so in the current era of cash-strapped local government, find it impossible to have their city or county attorney fund the litigation, given the circumstance that often there's a tremendous amount of investigation and fact gathering and discovery proceedings that precedes actually going to court. What these governmental entities have done—and certainly that's what was involved in the *County of Santa Clara* lawsuit—is hire private counsel who specialize in this type of lawsuit.

Here's the controversial part of it. The local entities certainly could not afford to pay the hourly rate of compensation to these usually high-priced private counsel any more than they could afford to expand their city attorney or county attorney office to handle this kind of litigation, so they entered into contingency-fee arrangements with private counsel whereby the compensation of private counsel is determined by the outcome—how much is secured by way of settlement or judgment after trial. The argument was made in this case that it is improper for privately retained attorneys to have a stake in the outcome, because the government and counsel representing the government are supposed to be neutral and not be influenced by such financial considerations. The law is quite clear about the government not being permitted to prosecute criminal cases through private attorneys retained on some kind of contingency basis, even though of course there usually isn't any substantial monetary recovery in a criminal prosecution. Here there were several local governmental entities around the state that had retained prominent plaintiffs' counsel, including Joe Cotchett and others, to file public-nuisance-abatement actions against manufacturers of lead paint. These business entities were national and even international corporations with enormous assets. The point was made by one of their attorneys at oral argument that here was the massive power of the government going against the individual business entity. I inquired, "These cash-strapped local governmental entities—aren't they more akin to the David in the David versus Goliath parable than to Goliath? It's the private entities that have the enormous assets."

Ultimately, there were certain safeguards that our court found were essential, especially requiring public officials to retain decision-making authority with regard to the conduct of the litigation. Decision making on fundamental aspects of the litigation couldn't properly be abdicated to private counsel. But with that safeguard and others ensuring adherence by private counsel to a proper and heightened standard of ethical conduct that's applicable to public officials, our court upheld this type of arrangement. In fact, were we not to have upheld it, I believe public legal actions to protect consumers, to protect the environment, and to take other action that's necessary in the public interest, would be crippled. I view this as a very important decision in terms of the functioning of government at the local level.

How well did the decision serve its intended purpose?

I don't know the outcome, and I suspect that proceedings in this litigation are still ongoing. But there was quite a negative reaction by some business interests—I believe especially the U.S. Chamber of Commerce—but of course the opinion was greeted very positively by various associations of local governments as well as consumer groups. A contrary decision by our court would have put much of local government out of business in terms of litigation initiated for the public interest. These last few cases you and I have been discussing all involve issues of process in one way or another, which are among the issues that always interested me as a judge at all levels of court.

Certainly the matter of a county or another local government entity hiring private counsel might not have come up too often, if at all, in years past. Yet I can see, with the kinds of situations local governments are faced with, that this might really be a rather large area.

Yes, a large area and one where the impact on the lives of individual residents of California is very substantial.

Were there other related cases, in terms of procedural issues, that stood out to you?

We have discussed just a few of those that may be of more general interest. There were many cases that I assigned to my chambers, involving rather arcane but minor points of procedure, that I sometimes found among the most intriguing but that probably aren't worthy of rising to the level of an oral history discussion.

I wonder if I might ask you about an earlier opinion that you did not author. We discussed most of the criminal procedure cases last time, but I got to thinking about the three strikes law, which came up when you were a new associate justice. The opinion was authored by Justice Werdegar, I believe. There have been so many interesting developments since her opinion of many years ago. Could you reflect on how that law has worked and what effect it's had on our system?

That law, the product of an initiative, has been very much in the public consciousness as a result of the public's general awareness that many criminals were released following relatively short periods of confinement after committing very serious offenses, and then went on to commit further serious offenses— sometimes murders and other offenses even more serious than they had committed previously. It has been said that 90 percent of the crime is committed by a very small percentage of the criminal population. I'm not a penologist and haven't studied the figures, but I believe this is true as a generalization, whether that's the exact figure or not. The three strikes law has had many consequences. First and foremost, it has, in my opinion, served to protect the public by keeping a lot of people off the streets who, given their rate of recidivism or likely recidivism, most probably would have been out committing serious and maybe life-endangering crimes.

On the negative side, because of what I consider to be a basic flaw in the law, it has contributed to the burgeoning population in our state prisons that has caused great difficulties to the state—both in terms of the cost of confinement and the issuance of federal court orders necessitating the release of persons from the state prison system if they can't be adequately housed within the state or if arrangements can't be made to house them in prisons in other states. There are efforts now underway in state government to confine more of the prisoner population at the local county jail level. That's a whole other problem. But much of the current problem of inadequate prison facilities reflects the fact that California has not had the kind of halfway-house facilities that many other states have. So in our state a prisoner may be released on a serious offense—with a small amount of cash and perhaps not much in the way of newly acquired job skills or incentive to become law-abiding. Then, if one is on parole, a relatively minor parole violation—which can consist of anything from failure to keep an appointment with one's parole officer or to test clean on a drug test—may result in a violation of parole and a remand to custody for several months, not to a halfway facility but back to the already overcrowded prisons at San Quentin, Folsom, and other institutions. I would like to see more use of halfway houses or other local types of facilities, both for persons exiting prison confinement and for those who are returned—which is almost inevitably for a very short period of several months—to serve an increment of time for violation of parole.

But the real flaw I see in the three strikes law is the following. The first and second strikes, appropriately in my view, have to comprise crimes defined in the Penal Code as "serious" or "violent." For some reason or other—and I never heard an explanation for this—the drafters of the three strikes initiative specified that the third strike could be virtually any kind of minor offense. So let's say you have a situation—and I'm not just speculating; I saw such cases come up before the Supreme Court—where someone committed a violent or serious offense in his or her youth, perhaps an aggravated assault arising out of a bar fight and then a burglary. After committing those two offenses in one's late teens or early twenties, the offender leads a crime-free life and then becomes a homeless person who steals a pizza or a bicycle or a minor item at a convenience store. These are actual illustrations. That third, minor offense qualifies, the way the law is drafted, as a third strike. The offender, then, is subject to receiving a sentence of

25 years to life and has quite a coercive threat hanging over his or her head. If the defendant exercises his or her right to go to trial, he or she may end up with a 25-year to life sentence for a very petty crime, after having been crime free for the last 20 years or so. If the defendant doesn't enter into a plea agreement for a lesser prison term the threat is, "We'll go after you as a third striker." In addition to having this disproportionate impact on those individuals subject to the three strikes law, the operation of the law contributes to the overcrowding—and rising expense—of California's prison system, filling it with many petty offenders who could more appropriately and economically be housed in local facilities.

Some individuals tried to remedy this situation by placing an initiative on the ballot that would have required that the third-strike offense be "serious" or "violent" like the first and second strikes. As a voter I was supportive of that until I realized that something else had more or less been snuck into this proposal—a redefinition of what constitutes a serious crime for purposes of the first or second strike. It became apparent that the offense of residential burglary was being redefined as no longer a "serious" crime. I know from our court's mandatory review of all death penalty cases that residential burglaries are among the very most dangerous crimes in their potential, because so many of the death penalty appeals that we saw on the court were the result of a homeowner surprising a burglar—or perhaps the burglar even knowing the homeowner was present—and then a struggle ensuing and the homeowner being stabbed or shot to death. I view residential burglary, in terms of the threat posed to the individual homeowner, as among the most serious of all life-threatening crimes. To provide that this offense would no longer be treated as a serious offense qualifying as a first or second strike was very disturbing and a fatal flaw in the initiative. My position as a voter was to vote against it. I think we'll see a more straightforward initiative that would not alter the definition of a serious or violent offense but would merely require that the third strike be a serious or violent offense as those terms are presently defined, like the first and second strike offenses. In that form, I believe this would be a substantial improvement in the three strikes law for the reasons I've outlined.

I'll try to tie this in to Justice Werdegar's opinion for the court in *People v. Superior Court* (*Romero*), which involved a constitutional challenge to the three strikes law. Various arguments were raised, including a separation-of-powers argument. It was claimed that—by providing the strike allegations were not to be dismissed by a trial court—the law improperly curtailed the fundamental discretion exercised by trial judges in sentencing matters, and that this curtailment, in turn, constituted a violation of the constitutional principle of separation of powers. There was a whole line of cases—one of them comes to mind, *People v. Tenorio*—that had invalidated various statutory restrictions on a judge's sentencing authority, restrictions that precluded him or her from dismissing charges when imposing a sentence. The question was whether the three strikes law was invalid on that basis. What came into play in our court's decision was one of the numerous maxims of jurisprudence that an appellate court will employ in performing its function of reviewing a lower court judgment and specifically in reviewing a statutory provision. Of course, first of all there is a presumption in favor of the constitutionality of a statute, notwithstanding that courts from time to time have to declare a statute violative of the state or federal constitution. Another maxim, which you and I discussed previously, indicates that if a statute is capable of being construed in more than one way and one construction would uphold its constitutionality, the statute should be interpreted in the manner that would preserve its constitutionality. There is, in other words, a presumption in favor of constitutionality that leads courts to assume the legislature would have drafted the statute with a constitutional result in mind in preference to having its enactment invalidated by the courts. Whether that assumption is theoretical or real, one can speculate, but it is one that appropriately guides the courts in performing their function of statutory interpretation. Applying that principle here, as I recall the court's decision, we concluded that the wording of the statute, the three strikes law, even though it was not entirely unambiguous, should be interpreted as preserving a judge's traditional discretion to dismiss allegations or charges—because if our court were to view the trial courts as having been deprived of that discretion, the three strikes law might well be unconstitutional as violating the separation-of-powers doctrine by denying a trial court its traditional and essential ability to perform its basic sentencing function. Such judicial discretion has to be exercised for legitimate reasons related to the particular case and not merely out of a general disinclination to impose the more severe punishments mandated by the three strikes law. Again, this was a case that I find interesting from the standpoint of process, totally apart from the subject of the three strikes law. Had the court not taken that approach in upholding judicial discretion to dismiss a strike allegation, we might very well have been compelled to invalidate the entire three strikes law as unconstitutional. The *Romero* opinion certainly suggests as much.

The news reports of this decision of the court in 1996 characterized it as weakening the three strikes law, but as you've just explained you were looking ahead to the constitutional challenge that you might face separately, that might knock the whole thing off the table?

It wouldn't really have been separately. Under this scenario, Justice Werdegar's opinion for the court in the *Romero* case probably would have had to invalidate the three strikes law because of that problem.

The U.S. Supreme Court got the opportunity to weigh in on California's three strikes law as well, rendering a decision in 2003 that it was not in violation of the Eighth Amendment provision on cruel and unusual punishment. Your thoughts about the court taking that case and making that ruling?

I don't have much insight into the U.S. Supreme Court's views on that issue except to say that had our court interpreted the three strikes law as mandating a 25-year-to-life term for a person who, let's say, was crime-free since his or her early twenties and two or three decades later committed a petty offense, it's possible that the U.S. Supreme Court would find the sentence to be grossly disproportionate and application of the three strikes law to be cruel and unusual punishment in the absence of discretion by a trial judge to dismiss a strike allegation in imposing sentence.[1]

As you said, in November 2004 voters got a chance to modify and limit the three strikes law. If the current attempt results in a ballot initiative for November 2012, they will eight years later get that chance again, but with the important distinction of retaining home-invasion-related burglaries as serious crimes. That would be enough to sway you personally, it sounds like. What do you think about the chances of the measure passing, either for differences from the earlier attempt or for reason of a different climate eight years later in our voting population?

I believe that, because of the changes in content and the different political climate, the proposal would be much more palatable to the public today. People are now more concerned with costs, including those attributed to the burgeoning population of our prisons. As I've said in other contexts, it's time to be not only tough on crime but smart on crime as well. I could see the proposal faring differently today, with the changed wording of the initiative.

There does seem to be great and broad concern about our prison system that is very much in our minds. Prison healthcare has been such a big issue, for example. Although that's really separate from your work on the jurisprudence side, I wonder how you see the prison population and what remedy might there be for our overburdened system?

---

[1] Ewing v. California (2003) 538 U.S. 11.

The federal litigation has certainly recognized that when a governmental entity incarcerates an individual, it is responsible for providing a certain level of care, including health care and mental health care. That's something that has to be part of the equation, I suppose, in terms of locking people up. California has an enormous incarcerated population; I believe there are about 160,000 people in prison and another 30,000 to 40,000 in local custody—meaning county jails—so basically 200,000 individuals in custody. The state is obligated to adequately feed and house and provide medical, including mental health, care for these individuals. We need to decide on a cost-benefits basis whether it's worthwhile to incarcerate some people for the less serious offenses, with all those costs involved. It's something that has to be given serious thought, at least in terms of whether some of them should be confined in local facilities instead, and for shorter terms, or be required to perform community service as part of their sentence.

In looking at your opinions, we thought we might move into the general area of civil rights and individual constitutional rights. Could we preface that with the "independent and adequate state grounds doctrine," a.k.a. state constitutionalism, and the whole history of that idea and practice for California? I gather a number of other judges, both in California and nationally, have been interested in the concept, I believe going back to Justice Brennan in the late seventies. How do you view the history of independent and adequate state grounds?

Yes, U.S. Supreme Court Justice William Brennan was one of the foremost exponents of independent state grounds, perhaps reflecting his prior experience as a judge in the New Jersey state judiciary, culminating with his service on that state's supreme court. By the way, I consider prior state judicial service to be a valuable—although rare—commodity among the persons appointed to the U.S. Supreme Court. Our own Justice Mosk has written articles on the subject of independent state grounds, in addition to authoring opinions in which he has discussed this concept. Former California Supreme Court Justice Joe Grodin also has written on that subject. One other person comes to mind as a national authority in this field, and that's a former justice of the Oregon Supreme Court, Hans Linde, who now is a law professor in Oregon. This is a concept that underlies so many important decisions, certainly of our court. Not every state chooses to place reliance upon its own state charter as an independent source of law, even though state courts have the right to do so under the principles of federalism that govern the American legal system. But some state high courts are content to just automatically imbue their parallel state constitutional provision with the same force and impact and content as the comparable federal constitutional provision.

California has been a leader in interpreting its own constitutional provisions, sometimes worded identically to the federal counterpart, in a different and more expansive manner. To put it succinctly, one could say that the federal constitution establishes a floor of rights and guarantees. The states may not offer less than that, in the sense that they are bound, whether they have a parallel state constitutional provision or not, to afford the minimum level of protection conferred by the federal constitution. But if the federal guarantees represent a floor, the state constitutional guarantees represent a ceiling that the states can expand upon and supplement with a greater level or additional type of guarantee. That is most graphically recognized in article I, section 24 of the California Constitution, which expressly provides, "Rights guaranteed by this Constitution are not dependent on those guaranteed by the United States Constitution."

The classic instance of that, and one that underlies some of the most notable decisions of the California Supreme Court, is the right of privacy. The electorate in 1972—among the basic rights set forth in article I, section 1 of the California Constitution, the article that comprises what is captioned "Declaration of Rights"—added, to the so-called inalienable rights, the right of "privacy." So the word privacy is explicit in the California Constitution. Interestingly enough, despite the fact that many U.S. Supreme Court opinions have discussed a right of privacy and have founded some of their rulings on recognition of that right in one context or another, the word "privacy" doesn't appear in the federal constitution. Some jurists and scholars quarrel with the analysis and formulation of privacy rights recognized in *Roe v. Wade*, even though they may agree that a woman's right of choice is constitutionally protected and should be upheld by the courts. As I said, a right of privacy is not explicitly set forth in the federal constitution, so it basically has been created through a blend of some due process, some equal protection, various provisions including the Fourth Amendment—including what's sometimes called a penumbra of rights. This term was famously used in the U.S. Supreme Court's opinion in *Griswold v. Connecticut*, although it did not originate there. I liken the concept, maybe a bit prosaically, to making a stew—a little of this, and a little of that, and a pinch of this, and here's a right of privacy. Whereas the beauty, here, of independent state grounds is that California did not have to go through any sort of legal gymnastics or legerdemain in recognizing a right of privacy. It is, since 1972, explicitly set forth as a provision in our state charter.

As an aside do you recall—when this inalienable right was added in 1972—what the judiciary at large thought of this? Was it clear how important this would be to your work?

I don't know that there was that much recognition. In the course of my authorship of various opinions for the court, I had occasion to look at some of the constitutional history of that amendment. As I recall from the ballot arguments that I examined, the real focus was on protecting privacy from wiretapping rather than recognizing a woman's right of reproductive choice. The voter information material and other available literature focused on electronic surveillance. The right of privacy had been recognized by our court in the context of abortion even before the 1972 constitutional amendment.[2] In one context or another, that right of privacy was recognized and expanded, including its application to persons under the age of 18 years. Additionally, the California state constitutional right of privacy has been interpreted to provide a broader and more protective right than its federal counterpart. This became important in the context of judicial decisions addressing abortion rights and specifically parental consent. The concept of privacy also was recognized in some of our decisions dealing with gay rights, although the bedrock of our decision in *In re Marriage Cases* was a different constitutional right—equal protection of the laws.

One can also view a decision that we discussed many sessions ago, *People v. Anderson*—invalidating the death penalty as cruel or unusual punishment under the state provision—as based on independent state constitutional grounds, with the California Supreme Court construing cruel *or* unusual as something different from what the U.S. Supreme Court was construing in the cruel *and* unusual punishment clause of the federal Eighth Amendment.

The concept of independent state grounds is very much part of the strategy that litigants have employed in various areas, whether it's abortion or the gay-rights area. Undoubtedly, the plaintiffs in *In re Marriage Cases*—not to get into a full discussion of the opinion yet, but just on this point—deliberately based their claims exclusively upon state constitutional rights, instead of federal constitutional rights, in order to evade federal court review. They felt, and I believe correctly, that in the event they were to prevail in our court having raised only state constitutional questions and not federal constitutional issues, as they ultimately did prevail, the U.S. Supreme Court would have no jurisdiction to review the resulting decision of the California Supreme Court in their favor. Once Proposition 8 passed, of course, our court was faced with a different state constitution to interpret than the one it had before it in *In re Marriage Cases*. Having upheld Proposition 8, our court was more or less out of any role in the gay marriage litigation for the time being. The focus of those supporting gay marriage shifted to the federal courts, and the plaintiffs felt it was then appropriate to raise

---

[2] People v. Belous (1969) 71 Cal.2d 954; 458 P.2d 194, relying on the U.S. Supreme Court's decisions in Griswold v. Connecticut (1965) 381 U.S. 479, and other cases.

issues under the federal constitution, because the state constitution no longer contained all of the protections it afforded at the time we rendered our decision in *In re Marriage Cases*.

Of course, now the litigation is going from the federal district court, where the plaintiffs prevailed, to the Ninth Circuit with an intermediate stop at the California Supreme Court just to deal with the issue of the standing of the Proposition 8 proponents. That is something we'll talk about, certification of questions of state law by the Ninth Circuit to the California Supreme Court. The case will be before the Ninth Circuit again once the California Supreme Court rules on the standing issue, and then, of course, the Ninth Circuit's decision will be subject to review by the U.S. Supreme Court—that is, potential review in the discretion of the U.S. Supreme Court. If the high court grants review, it may determine whether the adoption of Proposition 8 violated the federal constitution. Of course, if Proposition 8 is invalidated, our decision in *In re Marriage Cases* will be fully resurrected. So this case provides an interesting illustration of the whole concept of independent state grounds.

I should probably mention another point relevant to this discussion. There was a famous case in the 1960s involving the Rumford Fair Housing Act. That legislation provided that persons selling and renting out property would not be permitted to discriminate on the basis of race in carrying on those activities. The California Supreme Court, in the case of *Mulkey v. Reitman*, held that an initiative measure that sought to repeal the Rumford Act violated the federal constitution. There was no independent state ground for the decision of the California Supreme Court. The U.S. Supreme Court, therefore, had jurisdiction to review the decision of our court, and when it did so—and the case then was captioned *Reitman v. Mulkey*—the high court affirmed the decision of the California Supreme Court that the initiative, Proposition 14, which had sought to nullify the Rumford Act, did violate the federal constitution. That initiative had passed by a two-thirds vote of the electorate.

Attempts have been made to curtail the ability of the courts to base their decisions on independent state grounds. As I previously mentioned, there was one initiative that was so wide ranging that the California Supreme Court invalidated it in *In re Lance W.* on the theory that it was a revision to the constitution, not an amendment. This initiative sought to render all rights conferred by the state constitution subject to the same interpretation as their federal counterparts. The constitution provides that revisions can be initiated by the legislature but not by voter initiative. However, a more limited initiative enactment was upheld in the *Raven* decision. That initiative amended article I, section 28, of the state constitution to provide that in criminal cases, "relevant evidence shall not be excluded" except as required by the federal constitution. By enacting that initiative, the voters succeeded in barring the state courts from relying upon independent state grounds in ruling upon issues involving the law of search and seizure. Our state courts now are governed by the same standards as those guiding the federal courts in Fourth Amendment jurisprudence and are not free to extend greater rights in that particular area. Because this initiative dealt with a relatively narrow area of the state constitution, it did not run afoul of the "improper attempt to revise the constitution" argument that had been successful in the other litigation, and was upheld as a permissible amendment to the constitution.

As you say, as with privacy, that was one area where California's Constitution had differed in a way that would have significant effects?

Yes, although with wording that, except for minor stylistic differences, was identical in terms of the protection it provided against unreasonable search and seizure.

What was your own history with state constitutionalism? When did it enter into your work, and how did you view it?

I don't recall any personal involvement in that concept as a judge, other than my application of existing principles of independent state grounds. In the context of the cruel *or* unusual punishment versus cruel *and* unusual punishment differentiation, as we discussed previously, I worked as a deputy attorney general with then-Senator George Deukmejian to add an amendment to the California Constitution, article I, section 27, which basically provides that the death penalty should not be and cannot be deemed to be cruel or unusual punishment within the meaning of the state constitution. So that can be viewed as eliminating a certain component of the independent state grounds aspect of the prohibition against cruel or unusual punishment. I should also note, after the certiorari petition that I filed in the *Krivda* case was granted by the U.S. Supreme Court and oral argument took place following my appointment to the bench, the high court remanded the case to the California Supreme Court for a determination whether that court's decision was based on independent state grounds.

To what extent did you have an overarching philosophy about this, about the two different constitutions, and how California's differs, and how much weight that should have?

The philosophy that I have today is something that evolved over the years. I probably didn't have much occasion as a lower court judge to deal with it. But I have always believed in the wisdom of Justice Brandeis' observation that the then-forty-eight states of our union constituted laboratories and should be able—although he was referring primarily, I'm sure, to legislation—to experiment and try different solutions.[3] I assume his premise would extend to constitutional provisions as well. One example that comes to mind: we have one state, Nebraska, that has a unicameral legislature, so that's certainly constitutional experimentation.

Of course, the needs of different states may really vary according to their size and population and the kinds of legal issues they face.

Most definitely. You have some states that are more involved with agriculture and mining and, therefore, have different types of legal issues and perhaps different environmental issues than other states that are mainly urban. I'm very much a supporter of true federalism, as long as the basic rights set forth in the federal charter are recognized as providing a floor, and not a ceiling, for constitutional rights. I think that's part of the strength of our country, that we have been able to have various jurisdictions develop best practices which, as long as they meet federal constitutional standards, are recognized and respected in other states.

Knowing of Justice Mosk's interest in this matter of independent state grounds, I wonder what occasion you might have had to talk with him about this and about his very strong ideas about how important it was?

I know that it came up sometimes in conference. Interestingly enough, since you are asking about his view on this particular subject, although he was one of the main proponents of independent state grounds he was a dissenter in the opinion I wrote for the court in *American Academy of Pediatrics v. Lungren*, based on the state constitutional right of privacy, invalidating the requirement of parental consent for abortion.

Yes, and indeed had written the majority opinion that came before that went the other way. I'll look forward to talking about that.

I think that his approach on that issue and on some search and seizure issues involving minors reflected, perhaps—and I don't mean this to necessarily sound negative—more of a paternalistic approach toward younger people. That led him to feel that he could differentiate when it came to recognizing more rights for

---

[3] New State Ice Co. v. Liebmann (1932) 265 U.S. 262, 311 (Brandeis, J., dissenting).

adults than he was prepared to recognize for minors. That may just be speculation on my part, but I think his jurisprudence lends itself to that interpretation.
However, our court's case law has recognized for some time that California's
constitutional right of privacy extends to minors.

*Outside the membership of the court—in your time and from your own observa-
tion—which other advocates might have had a strong impact on this area of
adequate state grounds?*

In addition to noting the individuals I mentioned a few moments ago who
were leading advocates for recognizing independent state constitutional grounds,
I can say that our California Supreme Court regularly looks to other state courts
and their own holdings involving independent state grounds. Not to get ahead of
ourselves, but at the Conference of Chief Justices we were always eager to know
what each state was doing, the particular problems it was identifying and encountering, and what the solutions and best practices were. There was also a
certain amount of creative thinking germinated by discussions with the leaders
of other jurisdictions, whether it was in the formalized sense of looking at court
holdings from other jurisdictions or engaging in these discussions among the
Chief Justices.

*But your own view was that if the situation warranted going to the state consti-
tution in an area of real difference, you were willing and indeed bound to do so?
How would you characterize your view?*

. Yes, definitely willing and bound. When we look at *In re Marriage Cases* I
think that will become apparent. Much as the ruling may have come as a surprise to some persons, there was great reliance on the precedent established by
our own California Supreme Court in interpreting the state constitution as leading the way to the conclusion reached by a majority of the court.

*Very much so. Maybe we will now sally forth into your opinions in this broad
area of civil rights and individual constitutional rights, which will lead us in due
time to* In re Marriage Cases. *First, perhaps, we'll start in the area of public
accommodation, and I'll ask you to walk me through your decision in the 1995
case* Warfield v. Peninsula Golf and Country Club, *which raised the question of
whether the country club was a business establishment subject to the Unruh Act.*

The California public accommodations law, found in the Civil Code and also known as the Unruh Civil Rights Act, had an interesting evolution. As we all
know, there were civil rights battles fought in the southern states over the right

to be treated equally, regardless of race, at lunchroom counters, in public transportation, and so forth. California passed an act that mentioned a few types of public accommodations, and then more would have to be added to make sure that every type of establishment was covered, such as ice cream parlors, barbershops, and so forth, to the point where the statute became almost silly. So the solution was, the legislature took out that whole string of different types of businesses—the attempt to categorize every kind of venue in which a public accommodations claim might arise—and just substituted the words "in all business establishments of every kind whatsoever."[4] That, of course, gave rise to litigation as to what constitutes a business establishment. But I believe it was better to try to cover every type of establishment rather than omitting some in the catalog of such establishments and having to litigate or legislate whether they should or should not be included.

The court's encounter in the *Warfield* case with the public accommodations law was in the context of a wife who was, in a marital dissolution proceeding, awarded a regular family membership in what was considered a private golf and country club. She happened to be, by the way, an ace golfer. The bylaws of this club restricted membership to males only, and the club denied her request to transfer the membership to her name. So she brought a legal action urging that the club's refusal violated the Unruh Act. The trial court granted a motion for a directed verdict in favor of the club on the basis that the plaintiff, the wife, had failed to prove that the club was a business establishment within the meaning of the act. The case was one of the most interesting decisions I was involved in, trying to ferret this out. The opinion I authored for a six-justice majority of the court held that the legislature certainly never intended to cover, by the term "business establishment," something that would be a truly private social club. If you want to get together and form your own book club or other group and say you have to have red hair or be a woman to be a member or to be of this race or that, you're free to do that under the act. But once you qualify as a public accommodation business entity then you are subject to the strictures against discrimination on the basis of gender, race, ethnic background, and—now—sexual orientation. The question was whether this was a truly private social club. Our court concluded, based on the evidence contained in the record before us, that the business transactions that were regularly conducted on the premises of this golf and country club with nonmembers were sufficient to qualify the club as a business establishment, whether the club considered itself private or not, because the standard was, "Is this, in the words of the statute, 'a business establishment' of any kind whatsoever?"

---

[4] Cal. Civil Code, section 51.

There were direct and indirect financial benefits that inured to the club by reason of renting out its facilities for weddings and other events to nonmembers, on average once a week. The golf and tennis pro shops also would sell merchandise to nonmembers. Nonmembers were permitted to take paid lessons from the pros and use the club's facilities during such lessons. So the club, in many ways, was conducting itself as a business establishment within the confines of that term as it's been defined by law. Now, a very similar golf and country club, if it wants to be very strict about it—and some have made a point of doing this in the wake of our *Warfield* decision—can make itself immune from the application of that public accommodations law and be free to discriminate. It can be a club almost identical to the one involved in *Warfield* but one that doesn't allow nonmembers to rent the facilities, doesn't allow nonmembers to buy things at the pro shop, and so forth. That was the ruling, which also included a holding that applying the Unruh Act to the club did not violate the free associational rights of club members or their right of privacy. Again, what makes the law so interesting, especially at the level of a high court, is that we have concepts clashing with each other here: the members' right of privacy and freedom of association—a First Amendment right—and the excluded member's right not to be discriminated against because of her gender—a statutory right, and the court's effort to accommodate those competing rights.

You said this was one of the most interesting and satisfying decisions to you personally. Why?

I viewed the *Warfield* opinion as having broad application in the area of civil rights. Little did I know that many years later I would be relying on it in the context of gay rights, but it certainly was part of the continuum in this area. I also had a great interest in gender equality, an interest that was—I won't say created, but—certainly heightened by the assignment I received from my predecessor, Chief Justice Lucas, to chair the committee charged with implementing the recommendations of the gender bias committee.

Yes, I'm sure exposure to those issues would spark an interest that you could then trace over the course of many years. Since you mentioned Chief Justice Lucas, I'd like to ask if anything stands out about his reasons for dissenting, all by himself, on Warfield? *What might his thinking have been, if you recall?*

My best recollection is that he concluded that the club did not engage in sufficient business-like activities to come within the coverage of the public accommodations law. Of course, the court's view of this particular golf and country club as a business establishment does not comport with the traditional definition, certainly not the lay definition, of what we think of as a business establishment. Yet in my view the court's conclusion that this was a business establishment was not in any way a radical departure from the court's prior expressions. That is a subject where he and I obviously differed.

The court watchers of the time noted that when you first joined the California Supreme Court as an associate justice you voted rather closely with Chief Justice Lucas, at least in the first year or so, and then began to move away from him. Of course, that is a way of looking at patterns that you probably don't share. But I wonder how influential to you he was as a jurist at various points, if at all?

Certainly his leadership after the court had been in a period of several years of turmoil—heightened by the retention election at which three justices of the court, including Chief Justice Bird, were removed from office—brought stability and was very much respected for that reason. I think that by and large—and I may have mentioned this in one of our earlier discussions—the tendency of a new justice, with so much in the way of novel responsibilities to master, is, except where there's a clear disagreement, to go along with the majority and vote with the author of the tentative majority opinion who has the support of most of the justices. Having said that, it's ironic that my very first opinion in the official reports of the California Supreme Court was the *Rider* case that I referred to earlier. Although I signed the majority opinion of Chief Justice Lucas, I did write a concurring opinion putting forth what I thought was a superior approach to the tax problem involved in the case, an approach that, as I noted before, was ultimately adopted by the court in a later opinion. I believe that after a justice has served for a year or so and has mastered the extremely challenging responsibilities facing a new member of the court, he or she feels more inclined to explore different resolutions to these very complex legal problems, almost all of which afford more than one reasonable basis for a decision. Otherwise, for the most part, the case wouldn't be up there at our level.

What else influenced you in finding your own voice?

I suppose another factor is being exposed to the views of six colleagues instead of the sort of club-ish atmosphere of a division of four justices on the intermediate appellate court, of which two of the other three would be deciding any given case with you. There was in my own experience much more need for give and take on the high court than there was in Division Four of the Second District Court of Appeal, and a greater exposure to novel arguments, to academic authority, and to the potential ramifications of the court's decision. The high court's decisions rarely involve applying settled law, which is the typical fare in the Court of Appeal, but instead present unresolved questions of statewide importance, often involving cutting-edge issues in California. The Court of Appeal by contrast frequently is engaged in attempting to ascertain the existing applicable law and then applying that law, rather than making new law.

But on the Supreme Court it is your responsibility and, perhaps, constant effort to develop the law?

It is, even though it is sometimes stated somewhat simplistically that judges don't make law, they just apply law. I don't ascribe to the analogy that we're just umpires at a baseball game—or that we otherwise merely have to dig deep enough and we'll find the one true right way to resolve the dispute by discovering what the already established—even if inchoate—legal principle might be out there, perhaps buried in eighteenth-century constitutional text. Cases fall in between various precedents, and one has to chart one's way between and among them, and choose the course that seems the most appropriate under the law and that seems the most just in the given case, and to interpret statutes and constitutional provisions by examining available indications of the intent and policy objectives underlying their enactment. The answer isn't always that easy to come by. There are some areas of the law that don't involve the interpretation of specific constitutional or statutory or regulatory language but where virtually all of the law is judge created. The classic example of that is tort law. This is an area that, for the most part, has not been codified in statutes, so it's almost entirely a question of the court's interpreting its prior jurisprudence and incrementally adding to the evolving law. One area we discussed during our last session was the tort area of implied assumption of risk, where the court had to go back and look at its own precedents and consider the social and economic implications of the ruling it would make and other policy considerations. Our court was quite properly and unavoidably making new law, because it's not an area where there was a statutory or constitutional provision that directed the answer.

Thank you for reflecting on that. In this area of public accommodations I also want to touch on your opinion of 1998 in Curran v. Mount Diablo Council of the Boy Scouts of America, *another unanimous opinion in this case—again with reference to the Unruh Act, I might add.*

There were actually a couple of cases—*Curran* and then there was also the *Randall* case—that same year involving the Boy Scouts of America. In *Curran*, an applicant for a scoutmaster position in the Boy Scouts was rejected because he announced that he was a homosexual. He claimed that his rights under the

Unruh Civil Rights Act had been violated. Our court held that a regional council of the Boy Scouts of America did not come within the definition of a "business establishment" under the Unruh Act, and that it was basically a social and charitable and expressive association, as opposed to an entity that could properly be classified as a business establishment. The scouts' very minimal business transactions—if one could even call them that—with nonmembers were quite distinct from their core functions and did not render them a business establishment within the act.

You brought all your colleagues along on that one, as we said.

Yes. There were some concurring opinions, but we all came to the same conclusion there.

What kind of process did you have to go through to make the determination about the nature of the Boy Scouts, and how difficult was that?

We were provided a fairly complete record from the lower court proceedings in both the *Curran* scouts case and the *Warfield* country club case, with very specific evidence detailing the activities and functions of the two organizations in question, instead of just having to rely upon a gut feeling about the Boy Scouts as opposed to country clubs. Similarly in the *Randall* case. There, instead of having a scoutmaster as the plaintiff, we had a couple of scout brothers who declined to participate in religion-related elements of the scouting program. They declined to affirm a belief in God. Again, we held that a regional council of the Boy Scouts was not a business establishment of any kind whatsoever, in the words of the act. Because the scouts were basically a charitable organization and did not have any real involvement in promoting the economic interests of its members, and its membership didn't benefit from economic activity, the Boy Scout organization basically was not the functional equivalent of a traditional place of business or public accommodation.

In both Curran *and* Randall *there was another issue present, one that the court ended up not having to address by virtue of ruling that it was not a business establishment.*

Yes. Put very bluntly, purely private organizations have a right to discriminate. This is not a question of what's socially desirable. It's not a matter, necessarily, of their exercising a constitutional right—at least, that wasn't the basic factor in our decision. Our decisions in the two scout cases were premised upon our interpretation of the statutory provisions—specifically of what is and is not a business establishment of every type whatsoever in terms of whether an organization is covered by California's public accommodation law.

The Curran *case, at least, got a lot of attention for the other reason.*

Yes. Again, it's up to the legislature to define the scope of its public accommodations law, subject to any constitutional constraints.

I might just briefly mention that there was another quite different public accommodation situation that the court had to confront in an opinion I wrote in the *Angelucci* case. A supper club gave a lower entry fare to female patrons or, if you will, charged a higher admission to males. This was deemed to be violative of the Unruh Civil Rights Act, discriminating on the basis of gender. This is an example of one more context in which these public accommodations disputes can arise. Each one is very much determined by reference to the underlying factual setting in which it arises, namely the particular activities and nature of the business establishment.

If you're ready, we might move into another civil rights area, individual rights and public access. The opinion of 1997 you mentioned a few minutes ago, American Academy of Pediatrics v. Lungren, *is fascinating in any number of ways. Before you wrote that case, however, the California Supreme Court had already once considered it. Could you start with a bit of history?*

The court had considered the issue, and then there was a change in the composition of the court. Chief Justice Lucas and Justice Arabian retired, and Justices Chin and Brown joined the court. The court's opinion was not yet final, so its action in rehearing the case did not result in the court's literally overruling one of its prior decisions. Its decision, like all decisions of the court, was somewhat tentative in the sense that it was subject to the losing party's seeking and obtaining a rehearing. It is only when the time for seeking rehearing has lapsed or, if rehearing was granted, the ultimate decision has become final, that the opinion becomes a binding precedent.[5]

It's unusual for the court to grant rehearing, but it has done so for one reason or another on occasion over the years. The law clearly provides that the justices currently on the court at the time a petition for rehearing is acted upon would be the ones who would vote on that petition, even though in this case two

---

[5] A Supreme Court decision is final 30 days after filing, unless the court exercises its authority to extend the time to act up to as long as 90 days. Calif. Rules of Court, Rule 8.532. "An order granting a rehearing vacates the decision and any opinion filed in the case and sets the cause at large in the Supreme Court." Rule 8.536.

of these justices had not been on the court when the case was originally heard. This same situation existed after the 1986 retention election, when three new justices joined the court and participated in the rehearing of several cases that had been heard by the court as it was formerly constituted.

As you say, two justices had retired in the interim, Chief Justice Lucas and Justice Arabian. You were promoted to Chief Justice, and Justice Chin also joined the court. It was a different makeup by the time the petition for rehearing was granted, but you had seen it all the way through.

For obvious reasons, with two justices having left the court, it wouldn't have made sense to have an opinion issue and become final, reflecting the views of the prior court, if the current court was prepared to disavow those views— which turned out to be the case. Both of the new justices who had not participated in the original decision in the case, Justice Chin and Justice Brown, voted to grant rehearing, although after the case was reheard Justice Brown voted to uphold the parental consent requirement in accordance with the views expressed in the former majority opinion.

But you say such a granting of rehearing is unusual?

It is, although certainly not unprecedented. Apart from a change in the composition of the court, sometimes there are new developments in a case that warrant a rehearing. It may be a recent decision from the U.S. Supreme Court that constitutes controlling authority. It might be a persuasive decision from another jurisdiction. It may be something else newly called to the court's attention that is highly relevant.

As we talked about a few minutes ago, Justice Mosk had previously been the author of what would have been the majority opinion. You indicated that he was placing a great emphasis on the matter of privacy for a minor as distinct from that for an adult. Where did it go from there?

Those opposed to the decision, of course, would focus their attention upon however young one might be and be physically capable of conception, a twelve- or thirteen-year-old, and how such a girl would likely consult a parent, or certainly should consult a parent. A parent should certainly be involved in decision making of that sort. Those who viewed the requirement of parental consent as unconstitutional stressed the fact that, first of all, you could be dealing with a young person who was just weeks short of her eighteenth birthday, and that not infrequently the parent whose consent was being urged as necessary for an abortion might take very severe action against the pregnant person, even including physical violence. Another argument made was that, from time to time, the pregnancy was the result of sexual conduct by the father or some other member of the family. In that situation there would be a great amount of shame and anger involved, and the alternative of a judicial bypass proceeding might not be readily available to the young woman. It was also urged that the consequences of requiring a minor to carry a fetus to term were not only very momentous for the child that would be born, but could be an overriding concern in the entire future life of the pregnant young woman, and that this decision should not be made under the compulsion of having to obtain parental consent. Concern was also expressed that enforcing a consent requirement would lead some minors to seek illicit and dangerous means of terminating their pregnancies.

I've gone through some of the major policy considerations which, although of secondary concern to a court in performing its function of interpreting a constitutional provision, did infuse the assertion of an applicable right of privacy with real substance and meaning and made it more than an empty phrase. As I indicated to you earlier in our discussion today, there was clear precedent outside the abortion context of this case recognizing the application of California's explicit constitutional right of privacy to persons under the age of 18 years. Once the court recognized a right of privacy on behalf of pregnant minors, it was logical to apply that right in the context of a challenge to the parental-consent requirement.

I would note just as a matter of interest that there have been frequent attempts in subsequent elections to amend the California Constitution to override the parental consent decision in *American Academy of Pediatrics*, and all of those efforts have failed. I believe there is going to be another attempt next year to qualify another initiative proposal.

It's a difficult and complicated area. As with the earlier look the California Supreme Court had taken at the matter, the decision was four to three, so you were split on this. What memory do you have of how the different justices might have looked at this issue, having discussed Justice Mosk's view already?

I believe that Justices Kennard and Werdegar had been rather explicit in their views recognizing the right of choice of minors in this context. I also recall that Justice Chin, when his appointment to the California Supreme Court was announced by Governor Wilson, participated in a press conference at which he was asked about his views on abortion and responded that he was a supporter of a woman's right of choice. He and I both had antichoice activists testify against confirmation of our 1996 appointments to the high court, and immediately after my opinion for the court came out in 1997, in which Justice Chin joined, we both became the targets of an effort to deny us new twelve-year terms in the 1998 retention election.

I should mention one other aspect of the discussion contained in the court's opinion. The court observed that there were several California laws that authorized minors, without parental consent, to obtain medical care and make other important decisions in other contexts affecting their health and welfare. Also, physicians are accustomed to seeking an informed consent from minors in various situations, whether involving surgery or other procedures. There was nothing to suggest that a medical doctor wouldn't be equally capable of ascertaining whether a minor, in a given situation, was capable of giving an informed consent to an abortion, just as the physician would be required to make that determination in the context of other types of medical procedures and care.

Or other patients whose age or condition might affect the ability to give an appropriate informed consent?

Yes. In fact, because a question of mental competence is involved, a physician presumably would be more qualified than a nonphysician to make a determination of capacity to give an informed consent.

We didn't happen to touch on this, but this whole matter came up after the legislature enacted a statute requiring a minor in this situation to get permission before seeking an abortion. There is an area where the legislature was establishing something, and then it worked its way over to the judicial side. But it's a complex area of rights and responsibilities between the branches again.

That's true. Although I'm not saying this was necessarily the case here, often the attitude taken by persons in the legislative and executive branches is that they don't have to really consider whether or not what they are doing is constitutional, because the courts will decide that. Then when the courts do determine that the legislators' enactment violates the constitution, the court becomes the object of great criticism—often from legislators and executive branch officeholders. There are some scholars and even officeholders on the state and national level who have recognized that the legislative and executive branches have a responsibility—even though courts have the final word on questions of constitutionality—to make a determination whether there's a constitutional problem in a proposed enactment and that under the oath of office taken by legislators and chief executives, they should not be enacting legislation that they feel might very well be unconstitutional. I believe it is wrong for presidents or governors to sign bills that they basically have grounds to believe and maybe do believe are unconstitutional, and to just buck the legislation over to the courts to take the heat for invalidating it. All officeholders are duty bound to uphold the constitution, and I assume this duty encompasses their actions in enacting legislation.

Maybe we'll turn to a case that has come up before in these discussions in other connections, and that is NBC Subsidiary Inc. v. Superior Court, *a unanimous decision you authored in 1999 regarding the public's right of access to civil trials and proceedings.*

This was a case that arose out of litigation between two actors, Sondra Locke and her then-companion, Clint Eastwood. As often seems to be the case, many judges—maybe in Los Angeles more than elsewhere, because of the concentration of the entertainment industry there—appeared to feel, just as local law enforcement occasionally does too, that special accommodations should be made for celebrities. In this instance, the parties wanted to have their lawsuit tried in a public courthouse in a closed courtroom. Of course, they could have chosen, if secrecy was such an important consideration, to arbitrate their legal claims in a private setting. That, to me, is one of the best justifications for private resolution of disputes—when secrecy is an important consideration. You go to the public court, and you're going to have your proceedings aired in public. If you go to private ADR, then it will be done in private. In this case, the *Los Angeles Times* and other media groups had to bring a lawsuit to open up the court proceedings. The claim was made that, notwithstanding the well-established rule set forth in the 1980s by the U.S. Supreme Court in the *Press-Enterprise* cases that criminal proceedings are open to the public and that the press and the public have a constitutional right to attend and observe those proceedings, no such right had been clearly recognized in civil proceedings. The *NBC Subsidiary* decision established that those rights apply equally in civil cases, with very narrow exceptions—just as very narrow exceptions exist in the criminal area.

This was a case that had a lot of national ramifications for other jurisdictions and is one that I am particularly proud of, because I believe that openness and transparency are hallmarks of what we strive for in a court of law. They exist not merely to satisfy public interest or curiosity. Aside from accommodating the public's interest in the particular proceedings, permitting the public to observe the way court proceedings are conducted serves to cast light upon the competence, fairness, and efficiency of the trial judge. It may be relevant to the position people take in informing themselves how to vote when judges and judicial branch issues are on the ballot. It may be relevant to public perceptions, real or imagined, about corruption and the way the courts operate. So it's vital that the public have the opportunity to have that view—an opportunity that is vastly expanded when trial and appellate proceedings are televised.

The *NBC Subsidiary* opinion also is an illustration, as are a couple of other opinions—such as *Elkins* in the family law area, and the cases related to the Riverside criminal case backlog—of where there is an intersection between administrative action and opinion decision making. The *NBC* case led directly to the adoption of certain rules of court governing the sealing of exhibits and documents filed in court, requiring that there be a justification and specific findings made before such items are made inaccessible to the public and the press by court order.

What hand did you have in those new rules of court, if any?

I urged, in my capacity as chair of the Judicial Council, that the issue of access to court documents and exhibits be studied and that recommendations be made for rules changes in this area. I was pleased when the council adopted those changes.

We noted that the U.S. Supreme Court had made a parallel ruling on criminal matters nearly 20 years before, yet nothing had appeared on the civil side until you took it up in this very case. To what extent was that a glaring hole in the law—that it had not been ruled upon? Was that something that one could watch for, almost?

I think it was a natural development in the law to recognize that the right to open court proceedings in criminal cases extends to the civil area, but it took someone motivated enough to invest the funds to challenge this in court and take it up to a higher level of court. Frankly, that's something that I have heard in the years since *NBC*, that occasionally there are still judges in the trial courts who, in the vernacular, "don't get it," or don't want to comply and therefore engage in unwarranted court closures.

The media may call the attention of the judge, or perhaps a party does, to the holding in *NBC* and other cases applying *NBC*, and the judge disregards it, forcing the media to file a writ petition in an appellate court. I had complaints from the press concerning that problem when I had my get-togethers with them, to the effect that "We can't afford to hire appellate specialists in First Amendment law every time to run to the Court of Appeal to obtain a writ to open up a court proceeding."

Again, openness in court proceedings is something we're trying to promote not only through the bench-bar-media effort that we talked about earlier but also through judicial education. There should routinely be a very strong, almost irrebuttable, presumption of an open court, with a firm obligation to make the specific findings required in an extreme situation to justify why a court proceeding—or a portion of one—should be closed to the public. One example in the civil area would be court proceedings that disclose a trade secret—the formula for Coca-Cola, let's say. [Laughter] That part might be closed, but not the whole trial. Likewise, in a criminal case, there are certain phases of jury selection involving a highly intrusive but pertinent inquiry, such as when a prospective juror in a rape case might be asked whether she herself had ever been a victim of rape—something the juror probably would feel very uncomfortable or constrained in discussing in open court. Or perhaps a portion of the testimony of a witness might fall into a similar category, where the courtroom could properly be closed for a very limited portion of the witness' testimony. But it has to be the rare exception rather than the subject of an easy-to-come-by blanket order proclaiming that the trial is closed for the duration.

Clearly, you saw this as an important matter for all public access along the lines of this general openness of our judicial proceedings?

Yes, and this approach extended into some other opinions I wrote for the court involving the California Public Records Act. Here our court, in proceedings instituted by the media, ordered that local governments release the names of their employees and certain identifying employment data and salary information to the press, there being insufficient justification for keeping that information confidential. It's all part of openness in government in a broader way, including the judicial branch.

Another aspect of ensuring the openness of proceedings was involved in the decision I wrote for the court in *Adams v. Commission on Judicial Performance*, which held that the commission charged with acting on disciplinary complaints against sitting judges must conduct open hearings and that the provisions requiring open proceedings don't violate constitutional provisions mandating separation of powers.

How much difference did it make that it was the Commission on Judicial Performance that was the body in question in that case? That's an interesting mix.

It certainly is. Of course, there are so many considerations that suggest the need for openness in court proceedings that we've talked about. Certainly they apply equally—maybe even more to the commission's proceedings—in terms of the public having the assurance that this constitutional entity that they created, the Commission on Judicial Performance, in the sensitive manner of overseeing charges of misconduct or inability to perform duty on the part of judges, is conducting itself in a proper manner and is not showing favoritism toward the judges who are under investigation and being evaluated for possible disciplinary action.

You have often mentioned this broader idea of the importance of maintaining public confidence in the judiciary. Tie that in with this, if you would.

A judge is understandably concerned with his or her reputation, especially if the charges should prove unwarranted or less serious than originally thought. Despite this circumstance, the public has a vital interest in having confidence that its judiciary is being fairly managed, that such management extends to ferreting out individuals who merit discipline or, in extreme situations, removal from the bench, and that no favoritism is being shown by a body composed partly, although not exclusively, of judges passing judgment on their fellow judges. That's a vital interest in terms of ensuring the public's confidence in our court system. If the disciplinary proceedings against judges were being held in closed settings, such public confidence would be lacking. I'm very proud that California has such an exceptional commission and structure for overseeing the performance of its judiciary at all levels. I would mention parenthetically that justices of the U.S. Supreme Court are not subject to the type of oversight applicable to federal lower court judges and to all levels of the California judiciary, including justices of the California Supreme Court.

What is your view of that difference?

I think it's unfortunate that the governing standards are lower at the federal high court level.

You touched a moment ago on the Public Records Act. Is there more to add about the specific case Commission on Peace Officer Standards and Training v. Superior Court, *which you authored in 2007? As you indicated, the personal records were not confidential under the Penal Code? Is that the idea?*

Not under the Government Code or the Penal Code. Certainly the legitimacy of safety concerns is a factor, but peace officers in general—their safety and privacy concerns—were thought not to outweigh the public's interest in the disclosure of the information in question. The court recognized that you obviously could have undercover officers with a legitimate interest in privacy and confidentiality and that this interest should prevail. Of course, I'm well aware of that, going back to the *Los Angeles Free Press* case that I prosecuted many years earlier, as you and I discussed. But that's a different situation from having the public know that John Smith is a police officer. He may be at a desk job. He may be on patrol. The interest in keeping the fact of his employment private does not outweigh the public's interest in knowing who their peace officers are and having certain basic employment data. The same is true with regard to salaries. In the *International Federation of Professional and Technical Engineers* case the question was whether the trial court could order a city to disclose the salary information of all city employees who earn more than $100,000. The city resisted that, and the court found that there was no legitimate basis under the California Public Records Act for finding that such disclosure would invade the employees' privacy interests.

It's part of being a civil servant at any level?

Yes.

Shall we turn to a few opinions you authored in the area of employment discrimination?

Yes. One of the most interesting ones was *Aguilar v. Avis Rent-a-Car*. Something that I find most intriguing about this case, in which three justices dissented, was that it is a quintessential illustration of the fact that, at the high court level, justices are faced with clashing and competing constitutional and statutory rights that have to be resolved. In this case there were Latino workers employed at the San Francisco airport who brought an employment discrimination case against Avis Rent-a-Car. The allegations were that they had been the target of racial epithets that were repeatedly uttered by their manager in violation of the Fair Employment and Housing Act. It wasn't just an occasional reference. It actually was so pervasive that it constituted making the workplace basically intolerable because of the constant barrage of racial and ethnic epithets. Interestingly enough, the employer's defense was that these racially discriminatory epithets were protected by the First Amendment of the federal constitution and its California constitutional counterpart. But unreasonable as the manager's conduct may seem, it engendered a lot of legal debate in the lower courts and in our court in terms of the extent to which, if you will, verbal employment discrimination can amount to an exercise of free speech rights under the constitution. Our court hinged its ruling in part upon the fact that the restraining order ultimately issued by the trial court prohibiting the manager's use of these epithets was rendered only after a jury determined that the defendants, the manager and the corporation Avis Rent-a-Car, had engaged in employment discrimination. The order simply barred them from continuing in that behavior, so the fact that there had been a jury determination was viewed as an important element in this litigation in upholding the issuance of an injunction. The case presents a fascinating instance in which there was a clash between the right to be free of a discriminatory workplace and the right to exercise free speech and how a court is to resolve those competing considerations.

The federal Fair Employment and Housing Act comes up every now and then for this court?

It does. Here we were focused mainly on the Fair Employment and Housing Act of the state, set forth in our California Government Code, but the federal act comes up as well.

There was another one where that act came in that you authored later, in 2005, in a unanimous decision, Miller v. Department of Corrections.

Yes, that was one of a couple of decisions that I authored for the court that year in the area of sexual harassment committed in violation of the California Fair Employment and Housing Act. In *Miller,* the court held that an employee could establish a claim of sexual harassment by showing that widespread favoritism in the workplace resulted from a prison warden's engaging in sexual conduct with subordinate employees, and that it was pervasive enough in terms of affecting promotions and employment conditions to create a hostile work environment.

The other case I authored in this area was *Yanowitz v. L'Oreal.* There a sales manager refused to follow the order of her supervisor to fire a female sales associate, based on the head supervisor's assertion that the female sales associate was insufficiently physically attractive, even though the associate was one of the most successful salespersons in the chain of stores. Because of this refusal, the sales manager was the subject of constructive termination. She was harassed and received unwarranted negative performance evaluations and criticism rather than being fired outright. The sales manager basically believed that the directive she had received to terminate the employee constituted sex discrimination against the sales associate. We upheld the sales manager's position that she had been subjected to unlawful retaliation by her employer under the F.E.H.A.

This one was a split decision of four to three. What do you recall, if anything, about areas of disagreement or interpretation here?

I believe there were only two dissenters. The decision came down while we had a vacancy on the court. The dispute was basically about the nature of an employer's authority to hire and retain its employees and focused partly on the fact that this was a type of business where the physical appearance of the salespersons was thought to be more relevant than it might be in some other kind of business involved in selling other products—whether it's groceries or hardware—as opposed to beauty products and fashion.

In general, the Fair Employment and Housing Act is called upon to oversee a lot of tricky areas here. I wonder how well it's living up to its promise?

I haven't had enough exposure to the workings of the department to evaluate its overall performance, but certainly in the area of racial and ethnic discrimination there seems to be a lot of activity. The agency has quite a broad charge in terms of the matters entrusted to it. They include employment, housing, and public accommodation violations and other matters.

Employment cases alone are a fascinating area. How often did the California Supreme Court see fit to take such cases?

I know that there are many petitions for review in this area that the court did not accept. Frankly, the lower courts consider many of these lawsuits to involve bogus claims. A person who is terminated with cause may, in some instances, seek to invoke the protections that are afforded by the act by claiming that the real reason for termination was age or gender or race or religion. So the difficult task facing a claimant is to be able to make a record that will satisfy the trier of fact that there was no legitimate basis for the termination and that, in fact, a discriminatory factor was the operative one in the decision to terminate or demote or discipline. Evaluation of such claims can end up being somewhat subjective, but the *Miller* case was so egregious that all seven of us readily agreed in one opinion about that. The *Yanowitz* case was somewhat less clear in the minds of some of my colleagues.

Chief Justice George, would you like to talk about the marriage cases today, or shall we put it off until next time?

Yes, I'm fine to go on with that, and I think that we can have a cohesive discussion that won't go too far afield but put everything in context.

I've been eagerly awaiting this moment, in a sense. Perhaps I'll ask you to start by setting the stage as you saw it from your position as Chief Justice.

There are three marriage cases that I authored for the court. The first one, in retrospect, is given less attention but illustrates the origin of the whole series of cases that came before the courts. The mayor of the city and county of San Francisco, Gavin Newsom, decided that the restriction on issuing wedding licenses through the city clerk to opposite sex couples only, although reflecting statutory law—both a statute passed by the legislature and a parallel one adopted by voter initiative—was, in the mayor's view, unconstitutional. He therefore resolved to no longer enforce these statutes or allow his subordinates or other city officials to do so. The mayor directed that wedding licenses be issued to persons of the same gender, and immediately many same-sex marriages were performed, ultimately about 4,000 of them, until the California Supreme Court, in proceedings initiated before us—through a petition for writ of mandate—temporarily brought a halt to those marriages while we analyzed the legal claims that had been raised. The court's initial order was to direct officials to comply with the statutory requirements and limitations. We stayed various proceedings in lower courts, but made it clear that the issuance of our stay order did not preclude a separate legal action in a superior court to raise a constitutional challenge.

What was your thinking there, in making that so clear?

The basic thinking, and I believe it's reflected in the ultimate decision of the court, was that—not to sound too harsh—the decision made by local officials was, essentially, a lawless act and that we cannot have each and every one of the hundreds or thousands of local officials in the state of California determining for himself or herself which laws will be enforced, which will not be enforced, which ones in the view of the officeholder are constitutional, which ones are unconstitutional. We are a society governed by laws and if there is a genuine question by an officeholder or a member of the public about the constitutionality or other validity of a particular statute or ordinance, the means to determine that is to file a court action and not in effect to take the law into one's own hands. Basically, I did not view this first of the three cases, the 2004 case of *Lockyer v. City and County of San Francisco*, as a difficult case. In a sense, it wasn't truly even a gay marriage rights case so much as it was a rule-of-law case. Who determines which laws are constitutional or unconstitutional, who determines, as an official, which laws to enforce and which not to enforce once they have been enacted? In the absence of a clear judicial determination directing otherwise, the obligation of a local official is to enforce the law just as it's the province of local authorities within their sphere of authority to adopt laws—that's not the court's obligation. Clearly, it is not the function of local officials in our system of government to make judicial-type determinations as to the validity of various enacted laws but rather, consistent with their oath of office, to support and defend the constitution and the laws.

Within hours of our ultimate decision in *Lockyer* invalidating the actions taken by these local officials and invalidating the 4,000 marriages, the mayor and his subordinates did what they should have done at the outset, namely proceed with a lawsuit seeking to have the superior court determine the constitutionality of the marriage statutes. We viewed the city as having basically engaged in a wholesale defiance of the law. A so-called test case could have been filed, or an action seeking a declaratory judgment. There was a means available within our judicial system to make this determination rather than the improper method that was chosen by the local officials. Of course, the legal proceedings that were pursued in the trial court were the direct result of our opinion in *Lockyer*. They culminated, after various hearings and the consolidation of several lawsuits, in a lengthy superior court trial that was held before Judge Richard Kramer of the San Francisco Superior Court. He ultimately upheld the position of the city and county of San Francisco and held that the statutes in question violated the California Constitution by limiting marriage to opposite-sex couples. There was then an appeal, of course, to the Court of Appeal, which issued a two-to-one ruling reversing the trial court. Ultimately, the California Supreme Court received a petition for review. We knew that, whatever happened, this was a case that was going to end up in our laps. That was unavoidable.

That is exactly what I wanted to ask you, because by choosing this sequence of events rather than going for a court trial immediately, Mayor Gavin Newsom had made an enormous statement and had involved the personal lives of many, many people. How did you see this coming to you as it was developing, before it actually reached your chambers?

This is not a very original metaphor, [laughter] but it really was a gathering storm, appearing almost like dark clouds gathered across the street over City Hall and making their way over the Civic Center Plaza to the building in which the Supreme Court is housed.

It was playing out practically within arm's reach of you.

It was. Your comment brings to mind an editorial cartoon that appeared at the time in *The Recorder*, one of the legal newspapers. Two fairly identifiable figures are depicted, Mayor Newsom and myself. Mayor Newsom is standing on top of City Hall—as he swings a large wrecking ball toward the building across the street, namely the Supreme Court's quarters, with me on top of that building—and the caption is, "The ball is in your court." [Laughter]

At the Supreme Court's weekly petition conference, sometimes the justices spend a lot of time, occasionally as much as 15 or 20 minutes, debating whether a particular case should be granted review, whether there's a substantial question—or is there truly a conflict in the decisional law or not?—and it might be on a very minor matter, one of much less interest to the public and to the legal community than most other issues. On the same-sex marriage case it was so obvious that we had to grant review that, as I recall, when we went around the table, I heard the word, "Grant," "Grant," "Grant," "Grant," "Grant," "Grant," "Grant," uttered seven times, with no need to engage in any discussion whatsoever. The usual questions were absent: Did the case meet the standards for review? Should we grant review or not? Did the case present a substantial question of statewide importance? Did a conflict in the law exist? It was obvious we had to take up this case. We would have been derelict in our duty had we not done so. These consolidated cases were captioned *In re Marriage Cases*, the second of the three opinions I authored in the area of marriage equality.

We clearly were confronted with basic questions concerning state constitutional rights. We recognized there is a fundamental and well-established constitutional right to marry.[6] Although this right doesn't appear in those exact words, the jurisprudence of our court and, interestingly enough, of the U.S. Supreme Court, explicitly recognizes a constitutional right to marry—I believe going back to a case from the 1920s, *Meyer v. Nebraska*. In that case the U.S. Supreme Court recognized, in discussing the liberty interests protected by the due process clause of the federal constitution, that it includes a right "to marry, establish a home and bring up children." Although we were dealing with state constitutional rights, there was precedent even in the jurisprudence of the U.S. Supreme Court for recognizing that there was in fact a fundamental constitutional right of marriage, although we were called upon to evaluate basically the scope of that right under the California Constitution and whether there had been a violation of the state constitutional right to equal protection of the laws and to privacy by virtue of the state action in adopting the statutory differentiation between opposite-sex and same-sex couples.

Interestingly enough, our court's recognition of an equal protection violation was premised in large part upon the existence of a domestic partnership law

---

[6] The court's opinion concluded that this right encompasses a "core set of basic *substantive* legal rights and attributes . . . integral to an individual's liberty and personal autonomy that . . . include, most fundamentally, the opportunity of an individual to establish—with the person with whom the individual has chosen to share his or her life—*an officially recognized and protected family* possessing mutual rights and responsibilities and entitled to the same respect and dignity accorded a union traditionally designated as marriage." *In re Marriage Cases*.

in California, along with the conferral of many additional rights to same-sex couples. Aside from the differentiations made by federal law, virtually all the rights that one had as a gay couple were identical to the rights one had as a married heterosexual couple, subject only to the exception for the nomenclature of "marriage." Some persons, of course, have asked, "What's so important about a name?" Shakespeare observed, "A rose by any other name would smell as sweet." But our court hinged its decision invalidating the statutes very much upon the fact that the distinction was being made, in the court's view, in violation of the equal protection of the laws, based upon the gender of the couple who formed this basic primary association. The union of an opposite-sex couple was deemed a marriage and that of a same-sex couple was deemed a domestic partnership. The court concluded that the lack of demonstrated justification for this distinction was a sufficient basis for concluding that the differentiation in nomenclature did amount to a denial of equal protection of the laws. One can pose the question, "Imagine if marital relationships between a Black man and a Black woman were to be given the name domestic partnership and the same relationship between a Caucasian man and a Caucasian woman were to be called a marriage, would we find that this passed constitutional muster?" I don't think a court would uphold that.

Much of the court's analysis in *In re Marriage Cases* is based upon its landmark 1948 decision in the case of *Perez v. Sharp* that invalidated California's antimiscegenation laws. Many states, and not just in the South, had laws barring interracial marriage. I have friends, a Japanese-American man and a Caucasian woman, who felt compelled to leave Virginia in the 1960s, knowing that their marriage would have been illegal in that state.

Shortly after the opinion in the *Marriage Cases* was filed, I received a letter from Michael Traynor, a Bay Area attorney and former president of the American Law Institute. With reference to his late father, California Chief Justice Roger Traynor, who was the author of the opinion in *Perez v. Sharp*, he wrote to me: "In an imaginary conversation with my father, we agreed with your framing of the issue, strengthening the standard of review, and expanding the class to assure equal protection. Congratulations on a magnificent contribution to the law." He added, "I remember vividly the threats and diatribes my father described having received after *Perez* was decided."

Interestingly, Virginia was the source of the case that the U.S. Supreme Court took up.

Yes, the *Loving* case. It took other states, over the years, several years to follow California's lead, but there were, I believe, about a dozen states that still had antimiscegenation laws at the time the U.S. Supreme Court finally rendered its 1967 decision in *Loving v. Virginia*, 19 years after the California Supreme Court's decision in *Perez v. Sharp*.

By the way, our court has made it very clear there is no compulsion on behalf of any officiant, whether or not he or she is a formal member of a religious group or other entity, to perform interracial marriages or marriages of persons of the same gender. There the First Amendment right of religious freedom trumps other interests—because there are plenty of other individuals who can perform those marriages and are willing to do so. Our opinion respects that choice. That's made clear.

One of the most important aspects of the decision in the *In re Marriage Cases* is that the court applied the standard of heightened scrutiny to laws that cover gay and lesbian individuals. Customarily courts have applied that standard—which is a standard much less deferential to legislative determinations than is normally applied by reviewing courts—only in cases involving gender, race, national origin, and religion. Our ruling was very significant in extending that special standard of review to laws that differentiate on the basis of sexual orientation.

This case provides a graphic illustration of a point that I have had many occasions to make in public speaking, but here was able to include in our decision in the *In re Marriage Cases*. People raise the issue, "How can the court flout the people's will here? They passed this statute defining marriage by initiative. Their elected representatives also passed this limitation." My answer is always that the court, instead of overriding the people's will, is upholding the highest and ultimate expression of the people's will, the constitution that they themselves have enacted. In enacting their constitution and adopting it, the people have expressed their ultimate will and have imposed limits upon their own ability to legislate, either at the ballot box or through their elected representatives. That's a point that is made by the *Marriage Cases* opinion in rejecting the argument that the court was obliged to defer to the statutory definition of marriage.

Another matter I want to add at this point to the discussion of the case is that history and tradition were invoked in support of the statutory scheme limiting marriage to the formal relationship between a man and a woman. In other words, "It's always been this way." But I find that a rather hollow justification, and the court rejected it because one could say the same thing about, first of all, the subordinate position that was imposed upon women in terms of various rights. In effect, women were virtually considered the property of their husbands. Then, of course, racial discrimination is an arch example of something that goes back many, many years and was formerly recognized in the laws. Ul-

timately those traditional laws had to be held violative of constitutional principles.

I did cite the *Warfield* case as well as *Perez v. Sharp* in the *Marriage Cases*
opinion. That's the fascinating thing about the law, how these principles build
upon themselves. Interestingly enough, another justification for limiting marriage to persons of the opposite sex was that, in the eyes of some, the purpose
behind the official recognition of the status of marriage was to foster procreation
and the welfare of children. Yet we all know that there are married persons who
do not have children because they are incapable of having them due to the physical condition of the husband or the wife or their age. Of course, there are couples who are capable but unwilling and undesirous of having children. By the
same token, the law in California and many other jurisdictions permits gay persons and lesbian couples to adopt and raise children. In fact, the empirical data
indicates, if anything, a greater stability in domiciled gay and lesbian relationships than in the domiciled relationships of opposite-sex couples. In some geographical areas, the divorce rate is close to 50 percent among married opposite-
sex couples, and I believe there is a greater stability, if anything, among same-
sex couples and specifically among those who have formalized their relationship
by entering into domestic partnerships or civil unions, as they're called in some
states, as compared to married opposite-sex couples.

The California Supreme Court's decision in this case had quite a bearing on
developments in other states. Our court, unlike the court in some other jurisdictions, was faced with a specific statutory definition of marriage restricting that
term to opposite-sex couples. In the wake of Chief Justice Margaret Marshall's
groundbreaking decision for the Massachusetts high court, I believe there now
are seven jurisdictions that issue same-sex marriage licenses—Connecticut, Iowa, Massachusetts, New Hampshire, New York, Vermont, and the District of
Columbia. I'm not including the domestic partnership arrangements that are
created by law. I believe our opinion was quite influential not only in its result,
but in its reasoning. The court basically affirmed that marriage must be recognized by the law as one of the most fundamental of human relationships and that
therefore it is a denial of equal protection of the laws to restrict its definition to
opposite-sex couples.

*With regard to your result, what options did you have in terms of the reasoning
or the path to pursue to get there?*

Of course, one extreme solution when there's an equal protection violation
would be to say in this context that because everyone has to be treated the same,
in order to achieve this objective no one can get married. [Laughter] We didn't

take that possible solution seriously, but interestingly enough this is one of those areas in the law where the recognition of a right does not conflict with the rights of others and did not in any way diminish or take away from the rights of others. I included in the *Marriage Cases* opinion a quotation from a dissenting opinion of the now-retired Chief Judge of New York State, Judith Kaye, who wrote that there are enough marriage licenses to go around. There's no shortage of them. [Laughter] So recognizing the right of same-sex couples to marry doesn't diminish anyone else's rights. In fact, this line of thought evokes something that I saw only recently, a billboard that—simplistically perhaps, like most billboard messages—colorfully proclaimed its message but had an underlying truth to it: "If you don't like gay marriage, don't get gay married." [Laughter] That slogan does somewhat encapsulate the reality that getting married is a matter of individual choice and does not sacrifice the rights of one group at the expense of another.

You mentioned the political cartoon that showed Mayor Newsom heaving the wrecking ball in the direction of you personally. Perhaps you could talk about your decision to assign the case to yourself and how far ahead you knew that you would do so?

Although, as I do on other issues, I respect the right of reasonable minds to differ among judicial colleagues as well as among members of the public, I found it quite offensive that various groups and individuals, on occasion, would attempt to intimidate the court in the performance of its duties. Certainly that was the case on the parental consent case where, as we discussed earlier, there were individuals who showed up at my confirmation hearing threatening that I would be targeted for defeat at the polls should I rule a certain way. I made a point, therefore, of assigning both the parental consent case and the marriage cases to myself. I felt I should have the broad shoulders and should bear the controversy that undoubtedly would descend upon the court, whichever way it would rule, because I didn't know at that point how I was going to vote on the case. I felt I should assign the case to myself with that in mind, regardless of which way the case was going to go. I then focused very much on determining how I would resolve my own position on the case.

Again, although we don't customarily discuss, as justices, whom on our staff we worked with on a particular case, I do want to give credit—in the face of the customary anonymity that cloaks research attorneys at the California Supreme Court—to Hal Cohen, who worked with me on all three marriage cases, *Lockyer*, *In re Marriage Cases*, and *Strauss*, as one of the most brilliant minds that I've had the pleasure of encountering in any venue, and not just limited to

the California Supreme Court. His analytical and research skills and his thoughtful and open-minded approach to all matters were of enormous assistance to me
in resolving my own position and in preparing the opinion for the court.

Hal was open-minded about both possible outcomes in the marriage cases,
and we had numerous discussions on the case. As his research progressed, he
and I both became more and more receptive to the ultimate conclusion reached
by the court. What I ended up doing in preparing the case was unprecedented, as
far as my own experience is concerned, and rarely done in the past practice of
the California Supreme Court. At least I certainly didn't encounter it during my
19 years on the court, and I hadn't heard of this being done before. I worked
with Hal to prepare a calendar memorandum on the case reflecting two opposite
outcomes. As I indicated before, a calendar memorandum is a draft opinion.

I made an appointment—basically, informally, I asked to drop by—with
each of my six colleagues. I informed all of them, at these six separate meetings,
that I was giving serious consideration to recommending that the court invalidate the marriage statutes that limited marriage to the officially recognized relationship "between a man and a woman," and that I would, in the next day or
two, be circulating a draft with both options and would very much welcome and
await the views of each of them before finalizing my own views. I would want
to study their preliminary responses, their overall input on the issue, in formulating my own final position. I thought, given the momentous, novel, and controversial nature of the legal issues, that this approach would be appropriate and
would best serve to edify my own views. Of course, as chance would have it, I
ended up having three justices in favor of one version and three in favor of the
other, so I was—as came to pass on many occasions during my tenure as Chief
Justice—the deciding vote, the tiebreaker, on this issue.

What can you tell me about the differences between the two?

Actually, except for the most important thing, the end result, the two approaches were basically identical. As one would ideally aspire to in a Supreme
Court opinion, the draft went into great detail, given the nature of the case, in
describing all the preceding factual and procedural scenarios that had brought us
to the threshold of making a decision. The draft led us through an exhaustive
survey of the relevant law in California and elsewhere. An objective presentation in an opinion—certainly one of this magnitude—involved setting forth a
very thorough and careful statement of both sides of the arguments supporting
each side. Then, the two approaches set forth in the calendar memorandum part-
ed company in weighing the competing arguments and considerations, and in
finally putting forth each one's own respective conclusion.

I'm curious about your choice to go and visit each of them in person to warn them that two versions were coming. What can you tell me about the response you got?

The reason I did that was that it was highly unusual to put out alternate versions. Of course, normally the nonauthoring justices would welcome the author's taking a position. Here my colleagues didn't have that assistance, if you will, but they had what hopefully was an objective presentation of both sides. I wanted them to know what was forthcoming, instead of their just finding this in their chambers mail slot the next day. I don't recall any substantive discussion taking place at any of those six meetings. I remember a couple of the justices having their eyes very, very wide open at, I suppose, even the consideration of the outcome of same-sex marriage, notwithstanding the fact that it was only one of two alternatives being presented to them. But the reaction of my colleagues was basically one of wait and see, and "I'll be very interested to read this."

Then of course in the days that followed there were very helpful comments, there were disagreements, there were suggestions on how to make one conclusion or another more palatable. There was the usual process, although more extensive here than in most other cases, of back and forth and, in effect, informal negotiation. "This should be added." "This should be taken out." "This should be reworded." As I've described elsewhere in our conversations with reference to a much later stage in the decisional process, each little change made in a draft opinion circulated after oral argument, even if two or three words, would necessitate a round of these pink "okay" sheets, until we ultimately had a final product. As in any case, the author of an opinion had to be mindful of the risk that making an addition or deletion, in order to satisfy the concerns of one colleague, might cause you to lose the vote of one or more other colleagues.

During this part of the process, what did you reveal to your colleagues about your own position or which of the drafts you hoped to send forward into the final?

I didn't communicate any such preferences or leanings. I was just soliciting their views and helpful comments and suggestions.

What happened next?

I gave very careful thought to the points that they raised, some of them major in terms of the ultimate conclusion and others more technical, sometimes supporting or controverting certain legal points that were made in the draft. I engaged in additional discussions with Hal Cohen, although I also benefited from the input provided by some other members of my staff before finalizing my own views. After considering the input from the six justices, their staff, and my own staff, I decided to cast my vote as I ultimately did. I circulated a revised calendar memorandum before the case was set for oral argument, finding the statutes unconstitutional in limiting marriage to opposite-sex couples and concluding that drawing a legal distinction between the relationship between same-sex persons that was officially recognized as "domestic partnership" and the relationship between opposite-sex persons as "marriage" violated the constitutional guarantee of equal protection of the laws. Underlying my position, adopted by a majority of the court, was the circumstance that, had California withheld all of the rights from same-sex couples that it provided in the form of domestic partnership and other benefits, the court could not have engaged in the same type of equal protection analysis that it did.

The legal reasoning would have had to be different?

It would have had to be different because the ultimate decision, recognizing a constitutional right to marry, evoked equal protection and due process claims premised upon the distinction in legal nomenclature that was afforded the two types of otherwise comparable relationships that carried with them what were basically equal rights and responsibilities—"marriage" and "domestic partnership." This is another interesting aspect of the legal analysis. The infirmity in the statutory scheme was the result of the state's having afforded basic equality between the two types of relationships—and then treating equally situated persons differently in terms of nomenclature. Disparate treatment of equally situated persons goes to the heart of the federal and state constitutional guarantee of equal protection of the laws. The law can treat different entities or different categories of individuals differently, provided the classifications are not arbitrary, but generally cannot treat similarly situated individuals or entities differently.

What swayed you, in the end?

I was swayed by the last point—that underlying all of this was a very basic human right, the constitutional right to marry, and then to affix different labels to it denoted a second-class citizenship, very much akin to letting certain persons ride on the bus but making them sit in the back, in the context of racial segregation. I tried to be influenced just by these constitutional considerations, of course, although I certainly admit that the end result comported with my own sense of justice on a personal level. Much of this is really a generational matter too. I believe—notwithstanding the narrow passage of Proposition 8, which resulted in large part from the infusion of substantial amounts of out-of-state money and a not-that-well-run campaign by the defenders of gay marriage—that ultimately the popular view will change in California, especially as members of my generation die off. The idea of same-sex marriage is very much accepted by younger generations, just as interracial marriage—although highly controversial at the time of *Perez v. Sharp* in 1948—is now very much accepted and not really the subject of much commentary at all. Many people consider gay rights to be the civil rights issue of our times.

But of course there now are other obstacles to same-sex marriage, because the decision in the *Marriage Cases* was, to a substantial extent, overruled by the voters' adoption of Proposition 8. I say to a substantial extent, because people often overlook what some consider the most important part of the decision— subjecting the review of discrimination that is based on sexual orientation to the same heightened level of strict scrutiny as is applied under California law to discrimination against the traditionally recognized classifications that are based on gender, race, ethnicity, and religion. Application of that heightened standard to gay men and lesbians will pervade all sorts of areas and questions that go well beyond the issue of whether the word "marriage" is to be applied to formal same-sex relationships.

Indeed, that is one of the most fascinating aspects. I'm thinking about your process leading to your decision in the Marriage Cases *and the fact that you knew ahead of time that you'd have three votes with you either way. There you were, really, with a large responsibility and a much greater ramification all on your "broad shoulders." Was it lonely at the top?*

It was to a large degree, and it was somewhat ironic that every time I would sit in certain parts of my chambers I would be looking out at City Hall, where it all began. I was there on the day our decision was announced. As I said before, with the last-minute okay of changes to the opinion one sometimes doesn't know until a day or two before, when the decision is going to be released. I had agreed to give an interview to some television producers from New York, who were doing a documentary on the death penalty. When I learned of the filing date, it was too late to cancel the interview. The TV people were on their way out, and the filming was set for 10:00 a.m. on May 15, 2008, the exact time the decision was going to be announced. The clerk had carefully locked up all copies of the opinion the night before, and only the justices and staff were aware of the outcome of the decision that would shortly be forthcoming. The doors to our building were opened for people to file in from Civic Center Plaza and get copies of the opinion off the clerk's counter. When we had oral argument in the case, a giant television screen had been erected by the city right in front of City Hall, reflecting the great public interest. People were lined up again, this time to get a copy of the opinion, and the attorneys were there ready to give press conferences on the steps of our building. Simultaneously, the clerk released the opinion on the court's website. Sure enough, a couple minutes into the television interview, on camera, despite the double-paned glass, there was a roar that came up from Civic Center Plaza from members of the gay community who had gathered to learn of the result that would be announced at 10 o'clock.

I wanted to cover a couple other aspects of this case before we wind up on *In re Marriage Cases*. When oral argument took place, there were people not only outside in the Civic Center Plaza watching the proceedings on the large screen, but we had overflow rooms including the lower-level auditorium, where people were seeing it who couldn't make it into the courtroom because of the seating capacity. The arguments also were televised live by California Channel and later rebroadcast. The oral argument was truly excellent. I will say that the proponents of same-sex marriage made by far the most brilliant arguments, and I would single out Therese M. Stewart, the chief deputy in the San Francisco city attorney's office.

In addition to the briefs filed by the parties to the litigation, there was an extraordinary amount of input from amici curiae. There were literally dozens and dozens of amicus curiae who filed briefs. In fact, if you look at the published opinion in the official reports, the single-spaced listing of the amici covered more than 12 pages of print, just listing all the groups and their respective attorneys.

The reaction to the opinion among the public was quite interesting. Personally, I have been accustomed to the relative anonymity that judges have, even at the high court level. But still to this day I'm amazed that people occasionally still recognize me from press coverage of the case, as they especially did in the immediate aftermath of the opinion. I have been approached by strangers at business establishments, restaurants, and on the street. It was always by those who liked the decision. [Laughter] Fortunately, I wasn't confronted by people who disagreed, although there were many of them. But I received handshakes, slaps on the back, and hugs from couples who told me how meaningful it had been to be able to solemnize their relationship and have it officially recognized. Even today that happens occasionally when someone, not so much recognizing me but recognizing my name, expresses appreciation for the court's opinion and the direct personal bearing it has had upon his or her own life or that of a family member. Despite subsequent legal developments, including the third case that I'll cover in a moment, those 18,000 marriages statewide were upheld and remain valid today.

The third case, of course, was *Strauss v. Horton*. It involved the issue whether Proposition 8, which wrote into the state constitution a provision limiting marriage to persons of the opposite sex, was itself validly adopted and constitutional. Like the first case, *Lockyer*, the *Strauss* case did not pose a difficult legal question in my view. Although my colleague Justice Moreno found grounds to disagree as the sole dissenter, I did not find there were any very debatable issues here. The people of our state clearly had the right to amend the constitution upon which their Supreme Court had based its ruling in the *In re Marriage Cases*.

One of the passages I personally composed in the *Strauss* case provided an overview of this trilogy of cases as constituting, in a sense, one gigantic civics lesson. I wanted to make that point, not only in the context of the issue of gay marriage but as a reflection of the general concern that I have expressed in many of the discussions you and I have had about the public's lack of understanding about the judicial process. At an early point in the *Strauss* opinion I described our court's holdings in the *Lockyer* decision and in the *In re Marriage Cases*, and then noted that in the *Marriage Cases* a right had been recognized that was later amended out of the California Constitution by the enactment of Proposition 8. Then I made this observation: "In a sense, this trilogy of cases illustrates the variety of limitations that our constitutional system imposes upon each branch of government—the executive, the legislative, and the judicial." *Lockyer*, of course, showed the limitations on the executive—its lack of authority to decide which laws to enforce, its lack of authority to declare enacted laws unconstitutional. *In re Marriage Cases* illustrated the limitations on the legislative power—both as exercised by the legislature, and as exercised by the voters acting as legislators themselves in enacting an initiative measure. These constitutional limitations restrict their ability to pass laws when those laws don't pass muster under the constitution. Third, the case that I was then addressing, *Strauss*, illustrated the limitation on the judicial power, because the authority of the California Supreme Court was subject to the right of the people to amend their constitution, provided that the amendment did not run afoul of federal constitutional principles or of procedural requirements governing the initiative process. The opponents of Proposition 8 chose not to raise *federal* constitutional issues at this time, and those issues were therefore not before us.

I made a point of making the following observation at the outset of the court's opinion upholding the voters' enactment of Proposition 8: "In addressing the issues now presented in the third chapter of this narrative, it is important at the outset to emphasize a number of significant points. First, as explained in the *Marriage Cases*, our task in the present proceeding is not to determine whether the provision at issue is wise or sound *as a matter of policy* or whether we, as individuals, believe it *should* be a part of the California Constitution. Regardless of our views as individuals on this question of policy, we recognize as judges and as a court our responsibility to confine our consideration to a determination of the constitutional validity and legal effect of the measure in question. It bears emphasis in this regard that our role is limited to interpreting and applying the principles and rules embodied in the California Constitution, setting aside our own personal beliefs and values." Then I went on to note that the issues in *Strauss* were entirely distinct from those involved in the two other cases and that the court was presently faced with questions arising under the state constitution as it had now been amended. I felt it was important to point out these considerations to the public in what hopefully was fairly understandable language.

As you're acknowledging, those are distinctions that might be widely misunderstood or not at all understood by members of the public, who might have viewed your decisions in the Marriage Cases *and in* Strauss *as in conflict with one another.*

Exactly. There was no conflict. There was adherence to the law, to the constitution, in each instance.

It may be hard to make that point to the public. I know you were asked many, many times about that very matter.

Again, I have to go back to the observation I quoted from the *In re Marriage Cases* opinion. The ultimate expression of the people's will was upheld by that opinion—the constitution that they had adopted was being upheld by recognizing the limitations they had imposed on their own ability and the ability of their elected representatives to pass laws, but also by recognizing their right to amend their constitution. Once the people amended that constitution through their enactment of Proposition 8, their will was again upheld by our court.

On the occasion of my induction into the American Academy of Arts and Sciences in Boston, I was asked to give an address, in which I made an observation that I can't resist making here. I have repeated it in subsequent remarks and writings. It is that at the same election in 2008, alongside Proposition 8, was another initiative measure that illustrates something you and I will probably talk about at greater length—the odd mix of things that come before the voters by way of numerous initiative measures dealing with a wide array of subjects. That other initiative measure proposed to regulate the confinement of barnyard fowl in coops. That one also passed, along with Proposition 8. I could not resist making the observation to the Academy,[7] and also in a *Stanford Law Review* piece:[8] "Chickens gained valuable rights in California on the same day that gay men and lesbians lost them." I suppose that is more a commentary on the vagaries of the initiative process than on anything else, and is a separate topic for another session. Former Speaker of the Assembly Bob Hertzberg, with whom I worked closely on a number of judicial branch issues, told me later that my speech before the Academy "created quite a buzz" around the state Capitol.

---

[7] "The Perils of Direct Democracy: the California Experience," *Bulletin of the American Academy*, Winter 2010, p. 7 (delivered October 10, 2009).

[8] Keynote Address, *Symposium*, State Constitutions, 62 Stan. L. Rev. 1515 (2010).

Chapter 18

Comparisons between the California and U.S. Supreme Courts
November 11, 2011

We discussed at our last meeting the various same-sex-marriage-related cases, up to and including the challenges to Proposition 8. I wonder if you could finish by making some remarks on what happened with that issue after it left your court with your decision in May 2009.

As I mentioned previously, the persons who brought the initial litigation to invalidate the restrictions on marriage that confined the formal relationship to persons of the opposite sex, had deliberately chosen to invoke only state constitutional grounds. They had shied away from raising federal issues because of their strategy to avoid U.S. Supreme Court review in the event the California Supreme Court were to go their way, which it did. Consequently, no review of our decision was possible except at the ballot box. Of course, that is what transpired and the third case, *Strauss*, upheld the people's right to amend the state constitution, upon which we had based our decision in *In re Marriage Cases*.

The next step, given that sequence, was for those persons urging invalidation of the opposite-sex limitation on marriage to then raise the federal issues that they had put aside for the time being. They chose to raise the federal issues in the U.S. District Court for the Northern District of California. The matter was assigned to the Honorable Vaughn Walker, who was chief judge of the court. He has since then retired. After a very lengthy trial at which evidence was taken and very capable attorneys represented the two opposing positions, Judge Walker ruled in favor of the plaintiffs and invalidated Proposition 8, thereby reviving the right of same-sex couples to marry, as recognized by the California Supreme Court in *In re Marriage Cases*. Judge Walker's ruling, in turn, was appealed by the opponents of same-sex marriage to the Ninth Circuit U.S. Court of Appeals, which is the federal circuit that covers nine western states plus the Pacific territories. In the course of arguments made in that court, the three judges of the Ninth Circuit assigned to the case determined that a serious question had arisen whether the persons who were the proponents of Proposition 8 had standing to appeal from Judge Walker's ruling.

Standing is a somewhat technical legal concept that boils down to whether or not the person in question who is asserting a position in a court—in a trial court or, in this instance, an appellate court—is entitled to participate in the court proceedings to raise the issues involved. To put it bluntly, there are many situations where an ordinary citizen cannot go to court to challenge the constitutionality of a law, but someone else who has more of a direct interest may be able to do so. The problem of standing arose here because the governor of California and the attorney general of California chose not to appeal from Judge Walker's ruling, even though that ruling was technically adverse to those two officials, given their duty to uphold the laws of California. The Ninth Circuit, before the appeal could proceed, needed to determine whether there was standing on behalf of someone else—such as the proponents of Proposition 8—to argue in favor of upholding Proposition 8. The consequences of that determination are as follows. If the proponents don't have standing, there's probably no one else who has standing under this scenario that I've given you regarding the position of the governor and the attorney general. The result of no one having standing to appeal from Judge Walker's decision might well be that the Ninth Circuit would have to dismiss the appeal without ruling on the merits, having determined that no appeal could be taken. That would reinstate Judge Walker's ruling, although the ruling would be of much more limited effect in terms of just affecting the precise parties and perhaps the U.S. District for Northern California, as opposed to a case of greater application and precedent if decided by a higher court.

The Ninth Circuit, in determining whether or not the proponents of an initiative measure possess standing, interestingly enough has sought out the views of the California Supreme Court. My own view—and I haven't studied the matter in any depth—is that the question of whether or not standing exists in a federal appeals court ultimately is a matter of federal law, but that determination may take into account the rights that the proponents have under state law. The Ninth Circuit chose to ask the California Supreme Court for its views on the state's law on standing, as at least a factor for the Ninth Circuit to consider in determining the question of standing in federal court, even though the state court ruling would not be dispositive of the federal issue of standing. There was a case from Arizona that involved an English-only requirement where the U.S. Supreme Court questioned whether the parties had standing to urge the points they were making before the high court and before the lower courts, because the law of that state did not appear to give the proponents of an initiative any right to represent the state's interests.[1] So standing is an important consideration that can be dispositive of the litigation. Certainly a finding of no standing would be dispositive. The process by which the Ninth Circuit has sought the views of the California Supreme Court is one that I believe you and I will discuss later today when we discuss the general process of the Ninth Circuit's certification of questions of state law to the California Supreme Court. But suffice it to say at this point in our discussion that there is precedent for the Ninth Circuit having asked the state high court for its views. The California Supreme Court received briefing on that matter, chose to accept certification—it's not compelled to—and heard argument in September, which means that by the first week of December the state high court is expected to render its decision on the question of standing. That ruling on a question of state law will then go back to the Ninth Circuit, which will have to make its own determination about standing. Then, if it finds a lack of standing, the case—as I said earlier—would undoubtedly be remanded to the U.S. District Court and would have much more limited application or bearing as precedent. On the other hand, if the Ninth Circuit concludes that the proponents of Proposition 8 do have standing, the Ninth Circuit will then proceed to consider the substantive merits of the claims of the proponents of Proposition 8, to the effect that Proposition 8 is valid and that therefore the judgment rendered by Judge Walker should be reversed. The Ninth Circuit's ruling will be subject to a petition for writ of certiorari in the U.S. Supreme Court. The high court will, in the likely event a petition is filed, exercise its discretion in determining whether to take up the case. It could, if it grants review, rule on the matter of standing and hold that the Ninth Circuit was wrong in finding standing, which would have the consequences that I delineated earlier, or the high court could resolve the question of Proposition 8's constitutionality on the merits.

Of course, the one other piece that is part of this somewhat Byzantine puzzle is that, notwithstanding all of these court rulings, the people of the state of California are free at any time to qualify another initiative to undo Proposition 8. The legislature is powerless to repeal that initiative because it is a part of the constitution, but the voters of the state could do so. I believe there is a petition circulating to obtain the requisite number of signatures, which for a constitution-

---

[1] *Arizonans for Official English v. Arizona* (1997) 520 U.S. 43.

al amendment is 8 percent of the number of persons who voted in the last gubernatorial election. It would be 5 percent if it were merely a statutory initiative.
Once qualified, if a majority of the electorate vote in favor of a new initiative
repealing Proposition 8 and validating future marriages between same-sex couples, same-sex marriages would resume once again in the state of California—
adding to the 18,000 couples who were married between the time such marriages were authorized by the *In re Marriages* case and the time those marriages
were halted by the passage of Proposition 8. That's I guess as much of an overview as I'm in a position to give you.

*As you say, the California Supreme Court did elect this fall to accept this ques-
tion from the Ninth Circuit on legal standing. I wonder if I might ask you to just
expand a bit more on your thinking about the appropriateness of accepting that
question.*

I believe that it was very appropriate to accept the question, even though
whether to do so was fully within the discretion of the California Supreme
Court. In fact, I believe the court would have been almost derelict in its duty to
provide guidance and assistance to the federal courts had it declined this particular request.

*There are fascinating aspects of strategy here. How do you see those, as a for-
merly involved player who is now on the sidelines?*

It really boils down in many ways to political strategy as much as legal
strategy in terms of which court to file in, which issues to raise, and when. There
might have been a sense among the litigants that it would not have been advantageous to raise the federal issues before the California Supreme Court, but of
course that court—if both state and federal constitutional issues were raised—
could always decide to forgo a decision on federal grounds and rule only on
state grounds. The court has had occasion to do that sometimes in the past. I
believe that people who favor the legalization of same-sex marriage are, from
what I read in newspaper accounts, somewhat divided on the wisdom of the various courses of action that have been taken in the past history of this litigation.
So there isn't one uniform view, even among those who totally share a commitment to bring about same-sex marriage.

*As you say, there are many chapters yet to be played out, and the option of a
further initiative by the people is still and always out there. We know that sometimes those matters get a different reception at different times—different eco-*

nomic times, different political times. Thank you for reflecting on what has happened since your own involvement ceased.

We reviewed a number of your opinions and some other opinions of the court. To summarize that whole area, may I ask you to reflect on what we think of as the George Court, particularly those nearly 15 years when you led that body? What came out of that?

When I have been asked that question over the years, and even more so at the conclusion of my term of office, after I had announced my pending retirement, I always would say—and I mean it quite sincerely—that I have had great difficulty in making that evaluation. I didn't come to the position of justice of the Supreme Court—associate justice or chief—with any agenda or any vision of changing the law. I think I did come with some vision in terms of administrative goals, but the cases basically were decided as they each came before us, and based upon the record and the law and the underlying policies involved in the particular case, to the extent the court was concerned with such policies. I always told members of the press—and I'll repeat it now—that it's probably best left to academics and journalists to make overall evaluations, to perceive trends of the court as a whole, to ascertain trends in the jurisprudence of an individual justice over the period of his or her tenure on the court, or in the course of his or her service on the bench through multiple courts. Having said that, I suppose I'm able to make a very general commentary. That would basically boil down to the fact that I view the court during the time I served as Chief Justice as a moderate court guided by a pragmatic, nonideological approach. Of course, there are observers in both the civil and criminal arenas who would take issue with that premise—who sincerely believe that the court favored one side or the other. But I believe from the perspective of the hundreds of opinions I wrote and the many hundreds more in which I was a participant, that the justices truly committed themselves to resolving the issues before them in a neutral, dispassionate way, fair to the parties and fair to the public, and that the members of the court approached their task without any agenda. I believe there was a tendency, during the years I served as chief, to perhaps take a wider range or mix of cases, to get more involved in legal disputes that involved social issues and not as high a percentage of cases that dealt with the business community. Given the court's limited ability to render more than 110 to 115 opinions each year, the court by turning its attention to certain areas necessarily limited its ability to focus on others. I believe the court found itself taking a broader range of cases and having a caseload not so heavily weighted in favor of business and insurance issues.

To what extent was there an awareness at the time that that was happening or an intention for that to happen? Is that possible to put into words?

I'm not really capable of throwing any light on that. I can just say, speaking for myself, that I found many of the novel issues that came up in petitions seeking review to be intriguing and worthy of the court's consideration. The justices can only take up 1 or 2 percent of the cases in which review is sought, so it's always a choice. I don't know that any justice ever consciously felt we should be taking more of this or that type of case, and I certainly don't remember anything of that sort being said at conference when we would consider individual petitions for review. But it certainly worked out that way, that we got more and more into emerging areas of the law that have broad ramifications for society. Some of the changes in the California Supreme Court's caseload reflect changes occurring in society and accompanying changes in the statutory law. Adoptions by gay parents and the issues involved in the dissolution of formal relationships between gay individuals, whatever interest there could have been in the abstract in such issues in prior years, just couldn't arise given the state of society and of the law at that time. So some evolving issues reflect changes in society, which in turn create novel issues of law that just weren't on the table before. Over my 19 years on the court, I definitely saw shifts in the areas of the law in which the court got involved.

There is also, of course, the changing membership of the court over time.

Certainly, that's part of the mix too—changes in society resulting in changes in the law resulting in a different mix of petitions for review reaching us, and changes in the composition of the court itself.

What areas of the law, if any, did you feel the court had a responsibility to address but didn't really get the appropriate chance?

I don't believe any of the justices with whom I served ever felt that we had a quota that we had met for granting petitions for review, although I was told that on occasion Justice Frank Newman would say something like, "Look, we've already granted four today. That's enough." I can't say that on any occasion we felt, if only we had more time or resources, we would have taken *x* case—because if it truly met the standard for review we'd take it. Once in a while we'd have half a dozen cases granted off of a single, relatively short conference list, and often there were no grants from a long list. But in a general sense, if we didn't have mandatory jurisdiction over automatic appeals in death penalty cases, we obviously could be taking more civil and noncapital criminal cases in which there were substantial questions of statewide importance. Death penalty cases probably consume 25 to 30 percent of the court's time and resources. I'd like to think that we still have always taken up cases in those areas where there's a true conflict in the law. However, there were other cases that we might have found borderline as to whether the question posed was of substantial statewide importance, that we didn't take, given the limitation of how many opinions we can render in any given year.

You did mention on another day some of the cases you're most proud of that you authored yourself. We noted that they were across a variety of areas of the law. How do you think about your own body of work as a whole?

One theme that is probably joined in both my decision-making responsibilities and my administrative responsibilities is the overall concept of access to justice. I believe if we look at the opinions I authored in the area of civil rights and constitutional rights, all of those—whether they involved public accommodations, whether they involved access to the courts or to public records, whether they involved the right to be free of a hostile work environment, and certainly the *Marriage Cases*—involve access to justice in some fashion or another. As a result, these matters all had a direct impact on people's lives. Certainly, without rehashing them again, my priorities as Chief Justice of California—and in particular the steps I took to further access to justice in the area of services for unrepresented litigants, procedures to assist family law practitioners, expanding the services of language interpreters, dealing with the problem of bias in one form or another in our court system—were all basically access-to-justice issues. I suppose what has given me the greatest personal satisfaction are the efforts I was able to make both in case decision making and in administrative decision making to further the public's access to justice, which I regard as a basic underpinning of our democratic system of government.

Thank you. Even if you don't think in terms of the George Court, I know a lot of other people do—as you say the media and academics and other court watchers. Certainly there has been a lot of outside commentary on what transpired under your leadership. How do respond to those kinds of summaries?

I have received some very generous accolades from judge and lawyer colleagues of mine over the years. Justice Mosk, at the tribute that the court gave him for surpassing the record length of service as a justice of the Supreme Court, said of me: "No one, at least in modern times, has done more for judicial administration than our current Chief Justice."[2] And Justice Sandra Day O'Connor, in introducing me at an event, remarked, "The leadership of California's courts, for 15 years under the leadership of Chief Justice George, is as good as it gets." From an academic perspective, Professor Clark Kelso, who has studied the work of our court for many years, was very generous in writing an article in the September 2010 edition of the *California Bar Journal* summarizing his perception of my legacy.[3] It certainly is a very gratifying evaluation and one that I very much appreciate, especially coming from an academic who has substantial real-life experience in many different government positions.

Yes, and he has written at some length on many of the things he mentions. There were many such favorable evaluations of your tenure. He raises a particularly interesting one, and that is comparing California to other states, calling it once again a leading state court. There has been study of that very matter in recent years, and I wonder if you could talk about this idea of "following" the opinions of California and other states, as reflected in the study?

Yes, there was a study that was published in the *UC Davis Law Review* that's titled, "'Followed Rates' and Leading State Cases, 1940–2005."[4] It was written by two persons whom I've made prior reference to, Jake Dear, the chief

---

[2] 21 Cal.4th 1316, 1333.

[3] "Not since the great Chief Justice Roger Traynor has California been blessed by such a towering judicial figure. During his 19-year tenure on the Supreme Court, 14 years as its chief, Ron George successfully re-established the preeminence of California's highest court as one of the leading state courts in the country. The court's national reputation and prominence had taken a steep dive in the late 1970s and early 1980s, and the failure of three justices to win their retention elections in 1986 further damaged the court's prestige and credibility. In the aftermath of the 1986 election debacle, the court swung hard to the right. Chief Justice George slowly but surely led the court back to the center, and from that position of strength, the court reemerged in this decade as a jurisprudential and constitutional leader. Its jurisprudence has been marked by fundamental themes that express the very essence of a judiciary that is independent yet appropriately restrained and respectful of the people's political power and the powers of the other branches of government. . . .

"The chief has earned his retirement and our gratitude for his service. He will be leaving the California judiciary much stronger than when he joined the Supreme Court. The courts are more accessible and better prepared to meet the many challenges of the coming decades. Public trust in the judiciary remains at high levels. And Chief Justice George led the California Supreme Court back to national stature. Throughout his tenure, he was the most influential vote on the court, and he often took responsibility for authoring the court's most difficult and politically sensitive decisions. Ron George has been a leader in every sense of the word. We will not likely see his equal for generations to come."

[4] Dear and Jessen, 41 *U.C. Davis L. Rev.* 683 (2007).

supervising attorney of the California Supreme Court, and the reporter of decisions, Edward Jessen. It is the responsibility of Mr. Jessen and his staff to make sure the court's opinions are in uniform and accurate format in terms of citation and editorial style prior to their appearance in the bound volumes of the official reports containing the decisions of the California Supreme Court and the six Courts of Appeal. They undertook a study whose bottom line is that the decisions of the California Supreme Court in the period in question were followed by far more states than the decisions of any other state supreme court. In the wake of those very nice comments by Professor Kelso regarding the preeminence of the California Supreme Court under my stewardship, I suppose I could introduce my comments about the study by uttering the old truism, "Imitation is the highest form of flattery." By imitating or following decisions of the California Supreme Court, both before and during my tenure as Chief Justice, other courts around the nation have recognized the jurisprudential quality of our opinions. Of course, what was done in the study was not just simply count the number of citations to California Supreme Court opinions. Sometimes there's a survey of legal authority undertaken in a judicial opinion by a court that may agree or disagree with a decision of the California Supreme Court in a string of citations to cases in several jurisdictions. The methodology followed by the study instead counted up the number of times that decisions of high courts of the various states were followed in the sense of an opinion truly being relied upon and playing a direct role in shaping a decision in that other jurisdiction.

The authors' survey disclosed that in the 65 years ending in 2005, about 24,000 opinions from state high courts have been followed in other states at least once. California led with 1,260 of its decisions being followed. Now, one might state the obvious. Because California is so populous, isn't that the main factor? Although it has to be a factor, it certainly is not the determinative factor in the conclusions reached by the study, because the second-most-followed court is the Washington State Supreme Court with 942. Colorado is third with 848. You might expect, if population were the predominant factor here, that New York would be way up there, but New York came in only tenth, and numerically was only half as influential as California. The study attempted to explore why this is so. In fact the study itself was the subject of an article in the *New York Times* by Adam Liptak, who is the newspaper's Supreme Court legal reporter. His article suggests there is something about the state's legal culture and the jurisprudence of the California Supreme Court that's a major factor.[5]

---

[5] "Around the U.S., High Courts Follow California's Lead," *New York Times* (March 11, 2008).

What do you think?

I believe there are many factors. There has been favorable academic commentary from law professors, law deans, and other legal authorities about the quality and the conclusions reached in California Supreme Court opinions. Certainly, as I said, the size of California is a factor, but so is its diversity. When you have a populous jurisdiction with a variety of economic, cultural, and social attributes, there is a greater likelihood of producing a large volume and variety of litigation on important issues. That's part of it. Another factor is the way the California court system works. You have the appeals going first to the intermediate Court of Appeal, and not every state has an intermediate appellate court. The issues get thrashed out there, and perhaps in a more thorough way than they get thrashed out in other jurisdictions.

That gets me back to something I've mentioned previously in our discussions. Article VI, section 14 of the California Constitution, requires that all decisions of appellate courts be in writing with reasons stated. California's Supreme Court and Courts of Appeal can't put out memorandum opinions that say—after reciting the basic procedures and facts underlying the appeal—"A number of claims were raised and we find all of these contentions are without merit." An appellate court, whether it's the Court of Appeal or the Supreme Court of California, must of legal necessity explain in every case what contentions have been made and give some reasons in writing why the court has accepted or rejected the claims related to those issues. This constitutional requirement of a reasoned opinion in each and every case brings up for the consideration of the California Supreme Court a variety of issues that have been fleshed out by the intermediate appellate court. Additionally, our high court has very talented central staffs who ferret out these issues and see whether they truly meet the test of presenting a substantial issue of statewide importance or a conflict in the law or both. The court uses its discretion quite wisely in selecting significant cases in which to grant review from among the roughly 10,000 petitions seeking appellate review or writ review that are filed every year.

When we do grant review and write an opinion, we often survey trends and leading authorities in other jurisdictions. We take wisdom wherever we can find it. A court in a small state may have done something worthy of our consideration. If we find its reasoning worth emulating in deciding a given case, we will note it and credit it. We also benefit from a very specialized appellate bar, meaning that the lawyers arguing cases in the California Supreme Court—not always, but to a great extent, especially in the most significant cases—are persons who have specialized in appellate practice. They're generally not just the trial lawyer who handled the case in front of a jury and then is thrilled for the opportunity to be able to argue the appeal before the California Supreme Court but doesn't really have the talent to do so.

I would note, interestingly enough, that Washington State has the same requirement as California of issuing appellate opinions in writing with reasons stated. Maybe that's a factor why that relatively smaller jurisdiction is way up there in the number two position in opinions followed. What I find most remarkable about the study is not that California is number one, but who is number two and three and who is number ten. To me, that tells a lot more than just California being where it is.

You said as much in the interview with Mr. Liptak for this article.

Yes. I believe the full analysis provided by our opinions, especially on major novel issues, is a factor. Although issued subsequent to the period covered by the study, our same-sex marriage opinion is an example of a case cited in many jurisdictions. That case relied on *Perez v. Sharp*, in which California's high court was the first in the nation to invalidate antimiscegenation laws. State high courts followed our lead over a period of 19 years until the U.S. Supreme Court finally, in the case of *Loving v. Virginia*, came to the same conclusion. So there are many factors in California's leading role, but what's most interesting to me is why Washington and Colorado and Kansas are way up there.

What significance do you place, if any, on individual cases that placed high in this ranking of "followed" citations?

That's hard to say. I wrote an opinion that is cited in the study, *In re Alvernaz*, and it just deals with when a guilty plea can be challenged under certain circumstances. Why that one ended up being cited and followed so frequently in other jurisdictions I'm not really prepared to say. I just don't know. There are some other decisions from the Traynor Court establishing product liability that truly embarked on totally new ground. The basic standard employed by the study was whether under the Shepard's Citations Service—which has a unique coding system for the citation of cases—the letter "f" designating "followed" appears. That seemed to be an easy way of measuring the degree of reliance in an objective manner, the extent to which the case was in fact being followed. The study noted there is a lag time, because a case has to be out there a certain amount of time before it becomes known and absorbed and is more likely to be cited and followed by a court in another jurisdiction.

The study itself succinctly ascribed California's preeminence to what it called "the depth of inventory and a focused review selection system." That of course includes the constitutional requirement I referred to, having opinions "in writing with reasons stated," but also the style and culture of high court opinions in our state. We tend to write more extensively, with more explanation and analysis, than many other courts—in fact, some observers believe we do so to an excessive degree and that we're really writing law review articles. I suppose a court can explicate to excess, but we bear in mind that our primary responsibility in exercising discretionary review is not just to resolve the case before us for the benefit of the parties, but rather to settle the law, to establish principles to guide the lower courts, the bar and the public and rules that will serve as precedent. To the extent our opinions reflect the underlying analysis and ramifications of our review, we are, I believe, performing our function in a more suitable way. I believe the depth of our analysis and explanation makes it more likely that an opinion we issue will be considered persuasive authority in another jurisdiction.

Aside from the New York Times *piece, what response did you get—or should I say, did the authors get—from the study?*

I believe they received quite a bit of correspondence from legal authorities in other states, some defensive of their own standing as a less-followed state, others interested in having more information about the study. Apparently there is a whole cottage industry of analyzing the extent to which judicial decisions themselves are cited and followed. In the academic setting this was a major development. The law review article that was published generated a lot of interest, even though this field occupies only a very tiny niche in legal academic research.

I wonder what other indications you had over your tenure of the California Supreme Court influencing jurisdictions outside the state.

Anecdotally, when I would attend meetings of the Conference of Chief Justices in various places around the United States—which was twice a year—there frequently was keen interest in court decisions from California. Certainly that was true, equally so if not more so, in terms of administrative matters—how we were coping with our budget crisis, how we were dealing with access to justice issues, and various reforms. I found myself frequently being a presenter at educational panels on current developments involving the judiciary—for example, our complex litigation courts and our self-help electronic website. Sometimes we'd just have a roundtable of all the chiefs, pointing out how bad things were with the budget crunch. "What are you doing in California about it?" and so forth.

This whole idea of comparing jurisdictions leads me to ask if we could approach the subject of your views on the U.S. Supreme Court, its justices and its jurisprudence. I know that you were in a position to have a lot of both direct and indirect interaction with that court, going back to the time of Chief Justice Earl Warren and right straight forward to today's era under Chief Justice John Roberts. Before I ask you to reflect on that and perhaps draw comparisons, I wonder whether you ever aspired to or were considered for nomination to the U.S. Supreme Court?

At the risk of sounding somewhat parochial, I felt that as Chief Justice of the largest court system in the Western world and perhaps anywhere, I was in a better position to advance the cause of justice through administrative reforms than I would be as one of the eight associate justices on the U.S. Supreme Court. Although the U.S. Supreme Court has some cases of incredible significance and interest, I personally find a very large part of its caseload—and certainly this is subjective—much less interesting than the caseload of the California Supreme Court. There are so many cases that make their way up to the federal high court that involve administrative agencies and other matters that I personally find less challenging as the subject of writing an opinion than I do even the garden-variety types of cases that we have on the California Supreme Court. That covers, pretty much, my attitude as far as any aspirations.

It is true, however, that your name was bandied about occasionally for such a possibility. I assume you must have given it a fair amount of thought?

I was flattered to read in the newspaper—and that was the only communication to me about this—that Senators Dianne Feinstein and Barbara Boxer had put my name forward in a public statement they released to the press, describing me as a Republican whom they could support and whom they urged President George W. Bush to consider for the Sandra Day O'Connor vacancy on the high court. It was very gracious of the two senators to make that suggestion. They never consulted me beforehand, nor did I ever have a conversation with them subsequently about it. I had no contact from the Bush administration, and of course I knew I never would, given a couple of the more controversial decisions that I had rendered. I was quite confident I would not be the type of candidate this administration would want to consider for appointment to the high court, which did not trouble me in the least since I had no personal desire to join that court.

You have been in a position to watch the work of that court and on occasion interact with it. Having served for nearly 15 years as the head of our state's high court, what kinds of comparisons would you draw with the U.S. Supreme Court?

My conclusory response to your question would be that I believe on many levels the California Supreme Court compares quite favorably to the U.S. Supreme Court. More specifically—first of all in terms of productivity, although both courts receive roughly the same number of petitions seeking review or other relief, about nine to ten thousand each year—the California Supreme Court writes far more opinions than our federal counterpart. A couple years ago, the U.S. Supreme Court's term produced fewer than 70 opinions, and I believe they've since then been hovering in the low seventies. The California Supreme Court is virtually always above 100, and we've reached 115 opinions or more in recent years. This is notwithstanding the fact that the federal high court has nine justices as opposed to our seven, so we're issuing more opinions with fewer justices, and also notwithstanding the fact that about 20 to 25 percent of our caseload comprises automatic appeals, which means that in these death penalty cases we are coping with transcripts averaging 10,000 pages. Transcripts occasionally reach 50,000 to 70,000 pages, even approaching 100,000 pages in length, with literally dozens and dozens of issues. The U.S. Supreme Court does not have to deal with capital jurisprudence except when it accepts review in one of those cases in its own discretion. When that happens, the court generally limits its review to one or two issues and not the dozens of issues that we have to go through routinely. We also, having heard the automatic appeal, are faced concurrently or shortly thereafter with a new round of habeas corpus claims that often raise dozens of additional issues, opening up the case for the presentation of additional evidence. Although our orders in those habeas cases usually end up being one or two pages long, for the court to come to a decision on the habeas we have the authoring justice prepare an internal memorandum that can be up to 100 pages long. That's sometimes almost as much work as writing an opinion. Of course, there may be multiple habeas corpus petitions, not just one per case.

We are subject to the constitutional requirement that a decision be rendered within 90 days of oral argument or else have our salary withheld, except, as I said before, in the very unusual situation where there are grounds to delay submission or vacate submission of the case. That doesn't happen in even 1 percent of the cases. We do not have the luxury of hearing oral argument the first Monday in October and having until the last day in June to render a decision. Now, in all fairness, I want to point out that we have the opportunity to do what's called frontloading, to do more work on the case before we hear oral argument so that presumably we need less time after argument and can meet the constitutional requirement of resolving the case within 90 days. There's another advantage to frontloading. By the time oral argument takes place in the California Supreme Court, the justices are intimately familiar with the record—that is, the evidence—and the legal issues. The U.S. Supreme Court justices, as I understand their practice, have their first truly substantive discussion on the case only after oral argument, and consequently they may not be as informed about the case at oral argument as the justices of the California Supreme Court. I remember from cases in my own experience at the U.S. Supreme Court as a deputy attorney general, while waiting for my case to be heard, that the justices would sometimes ask very basic questions about the posture of the case. I don't fault them. It was just that they were only then delving into the case, whereas we are steeped in a case, having studied it and exchanged views on it for months preceding oral argument. That made for a style of oral argument in the California Supreme Court that caused the court to be called a "hot court," not perhaps in the current vernacular's use of that term, but one that reflected a very full awareness of all the underlying aspects of the case and an eagerness to engage counsel in informed debate.

The circumstance that the U.S. Supreme Court can accept review of a case with the vote of only four justices—less than a majority of the court, unlike California's high court—can lead to difficulties in deciding the merits of the case after oral argument. As is true in embarking upon most journeys, it is usually advisable to have at least a general idea of where you are headed before setting off.

Another area of comparison might be—and this goes beyond the high courts themselves—the area of administrative reform. Authorities such as Dean Roscoe Pound and Chief Justice William Howard Taft wrote about the lack of cohesion in the federal judiciary many years ago. The federal judiciary is not as much of a cohesive branch of government as I believe our California judiciary is. I believe the Judicial Conference of the United States, headed by the Chief Justice of the United States, has a much less hands-on role in a managerial sense than the Judicial Council of California. It was of interest to me that, just a few years ago, the federal administrative office of the courts, which serves as the staff of the Judicial Conference of the United States, sent a small delegation to California to examine how our own A.O.C. was functioning. When I chatted briefly with Chief Justice Roberts at an event in Washington, he complimented California's judiciary on the success that I and others had had in engaging our system in administrative reform.

As we previously discussed, another area of comparison would be the televising of oral arguments, which I consider very important. The California Supreme Court's commitment to this practice has led to more openness in our proceedings, more transparency, and has served to instill public confidence and trust in the judicial system, whereas the U.S. Supreme Court has been quite resistant to that possibility. In fact, when Judge Vaughn Walker sought to open his courtroom to televised proceedings in the Proposition 8 case—and the Ninth Circuit had adopted some ad hoc rules to authorize that—the word came down from Washington that he had acted outside his authority. He was prevented from opening up his own courtroom to television cameras. I was a bit surprised that the high court would intervene in that circumstance, even though there was some dispute over whether the rulemaking process had been fully followed. It was surprising there would be that much exercise of authority over a lower federal court, telling it whether it could or should or would be able to televise its own proceedings, because much as I've been a proponent of statewide standards—and we've had our own study on cameras in the courtroom conducted by the Judicial Council—the California court system recognizes a certain amount of discretion, as long as it's exercised according to neutral principles, reposed in individual trial judges on this subject.

There even have been moves in the U.S. Congress to pass legislation mandating the opening of federal courts to television cameras. I find the prospect of such legislation very troubling, even though I favor greater consideration of televising particular proceedings when they are of public interest. The reason I find it disturbing is that it invites another branch of government to regulate a judicial function. That's really getting the camel's nose under the tent, I feel—having one or both of the other two branches make such a decision for the judicial branch. To me, it's quite clear that it is the judicial branch at some level or other that should make the determination whether public courtrooms in the judicial branch may admit television cameras. I could see that if Congress ever attempts to do that, a genuine constitutional issue might very well arise—which is whether a congressional mandate that federal courts be open to televised proceedings would violate the separation of powers by infringing upon the independence of the judiciary and the ability of the judiciary to govern itself. This dispute, if the judicial side remains resistant to opening courtrooms to the electronic media, could end up in a constitutional confrontation. Opening judicial proceedings to the electronic media is important because often it's only 30 persons or so who can fit into a courtroom. The public really has to depend on the press in one form or another, especially the electronic media, for being its eyes and ears for the judicial process. I won't repeat what I said when you asked me about my decision for the court in *NBC Subsidiary*, but there are reasons beyond the interest in the particular case, systemic interests, why I think it's so important to have these proceedings open, and open electronically as well—including at the U.S. Supreme Court level. It will be interesting to see what happens in this whole debate.

What other separation-of-powers issues has the U.S. judiciary faced that have been of particular interest to you?

Some federal judges have raised issues concerning judicial compensation. I believe there was a decision titled *United States v. Will*, where the issue was raised whether the failure of federal judicial salaries to keep up with the rate of inflation amounted to a reduction in judicial compensation in violation of the constitutional provision that forbids a diminution in such compensation.

Some have raised issues concerning Congress' failure or refusal to provide judicial nominees with a floor vote in the Senate, up or down. This has left a great number of vacancies on the federal bench, resulting in a negative impact on the public's access to justice due to the burgeoning caseload and an insufficient number of judges to handle the caseload. In addition, there is a need to create additional federal judgeships.

That whole process of confirming judges at any level of the federal system has become a different question today than it once was.

Yes, the process for confirming federal judicial nominees in the U.S. Senate has become highly politicized. By contrast, I would say, in terms of judicial selection, that although there are ways in which California's system could be improved, it is basically an apolitical system except that the appointing authority, the governor, obviously can consider, among the mix of qualities, the political leanings of the candidate. About 45 percent of the judicial appointments of the last administration, that of Governor Arnold Schwarzenegger, came from the opposing major political party. These appointments included a broad mix of individuals from the standpoint of gender, race, and ethnicity. When asked about which I believe to be the better system for selecting judges, I fall back upon the fact that the way the federal system is working or not working now, I'd rather take my chances before the electorate with a yes or no vote as a justice of the California Supreme Court every 12 years than run the political gamut of confirmation hearings, like those in the U.S. Senate, with their very intrusive and often inappropriate inquiries, and then languishing there without sometimes even having a vote for a year or two if ever. I'm convinced that if California were ever to switch to an appointment process that substituted legislative confirmation for voter confirmation, the state legislature would be no more exemplary in performing the task than the U.S. Senate.

This is jumping ahead, but the new justice on the California Supreme Court this year, Justice Goodwin Liu, had that very situation didn't he, waiting for quite some time and several rounds for a possible federal appointment and then ulti-

mately removing his name from consideration and accepting the appointment here in California?

Yes, his nomination to the federal Ninth Circuit was pending 15 months before the U.S. Senate and never received a vote. When Governor Brown appointed him to the California Supreme Court, he received an "exceptionally well qualified" rating from the State Bar and was confirmed unanimously and easily by the Commission on Judicial Appointments. The federal judicial system's loss was a gain to the California judiciary.

Getting back to your question about comparisons between the federal high court and the state high court, what I'm about to say is meant in a very general sense and not about each and every member currently or recently serving on the U.S. Supreme Court. I do, in fact, know several of the current and former members of the federal high court, three of them fairly well, Justices O'Connor, Kennedy, and Breyer. But as a generalization, I would say that the high degree of collegiality that I described to you previously, that exists on the California Supreme Court, is not equaled by what at least outsiders see on the U.S. Supreme Court. There is much talk nationwide among judges about the need for civility and how civility has declined—civility among judges and civility between the bench and the bar. I would observe, from reports of exchanges at oral argument and some of the exchanges I have read in the high court's written opinions, that there sometimes seem to be sarcastic and perhaps occasionally almost ad hominem attacks by one justice against another. Again, this is at a time when judges around the United States have called for more civility, so I'm not sure the best example is always being set. The same negative example is certainly set by the high courts of some other states.

Another area where I believe we compare quite favorably to the U.S. Supreme Court is our view in California of the type of conduct that requires a justice's recusal from hearing a case. There are relations and actions that we read about pertaining to the justices of the U.S. Supreme Court that would certainly necessitate recusal in California and—in the absence of recusal—might very well result in disciplinary action by our constitutional agency, the Commission on Judicial Performance. Interestingly enough, lower federal court judges are subject to a disciplinary mechanism, not as cohesive and effective as what we have in California, but one that nonetheless does exist. Although a statutory restriction that addresses financial conflicts of interest applies to all federal judges, including those on the U.S. Supreme Court, the Code of Conduct for United States Judges, adopted by the Judicial Conference of the United States, explicitly applies only to lower federal court judges. However, some of the high court justices have said that they nonetheless follow it.

A collateral aspect of this situation is that when a recusal does occur on the U.S. Supreme Court, there is no process for the appointment of a justice pro Tem the way there is in the California Supreme Court. So when one high court justice disqualifies himself or herself due to perhaps an investment in the stock of one of the parties or some other conflict of interest and the decision is four to four, the result is a very brief order or memorandum that indicates that the lower court decision is affirmed by an equally divided court. This resolution of the case holds absolutely no precedential value. It affects no one other than the parties themselves.

The issue concerning conduct that would require recusal is something that came up in one of the decisions of the U.S. Supreme Court that I'd like to touch upon. This is the high court case of *Caperton v. Massey Coal Company*, a 2009 decision that also reflects the ethical standards that do or do not apply in West Virginia. A West Virginia jury had found in favor of a plaintiff and awarded $50 million in damages against the Massey Coal Co. That state has no intermediate court of appeal, so the case went straight to the West Virginia Supreme Court of Appeals, as it's called, and what happened was the following. The CEO of the losing party coal company created a nonprofit entity through which he contributed more than $3 million on behalf of a fairly obscure West Virginia lawyer to run against a justice of the West Virginia high court. It was fairly obvious from past rulings that the West Virginia high court would be likely to affirm the $50 million judgment by a three-to-two vote and that the targeted incumbent justice was likely to be part of the majority that would rule against the coal company. This very sizable contribution to the challenger amounted to much more than the total amount spent by the candidate's other supporters in this election, and the plaintiff petitioned the newly elected justice to recuse himself. But the justice declined and was part of a three-to-two majority that overturned the $50 million verdict. There was another justice who did recuse himself because he was found to have been vacationing with an officer of the Massey Coal Company on the French Riviera, as documented by photos that appeared in the media. The question was raised, with regard to the newly elected justice, whether the contribution from the coal company raised an appearance of partiality. But the justice said no, he wasn't biased and there was no need for him to recuse himself.

The U.S. Supreme Court did the right thing, in my view, by finding that the failure on the part of the justice who was the recipient of the contributions to recuse himself did deny the plaintiff due process of law. But justice wasn't fully achieved in *Caperton,* because after the high court remanded the case to the West Virginia Supreme Court, that court, again three-to-two, voted in favor of Massey Coal on the ground that the plaintiff shouldn't have brought his lawsuit in the first place in West Virginia but instead in Virginia. So the plaintiff lost out anyway after all of this.

What shocked me was that the U.S. Supreme Court's decision was not unanimous. It was a five to four decision, with Chief Justice Roberts writing a very lengthy and strongly worded opinion for the four dissenters in which he attacked the majority opinion for providing insufficient guidance and posed a series of 40 questions. I'll mention the first question posed by the Chief Justice, because of the implications it has for the independence of the judiciary in conjunction with some of the high court's other decisions. This was the first of the 40 questions posed by the dissent, questioning the majority's test of the probability of bias and appearance of bias on behalf of the newly elected justice. Question number one: "With little help from the majority, courts will now have to determine how much money is too much money. What level of contribution or expenditure gives rise to a probability of bias?" I don't think we have to get into—if $3 million is too much—whether $2.5 million is too much. This amount clearly was too much. The dissent also posed the question of why the majority was so convinced that this was an extreme case, and noted that the justice newly elected to the West Virginia high court and his campaign had no control over how the money was spent, and so on.

Again, compare this to California. Our Code of Civil Procedure provides that a judge shall be disqualified and be compelled to recuse himself or herself if for any reason a person aware of the facts might reasonably entertain a doubt that the judge would be able to be impartial.[6] Again, it's a public confidence test. I found it quite surprising that this was a question that divided the U.S. Supreme Court right down the middle. Our statutory provisions state that a judge shall be disqualified if the judge or the judge's spouse has a financial interest of more than $1,500 in a party or in the subject matter of the litigation or has a position or is an active participant in some way with a party,[7] so there are clear guidelines in California that keep us from getting into the kind of position that was almost countenanced by a majority of the U.S. Supreme Court in the *Caperton* case. Campaign contributions to a judge are required by California law to be reported, identifying each donor of a cumulative amount of $100 or more, and these disclosures become publicly known.[8] My test, by the way, on something you'll probably ask me about before we're done, my 1998 retention election campaign, was that if anyone made any donation, I of course reported it as required by law and also would not hear any case involving the party or the lawyer

---

[6] Cal. Code Civ. Proc., sec. 170.1(a)(6).

[7] Cal. Code Civ. Proc., sec. 170.1(a)(3), 170.5(b).

[8] Cal. Gov. Code, sec. 84211.

for a period of two years following that contribution. Obviously, less stringent standards may be perfectly appropriate.

I instituted a procedure at the California Supreme Court that was endorsed by my colleagues, designed to make sure that the justices were not overlooking a conflict of interest that might not be apparent given the ebb and flow of mergers and acquisitions in publicly owned corporations. Certain companies might be a parent or a subsidiary of a company whose shares were held by a justice without him or her knowing this. Our court now requires that within 15 days of review being granted in any case, all of the parties file a disclosure statement specifying all of those relationships—parent, subsidiary, and related relationships—that brings to the court's attention a full panoply of ownership interests that could give rise to a conflict. Our court's practices are, I believe, totally above board. Early in his legal career, our son Eric worked at a very large multinational law firm, Skadden Arps. The test would be, if a lawyer in the New York office or some other office of Skadden Arps had a case that at some level or other was in the California court system and that case came up to the California Supreme Court for possible review, I would recuse myself even if my son had nothing to do with the case and knew nothing about it. I believe that, given the vital need to maintain public trust and confidence in our court system, it is essential that there be an expansive approach to avoiding conduct that brings the impartiality of the court in question in the public eye, and that if there is conduct or contact that would suggest there might be an appearance of impropriety—which, as I said, is the California standard—then the justice in question should recuse himself or herself. As I said, the California disciplinary system, administered by the Commission on Judicial Performance, takes such matters very seriously.

Those are some preliminary observations I would make in response to your question inviting me to draw some comparisons between the U.S. Supreme Court and the California Supreme Court. I have some additional observations about some of the jurisprudence of the current U.S. Supreme Court that I would make—not necessarily because of any personal intellectual difference of opinion on my part with the decisions, but more out of concern that the methodology employed by the court in some instances lends itself to the perception that the court's decisions may be result oriented, a perception that can place the court in the public eye as being yet another political institution of government. That to me would be very harmful even if it's just a perception. I believe there are decisions that a majority of the court has issued that give rise to that perception and therefore have a very deleterious effect upon the public's confidence and trust in the court system. If we lose that trust and confidence, and recent surveys indicate it's down to less than 50 percent, respect for the rule of law is undermined.

And it is the rule of law that many of us feel lies at the basic foundation of our democratic system of government.

You've noted that the decision in the West Virginia case was five to four, and indeed the U.S. Supreme Court has issued many decisions with that very close split. What does that, in particular, say?

Sometimes that may be unavoidable, but equally unavoidable is the perception that a pronouncement of law is less likely to be readily accepted by the population when the justices are so closely divided. That was always something that concerned me when it would occur on the California Supreme Court. I'm not suggesting that a justice on our court or the U.S. Supreme Court should give up a firmly held belief in the validity of his or her position just to avoid a narrowly decided decision. But to the extent that such divisions can be minimized, a court strengthens the persuasive force with which it speaks in rendering a decision and makes its ruling more readily acceptable by the parties and by the public. The point you bring up is, I think, very important indeed. Some of these observations I'm about to make I'm expressing for the first time outside a purely private setting, but now that I'm retired I am no longer a second-class citizen when it comes to First Amendment rights, and now enjoy a freedom to comment upon the decisions of other judges and courts. [Laughter] I would say that, as you point out, there are far more split decisions, decided by one vote, in the U.S. Supreme Court than there are in the California Supreme Court—five-to-four decisions are frequently rendered in the high court, with there being far fewer four-to-three decisions in our court. Our court has far more unanimous decisions, and again, when a court can speak with one voice, it speaks in a far more authoritative way and there is far greater likelihood of acceptance of its rulings. Look how hard Chief Justice Earl Warren worked to have the school desegregation case, *Brown v. Board of Education*, be a unanimous opinion. My understanding is that during the preceding term of the U.S. Supreme Court, Chief Justice Fred Vinson was unable to get his colleagues together on any resolution of the case, and it had to be put over to the court's next term. During the intervening year, Chief Justice Vinson passed away, and Warren made a conscious effort to have the court speak on this highly divisive social issue with a single voice. Even though the path of desegregation and racial tolerance has not been an easy one since *Brown*, think how much more difficult it would have been had *Brown v. Board of Education* been rendered as a five-to-four decision or, worse yet, perhaps a decision in which there were multiple opinions and fewer than five votes for any single opinion. I believe that it is a basic function of a high court, a court of last resort, to try to speak whenever possible in a way that provides the guidance afforded by a single voice. Again, there are cases where one legally or morally feels compelled to dissent—although interestingly enough, as I previously mentioned to you, there are some foreign jurisdictions where the culture of the court does not entertain dissenting opinions, so if in fact the court was divided one never learns of any dissenting views. There is *an* opinion, one opinion, issued for the court so as not to detract from the persuasiveness and the authority of the high court's decision.

But let me mention at this point some examples where again, putting aside any disagreement I might have with the opinion issued by the high court on a personal or intellectual level, I believe the opinion clearly fails to provide the guidance that is a basic function or purpose of a high court. When one looks at *Bush v. Gore*, a one-time decision that in the views of some commentators is probably destined never to be cited as authority or precedent for anything, it does bring to mind an observation made in the 1940s by the other Justice Roberts, Justice Owen Roberts. He said in dissent in the case of *Smith v. Allwright*: "The reason for my concern is that the instant decision, overruling that announced about nine years ago, tends to bring adjudications of this tribunal into the same class as a restricted railroad ticket, good for this day and train only. I have no assurance, in view of current decisions, that the opinion announced today may not shortly be repudiated and overruled by justices who deem they have new light on the subject. In the present term the court has overruled three cases." Does this mean there should never be an overruling of precedent? No, obviously not. *Brown v. Board of Education* overruled precedent and is a prime example of a case in which it would have been wrong to adhere to precedent. The same is true of the majority opinion in *Allwright*, to which Justice Owen Roberts took exception. But such action by the court should be an extreme situation founded upon a compelling need, a change of circumstances, a reexamination of some very fundamental values and not have the appearance of being a casual change of course.

There have been some situations where the lack of guidance provided by the high court is truly egregious. In our earlier discussions, we referred to the case of *Furman v. Georgia*, which invalidated the application of the death penalty as imposed in that particular case and the related cases before the court. In arriving at that conclusion, the court found that in those cases the death penalty was arbitrarily and inconsistently imposed and constituted cruel and unusual punishment in violation of the Eighth and Fourteenth amendments. Unlike *People v. Anderson*, this was not a wholesale rejection of the death penalty as inevitably cruel and unusual—or cruel *or* unusual punishment, as held by *Anderson*. It was found to be cruel and unusual only as applied in these particular cases, *Furman* and the two companion cases. So what guidance did the high court provide? *Furman* is described as a five-to-four decision, but the opinion rendered by the court consisted of a one-page per curiam opinion holding only that the imposition of the death penalty in those cases constituted cruel and unusual punishment in violation of the Constitution. There were also seven separate opinions in the case—three concurring opinions and four dissenting opinions totaling more than 200 pages—and not one of them was able to garner the votes of more than four justices. The majority could not agree on a rationale and did not produce any controlling opinion, so what kind of guidance did this supply to lawmakers and judges trying to comply with the court's decision? In the four years that followed *Furman*, 37 states had to enact new death penalty laws. Some of these statutes mandated bifurcated trials with separate guilt and penalty phases. Some imposed various standards of some sort or another. Some of these efforts were upheld in later U.S. Supreme Court decisions and others were not, and very little guidance was provided by the monumental ruling in *Furman*.

The U.S. Supreme Court's opinion in *United States v. Booker*, another significant case—invalidating portions of the federal sentencing guidelines—was preceded in the official reports of the court's decisions by the customary syllabus prepared by the court's reporter of decisions. This official summary—pardon my lack of respect—is almost comically complex in setting forth the lineup of the justices. It reads verbatim: "Stevens, J. delivered the opinion of the court in part, in which Scalia, Souter, Thomas, and Ginsburg joined. Breyer delivered the opinion of the court in part, in which Rehnquist, O'Connor, Kennedy, and Ginsburg joined. Stevens filed an opinion dissenting in part, in which Souter joined and in which Scalia joined except for Part 3 and Footnote 17. Scalia and Thomas filed opinions dissenting in part. Breyer filed an opinion dissenting in part, in which Rehnquist and O'Connor and Kennedy joined." Professor Gerald Uelmen has written that, in order to accurately figure out the holding of one U.S. Supreme Court decision, the reader would need a slide rule.[9] In the end, perhaps, all the reader can conclude is that the court reversed or affirmed the judgment of the lower court, but you don't really know the reasoning of a majority of the court, or at least you can't readily discern it.

These last two examples happen to have been during Chief Justice Rehnquist's time leading the court. Without thinking specifically of him, to what extent in your view is it a matter of leadership at the top?

I believe that can play a part. It obviously did in *Brown v. Board of Education*. It certainly is reflected in the degree to which a Chief Justice is willing to

---

[9] Gerald Uelmen, "The George Court's 8th Year," 24 *Calif. Lawyer* 26, 28 (July 2004).

try to persuade the justices to speak with one voice or fewer voices or at least to have, in the case of the U.S. Supreme Court, at least five names on an opinion, a majority of the court, however many additional separate opinions might be issued by those five justices and perhaps by dissenters. Whenever I saw fewer than four names on a proposed opinion of our court, I undertook an effort to achieve a compromise that four or more justices could put their names on, even if they had to offer additional explanations in concurring opinions.

What form would that effort take on your part?

Just reminding them of what our basic function is, to provide guidance, that the writing of separate opinions is not supposed to be an exercise in venting one's spleen; that sometimes you hold your nose and you sign something that isn't exactly the way you would have it; and that the greater interest—that is, an interest greater than the purity of one's own intellectual views—is at stake in this process. It's not just an exercise in ego.

But sometimes, due to the multiplicity of the opinions issued in a particular case or the convoluted nature of the case combined with the inability or unwillingness of the justices to coordinate their expressed positions, a court does not succeed in providing clear rules to guide lower courts and parties in future situations. This is not a new phenomenon. There is a colorfully written passage in an opinion rendered by the California Supreme Court in 1914 titled *Albert Pick and Company v. Jordan*. In this case, Justice Frederick W. Henshaw, one of my predecessors from almost 100 years ago, with reference to the jurisprudence of the U.S. Supreme Court in a particular area of the law, pointed out that several high court decisions were hopelessly irreconcilable. Justice Henshaw wrote: "We are constrained to admit our inability to harmonize this language in these decisions, though we make haste to add that undoubtedly the failure must come from our own deficient powers of perception and ratiocination, and for this deficiency it is no consolation to us to note that our brethren of the Supreme Court of Montana are similarly afflicted." [Laughter] I thought that was a wonderful way of making a point about the lack of guidance coming from the nation's high court.

Sometimes the problem is not just one of a lack of guidance. I believe that what occasionally occurs can truly be termed judicial activism. That's a subject that is probably worth spending a couple of moments on. It's a pejorative term that perhaps is most often used by conservatives in attacking what they view as liberal jurisprudence. But I truly believe it works both ways and can apply just as well to conservative jurisprudence. Some say judicial activism is a meaningless term that exists only in the eye of the beholder, and only describes an opinion you don't agree with. But I think it is more than that. There are instances where a court exhibits no reluctance about abandoning settled precedent, or intruding upon states' rights in violation of our federal union, or disregarding the original understanding of the Constitution, and other instances where it reaches out to decide an issue when there's no need to do so, even when the parties may not have called upon the court to address the issue.

What's a prime example of that?

One illustration, of course, might very well be *Bush v. Gore*, where another principle, arguably ignored in that case, comes into play—avoiding political issues. Previously I made reference to Justice Felix Frankfurter's famous warning, in the context of judicial intervention in legislative redistricting, of the dangers of entering into the "political thicket." Interestingly enough, although I like the phrase and think the concept is an important one, entering into what might have been a political thicket in *Baker v. Carr* was probably absolutely necessary because—due to gerrymandering and the absence of proper redistricting for about half a century—one legislative district in Tennessee had 10 times as many residents as some of the rural districts of that state. The claim was made by the plaintiff that the votes of rural citizens were worth so much more than the votes of urban citizens because urban citizens like himself were not receiving equal protection of the laws under the Fourteenth Amendment. There I disagree with Justice Frankfurter's view that the remedy for malapportionment had to be found through the political process. How can you achieve that if the political process itself is unresponsive because of the districting and the obvious interest of "unrepresentative" representatives in protecting their own self interest?

But I believe the concept of improper judicial intervention in the political process does apply in some instances, and certainly *Bush v. Gore* legitimately may be viewed as an instance of the high court's reaching out into a political area. Justice O'Connor has stated that this decision was viewed by the public as political and may in part be responsible for the drop in the approval rating for U.S. Supreme Court justices from 66 percent in the late 1980s to 44 percent. Now, I'm trying to be objective here and therefore pose the question, who am I as author of the court's opinions in the parental consent and gay marriage cases to accuse anyone of judicial activism? A law review article that was brought to my attention actually undertook a comparison of the opinions in *Bush v. Gore* and the *In re Marriage Cases*. The author concluded that the decision in the *Marriage Cases* was totally consistent with the California Supreme Court's past development of its own jurisprudence in the area of the right of privacy and specifically the fundamental right to marry and to form a family—rights recognized over the years by the U.S. Supreme Court. In contrast, in his view, *Bush v. Gore* absolutely ignored precedent in many crucial respects. The law professor who was the author of this law review article states that in conducting an exercise with his class comparing these two decisions, "I argue that *Bush v. Gore* makes *In re Marriage Cases* look tame. In fact, while the California Supreme Court's conclusion was not inevitable in light of existing constitutional text and case law, it does not represent a radical departure from precedent. Instead it extends the logic of existing cases. By comparison, *Bush v. Gore* was a product of whole cloth and a dramatic departure from precedent."[10]

There are two sides to that question, but I thought this was worth pointing out. The author also notes that, according to his count, Justices Scalia and Thomas have voted to strike down statutes more frequently than the court's more liberal members.

Another case that in my view will have a dramatic impact on the political landscape of the United States and, unfortunately, on judicial elections is the *Citizens United* case, which held that certain provisions of the political campaign finance law are unconstitutional under the First Amendment because corporations are persons and thus are entitled to the exercise of free speech rights under the First Amendment. The court's perception of corporations led one observer to remark that he would believe corporations are people when Texas executes one. The court's opinion is an example of what I mentioned a moment ago—the sometimes unfortunate act of reaching out to decide issues that were not raised by the parties. The parties had raised much narrower issues in the *Citizens United* case. The court put the case over to the following term for reargument, which is highly unusual, and not only reached issues that the parties had actually sought to avoid but ruled on constitutional issues when it could have ruled for the prevailing party on much narrower grounds. Various maxims of jurisprudence that have guided the high court and other courts direct courts to rule on the narrower available ground, not to reach out for issues, and to avoid ruling on constitutional grounds when the court can rule on a nonconstitutional ground, even if this involves interpreting a statute in a certain way—when a court properly can do that—so as to avoid the statute being held unconstitutional. Proceeding in this manner is viewed as less intrusive on the other branches of government than invalidating the measure.

The *Citizens United* case overruled a recent precedent without the customary justification that's invoked when this somewhat radical course is taken—the justification of reliance on changed circumstances, a misapprehension about underlying conditions or consequences, or something else of that sort. Interest-

---

[10] Michael Vitiello, "Lies, Damn Lies, and Claims of Judicial Activism," Chapman University School of Law, *Journal of Law and Public Policy*, 14 Nexus J. Op. 55 (2009).

ingly enough, Justice O'Connor made a comment reported by the *New York Times* about the 2010 *Citizens United* decision having partially overruled her own 2003 decision for the court in the *McConnell* case, which had upheld the same provisions that were struck down in *Citizens United*. Her words, quoted by the *New York Times*, were: "Gosh, I step away for a couple of years and there's no telling what's going to happen."[11]

Indeed, that decision was thought to overturn precedent of a much longer period, was it not?

The *Austin* case as well as a whole slew of other cases. Justice Stevens' dissent went beyond those precedents and raised the question of whether the majority's view of corporations was inconsistent with the historical understanding of the scope of the First Amendment. I know commentators have been highly critical of the decision, especially for not choosing among, as one of them put it, several narrow remedies recommended in Justice Stevens' dissent and instead overturning dozens of court cases and statutes promulgated over the past 100 years, even though the parties had not asked them to issue such a broad ruling.

Again, it was a five-to-four decision. Aside from the constitutional aspects you mentioned, what is most troubling to you about this one?

The most disturbing aspect to me is the basic effect of opening the floodgates to corporate donations with the resulting impact on the public's exercise of its right to vote. It is still their own vote—but if there's a deluge of expensive advertising on one side, that's likely to have an impact. Now, to be even-handed about this, it opens the same door to labor unions. But as a practical matter there is no doubt that corporations will be able, in the eyes of most commentators, to contribute far more than labor unions. Some of these corporations, by the way, may be foreign corporations, which are not permitted by law to get involved in American elections. But with corporations crossing national boundaries and having subsidiaries and parent corporations, it is quite possible—and not unreasonable to anticipate—foreign corporate money being used to affect elections in the United States.

That was my preliminary concern, and here is my parochial view as a judge. I believe this decision has the potential to be devastating in judicial elections. *Caperton v. Massey Coal Company*, the West Virginia case you and I discussed, provides an illustration of the willingness of a corporate entity to throw millions of dollars into a relatively small race for one Supreme Court position in a small

---

[11] Adam Liptak, "The Caucus Blog" (*New York Times*, Jan. 26, 2010).

state. You need to take *Citizens United* together with the illustration provided by *Caperton* and then add on another factor, another decision of the U.S. Supreme Court titled *Republican Party of Minnesota v. White*. This decision held that the codes of judicial ethics that prevent judicial candidates, whether they're incumbents or challengers, from announcing their views on legal issues, on how they should be resolved by a court, are unconstitutional because those ethical constraints constitute an abridgment of freedom of speech under the First Amendment.

Let's say a judge or a candidate for judicial office announces his or her views on a civil issue or a criminal issue—perhaps the appropriate punishment in all cases involving a particular offense. Someone running for office says, "I believe that the economy is being destroyed by shoplifting. I think that anyone who is found guilty of shoplifting should receive the maximum punishment, even as a first offender, no matter what the circumstances." Or: "Drunk driving is such a hazard that anyone who engages in drunk driving and is found guilty of that offense should be sentenced to a full year in county jail." I would ask, who would want to have his or her family member or friend go before a judge who had announced such preconceived views? And yet the judicial canons of ethics have in part been invalidated by this decision of the U.S. Supreme Court. So you take the ruling in the *White* case, together with *Citizens United* and the illustration provided by *Caperton*, and you have the perfect storm—a true danger posed to judicial independence, to fairness and integrity in our state courts, as a direct result of these rulings by the U.S. Supreme Court. *White* was another five-to-four decision, with Justice O'Connor a member of the five-justice majority. She has stated—and I've heard her do so publicly on at least two occasions—that she regrets her vote on that case, which is a rare thing for a justice of the U.S. Supreme Court to say.

Did she elaborate?

I did not hear her elaborate, no. But I got the impression from the context in which her remarks were made, at least on one of those occasions, that she was very concerned about the practical consequences of the ruling for state judicial elections. It's one thing for a court to come up with these abstractions and niceties on a theoretical level in terms of what is free speech and what it shouldn't include, but it's another thing to consider the practical ramifications of the court's decision. The justices in the *White* majority clearly gave the impression that they disfavor judicial elections, and that if the people of the state don't like the *White* decision, their remedy is to abolish such elections. I believe that's a somewhat arrogant justification for the high court to invoke for its ruling, even though I happen to share the view that there may be better ways to select judges. But as a practical matter and a political reality, the people are unlikely to give up their right to vote for judicial candidates.

Since I'm being expansive in sharing my views concerning the First Amendment jurisprudence of the U.S. Supreme Court, I might as well indicate that I have long disagreed with much of the law made by the high court in this area. I believe very, very strongly in the protection of First Amendment rights, and I believe the opinions I've written for the California Supreme Court and other actions I have taken have illustrated that commitment on my part. Certainly the *NBC* case is one case that we've discussed that I'm most proud of. But I believe it debases and cheapens one of our most fundamental rights, the right of free speech and the other First Amendment protections, to expand that right beyond what we would call "pure speech" to "commercial speech," which may involve advertising, and to other efforts to enhance corporate profits, equating these two forms of speech—and to expand the cherished principles of free speech to what the high court sometimes views as "expressive conduct." Confounding the concepts of "commercial speech" and "expressive conduct" with "pure speech" is in my view—to borrow the phrase used by one of my law school professors in another context—like mixing a dog's dinner.

The most glaring examples I can give are the decisions of the U.S. Supreme Court invalidating statutes passed by 48 states and Congress that banned flag burning.[12] To consider burning a flag an exercise of First Amendment rights, in my view, diminishes the stature of free speech—one of our most cherished rights and one deserving of the highest protection. The high court's *Bates* decision striking down the regulation of lawyer advertising—a practice that has not been a great boon to the integrity of the legal profession—is another high court First Amendment ruling that tarnishes our veneration of what truly constitutes free speech, in my view. This expansive view of the First Amendment, carried to its logical extreme, probably would cause the high court to reverse a couple decisions I was involved in that you and I discussed—the opinion in *Aguilar v. Avis Rent-a-Car* upholding prohibition of the pervasive use of racial epithets by supervisory personnel in the workplace, and the conviction of the *Los Angeles Free Press* for receiving and publishing a stolen roster containing the names and home addresses of all the state justice department narcotics agents.[13] That's my riff on my disagreements with the First Amendment jurisprudence of the U.S.

---

[12] United States v. Eichman (1990) 496 U.S. 310; Texas v. Johnson (1989) 491 U.S. 397.
[13] People v. Kunkin (1973) 9 Cal.3d 245; 507 P.2d 1392 (reversing the convictions on a different, nonconstitutional ground).

Supreme Court, in addition to what we're talking about here specifically in terms of activism and disregard of precedent.

There's another area of the law where the high court overruled rather recently decided precedent. I mentioned it previously, when we were discussing the high court's jurisprudence in capital cases, so I won't discuss it now at any length. I noted the ruling admitting victim-impact evidence, voicing some concern about the substance of this ruling, but an additional concern is that it overruled the high court's decisions to the contrary of just a few years earlier.

I would also add that sometimes the rulings of the high court appear to some observers to be selective in their application of various principles of decision making. There are some commentators who view the current court majority as likely to invoke principles of federalism and states' rights when those justices apparently approve of what the states are doing or disapprove of what Congress is attempting to do. But, in the view of those commentators, the same justices on occasion appear to disregard those very same principles when the opposite is true—when the court majority seems to support the result of what Congress is doing and to not like what the states are doing, leading the court under those circumstances to find that federal law preempts state regulation.

To what extent do you agree with that?

Sometimes it is difficult for me to find consistency in the high court's approach to cases that raise issues of federalism. Of course it's very difficult—it's impossible, actually—to ferret out the motivation of a justice, conscious or subconscious, unless he or she is quite candid in expressing it, either in an opinion or in a speech or other public manner. But I don't believe it's unreasonable for commentators to have drawn that conclusion on the basis of their comparison of various rulings and it being difficult to come up with a reasoned way of reconciling the different results. All of that can give rise to a perception that the court is being selective in its approach, in its invocation of standard principles of jurisprudential decision making.

Another area of classic debate lies in the much-discussed and closely related approaches to decision making that have been called originalism and textualism—attempting to ascertain the original intent of the Founders or, as I might call it, a somewhat literal approach to the interpretation of the federal constitution.

The right to bear arms, for example?

Exactly. I'd like to focus on that for a moment. Obviously, as a constitution our charter was intended to be susceptible of adaptation to changing circumstances. Some have taken objection to the label "a living constitution," and I don't think we have to necessarily adopt that particular verbiage. But obviously the charter was intended to provide guidelines for future times and unanticipated situations. Clearly, our founding fathers could not have contemplated the need to apply their Fourth Amendment constraint against unreasonable search and seizure to future modes of transportation such as automobiles, or to wiretapping and electronic eavesdropping. Those are things that, because they didn't exist in the eighteenth century, couldn't have been within their anticipation, no matter how clairvoyant they were.

But apart from whatever merit the textualist approach might have, I find it very odd that some of its strongest advocates on the court could appear to so easily abandon it in their opinion for the court in *District of Columbia v. Heller*, the case that you alluded to that struck down gun-control laws on Second Amendment grounds. Even conservative federal appellate judges such as Richard Posner and J. Harvie Wilkinson have been very critical of the *Heller* decision as creating a constitutional right that did not previously exist. The *Heller* opinion concluded that the Second Amendment confers on individuals the right to bear arms, rather than recognizing the right of each state to maintain a militia—despite the wording of the prefatory clause of the Second Amendment, which reads in its entirety: "A well regulated militia, being necessary to the security of a free state, the right of the people to keep and bear arms, shall not be infringed." Now, aside from the fact that this ruling has the practical effect of hampering local government and law enforcement in their attempts to deal with violence at a time when there seems to be quite a need for gun control, it certainly seems that this opinion represents a selective application of the textualist approach to constitutional interpretation. Even though the court's opinion made an attempt to rationalize its interpretation of the "militia" language, I believe that to basically disregard it can't help but fuel a cynical attitude on the part of the public that the nation's highest court is just one more political entity in our government and that its decisions are result oriented rather than based on a neutral and consistent application of legal principles.

These are some of the reasons for the reservations and concerns I have about the decisions that we've been discussing the last several minutes—apart from whatever intellectual disagreements I may have with their reasoning. What's truly important to me is that these opinions may serve to undermine the public's confidence in our judicial system, which—I think I've tried to make clear time and again in our discussions—is a matter of paramount concern to me, given the role of the judiciary in American society. I would add that public confidence in these U.S. Supreme Court decisions—*Bush v. Gore, Furman, Booker, White, Caperton, Citizens United,* and *Heller*—undoubtedly has been further lessened by the circumstance that each of the seven cases was decided by a five-to-four vote of the nation's highest court.

As you said, the public's view of the system and how well it works ties so strongly with this related matter of the independence of the judiciary and the public's willingness to recognize and support that.

Yes. The chickens all come back to roost, I think, if the court puts itself in a role that's perceived as political. It's a matter of great concern to me.

There's something that further exacerbates the effect of these rulings, and that is the near impossibility of reversing them by amending the Constitution of the United States. In the case of California it's easy—all too easy some might argue—to amend the state constitution. California's current constitution has been amended more than 500 times since its adoption in 1879. That was the second constitution we had, after the one of 1849. The United States Constitution, which is almost a hundred years older than the current California Constitution— and not counting the first 10 amendments, which were the Bill of Rights adopted shortly after ratification of the federal constitution—has been amended only 17 times. It's very difficult to amend the federal constitution. One needs a two-thirds vote of each house of our national legislature, the House of Representatives and the Senate, or an application by the legislatures of two-thirds of the states, and then ratification by three-fourths of the states. If the U.S. Supreme Court does something that the people truly object to and think is wrong—and I think we can say that *Citizens United* falls in that category, from the articles I've seen and the public opinion surveys—it's almost impossible to do anything about it, unlike the situation in California where a slim majority of the electorate exercised its right to overrule our court's decision in the gay marriage case and enact Proposition 8. They had a remedy, but there's almost no remedy for a decision of the U.S. Supreme Court. A justice of the U.S. Supreme Court once said something to the effect that the high court's decisions are not unreviewable because the justices are infallible. The justices are infallible only because they are unreviewable.[14] [Laughter]

Semantically entertaining, but with a germ of serious truth, perhaps?

---

[14] Concurring opinion by Justice Robert H. Jackson in Brown v. Allen (1953) 344 U.S. 443, 540.

Yes. So those are my reasons for expressing these concerns when you ask me to compare the court on which I sat and the court before which I argued cases many decades ago in Washington.

What further reflections do you have, if any, on this matter—this phrase used so often—of judicial activism? What is a way that the public can look at these matters more clearly?

I think it's really a mix of many factors. Again, the *Marriage Cases* was founded on precedent, whether or not one agrees with the decision or its precedents. But if a case reaches out of the blue to resolve issues that weren't posed by the parties and overrules recent precedent without adequate explanation; if it delves into an area that is basically political in nature and that would customarily be viewed as a political question, then I think a court is vulnerable to accusations of judicial activism. I don't think there's any neat formula, at least none that I can come up with, but there are many potential manifestations of judicial activism—whether they arise in a court's approach to political questions, to federalism, or to originalist or textualist interpretation of the Constitution. I believe that perhaps an underlying thread would be—whatever principles are invoked in decision making—are they being applied in a consistent manner or are they being selectively invoked and applied, thereby giving rise to the perception that various principles of jurisprudence are just being employed as tools to achieve a given result, in other words that a court is engaged in result-oriented jurisprudence? I think that one of the deadliest perceptions one can have about a court is to believe it is engaged in result-oriented jurisprudence, because that undermines the integrity of a court or of an individual judge or justice in the eyes of the public and certainly can destroy the essential confidence that the public must repose in its judicial system.

Perhaps we'll turn to some other areas of federal and state relations. As we said, you had a chance to serve on the California State-Federal Judicial Council as one of the venues for interacting with your colleagues in other jurisdictions.

Yes. Some but not all states have these joint councils that typically are comprised of members of the particular state's judiciary and the federal judiciary sitting in that state. These councils serve a very worthwhile purpose. California has a far more active council than many other states, and some states have no such council. We have, in the United States, a truly federal system in which both the federal and state judiciaries are quite active and have roles that on occasion can overlap. This is probably a good time to note that roughly 95 percent of the cases heard in American courts are heard in state courts. The bulk of our law is made in state courts, not in federal courts. The state courts really do not receive as much attention as they should, in terms of the role they play as sources of law. Many lay observers, and especially foreigners, are quite amazed and perplexed by the diversity of American judicial jurisdictions. They can't understand, for example, how it is that numerous states have the death penalty but many other states do not. How can you have this lack of uniformity? They don't understand that our national government does not extend down to the local level the way it does, for example, in France. Instead, we have a truly federal system that depends in large part upon each level of government according proper respect and deference to the other.

But inevitably there are areas that overlap, where we not only need a mechanism to smooth over any friction, but where we can learn from each other. The Chief Justice of California cochairs the California State-Federal Judicial Council and appoints the state-judge members, who comprise half of the council. The chairmanship has been shared over the years with the chief judge of the Ninth Circuit or his or her appointee, and I've had the pleasure of serving with some exceptional cochairs, Clifford Wallace and Arthur Alarcon, as well as Ninth Circuit Chief Judges Mary Schroeder and Alex Kozinski. We have committees of the council that are focused on various areas where there is an interplay. One obvious area is the Native American tribal courts. Those courts are a separate entity. The state courts need to coordinate their own functions with those of the tribal courts, as do the federal courts. There are complex issues of overlapping jurisdiction. My work on the California State-Federal Judicial Council caused me to convene a meeting of tribal judges—I had visited the tribal courts on my visits around the state in 1997—and to establish, as a result, a working group with the Native American judges, which was very much appreciated. We've all learned from each other and have tried to smooth out the relationship in situations where two court systems are attempting to exercise jurisdiction. Even substantively, I remember one very nice story that a Native American tribal judge told me, attempting to explain the Native American approach to justice and differentiate it from our adversary system. He used the parable of a Native American father who came home to find his two daughters squabbling over an orange. Each one wanted the single orange that was in the home. The father, instead of doing what his Caucasian counterpart might have done—namely taking a knife and cutting the orange in half so that each daughter would have half an orange— took the trouble to find out what each of his daughters desired, what was her objective in wanting the orange. One daughter wanted to create an art project for her class out of the rind of the orange, and the other one wanted to eat the fruit. He used this is a parable to illustrate how, through the Native American approach to justice, the needs of both parties in a dispute often could be fully satisfied. This is just a minor illustration of something enlightening, rather than a specific reform, that came out of these contacts.

The California State-Federal Judicial Council has a joint committee on judicial education, also one on unrepresented litigants, because the federal courts have problems similar to ours in this area, and we each were able to learn from each other's experience. And on jury reform. Especially fruitful has been the discussion on handling capital cases, because we viewed each individual case as basically an item moving through the python [Laughter], starting off with state charges, going through state automatic appeal, potentially to the U.S. Supreme Court, having state habeas corpus proceedings, then having federal habeas. Out of that came the proposal to have joint state-federal habeas counsel, which we've talked about, and trying to obtain some congressional funding for that. Each individual capital case basically coexisted in the two systems. Those were examples of some of the things that we were able to discuss. We learned from each other and from the judges and lawyers who came to address us, including Michael Laurence of the Habeas Corpus Resource Center. The federal judges had been largely unaware of his efforts encompassing the collection of briefs, legal authorities, and testimony from expert witnesses, which could then be shared with the federal defense counsel.

Another area of state-federal cooperation and coordination is a process that originally was called certification of issues of state law from a federal court to a state court. I believe this process exists in the majority of American jurisdictions, but California was one of the states that declined to enter into it until relatively recently. It certainly is a voluntary process. There's no ability on the part of a federal court, despite the supremacy clause of the federal constitution, to require a state court to answer a question of law from a federal court. But under this process the federal Ninth Circuit Court of Appeals can ask the California Supreme Court to answer a question of state law that is pending in a federal court case.[15] I mentioned earlier the Ninth Circuit's certification of the question of standing in the Proposition 8 federal court appeal from Judge Walker's ruling in the marriage equality case.

What do you know of the history of California's decision not to enter into the certification process before now?

Part of the institutional knowledge of the court during most of my time on it resided in Justice Mosk. When he resisted certification, he put it rather succinct-

---

[15] Cal. Rules of Court, rule 8.548.

ly, "Why should we as justices of the California Supreme Court serve as the research attorneys for Ninth Circuit federal judges?" [Laughter] Less colorfully, some of the other justices also felt that this process would add a lot to our work. In many, if not most, states where this process has been accepted, it encompasses U.S. District Court judges being able to certify questions to the state high court. California, being uniquely large in population, has dozens of U.S. District Court judges, so that would have imposed an enormous burden on our court.

I was a firm proponent of our joining the other states that have adopted this process. The reason I favor it is that it furthers the vital element of comity between our two court systems and thereby lubricates the relationship in what could otherwise be a somewhat dysfunctional system, having these two tiers of judiciary of general jurisdiction in our nation, unlike most other countries. First of all, this process serves the valuable function of furthering comity on the part of the state courts toward the federal appellate court. The federal courts on occasion express a need for guidance on an unresolved question of state law that is pending in a federal court proceeding.

I should explain that, although federal courts can't get involved in cases that involve only questions of state law unless there's some kind of diversity jurisdiction or some other special subject-matter jurisdiction that comes into play, there are often cases that are basically federal law cases where federal issues are intertwined with issues of state law that can have a strong bearing on how the federal court resolves what is primarily a question of federal law in the litigation before it. On occasion, the federal court needs to know what the state law is when that is unclear from existing state court decisions. The state high court shows respect and deference to the federal court through accommodating it by providing guidance. After all, that is our field. We're in the business of interpreting state law and have the final word on it. We may have had analogous rulings in that area of the law and possess relevant expertise. On the other hand, the federal court is furthering comity toward the state court by obtaining its views, instead of going ahead with the attitude, "We're going to decide this question of state law even though it's your jurisprudence. We're stepping into your field."

So it works nicely both ways. It also is efficient in facilitating the resolution of legal disputes by avoiding having a federal court guess on a question of state law and then perhaps be proved wrong when the state court in a later case decides the question of state law differently from the way the federal court did. Although the process can and does delay federal litigation somewhat, overall I think it's an efficient and sensible use of the resources of both courts. To meet the concern of burdening the state high court, I suggested we make the following modifications in the proposal. First we limited the process for accepting certification of questions of state law to requests from the federal circuit Courts of

Appeals or the highest court of the various states in order to avoid opening our-selves up to the dozens of U.S. District Court judges sitting in California send-ing us requests to resolve hundreds of legal questions. Even if we decline those requests—and there's never an obligation to accept them—it involves a certain amount of work to evaluate the request and decide whether we want to exercise our discretion to accept the request. Another requirement we wrote into our pro-cedure is that our court's answer to the question posed by the federal court has to be dispositive of the litigation. If it wouldn't be dispositive, then it's frankly not worth our while to undertake that task for them and render a purely advisory opinion. Third, and very importantly, we have made it clear that we retain the authority to rephrase the question that is referred to us. We may realize from our perspective that the question is phrased more narrowly than it need be and is really part of a somewhat larger question whose resolution would be far more helpful to the development of the law, benefitting not just the federal court in that case but also facilitating our own court's task of developing a jurisprudence of state law in that area. When we rephrase the question, it's up to the requesting court to accept our redefinition of the question or to withdraw its question. I don't know of any instance in which a federal court has ever withdrawn a re-quest because of our action in redefining the question.

I believe all of the certifications that we have accepted have been from the Ninth Circuit, except for one from the District of Columbia circuit. I could also see a situation arising, for instance, where the high court of New York is faced with a question of community property law. New York doesn't have community property law, so—in a marital dissolution proceeding that might involve New York parties who own community property in California—before the New York court would decide that case, it might very well want to have an answer to a complicated unresolved question of California community property law. The New York high court would want the California Supreme Court's answer, in-stead of their guessing at it and having a marital property division that turns out not to be equitable because they guessed wrong as to what was or was not com-munity property or the consequences of something being community property or not. That's the kind of example that could easily arise in a future case referred to us by another state high court. Roughly two-thirds of the requests submitted by the Ninth Circuit to the California Supreme Court to resolve a question of state law have been granted. We've rejected some requests where certification would be basically a theoretical exercise and our expending the effort to answer the question wouldn't truly resolve the federal dispute in question.

You're accepting approximately two-thirds of the requests. About how many requests are you getting—from the Ninth Circuit mainly?

There aren't all that many. I don't have up-to-date figures, but I can give you an approximation and indicate that we've probably had in the neighborhood of 40 requests from 1998 through last year.

How much of a task did you have persuading other colleagues that this was worth taking on?

There was some reluctance, but I think these limitations—in terms of confining it to the level of the federal circuit Court of Appeals or the high court of a state and letting us redefine the question—are what persuaded my colleagues. I'm glad we added those limitations, not just because they enabled us to all agree to adopt the certification process, but because they improve the system. I wouldn't want a system where the California Supreme Court was being barraged with questions from dozens and dozens of federal trial judges whose jurisdiction lies within California, let alone from district courts in other states.

What was the response of the greater legal community to this change?

Very pleased. There was an attorney, Jerome Braun, from San Francisco who was the leading advocate for certification. He met with me to persuade me to take up the cause and made a very convincing case for California joining the majority of state jurisdictions that accept such requests.

We talked about independent and adequate state grounds, but is it worth exploring as a separate question how your court and your colleagues, over the time that you served, viewed the U.S. Supreme Court and its rulings as worthy of attention compared to state precedents and rulings?

Certainly decisions of the U.S. Supreme Court were viewed as very important sources of precedent, but I should distinguish between the situation where a ruling by the federal high court was binding precedent on us and where it might only be something that was perhaps persuasive or perhaps not persuasive. I know that there were cases where we had U.S. Supreme Court authority cited to our court and declined to follow it where it wasn't binding. It was something that we looked at closely, but if we didn't feel it was persuasive we would not follow it, just as we might be faced with a situation where the overwhelming number of state high courts that had ruled on an issue had ruled a certain way and we found reason to go with the minority view.

How much variation was there among your colleagues in how they approached that matter of looking to the U.S. Supreme Court if it was an option rather than a requirement?

I don't recall any predisposition or propensity on the part of any individual justice to either slavishly or otherwise follow the lead of the U.S. Supreme Court. [Laughter] I think my colleagues and I all approached it on a case-by-case basis. "Well, fine, it comes from the U.S. Supreme Court. It's worth looking at, certainly, and in this case it makes sense to follow the high court but in that case it doesn't." We followed the same approach in considering the persuasiveness of rulings from the lower federal courts and from the high courts of other states. As I said previously, we would take wisdom from whatever source we could find it.

You were appointed to other committees at the federal level. Could you describe those briefly?

Yes. I had interaction with federal judges on many levels. In addition to co-chairing the California State-Federal Judicial Council, I was invited to address the Ninth Circuit judges at their annual meeting from time to time. We've already talked about the pro bono press conferences that I had with the chief judges of the U.S. District Court for the Northern District of California, where private firms signed up to commit billable hours to pro bono activity. I've mentioned, on the international level, Chief Justice Rehnquist appointing me to the joint Anglo-American Legal Exchange. I also was invited to participate in the Canadian Legal Exchange, but it didn't fit in with my schedule. Judge Clifford Wallace, a senior chief judge of the Ninth Circuit, and I participated in a video conferencing educational program with judges in Thailand. The State Department sent numerous delegations from China, Yemen, Australia, Canada, and other countries to California to meet with state and federal judges.

My most extensive contacts with the federal judiciary were through my service, by appointment of Chief Justice Rehnquist, on the Committee on Federal-State Jurisdiction, first of all. The name of the committee obviously illustrates its purpose—to attempt on a national level, somewhat paralleling what I described as the work of the California State-Federal Judicial Council, to coordinate the areas of common responsibility of federal and state courts. Three other Chief Justices of state courts and I served on this committee with a number of federal judges. We studied various matters and made recommendations, and because we were a committee of the Judicial Conference of the United States, our recommendations made their way up to the entire Judicial Conference for action and possible implementation. Subsequently, Chief Justice Roberts appointed me as the sole state judge on the Committee on Rules of Practice and Procedure of the Judicial Conference of the United States. That involved a lot of esoteric federal legal procedure that I hadn't had much occasion to give thought to since my law school days. I enjoyed working with quite an erudite group of federal judges. There were also interactions at our meetings of the Conference of Chief Justices where we would invite a couple of federal judges and they would make presentations to us.

Talk a bit more about that body if you would. I know we mentioned it in other sessions, but first of all how did you come to be selected as head of that group for a time?

I served one year as president of the Conference of Chief Justices, and I don't really know why I was selected, but I had made various presentations to them and was urged to put myself up for that position. As I said to you, I engaged in the difficult task of also hosting the annual meeting of the group at the same time, so that was a very, very busy year.

It is a body in which the Chief Justices truly learn a lot from each other in terms of mutual problems, solutions, and best practices. I told you about my convincing Governor Schwarzenegger to address the group. There were many enjoyable social activities in the evening in addition to the educational programs involving exchanges of views on substantive legal questions, dealing with budget crises, administrative reforms, and a variety of access-to-justice issues. We met at the same time, for one of our two annual meetings, with COSCA, the Conference of State Court Administrators. I found that working together with them was very worthwhile. They are professional administrators, and many of the chiefs—probably most of them—are chiefs for a very short period of time and haven't necessarily acquired much administrative experience during their judicial career. In California, the Chief Justice of the state occupies that position for the duration of that person's tenure on the California Supreme Court. However, in some states, the Chief Justice position rotates every two years among the justices of the court, which is unusual, but four or six years is not uncommon. West Virginia is one year only. I think it's probably not by accident but rather by design that in some states, in order not to give the judiciary the role of an equal partner in the tripartite arrangement among the three branches of government, the Chief Justice position by law is one that is of short duration. That's maybe a cynical view, but I came to that conclusion.

*What use did you make of the presidency of the Conference of Chief Justices as
a bully pulpit?*

I certainly did make use of that. I believe the presentations I made helped
convince some of my colleagues to take certain action regarding CCJ's access-
to-justice committee, such as furthering the efforts of what are called collaborative justice courts, and also in setting up complex-litigation courts. I shared
some of the California judiciary's occasionally innovative budget crisis solutions with other justices, and received numerous phone calls and several visits
from some of them to California to see what we were doing. It was a nice illustration, again, of what I have mentioned a couple times—Justice Brandeis' observation of the then-48 states serving as laboratories. We all learn from each
other—shared experiences, best practices, solutions.

I don't want it to seem as if the Conference of Chiefs was all hard work.
The host states always went through a lot of effort to have daytime programs for
spouses and very enjoyable evening events after our educational programs. I
attended the winter meeting of the Conference of Chief Justices in Indianapolis
shortly after I had become chief. Being an active runner, the thought had immediately occurred to me of trying to get permission to run the Indy 500, just a lap
or two. I was turned down when I called. Then I wrote a letter and was turned
down. I said to Barbara, "Nothing ventured, nothing gained," and brought along
my running shoes, running shorts, and tank top when the chiefs were brought to
the race site in Indianapolis as one of our social outings. Once there, I persuaded
the authorities to let me run "the bricks." Although they relented, they said,
"There's one condition. We have to send a pacer car around with you." I said,
"That's fine. My condition is that my wife gets to sit in the pacer car and take a
photo." [Laughter] So I have a wonderful photograph of me rounding the slightly banked bend where they have a tall pole listing the numbers of the passing
cars. My main impression was seeing this august group of Chief Justices, predominantly gentlemen older than myself, bundled up against the cold, shaking
their heads and clucking away, "All right, who's this nutty new Chief Justice
from California?" [Laughter]

Through the Conference of Chief Justices I also had some dealings with the
American Bar Association. There was a good working relationship between the
two organizations. Generally speaking, I would say that California was truly
viewed as a leader, not just because of its size and population, but more importantly in its role as often being on the leading edge of questions of law and in
dealing with budget crises and engaging in innovative measures to increase access to justice.

You asked a moment ago about a bully pulpit, and some of my activities at the Conference of Chief Justices and the National Center for State Courts led to my being invited to visit and address the judiciary of other states. I was asked by the Chief Justice of the Massachusetts Supreme Judicial Court, Margaret Marshall, to address an assemblage of Massachusetts judges, and I also addressed a conference of Arizona judges. I believe that the Chief Judge of New York State, Judith Kaye, was instrumental in having me invited to deliver the Brennan Lecture at NYU.

Talk a little about that speech, if you would.

It emphasized many of the themes you and I have talked about in terms of independence of the judiciary and the fact that, although we usually speak of independence of the judiciary from the standpoint of decisional independence, that's just one side of the coin. The other side is institutional independence, which implies the need for stable and adequate funding and lack of interference by the other two branches of government in the operations of the judiciary. I related some of the experience of California in that regard, in terms of how the judiciary has interacted with the other two branches. The Brennan lecture gave rise to some other speaking engagements and recognitions. I already mentioned my address to the American Academy of Arts and Sciences, which touched upon some aspects of judicial independence but focused largely on the initiative process in California and what was to be learned from it and what was to be avoided.

Congratulations, by the way, on your induction into the AAAS. What did that signify to you?

It was a very impressive ceremony in a wood-paneled hall, an institution that was founded by John Adams, our second U.S. President, and that apparently is quite select in its membership, which encompasses a broad array of disciplines in the arts and letters and sciences and includes many individuals of national and international renown. I was honored to be asked to be one of the three or four members of my entering class to give an address to the group on a topic of my choosing. Preparing for that presentation led me to examine and develop my views in the area of initiative reform, which I know is something that you and I will talk about before our sessions are completed.

Some of this exposure, through the Conference of Chief Justices and otherwise, ended up bringing about some very nice awards and recognitions. It really took me out of my own jurisdiction which, given the size of California, was quite large enough for me, and put me on a larger stage for a number of years.

Which of these awards and honors and writings of yours stand out in your own mind as important?

In terms of the writings, the *NYU Law Review* did publish my Brennan Lecture. I wrote on some similar themes in *Daedalus*, the journal of the American Academy of Arts and Sciences, and the Boalt *California Law Review* and the *Golden Gate University Law Review*. My *Stanford Law Review* piece was focused on the initiative process, and I ended up writing an op-ed piece in the *San Francisco Chronicle* on that topic. I also was asked to co-author an op-ed piece in the *New York Times* with the Chief Justice of New Hampshire, John Broderick, on access-to-justice issues and the problem of unrepresented litigants in civil cases. These were time-consuming tasks, but I felt a certain responsibility to speak out on such issues.

You asked about awards and honors. There were dozens, and I won't drag us through all of them. I'll mention some, primarily those that involved recognition on a national level. The Rehnquist Award may have been the first one on a national level. The ceremony was very impressive, as it was held in the Great Hall of the United States Supreme Court in front of the open doors to the courtroom, with Chief Justice Rehnquist personally conferring the award. I found it rather interesting to come back to the high court in that capacity. I don't believe I'd been back there since I had argued cases before that court as a young deputy attorney general in the late 1960s and early 1970s. I could not resist, after Chief Justice Rehnquist made his opening remarks, responding that it was a pleasure to be back in that magnificent structure and be able to speak without interruption for 15 minutes, without being questioned, [Laughter] and second, not have to worry about my knees shaking either. He took that in good humor.

What sort of person was he, in your view?

He was very self-effacing and had a wry sense of humor. He was not by any means humorless. He seemed to have great affection for the state courts—that was quite apparent.

Among the other awards I received from national organizations are the American Bar Association's John Marshall Award; induction into the Warren E. Burger Society; the Legal Writing Institute's Golden Pen Award; the American College of Trial Lawyers' Samuel Gates Award; a couple of awards from the American Judicature Society—the Opperman Award and in another year the

Herbert Harley Award; and one from the National Association of Women Judges. I'll just mention some of the other awards that are particularly meaningful to me. I received one just this year from the California Newspaper Publishers Association, recognizing my efforts to open up court proceedings and records. Of course, your own Institute of Governmental Studies' Distinguished Service Award was another significant recognition I received this year. The Consumer Attorneys of California conferred a couple of awards on me, a civil justice award and a justice of the year award. I twice received the California Judges Association President's Award, in 2010 and 30 years earlier; the Roger Traynor Award from the Consumer Attorneys Association of Los Angeles; the Champion of Justice Award from the Bar Association of San Francisco; the St. Thomas More Law Honor Society's Medallion Award; the State Bar of California's Bernard E. Witkin Medal; another award from the press, the James Madison Freedom of Information Award from the Society of Professional Journalists; the Judge Learned Hand Award—anyway, I've gone on more than I should have.

I guess it is a particular tribute that there are six awards that bear my name as the Chief Justice Ronald M .George Award conferred by various organizations—for example, the State Bar's Ronald M. George Public Lawyer of the Year Award, a Beverly Hills Bar Association award, and from a Central Valley legal services organization the Ronald M. George Equal Justice Award—and now a couple buildings. [Laughter]

I wanted to ask you about that very thing. While you were off in Antarctica last December, Governor Arnold Schwarzenegger took steps to name the Civic Center Complex here in San Francisco after you. Please tell me, first of all, how you learned the news.

Actually, I learned of it while I was in Antarctica. The governor's office managed to get an e-mail to me, and I read about the naming two days after the governor issued the December 21 executive order—a wonderful gesture! I'm deeply appreciative of it. That was quite a surprise to me, to be off in Antarctica and find out that one square block of the San Francisco Civic Center, in the form of these two buildings, would bear my name. Just about two weeks ago there was a formal ceremony officially rededicating the buildings with signage on the exterior of the buildings at both the McAllister Street and Golden Gate Avenue entrances and plaques in the interior. As I said at the ceremony in my somewhat irreverent remarks, "Given the reality that many individuals who are accorded recognition for their professional achievements do not receive it during their lifetime, it's particularly gratifying to me to receive this honor premortem rather than postmortem." It was a very nice ceremony.

Your successor as Chief Justice and her colleagues and the members of the Judicial Council were on hand to help dedicate that.

They were there and were very generous in their remarks about me and about the governor's action. My successor officiated at the ceremony. I want to voice my great appreciation to Governor Schwarzenegger and the Department of General Services for carrying out this project and allocating executive branch funds for it, as well as to legislative members and staff who supported it, and to those persons in the judicial branch who helped design and install the plaques and inscriptions.

Having been a "lobbyist" in your time, you know how hard these things are to accomplish. Hearty congratulations for the naming of the building. Is there anything else you'd like to mention in that vein?

No, I've probably talked about it too much already, but I'm very moved by having this recognition—hopefully not to the point of acquiring—as one of my college roommates, now a psychiatrist, humorously cautioned—an "edifice complex."

I sincerely feel that these awards and the renaming of the Civic Center Complex reflect achievements in which I may have been the first person in the parade, but they represent the hard work, dedication, and loyalty of countless individuals with whom I was privileged to work—in the California Supreme Court, the Judicial Council, the Administrative Office of the Courts, and the statewide judicial branch as a whole, as well as with members of the legislature and their staff, various governors and executive staff, and our justice system partners, whom I've identified in our earlier conversations. These various awards recognize collective efforts that have brought great and enduring benefit to the judicial branch and, most importantly, to the public we serve. To me, that's what this is all about in the end, providing fair and accessible justice to the people of California.

###

Chapter 19

The Historic Supreme Court Building and Art Collection; The Decision to Retire
November 16, 2011

I'd like to start off today with a different kind of subject and ask you to talk a little about the career and contributions of your wife, Barbara George.

Yes, I'd be happy to. Barbara certainly turned out to be the right person at the right place at the right time, not only in my personal life and my professional career, but for her major role in enhancing the structures that house the California Supreme Court and the Judicial Council. Barbara's involvement with the court buildings began in the early 1990s when Chief Justice Lucas asked whether she would be willing to install the Supreme Court's photography collection in the temporary quarters that were occupied by the court on Folsom Street for a ten-year period following the 1989 Loma Prieta earthquake. This was a display of photographs of each of the more than 100 individuals who had served as justices of the court since its inception in 1850, as well as a number of historic group photographs. When this collection was later reinstalled in the court's historic quarters, it stretched the length of a city block along both sides of the fourth-floor corridor.

It bothered me that the court had been unable to locate a photograph of one of the justices, Justice Charles Bryan, who served from 1854 to 1855, when he was succeeded by Justice—later Chief Justice—David Terry, whom I previously mentioned in conjunction with our discussion of his colorful career involving his fatally shooting U.S. Senator David Broderick in a duel. Soon after I became

Chief Justice, I assigned one of my eager research attorneys, David Miller, to try to track down a photograph of Justice Bryan, assuming one in fact existed.

I understand it was quite a feat to locate this photograph.

It was. The tale of this effort to trace the path of Justice Bryan was full of false leads through correspondence, phone inquiries, and other research that involved various states. At one point it yielded a photograph that turned out to be of another Charles Bryan. This detective work finally did lead us to an authentic photograph of the elusive justice. The course of David Miller's laborious and ultimately successful efforts proved to be most interesting and was published in a monograph titled "The Search for Justice Bryan," which was included in the annual yearbook of the California Supreme Court Historical Society. As a result of this endeavor, the court acquired a photograph that replaced the framed piece of cardboard bearing biographical data related to the absent Justice Bryan.

During the court's ten-year absence from the historic Earl Warren Building that structure was retrofitted, and the Hiram Johnson Building rose as a new fourteen-story structure housing the Administrative Office of the Courts and local offices of the governor and other elected state officials. The retrofit of the historic building was a truly herculean effort, with great credit due to everyone involved: the architectural firm of Skidmore, Owings & Merrill and the project architect, Craig Hartman, Clark Construction Group, Hines Interest Group, HSH Design/Build Inc., Page & Turnbull, the San Francisco State Building Authority, and the California Department of General Services. They all balanced the need to preserve what was historically worth keeping and at the same time rendered the building suitable for twenty-first-century use in terms of safety, technology, and other needs. They succeeded in blending in the historic structure with the construction of the new fourteen-story building. I thought they did a masterful job.

I'll mention briefly—because I think it's relevant to what Barbara accomplished in the two buildings—that she had 27 years' experience in her Los Angeles business, which was called George and Jacobson Interiors, with her longtime friend and business partner, Nancy Jacobson. The partnership was known for its interior design and art consulting services. Her participation in that business terminated upon our move to San Francisco. Barbara also had involvements with the Art Museum Council of the Los Angeles County Museum of Art, while bearing the major responsibility for raising our three sons. After our move up north, she entered the two-year training program of the San Francisco Fine Arts Museums, the de Young and the Legion of Honor, in order to become a docent. Barbara received an appointment in 1994 from Governor Wilson to the California Arts Council, a governmental agency to which she was reappointed by Governor Davis, serving a total of three terms.

May I ask for more detail about how she became involved with the California Arts Council, as you say, appointed by two governors? How did that affiliation begin?

Governor Wilson knew Barbara from the prior relationship that I had with the governor and that had developed into a social relationship between the Wilsons and us. The governor was well aware of Barbara's education, interest, and experience in the arts, so I suppose she seemed to be a natural appointment. Her peers elected her chair for three successive years, and she completed her service on the council in 2006. Under her stewardship, the California Arts Council adopted a policy favoring the installation of publicly accessible art in all future state buildings. In fact, Barbara acted as an unpaid volunteer, not only in her efforts to bring art into the two buildings that now bear my name, then known as the San Francisco Civic Center Complex—the Earl Warren Building and the Hiram Johnson Building—but she also was asked by state agencies to participate on the art committees for other state buildings. I recall the principal ones were the new Los Angeles headquarters of the California State Department of Transportation and the renovated Junipero Serra State Office Building, also in downtown Los Angeles. Barbara volunteered her services for these projects, receiving no compensation.

I previously described to you in our conversations the experience I had in Sacramento as she left Senator Burton's office and I simultaneously entered that office, both of us engaged in parallel, and hopefully not conflicting, lobbying efforts, trying to secure funding for our respective entities. Aware of the benefits of legislative involvement in obtaining adequate funding for the Arts Council, legislators were invited to participate in presentations of grants in order to observe first hand and hear stories from the grateful recipients throughout the state. Senate President pro Tem Don Perata and Barbara held a joint press conference announcing California Arts Council grants that had been awarded in his district. He was very pleased to do that and ended up personally bestowing the awards, as did another legislator, Mark Leno. Barbara still remembers how extremely moved some of the legislators appeared to be by these ceremonies.

Barbara's direct involvement in our buildings began after I became chief in 1996, well before the court began preparing to move back to the historic building on McAllister in 1999. Barbara asked me with a professional interest, "Is there an arts budget for this building?" I said, "I don't know. I'll have to inquire." Public projects involving the federal government, county and local government, and the private sector generally allocate a certain percentage of the cost of construction and furnishings to art. I made inquiry, and I got back to Barbara with the answer: "Zero." Asking advice from the staff of the California Arts Council on whom to approach, Barbara discussed with the contractor and the developer how to obtain an allocation of funds. She eventually received $1.5 million through various funds that had been allocated for the project through the issuance of bonds and organized an art selection committee for the two buildings. She chaired that committee, and among its members were my Supreme Court colleague Justice Ming Chin, and Presiding Justice Anthony Kline from the First District Court of Appeal, Janet Dreisen-Rappaport from the California Arts Council, Stan Moy of Finger and Moy Architects representing the San Francisco State Building Authority, James Buie from the Hines Interest Group HSH Design/Build, and Craig Hartman of Skidmore, Owings & Merrill. Michele DeAngelus and Marc Pally were hired as art consultants to the committee. The committee proceeded to purchase, in some cases commissioning, various works of art, also in some instances obtaining donations of artwork. The art included paintings, photography, sculpture, and historic items. Our son Andrew contributed several framed photographs from some of his gallery exhibitions.

In the course of the retrofit of the Supreme Court's courtroom between 1989 and 1999, the demolition and roof reconstruction uncovered some of the remodeling that had taken place in the 1950s. At that time, the new United Nations building in New York was the architectural inspiration of the decade, which unfortunately led to the lowering of the beautiful coffered high-domed ceiling constructed in the 1920s, and to blocking the skylight. The walls of the courtroom were covered with naugahyde and brass reveals were inserted. A huge mural extended across the area behind the bench, painted in the classical style of the 1920s by noted artist Arthur Mathews. The mural had been taken down and replaced by a royal blue velvet curtain. The Commonwealth, as the mural was called, was misplaced and has not been found to date. The art committee organized a competition to commission a new mural. More than 80 applications were received; three finalists were chosen, and the final decision was left to the justices of the California Supreme Court. They chose Marin artist Willard Dixon's depiction of the eastern face of the Sierra Nevada as a suitable metaphor for the strength and fortitude of the court. It is a majestic painting of a scene that is conducive to having a calming effect on the sometimes anxious attorneys who face the mural during their oral arguments before the court— more calming than some frenetic abstract modern piece of art might be.

The artwork selected by the committee appears throughout the two buildings, both in public and private areas. The efforts of Barbara and her committee members were very much appreciated by the more than 2,100 persons who work there. On one occasion when she was there with the crew installing some art in the Great Hall that connects the two buildings, an employee from an executive branch agency approached Barbara enthusiastically and asked if she could give her a hug, telling her, "You have transformed a cold impersonal structure into a warm and friendly working environment." The art installation really has meant a lot to the individuals who work in the buildings—I have heard that countless times.

What's the secret to her success?

Barbara is extremely creative and also receptive to the views of others. She worked well with a committee that had very strong personalities on it and strong views when it comes to art. However collegial individuals may be in their professional relations, when it comes to selecting artwork the road can be quite rocky. In addition, there were 2,100 opinions from the employees—if there was something they deemed unacceptable, they were not reticent in expressing their views. The result was a very fine collection of art for the buildings. Barbara had encountered that trait in her clients while engaged in her own private decorating business. When she installed art for various firms, and especially law firms, the most heated disputes would erupt among people over the artwork—apparently more than over the professional differences they might have.

A small book was published that encompasses most of the artwork and some of the architectural modifications, entitled *Art & Architecture—San Francisco Civic Center Complex*. It's filled with illustrations of the art and a description of what the retrofit involved. Governor Gray Davis wrote a welcome, and I wrote a foreword to the booklet. I should mention by the way that much of the art acquired by the committee has appreciated greatly in value, so it turned out to be a very fine investment for the State of California.

I mentioned to you previously that when Barbara learned of the extensive and fast-paced schedule of my intended visits to the courts in the 58 counties, she quickly dropped her plan to accompany me and substituted an offer to assemble a collection of photographs of historic courthouses from each of the counties. She was greatly assisted in this endeavor by A.O.C. staff member James Carroll and by the late James Pfeiffer, the husband of the A.O.C.'s Bonnie Hough, to whom I've made reference in conjunction with our self-help programs for unrepresented litigants. Jim Pfeiffer was also the former director of the Foundation of the State Bar and of the California Supreme Court Historical Society. Their task, in assembling this collection of photographs, proved to be both difficult and time-consuming. Writing letters requesting a black-and-white photograph of each county's historic courthouse yielded frustrating efforts—

often a few glossy, full-color photos of modern structures. Ultimately it took as long for Barbara to assemble a complete 58-county collection of an historic courthouse photograph from each county as it did for me to actually complete my round of visits—namely one entire year.

The collection is displayed in duplicate at two locations, outside the Judicial Council's boardroom and also in the fifth-floor hallway of the Supreme Court. That collection was published by the California Supreme Court Historical Society in another small booklet that I referred to when we were discussing my visits to the 58 counties. It's entitled simply *California Court Houses*. I already mentioned another contribution Barbara made to the aesthetics of our quarters at the court by acquiring artwork on loan from the Oakland Museum of California for the Chief Justice's chambers.

Barbara developed a close working relationship with many of the court staff, in particular with Carmen Kissinger, the deputy court administrator/clerk of the California Supreme Court. That relationship encompassed not only continuing care of the artwork but also a role in the general upkeep and improvement of the two joined buildings and their landscaping. Betsy Everdell, a private landscaper, produced an excellent design for the gardens on McAllister Street that was very much in keeping with the beaux arts architecture. Barbara also became involved with the Northern California Cancer Center, now known as the Cancer Prevention Institute of California, an organization dedicated to disseminating cancer and health education information. Every six weeks she and the center would arrange for a lecture to be given by outside experts—some of the finest physicians in the Bay Area—for the employees of the buildings and other persons from the surrounding area.

Barbara had another involvement arising out of our relationships with the governors whom we came to know. She attended the annual governor's women's conference organized by three of California's first ladies, Gayle Wilson, Sharon Davis, and Maria Shriver Schwarzenegger—and, as I mentioned, served on Maria Shriver's Minerva Committee that nominated women of achievement for special recognition at the California Museum for History, Women, and the Arts. Through her work on the California Arts Council with Malissa Feruzzi Shriver, the wife of Bobby Shriver—a city councilman in Santa Monica and the brother of Maria Shriver—I came to know him and participated in a Rand Institute conference that he and former Los Angeles County Supervisor Ed Edelman organized on the subject of the homeless and their interaction with the court system. I mention this in part to show how there were these intersecting relationships that both Barbara and I developed that went back and forth between her interests, specifically in art and design, and mine involving the judiciary, the law, and government. Also Barbara and her friend Phyllis Epstein founded a nonprofit organization called the California Music Project, an ongoing effort to restore music education to California's public schools.

One thing that pleased me very much and certainly has pleased Barbara as well is the fact that, in grateful recognition of Barbara's many contributions to the art in the two adjacent court buildings, a plaque was installed in the Great Hall. It bears a photograph of Barbara and me under the caption "Art and Justice." I want to read these two paragraphs of it to you:

> The art collection that graces these buildings has its origins in the leadership of one individual, Barbara George, wife of Chief Justice Ronald M. George and former chairperson of the California Arts Council. Mrs. George assembled an unprecedented collection of court related material culminating in a series of photographs of California's historic county courthouses. Her leadership as chairperson of the art committee for this complex resulted in a magnificent public art collection by California artists whose visions and styles reflect the rich diversity of our state. Thank you, Mrs. George.

> Dedicated October 28, 2010. This recognition was made possible by contributions from the California Supreme Court Historical Society, the California Bar Foundation, and the Ralph and Shirley Shapiro Family Foundation.

A few weeks ago, the Administrative Office of the Courts renamed a competition that had been organized for children who have had experience in California's court system as "The Barbara George Art and Poetry Contest." Just as recently as yesterday, Barbara was at the A.O.C. playing the role of judge herself—on this occasion, of the art and poetry submitted to the competition that now bears her name.

I would conclude, with regard to Barbara's contributions, that the plaque really symbolizes—under "art and justice," but in so many other ways—the fact that Barbara, for 46 years of marriage, and throughout my professional career, has certainly been the closest of partners in so many ventures and ways.

It's striking that several of her recent efforts have focused on public education. You mentioned the music project and the recently renamed art and poetry contest as examples. That's been a strong thrust of your own interest in recent years—public education, civics education—and I note what a close partnership you have had, one that crosses over in so many ways. How do you think about that yourself?

I doubt that we came to our marriage decades ago having identified all these similar interests that we shared. It's likely that through our communication, through our shared experiences, we have concurrently developed and evolved interests that have crossed the lines of our own primary endeavors, and that we each have grown and benefited from that exchange of shared interests.

What is she working on now, may I ask?

She is back to interior design in terms of our own home expansion project of this year. That has almost been a full-time activity, although she is still busy with the California Music Project and currently with this art and poetry contest. She is constantly being asked to involve herself in various community efforts. I am confident that she's not destined to have a whole lot of free time, just sitting back, although she manages to do an incredible amount of reading, being a member of book clubs both in San Francisco and Los Angeles. But we love, of course, to travel, to engage in various cultural pursuits together, and to spend time with our two young granddaughters, so it's a very full life, that's for sure, for both of us.

There are some other substantive things we want to talk about before we close our series of interviews. Let us begin to broach the subject of how and when you began to contemplate the possibility of retiring as Chief Justice of California. What is that story from the very beginning?

The approach of my seventieth birthday last year in March focused my attention on a question that had recently been posed by my family. This was basically, "What more do you hope to accomplish if you file for reelection this year for another twelve-year term?"

As we know, that reelection would have happened in November 2010. Who asked you this question, specifically? Do you remember how it first came up?

It was posed by our eldest son, Eric, but I think we all began to talk about that. What would be the benefits of re-upping? I tend to approach many things on a cost-benefits analysis and started mulling over the pros and cons. When pressed for an answer by Barbara and our sons, all I could really come up with was: "Well, yes, I've authored hundreds of judicial opinions and overseen major administrative reforms in the judicial system. I suppose I'll enjoy writing more opinions and continuing to refine and preserve what I've already done administratively." But I also began to think—without being overly dramatic—of the increasingly demanding sacrifices that I felt I had had to make not only for myself but also for my family, the things that I had given up because, basically, serving as Chief Justice of this state, in addition to my responsibilities at the court in doing my one-seventh share of the opinions, had been almost a 24/7 type of total commitment, at least the way I had defined the duties of Chief Justice in terms of how I chose to perform them. I didn't see any way that this schedule, this workload, would lessen. It was going to continue, with all the difficulties in Sacramento reflecting the state's economic situation and its impact on the judicial branch. I had always loved to read, and I found myself fortunate if I could steal away five or six minutes of pleasure reading unrelated to the law before I turned the lights off, doing so mainly to try to clear my mind from the day's events and tomorrow's. I knew there would continue to be a steady stream of crises in the affairs of state in Sacramento. I realized that although I always managed to carve out vacation time to engage in my love of travel, usually it was with legal briefs and administrative memos packed in the suitcase and receiving FedEx packages, e-mails, and cell phone calls on my time away from court.

I just didn't see that schedule improving, including not having as much time as we wanted with family—our three sons and other family members, including but not limited to our little granddaughters. With all that in mind, the bottom line became: I've engaged in 45 years of public service, 38 of which have been as a judge; now it's time for self-service! Although I really gravitated in that direction, I felt I could only take that step if I could leave the judicial branch in a condition in which it was not in great peril, given the very drastic cuts that had been imposed in the judicial branch budget during the preceding year and that year, 2010, as well. I felt I could not otherwise pursue the thought of retiring.

As I mentioned previously, with the hard efforts of myself and others, and with good fortune, we were able to restore about $300 million to the 2010–2011 budget of the judicial branch through a combination of my rather impassioned plea to Governor Schwarzenegger and concurrent action by the legislature. I then was satisfied that I would not be leaving the judiciary in a lurch and that I could depart in good conscience. Once I accomplished what I set out to do concerning the cuts to our budget, I truly felt free to do what I could already tell was very much my inclination—to go while I thought I was in a position to do so, and to leave things in the good hands of a worthy successor. I felt I would be leaving when I was at the top of my game or—to use one of the many favorite expressions I recall from my late mother-in-law—leaving while the music was playing.

What were your family members saying?

The only ones I consulted were Barbara and our three sons, no one else. They urged me to move on. They thought I had accomplished everything I might wish to accomplish and that it was time to kick back and enjoy the other aspects of life that went beyond one's work responsibilities and professional commitments.

As I stated in the written notice of retirement that I ultimately issued, I found it both difficult and liberating to relinquish a position of responsibility of this sort. I'm sure that is usually the case in both the public and the private sphere. I certainly felt there were no greener pastures of employment beckoning me. I always stated that and felt that way. But the prospect of leisure time to enjoy these other aspects of a full life was truly irresistible at this point. Retirement would have been a difficult choice only if I were one of those persons who lack a life—and lack interests—outside of his or her professional life.

I felt that the age of 70 years was certainly not too old for someone blessed with good health to perform the functions of Chief Justice of California, but at the same time it was an age young enough to pursue the richness of a life outside the law that I truly relished having before me. That was the perspective I had. I had served the third-longest tenure among those 27 persons who had occupied the office of Chief Justice in the history of California.

What were the personal negatives to this plan, if any?

I reflected upon whether I would miss the stimulation of working on the complex and significant legal issues that reach the California Supreme Court, and whether I would miss working with legislators and governors in Sacramento. Because even though it was onerous to lead the judiciary through constant crises in the state Capitol, the victories brought about reforms that will benefit the judiciary and the people of the State of California for many decades to come. There have been few things as satisfying as winning some of those hard-fought battles. I wondered, would I miss that?

And yet, I knew that I could fill my life with many other interesting pursuits that I had had to put aside. All I had to do, I realized, was pursue the existing interests in my life that I had had to subordinate due to the press of my professional responsibilities. All those other things were out there waiting for me, and I knew that, for me, in the end, the transition would not be difficult. I knew that if I left, I would have no desire to sit as an assigned judge or a private judge, or to engage in the private practice of law or alternative dispute resolution. Already, I don't have enough time to do as much of all the many wonderful things that I want to do in retirement. It has been an easy adjustment getting back into a life of carefree travel, hiking, reading, and cultural events. I'm not at all worried about filling up my time.

Barbara says my new life, with the absence of stress and pressures, is typified when I check my cell phone every two or three days and receive the prerecorded message: "You have no messages." [Laughter] That is in sharp contrast to the string of six or seven long messages that I used to find several times a day.

You mentioned that, last year as you were considering retirement, there was a forthcoming retention election. How did you go about deciding the timing of your retirement?

I felt that with his track record of taking very seriously the task of appointing judges to the bench, Governor Schwarzenegger would appoint a suitable successor. I had total confidence that he would take this task very seriously and in a nonpolitical manner, and I wanted to give him enough time to make the appointment of the new Chief Justice. In that regard, I should mention the somewhat unusual provisions that govern the appointment not only of a Chief Justice but of any member of the California Supreme Court or the Court of Appeal. The procedure is set forth in article VI of the constitution, section 16. It provides, in this language:

> Within 30 days before August 16 preceding the expiration of the judge's term, a judge of the Supreme Court or a court of appeal may file a declaration of candidacy to succeed to the office presently held by the judge. If the declaration is not filed, the Governor, before September 16 shall nominate a candidate. At the next general election, only the candidate so declared or nominated may appear on the ballot, which shall present the question whether the candidate shall be elected. The candidate shall be elected upon receiving a majority of the votes on the question.

The same requirement of an evaluation of the judicial candidate applies, to be conducted by the Commission on Judicial Nominees Evaluation of the State Bar, and for its report to be considered at a hearing to be held by the Commission on Judicial Appointments, which as we'll discuss had to convene to consider the nomination before my successor's name could be placed on the November 2010 ballot.

Your thinking, in other words, was to allow enough time for all of this to transpire before the election?

Yes. By the same token, I did not wish to create an excessively long period of uncertainty in terms of the succession of a new Chief Justice. I also wanted to minimize the period during which I would be a lame duck with the usual disabilities that attend that situation. All of these factors came together as I mulled things over. I made a tentative decision that I would let my term expire without filing for reelection, and allow Governor Schwarzenegger to nominate my successor. But I thought since this would be a very significant decision for me and my family, I wanted to let it gel in my mind for a few weeks before finalizing it. With all of those considerations in mind as well as the circumstance that the filing period was to commence Monday July 19, I decided to leave the announcement of my retirement to the last Wednesday preceding that date—so that I could collectively inform my six colleagues at the court's weekly petition conference before notifying the governor and making a public announcement.

Before you describe that—and I would very much like to hear it—you stated on other occasions that the trip to Lake Tahoe with your family, the week before that, was the moment to decide for sure. But how sure was it in your own mind by then, and what happened up there?

It was probably sure beyond a reasonable doubt. [Laughter] But there was still the need for me to finalize it as absolutely certain. The opportunity to be up there, away from the press of daily court business, confirmed to me intuitively that this was the proper time for me to leave office and enjoy other aspects of life, and the proper time to announce this decision. The next petition conference—which was the last one before the start of the 30-day filing period—was July 14. Of course, I found this timing to be quite fortuitous, that date being Bastille Day, a day of liberation—with the added element of a nod to the heritage of my late French father, who had passed away at the age of 101 a few years earlier. It just worked out that way. I mentioned to you previously that he was very much on my mind, as was my late mother. They both traveled to San Francisco to see me sworn in as Chief Justice, which of course was a rare joy for a parent. Everything just came together at the right time.

Whom did you tell first of this decision?

Of course, I told Barbara and our three sons in advance of the July 14, 2010, conference. I also tipped off, just the evening before, a couple of my senior attorney staff members and both of my judicial assistants, so they wouldn't learn of it only as my judicial colleagues filed out of the petition conference astounded at the news, as I knew they would be. I also alerted the court's Clerk/Administrator, Fritz Ohlrich, and the A.O.C. leadership, Bill Vickrey and

Ron Overholt, that preceding evening. I knew that my announcement would be a shock to most persons, because all of my colleagues on the court and on the Judicial Council, and everyone in the hierarchy of the A.O.C., had always assumed that I would probably be the last person to go, that I would leave feet first with my boots on and never retire as long as I could perform my duties. But for all the right reasons, this was the right time to go, so I did pick the July 14 conference day on which to announce my decision.

I deliberately did not bring up my retirement during the informal part of the weekly conference that I always reserved for exchanging news and views, because I felt it would distract all seven of us from focusing and voting on the 200-300 petitions that we had before us that morning. When we finished up with our work and my six colleagues were gathering up their papers and starting to get out of their seats at the conference table, I said, "Wait a moment. There's one other matter I need to discuss with you." When I informed my colleagues of my news, they all thought that this was one of the little jokes or quips that I often would share with them. I know Justice Kennard voiced that sentiment. It was only when I repeatedly assured them I was not joking and handed them each a copy of the written statement I had prepared for release and asked them to read it—which they silently did for the next couple of minutes—that the six of them realized I would not file for reelection by the fast approaching mid-August deadline and would let my term expire on January 2, 2011. It took reading the statement to overcome their initial disbelief and to realize that this was for real. The statement that I handed to my colleagues had been crafted in the preceding couple of weeks without any hints to my staff, so I had enlisted Barbara's typing skills. The resulting reaction was quite emotional and, I will say, heartwarming. There were actual tears, and I don't use that word loosely, as well as some hugs and generous words of praise. I need to add—without wanting to be grandiose about this—that there was an immediate sense of impending historic change in the court. I realized, as I discussed with you previously, that any change in the composition of the seven-justice court inevitably alters the atmosphere, the dynamics, and the chemistry of the court in very subtle, undefinable ways, whether it's the departure of a Chief Justice or of an associate justice of the court—even a new associate justice joining the court alters the entire court in undefinable ways.

What did your written statement say?

It covered much of what I just went over with you. It started out by noting that I would be informing the governor that day that I would conclude my service with my current term of office and would not be seeking reelection. I expressed my gratitude for the privilege and opportunity of serving the people of the state and my great appreciation to the four governors who had entrusted me with the responsibility of judicial office, Governor Reagan, Governor Brown, Governor Deukmejian, and Governor Wilson. I stated that I couldn't imagine a more rewarding experience than engaging in a common effort to give meaning to the rule of law by collaboratively crafting judicial opinions, which by the conclusion of my term would span 50 volumes of the official reports. The written statement also noted that I took great pride in my achievements on the administrative side of my duties as Chief Justice, that since my appointment as Chief Justice it had been a great pleasure for me to work directly with three governors—Governor Wilson, Governor Davis, and Governor Schwarzenegger—as well as with successive legislatures, and that with their assistance we had truly created a judicial branch in meaning and function as opposed to what had existed merely in name and theory. Then I noted the personal considerations that I just went over with you. My written statement concluded with the observation that I was leaving office at the expiration of my current term but with complete confidence that Governor Schwarzenegger would appoint a successor as Chief Justice who would meet the very high standards of the judicial appointments he had made during his tenure as governor. That summarizes the statement that I gave to my colleagues and issued publicly later that day.

What was it like to get their response to your news?

It was, as I said, very emotional and heartwarming. There was genuine affection and friendship reflecting all that we had worked on together and accomplished and gone through, and a palpable sense that this was a moment of true change at the Supreme Court and in the state's court system, as inevitably it would be. But I have always felt—and I mentioned this to my colleagues that morning—that each person entrusted with the position of Chief Justice builds upon the accomplishments of his or her predecessors, and that I was confident that my successor, whoever he or she might be, would do the same, as would future Chief Justices.

I had quite a quick timetable in mind for that day. I wanted to publicly release the same written statement that I had given to my colleagues, as an attachment to a press release that I would ask Lynn Holton, our public information officer, to issue for the court later that morning. But I first wanted to meet with my entire chambers staff, then to contact the governor to give him the courtesy of notifying him of my decision, and finally to send an electronic copy of the announcement to the entire staffs of the Supreme Court and of the Administrative Office of the Courts before publicly releasing it. As soon as my colleagues left my chambers, I placed a call to the governor's chief of staff, Susan Kennedy, to ask her to inform Governor Schwarzenegger of my decision not to file for reelection, emphasizing the fact that this imposed on him the obligation to select and nominate my successor before September 16.

How did he respond when you reached him?

I placed the call to his chief of staff, and after I chatted with her she said she was sure that the governor would want to speak to me. He called me back a few minutes later and was very gracious in telling me how much he had enjoyed working with me on issues involving the judiciary and the administration of justice, and he included some very generous words of praise. He added that he would like to speak with me concerning my recommendations for the appointment of a successor. When I said that I planned to travel to Los Angeles in a couple of days, we agreed that we would speak again in a week or so. However, very early the next day—the Thursday morning following the Wednesday conference and my telephone conversation with the governor—I received a call at home from Chief of Staff Susan Kennedy stating that the governor was very eager to see me as soon as possible that very morning. I responded that I could only be in his office at the state Capitol about one o'clock that afternoon. We agreed to meet then.

The reason I didn't want to meet before one o'clock was that I wanted to spend the morning, or a good part of it anyway, preparing a binder for the governor, with a copy for Susan Kennedy, that would contain first of all the constitutional provisions governing his authority to appoint my successor, pointing out the timeline and so forth—especially because the procedure was unusual in this instance, where I was not resigning but merely declining to file for reelection at the end of my term. Of course, my term would end at midnight on January 2, the same time the governor's term would end, and yet under this unusual constitutional provision he would have the authority to appoint my successor, even though that successor would not take office until after the governor himself had left office. I also placed in this binder the applicable provisions that related to the respective roles, under these circumstances, of the State Bar's Commission on Judicial Nominees Evaluation and the Commission on Judicial Appointments. Second, I included in the binder some biographical information on four individuals whom I was recommending that the governor consider for appointment as Chief Justice of California. I ranked the four individuals, and number one in my ranking was Justice Tani Cantil-Sakauye, an associate justice of the Third Appellate District who, as soon became apparent, ended up being the governor's nominee.

How early had you begun considering and compiling this list of four names?

I did not know whether I would be asked to make a recommendation. I had in my mind, in the weeks that led up to July 14, that Justice Cantil-Sakauye would be in my view—and for reasons that I'll express to you momentarily—an ideal person to occupy the position of Chief Justice. Having received a formal request from the governor on July 15 to confer with him that day on the subject of a successor, I felt it would be appropriate to go up there well organized, with alternatives to place before him. Not having known whether he would ask me for a recommendation, I certainly didn't know that if he did, he would go with my first choice—or with any recommendation of mine. I thought that under those circumstances I really should present him with more than one alternative recommendation. That's why I needed the time to actually get to the court and photocopy and assemble biographical material on these four individuals, before being driven to Sacramento.

When I met with the governor, only he, his chief of staff, Susan Kennedy, and I were present in his office. I told him that I was providing him and Susan with binders containing material on the procedural aspects of the appointment as well as biographical material pertaining to persons whom I thought were the most suitable and qualified in the State of California to perform the duties of Chief Justice of California. He invited me, then, to describe the background and qualifications of my first choice. I went through my impressions of Justice Cantil-Sakauye, indicating that I had focused on her because, having appointed her to the Judicial Council, I had come to believe that she was truly a star in the area of statewide court administration. I stressed her knowledge and intellectual ability, as well as her willingness to apply herself in confronting new situations, even crises, in a calm and reasoned way and to work constructively with others in a collegial manner. At the same time she had a backbone of steel and was highly articulate. I told the governor that in formulating my plans in the preceding weeks, I had made a point of reading many of her judicial opinions to satisfy my interest in her suitability to serve on the Supreme Court and was very impressed with the high quality of her written analytical work. I also noted that her experience was quite remarkable and involved all three branches of state government. She had three years' experience in the district attorney's office prosecuting violent crime before serving as an assistant legal affairs secretary and deputy legislative secretary for Governor George Deukmejian. Following that experience, she served 20 years as a judge, first at the municipal court and superior court, where she set up the first court in Sacramento dedicated exclusively to domestic violence issues, and then on the Court of Appeal.

I also mentioned her very compelling life story, which, in addition to her professional qualifications for office, would bring many advantages to the performance of her duties as Chief Justice of our large and multicultural state. She was the daughter of immigrants from the Philippines who were farm workers. She had to waitress her way through college, to help earn money for her tuition and, after going to law school, spent some vacation time working as a blackjack dealer in Reno before starting her legal career. She had a wealth of life experience that I thought would be of great benefit.

I stressed how the Chief Justice's position in today's era requires, in addition to the intellectual abilities involved in writing judicial opinions for a state court of last resort, a unique blend of administrative, diplomatic, and political skills in order to manage what is probably the largest law-trained judiciary in the world. Those special skills are needed to enable the Chief Justice to work effectively with the executive and legislative branches in securing and overseeing a budget of almost $4 billion while maintaining the independence of the judicial branch as a separate and co-equal branch of government. I felt she had all those requisite skills and, very importantly in my view, shared my unwavering commitment to a strong statewide administration of justice for California's judicial system. With all of that, she was only 50 years of age at that time. I was eager for Governor Schwarzenegger to nominate someone who would be young and energetic enough to remain as Chief Justice for many years to come in order to maintain continuity with what I had sought to accomplish.

When I had finished describing Justice Cantil-Sakauye's qualifications, the governor appeared to be very favorably impressed. Of course, he had previously appointed her to her position as an associate justice of the Court of Appeal and undoubtedly had heard favorable reports about her from various sources in one context or another. But the governor gave the impression of not having given any prior thought as to whom he might be inclined to consider appointing to the upcoming vacancy that he had learned of only 24 hours ago. Interestingly enough, the discussion I had with the governor never advanced to the second, third, or fourth names in the binder. As I left the governor's office, he turned to Susan Kennedy and stated that Justice Cantil-Sakauye should be called in for an interview. A very few days later, Susan Kennedy called me back to inform me that the interview had taken place, that Justice Cantil-Sakauye had conducted herself in an outstandingly impressive way during the interview, providing brilliant answers to difficult and hard-to-anticipate questions, and that the governor had selected her to be his nominee as Chief Justice.

I was invited to participate with the governor and Justice Cantil-Sakauye in a ceremony that would be held in the rotunda of the state Capitol. The governor asked me to be there July 22, which was only seven days after my meeting with him and eight days after I had announced my retirement. That ceremony, of course, would announce her appointment as my successor as Chief Justice.

How did this whole process square with what you already knew of Governor Schwarzenegger from working so closely with him?

Well, I knew that he was very much inclined to listen, to take in a great amount of input, and to make his own decisions and do so quickly. Despite those anticipations on my part, I was taken by surprise at how quickly and efficiently the whole process moved forward. I was quite amazed to be standing there with him and my successor eight days after having first broached to the governor and to anyone else outside immediate family my intention not to file for reelection.

By the way, I had never told Justice Cantil-Sakauye that I would recommend her appointment, nor did I have any conversation with her about it until after the governor made the appointment and publicly announced it.

Please describe that event, if you would.

Certainly. I just want to add, before I do, that I know from Tani herself that the governor's call for her to meet with him came as a total surprise to her, as had my own announced retirement—she was quite shocked by that. She told me later that she and her husband Mark had been speculating, when she heard the news of my impending retirement, who might be considered for the position of Chief Justice and who would be jockeying for the appointment. So she was quite surprised to be called into the governor's office and told that she was under consideration.

On to your question about the events of July 22. The three of us—the governor, Justice Cantil-Sakauye, and I—walked from the governor's office, through corridors that had been specially decorated with California and American flags, to the Capitol rotunda. The governor first said some very kind words about my own judicial career, and then he added a comment pretty much in these words: "Well, this Chief Justice certainly won't be retiring to a rocking chair." Being on fairly familiar terms with the governor by then, I took the liberty of leaning into his microphone while he was speaking, and interjected: "Maybe we'll make some movies together." This was a reprise of the comment he had made when I introduced him at the San Francisco meeting of the Conference of Chief Justices in 2004. [Laughter] The governor responded, "Yes, Chief Justice action hero!" After the governor announced his reasons for appointing Tani, including, of course, well-deserved praise that he gave for her abilities, she responded in her customarily eloquent manner and, as is her practice, without the aid of any notes.

What followed, of course, was a very easy and rapid confirmation process. An investigation by the State Bar's Commission on Judicial Nominees Evaluation resulted in, first of all, the State Bar's giving her the highest possible rating, "exceptionally well qualified." The report supplied to the commission by the attorney general's office was equally positive. I chaired a very easy hearing of the commission, ending in her unanimous confirmation. Subsequently, the voters overwhelmingly approved her nomination at the November 2010 election for a term to commence on January 3, 2011. Between the election and my departure on vacation December 16, my successor and I had some private meetings, without staff, at which I tendered information and some of my views, all of which she immediately grasped and absorbed. I did tell her that I would always be available to her as a resource but that I was not going to intrude by volunteering suggestions.

I understand those meetings were private between the two of you, but I wonder, in general, what kinds of things did you think it was most important to communicate to her at that point?

Our discussions covered a wide array of matters, from some of the more arcane procedures at the California Supreme Court, including the routine followed at the petition conferences, in the circulation of court memoranda and draft opinions, and court administrative matters, and information related to chairing the Judicial Council and to the structure of the Administrative Office of the Courts. These discussions also encompassed the duties of the Chief Justice as chief lobbyist in Sacramento. They covered everything that I thought would be of possible interest to her, plus anything and everything that she wanted to bring up. Then we scheduled one additional meeting for mid-January, so she could review anything that she wanted to from the perspective of her actual experience on the job.

May I back up to July 14, your announcement day, and ask you to talk more about how your own staff members received the news of your retirement?

Everyone, uniformly, was shocked. I never received an indication from any of them that day or—subsequently, in the months that followed—from anyone else in the judiciary or in the legal profession of anything other than total surprise. Ultimately, I believe, there was a fairly uniform understanding of how, after 14 years as Chief Justice, one would want to pursue the other things that life has to offer that really had to be put aside with those full-time responsibilities.

Many persons—given the difficulties that have further complicated life in California government in the year 2011—have complimented me on my supposed brilliance and foresight in leaving when I did. My reply has been, "I can't take credit for all of that. It was mainly fortuitous."

I got things in as good a shape as I thought I could, but of course had no way of knowing what would happen in the year 2011, although I did anticipate that this year, as well as 2012 for that matter, would be characterized by continuing difficulties in operating California state government, with the resulting limitations on providing the judicial branch with adequate funding.

How did you go about thinking of and carrying out your last tasks over those last few months? What did you need to finish?

The last few months, and especially the last several weeks before the end of my term, were particularly frenetic, even though I guess in retrospect the whole pace of my time as chief had been frenetic. It was important to me to make the rounds to different divisions of the Administrative Office of the Courts, including their three regional offices, to express my gratitude for all the hard work and, often, unrecognized contributions made by those toiling in the administrative ranks. There were numerous farewell events given by various judicial and bar associations, so many that I can't even mention them all. Among the highlights was the Judicial Council's having commissioned an artist to create a terrific oil painting of me based on photographs. It was a true surprise. That now hangs outside the Judicial Council boardroom.

Speaking of the council, one of the more notable recognitions I received, I guess, was being presented with a bobblehead in my likeness. Being bobbled is a true form of immortality, maybe as much as an oil painting. [Laughter] It was presented at a Judicial Council meeting by a former president of the State Bar, Tony Capozzi. Funny enough, because the legal newspapers cover Judicial Council meetings, they published a photograph of the bobblehead, and Tony started getting order requests for bobblehead likenesses of me from people around the state. [Laughter]

There were many recognitions conferred on me at the annual State Bar convention, which as you know I had attended and spoken at every year. There were some awards that were then named after me, including the bar's Public Lawyer Award. The Los Angeles Lawyers Philharmonic Orchestra flew up to Monterey, where the State Bar's annual meeting was being held, to perform at a tented party held in my honor, hosted by former Judicial Council member Tom Girardi, that featured Paul Anka serenading me on stage with specially composed lyrics to the song *My Way*. That rendition prompted an onstage but nonmusical reply from me that quoted the Kenny Rogers refrain: "You've got to know when to hold 'em, when to fold 'em, and when to walk away." It seemed to be an appropriate response, given the nature of the event. My colleagues on the Supreme Court also hosted a very enjoyable dinner just for the seven of us and spouses in a private room at the St. Francis Yacht Club.

And Justice Kennard surprised me December 8, my last day on the bench hearing oral arguments, with some remarks on behalf of my six colleagues which are set forth in the official reports of the court's decisions, commemorating my retirement.

I had announced that I would be leaving on vacation the morning of December 16 for Antarctica, having decided that I didn't want to watch the hands of the clock ticking away the last hours of my 38-year judicial career as it drew to a close at midnight on January 2. My planned vacation accelerated the process of Governor Schwarzenegger's appointments to other judicial vacancies that existed, mainly on the Court of Appeal. Action by the Commission on Judicial Appointments, which I chaired, would be required if these appointments were to be confirmed before the end of the governor's term. I scheduled—after working it out with the other members of the commission—six confirmation hearings of the Commission on Judicial Appointments for December 10, which was unprecedented. The other two members of the commission were Attorney General Jerry Brown, who of course was governor-elect at that time, and the senior presiding justice of the affected district of the Court of Appeal. When the last of those hearings was conducted that day, I tallied up the total—knowing that would be the last such hearing over which I would preside—and realized that I had presided over 105 confirmation hearings of the Commission on Judicial Appointments for appointments to the Court of Appeal and the Supreme Court.

On the evening of December 15, which was my last day at the court, the Supreme Court held its annual holiday celebration. This year those in charge had decided that the festivities would also honor Barbara's and my departure. It was a wonderful farewell that included warm tributes from judicial and staff colleagues and even a musical composition sung by Justice Moreno, his staff, and Justice Corrigan. When it was all over with—or maybe even before it was all over—Barbara and I left at 10:00 p.m. and walked from the Green Room at the Herbst Theater building, passing Civic Center Plaza, accompanied by Officer Terry Tracy. The three of us proceeded to my chambers to complete packing up the last of my personal effects, a task that I had been unable to complete until then due to the press of final official responsibilities. We were quite weary when, about midnight, we left chambers to go home to complete some final packing for our trip. Terry drove us to the airport later that morning to begin our long journey to Antarctica.

You had been to Antarctica once before. How did you decide to go back at this particular time?

It is a very special place in terms of spectacular scenery and animal life. I wanted to expand our exploration beyond Antarctica to include some of the neighboring islands, especially Elephant Island and South Georgia Island, because I had read a great deal about the explorer Sir Ernest Shackleton and his heroic adventures in the early 1900s. It was also a place where I was confident I would be out of reach. I had left things in the hands of an Acting Chief Justice, Joyce Kennard, until my successor would take office January 3. I wanted this to be a real wind down and relaxed transition.

One of the things I was asked for, during the weeks leading up to my departure from office, was to furnish a prognostication for the year 2011 for the magazine *California Lawyer*. My published prognostication was as follows: "My end-of-year voyage to Antarctica will facilitate a unification of penguin colonies, accomplished with greater ease and acceptance than that achieved by their black-robed colleagues on the California bench." That was my little farewell.

How did the trip proceed from San Francisco?

It was a series of flights to Buenos Aires and then about three hours flying time from Buenos Aires, which is already quite south, to Ushuaia, the southernmost city in the world and a very interesting place in its own right. It had been the site of an Argentinian penal colony where political prisoners and journalists were imprisoned for many decades, even into the 1950s. It's right on the Beagle Channel on the southern coast of Tierra del Fuego. We took a ship from there and went first to the Falkland Islands and then on to South Georgia Island—which is a truly amazing place, probably the most beautiful I have been to anywhere—before heading to Elephant Island, Deception Island, and Antarctica.

We were interrupted with only one communication in the course of the trip, which was the e-mail notifying me that Governor Schwarzenegger had issued the executive order on December 21 naming the San Francisco Civic Center Complex the "Ronald M. George State Office Complex." Barbara and I and our son Eric, who was with us, toasted the news with champagne on board.

How did that trip compare, with the added stops you described, to the earlier one?

I can't come up with any word other than spectacular. It truly was. The vastness of the area is hard to describe. Some massive icebergs were as high as 30- or 40-story buildings. There were enormous colonies of marine animals and birds. There is one place on South Georgia Island called the Salisbury Plain that had a colony of King penguins that stretched as far as the eye could see, from the shore onto the bluffs, and into the hills. The population of the colony was estimated by our guide as upwards of 300,000 King penguins, all huddled together, with mothers going to sea, catching fish for their offspring, and locating them in this gigantic colony of penguins solely through vocalization recognition. There were many other species, from whales to sea lions to giant albatrosses, a total richness of life and spectacular glaciers rising up from ice-churning seas to between 9,000 and 10,000 feet altitude in South Georgia.

What a dramatic transition from your working life. When did it begin to sink in that you really had retired?

I suppose in the aftermath of the ship voyage, when we went to Patagonia and saw an enormous glacier called Perito Moreno, on the Argentinian side, and then on the Chilean side went to Torres del Paine National Park and engaged in some fairly rigorous hiking. I realized that I really wasn't in as good a shape as I had been before. In fact, it took me six months—until I was hiking in July of this year in the Sawtooth Mountains in Idaho—before I really felt I had regained my vim and vigor, demonstrating to me that there certainly had been a lot of wear and tear in terms of my energy level, resulting from the performance of my duties as Chief Justice.

I wonder how much you had given thought to other things that you might do in retirement, aside from the full life that you already intended to pursue. What kinds of other offers did you get or activities did you consider?

I made it fairly clear in my official statement that I was not going to engage in the practice of law or private or assigned judging or alternative dispute resolution. Most people took me at my word. Notwithstanding that, I had various offers, which I have politely declined, relating to the practice of law. Interestingly enough, two of them came from politically affiliated law firms, one Republican and one Democratic. Also some offers regarding private dispute resolution. I was also told that I had been suggested by a major headhunter firm as a finalist in a search for a new law school dean. I also had invitations to join the boards of a couple of public policy institutes, which I also declined. I did try to make it clear that if I ever were to become interested in engaging in the private practice of law—which I frankly doubt I ever will be—I certainly would accept the offer of our eldest son Eric to be "of counsel" to his Los Angeles firm of Browne George Ross.

Even though I'm rejecting other commitments as such, I have received calls from all sorts of persons bouncing ideas off me and asking for my views informally—not on a professional or retained basis. A couple of legislators also have called me. I had a phone call from Governor Brown—we talked about that—when I was on my way to the museum with my two little granddaughters, seeking my views regarding an initiative reform. I also had an invitation from a member of the Los Angeles County Board of Supervisors asking me to consider an appointment to chair a commission to investigate the Los Angeles County jail system, which I've also declined.

I've also declined several requests for press interviews, even though I made myself very accessible when I was still in office. I have felt that it was certainly my successor's turn now to not only be in charge but to be in the spotlight. I would never want to appear to be speaking over her shoulder, so to speak. I was even asked to appear on the Jon Stewart *Daily Show*. [Laughter] They are apparently going to do a program on California's initiative process. I declined that too.

I have tried to really commit myself to retirement in a serious way, even to the point of not subscribing to any of the legal newspapers or other publications on the law and the judiciary, and trying to get back instead into reading history, biographies, memoirs, and fiction—and traveling and spending time with my family. Probably as a result of having indicated in my retirement statement that reading was one of the activities I was going to pursue, I received a remarkable number of books from various persons, including a journalist employed by a major California newspaper and a retired legislator. The only formal activities in which I've agreed to participate in retirement are this oral history project and membership on the Think Long Committee for California, which I'll be glad to discuss with you.[1]

Yes. Particularly knowing that the committee's report is due to be released very soon, I am quite interested in hearing about your experiences there. Could you start off describing when and how you were recruited and how the mission of the committee was communicated to you?

---

[1] Subsequent to these oral history interviews, Chief Justice George was appointed as a member of the Commission on Global Ethics and Citizenship, charged with reviewing the United Nations' Universal Declaration of Human Rights and recommending any revisions.

I was asked in the spring of this year to make a presentation to the Think Long Committee for California, as it's officially known. I didn't know much about it. I guess I had seen a couple of things in the press. The committee was interested in hearing my views concerning the initiative process and any reforms that were needed. I learned that the committee had become aware of my interest in this subject as the result of articles I wrote for the *Stanford Law Review* and the *San Francisco Chronicle*. My presentation to the committee did not urge that the initiative process be abolished, but suggested how its excesses could be remedied. I felt that the current process was contributing to the dysfunctionality of California government and that the process needed to be reformed in its own right.

The Think Long Committee was created by one individual, Nicolas Berggruen, and the institute that bears his name, which is headquartered in New York. Mr. Berggruen is described in the press, tongue-in-cheek, as "the homeless billionaire," because he flies around the world in his own airplane staying at hotels but doesn't actually have his own residence. He is of European extraction, but went to college in the United States and has had many dealings with California and a great affection for the state. He seeks nothing from the efforts of his committee except to try to restore functionality to California government. Quoting from the mission statement of the committee,

> . . . the Nicolas Berggruen Institute envisions establishing a nonpartisan Think Long Committee for California of eminent Californians, not more than 10 or 15 people, that can apply their experience, stature, and knowledge toward the goal of getting the state back to governability. The recommendations of the committee will be presented to the next governor and the legislative leadership or, as necessary, taken to the public in ballot initiatives. Nicolas Berggruen will provide $20 million in funds to finance the endeavor. Unlike any other reform efforts, this fund will not support a single candidacy or single issue but only those structural and constitutional changes that will break the present gridlock and make government more responsive and efficient, while at the same time putting in place the incentives and institutions vital for California's long-term future.

The committee's membership is comprised of a bipartisan, well-respected group of 15 Californians, including former U.S. Secretaries of State George Shultz and Condoleezza Rice, former Governor Gray Davis, former Speakers of the Assembly Willie Brown and Bob Hertzberg, and some of the state's leaders in business, finance, labor, and philanthropy. The consultants to the committee include the directors of finance under Governor Davis and Governor Schwarzenegger and a member of Governor Wilson's cabinet.

Once you became involved, what was Mr. Berggruen's approach to this very complicated mission?

I've been very impressed with his lively mind and interest in all of the subject matters encompassed by the charge given to the committee that he established. But unlike other individuals whom I've encountered in similar situations, he is not in the least overbearing, nor does he treat the committee as his personal creation or fiefdom. He's quiet, sits back, and speaks up when he feels it's appropriate to do so but doesn't try to take charge or to run an agenda. Clearly, he has no parochial or selfish interest in the outcome. All he wants is the betterment of California government. I've been very gratified by his commitment. After hearing my presentation on the initiative process, he felt it would be useful for me to be a member, not only because the committee might propose reforms in the initiative process and try to advance its other reform proposals through that process, but also because someone with a judicial perspective on legal and constitutional issues that might arise in the course of the work of the committee would be an asset to its efforts.

How far along had that work progressed at the time you joined? What were they focusing on by then?

The committee at various stages of its work has dealt with subjects encompassing tax reform, education, the creation of a citizen's council to coordinate policies, both economic and environmental, taking positions on initiative measures advanced by others so that voters would have access to our neutral evaluation—which would be included in the secretary of state's voter information pamphlet—and, quite innovatively, for the citizens council itself to be able to propose initiatives for placement on the ballot without having to obtain the hundreds of thousands of signatures required under present constitutional provisions in order to qualify a measure for consideration by the voters at the polls. My presentation on the initiative process had focused on the length and complexity of California's Constitution and how often our constitution has been amended. We have all sorts of odd things in our state constitution that don't belong in a constitution and cause it to rival the constitution of India in its length and complexity. Although the majority of these more than 500 constitutional amendments were placed before California voters by the legislature rather than through the initiative process, those that have been most disruptive to governmental functions have emanated from the initiative process. In recent years there seems to be a focus on the animal kingdom as a favorite subject of California's initiative process. Statutory measures banning the hunting of mountain lions and regulating the size of chicken coops have been enacted by initiative, as have constitutional provisions regulating the use of gill nets to catch rockfish.

Perhaps on a more fundamental level, much of California's dysfunctionality has resulted from the fact that initiatives have enacted spending mandates for admittedly worthwhile causes such as education—Proposition 98—and transportation, and yet by the same initiative process the people have imposed restrictions under the constitution on their ability to raise the revenue to pay for those very same mandated expenditures. There is another factor that I illustrated when we were discussing my opinions for the court, specifically one of the *Kelly* cases, which holds that unless an initiative has provided otherwise, the legislature is unable to fix or alter—even consistently with the objectives of the initiative—a problem posed by the measure, and that the only solution is to seek the approval of the voters at a future election.

All of this has combined with the effects of term limits, the two-thirds-vote requirement for raising taxes, the two-thirds-vote requirement for passage of the budget, and legislative districting—although there have been some recent changes in the last two areas—to increase the dysfunctionality of California's government in difficult economic times. Perhaps above all, California's initiative process—which exists here in its most extreme form among the two dozen states that have it, and is responsible for many of the restrictions I just mentioned—seems to largely deprive the other branches of government, especially the legislature, of true accountability, because so much legislative action and so many of the legislature's options are curtailed by the initiative process. Then throw in term limits—legislators are out of there in a few years. The long-term perspective that previous governors, such as Governor Edmund G. Brown Sr., had of looking at the needs of the state in terms of infrastructure—the University of California, the freeway system, the water system—has largely vanished from the scene facing incoming legislators. Those are some of the concerns that were put before our committee.

There's a full-scale industry now that is directed at qualifying and then passing initiatives—and in some instances conjuring up initiative proposals just to be able to shop them around to special interest groups in various states. This situation makes it very difficult to change the process. I'm glad, though, that the governor signed a bill providing that initiative proposals can now be placed by the Secretary of State on higher-turnout November general election ballots instead of proponents being able to cherry-pick measures for either a low-turnout June primary or the higher-turnout November election. I'm also heartened by the change in the reapportionment scheme, permitting the electorate, freed from the constraints of gerrymandering, to pick their legislative representatives—instead of the representatives picking their electorate. I'm hopeful that we have some change on its way in California.

You mentioned the citizens council that the Think Long Committee proposes. With the report due out in several days' time, what can you tell about specific recommendations?

The committee at some point is going to go forward with this citizens council, whose functions I have mentioned to you. It also wants to pursue a tax reform proposal, which would basically seek to lower the income tax liability of taxpayers in all income levels. The proposed tax reform would also slightly reduce the sales tax for goods and reduce the corporate tax to a level where it would be more competitive with the corporate tax imposed by other states. To make up for this loss in revenue, the committee's proposal would extend the sales tax to what's roughly the other half of California's gross product, namely the services—as opposed to the goods—that are produced in California. The committee and its financial and tax consultants believe that this extension of the sales tax would make up for the loss of revenue and, in fact, not only be revenue-neutral but enhance the revenue received by the State of California. I believe the committee has decided not to bite off too much to begin with, and reforms in the area of education will be left for a different election cycle. I expect the committee to place the first of its proposals on either the 2012 ballot or the 2014 ballot.

Knowing that Governor Jerry Brown gave a presentation to the committee at the time you did, to what extent has the committee consulted him about this proposed tax reform?

There have been communications between the committee and the governor's Department of Finance. I'm hopeful that the governor and our committee will ultimately coordinate their objectives in seeking tax reform.

Other reforms in the initiative process are being considered in legislation that is proposed from time to time. That could involve increasing the number of votes required to pass a measure, especially one that imposes a supermajority-vote requirement upon the legislature. In other words, if an initiative were to require a two-thirds vote to do something or other in the legislature, the initiative itself would have to pass by a two-thirds vote. Another idea discussed by the committee was to increase the number of signatures required to qualify an initiative measure for the ballot. Presently five percent of the number of persons who voted in the last gubernatorial election is required for a statutory Initiative enactment and eight percent for an initiative constitutional amendment. One proposal is to instead apply those percentages to the number of persons registered to vote in the last gubernatorial election as distinguished from the persons who actually voted in that election.

There have been suggestions that initiative supporters not be allowed to pay petition signature gatherers based on the number of signatures obtained. The current practice allowing this form of compensation sometimes results in undesirable approaches and tactics, and can give rise to a conflict of interest. There's a U.S. Supreme Court decision, I believe *Meyer v. Grant*, that held it is a violation of the First Amendment to prohibit any payment to signature gatherers. I guess I could add this decision to the other disagreements I have with the First Amendment jurisprudence of the U.S. Supreme Court that I expressed at our last session. Earlier this year the legislature passed a bill requiring that if a signature gatherer is paid, he or she must be paid by the hour and not per signature, but Governor Brown vetoed the bill. Hopefully such a bill would pass constitutional muster if enacted into law.

It's not unusual to have dozens of initiative measures circulating, some of them wildly absurd, and some of the absurd ones even qualifying, putting the question of their validity back in the lap of the courts to sort out their provisions and, on occasion, keep them off the ballot if they haven't complied with procedural requirements—resulting in the courts incurring the displeasure of the electorate.

How would the proposed citizens council be selected?

The council would consist of individuals appointed by various officeholders but only individuals who had not made political contributions to the appointing officeholder during a specified period preceding their appointment to the council. It is proposed to have the council's membership include a broad range of persons. Among the thirteen voting members, nine would be appointed by the governor. The Senate Rules Committee and the Speaker of the Assembly would each appoint two members, one from each of the state's two largest political parties. At least two of the governor's appointees would not be registered to either of the state's two largest political parties. In addition to the nine appointed members, there would be four ex officio members who would be nonvoting members. They would include the director of finance, the state treasurer, the state controller, and the attorney general. The citizens council would also be charged with trying to coordinate and cooperate with the actions taken by all the state agency heads. Members of the citizens council would be limited to two terms of six years each, and the terms would be staggered. A simple majority of the council would be required to place a statutory proposal on the ballot, but a two-thirds vote would be required for a constitutional amendment.

This Think Long Committee is a group of illustrious and rather powerful individuals. What more can you tell me about their process of working together? That must have been fascinating.

It really was. In yesterday's conference call, former Secretary of State George Shultz complimented all of the members of the committee and its staff. "When we began our efforts last year," he said, "I never thought that we could come together and work out—with a wide diversity of political and other views—so many constructive proposals for the betterment of the people of the State of California."

Coming from Secretary Schultz, that is quite a statement.

That's exactly what Mr. Berggruen said. He said to George Shultz, "Coming from you that is the ultimate compliment."

What were the trickiest parts for the committee in working together?

I'd say tax reform, because it's such a sensitive issue and requires trying to work out something that would be fair across the broad span of income levels, and at the same time provide the assurance of sufficient revenue for the state and stimulate economic growth in California, which is a major concern of the committee.

How fully can you personally support the recommendations coming out in this report?

Personally I can say I am totally in favor of them as they now stand. Now that I am retired, I am free to voice a preference and endorse the bipartisan work product of the committee.

As you said, consideration of education reform in California will come at a later stage. What else lies ahead? Just briefly and in your own words is fine.

There are matters in addition to education that involve the environment and local government as well that I think may be further examined by the committee and find themselves included in one or more future initiative proposals.

What did you get out of serving on this body?

It was truly a privilege to be exposed to the views of such a highly qualified, highly experienced group of individuals with service in the public and private sectors, and to be able to engage in discussions with them in a most worthy effort to restore the somewhat faded luster of California government. I enjoyed the collaborative efforts and have nothing but praise for the committee and its very capable staff, who were of great assistance to all of us. I hope and expect that much good will come out of the committee's efforts.

###

Chapter 20

Reflections on Past and Future Challenges Facing the Courts
November 16, 2011

Chief Justice George, for our second interview today may I ask you to talk about what you see as some of the future challenges for the judiciary and, in some cases by extension, for the state, starting with the matter of funding?

I would certainly count adequate funding as one of the foremost major challenges facing the courts in the coming years. It is something that is a constant concern.

There's no doubt that the switch from county-based funding to state-based funding was a vast improvement. In today's economic crisis—just as in the previous downturns we have cyclically had in California—the courts would be far worse off if they were forced to weather those storms under the old system. County governments are, in some instances, on the verge of going bankrupt and see intense competition for the various types of services they provide, whether it's law enforcement, parks, various health and social services, and so forth. It would be more difficult for the courts to compete in that county domain than it is on a statewide level under our current statewide funding system. The legislature and the governor authorize and appropriate funds that are basically entrusted to the Judicial Council to distribute to each court, with a fairly minimal degree of micromanagement by the other two branches of government. Contrary to the misinformation disseminated by some judges, this distribution of funds is not done willy-nilly by the A.O.C. In disbursing these funds to the 58 trial courts, the Judicial Council relies heavily on the recommendations of a committee of all the presiding judges as well as one composed of all the court executive officers. The Judicial Council remains accountable to the executive and legislative branches for these public funds—just as the individual trial courts remain accountable to the Judicial Council.

Admittedly, there are some courts that are in worse shape than others, for a variety of reasons. One of them is historic underfunding. If a county, over many years or decades, was chronically remiss or perhaps unable to provide adequate funding to its courts, the switch to state funding was incapable of remedying the deficiencies over a short period of time. There is a formula built into the allocation of state funding through the Judicial Council that takes into account historic imbalances. But it will take years for some courts to fully catch up.

Second—I don't know of any delicate way of putting this—some of the funding difficulties experienced by specific courts, in the past or currently, reflect mismanagement on their part. There were a couple of counties where the A.O.C., at the request of the local court, had to take over the responsibility for the court's funds when the particular courts went way over budget and had no means of meeting their financial obligations other than by seeking a bail-out from the Judicial Council, which the council provided along with an overhaul of the court's procedures. There have been a variety of circumstances that have contributed in recent years to poor management practices by a few of the state's trial courts. Given the publicity the San Francisco Superior Court has sought and obtained in the press regarding its financial situation, it's worth discussing the situation of that court. Earlier this year, the San Francisco court's chief executive officer was candid in admitting that poor practices had caused that court to incur a deficit. My understanding is that the San Francisco court pays about 20 percent more in salaries to its employees than other comparable courts. Although the cost of living in the Bay Area is higher than in most other areas of the state, this circumstance already is taken into account in making the assessment that those salaries still are 20 percent more than they need to be. I also have been informed that the San Francisco court has been remiss in some of its collection responsibilities—in not obtaining funds that are owed to it by various public and private entities. Also, it is widely understood that the San Francisco court, like the Los Angeles court and several other trial courts, has retained many millions of dollars in reserves.

The law permits trial courts to carry over unexpended funds and savings from one year to another in reserve, an authority not possessed by the Supreme Court, the courts of appeal, the Judicial Council, or the Administrative Office of the Courts. In light of that situation, I think it was very inappropriate that the leadership of the San Francisco court saw fit to attack the Judicial Council and the Administrative Office of the Courts and at the same time demand bailout money, which the council ultimately provided the San Francisco court, but in the form of a loan that has to be repaid instead of the requested dole. To the extent the Judicial Council, with the very limited amount of funds available to the judicial branch in these difficult economic times, rides to the rescue of some local court, it is in a sense being unfair to other courts that have engaged in more appropriate and disciplined management practices.

As I mentioned before, adequate court funding is tied into the crucial concept of institutional judicial independence. Again, I stress that "judicial independence" does not mean unaccountability. The judiciary is accountable for how it performs its function of administering fair and accessible justice and is accountable for the taxpayer dollars it receives from the legislature. The legislature by and large treats us as a co-equal branch of government by not micromanaging the local courts but instead leaving to the Judicial Council the responsibility of distributing these funds in an appropriate manner. Some misinformed judges yearn for what they claim were "the good old days" of county funding—days that I and others who served in that era know were not in fact so good. A return to that discredited system would place the judiciary in an even worse condition in today's fiscal situation. The real goal of these throwbacks is to escape the accountability that comes with receiving statewide funding, and to return to the time of unaccountable judicial fiefdoms.

The reason I bring up the concept of judicial independence is that—as I mentioned before—this coin has two sides. One is the side we hear most about, decision-making judicial independence. The other side is institutional or structural independence, which is quite fragile. That aspect of judicial independence is quite dependent upon the other two branches, the executive and the legislative, doing their job and providing adequate support and resources for the functioning of the courts and the administration of fair and accessible justice. The reality is that those other two branches do possess the power of the purse and occasionally, as we've mentioned in our discussions, employ that power in a retaliatory or punitive manner because of their disapproval of a particular decision—or of a particular mode of decision making—on behalf of a court, especially the state high court. Some legislators, either out of ignorance or for political reasons, overlook the distinction between the Chief Justice's role as one of seven decision makers on the high court, and on the other hand his or her administrative and advocacy role as Chief Justice of California and head of the judicial branch. This attitude can lead some legislators to engage in "payback" to the entire judicial branch because of a single court decision of which they disapprove.

I've tried to make the point—and I did so in my final State of the Judiciary address to a joint session of the legislature last year—that courts are not a luxury to be funded in good times and ignored in bad times, that justice cannot be made available only when it is convenient to pay for it. On many occasions I've had to deliver this message loud and clear to the other branches of government, because the courts can't go up to the state Capitol being perceived as just one more special interest. With the assistance of our justice system partners, we have to convince the other two branches that the funds we seek are not for the benefit of the courts or the judges who serve on them, but are sought for the benefit of the public to provide it with access to justice. We cannot and do not join the horde of lobbyists attending the dozens of political fundraising events held by legislators each year in the capital and in their districts. We have to sell the concept of access to justice just on the basis of its own merit.

One of the long-term goals the Judicial Council has worked on to meet the continuing challenge of adequate court funding—but the political climate hasn't been right for it yet—is a proposal we approved to amend article VI, the judicial article of the California Constitution. This proposal was supported by the administrative presiding justices of the Courts of Appeal, the executive committee of the Judicial Council's presiding judges advisory committee, the court executive officers advisory committee, and the chairs and vice chairs of the council's advisory committees, the State Bar of California, and the executive board of the California Judges Association. I hope this proposal will move ahead at an appropriate time. Much of this effort would deal with court budgeting, guaranteeing financial stability for the courts by placing the judicial branch's funding mechanism in the state constitution itself. The proposed constitutional amendment also would require the legislature and the governor to provide a number of judges sufficient to ensure public access to the courts by reference to specified objective criteria, and would establish an independent commission charged with setting judicial salaries. The constitutional amendment also would clarify the Judicial Council's budgetary responsibilities, administrative duties, and authority in overseeing the various courthouses that are now owned by the state and managed by the council and clarify the Supreme Court's authority over bar admission and the discipline of attorneys, as well as the State Bar's function as an administrative arm of the high court.

How long have you been working on that?

Approval by these entities goes back to about 2005, when we publicly announced the proposal, but there were efforts that preceded that.

This is an ambitious set of ideas in the proposed judicial amendment, knowing the economic situation of the moment. What would be the right timing to bring this forward and try to get it enacted?

This proposal needs to be pursued by the judicial branch and its supporters during an uptick in the state's economic fortunes. It involves additional costs to the state and certainly will be attacked for that reason, even in good economic times. It also, of course, will be resisted by some who will see it as a diminution of the authority held by the other two branches of government.

What are the practical effects of having the budget addressed in this way rather than the way it is now?

The other two branches' control over the judicial branch would be reduced. Some legislators would like to maintain or even increase their control over the judicial budget. We often speak of the separation of powers, but as I mentioned in our discussion of one of the opinions I wrote for the court—*Superior Court v. County of Mendocino*—there isn't an absolute separation. What we have is a certain interdependence among the three branches of government, with checks and balances, and not a true and total independence.

Even recognizing that qualification, I don't believe the proposed constitutional amendment would run afoul of the traditional concept of separation of powers. In any event, if this proposal is adopted, it would have to be by way of a constitutional amendment, which would itself modify or, if you will, carve out a bit of an exception to any concept of a complete separation of powers. There are other entities whose structure blurs the lines of separation of powers, such as the Coastal Commission, the State Bar Court, and the Public Utilities Commission that we discussed in conjunction with some of my opinions for the court. I don't think it would be inappropriate to proceed with this proposed constitutional amendment, whose approval by the voters of course would be required in order to make the changes.

Given that the economic time is not right now, what kind of a partner do you have in Governor Jerry Brown in general for these ideas?

I really do not know. Of course, the governor plays no direct role in the adoption of a constitutional amendment. It would be proposed and placed on the ballot either by a two-thirds vote in each house of the legislature or by the requisite number of signatures from the voting public. Similar to our successful proposal of the constitutional amendment unifying the superior and municipal courts, it's not something that a governor has a direct hand in, although obviously the governor could make his wishes known to the legislature. But I have no idea, in any event, to what degree Governor Brown or any future governor would support or resist this proposal.

The legislature itself would be another matter entirely.

Yes. Our proposal represents good government, but it has political ramifications that would have to be confronted. But many of our other reform proposals encountered such obstacles and overcame them.

What are the other challenges you see ahead for the judiciary in this state?

A second challenge, one of the greatest long-term challenges that will continue to confront the courts for a long time, is something that you and I have spoken about at substantial length and that I will dwell on only briefly here—the fact that legal representation for Californians in civil cases is becoming increasingly out of reach. I don't mean only for the lowest economic levels of our society but for middle-class individuals, who have to consider going into great debt or bankruptcy to fund a lawsuit that may not secure an award equal to the expenditure required to obtain that award. We've talked about the alternatives: legal services organizations, which can't accommodate more than a fraction of the people needing their assistance, pro bono work, self-help locations and the related website, the *Elkins* task force family law recommendations, and the Sargent Shriver Civil Counsel Act pilot program. We're going to have to look at all sorts of solutions. There are certain areas of litigation involving marital or child support, division of community property, or domestic violence restraining orders, in which 80 to 90 percent of Californians—at least in some parts of the state—have their cases heard without the assistance of an attorney. The same is true with landlord-tenant disputes. This is a major challenge that we'll have to confront, because unlike the area of criminal law, where there's a constitutional right to counsel, with the rarest of exceptions no right to counsel exists in civil proceedings.

I want to talk about the independence of the judiciary—which you touched on a moment ago with respect to the judicial article amendment—both decisional and institutional. This is a broad area that you showed great interest in, in recent years. May we start with the matter of retention elections?

Certainly. A third major challenge continuing to confront the judicial branch will be preserving decisional judicial independence. Just to set the stage for that topic, judicial independence is not just an abstract principle. Article III, section 3, of the California Constitution states as follows: "The powers of state government are legislative, executive, and judicial. Persons charged with the exercise of one power may not exercise either of the others except as permitted by this Constitution." Note the qualification "except as permitted by this Constitution," and also note—as I indicated a moment ago—that in the *Superior Court v. County of Mendocino* case there is a recognition that in many ways there is no absolute separation and that a mutual dependency exists between and among our branches of government. This in a way is analogous to the First Amendment's prohibition against the establishment of religion, concerning which there is often mention of a "wall of separation between church and state." I don't believe that term appears anywhere in the U.S. Constitution; instead it reflects a concept that Thomas Jefferson referred to in his correspondence and his other writings. There too, with regard to religion as with separation of powers, there is no rigid wall. We all know that there are certain overlappings or intrusions or accommodations between church and state just as there are among the three branches of government. These concepts are not absolute.

There is a concern I have always had with judicial elections that involves both aspects of judicial independence—the decision-making side of judicial independence, and the structural or institutional side of the independence of the judiciary vital to its survival as a co-equal branch of government. Judicial independence exists not to benefit judges, but to benefit the public and the rule of law. It is therefore somewhat ironic that one of the challenges to judicial independence can come from the manner in which the public exercises its right to vote in judicial elections.

These elections, by the way, have an interesting history. I believe that when the thirteen colonies formed the United States of America, there was only one of them, Vermont, that had a practice of judicial elections. In many states, the judicial appointment power resided in the legislative branch. There are still some states, like South Carolina and Virginia, where the legislature appoints the Supreme Court justices. The reaction against this legislative predominance in the judicial selection process certainly was fueled by the onset of Jacksonian democracy, which brought about a general expansion of the electorate's role. There was a movement in the United States in favor judicial elections. I believe that 39 states currently elect their judges in some form or another, either through a contested partisan election or a contested nonpartisan election, or through an uncontested retention or "yes or no" type of election. What has bothered me, of course, is the fact that increasingly special interests and others—often persons and groups with a so-called social or economic agenda—have attempted to alter the course of the law by playing a direct role in judicial elections. This situation has expanded to the point where funds come in from out of state to influence a judicial election in a given jurisdiction. In a similar vein, a lot of money came into California from Utah and other states to overturn a judicial decision, our ruling in the *Marriage Cases*, by supporting the successful campaign to pass a constitutional amendment, Proposition 8. Increasingly such expenditures are made by special interests, and it's obvious that recent decisions of the U.S. Supreme Court that you and I discussed have aggravated this situation.

The *White* case removed the ethical shield that protected an incumbent judge or judicial candidate—and the public—from the contestant's being permitted, or feeling compelled, to announce his or her views on a legal issue that is likely to come before the courts. The *Citizens United* case opens the floodgates of corporate donations to judicial elections, and I predict that you will see a lot more corporate money being thrown into judicial races from out-of-state sources. Now admittedly, it opens such elections equally to labor union funding—which I find equally undesirable—but in any event as a practical matter corporations generally will be able to greatly outspend unions. Then we have the *Caperton* case, which illustrates the degree to which special interests can and will invest in judicial candidates to further their own interests, and specifically their interest in a lawsuit to which they are a party. In that case, a coal company's donation of more than $3 million to the campaign of a lawyer, who successfully challenged an incumbent West Virginia Supreme Court justice, enabled the challenger to cast the tie vote to overturn a $50 million verdict rendered against the coal company. It was only by the narrowest of margins, five to four, that the U.S. Supreme Court held, as we discussed recently, that it was a violation of due process for the recipient of the donation to sit on the state Supreme Court in judgment on the validity of the verdict rendered against the corporate donor. It is apparent that there were five votes to overturn the state court decision only because the federal high court characterized this as an extreme case, involving a donation of millions of dollars. Presumably if it weren't quite that extreme, in the court's words, the high court would not have invalidated the state court decision. I view *Caperton* more as an illustration of the dangers of what lies ahead than as a reassuring restraint on corporate expenditures in judicial elections.

Of course, I had personal experience with a contested confirmation election, namely the 1998 election to retain my position for a full 12-year term as Chief Justice. This was my first confirmation election that was contested. I had been on the ballot previously as an associate justice of the Supreme Court, as an associate justice of the Court of Appeal, and as a trial judge. Interestingly enough, justices on both appellate levels have found that traditionally, with no issue or campaign money raised, there always seemed to be a good chunk of the population that would automatically vote no on the question of whether a justice should be retained in office. Some have theorized that it was because of the lack of information that people had before them in being asked to vote yes or no and seeing, if it was a full term that was up, a twelve-year term and thinking, "Why should I sign off on that? I know nothing about this individual." One trial court incumbent was believed to have lost to a challenger who ran a bagel shop and had no legal experience, largely because of the judge's difficult-to-read Eastern European name. I know that when Justice Arabian was on the ballot he received fewer votes than his colleagues, and the general view was, in that year of troubles in the Persian Gulf, that many voters assumed that someone with the name Arabian was, in fact, an Arab, although Justice Arabian was of Armenian-American descent. On the other hand, in a retention election at which no issues were raised against any of the numerous appellate justices who were on the ballot, the candidate with the all-American name of Justice Jack Armstrong led the vote.

By the same token, it used to be that judges standing for retention could more or less sit back at election time, unless there was some enormous controversy, without doing a lot about campaigning or financing.

That's basically true, although again they'd still get a hefty number of no votes for any reason or no reason. With that in mind, as I mentioned previously, in 2008 I met with Secretary of State Debra Bowen, whom I knew from her former days in the legislature, and told her, "Statements for all sorts of officeholders appear in the voter information pamphlet, and here are Supreme Court justices, a statewide position. Why not include some biographical information for them as well?" She supported legislation that was enacted into law that year, amending the Elections Code and the Government Code to provide that the ballot pamphlet must contain a written explanation of the confirmation process that precedes a Supreme Court retention election, accompanied by biographical information on the justices whose names appear on the ballot so that voters will understand how and why they're being called upon to vote in the election. This legislation has served to improve the process quite a bit. Previously, voters may have been approaching judicial retention elections similarly to the way they consider a lot of these propositions on the ballot, concluding, "Here's something I know nothing about. How can I meaningfully and intelligently vote yes or no? I'll just vote no on the justices if I don't know anything about them." I believe that with the information now being provided, fewer voters will vote no or leave their ballot unmarked in judicial retention elections.

But in any event, I believe your question calls for me to explain the underlying situation with regard to my own 1998 retention election. You will recall from our discussion of my confirmation hearing before the Commission on Judicial Appointments on May 1, 1996 for the position of Chief Justice, that there were persons who exercised their right to appear and testify in opposition to my appointment. With the exception of a disgruntled litigant whom I had ruled against, this opposition was based entirely upon my position in the *American Pediatric Society v. Lungren* case, which ultimately invalidated the parental consent requirement for a person under the age of 18 years to obtain an abortion. Justice Chin, in answering one or more questions at a news conference held by Governor Wilson to announce Chin's appointment, had stated his position in favor of abortion rights. Accordingly, he and I both faced an organized political campaign to deny us retention for our positions on the California Supreme Court.

How far ahead of the 1998 election did you have to be concerned about this?

I certainly saw the storm clouds on the horizon. I had been warned back in 1996 at my confirmation hearing. Of course, my answer, as I said before, was to demonstrate that the court would not be intimidated, so I assigned the case to myself rather than duck responsibility for the criticism that would follow. As the year 1998 began, because I didn't want to get involved with political or fundraising activities before then—and I didn't particularly relish getting involved with them at all—I hired a political campaign organization, McNally Temple Associates, headed by Ray McNally, a moderate Republican with offices in Sacramento, and also engaged the services of Muffie Meier, a Democratic fundraiser located in San Francisco. She told me she would never take a Republican for a client, but she ultimately relented and did. [Laughter] Governor Deukmejian and Senator Feinstein agreed to serve as bipartisan honorary co-chairs of my retention election campaign. My son Eric also became involved in assisting my campaign. In the course of the efforts to defend my seat on the Supreme Court, I ended up raising about $900,000—because there's a certain amount of electronic media that one must engage in, in California, given the size and nature of the electorate. I imposed upon myself a two-year period of disqualification from hearing any case in which any party or lawyer who contributed to my campaign would appear.[1]

---

[1] An amusing perspective was provided by a conversation Barbara had, years later, with Ann Gust, the wife of then-Attorney General Jerry Brown, at a brunch honoring First Lady Maria Shriver, hosted by Governor Schwarzenegger's Chief of Protocol Charlotte Shultz, wife of former Secretary of State George Shultz. As Barbara and Ann dis-

I ended up visiting a great number of editorial boards and editorial writers around the state. My basic pitch was that a voter's decision whether to confirm or not confirm an appellate justice should not be based upon a single decision made by the justice, nor upon the political views of the voter, and that I felt the press had a moral obligation to make this clear to its readership. I found it disturbing that many newspapers endorsed on every office from President of the United States down to the local dog catcher but in effect left California Supreme Court justices twisting in the wind. I told them they should make a point of taking a position, recommending either a yes or no vote, but not just leaving it to chance. Voters, in my experience, would vote no if they had no information and most of them, although not all, would vote yes if they were just provided with some basic information, such as the candidate's legal education and experience and a description of the retention process. A short paragraph putting some flesh on the bare bones of the office held by the incumbent and his or her background would enable the voter to feel that he or she was casting an informed vote.

What kind of response did you get from the editorial community?

It was positive. I believe they realized there was a gap in terms of fulfilling their journalistic responsibilities. Some of them tried to engage me in a discussion of my views on various topics, and of course I wouldn't announce or commit myself to any particular decision. [Laughter] But I explained generally the decision-making process that a judge or court goes through. In the course of this round of visits, I met with editorial boards and editorial writers from the *Los Angeles Times*, the *Oakland Tribune*, the *San Diego Union*, the *San Francisco Chronicle*, the *Los Angeles Daily News*, the *Contra Costa Times*, the *San Jose Mercury News*, the *San Francisco Examiner*, and the various legal newspapers. I spoke at the Sacramento Press Club. I had quite a few interviews with newspapers and magazines.

At the same time, these visits provided me with an opportunity to do two things not narrowly confined to enhancing my own election prospects: first of all, to basically provide another civics lesson concerning what our court system is all about and why it is such a crucial part of our democratic process; and second, to talk about my agenda and vision for the courts. I'm not talking here

---

cussed the challenges posed by their husbands' elections, Barbara observed that at least Ann had to be well aware of what she was getting into, given Brown's lifelong career in politics. "What about me," Barbara asked, "Do you think I ever anticipated we would have to raise nearly one million dollars for Ron's 1998 retention election?" With that, Maria looked at both Barbara and Ann and exclaimed, "What about me? I married the one man I knew for sure would never run for political office."

about decisional objectives but rather structural reforms that I had implemented and planned to implement, along with the other subsidiary reforms—whether it was jury reform or technology or whatever.

I also appeared on various television and radio programs, being interviewed a few times by Michael Krasny and Scott Shafer on KQED, speaking at the convention of the California Broadcasters Association, the Cable Television Associates of California, and many others. Additionally, I met with a wide range of groups, from the California Manufacturers Association to a group of African-American ministers and political leaders that was organized by Congresswoman Juanita Millender-McDonald. There was even a Sunday when, at her invitation, I spoke at several South Central Los Angeles churches in her district, which had a primarily black population. I addressed the Los Angeles Police Officers Protective League, did a video for labor groups, spoke to the teachers union, all sorts of bar associations, lawyers groups, business executives, the California Chamber of Commerce, the Lincoln Club, the California State Sheriffs Association, Kiwanis, a crime victims' group, the California Council for Environmental and Economic Balance, and the Federalist Society. Those are just some of them.

Given the fact that abortion was the major issue, I arranged to have private meetings with two of the leaders of the Catholic Church in California, urging them not to take any official position against my confirmation and to at least remain neutral. They were Archbishop (later Cardinal) William Levada, whom I met with in San Francisco, and Cardinal Roger Mahony, whom I met with in Los Angeles. It was quite an experience getting out on the campaign trail.

It would have been very easy to feel overwhelmed by the need to conduct a political campaign to retain my position as Chief Justice, given all the other duties that I felt obliged to continue performing during the year. I tried to maintain a positive attitude and, as I said before, use this experience as an opportunity to put forth my views on the rule of law, why we have judicial elections, how judges and courts decide matters, the need for the judicial reforms that we were trying to advance, and how important it was to promote access and fairness in our system. I believe there were many benefits that I reaped, and that benefited my ultimate agenda, totally apart from the political aspect of promoting my own retention in office.

What kinds of promises could you extract from the two cardinals?

They just heard me out, but ultimately I avoided having any announcements from their pulpits the Sunday before election day urging a "no" vote on myself and Justice Chin. [Laughter]

You were leaving no stone unturned and doing double duty, not only in advancing your election prospects but also making this larger education effort on behalf of the judiciary. While all this was going on, those who wanted to unseat you were active as well. What were they doing?

They aired some radio ads in the Central Valley. There were a lot of mailings, and there were some Sunday-before-the-election pulpit announcements and flyers in parking lots of churches. There were some political entities that took a position against our confirmation. But aside from my own self-interest, I truly felt there needed to be a defense of judicial independence and that it would have been totally wrong to just leave it to chance, quite apart from my desire to continue serving on the bench.

What was Justice Ming Chin doing before his own retention election that year?

He was doing some similar things. We didn't coordinate our strategy efforts very much, and I recall that was a view we both shared, that it would be better not to be running as a ticket but to just promote our own separate but similar messages. Our efforts bore fruit. I was very pleased to have more than 75 percent of the electorate vote to confirm me, notwithstanding the fact that there was opposition that had spent funds to deny me retention in office, and to see that Justice Chin fared similarly well himself.

This all transpired in the context of political developments in judicial elections elsewhere in the nation, which also concerned me totally apart from my own election. These developments illustrated for me that the situation was not "all about me" and that this was a national phenomenon that the courts had to take seriously and that the people in the various states had to take seriously. The press also began to take the situation seriously, as did various organizations. The Conference of Chief Justices got quite active too, because there were some truly outrageous efforts that got underway in various states.

Before we move on to the national scene, which was particularly important last November, let's acknowledge that we had a history with retention elections here in California. Future historians will want to know your thoughts about the 1986 election here, in which Chief Justice Bird and Justices Grodin and Reynoso were ousted from their seats on the California Supreme Court. Could you reflect on that for a moment?

I believe it was unfortunate that the 1986 retention elections became focused on political issues rather than on the personal qualifications of the three justices to hold office. The practical consequence was that Chief Justice Bird became a lightning rod for political attacks and dragged down Justice Grodin and Justice Reynoso to defeat. I have since come to know Justice Grodin and consider him to be an excellent jurist. The defeat of all three justices illustrates the problem that occurs when there's a perceived ticket of candidate justices running together. The opposition doesn't differentiate or individualize among them and runs a campaign based upon generalities. I do think that Chief Justice Bird did nothing to maximize her chances of being successful at the retention election and, in fact, made certain choices as to on how to conduct or not conduct her campaign that I think really doomed her and the other two justices at the same time. Justice Mosk, however, was very clever in dissociating himself from the justices being targeted and managed to get by with no problem.

How did he pull that off, as you saw it then?

He remained coy about whether he would or would not stand for election but made it clear that he wasn't about to be forced into not filing for reelection—the assumption being that perhaps if he was just left alone he would gracefully retire on his own terms. Then, of course, he proceeded to finance a campaign that consisted of the cost of first-class postage for mailing in his election papers for filing, although I understand that he waited a little bit too late and thought it more prudent to send a messenger up to file the papers. He later ended up receiving a lot of first-class postage stamps, one at a time, from friends and other people who admired the way he had handled his retention.

I have mixed feelings about that election and about Chief Justice Bird. I did find it remarkable that she could vote 100 percent of the time—in more than 60 cases—to overturn the death penalty, suggesting to the opposition that she was following her own personal views rather than applying the law. That was certainly the major focus of the campaign against her, but on the other hand I'm also troubled by reports that major funding, and perhaps *the* major funding, for the campaign against her came not from persons concerned with the issue of the death penalty but rather from corporate interests who presumably did not favor her rulings in areas that affected their economic well-being. Such a scenario sounds, in a way, like a preview of the coming attractions that manifested themselves in the *Caperton* case, although not with a direct party in a pending lawsuit playing the major role in the judicial election. Events in California and in other states have caused some of my views about judicial selection to evolve in ways that I'll share with you at the end of our discussion on this topic. Over the years, especially once I joined the high court, I did hear many negative reports about Chief Justice Bird's role as an administrator and the difficult relations she had with other justices and staff at the court and with persons outside the court, whether they shared her views or didn't.

Can you share your own response to that 1986 election, once it had taken place and you learned that the three justices would leave the court, while Justice Mosk would, of course, stay on?

I hadn't really followed the details of the campaign very closely. It was obvious that Chief Justice Bird and maybe one or two of the other justices were in jeopardy. Not having a great insight into the election, I recall my assumption was, "Well, they'll squeak through." Ultimately I was quite astonished to learn they had been swept out of office.

What's the lesson in all that?

One lesson is that—without letting the circumstance affect one's judicial decisions in the least—if one is a judge or a justice, one has to be prepared to be challenged. This is because judicial officers hold a position that is political in the sense that one appears before the electorate as a candidate, even though the performance of one's official duties is strictly nonpolitical. You have to be prepared to engage in the efforts that one engages in, in a political campaign, modified to be consistent with proper judicial decorum and standards. That is one lesson. Another lesson is recognizing that there needs to be more civics education about the process of judicial elections. People have to understand how and why they are called upon to participate in the judicial selection process. We still haven't really done that job thoroughly enough, even though the secretary of state's legislation has improved the situation substantially for state Supreme Court justices.

There's also the lesson that demonstrates that special interests will involve themselves in a judicial election to further their own financial objectives. Perhaps they will do so without coming right out and indicating what their points of disagreement might be, but they may enter the fray in a way that may not disclose to the voting public the true involvement and motivations of those special interests.

As you say, the general election of November 2010 was of great interest in judiciaries across the country. You mentioned the influence of money from out of state, and I was thinking about the three Supreme Court justices in Iowa who met their fate in that election.

Yes, they were ousted because of their vote on a gay marriage case that reached the Iowa Supreme Court. In fact, there was even a follow-up effort—I don't know whether it's gotten anywhere—to impeach the other four justices who had not been on the ballot but who had also participated in the case.

One of the most egregious measures to make it onto a ballot in recent years was South Dakota's "JAIL 4 Judges" Initiative, the acronym standing for Judicial Accountability Initiative Law, if I recall correctly, and spelling out JAIL. This measure would have literally posed the possibility of incarceration for judges who didn't follow the proponents' concept of the law, and would have imposed a lifetime disability on holding judicial office. Roving special grand juries would evaluate the decision making of judges. The ballot measure was ahead in the polls until the press publicized what the initiative would do. Then it was voted down.

In some states the judicial elections traditionally are highly politicized. In Ohio there are contested elections for the Supreme Court, often with one candidate backed by the Chamber of Commerce and another opposing candidate backed by the labor unions. I was told by the Chief Justice of Texas that a few years ago, when one party swept the elections nationally, virtually all of the trial judges of the other party were voted out of office in the Dallas-Fort Worth area. In fact, one year apparently there was an election for the Supreme Court of Texas in which competing candidates for justice of the Supreme Court were backed by competing oil companies. Now, is that a way to select a Supreme Court? There have been very recent efforts in Tennessee to prohibit "activist" judicial philosophy and, in Arizona, to prohibit courts from relying on foreign or international law or, specifically, Islamic sharia law or canon law.[2]

In light of this election environment and the overlay of these high court decisions—*White, Citizens United*, and the situation illustrated by *Caperton*—the future of judicial selection in state courts is a matter of real concern. A reading of the opinion in *White* suggests that the justices of the U.S. Supreme Court share an antipathy to judicial elections. Believe me, I'm not a fan of judicial elections either, but given my experience and observations, I would much prefer—even having had a contested retention election in 1998—to face the voters every 12 years with a yes or no vote than go through the highly politicized confirmation process engaged in by the U.S. Senate in recent years in acting upon presidential nominees for federal judicial positions. Look at someone like California Supreme Court Justice Goodwin Liu, whose nomination couldn't even get a floor vote in the U.S. Senate for 15 months and then had to be withdrawn by the president. He subsequently joined the state system by appointment of Gov-

---

[2] "Courts under Attack," editorial, *Judicature* (Vol. 94, No. 6, May-June 2011).

ernor Brown, was rated exceptionally well qualified by the State Bar, and easily sailed through his confirmation hearing. The process took five weeks from the date the governor announced his appointment, to his taking the oath of office.

I think what is significant about the U.S. Supreme Court's attitude is that it shows a certain naïveté in assuming that states readily can and will get rid of judicial elections. People will not readily vote in favor of relinquishing their power at the polls—a problem also faced by proposals for initiative reform. It certainly will be difficult to try to persuade the people that they shouldn't be able to vote for or against judges. It's unrealistic of the high court to make it so much more difficult to attract and retain people qualified to serve in state judicial office by coming down with this body of jurisprudence, and then to assume that, okay, if the states don't like it, let them switch to a nonelected judicial selection process. This just isn't that likely to happen. There are more than 10,000 state judges serving in courts of general jurisdiction in the United States, and in 39 states some or all of them face elections of some type, whether it's a contested partisan or nonpartisan election or a retention election.

The U.S. Chamber of Commerce and the National Association of Manufacturers are becoming major players in these elections. Recent reports by the respected American Judicature Society and the Brennan Center for Justice at N.Y.U.—the latter with a forward by Justice Sandra Day O'Connor—detail the growing role played by special interests in targeting campaign contributions to judicial elections at the state high court level and now at the trial court level as well. These reports predate *Citizens United*, which, it is believed, will greatly exacerbate the problem. The articles note examples of judges rendering rulings that were favorable, in significant cases, to large contributors to their judicial election campaigns. In one large-scale survey, a majority of respondent judges conceded that campaign donations had an influence on their decision making.[3] Subsequent articles and studies document the continuing trend toward even greater financial involvement by special interests—corporate, as well as plaintiffs' lawyers—in judicial elections, further eroding the public's confidence in the impartiality of its courts. To put it bluntly, I believe that the increasing efforts of special interests to buy seats on state supreme courts and lower state courts have been facilitated by the high court decisions I have mentioned.

Many high court judges have fairly short terms, and their judicial election campaigns end up being treated just like ordinary political campaigns, which really undermines the whole role of the judiciary and encourages these judges to act like politicians. One solution, in part, is to lengthen the terms, but that's not a

---

[3] *The Judges' Journal* (Vol. 46, No. 1, Winter 2007, published by the American Bar Association).

full solution. Missouri had a response to the *White* decision. It just broadened the rules for recusal. Missouri said, in effect, "Fine. The U.S. Supreme Court has held that you can go ahead and announce your views in violation of the existing code of judicial conduct, but if you go ahead and do this you must recuse yourself." This may remove the incentive for someone to press a judicial candidate to express or announce his or her views on matters likely to come before the court.

Speaking of other states and how they are coping, to what extent were these issues dwelled upon in the Conference of Chief Justices?

Very much so. It's been quite a clearinghouse. We've exchanged views on how to cope with unfair attacks, what judges can and cannot do in response, and how to improve the system of judicial selection.

You may wonder about the so-called merit system. The use of that nomenclature assumes a certain characteristic, merit to the exclusion of political considerations, which isn't necessarily borne out in reality. In my view, so-called merit selection generally just substitutes lobbying directed at a fairly anonymous group for lobbying directed at an accountable, elected official who is the appointing authority—usually the governor. Members of the merit selection committees often are fiercely lobbied, from what I've been told, and it gets to be a bit of an insider's game, so I'm not sure that's really the best way of selecting judges. One of the most important responsibilities of a governor or president of the United States is to select judges who will serve for many, many years, well after the incumbent executive has left office. If he or she—as one in the mix of factors—considers the political and philosophical leanings of the appointee in making a judicial appointment, I don't think that's inappropriate. By the way, if you look at Governor Schwarzenegger's appointments to the bench, I believe that about 45 percent of the judicial appointments by that Republican governor were Democrats.

Of course, on the federal side there is a lifetime appointment for judges, but again, in my view, I don't think obtaining a lifetime appointment is worth going through all of the rigmarole that the U.S. Senate puts people through. I know from my experience chairing a federal judicial selection committee, and from other things I've heard, that there are many highly qualified individuals who have forgone consideration for appointment to the federal bench because they just didn't want to go through that process.

Or others that do go through it and are left hanging, as with now-Justice Goodwin Liu of our California Supreme Court. What occasion did you have to discuss Justice Liu's nomination to our court with him?

I'll first add one other thing. There are persons, unlike Goodwin Liu—who was in an academic environment and could bide his time, so to speak—who have had their law practices virtually destroyed because their clients and the public at large knew they were up for a judicial appointment, and clients did not want to have their lawyer in limbo month after month, more than a year. It's very difficult to maintain a law practice in that situation.

When Goodwin Liu was selected by the governor, Liu asked if he and I could get together for the purpose of his hearing my impressions concerning the work of the California Supreme Court. We had not previously discussed his pending appointment to the bench. We went out to lunch and had a very nice discussion. He was quick to grasp the various nuances of what we discussed. This was about two days before his confirmation hearing, and I shared my impressions of that process with him. I also knew that the very next week he would have to sit on the bench, as I did as a new associate justice, and face a very widely watched and significant case. In my instance it was the term limits initiative. In his it was the Proposition 8 "standing" issue, involving the question of gay marriage, certified to our court by the Ninth Circuit U.S. Court of Appeals. I've since heard very positive reports of how thoughtful his questions were from the bench and about his intelligence, diligence, and very collegial manner.

Thank you. We were talking about the merit system idea of bringing judges into their roles. I know that you had the chance to give considerable thought to this and other alternatives. What more can you tell me about the journey you've taken on the matter of judicial independence and some good alternatives for improving the way things are now?

You and I already discussed my visit to the secretary of state and the ensuing 1998 legislation related to Supreme Court retention election ballot materials. I also appointed a Commission for Impartial Courts, asking Justice Ming Chin to chair it. The commission rendered its final report in 1999 in the four areas of public information and education, judicial campaign finance law, judicial campaign conduct, and judicial selection and retention. The report included a number of thoughtful recommendations that I hope will bear fruit eventually and that are designed to enhance the judicial selection process in various ways to make it more meaningful for the public and at the same time, while holding judges accountable, to keep them above the political fray. Justice Chin's stewardship of this commission was a significant contribution, in addition to all his work chairing the technology committee, his involvement in developing the case management system, and his leadership of our "science and the law" educational efforts.

Indeed, Justice Chin has taken quite an interest in the matter of judicial independence, even beyond chairing this commission. How do you characterize his view of all this?

Yes, he has. I believe his interest comes not only from his having had the opportunity to study the issue in the course of his work heading the commission but also as someone who knows, from the real-life perspective of going through a contested retention election, what in fact it's all about. That's a very helpful blend of experiences and insights to bring to this subject. I'm sure his own thinking has evolved as a result.

My own views, and I haven't talked with Justice Chin about this, have themselves evolved—not only in light of judicial election events on the national scene, but specifically in light of the climate created by the *White* and *Citizens United* cases as, again, illustrated by the situation posed in *Caperton*. I've come to the conclusion that, even though I believe California's judicial selection system is probably the best that exists in the United States—a lengthy term with a yes or no vote by the electorate that follows a confirmation process conducted by a neutral commission after evaluation by the State Bar—our system still is not immune from the very destructive forces that have been unleashed in recent years and that are on the rise nationally. This situation unfortunately will be further fueled by the decisions of the U.S. Supreme Court that you and I have discussed. If I were designing a judicial selection system from scratch, I would provide that a justice would be appointed to the Court of Appeal for a 12-year term pursuant to the existing procedure of appointment by the governor, with evaluation by the State Bar commission, confirmation by the Commission on Judicial Appointments, and confirmation by the electorate, although only after an opportunity to serve at least two years on the appellate bench before facing the electorate, so that there would be a track record upon which to judge the justice. I would provide that those same procedures be followed for appointments to the California Supreme Court with the exception that the appointee be limited to a single term of 15 years and not appear before the electorate for confirmation. The elevation of an associate justice of the Supreme Court to the position of chief justice would not extend the 15-year limitation.

Why 15?

I believe that's a reasonable trade-off for permitting a gubernatorial appointment without legislative or electoral confirmation. There is precedent, of course, in the existing length of term of 12 years, which is close to what I propose, and there are some states that have 15- or 16-year terms—which I believe to be the longest terms provided by any American jurisdiction. This approach refrains from giving someone a life term. Perhaps a life term could be justified and would be politically feasible if there were to be a confirmation process that involves the California Senate, as exists now for U.S. Senate confirmation of federal judicial appointments. But I'm convinced that if California had a process requiring confirmation by the state Senate for appointments to the Supreme Court, legislative confirmation of these appointments would become just as politicized in Sacramento as it is in Washington, D.C., and we would all be the worse off for it. I believe that the price of receiving a life appointment is legislative confirmation, and that a life appointment is not worth that price. But I believe a term of 15 years is not too long to justify an appointment without legislative confirmation, and at the same time it doesn't present the rather awesome situation of a life appointment with no confirmation by a legislative body or the electorate. I would limit a person to 15 years on the Supreme Court, whether as an associate justice or Chief Justice, even though I ended up serving 19 years on the court and wouldn't have been able to do that under the approach that I'm suggesting. I believe, putting aside personal considerations, that this limitation on judicial service would be justified by the benefit of removing justices from the political process, from the retaliation of an electorate fueled in the wake of *Citizens United* by campaign donations from special interests located within and outside California. Although the judicial service of some individuals might be shortened, we used to have a severe retirement-benefit penalty for serving on the bench beyond age 70 in California, which caused many jurists to shorten their judicial service, and we tolerated that before it was repealed, largely due to the efforts of Justice Mosk. I believe it is worth forgoing the possibility of a few more years of service from associate justices and from chief justices if that is the price to be paid for eliminating politics from the determination whether they should continue their service on the high court. Many justices, because of considerations of age and preference, would not end up having their service on the high court shortened by such a 15-year limit on their term.

Judicial elections are going to become more and more politicized through the activities of special interest groups motivated by social or economic agendas. It is unlikely that the public will agree to forgo these elections for an alternative selection process that is more drastic than what I am proposing. So, even though I believe that the detriment of term limits for legislators far outweighs the benefits, the type of term limit I suggest for California Supreme Court justices would be beneficial in removing them from the electoral political process that appropriately governs the election of legislators but that should not affect judicial selection at the high court level. Justices of the high court are far more likely to be targeted by special interests than are the justices of our intermediate appellate courts, so I see much less need at the present time to change the existing electoral process for those positions.

What kind of response have you received to this idea?

Other than mentioning this suggestion briefly and having it picked up in one article, I haven't had any response because I haven't really aired it publicly.

This is your chance. [Laughter]

That's right.

Much as I've been concerned about the threats to judicial independence that come from special interests—whether they're based in California or out of state—and the threat to judicial independence that arises from the use or misuse of the electoral process in our selection of judges, I believe that a significant threat to judicial independence actually comes from another source—one that, perhaps surprisingly, emanates from within our very own ranks, that is, the ranks of California's judiciary itself. This recalls, at least for those of us who used to read the comics pages some time ago, the possum philosopher Pogo, who made the famous pronouncement, "We have met the enemy, and he is us."

My reference is to those relatively few rogue judges, whether operating through their own local court or as part of what I believe they call the judges alliance, who seize upon any issue that arises—and it's a shifting target from one thing to another; they cannot be appeased—as a device to urge the dismantling of the statewide administration of justice and a return to what they view as the good old days, when local courts operated as individual fiefdoms with no true accountability to the counties or to the state for the court's actions or for the court's expenditure of public funds provided by the taxpayers. There are judges who just have never gotten over the changes made by our structural reforms, which some of them fought—and I certainly admit that we have put the judges through a lot of change. As President Woodrow Wilson once observed, "If you want to make enemies, try to change something."

Over the years, I have heard several of the judicial branch's strongest supporters in the legislature voice their concern, publicly and privately, about how destructive these cannibalistic efforts are, and how the interests of our branch of government will be trampled on if we speak with a fragmented voice. If we have the Judicial Council go up to Sacramento with one position, and the California Judges Association go up with another, if individual courts like Los Angeles hire their own lobbyists, and if we have other individuals and groups that purport to represent different segments or fragments of the judiciary myopically seek to further their own parochial positions in the state Capitol, the consequences for the judicial branch can be disastrous. Those same legislators have also remarked how some uninformed, renegade judges have managed the difficult feat of being both cynical and naïve in their efforts to advance their own political agenda, and how hazardous it is to invite legislative intervention in the internal affairs of the judicial branch instead of resolving those matters ourselves. Even if they succeed in achieving a given goal, it is a Pyrrhic victory, very disadvantageous systemically—even to them—in the long run. It's really a classic case of getting the legislative camel's nose under the judicial tent.

Some judges still resent the peer pressure generated by my successful call in 2009 for judges to do their part in coping with cuts to the judicial branch budget by participating in a voluntary short-term salary waiver one day each month. This waiver amounted to a reduction of 4.6 percent in judicial salary for several months and was designed to roughly parallel the mandatory pay cut incurred by judicial branch employees resulting from work furloughs necessitated by the one-day-a-month court closures authorized by the legislature and implemented by the Judicial Council. By the way, all California judges had received pay increases of about 24 percent in the preceding five-year period, due not only to automatic salary adjustments but also to special efforts that I and the Judicial Council had made, prompting a senior Senate staffer to e-mail my principal attorney the message, "I want Ron negotiating my next paycheck."

The so-called judges alliance appears to be basically not much more than an e-mail string on the fringe of the judiciary. Other than the nine or 10 names listed on a letterhead identifying themselves as a board of directors, their alleged membership has been kept secret—believe it or not out of a supposed fear of reprisal by the Administrative Office of the Courts, the Judicial Council, and the California Supreme Court. When someone first told me about this, I said, "My gosh, we're not living in the Soviet Union. How can anyone reasonably believe this?" Apparently no one pays any dues, at least currently. I've been told that's what they say on their website. So merely by receiving e-mail missives because you may want to know what they're up to, you will be included on their inflated membership roster. At times, I have wondered whether the group offers reciprocal membership in the Flat Earth Society. The official directors of the group have spent countless hours composing and distributing rather strident written manifestos on one topic after another—hopefully without employing public resources or their time on the public payroll to engage in these efforts and to travel to attend Judicial Council meetings and lobby at the state Capitol.

There actually have been some rather comical elements in the activities of these judges. A judge who identified himself as a member of the group's board of directors inadvertently sent me and the Administrative Director of the Courts,

Bill Vickrey, the following e-mail, which was intended only for another judge: "Internal debate among judges, my ass. How about a war on judges started by the A.O.C. wherein some judges have become collaborators, others still won't drink the Kool-Aid. I like that take better." What happened after this inadvertent transmittal was a series of phone calls, which one of my secretarial assistants, Gale Tunnell, described as desperate in tone, in which the sender of this e-mail unsuccessfully pleaded with her to erase the e-mail message from my computer before I could get back to town and read it. Then there was a second e-mail, this one intentionally addressed to Bill Vickrey, that read as follows: "If you received an e-mail from me today it was sent in error and was a situation of hitting 'reply all' rather than 'reply sender only.' The e-mail was obviously not intended for you. My apologies for any confusion." Vickrey wrote back a funny response saying he wasn't confused—but that he didn't know about his other reactions. [Laughter] Then came the third part of this trilogy, an e-mail message—this time intentional—that was addressed to me. This was on a Saturday, two days after the last one. It stated: "Soon you will receive a lengthy letter of apology from me. It's already been sent, and I expect that it will arrive by overnight mail on August 21. In my rush to get it out today, there is a possible ambiguity that I have corrected in a follow-up letter that may not arrive until a day later, so I wanted to get this to you now. On page 2, line 8, where it reads, 'resignation letter based on frustration he shared with you both,' it should more correctly read, 'based on frustrations he had shared with you both,' i.e., not that he was frustrated with you but that he had frustrations and had shared them with you both in his letter."

This was the somewhat comic series of communications from a director of this group. Typical of the grandiose rhetoric of their spokespersons is an e-mail message that was sent by one of their board members to my successor—only four months after she assumed the office of Chief Justice. This was widely circulated, so I feel I can make reference to it. "We are concerned that if you succeed in defeating Assembly Bill 1208"—that's the so-called Trial Court Rights Act—"there will be a terrible cost. What has happened in the last 18 months is a Prague Spring for the judiciary of this state. Judges realize that the complete centralization of authority in our branch is a failure. We demand democracy. The genie will refuse to go back into the bottle." The pronouncements of this group also often include wild accusations, such as a reference to "judges willing to put their neck out there and face the wrath of the A.O.C. empire."

When I was asked by the press whether these malcontents were a major source of concern to me, I responded that if I were to let that happen it would be like canceling a trip to Yosemite because there were ants on the trail. [Laughter] That caused a further complaint that, "We have been called insects by the chief!" Frankly, I think I was being rather charitable in making a comparison to creatures that occupy a much higher rank in the insect hierarchy than I might have referenced.

I laughed at the fantasies, conspiracy theories, and frequent references by these complainers to me as King George, with their protests to things such as Bill Vickrey's having electronically distributed to the judiciary my State of the Judiciary address, and I found it curious that their complaints about the Judicial Council and about me usually were focused on the very things that had generally earned the most praise. But I did take more seriously the vicious, false personal attacks that they have leveled against others, in a cowardly fashion, through often anonymous blogs. Their targets have included Judicial Council members—for instance Justice Richard Huffman, who was one of the most dedicated and productive members of the Council—and the talented and hard-working members of the A.O.C. staff, from Bill Vickrey on down. They even found fault with the Shapiros' philanthropy in establishing the Administration of Justice Fund.

I also believe that these judges were quite wrong to rebut the overtures made by my successor shortly after she assumed office, not even giving her a chance to engage them in dialogue before launching unfair criticisms. I do believe that they may be seeking to exploit the transition to a new Chief Justice, as well as the critical funding situation that lies ahead for the courts in the state's current economic downturn. I view them as the Tea Party element of the California judiciary. I think the tone of the criticism that they level against anyone who doesn't go along with their agenda seriously calls into question the judicial temperament of some of these critics to the extent that I would counsel a friend against having even a dog-leash violation tried in one of their courtrooms. I have been informed that some judges have attempted to intimidate their judicial colleagues, especially those serving in the Sacramento Superior Court, by threatening to support an opponent when they are next up for election, if the incumbent does not go along with the critics' agenda. Some judges have ties to political operatives that have enabled them to engage in opposition research, political dirty tricks,[4] and the knowing distribution of false information or disinformation.

As observed by one of the characters in a book I read recently, *The Cellist of Sarajevo* by Steven Galloway, "There is a lot less tolerance for tolerance right now. I hope this will change." I only hope that these destructive efforts do not impair the cooperative relationships that have developed and functioned so well among judges and our justice system partners—including the California Judges Association and the various bar groups—and with the other branches of gov-

---

[4] For example, posting on a website the home address and a Google Earth photograph of the home of a senior member of the A.O.C. staff, accompanied by false accusations, necessitating protective law enforcement surveillance of his home.

ernment. The time, energy, and resources expended by these critics and unfortunately, by necessity, by the A.O.C. in responding to the false information contained in their diatribes and manifestos, and to countless oppressive demands for
information under public records provisions, could be put to much better use in
dealing with the challenges currently confronting our judicial system and the
public it serves.

The critics of our successful efforts to establish a statewide system of court
administration and a true judicial branch of government, in function and not just
in name, have been rebutted by countless judges and court administrators and
court staff and leaders of the community. This support has been communicated
to the Judicial Council and the A.O.C. verbally and in writing. I have received
many of these communications and have been informed of others received by
the Council and the A.O.C. I do want to quote one such communication from
Justice Donald Franson of the Fifth District Court of Appeal, which puts some
of this foolishness in historical and national perspective. This is from a letter he
wrote to me earlier this year: "I'm in the middle of a biography of Justice [Wil-
liam] Brennan, who spearheaded a reorganization of the New Jersey court system in the 1940s, which was fought by all the entrenched interest groups. He
described it as an 'unwieldy labyrinth of courts with overlapping jurisdiction
ruled by judges seemingly answerable to no one. The system was notorious for
long delays.' Like you, he eventually won over the opposition and greatly improved the New Jersey court system."

I guess the last point I'll make on this subject is that when I recently saw
Justice Kathryn Werdegar, she graciously described my stewardship of the judicial branch as a golden era. My hope and my expectation is that the glow of that
era will continue into the stewardship of my successor and her successors. It has
been gratifying to read of Chief Justice Cantil-Sakauye's commitment to preserving what she frequently calls "the house that George built."

I regret having had to dwell to this extent on the negative, but I did so because—in response to your inquiry about challenges facing the judicial branch
and your focus on judicial independence—I truly believe that among the various
hazards faced by the judicial branch, it is important to keep in mind that a substantial threat to judicial independence comes from within our own ranks. That's
something that I believe demands courage and vigilance by the approximately
1,700 judges in our California judiciary if we are to remain the best, the fairest,
and the most accessible of judicial systems, as I believe us to be.

*Knowing that you have remained available for consultation but otherwise
hands-off with your successor, what observations do you make about her first
year, almost, on the job?*

I regret for her that she immediately had to be confronted with such severe budget problems. I recognize based on my own experience as chief for 14 years that the state's budget difficulties—and therefore those of the judicial branch—are cyclical. The state has a boom-and-bust structure, in part due to our tax system that depends so much on fluctuating sources of revenue. Chief Justice Cantil-Sakauye took office during a period of severe downturn instead of when there was an uptick in the economy and in the welfare of the state's judicial budget. I'm sure the latter situation will return, but the interim will be difficult.

It's unfortunate that as she was faced with an immediate fiscal crisis, she had to deal with dissident judges who didn't even give her the courtesy of letting her get her feet on the ground before they made demands and launched criticisms while she was mastering the operations of the California Supreme Court, dealing with a myriad of administrative responsibilities, and establishing her relationship with the legislature and the governor. Having said that, I cannot imagine anyone better equipped by temperament and experience to confront these challenges than she. She's done a remarkable job performing a great variety of duties and at the same time being accessible—speaking all over the state to her constituencies in the justice system, judges and lawyers alike, and the public, in a tireless fashion while also engaging the executive and legislative branches in dialogue on matters of crucial importance to the judiciary. I have the highest admiration for her and for her adaptation to the enormous responsibilities that she has willingly, enthusiastically, and even cheerfully assumed.

I note that you had an opportunity to become involved in the Sandra Day O'Connor Project on the State of the Judiciary at Georgetown Law School. Could you preface that by talking about Justice O'Connor herself and her interest in this area?

Yes. Your question concerning the Sandra Day O'Connor Project brings me to the fourth major challenge facing the judiciary in the coming years—the need to ensure sufficient awareness among our student and adult population, through civics education, of their rights and responsibilities and of the role of the courts in our society.

I did get to know Justice O'Connor from my involvement in the Conference of Chief Justices, where she addressed us. She subsequently came to California, spoke at some events sponsored by our Judicial Council and other groups, and participated in conferring a couple awards on me. We were both called upon to participate in the rededication of a courthouse, namely the building in which I had served as supervising judge of the criminal divisions of the Los Angeles

Municipal and Superior Courts. It was called the Criminal Courts Building and is a block-long building of 17 stories with more than 60 courtrooms, all devoted exclusively to hearing criminal matters arising just in the downtown area of Los Angeles County. More judges preside in that one building than comprise the entire statewide judiciary of general jurisdiction judges in any one of at least 10 individual states. One of the few things that the L.A. District Attorney and the L.A. County Public Defender agreed upon was that the building should be re-named to honor the first woman lawyer in the state of California. They con-vinced the L.A. County Board of Supervisors to take this action, and the build-ing is now known as the Clara Shortridge Foltz Criminal Justice Center. Foltz was quite a remarkable woman, a single mother who studied law in a law office. She had to bring a lawsuit to be admitted to practice, because the legal profes-sion was restricted by statute to males. She set up the first public defender's of-fice and ultimately ran for public office.

I was asked to speak at a luncheon attended by several hundred people, pre-ceding the official ceremony, and in the course of my remarks to introduce Jus-tice Sandra Day O'Connor. I asked my staff to come up with something interest-ing about her. I was able to tell the following story. Justice O'Connor had at-tended the law school that I later attended, Stanford Law School, where she was number three in her class. I believe Chief Justice Rehnquist was number one in the same class. When it came time to apply for a position as an attorney in a law firm, Justice O'Connor was turned down routinely. She could not get a perma-nent job offer anywhere. Many of the prospective hiring firms just told her bluntly, "I'm sorry, we don't hire women." This included a large multinational firm, Gibson Dunn & Crutcher. The managing partner said, "I'm sorry, Miss Day. We just can't hire you, because you're a woman." But he said that if she typed well enough, the firm might hire her as a legal secretary. Justice O'Connor, being the polite woman she is, didn't respond in the manner I'm sure she was tempted to, and ultimately made her way back to Arizona, where she did obtain employment in a law firm. She later was elected to the state legisla-ture, becoming, I believe, the Republican leader in the Arizona Senate before being appointed to Arizona's intermediate appellate court.

The day then came when President Reagan had his attorney general phone Arizona Court of Appeal Justice Sandra Day O'Connor and, as I understand it, more or less the following conversation occurred. "Justice O'Connor, I have the distinct honor, on behalf of President Reagan, of offering you a position on the United States Supreme Court." This is where the story gets quite amusing. It was Attorney General William French Smith, the former Gibson Dunn & Crutcher managing partner who had told her that he could only offer her a posi-tion as a legal secretary. Justice O'Connor's response, which I'm sure she was very pleased to give after this interval of many years, still recalling the earlier conversation, was, "Oh, a position on the U.S. Supreme Court? Is that as a legal secretary?" [Laughter] In any event, Gibson Dunn & Crutcher made amends and held a reception in honor of Justice O'Connor. When I told this story, the audience burst into laughter and drowned out Justice O'Connor, whom I could see at one of the tables below the dais, gesticulating as if to indicate, "Yes, that's it. That's what happened." We both then proceeded to the site to cut the ceremonial ribbon.

I believe I did not see Justice O'Connor again until U.S. Supreme Court Justice Stephen Breyer asked Barbara and me over to dinner at his Georgetown home. Because the dining room door was somewhat ajar, I could see that this was to be a dinner for six and was curious as to who would be the other couple. When the doorbell rang, Justice Breyer jumped up and said, "Oh, good. Here's Sandra with the potluck." It was Justice O'Connor, who was accompanied by her husband, John. Over dinner we talked about the project that later became known as the Sandra Day O'Connor Project on the State of the Judiciary at Georgetown University Law Center. I was asked to serve on the steering committee, and I went back to Washington four years in a row in that capacity.

There were some excellent presentations at these sessions. One of the most remarkable speeches was delivered by Justice David Souter, who eloquently spoke of learning about the separation of powers and the role of the judiciary through his experiences growing up in a small town in New Hampshire. An excellent talk by Justice Breyer focused on three very significant cases in the history of the U.S. Supreme Court that illustrated America's growing acceptance of the rule of law. It started with a discussion of the case involving the Cherokee Nation in Georgia, and President Andrew Jackson saying basically, "Chief Justice John Marshall has made his decision. Now let him enforce it." Justice Breyer went on to the Little Rock, Arkansas, Central High School desegregation case, and President Eisenhower sending troops to enforce the decision of the U.S. Supreme Court. He then got to *Bush v. Gore*, which—despite a lot of public disagreement and consternation about the process and the resulting opinion, issued over his dissent—was accepted with no manifestations of civil disorder, such as undoubtedly would have occurred in many other nations with a court weighing in on a presidential election. The way he wove these themes together—and they are illustrated in a very fine book he wrote—was quite captivating.

One of the conclusions reached during the course of the O'Connor Project was that Americans are woefully unaware of how their government operates and of their constitutional rights and civic responsibilities. I'll mention a few of the findings, which all came from polls or surveys conducted in recent years, because Justice O'Connor viewed them as very significant, and they contributed to the ultimate recommendations that came out of her efforts. The majority of Americans do not know what the Bill of Rights is and could not define it, and one-third of native-born Americans can't pass the civics portion of the naturalization test that legal immigrants are required to pass to become full citizens. Some of the constitutional rights set forth in the Bill of Rights, if put before potential voters today as abstract propositions, would be defeated. Two out of three adult Americans could not name the three branches of government, and one out of three could not name even a single branch. More could name the Three Stooges than the three branches of government. Some identified the three branches as the Republican, Democratic, and Independent. Fifty-four percent of those polled could name the judge on the television program *People's Court*, but only 9 percent could name the Chief Justice of the United States. There were far more people who could identify the star of the motion picture *Titanic* than identified the vice president of the United States. Justice O'Connor has stated that she views political attacks on judges as an offshoot of such civic ignorance.

More recently I learned that 45 percent of the high school students in one survey thought that our country had fought alongside Germany against the Russians in World War II, and that although most of them could not name any five U.S. presidents, they could name five brands of designer jeans.

By the way, while we're talking about television, I want to mention that the California Commission on Judicial Performance occasionally receives complaints about the rulings rendered by Judge Judy on TV, asking that she be disciplined—not being able to differentiate between real life and entertainment. [Laughter] Conversely, there are some who write in to complain, "Judge So-and-So ruled incorrectly. He should have ruled the way Judge Judy would,"—so either holding her up as a model or as a jurist meriting discipline.

What do you think of People's Court and like TV shows?

To the extent they illustrate real-life situations and people's rights, I suppose they perform somewhat of a positive role, but from what I understand many of the episodes are fictionalized or overly selective in terms of what they portray. Anything in motion pictures or television that distorts the public's perception of how and why judges and courts decide things is in my view quite misleading and harmful. Some of the things that you see going on in courtroom entertainment are the equivalent of a medical drama's having Dr. Kildare flick cigarette ashes into an open body cavity. They're just totally off the mark. I think that's very unfortunate.

Justice O'Connor herself, I remember, told us that during a visit to a high school, she asked a class of students to tell her the purpose of the Declaration of

Independence. She said they were unable to answer. As she exclaimed to us, "My gosh. It's in the title. You'd think that would be pretty obvious."

That's like asking who's buried in Grant's tomb.

Exactly. I found all this ignorance particularly disturbing at a time when we are purporting to export our democratic system of government, whose foundation is a fair and impartial and independent judiciary, to new and emerging nations while not fully understanding or appreciating it ourselves.

Justice O'Connor, with the aid of experts, came to the conclusion that the best way of dealing with this educational gap is actually to focus on middle-school kids through devices that they spend so much of their time with, namely electronic games—which can be very educational. She founded "iCivics," which has produced more than a dozen educational video games and various teaching materials that are now used in classrooms in every state. In one game, you're a clerk to a Supreme Court justice. In another, you're a law partner. You may be a deputy public defender, or counsel to a corporation. There are electronic games with role-playing, and the kids have been wildly enthusiastic about them. The games include all sorts of different scenarios. What is very heartening to hear is that apparently they bring these games home and instruct their parents, who also end up learning something valuable.

I think we have a big hill to climb here, but this seems to be a very productive approach. I truly admire Justice O'Connor—at any age, but especially at her 81 years, in retirement—for traveling throughout the United States tirelessly promoting her program for civics education.

What else came out of the O'Connor Project before it finished, what kinds of recommendations or ideas for improving the independence of the judiciary and civics education?

My recollection is that the main focus ended up being on civics education in terms of practical recommendations as to what we actually can do. There were numerous observations and illustrations of what needs to be done to improve the current state of public awareness and judicial selection. I also remember that some judicial campaign television ads were screened, and they were as bad as you could imagine. There was some discussion of so-called merit selection, but as I recall there certainly were no uniform views on that option. Everyone focused on the educational element and the need for each state, through its Chief Justice or otherwise, to set up some sort of effort to engage in civics education and to take steps, according to the needs of the particular state jurisdiction, to protect judicial independence, which the participants viewed as very much under threat. This was one of the occasions on which I heard Justice O'Connor express dismay at her own vote in the *White* case. She said she had not realized what a negative impact it would have on judicial independence. Who knows, perhaps these sentiments had a bearing on her desire to become involved in what became known as the Sandra Day O'Connor Project.

What are the ramifications for California in this area?

We have a very fine civics education program, which parallels and emulates what is urged by Justice O'Connor. Some of it was developed independently, but we're certainly taking advantage of her efforts. The California judiciary is firmly committed to achieving the objectives put forth by the O'Connor Project.

As I mentioned in one of our prior discussions, I made it a point every year to greet a number of civics teachers who came to the Administrative Office of the Courts to receive a few days of intense training on how to teach civics and how to teach other teachers to teach civics. This is a vital effort because—with the current emphasis on achievement in math and science and the federal monetary reward to schools for high scores in those subjects—there's been a real tendency to neglect other subjects, whether it is civics education, grammar, or arts and music education—an area that Barbara has focused her attention on.

I would add, as I said in another context in one of our earlier sessions, that if the public doesn't understand what we're doing as judges they will mistrust the judicial system—and that is something that comes back to haunt us in terms of how people act on issues involving the judiciary and our legal system, how they will exercise their right to vote in judicial elections and on ballot measures affecting the courts, what they communicate to their legislators when issues come up involving the judicial system, and how they perform their duties as jurors. These matters are all dependent upon our citizens' having a basic understanding of their government, including their courts, and of their own rights and responsibilities.

What about some other actions that Justice O'Connor has expressed interest in, in her writings, such as more education of the media and directly of voters about judicial elections and then providing more information to voters. You did touch on that.

Justice O'Connor expressed strong interest in the areas you mention. I believe we need to engage in more of those efforts by encouraging the press to explain what courts do and how they decide cases, and to make endorsements—pro or con—in judicial elections, and not just ignore them. California has an active Bench-Bar-Media Committee that I established to foster better understanding, not only by members of the media in terms of how the courts operate but—it's bilateral—for judges to have a better understanding of how journalists work and the conditions under which they operate.

For instance, I've always marveled that a reporter, usually not trained in the law, has to assimilate one or more of our opinions—and occasionally they are rather turgid and lengthy to boot—and understand and be able to describe the reasoning and holding in time to meet that day's deadline. Reporters who write for one of the wire services such as Associated Press have to do this under an even shorter deadline, because they're supposed to be out there in advance of the deadlines of the regular newspapers. The legal newspapers also have a deadline that is earlier than the general circulation papers, which still have to have something out by the end of the day. So we decided to give advance notice by a day or so of impending filings to enable the reporters to get their notes together from oral argument, if they were in attendance, or to electronically retrieve a recording of the oral argument. They can go to the briefs if they haven't already, and can start getting ready to assimilate the opinion and to locate the attorneys on the winning and losing sides to arrange to obtain reactions to the opinion once it is released. All of this helps enable the press to do its job of informing the public. There's a lot that judges can do, instead of just saying, "No comment. I'm afraid of getting involved with the press," and still comport with proper standards of judicial decorum.

We've touched on a number of current and future challenges for the judiciary. Where do you think the most important emphasis should be? What concerns you most among these various challenges that lie ahead?

I would say that each of the four areas that we've just discussed—the perennial problem of securing sufficient funding for the operation of the courts; the problem of lack of legal representation for parties in civil litigation; the problem of judicial independence; and the fourth area, civics and the lack of awareness by our public of how the courts operate—is vitally important.

Knowing you have had nearly a year of retirement, how do you evaluate your own career looking back on it?

I consider it, of course, an enormous honor and privilege to have been entrusted by four governors with different levels of judicial office and, in particular, for Governor Pete Wilson to have appointed me first as an associate justice and then as Chief Justice of the California Supreme Court and of the State of California. It was an opportunity that in my view was without equal or parallel in any sphere of public or private endeavor. I cannot imagine any position in either sector that I would have been happier to serve in or felt as challenged in serving. It was an exceptional experience to work with an outstanding chambers staff and other legal, administrative, and clerical staff serving on the Supreme Court, on the lower courts, and in the Administrative Office of the Courts; to formulate policy with members of the Judicial Council, which included exceptionally dedicated justices, judges, lawyers, and court administrators; to collaborate with judges throughout the state in efforts to improve the administration of justice; and to form working partnerships with some of our finest public servants in the legislative and executive branches in Sacramento.

Occasionally in our discussions, I have mentioned some of the negative and more challenging aspects of my role as head of the judicial branch in interacting with our two co-equal branches, but I don't want to overlook in any way the circumstance that whatever we accomplished would not have been possible without the dedication and commitment of outstanding leaders and staff in the State Senate, the State Assembly, and the Office of the Governor, as well as local governmental entities and judicial and bar associations throughout the state—all of our justice-system partners. This collaboration has been a wonderfully gratifying experience, as has been, of course, my primary responsibility of authoring opinions for the court that will have a profound effect on people's lives for many generations to come. A true privilege.

Any regrets?

No regrets. I wish some things that occurred or that were accomplished had transpired more easily, but in retrospect I consider myself very fortunate with regard to how well things have gone in terms of my career, my family life, my ability to set out to accomplish certain things for the judiciary and the public it serves, and the success those efforts have met.

I was thinking about how you described your father as a risk taker in his work and that you might be a risk taker of a different sort. You did have to go out on a few limbs along the way.

I often do reflect on my father and mother and on how much in the way of values they instilled in me. They also made it possible for me—by enabling me to obtain an excellent education—to undertake some of these tasks over the years, starting with my career as a deputy attorney general and advancing through four levels of the judiciary to the position of Chief Justice of California. In reflecting on my parents, I realize how I truly did inherit traits from both sides—the intuitive, creative, and risk-taking element of my father and the more cautious, conservative, and analytical approach of my mother. I'd like to think this mix has served me well and hopefully served well the tasks that I undertook in public service.

You certainly put that mix to work for all Californians. Are there any other observations you'd like to offer before we close?

In preparation for this last of our interview sessions, I spent some time thumbing through two very large notebooks assembled by the very able staff of the court library. These notebooks chronicle stories in newspapers and journals that are related to my fourteen-year service as Chief Justice of California. Each article covers some aspect of that service, whether it's a personal profile or something relating to a judicial opinion or to an administrative reform.

My purpose in undertaking this little effort last night was to see whether you and I had missed any major loose threads in what we've covered in these discussions over the past six months. You'll be very relieved to hear me report that we did not overlook anything. But going through these clippings has reminded me of an observation that's been made: journalism is the first rough draft of history—which, by the way, is one of several reasons I always made it a practice to attempt to accommodate the needs of the press in the course of my professional career. Others have made the additional observation that most people today have a very minimal sense of history, only a sense of nostalgia. So, Laura, I feel confident that our 20 very enjoyable and productive sessions will provide a second draft of history of use to persons in the present and the future with an interest in our judicial system. I thank you very much.

You're so welcome. Let me thank you for the honor of working with you this year to document your life and career. Is there anything you'd like to say more about or to bring up for the first time?

No, nothing at all.

Thank you again.

My great pleasure.

###

Appendix 1

Areas of Chief Justice's Responsibilities
(Prepared by Chief Justice Malcolm M. Lucas' staff)

1. Administrative Presiding Justices meetings and appointments
   Budget allocation, review, and advocacy
   Personnel issues
   CAP oversight (AIDOAC committee—including appointments)
2. California Constitution Revision Commission
3. Commission on Judicial Appointments
4. Commission on Judicial Performance
   Disability Retirements
   Oversee appointment of masters at CJP request
5. Judicial Emergencies
6. Judicial Council
   Appointments
   Presiding
   Committee Meetings
   Budget
7. Judicial Assignments
8. Judicial Retirements
9. Administrative Office of the Courts
   Overall supervision
10. Litigation against the court
11. State Bar/State Bar oversight
12. Supreme Court
    Presiding over conference
    Assignment of cases
    Review of salmon and blue sheets
    Personnel
    Regular review of court production statistics
    Stays
    Capital Appeals procedures
    Administrative Conferences
    Central Staff Committees
    Administrator/Clerk's Office supervision
    Library issues
    Reporter of Decisions (Publication of official reports)
    Internal budget
    Maintenance of internal procedures and practices
13. CJER Governing Committee appointments

Appendix 1

Other duties and involvement
1. ABA task forces as requested
2. Conference of Chief Justices
3. Coalition for Justice
4. Federal State Jurisdiction Committee
5. Future studies
6. National Center for State courts
7. Assorted National Conferences
8. State/Federal Judicial Council
9. AOC Public Information Office

Appendix 2

Wednesdays with the Chief
(A Charming and Multi-Tasking Micro-Manager)[1]

As most court observers know, the seven justices of the California Supreme Court meet every Wednesday morning (except during oral argument week) at 9:15 a.m. around a large dark walnut table in Chief Justice Ronald M. George's fifth floor chambers in the Earl Warren Building, alone behind a heavy oak door. Standing outside, during the first few minutes of the meeting, one hears muffled conversation from inside, often punctuated by group laughter, before the justices get down to business.

First they discuss the progress of granted cases working their way through the court—does Justice X's circulating draft opinion in *People v. Jones* adequately respond to Justice Y's concurring and dissenting opinion such that it retains a majority vote of four justices? Is there sufficient agreement with Justice Z's "calendar memorandum" in *Williams v. Smith* that we can set it for the next oral argument calendar? And so on. Next they tackle the "conference list"—typically 200–400 petitions for review and for writs, and an accompanying four-inch stack of internal memos prepared by court staff, describing, analyzing, and making recommendations in each matter. From this list and these memos they decide which few cases merit full review by the court (oral argument and opinion), and they dispose of the rest in a variety of ways, mostly by straight denial. Then the meeting breaks up, the door to the Chief's conference room opens, and the justices emerge into the anteroom, animated, chatting, making small talk with each other and the Chief's secretaries and any of his legal staff who happen to be there, before walking the halls back to their own chambers.

Except on July 14, 2010, when the justices emerged from the Chief's chambers looking ashen and with reddened, moist eyes. He had waited until the end of conference to mention, with a glimmer in his eye, that it was Bastille Day, and that, by the way, after considerable reflection, he would not seek reelection to a new 12-year term and would instead retire, after 38 years as a judge, and 14 as Chief.

The shock has since been absorbed up and down the halls of the court, and throughout the state. Editorial writers have lauded the Chief's vision and recounted his many administrative accomplishments: among other things, stabilized trial court funding; unification of the municipal and superior courts into one superior court in each county; and state/judicial branch own-

---

[1] This article originally appeared in the *California Supreme Court Historical Society Newsletter* (Fall/Winter 2010), 2–4.

ership and control of county courthouses. And of course many have focused on his courage and craft in authoring more than a few landmark decisions. In the same vein, numerous bar groups have bestowed ever more engraved honors—crystal or glass sculptures, and plaques that threaten to overwhelm his commodious chambers—along with letters and bouquets from judicial and political leaders statewide and nationwide. Most recently, in late October, the Judicial Council sponsored a two-hour tribute memorializing the Chief's career and tenure.

To that broad macro view of the Chief's public accomplishments, I'll add some brief personal observations about the Chief's hands-on approach to the behind-the-scenes daily workings within the California Supreme Court itself.

In addition to all of the systemic reforms for which he has become and will long be known, the Chief also is one of seven justices on the California Supreme Court, and in that capacity he has opinions to prepare and a court to run. Those tasks require focus on two matters, simultaneously: quality and productivity. He is proud of the court's tradition as a leading and influential judicial body, and he has always made it clear that the quality of his, and the court's decisions is paramount. At the same time, he is aware that matters before the court must be resolved at a reasonably efficient pace, and that the court needs to maintain a respectable level of productivity, measured by, among other things, its annual output of filed opinions. In this regard, I'll focus on something that others have not discussed—my perspective of the Chief as a persistent, yet charming, multitasking nudger with a keen attention to detail.

His operating principle is an extreme version of the maxim "Don't put off for tomorrow that which you can do today." As his administrative and attorney staff can attest, when he receives a draft memo, he often returns it within hours. Very lengthy memos may stay with him for a few days or longer—after all, there's a lot of competing paper in his rolling briefcase—but once he's made his edits, he's in no mood for further delay. And what edits they are. In addition to refining clarity and improving focus, he has an uncanny ability to spot (or sniff out) errors, large and small, in any material that's presented to him. He calls you into chambers, discusses the changes, and then nicely lets it be known that he wants the revised memo to circulate as early as possible that afternoon (after he approves and personally proofreads the revised version) so that it will be logged into the court's internal tracking system as of that time and date, and hence start the clock running for other chambers to respond. This get-it-done-correctly-and-promptly approach, and variations of it, is how he manages the huge amount of material that overflows his inbox hourly.

My most direct observations of the Chief in "manager mode" relate to our private meetings following each Wednesday conference. After the conference concludes and the justices leave his chambers, I receive a call from one of his two secretaries: "The Chief is ready to see you now." I gather some papers and walk a few steps down the hall to his chambers, to go over the conference results and related matters concerning cases pending within the court. Our meeting lasts between 15 minutes to one hour, depending on his schedule, and it provides a glimpse of the Chief in high administrative/multitasking form.

"First, the salmon course," he says. We pick up the "salmon list" (so-called because of the color of paper on which it's printed), setting out the status of each case that's been argued, and for which an opinion is due to circulate. Our discussion is punctuated with substantive asides about a few problematic cases, and then the phone rings. He's informed that "Senator 'A' is on the line." He tells me "this will take just a minute," takes the call, finishes, and without missing a beat, moves to the next case on the list. It proceeds like this, with other interruptions: "Court of Appeal Justice 'B' is calling . . . ." Two minutes later we are back to the salmon sheet. He's concerned that Justice "X" still has not circulated an opinion in an overdue matter. He mentions that he's already touched on this with his colleagues at conference, but could I please also gently contact that justice's staff, and ask about the status? I make a note to do so. And by the way, that reminds him—he digs into his left pants pocket and out comes his wad of paper scrap notes—an inch thick, organized in a fashion that only he understands, and he sifts through them: It's a jotting that he wrote at least a week ago, about a wholly separate matter. "Could you please look into this [case, statute, news article] and follow up on that?"

We then review the "blue list" (again so-called because of the color of paper on which it's printed), detailing the status of each case in which a pre-argument "calendar memo" has been circulated, but that has not yet been argued. We discuss a case in which Justice "Y" is a bit overdue in circulating an internal "preliminary response"—necessary before the court can set the matter for argument. There was some discussion of this matter at conference, and the justice promised to issue his response soon. The Chief, ever vigilant, says, "If that doesn't happen within the next few days, will you please follow up with his staff?" I make a note to do so. The phone rings; a trial judge in on the line, can the Chief speak with him now? Two minutes later we resume, only to be interrupted again by his private phone. His wife, Barbara, is calling. "I'm just going through the conference with Jake," he says. A minute or two later, after he quickly discusses plans for that evening's social engagement (tonight, opera; other times it's a charity or bar event, the ballet, a dinner party, or a visit by one of his three sons), we return to the list. Two cases have progressed sufficiently that the court has agreed to set them for the annual "on the road" oral argument session, to be held this year in the Central Valley, but another case, also targeted for that special session, has stalled. "Let's add a note to the next calendar conference memo that the court is targeting this case for the special session, and asking all chambers to act on it in time to make that calendaring decision in the next two weeks." I'll incorporate that notation to the "calendar conference memo," setting the agenda for next week's calendaring discussion, which the Chief will circulate within the court later that afternoon.

In the meantime, one of his secretaries brings in lunch—frequently, in recent months, it's tuna, often without bread. At this point I run to the staff fridge to get my own half sandwich, and we picnic at the big table, talking briefly about family issues ("so how's Adam?") or former court employees, restaurants, and politics—United States and international. If I say something that he wants to follow up on, he takes out his wad of paper scraps, finds an appropriate clear area, and jots down some words. At that point he gets up and walks over to his rolling brief case, parked near the door: "That reminds me, I have an article for you from over the weekend." It's from the *New York Times* business section, and has been carefully cut out, with an arrow pointing to my circled name in red ink in the upper right corner. After I share with him a slice of apple or pear, he says, "All right, let's turn to the conference list."

This third internal court document of the day sets forth all of the 200–400 matters acted upon by the court earlier in the morning. We go through the 20–40 most important cases on the list, noting the votes ("denied; Justices 'X' and 'Y' would have granted"), and he relays pertinent comments by the justices concerning certain cases, or about the internal memo prepared by staff for the court concerning the case. Concerning one matter that the court transferred back to the intermediate appellate court, the justices revised the proposed order language— could I please bring that change to the attention of the appellate clerical and attorney staff for future reference? The phone rings; a journalist is calling to interview him for a story about a recent Judicial Council matter. Ever cognizant of the 4:00 p.m. press deadline, he takes the call, and addresses the questions with carefully-worded candor. Back to the conference—where were we? Item number 20, *Smith v. Jones*—the court granted review after a spirited discussion and despite a recommendation by the writer of the internal memo, that the matter be denied. He's thinking of assigning the case to Justice "X," but has some hesitation; maybe it would be a better fit for Justice "Y"? He'll finalize that decision by the end of the day (after consulting his own hand-written tally of matters, already assigned to each justice) when I give him a draft of the assignment memo, which he will edit and then promptly send out to his fellow justices. And finally, concerning another matter in which the court granted review: "We want to make sure that the assigned justice considers, and promptly prepares a memo for the court concerning whether we should expand briefing to address the additional issue mentioned on page 7 of the conference memo"—and so he asks me to incorporate that notation into the draft assignment memo. And how about that?—only one interruption in the past 15 minutes.

Back to Bastille Day 2010: I'll never forget that post-conference meeting with the Chief. Because of his surprise announcement, there were more than the normal number of interruptions that afternoon—including a couple calls from the Governor's office—and our meeting progressed in fits and starts, sandwiched between in-person and telephone interviews that he'd spontaneously agreed to give to various members of the media. Instead of finishing at our normal time of about 12:30 or 1:00 p.m., I was still at the conference table with him at 4:50 p.m. We were concluding our discussion of the conference list, when we were interrupted: Yet another radio station was on the line, requesting a live interview—at least the fourth that afternoon. "All right," he said, "as long as the questions will be from the reporters, and not call-in listeners." We continued to work through the conference list as we could hear, on speakerphone, the radio station producer cueing the two radio station anchors, while in the background we heard the end of a commercial for a roofing business. And then we went live for an eight-minute interview. As the Chief spoke—naturally, extemporaneously, and yet carefully, elegantly answering wide-ranging questions about court unification, state funding for courthouses, and of course the marriage decisions—he continued to jot notes about matters from the petition conference, and slide them across the big table to me. When I commented afterward that I'd not expected that even he could multitask like that while being interviewed by two journalists live on radio, he responded that he knew I hoped to catch a 5:10 bus and didn't want to delay me.

That's the kind of frenetic approach and pace the Chief kept, and that's how and why he got so much done—inside and outside the court. He's one of a kind—the most effective and charming multi-tasking micro-manager that anyone could ever hope (or dare) to meet.

Jake Dear
Chief Supervising Attorney, California Supreme Court

Appendix 3

Retirement Statement

I have informed Governor Arnold Schwarzenegger that I shall conclude my service as Chief Justice of California with my current term of office, and shall not seek re-election during the approaching filing period. On January 2, 2011, after 38 years of service, including 19 years on the California Supreme Court, I shall leave California's judiciary.

It is with enormous gratitude for the privilege and opportunity to serve the people of California that I shall conclude my time in public office.

My gratitude begins with the four governors who respectively entrusted me with the responsibility of serving at each level of California's court system: appointment by Governor Ronald Reagan to the Los Angeles Municipal Court in 1972, Governor Edmund G. Brown, Jr., to the Los Angeles Superior Court in 1977, Governor George Deukmejian to the Court of Appeal in 1987, and Governor Pete Wilson to the Supreme Court as an Associate Justice in 1991 and as Chief Justice in 1996.

Most of all, I am grateful to have served each day with a group of colleagues—justices and staff alike—unmatched in their judgment, scholarship, professionalism, and collegiality. No person could ask for a more rewarding experience than engaging in a common effort to give meaning to the rule of law by collaboratively crafting judicial opinions which, by the conclusion of my term, will have spanned 50 volumes of the Official Supreme Court Reports, resolving issues important to all Californians and to the nation.

I take great pride also in achievements on the administrative side of my duties as Chief Justice. It has been a great honor and privilege to lead, for 14 years, what is often recognized as the finest judicial system in the world and—with about 1,700 judges, hundreds of subordinate judicial officers, and 20,000 court employees—perhaps the largest. Heading California's judicial branch and its efforts to carry out our mission of providing fair and accessible justice to all Californians has been a particularly rewarding experience during these times of great challenge, opportunity, and reform. My gratitude extends to literally thousands of persons—judges, court executives, lawyers, and others—for their service on the Judicial Council, on its many advisory committees and task forces, and in the Administrative Office of the Courts, in strengthening the quality, independence, and accountability of our judiciary as a co-equal, separate branch of government.

Since my appointment as Chief Justice, it has been my responsibility and pleasure to work with three governors—Governor Wilson, Governor Davis, and Governor Schwarzenegger—as well as successive legislatures, in representing and administering our third branch of government. Each of these three governors, together with legislative leadership and our partners in the justice system, has been instrumental in making California's court system what it is today, through the adoption and implementation of fundamental structural reforms that followed my visits to the courts in all of California's 58 counties soon after I became Chief Justice: (1) vesting the responsibility for funding our trial courts in the state instead of the counties, (2) unifying California's 220 municipal and superior courts into a single level of trial court consisting of one superior court in each county, and (3) transferring ownership of the state's 533 courthouse facilities from the counties to the state, under judicial branch management. Added to these achievements are dozens of other improvements in our court system. These include jury reform, expanded interpreter services, accommodations for self-represented litigants, the launch of a statewide case management system, the development of court community outreach programs (including special sessions of the Supreme Court held around the state and focused on student participation), the creation of new judgeships, and an ambitious courthouse construction project to replace or retrofit unsafe facilities.

My 70th birthday this year focused my attention on a question recently posed by my family: why file for re-election for another twelve-year term, after having authored hundreds of judicial opinions and overseen major administrative reforms in the judicial system; what more do you hope to accomplish other than refining and preserving what has been achieved? Reflection convinced me that now is the right time—while I am at the top of my game—to leave while the proverbial music still plays, and return to private life.

It is both difficult and liberating to relinquish a position of responsibility in the public or private arena. I would find it impossible to cut back on what is virtually a daily full-time commitment to administrative and case-related duties. I have often said there are no greener pastures of employment that pose any attraction to me, but the prospect of leisure time devoted to family, reading, and travel is irresistible at this point in my life. Seventy years is not an age too old for a person to occupy the office I hold; at the same time, it is young enough to enable me to pursue the richness of a life outside the law that I relish having before me.

Despite these considerations, I resolved that I could not in good conscience depart this post if California's judiciary remained enmeshed in a severe budget crisis. But through the tireless and creative efforts of many individuals within and outside the judicial branch, the issues facing the courts have been resolved in a manner that will get us through the difficult budget year that lies ahead, without compromising our ability to provide the public with fair and accessible justice.

And so, with 14 years as Chief Justice—and soon reaching the third-longest service among those 27 individuals who since statehood have served in that role—I shall not be filing a declaration of candidacy for re-election during the 30-day period preceding the August 16, 2010 deadline provided by the California Constitution. It is now time for someone else to assume those responsibilities and, as I have done, to build upon the work of his or her predecessors. The governor accordingly will have the opportunity to nominate, before September 16, 2010, my successor as Chief Justice in accordance with Article VI, section 16, Subdivision (d), of the California Constitution.

It is with an enormous sense of gratitude for the opportunity to serve the people of California that I announce my intention to leave office at the expiration of my current term on January 2, 2011. I do so with complete confidence in Governor Schwarzenegger's commitment to appoint a successor who meets the high standards reflected in the judicial appointments he has made during his tenure as governor of California.

Appendix 4

From California Courts and Judges Handbook

GEORGE, Ronald Marc

RETIRED CHIEF JUSTICE, SUPREME COURT OF CALIFORNIA

Appointment/Election: Appointed [succeeding Chief Justice Malcolm M. Lucas, retired] by Governor Wilson March 28, 1996, confirmed by Commission on Judicial Appointments May 1, 1996, oath of office same day and confirmed by electorate November 3, 1998 to 12-year term, which concluded on Jan. 3, 2011. Chief Justice George did not seek another term.

Other Judicial Offices: Associate Justice, Supreme Court of Calif., appointed [succeeding Associate Justice Allen E. Broussard, retired] by Governor Wilson July 29, 1991, confirmed by Commission on Judicial Appointments Sept. 3, 1991, oath of office same day, confirmed by electorate Nov. 8, 1994 to 12-year term commencing Jan. 2, 1995 and succeeded May 1, 1996; Associate Justice, Court of Appeal, Second Appellate District, Division Four, Aug. 27, 1987 (date of confirmation by Commission on Judicial Appointments and oath) to Sept. 3, 1991, appointed [succeeding Associate Justice John A. Arguelles, elevated] by Governor Deukmejian July 23, 1987, and confirmed by electorate Nov. 7, 1990; Judge, Superior Court, Los Angeles County, Jan. 20, 1978 (date of oath) to Aug. 27, 1987, appointed [succeeding Judge Steven S. Weisman, retired] by Governor Brown, Jr. Dec. 23, 1977, elected in 1978 (unopposed), and reelected in 1984 (unopposed); Supervising Judge, Criminal Division, 1983-84; Civil assignments, 1985-87. Member, court's Executive Committee, 1983-84 (ex officio); Judge, Municipal Court, Los Angeles Judicial District, Los Angeles County, April 21, 1972 (date of oath) to Jan. 20, 1978, appointed [succeeding Judge Peter E. Giannini, elevated] April 20, 1972 by Governor Reagan, and elected in 1976 (unopposed). Supervising Judge: Criminal Courts Division, 1977, and West Los Angeles Branch Court, 1974-75.

Past Public Position: Deputy Attorney General, Calif. State Dept. of Justice, Los Angeles, Calif., 1965-72 (Administrative Assistant in charge of Los Angeles office, 1971).

Memberships: Member: Commission on Global Ethics and Citizenship (charged with updating United Nations' Universal Declaration of Human Rights), 2013—; Think Long Committee for California, 2011—; Chairperson, Commission on Judicial Appointments, 1996-2011; Chairperson, Calif. Judicial Council, 1996-2011 (Executive Committee, 1993-96), 1989-91 (Chairperson, Committee on Gender Bias in the Courts, 1990-94, and Advisory Committee on Voir Dire, 1988); Co-Chairperson, Calif. State-Federal Judicial Council, 1996-2011; President, Conference of Chief Justices, 2003-04; Chair, Board of Directors, National Center for State Courts, 2003-04; Judicial Conference of the U.S.,

Committee on Rules of Practice and Procedure, 2006-09; Judicial Conference of the U.S., Committee on Federal-State Jurisdiction, 1999-2002; Anglo-American Legal Exchange (U.S. State Dept. program), 1999-2000; Governor's Commission on Building Calif. for the 21st Century, 1999-2002; American Law Institute, 1996-2011; Calif. Judges Assn., 1972— (President, 1982-83); American Judicature Society; American Bar Assn. (Committee on Continuing Appellate Education, Judicial Administration Division, 1993-96); Los Angeles County Superior Court Committee on Standard Jury Instructions, Criminal (CALJIC), 1977-87; Los Angeles Countywide Criminal Justice Coordinating Committee, 1983-84; Calif. Attorney General's Commission on Crime Victims, 1980-82.

Awards: Lifetime Achievement Award, California Newspaper Publishers Association, 2011; Distinguished Service Award, University of California Berkeley Institute of Governmental Studies, 2011; Award for Judicial Excellence, Beverly Hills Bar Association, 2011; renaming of the San Francisco Civic Center Complex, comprised of the Earl Warren Building and the Hiram Johnson Building, as the Ronald M. George State Office Complex, 2010; The Diversity Award, State Bar Council on Access and Fairness, 2010; Inducted, Member of Warren E. Burger Society, 2010; Joan Dempsey Klein Award, National Association of Women Judges, 2010; Champion of Civil Justice Award, Consumer Attorneys of California, 2010; President's Award, California Judges Association, 2010 and 1981; President's Award, California State Association of Counties, 2010 and 1997; Inducted, Fellow of the American Academy of Arts and Sciences, 2009; American Academy of Matrimonial Lawyers' Family Law Person of the Year Award, 2009; Asian Law Alliance's Legal Impact Award, 2009; Friends of the Los Angeles County Law Library's Beacon of Justice Award, 2009; Los Angeles Consumer Attorneys Association Roger J. Traynor Memorial Award, 2008; Bar Association of San Francisco's Champion of Justice Award, 2008; American Bar Association's John Marshall Award, 2007; Legal Writing Institute's Golden Pen Award, 2007; American College of Trial Lawyers Samuel Gates Award, 2007; American Judicature Society's Opperman Award for Judicial Excellence, 2006; Consumer Attorneys of Calif. Justice of the Year Award, 2006; San Francisco Trial Lawyers Assoc.'s Justice of the Year Award, 2006; Burton Reform in Law Award, 2006; Ronald M. George Equal Justice Award, Central California Legal Services, 2006; Los Angeles Inner City Law Center's Humanitarian Award, 2006; Mathew O. Tobriner Public Service Award, Legal Aid Society of San Francisco, 2006; Children's Advocacy Award, Los Angeles Legal Services for Children, 2006; State Bar of California's Bernard Witkin Medal, 2005; Foster Care Awareness Campaign Recognition, 2005; Public Counsel's William O. Douglas Award, 2004; George Moscone Award for Outstanding Public Service, Consumer Attorneys of Los Angeles, 2003; James Madison Freedom of Information Award, Society of Professional Journalists, 2003; William H. Rehnquist Award for Judicial Excellence, 2002; Legal Aid Foundation of Los Angeles' Maynard Toll Award for Distinguished Public Service, 2001; Foundation of the State Bar's Justice Award, 2000; Judge Learned Hand Award, 2000; National

Assoc. of Drug Court Professionals' Leadership Award, 2000; American Judicature Society's Herbert Harley Award ("for services in promoting the effective administration of justice"), 1998; Los Angeles County Barristers' Special Recognition, 1998; St. Thomas More Law Honor Society's Medallion Award ("for outstanding moral, intellectual, and professional contributions to the law and society"), 1997; "Justice of the Year," 1997, by Consumer Attorneys of Calif.; "Person of the Year," 1996, by Los Angeles Metropolitan News Enterprise; "Appellate Justice of the Year," 1991, by Los Angeles Trial Lawyers Assn.; "Trial Judge of the Year," 1983, by Los Angeles Metropolitan News.

Teaching/Lectures/Panelist: Georgetown University Law Center's Sandra Day O'Connor Project on the State of the Judiciary, Steering Committee (2007-2010); Faculty: American Bar Assn., Appellate Judges Seminar Series, 1992; Calif. State-Federal Judicial Council Capital Case Symposium, 1992; San Diego Law Library Justice Foundation, 1992; Criminal Justice Legal Foundation, 1992; 2020 Vision Symposium on the Future of California's Courts, 1992; Calif Judicial College (CJER), Berkeley, 1982; Calif. Continuing Judicial Studies Program (CJER), 1982 and 1981; and 4th Annual Calif. Institute for Trial Advocacy Skills, 1979; Served as lecturer at various law schools, bar associations, media seminars and law enforcement agencies.

Publications: Author: "The Perils of Direct Democracy: The California Experience" (Bulletin of the American Academy of Arts and Sciences) Winter 2010; Keynote Address, *Symposium*, State Constitutions, 62 *Stanford L.Rev.* 1515 (2010); "A Nation of Do-It-Yourself Lawyers" (New York Times Op-Ed article co-authored with John T. Broderick, Jr., Chief Justice of New Hampshire), January, 2010; "Dysfunctional California: Initiatives Straitjacket the State" (San Francisco Chronicle Op-Ed article), November, 2009; "In California, Justice Takes a Day Off" (Los Angeles Times Op-Ed article), September, 2009; "California Criminal Trial Judges Benchbook and Deskbook (West Publishing Co.), 1985-87; "Common Crimes and Punishments Bench Blotter" (Los Angeles Daily Journal), 1985-88; "Determinate Sentencing Manual" (Los Angeles Daily Journal), 1987; Co-author (with Judge William H. Levit), California Judicial Retirement Handbook (Calif. Judges Assn.), 1985 (3rd ed) and 1989 (4th ed).

Noteworthy Cases: Significant majority opinions authored as a Supreme Court Justice include: *People v. Engram* (2010) 50 Cal.4th 1131 (upholding trial court's dismissal of criminal cases in the face of chronic court congestion due to provision of insufficient resources); *Professional Engineers in Calif. Gov't. v. Schwarzenegger* (2010) 50 Cal.4th 989 (upholding the Governor's 2009-10 furlough of state employees); *St. John's Well Child & Family Center v. Schwarzenegger* (2010) 50 Cal.4th 960 (upholding the Governor's use of his line-item veto authority to further reduce funding levels set forth in the Legislature's midyear reductions); *County of Santa Clara* (2010) 50 Cal.4th 35 (permitting public entities to pursue public-nuisance-abatement litigation assisted by private counsel retained on a contingency-fee basis); *People v. Kelly* (2010) 47 Cal.4th

1008 (holding invalid a legislative enactment amending the medical marijuana initiative without approval of the electorate); *Strauss v. Horton* (2009) 46 Cal.4th 364 (involving the constitutionality and retroactivity of Proposition 8, which amended the California Constitution to restrict marriage to opposite-sex couples); *Silverbrand v. County of Los Angeles* (2009) 46 Cal.4th 106 (applying the "prison delivery" rule to an inmate's filing of a notice of appeal in a civil case); *Vargas v. City of Salinas* (2009) 46 Cal.4th 1 (setting standard for lawfulness of city's expenditure of public funds on election campaigns); *In re Lawrence* (2008) 44 Cal.4th 1181 and *In re Shaputis* (2008) 44 Cal.4th 1241 (both involving the standard by which courts review the Governor's reversal of the Board of Parole Hearing's grant of parole); *In re Marriage Cases* (2008) 43 Cal.4th 757 (holding unconstitutional the California statutes limiting marriage to a union of a man and a woman); *Commission on Peace Officer Standards and Training v. Superior Court* (2007) 42 Cal.4th 278 and *Int'l Fed. of Prof. & Tech. Engineers v. Superior Court* (2007) 42 Cal.4th 319 (both holding that names and salaries of public employees are subject to disclosure under the Public Records Act); *Elkins v. Superior Court* (2007) 41 Cal.4th 1337 (invalidating local court rules that eliminated direct testimony and limited other evidence in marital dissolution trials); *People v. Black* (2007) 41 Cal.4th 799 and *People v. Sandoval* (2007) 41 Cal.4th 825 (both involving reformation of California's determinate sentencing laws in the wake of U.S. Supreme Court holdings); *City of Santa Barbara v. Superior Court* (2007) 41 Cal.4th 747 (invalidating release of liability for recreational activities involving gross negligence); *Kearney v. Salomon Smith Barney, Inc.* (2006) 39 Cal.4th 95 (involving applicability of California privacy laws to telephone calls made to Californians from out of state); *Ind't Energy Producers Assn. v. McPherson* (2006) 38 Cal.4th 1020; *Californians for an Open Primary v. McPherson* (2006) 38 Cal.4th 735; *Costa v. Superior Court* (2006) 37 Cal.4th 986 (all three cases involving the propriety of various pre-election challenges to voter initiatives); *Frye v. Tenderloin Housing Clinic, Inc.* (2006) 38 Cal.4th 23 (involving the authority of nonprofit legal services corporations to practice law); *Yanowitz v. L'Oreal USA, Inc.* (2005) 36 Cal.4th 1028 (holding that sales manager suffered improper retaliation under F.E.H.A for her refusal to terminate the employment of a female employee who was considered by the manager's male supervisor to be insufficiently attractive); *Miller v. Department of Corrections* (2005) 36 Cal.4th 446 (holding that pervasive favoritism toward female employees engaged in sexual affairs with male supervisor created a hostile work environment and violated F.E.H.A.'s prohibition against sexual harassment); *Delgado v. Trax Bar and Grill* (2005) 36 Cal.4th 224, and *Morris v. De La Torre* (2005) 36 Cal. 4th 260 (both allowing liability to be imposed upon business proprieters for failure to take reasonable action in response to ongoing criminal conduct on the premises); *Marine Forests Society v. California Coastal Comm.* (2005) 36 Cal.4th 1 (holding that Legislature's appointment of some of the members of this executive agency does not violate state constitution's separation-of-powers clause); *Lockyer v. City & County of San Francisco* (2004) 33 Cal.4th 1055 (holding that local officials acted outside of their authority in issuing marriage licenses to single-sex couples in violation of state statutes); *Bronco Wine Co. v. Jolly* (2004) 33 Cal.4th 943 (holding that federal law does not preempt state statute regulating "Napa" designation on wine labels); *Dept. of Finance v. Comm. on State Mandates* (2003) 30 Cal.4th 727 (interpreting constitutional requirement that local entities be reimbursed for state-mandated costs); *White v. Davis* (2003) 30 Cal.4th 528 (determining authority of State Controller to disburse funds during a budget impasse); *In re Rosenkrantz* (2002) 29 Cal.4th 616 (setting forth the standard for judicial review of Governor's reversal of parole board decisions); *People v. Mar* (2002) 28 Cal.4th 1201 (establishing the limited circumstances under which a defendant may be compelled to wear an electronic stun belt during a criminal trial); *People v. Mower* (2002) 28 Cal.4th 457 (interpreting Proposition 215, the medical use of marijuana initiative, to grant qualified patients and primary caregivers a limited immunity from prosecution for possession and cultivation of marijuana); *Zelig v. County of Los Angeles* (2002) 27 Cal.4th 1112 (holding that county and sheriff have immunity from liability for failure to protect litigant from shooting committed by other litigant inside courthouse); *Manduley v. Superior Court* (2002) 27 Cal.4th 537 (upholding constitutionality of Proposition 21, the Gang Violence and Juvenile Crime Prevention Initiative, which confers upon the prosecutor the discretion to file specified charges against certain minors directly in criminal rather than juvenile court); *Lugtu v. Calif. Highway Patrol* (2001) 26 Cal.4th 703 (holding that a law enforcement officer owes a motorist a duty of reasonable care in pulling over a vehicle during a traffic stop); *People v. Williams* (2001). 25 Cal.4th 441 (holding that there is no right of jury nullification); *In re Marriage of Bonds* (2000) 24 Cal.4th 1 (holding that in determining whether a premarital agreement was entered into voluntarily, the circumstance that one of the parties was not represented by independent counsel is only one of several factors to be considered); *Alvarado v. Superior Court* (2000) 23 Cal.4th 1121 (holding that the defendants' rights of confrontation and cross-examination were violated by a trial court order permitting the crucial witnesses against them to testify anonymously at trial). Significant opinions as a Court of Appeal justice include: *Di Donato v. Santini* (1991) 232 Cal.App.3d 721 (holding that rules prohibiting discriminatory use of peremptory challenges apply in a civil trial to the exclusion of prospective jurors based on gender); and *People v. Simmons* (1989) 213 Cal.App.3d 573 (holding that evidence of rape victim's prior consensual sexual conduct with the defendant is, itself, insufficient to require instruction that the defendant's good-faith belief in consent is a defense). Notable cases over which Chief Justice George presided as a trial judge include *People v. Buono* (Hillside Strangler case), which lasted two years (1981-83), after he denied the prosecution's motion to dismiss the charges and in which a jury convicted the defendant of 9 murders. While in Calif. Attorney General's office, Chief Justice George represented Calif. in six oral arguments before the U.S. Supreme Court, one of which involved the constitutionality of the death penalty under the cruel and unusual punishment clause, as did one of his numerous appearances before the Calif.

Supreme Court (see *People v. Anderson* (1972) 6 Cal.3d 628); also represented the State of Calif. on the appeal of the Sirhan Sirhan case (prosecution for assassination of U.S. Senator and presidential candidate Robert Kennedy (see *People v. Sirhan* (1972) 7 Cal.3d 710)).

Education: J.D. (June 1964), Stanford Univ. Law School; B.A. (June 1961), Woodrow Wilson School of Public and International Affairs, Princeton Univ., Princeton, New Jersey; Attended: Beverly Hills High School, Beverly Hills, Calif., 1953-55, 1956-57 (graduated in 1957); International School, Geneva, Switzerland, 1955-56 and 1952-53; Hawthorne Elementary School, Beverly Hills, 1945-52.

Personal: Born March 11, 1940; Los Angeles, Calif. Married. Three sons.

Interests: Enjoys skiing, hiking, and running (ran in San Francisco, Boston, New York, and Big Sur Marathons).

Admission: Admitted to Calif. Bar in 1965; to U.S. Dist. Court, Central Dist. of Calif., in 1965; to U.S. Court of Appeals, Ninth Circuit, in 1966; and to U.S. Supreme Court in 1969.

Political Affiliation: Republican

Appendix 5

Introduction

The great British Prime Minister Winston Churchill observed that "We shape our buildings, thereafter they shape us." So it is with the historic courthouses of California.

Inspired by the visits of my husband to all of California's 58 counties during his first year as Chief Justice, this collection includes a photograph of a courthouse in each county, and each tells a small part of the state's history. In the stories of these buildings, we see the evolution from Spanish colonialism to pioneer society to statehood and to the realization of a culture unlike any that had come before.

These courthouses are monuments to the way the people of California saw themselves at an earlier time, when the state was young and the ideals of the democratic society were not only embraced, but also enshrined in what was often the grandest building in town. "It is our temple of justice," said Judge J. E.

Prewett at the dedication of the Placer County Courthouse on Independence Day 1898. "It is the repository of our titles, the fortress of our personal and property rights, the fountainhead of our school system, the registry of our births, marriages and deaths, and its inmates stand guard by day and night over the peace and good order of our communities."

Of the 60 courthouses included here, just 32 remain standing, the others victims of earthquake, fire, neglect, and modernism. Of the buildings that remain, 21 are designated National Historic Places and 22 are still used as courthouses. The Mariposa County Courthouse, a Greek Revival treasure built in 1854 by those who had come in search of gold ore, has the honor of being the oldest courthouse in continuous use in the state.

All these buildings are remarkable for the places they hold in the short history of California, and all are reminders of the ideals of generations past.

It is not possible to thank all those individuals throughout the state who assisted in this project. For their diligent work on the original exhibit that hangs in the Judicial Council Conference Center in San Francisco, we are especially indebted to Michael Ginsborg and Gale Tunnell of the Supreme Court staff and to James Carroll of the Administrative Office of the Courts. Special thanks are also due to James Pfeiffer of the Supreme Court Historical Society for making this book possible.

Barbara George
Chair, Supreme Court Art Selection Committee

Appendix 6

Oral History Table of Contents[*]

SESSION I

Father's family background and career in France, Mexico, and Southern California; mother's Hungarian origins and European sensibilities; upbringing and schooling in Beverly Hills, California, and at the International School in Geneva, Switzerland; meeting and marrying Barbara Schneiderman; plans for a career in the Foreign Service; European and African travel; sister's art career and art restoration business; college years at Princeton's Woodrow Wilson School of Public and International Affairs; "college capers," including brief escapade with President Kennedy's campaign.

SESSION II

Returning to California for Stanford Law School, 1961; interest in constitutional law; influence of Professor Gerald Gunther; early views of California's judiciary; applying to the California Department of Justice, 1964; hiring by Attorney General Stanley Mosk; beginning legal career as a deputy attorney general in Los Angeles; representing California in criminal matters on appeal, with occasional trial work; first oral argument before the U.S. Supreme Court, 1969.

SESSION III

Arguing additional matters before the U.S. Supreme Court and the California Supreme Court; appeals and writs before the state and federal appellate courts; oral argument techniques; legal reasoning and personal views of the death penalty; research visit to death row at San Quentin Prison, 1971; California Supreme Court's decision in *People v. Anderson* ruling the death penalty unconstitutional; subsequent death penalty ruling by the U.S. Supreme Court, 1972; preparing the Department of Justice response to the California Supreme Court's invalidation of the death penalty; assisting Senator George Deukmejian with a proposed constitutional amendment to restore California's death penalty; assignment to represent California on appeal in Sirhan Sirhan's assassination of Senator Robert Kennedy, 1972; acting assistant attorney general in the Department of Justice's Los Angeles office; State Bar committee on criminal law and procedure; appointment to the Los Angeles Municipal Court by Governor Ronald Reagan, 1972.

---

[*] The numbering of the 20 oral argument sessions corresponds with the numbering of the respective chapters in this volume.

SESSION IV
Trying cases in the Los Angeles Municipal Court; judicial colleagues and Presiding Judge Alan Campbell; developing judicial skills through criminal trials; judges college, 1972; disciplinary removal of judges; observations on the Los Angeles County district attorney and public defender offices; assignment to misdemeanor master calendar court; notable first court visits by father and mother; becoming supervising judge of West Los Angeles branch and initiating major reforms there; brief assignment to San Fernando Valley courthouse; new downtown Los Angeles assignment as supervising judge for all criminal operations; performing weddings in and out of court; seeking elevation to the Los Angeles Superior Court by Governor Jerry Brown, 1978.

SESSION V
Elevation to the Los Angeles Superior Court and criminal trial assignment to the East District in Pomona, 1978; immersion in serious felony trials; unusual juror activity; assignment to downtown Los Angeles; master calendar system; memorable trials; security concerns; personal emphasis on creating a proper record; superior court committee charged with drafting jury instructions; assignment as supervising judge of the criminal division; appointment as chair of U.S. Senator Pete Wilson's Judicial Selection Advisory Committee; later service by son Eric on judicial selection committees; editing guides to criminal trial judging; testifying before congressional committees; roles in the California Judges Association (CJA), including president 1982-1983; study of judges' retirement system; CJA advocacy in Sacramento; work with the Judicial Council.

SESSION VI
Presiding over the then-longest criminal jury trial in U.S. history, the two-year Hillside Strangler case (*People v. Buono*), 1981-1983, along with other trial and supervisory duties; district attorney's request to dismiss, co-defendant's plea agreement, media attention, hypnosis, jury members, reporting verdicts as decided, and other notable features of the trial; taking up running as a personal coping mechanism (and later becoming a marathoner); trial's effect on family; book about the trial (*Two of a Kind*); seeking civil assignment on the Los Angeles Superior Court after Hillside Strangler trial; trying civil cases; mandatory settlement panel; role of settlement in the state trial system.

SESSION VII
Short-term superior court assignments to law and motion and juvenile court; sentencing laws in California (in contrast with federal sentencing); judicial discretion vis-à-vis the California Evidence Code and other statutory provisions; serving on Attorney General Deukmejian's Crime Victims Commission and on the Los Angeles Countywide Criminal Justice Coordinating Committee; working with district attorneys, public defenders, and supervising judges to solve joint problems; elevation by Governor Deukmejian to the California Second

District Court of Appeal, 1987; transition to appellate work; Presiding Justice Arleigh Woods, colleagues, and staff in Division Four; crafting opinions and dissents; role of collegiality; oral argument; views of appellate counsel; publication and depublication of opinions; selected opinions; retention election; qualities of an appellate justice; personal experience as a crime victim.

SESSION VIII

Before being appointed to the California Court of Appeal, applying for appointment to the U.S. Ninth Circuit Court of Appeals; structural and caseload differences of California and federal judiciaries; U.S. Senator Wilson's judicial selection committee and record of appointments to district court; desirable qualities for service on the bench; views concerning elevation to the California Supreme Court; appointment to that court by Governor Pete Wilson, 1991; confirmation as associate justice; move to San Francisco and Barbara George's new roles in civic affairs and arts; lives of parents and of three grown sons; colleagues on the California Supreme Court: Chief Justice Malcolm Lucas and Justices Stanley Mosk, Edward Panelli, Joyce Kennard, Marvin Baxter, and Armand Arabian; weekly petition conferences; central staffs; first key oral argument in *Legislature v. Eu*, challenging term-limits initiative; court's tests for evaluating challenges to voter initiatives; political prism of legislators; exploring court's "inherent powers"; value of careful wording in judicial opinions; ameliorating relations with legislative branch; national interest in term limits; judicial task of resolving reapportionment deadlock in *Wilson v. Eu*, 1992; execution of Robert Alton Harris, 1992.

SESSION IX

Early years on California Supreme Court: quarters at Marathon Plaza; opinion writing for panel of seven; leadership by Chief Justice Lucas; aiding liaison in Sacramento; colleagues; Chief Justice Lucas' retirement; becoming Governor Wilson's choice for Chief Justice, 1996; confirmation hearing and swearing in (including concern by some about court's recent but not final parental-consent abortion opinion); appointment of Justice Janice Rogers Brown and presiding over her confirmation hearing; key points of her tenure, including affirmative-action opinion; first State of the Judiciary address and pledge to visit courts in every county; Barbara George's companion photographic history of California courthouses; need for recognition of judiciary as a co-equal independent branch of government; federal-state relations; tribal courts; county court visits; water skiing accident; a view to unifying trial courts; court employee status; transferring court facilities to state ownership.

SESSION X

Views and approaches as Chief Justice; assignment and writing of opinions; relations with other branches of government; Trial Court Funding Act, 1997; research attorneys and executive judicial assistants; guidance to staff working on opinions; central staffs; meeting with each chambers; administrative operations; major areas of responsibility for a Chief Justice; constitutional basis for California's courts and Judicial Council; judicial emergencies; judicial assignments pro Tem; recusal and stock divestiture to eliminate conflicts of interests; chairing the Administrative Presiding Justices Committee of the Courts of Appeal; structure of California's six Courts of Appeal; mandatory continuing education for judges; appointments to the Judicial Council; list of duties prepared by predecessor's staff; authority and duties of Commission on Judicial Appointments and Commission on Judicial Performance; judicial emergencies; assigned judges program; the power of assignment; budget of judiciary and fiscal responsibilities; expansion of Judicial Council role consistent with constitutional provisions; the Administrative Office of the Courts; advice from legislators; presidency of Conference of Chief Justices and hosting conference; international judicial exchanges.

SESSION XI

Changes in California Supreme Court's membership; presiding over weekly petition conferences; deciding on petitions to grant review; tracking caseload; instituting time limits for circulating dissents; "preliminary responses" and other phases of opinion preparation; setting cases for oral argument and regulating the allocation of time among counsel; the "art and science" of assigning authorship of opinions; time limits for opinions; possible reasons for delay of individual opinions; options for acting on petitions other than outright "grant" or "deny"; depublication of Court of Appeal opinions vis-à-vis constitutional responsibility to develop state law; appointing committee to review publication practices; new practice of circulating unpublished Court of Appeal opinions electronically for ninety days; monthly administrative conferences; appellate judicial assignments pro Tem; revising antiquated procedure for case participation by justices traveling out of state; annual outreach sessions of oral argument; other special court sessions.

SESSION XII

Liaison meetings within the Supreme Court, the judicial branch, and with "justice system partners"; Administrative Office of the Courts staff and functions; California's specialty courts; trial court innovations; appointments to Commission on Judicial Performance; State Bar Court; concerns of capital-defense-related associations; increasing pay for capital appellate defense counsel; sheriffs versus marshals providing court security; statewide court security costs; interactions and speeches for law-related groups; building relations with legislators and pushing for judicial unity in Sacramento; meeting with law students and other student groups; State Bar meetings; bestowing awards and other recognitions; State of the Judiciary addresses to the bar; urging all bar members to consider pro bono efforts; changes to State Bar and use of member dues; media relations and views of press; authoring articles in legal and popular press; liaison with press groups and editorial boards; legislative branch and key legislators in term-limits era; legislative and executive branch staff; learning to succeed in Sacramento; role of strong legislative leadership.

SESSION XIII
Effects on legislature of redistricting, term limits, and initiative process; related imposition of spending mandates; individual legislators and their views of the judiciary; political prism of legislators contrasted to judicial views and methods; threats to judicial independence; need for judicial orientation of legislators; working with key legislators and legislative staff; liaison with Governors Pete Wilson and Gray Davis and their staffs on budget, legislation, and special projects such as complex-litigation courts; gubernatorial recall election, 2003; working relationship with Governor Arnold Schwarzenegger; inviting him to address the Conference of Chief Justices; details of hosting CCJ meeting; urging governor's support of "civil Gideon act" with promise to name it "Sargent Shriver Civil Counsel Act"; forceful advocacy under threat of $300 million budget cuts, 2010; Governor Schwarzenegger's later renaming of the San Francisco Civic Center Complex as the Ronald M. George State Office Complex; history of working relationship with Governor Jerry Brown.

SESSION XIV
History and changes in Judicial Council and Administrative Office of the Courts and its main committees: executive and planning, policy coordination and liaison, and rules; view by some that council acts with little debate; reality of debate and compromise in committee; value of consensus in policy matters and in opinions; instructions to potential council members; AOC structure and staffing levels appropriate to disburse statewide court funding and manage court facilities; history of Court Case Management System; importance of effective statewide electronic case management; technology committee; AOC's Administration of Justice Fund ("Shapiro Fund"); Trial Court Funding Act of 1997 and subsequent challenges; task force study and later reform of court employee status; unification of trial courts via constitutional amendment on local-option basis; Trial Court Facilities Act; later role of Senate President pro Tem Don Perata in $5 billion revenue bond; AOC's Office of Courthouse Management and Construction; court interpreter services; efforts toward diversity in judicial appointments; growth of self-help centers; access to justice for unrepresented litigants; future ways to improve access to justice; jury reforms: service, pay, facilities; revising jury instructions; views of private judging; adopting code of judicial conduct; judicial pay and retirement benefits; alternative dispute resolution issues, including mandatory arbitration.

SESSION XV
Other court administration reforms accomplished by the Judicial Council; standardizing statewide rules and practices; establishing new judgeships and raising

salaries; collecting fees and fines; evolving views of chief's role and duties; cameras in the courtroom, weighing judicial discretion against public's right of access; extending right to public judicial proceedings to civil cases in *NBC Subsidiary* on First Amendment and statutory grounds; closing courts one day a month due to budget crisis; administration of capital punishment in California; constitutional basis of Supreme Court's appellate jurisdiction; rotating assignment of capital cases; lengthy transcripts and varied legal issues; capital jury selection and *Wheeler-Batson* doctrine; personal role in appointing attorneys for automatic appeals; Senator Bill Morrow's help in cutting delay in transcript preparation; California Appellate Project; urging separate counsel for automatic appeal and habeas corpus proceedings; federal court review of death penalty cases; role of Habeas Corpus Resource Center; dysfunction of taking years to carry out or set aside death judgments; public concern with cost of administering death penalty; legislators' criticisms (and unwillingness to appropriate funds for reforms); areas of successful capital reform, including establishing a capital central staff; capital cases; ideas for capital reform, including those presented to the Commission on the Fair Administration of Justice; history of death as a punishment for crime, and personal views of it.

SESSION XVI
Views of oral argument and 90-day submission rule; considerations of venue in setting cases for argument; advice on oral argument; presiding over oral argument and post-argument conferences; value of oral argument; oral argument participation by justices; working out conflicts in draft opinions with justices and staff; considerations in assigning casework to staff; mentoring of staff attorneys; deciding cases on non-constitutional grounds where possible; footnotes in opinions; length of opinions in California and elsewhere; constitutional requirement that appellate opinions shall determine cause "in writing with reasons stated"; summary of some of own appellate opinions in the Court of Appeal, and in the California Supreme Court spanning fifty bound volumes, 1991–2010; selected opinions on tort law; negotiating to carry a majority; key opinions in criminal, family, election, and government law and interbranch relations; single-subject rule for initiatives; State Bar cases.

SESSION XVII
Miscellaneous opinions on right to present oral argument on appeal and on wine labeling (and latter holding's "presumption against preemption"); case on contingency-fee retention of private counsel by public entities; reflections on California's three-strikes law; independent and adequate state grounds doctrine; initiative restricting courts' reliance on independent state search and seizure law in excluding criminal evidence; opinions authored on civil rights and individual constitutional rights, public accommodations, and public access; key case of *American Academy of Pediatrics v. Lungren*, 1997; *NBC Subsidiary* case ex-

tending public right of access to civil proceedings and trials, 1999; employment law cases; detailed account of *In re Marriage Cases*, 2008.

SESSION XVIII

Same-sex marriage after *In re Marriage Cases*; federal issues beyond state constitutional grounds; U.S. District Court invalidation of Proposition 8; "standing" of Proposition 8 proponents; possible future reviews; characterization of "George Court" as a moderate body addressing a range of issues; societal changes that create novel issues of law; death penalty caseload as factor limiting review of civil and non-capital criminal cases; "access to justice" as personal priority in opinions and judicial administrative actions; Dear and Jessen's study of "followed rates"of state high courts; California's influence on other jurisdictions; benefits of staff work and specialized appellate bar; views of U.S. Supreme Court and how the California Supreme Court compares; federal separation-of-powers issues and judicial selection; recusal in U.S. Supreme Court and California; reflections on U.S. Supreme Court jurisprudence and frequency of split decisions; role of court decisions in providing public guidance; ethical issues; First Amendment rights; "originalism" approach; amending U.S. and California Constitutions; "judicial activism" and result-oriented jurisprudence; the California State-Federal Judicial Council; allowing federal judges to certify questions of law to the state high court; California's use of federal case law; serving on federal committees; presidency of Conference of Chief Justices.

SESSION XIX

Restoring California Supreme Court's home in San Francisco after Loma Prieta earthquake; Barbara George's interior design career and later contributions to art and architecture in California: chairing the California Arts Council, selecting artwork, editing the books *California Court Houses* and *Art and Architecture—San Francisco Civic Center Complex*, founding the California Music Project; Chief Justice's decision in 2010 to retire rather than seek another term; consulting family and deciding timing of retirement; constitutional time constraints for selecting a new Chief Justice; announcing retirement to Supreme Court colleagues, staff, and the public; Governor Schwarzenegger's request to advise him on a possible successor; governor's nomination of Justice Tani Cantil-Sakauye from the California Court of Appeal as successor; final months as Chief Justice; recognition at State Bar convention and retirement events; immediate travel in Antarctica; post-retirement offers and decision to join Think Long Committee for California.

SESSION XX

Future challenges facing the judiciary and California; proposal to amend the Constitution's judicial article (article VI); lack of adequate legal representation for Californians in civil cases; separation of powers as a key issue for the judiciary vis-à-vis performance of its constitutional responsibilities; special-interest funding of ballot initiatives and judicial elections; confirmation election of 1998 and issue-related opposition; reflections on 1986 election that unseated Chief Justice Bird and Justices Grodin and Reynoso; civics education relating to election of judges; recent judicial elections nationwide; process for contested judicial elections in other states; the respective experiences of Justice Goodwin Liu with federal and state judicial nominations; "merit selection" of judges; judicial independence; comparing California to other states and to the federal judiciary; ways to improve California's system of selecting high court justices by amending article VI; working with Justice Sandra Day O'Connor on civics education project; public misperceptions about courts brought about by the entertainment industry; civics education in California and role of media; public understanding of court system as key to public trust; challenges to judicial independence posed by the actions of some members of the judicial branch; Chief Justice Cantil-Sakauye's success; reflections on career.

Acknowledgments

Grateful acknowledgment is made to the following individuals, firms, and foundations for generous support between 2009 and 2012 of the oral history of the Honorable Ronald M. George, *California Supreme Court Oral History Project*, Institute of Governmental Studies:

California Supreme Court Historical Society
Administration of Justice Fund of the Administrative Office of the Courts
Cotchett, Pitre & McCarthy LLP
David and Diane Paul
Girardi Keese
Munger, Tolles & Olson
The Shapiro Family Charitable Foundation
The Eli and Edythe Broad Foundation
Greines, Martin, Stein & Richland LLP
Stanley Zax
Willie L. Brown, Jr.
Bingham McCutchen LLP
Farella Braun & Martel LLP
Horvitz & Levy LLP
Elwood Lui
The Maier Family Foundation
Michael Belote
Peter Glaessner

Index of Cases Cited

Subject Index

State Bar Court, California, 243, 324,
327, 382, 395, 589, 727
state constitutionalism, 606, 610
State of the Judiciary addresses, 234,
285, 406, 422
Steinberg, Darrell, 148, 393, 410, 424,
469
Stephens, Clarke, 59
Stevens, John Paul, 668, 672
Stewart, Jon, 714
Stewart, Potter, 539
Stewart, Therese M., 640
Sullivan, Raymond, 365
Symington, Stuart, 29
Szalay, Steve, 384
Tacha, Deanell, 329
Taft, William Howard, 659
Taylor, Marcia, 328
term limits, California (relating to
Proposition 140 of 1990), 149,
239, 241–42, 244, 247, 406–07,
415, 433, 452, 502, 585, 717, 741,
743
Terry, David, 282, 691
Tevrizian, Dickran, 96
Think Long Committee for California,
8, 433, 444, 586, 714–15
Thomas, Clarence, 329
three strikes law, California (relating to
Proposition 184 of 1994), 318,
592, 594, 601–05
Torre, Kiri, 275
Tracy, Terry, 277, 366, 411, 711
Traynor, Michael, 632
Traynor, Roger, 254, 505, 632, 652,
689
Trial Court Facilities Act, 6, 375, 410
Trial Court Funding Act of 1997, 6,
296, 324, 462
tribal courts, California, 277, 280–81,
288, 329, 679
Truman, Harry, 29
Tulleners, Paul, 166
Tunnell, Gale, x, 299, 746
unification of municipal and superior
courts, 147, 292–93, 326, 376,
409, 420–21, 427, 429–30, 454,
466–69, 470, 497, 712
Uelmen, Gerald, 530, 668

United States Court of Appeals
Ninth Circuit, 35, 38, 59, 96, 204,
216, 223–25, 329, 521, 532,
594, 609, 646, 648, 660, 662,
679–84, 741
United States District Court, 226, 522
Central District of California, 96
Eastern District of California, 227
Northern District of California, 225,
645, 684
Southern District of California, 227
U.S. Information Agency, 23
University of California, xi–xii, 39, 42,
113, 211, 262, 376, 403, 717
Berkeley, ix–xii, 9, 39, 82, 95, 175,
262, 369, 376, 393, 403, 461
Los Angeles (UCLA), 103, 113, 211,
232, 394, 460
Unruh Civil Rights Act (California
Civil Code), 612, 617–18
Unruh, Jesse, 247
Van de Kamp, John, 164, 194, 530, 534
Vanderbilt, Arthur, 254
Ventura, County of, 69, 287
Vickrey, William C., 421, 446, 460,
462, 702, 746
victims' rights, 192–93, 214–15, 220–
22, 283, 389, 461, 525–26, 540–
42, 572, 624, 734
Villaraigosa, Antonio, 427
Villines, Michael, 426
Vinson, Fred M., 666
Vogel, Charles S., 141
Vogel, Miriam A., 462, 489
Volunteers in Legal Services, Bar of
San Francisco, 391, 476
Von Bismarck, Otto, 413
Voting Rights Act, 467
Vox Pop Influentials, 390
Wagner, Lauren, 176
Walker, Vaughn, 476, 645, 660
Wall Street Journal, 126, 403
Wallace, Clifford, 679, 684
Ward, James, 485
Warren, Earl, 8, 51, 64, 75, 443, 547,
657, 666, 692–93
Washington Post, 30, 31
Washington, Yolanda, 176
Waters, Mary, 128